THE ENGLISH BIBLE AND THE SEVENTEENTH-CENTURY REVOLUTION

Christopher Hill

The English Bible and the Seventeenth-Century Revolution

ALLEN LANE
THE PENGUIN PRESS

For Edward and
Dorothy Thompson,

who know that history is about people not things,
and that all our work is about the present as
well as the past. In gratitude.

ALLEN LANE
THE PENGUIN PRESS

Published by the Penguin Group
Penguin Books Ltd, 27 Wrights Lane, London W8 5TZ, England
Penguin Books USA Inc., 375 Hudson Street, New York, New York 10014, USA
Penguin Books Australia Ltd, Ringwood, Victoria, Australia
Pengiun Books Canada Ltd, 10 Alcorn Avenue, Toronto, Ontario, Canada M4V 3B2
Penguin Books (NZ) Ltd, 182–190 Wairau Road, Auckland 10, New Zealand

Penguin Books Ltd, Registered Offices: Harmondsworth, Middlesex, England

First published 1993
1 3 5 7 9 10 8 6 4 2

Typeset by DatIX International Limited, Bungay, Suffolk
Set in 11/13 pt Lasercomp Bembo
Printed in England by Clays Ltd, St Ives plc

A CIP catalogue record for this book is available from the British Library

ISBN 0–713–99078–3

Contents

===

V. THE END OF THE REVOLUTIONARY BIBLE

Preface

My object in this book is to try to assess the part played by the Bible in the lives of Englishmen and women during England's revolutionary seventeenth century. The Introduction to the 1603 edition of Tomson's Geneva Bible, written by T. Grashop, tells us to remember that the Scriptures contain matter concerning commonwealths and governments, good and evil, prosperity and plagues, peace and war, order and disorder. They cover the common life of all men, rich and poor, industrious and idle. The ideas which divided the two parties in the civil war, and which divided conservatives from radicals among the victorious Parliamentarians, were all found in the Bible. But I shall not restrict myself to the religious and political ends to which the Bible was used; I shall also consider its effects on economics, on literature and on social life generally. I shall try to suggest some of the reasons for the ultimate decline of the Bible from the central place which it held in cultural life at the beginning of the century. When I speak of 'the Bible' I mean the text as it was accepted in the sixteenth and seventeenth centuries. Biblical criticism since then has called in question some attributions of authorship of books of the Bible, and the authenticity of some passages, including ones which I quote. But for my purposes this is neither here nor there. A few way-out radicals anticipated the higher criticism; but as far as we know they were statistically insignificant.

For this book I have read widely but not very systematically. If I still had fifty years to spend on serious study of sermons, Biblical commentaries and theological treatises, I might – just – be able to cover the ground. But as I have not, I have done the best I can on the basis of many years of desultory general reading in and around the subject.

I had the good fortune to be a member of the group under whose auspices it was proposed to reprint a number of seventeenth-century pamphlets. We did not get very far, but the Fast Sermons preached to Parliament in the 1640s were admirably edited in thirty-four volumes by Robin Jeffs and published in 1970–71. They stood me in good stead for Chapter 3 and elsewhere in the present volume. My other reading has tended to be in Puritan and radical writings, and Anglican commentaries on the Puritan wing. For my purposes the more traditional views of Catholics and high Anglicans seemed less relevant.

I tried out some of my ideas in a Tanner Lecture which I was honoured to be invited to give at the University of Michigan, Ann Arbor, in October 1991. I much benefited from discussions there, especially with Cynthia Herrup. I have enjoyed the help of many other friends. Professor Peter Hinchliff of Christ Church guided my reading on Biblical history. Marcus Rediker of the University of Pittsburgh saw the relevance to my theme of Liberation Theology today, and introduced me to the literature. Professor Onofrio Nicastro of the University of Pisa generously let me read the typescript of a paper on 'Usi Radicali della Bibbia nella Rivoluzione Inglese' given at a conference in Modena in September 1988. Frank Bremer kindly sent me papers given at the 1991 Millersville University Conference on Puritanism in Old and New England, which I was unfortunately unable to attend; and he allowed me to read in typescript his own forthcoming book, *The Congregational Connection: Friendship and Religion among the 17th-Century Clergy in the Atlantic Community*. From all of these I learnt a great deal. David Daniell gave of his time to read and correct several pages on the subject of his special expertise, the history of the English Bible in the sixteenth century. Robin Clifton generously read the whole book in proof, and spotted many errors.

I have tried to acknowledge specific debts in footnotes. But I have received help from Simon Adams, Valentine Boss, Norman O. Brown, Norah Carlin, Patricia Crawford, the late Margot Heinemann, Tim Hitchcock, Gerald MacLean, Steve Mason, David Norbrook, Tatiana Pavlova, Ivan Roots, Raphael Samuel, Valerie Taylor, Joan Thirsk and Elizabeth Tuttle. I have depended greatly on the work of classics like Perry Miller, W. K. Jordan, Arnold Williams and G. H. Williams. As always seems to be the case when I take up what is for me a new subject, I found myself continually treading in the footsteps of that great historian L. B. Wright. Among contemporary English historians whose work I have found particularly helpful is Bernard Capp, a writer no less versatile than Louis Wright. David Underdown's splendid *Fire from Heaven: Life in an English Town in the Seventeenth Century* unfortunately appeared too late for me to profit by its many insights into the complex links between Biblical religion and society.

Jo Whitfield proved a swift but sure typist, even when confronted with my illegible hieroglyphics: it is entirely thanks to her that I very nearly finished on schedule. Julia Hore and the office staff of Balliol College were continuously generous with help on all occasions, beyond any call of duty. It is also time that I paid tribute to the hard-pressed staff of the Bodleian Library for considerate service over many years.

Peter Carson of Penguin Books gave generous and encouraging support. Judith Flanders was the perfect copy-editor — well-informed, wise and patient. I owe a great deal to her supportive tolerance.

My greatest debt is as always to Bridget, who also was brought up in a Bible-reading family. She gave constant knowledgeable advice, help and encouragement. She read much of the book at various stages of its evolution, corrected my spelling, pointed out my repetitions, restrained my enthusiasms and verbosity and helped with the drudgery of indexing. She, like the others whom I have thanked, is not to blame for what emerged; but without her it would have been far longer and far worse.

I have observed the usual conventions. Seventeenth-century spelling, capitalization and punctuation have been modernized except in titles of books. Place of publication of books is London unless otherwise indicated. In Biblical quotations I have normally used the Geneva Bible, which I believe was more widely used among radicals than the A.V. But in non-controversial passages there is rarely much difference between the two versions: the A.V. normally took over the Geneva wording, just as the Geneva translators had followed Tyndale. I originally intended to give full Biblical references for what I regard as being key names and words — Cain and Abel, idols and groves, wilderness and garden, covenant, idolatry and the millennium. But this would have taken up too much space: the interested reader can find them for himself with the help of a concordance.

6 September 1992   C.H.

Abbreviations

===

The following abbreviations have been used in the notes:

A.V.   Authorized Version of the Bible
BMW   John Bunyan, *Miscellaneous Works* (Oxford U.P., 13
                vols., 1976–)
CSPD   *Calendar of State Papers, Domestic*
DNB   *Dictionary of National Biography*
EHR   *English Historical Review*
FS   *Fast Sermons to Parliament*, November 1640–April 1653
                (ed. Robin Jeffs, Cornmarket Press, 34 vols., 1970–71)
HMC   Historical Manuscripts Commission
Millersville   Papers delivered at the 1991 Millersville University
                Conference on Puritanism in Old and New England
MCPW   *Complete Prose Works of John Milton* (Yale U.P.,
                1953–82)
MER   C. Hill, *Milton and the English Revolution* (1977)
Offor   *The Works of John Bunyan* (ed. G. Offor, 3 vols., 1860)
OED   *Oxford English Dictionary*
P. and P.   *Past and Present*
PL   Milton, *Paradise Lost*
PP   Bunyan, *The Pilgrim's Progress*
PR   Milton, *Paradise Regained*
Sabine   *Works of Gerrard Winstanley* (ed. G. H. Sabine, Cornell
                U.P., 1941)
TRDM   Keith Thomas, *Religion and the Decline of Magic* (1971)
TRHS   *Transactions of the Royal Historical Society*
U.P.   University Press

Some Dates

This book assumes a narrative of events in Great Britain between the Reformation under Henry VIII and the end of the seventeenth century. The following dates may help the reader to keep this narrative in mind when I sometimes make confusing leaps. For the same reason I have normally given dates of publication for sixteenth- and seventeenth-century books quoted.

1509–47	Henry VIII, King of England.
1526–34	William Tyndale's translation of the New Testament into English.
1529–36	Reformation Parliament.
1547–53	Edward VI, King of England. Attempted conquest of Scotland.
1553–8	Mary I, Queen of England, married to Philip II of Spain. Catholicism restored, heretics burned.
1558–1603	Elizabeth I, Queen of England. Protestantism restored.
1560	The Geneva Bible.
1563	John Foxe's *Book of Martyrs*.
1567–8	Mary Stuart, Queen of Scots, deposed and flees to England.
1568	The Bishops' Bible.
1575–83	Edmund Grindal, Archbishop of Canterbury.
1583–1604	John Whitgift, Archbishop of Canterbury.
1587	Mary Queen of Scots executed in England.
1588	The Spanish Armada.
1589–90	The Marprelate Tracts.
1603–25	James VI of Scotland becomes James I, King of England: union of crowns.

1604–10	Richard Bancroft, Archbishop of Canterbury.
5 November 1605	Gunpowder Plot.
1610–33	George Abbot, Archbishop of Canterbury.
1611	Authorized Version of the Bible.
1618–48	Thirty Years War.
1624	Prince Charles marries Princess Henrietta Maria of France.
1628	The Petition of Right.
1629–40	Personal government of Charles I. No Parliaments.
1633–45	William Laud, Archbishop of Canterbury.
1634–9	Ship Money collected without authority of Parliament.
1638	Scottish National Covenant.
1639–40	War between England and Scotland.
April – May 1640	The Short Parliament.
November 1640 – April 1653	The Long Parliament.
May 1641	Execution of the Earl of Strafford.
1641	Abolition of Star Chamber and High Commission Courts.
November 1641	Revolt in Ireland.
1642–5	First Civil War.
September 1643	Solemn League and Covenant between England and Scotland.
January 1645	Execution of Archbishop Laud.
June 1645	Battle of Naseby.
June 1646	Charles I surrenders.
October 1646	Abolition of episcopacy.
1647	The New Model Army intervenes in politics, occupying London.
1648	Second Civil War.
December 1648	Army purges Parliament; the Rump of the Long Parliament orders the trial of Charles I as a traitor.
January 1649	Trial and execution of Charles I.
1649–60	The Commonwealth.
May 1649	Cromwell suppresses revolt at Burford.

1649	Cromwellian conquest of Ireland.
1650–51	Suppression of Diggers and Ranters.
1650	Compulsory attendance at parish church abolished.
October 1651	The Navigation Act – leads to
1652–4	War between England and The Netherlands.
1652	Union of England and Scotland.
April 1653	Cromwell expels the Rump of the Long Parliament.
July – December 1653	Barebones Parliament.
December 1653 – September 1658	Oliver Cromwell, Lord Protector.
1655	War against Spain. Conquest of Jamaica and Dunkirk.
September 1658 – May 1659 1658	Richard Cromwell, Lord Protector.
May 1659	Rump of Long Parliament restored.
1660	Restoration of Charles II, bishops and censorship. Star Chamber and High Commission not restored. Dissenters excluded from Church of England. Union of England and Scotland dissolved.
1661	Navigation Act confirmed.
1672	Declaration of Indulgence to Catholics and Protestant dissenters.
1678–81	Popish Plot: attempt to exclude James Duke of York from the succession. Temporary relaxation of censorship.
1685	James II, King of England. Monmouth's rebellion.
November 1688–9	James II replaced by William III, King of England, 1689–1702.
1689	Toleration Act.
1695	Licensing Act lapses.
1707	Union of England and Scotland.

I. INTRODUCTION

1. A Biblical Culture

Our holy prelates [say that God's Word] causeth insurrection and teacheth the people to disobey, . . . and moveth them to rise against their princes, and to make all common, and to make havoc of other men's goods.

William Tyndale, *The Obedience of a Christian Man* (1528), in *Doctrinal Treatises* (ed. H. Walter, Parker Soc., Cambridge U.P., 1848), p. 163.

> The Bible; that's the Book. The Book indeed,
>   The Book of Books;
>   On which who looks,
> As he should do aright, shall never need
>   Wish for a better light
>   To guide him in the night. . . .
>
> God's cabinet of reveal'd counsel 'tis;
>   Where weal and woe
>   Are ordered so
> That every man may know.
>   Nor can he be mistook
>   That speaketh by this Book.
>
> It is the Book of God. What if I should
>   Say, god of books?

Christopher Harvey, *Complete Poems* (ed. A. B. Grosart, 1874), pp. 19–21. This poem first published 1640.

> Richard Gloucester –
>   But then I sigh; and, with a piece of Scripture,
>   Tell them that God bids us do good for evil:
>   And thus I clothe my naked villainy
>   With odd old ends, stol'n forth of Holy Writ.

Shakespeare, *The Tragedy of King Richard III*, Act I, sc. iii.[1]

1. Similar examples of hypocritical use of the Bible abound in Marlowe's plays.

I

The story is told of an exchange between the legendary economic historian Jack Fisher and an importunate pupil who was pressing him for a reading list on sixteenth- and seventeenth-century English economic history. He said 'If you really want to understand the period, go away and read the Bible.'[2] The advice was no doubt especially appropriate for economic historians, but it has its relevance for political and literary historians too. The Bible was central to the whole of the life of the society: we ignore it at our peril.

The Bible is a large book, and most of the innumerable Biblical commentaries of the period, as I have learnt to my cost, appear to be as long as the Bible itself. I cannot claim to have read every word of all of them. This book focuses on a few areas in which the Bible was directly influential in matters other than – in the modern sense – the strictly religious. It is a collection of essays rather than a monograph. My object is to consider the impact of the Bible on seventeenth-century society – its use for political and other purposes, and its unforeseen effects on literature, political theory, social relations, agriculture and colonization, among other matters.

The vernacular Bible became an institution in Tudor England – the foundation of monarchical authority, of England's protestant independence, the text-book of morality and social subordination. Its centrality made it the battle-ground of several ideologies – English nationalist versus Roman Catholic, episcopalian versus presbyterian and sectarian. Society was in turmoil, and the Bible was expected to supply solutions for pressing problems. Translation of the Bible into English had made it available to new and far wider social groups than hitherto, including artisans and women, and they read their own problems and solutions into the sacred text. Consequently, in this book I am dealing with opinions and beliefs as well as 'facts'. So I have not hesitated to use literary evidence to tell us about opinions and beliefs. Such evidence varies, and needs to be critically assessed. But its existence is a fact.

The Bible was not monolithic – far from it. The accepted canon has been built up over the centuries; it incorporates many different and sometimes conflicting ideas and attitudes. The first two chapters of Genesis contain two different stories of the creation and fall, which it taxed scholarly ingenuity to reconcile; the books of Moses were not written by Moses, as

2. Negley Harte, 'In Memory of F. J. Fisher', in Fisher, *London and the English Economy, 1500–1700* (ed. P. J. Corfield and N. B. Harte, 1990), p. 28.

Thomas Hobbes showed in the seventeenth century,[3] nor the Psalms of David by David. The prophecy of Isaiah is a compilation of the works of at least three poets. The text is a palimpsest, which has been over-written and re-written in ways that modern scholars find very difficult to sort out. The re-writing of what we call the Old Testament almost certainly reflects political and social conflicts among the children of Israel; the canon was established by the Jewish priesthood. The text itself shows that prophets and kings were often at odds; the Bible's assessment of individual rulers usually reflects the values of the priestly editors.

The New Testament narrative is the product of a social upheaval. The canon as we know it was the end-product of bitter controversies over what was 'heretical' and therefore 'apocryphal', what orthodox. This canon evolved over centuries, as the original doctrines of Christianity were adapted first to the Graeco-Roman culture of the Gentile world, then to the acceptance of Christianity as the official religion of the Roman Empire. Decisions on what should be included and what excluded were fierce and sometimes bloody. Compromises were inevitable. Should the radical Epistle attributed to James be part of the canon? Should the explosive Revelation of St John the divine? The unity of the two Testaments was laboriously created by theologians of the Middle Ages, working on their palimpsest.

The Bible could mean different things to different people at different times, in different circumstances. It was a huge bran-tub from which anything might be drawn. There are few ideas in whose support a Biblical text cannot be found. Much could be read into and between the lines. When Luther challenged the Roman church's authority to define doctrine, and produced his own vernacular translation, he had to accept that 'the Gospel cannot be truly preached without offence and tumult'. 'The Word of God comes, whenever it comes, to change and renew the world'.[4] The result was disagreement and fragmentation. Lutherans against Zwinglians and Calvinists, Anabaptists and libertines against all the respectable – each group of heretics thought they found justification for their positions in the sacred text; nearly all proclaimed the over-riding authority of the Bible.

The Bible is one thing in a stable society, with an accepted machinery for controlling its interpretation. Control was never complete at any period – certainly not after the upset of the Reformation and the translation of the Scriptures from a language which only scholars could read and understand

3. R. Lane Fox, *The Unauthorized Version: Truth and Fiction in the Bible* (1991), p. 96.
4. *Selections from Luther's Table Talk* (trans. H. Bell, 1892), p. 133; *Luther and Erasmus: Free Will and Salvation* (ed. E. G. Rupp and others, 1969), p. 129.

into vernaculars which could be read by all the literate, and understood by all who heard them read aloud. Some mediaeval heresies – often based on unauthorized translations of the Bible – survived because they became associated with political units which established a precarious continuity – Waldensians, Hussites, Lollards in England.

Henry VIII was mainly concerned to secure England's political independence from the papacy when he authorized translation of the Bible into English. After the trauma of Mary's reign, something like consensus appeared to exist under Elizabeth. But in the turmoil of the seventeenth century, the Bible became a sword to divide, or rather an armoury from which all parties selected weapons to meet their needs. And what an armoury! The great advantage of the Bible was that it could be quoted to make unorthodox or unpopular points. The Greek and Roman classics were sometimes cited to similar effect, because they were recognized as impeccable authorities difficult to refute and yet which it was unwise merely to reject. But knowledge of the classics was restricted to learned scholars, or at any rate men of some education; the Bible in the vernacular was open to all, even the lower classes, to pillage and utilize.

In seventeenth-century England, a century of revolution and civil war, all parties appealed to the Bible for support. Heresy hunters like Thomas Edwards and Ephraim Pagitt pointed to similarities between the heresies of their time and those of the early church, but these similarities were rarely the consequence of antiquarian research by the heretics, though some no doubt inherited traditions from Cathars, Waldensians and Lollards. Seventeenth-century radicals claimed to find their ideas in the Bible. And they were right. All heresy originates from the Bible, because the Bible itself is a compilation, a compromise; orthodoxy changes as it incorporates or over-reacts against a heresy – which itself originated from the Biblical text.

Milton, and very many others like him, believed that – given free discussion – agreed truth would emerge among honest and fair-minded Christians; and he spent many years of his life compiling the Bible-based *De Doctrina Christiana* (*Of Christian Doctrine*) aimed at reuniting all protestants. What he produced was so radically heretical that it could not be published in England, even in Latin, and when attempts were made after his death to publish it in The Netherlands the whole power of British diplomacy was brought to bear to prevent it. It shattered the idea of a single Biblical truth acceptable to the rulers of his country.

Milton's *Of Christian Doctrine*,[5] his 'dearest and best possession', is

5. Henceforth I shall refer to it by its English title.

symbolic. The Latin text languished for 150 years among state papers in the Record Office. It was finally published, in 1825, on the orders of the King of England, translated by a Bishop of the Anglican church; and its publication excited only mild historical interest. The dynamite of the mid-seventeenth century had become a damp squib. The Bible was no longer the source of all truth; the eighteenth-century Enlightenment had virtually ignored it. Nor was it any longer the revolutionists' handbook. French revolutionaries relied on secular philosophers like Voltaire and Rousseau. My book is in one sense about the decline and fall of the political and *cultural* empire of the Bible in seventeenth-century England.

II

The Bible played a large part in moulding English nationalism, in asserting the supremacy of the English language in a society which from the eleventh to the fourteenth century had been dominated by French-speaking Normans. The translation of the Bible into English coincided in time with the spread of the new invention of printing. The printed vernacular Bible was something very different from the manuscript Vulgate, the private property of the clergy. As George Hakewill put it, books formerly imprisoned in the libraries of monasteries 'were redeemed from bondage, obtained their enlargement, and freely walked about in the light'.[6] The vernacular Bible was the property of all the literate laity, and radical protestant preachers made a point of trying to extend knowledge of it to all levels of society. By the seventeenth century the Bible was accepted as central to all spheres of intellectual life: it was not merely a 'religious' book in our narrow modern sense of the word religion. Church and state in Tudor England were one; the Bible was, or should be, the foundation of all aspects of English culture. On this principle most protestants were agreed. If we do not grasp this we shall fall into the anachronistic trap of speaking of 'a more religious age' than our own. In many senses it was a less religious age than ours.

Historians often comment on the fact that the English Revolution had no ideological forebears. None of the participants knew that what they

6. Hakewill, *An Apologie or Declaration of the Power and Providence of God in the Government of the World* (3rd., revised, ed., 1635), p. 316. First published 1627. For Hakewill see also pp. 349–50 below.

were living through was a revolution. The word was to acquire its modern meaning only in and because of the English Revolution,[7] the first great European revolution. American revolutionaries consciously looked back to seventeenth-century English experience, described by Catharine Macaulay in her eight-volume history – to Hampden, Milton, Marvell, Nedham, Sidney. Mirabeau organized a French translation of Catharine Macaulay's *History*, which had been studied equally carefully by leaders of the American revolution, many of whom corresponded with her.[8] Girondins and Jacobins, Mensheviks and Bolsheviks, regicide and republic, fitted into the pattern set by the English Revolution. French revolutionaries feared the advent of a Cromwell, and they got Napoleon; Russian revolutionaries worried about Bonapartism, military dictatorship, and did not notice Stalin creeping up from within.

Englishmen had to face totally unexpected revolutionary situations in the 1640s and 1650s, with no theoretical guidance such as Rousseau and Marx gave to their French and Russian successors, and no experience of any previous event that had been called a revolution. They had to improvise. The Bible in English was the book to which they naturally turned for guidance. It was God's Word, whose authority no one could reject. And it was central to the inheritance of the protestant English nation. It was available in print only because of the conflicts and martyrdoms of the English reformation, an essential part of the Revolution's pre-history.

The first recorded use of English in a government proclamation occurred in 1258, when Simon de Montfort controlled King Henry III. Official use of the vernacular died with Simon and his cause.[9] But the language had not died. As early as 1801 George Ellis noted connections between the development of the English language and the rise of towns.[10] The oldest piece of Parliamentarian English known is a petition from the Mercers' Company to Parliament, dating from 1386. By this time grammar schools were dropping French and teaching in English. Gentlemen had stopped teaching their children French. Private legal documents in English survive

---

7. See my 'The Word "Revolution"' in *A Nation of Change and Novelty: Radical Politics, Religion and Literature in Seventeenth-century England* (1990).
8. For Catharine Macaulay and the American and French Revolutions, as well as for her influence on English radicalism, see Bridget Hill, *The Republican Virago: The Life and Times of Catharine Macaulay, Historian* (Oxford U.P., 1992). I am much indebted to discussion with her.
9. I rely here on Basil Cottle's valuable book, *The Triumph of English, 1350–1400* (1969), p. 15.
10. Ellis, *Specimens of the Early English Poets*, I, pp. 76–81.

from the same period, wills and documents of city gilds from the late 1380s. Henry IV – an usurper – spoke English as his first language; and Shakespeare was right to show Henry V as having little French. Perhaps Shakespeare was reproducing something he had overheard when he made Jack Cade say 'he can speak French, and therefore he is a traitor'. He 'speaks with the tongue of an enemy'.[11]

Richard Rolle, the first significant poet to write in what is recognizably English, died in 1349; religious lyrics in English proliferate from the second half of the century. English literature appears in a rush, all at once – Chaucer, Langland, Gower, the poet of *Gawain and the Green Knight* and *Pearl*. Exactly contemporary is John Wyclif – a theologian who aggressively used English when Latin would have been more traditional.[12] The Hundred Years War against France no doubt accelerated the switch to English. No French vernacular version of the Bible circulated in England, though some did in France. Bible-reading was associated with the rise of an educated urban and rural middling sort: we meet with Lollard merchants and Lollard knights. Chaucer knew his Bible well. The Lollard Nicholas Hereford proposed that the wealth of the Church should be used to found fifteen universities and a hundred almshouses – an educational hope that revived in the sixteenth-century Reformation and again during the seventeenth-century Revolution.[13] John Rastell in 1527 observed that Henry VII had ruled that 'statutes and ordinances . . . made for the commonwealth of this realm in his days' should be printed, so that 'the people . . . might soon have the knowledge of the said statutes and ordinances which they were bound to observe'. Henry VIII followed his father's practice. Rastell translated from the French *The Abbreviation of the Statutes*, published before Henry VII's reign. For he knew that 'the universal people of this realm had great pleasure and gave themselves greatly to the reading of the vulgar English tongue'. If the statutes could be published so that people might 'avoid the danger and penalties of the same', why not the Bible?[14]

John Foxe attributed 'this gift of printing' to direct divine intervention. He quoted the Catholic Rowland Phillips in Henry VIII's reign: 'either we

11. *II Henry VI*, sc. ii; Cottle, op. cit., pp. 17–22.
12. Cottle, op. cit., pp. 23–4, 169, 221; cf. Anne Hudson, *The Premature Reformation: Wycliffite Texts and Lollard History* (Oxford U.P., 1988), esp. Chapter 2.
13. Cottle, op. cit., pp. 222, 226, 267.
14. Rastell, *An Abridgment of the Statutes*, quoted in *The Thought and Culture of the English Renaissance: An Anthology of Tudor Prose. 1481–1555* (ed. E. M. Nugent, Cambridge U.P., 1956), pp. 173–5.

must root out printing, or printing will root out us'.[15] Thomas Beard, Oliver Cromwell's mentor and friend, followed Foxe in seeing divine Providence behind the coincidence in time of the invention and development of the printing press and the translation of the Bible into English.[16] For John Preston the invention of printing was an additional proof of the existence of God, of his care for his creatures. Freedom of printing, Henry Robinson observed, had made possible both the Reformation and wider concepts of religious liberty.[17] For more than a century before Henry VIII's reign Lollards had been circulating manuscript versions of the Scriptures. They found profoundly subversive messages in the Bible. Lowly social elements gathered furtively in illegal groups to hear the vernacular Bible read and discussed. Among them perhaps God's word struck its deepest roots.

Wyclif justified his opposition to the temporal possessions of the church by the commandment 'thou shalt not steal'.[18] For him the Bible was the key to human understanding of truth; hence all laymen had a right and a duty to study it for themselves.[19] In the fifteenth century the mere fact of owning and reading the Bible in English was presumptive evidence of heresy. The church indeed seems to have been more worried about vernacular translations, and more severe in rooting them out, in England than elsewhere in Europe, except perhaps in Bohemia. Bale knew of vernacular Bibles in Brabant, Holland, Flanders, France, Spain, Italy and other countries.[20]

Many of those who engaged in the dangerous work of translating the Bible in the early sixteenth century became martyrs – Tyndale, John Rogers, Cranmer. Tyndale, whose superb version would be better known if he had survived to become an Edwardian bishop, declared that it was 'impossible to establish the lay people in any truth, except the Scriptures were plainly laid before their eyes in their mother tongue'.[21] He was financed by merchants whilst translating the Bible, and he anticipated the

15. Foxe, *Acts and Monuments* (ed. J. Pratt, n.d.), III, pp. 718–21; cf. IV, pp. 252–3. See also W. Haller, *Foxe's Book of Martyrs and the Elect Nation* (1963), p. 180.

16. Beard, *Antichrist, the Pope of Rome* (1625), pp. 181–2.

17. Preston, *Life Eternall* (4th ed., 1634), pp. 10–13; [Robinson], *John the Baptist, precursor of Christ Jesus: Or, a necessity for liberty of conscience* (1644), p. 74.

18. Ann Hudson, op. cit., p. 4.

19. M. Keen, 'Wyclif, the Bible and Transubstantiation', in *Wyclif in his Times* (ed. A. Kenny, Oxford U.P., 1986), pp. 3–4.

20. Bale, *The Image of Both Churches* (1550) in *Select Works* (Parker Soc., 1849), p. 336.

21. Quoted in *The Bible in its Ancient and English Versions* (ed. H. Wheeler Robinson, Oxford U.P., 1940), p. 156.

opposition of the clerical establishment: 'A thousand books had they lever to be put forth against their abominable doings and doctrine, than that the Scripture should come to light'.[22] Tyndale's analysis was confirmed from the opposite point of view by the Cornish rebels of 1549, who demanded that the English Bible should be called in, 'otherwise the clergy shall not of long time confound the heretics'.[23] The Roman church came to recognize that since it could not suppress English translations it must compete: the Rheims New Testament appeared in 1582, because 'divers things are either profitable and medicinable now, that otherwise in the peace of the church were neither much requisite nor perchance wholly tolerable'.[24]

The availability of the Bible in English was a great stimulus to learning to read; and this in its turn assisted the development of cheap printing and the distribution of books. It was a cultural revolution of unprecedented proportions, whose consequences are difficult to over-estimate.[25] Direct access to the sacred text gave a sense of assurance to laymen which they had previously lacked, and so fortified long-standing criticisms of the church and its clergy.[26] Henry VIII soon found it necessary to abolish 'diversity of opinions' by Act of Parliament, not very successfully. Women (except noblewomen and gentlewomen), artisans, husbandmen, labourers or servants were forbidden to read the New Testament, or to discuss it in public. Early reformers like Tyndale were well aware of the importance of widening the social area of theological discussion – though it is worth recalling that even at the end of the seventeenth century Richard Baxter said that the 'rabble' of 'tinkers and sow-gauters and crate-carriers and bargemen' never read the Bible at all.[27]

We might usefully ponder the economics of printing. Tyndale's New Testament cost 3/- – not a small sum. But manuscript Lollard Testaments had cost from seven to eighteen times as much.[28] That was a revolution.

22. Tyndale, Preface to *The Five Books of Moses* (1530), in *Doctrinal Treatises*, pp. 393–4.
23. F. Rose-Troup, *The Western Rebellion of 1549* (1913), p. 221; cf. Foxe, op. cit., IV, pp. 225, 239, VI, pp. 723–4.
24. Preface to the Rheims New Testament, quoted in *Records of the English Bible* (ed. A. W. Pollard, Oxford U.P., 1911), p. 302.
25. See Elizabeth Eisenstein, *The Printing Press as an agent of change* (Cambridge U.P., 1979), *passim*; S. Greenblatt. *Renaissance Self-Fashioning: From More to Shakespeare* (1980), Chapter II; Joseph Martin, *Religious Radicals in Tudor England* (1989), *passim*.
26. Martin, op. cit., pp. 71–3, cf. pp. 14–15 below.
27. Baxter, *The Poor Husbandman's Advocate to Rich Racking Landlords* (ed. F. J. Powicke, Bulletin of the John Rylands Library, 10, 1926), p. 182.
28. D. Zaret, *The Heavenly Contract: Ideology and Organization in Pre-Revolutionary Puritanism* (Chicago U.P., 1985), p. 35.

And once it had started, it was unstoppable. Professor Eisenstein has brilliantly demonstrated the stimulus which printing gave to anti-clericalism: what had been muttered in ale-houses could now be read by anybody. Indulgences for sins were *printed*: the fact that they brought substantial profits to entrepreneurs shocked serious believers. Lutheran attacks on indulgences were printed too: religious controversy was forced out into the open. Luther's sales would delight a modern pulp novelist.

The Reformation and the rise of free towns went together, with printing as the link. Printers, publishing both for the home market and for export, made vast – and new – profits – for example the Antwerp printer of Tyndale's New Testament. Geneva's main export was printed books, mostly written by religious refugees, who thus more than paid for their acceptance. Nor were printers too choosy about what they were now free to print: Sarpi had his *History of the Council of Trent* (1621) printed in Geneva, and it was reprinted in other protestant regions. 'From the days of Castellio to ... Voltaire, the printing industry was the principal natural ally of libertine, heterodox and oecumenical philosophers.' Small protestant countries, anxious to expand their markets, now had nothing to fear from the repressive power of Rome.[29]

Professor Eisenstein is right to see this as a cultural revolution. She quotes the utopian pamphlet *Macaria*, published by the Hartlib circle in 1641: 'The art of printing will so spread knowledge that the common people, knowing their own rights and liberties, will not be governed by way of oppression, and so, little by little, all kingdoms will be like to Macaria' – i.e. will be utopian.[30] That was only slightly premature in 1641.

In the long run there were also economic consequences for writers. Professor Eisenstein remarks that Erasmus showed how men of letters could be emancipated from client status, though it took a century and a half before any but the most eminent could win such freedom. Thanks to printing, Professor Eisenstein points out, there could be reform movements even among Catholics without waiting for papal permission to form a new order or to reform an old one, without even having to go and lobby the authorities in Rome. Theology was now open to the laity, from Calvin to Bunyan. Printing stimulated accurate scholarship, first Biblical, then scientific.[31] The Council of Trent's decision that the Vulgate was the only authoritative version could not be maintained.

29. Eisenstein, op. cit., I, pp. 404–19. I owe Tyndale's printer to David Daniell.
30. Ibid., I, p. 305.
31. Ibid., I, pp. 401–2; II, p. 568: Joan Simon, *Education and Society in Tudor England* (Cambridge U.P., 1966), pp. 56–8.

Quarrels between protestants and catholics, and between protestants, intensified the move back to the Bible, to question the accuracy of its text, and so stimulated a great wave of Biblical scholarship. William Bradshaw in his *English Puritanisme* (1605) insisted that Biblical scholars 'ought to follow those rules only that are followed in finding out the meaning of other writings': no more allegorizing, no more interpretation of the text in the light of ecclesiastical tradition.[32] The *Treatise of the Corruptions of Scripture* (1612) by Thomas James, Bodley's first Librarian, was a landmark here. Since the Bible was the ultimate arbiter, an authoritative text must be established by the severest scholarly tests. The authority of the Fathers, to which Romanists appealed, could be disregarded. James denounced all '*indices expurgatorii*', and is said to have used the papal Index to help him to decide which books to buy for the Bodleian Library.[33] James's penetrating analysis of texts and exposure of forgeries ultimately contributed to undermining confidence in the Bible's authority.

I find myself in agreement here with Elizabeth Eisenstein, against the conclusions of Gillian Brennan's article 'Patriotism, Language and Power: English Translations of the Bible, 1520–1580'. The latter wants us to think of 'a split in the intellectual élite between the conservatives who wanted to preserve their monopoly of access to knowledge through the use of classical languages; and the progressive thinkers who realized that it would be easier to control the ideas of the masses [*sic*] by using the vernacular'. This seems to me to be carrying the recent obsession with the links between literature and power to absurdity. I do not think that those 'progressive thinkers' who risked, and often sacrificed, their lives in order to put the vernacular Bible before their countrymen were primarily concerned with 'the manipulation of language as a form of power'.[34] *After the event*, after seeing what ordinary people got out of the vernacular Bible, many like Luther came to think that catechizing by ministers was safer than unrestricted Bible-reading. But there would be no point in translating the Bible *in order to* control a restless population. That there was a demand for an English Bible is one of the facts of the case, and must be explained in terms of social and economic developments since Wyclif's time. But Tyndale was hardly a

---

32. I cite from the 1640 reprint, p. 16. Cf. John Jewel, *An Apology of the Church of England* (Parker Soc., 1848), pp. 86–90: first published 1564.
33. James, op. cit. (Parker Soc., 1843), pp. 1–74, 233–315, 327. Cf. William Whitaker, *A Disputation on Holy Scripture against the Papists* (Parker Soc., 1849), *passim*: first published 1588.
34. Brenner, op. cit., in *History Workshop Journal* 27 (1989), pp. 32–3; cf. Eisenstein, op. cit., I, pp. 362–3.

calculating politician. We should not read back into the minds of early reformers considerations which occurred to some of their successors only after a generation or two of experience.

III

For Catholics images had been the books of the illiterate. Protestants and printers demonstrated that more people could be taught to read: and so created a new culture[35] and a new interest in popular education, both in the educators and in those to be educated. 'We allure the people to read and to hear God's Word', wrote Bishop Jewel. 'We lean unto knowledge, they [Catholics] unto ignorance'.[36] But later bishops lost this confidence. 'Error', wrote Joseph Hall under Charles I, 'that could but creep then [before the Reformation] doth now fly'. 'We might learn of our wise adversaries, that guide the helm of the Roman church' and straitly enjoin silence.[37] As late as 1643 Francis Cheynell thought 'it were better to confute Socinianism in Latin' rather than in English. But on second thoughts he recognized that by then it was too late to prevent the common people reading theological controversies.[38] Andrew Marvell, writing after the experience of the Revolution, ironically imagined a future bishop telling himself that 'the press . . . hath done much more mischief to the discipline of our church than all the doctrine can make amends for. 'Twas an happy time when all learning was in manuscript, and some little officer, like our author [Samuel Parker], did keep the keys of the library . . . . But now . . . a man cannot write a book, but presently he is answered . . . . There have been ways found out to banish ministers' (and to ban meetings of popular congregations), 'but no art yet could prevent these seditious meetings of let-ters'.[39]

The Elizabethan *Homily against Disobedience and Wilful Rebellion* had contrasted papal determination to keep 'specially the common sort' in ignorance with the availability of the vernacular Bible in England.[40] John

35. Eisenstein, op. cit., I, pp. 66–7.
36. Jewel, op. cit., pp. 92–3.
37. Joseph Hall, *Works* (Oxford U.P., 1837–9), VII, pp. 90, 102.
38. Cheynell, *The Rise, Growth and Danger of Socinianism*, quoted in H. J. McLachlan, *Socinianism in Seventeenth-Century England* (Oxford U.P., 1951), pp. 106–7.
39. Marvell, *The Rehearsal Transpros'd* (ed. D. I. Smith, Oxford U.P., 1971), pp. 4–5: first published 1672.
40. *Homilies* (Oxford U.P., 1802), pp. 507–8.

Jewel elaborated: 'unless thou know thou canst not judge: unless thou hear both sides, thou canst not know'.[41] 'When God gave [Adam] reason, he gave him freedom to choose, for reason is but choosing', said Milton in *Areopagitica*, demanding liberty of the press on political as well as religious grounds.[42] Bishop Jewel also declared that the authority of the Bible was above that of a General Council of the Church, was the ultimate interpreter in disputed doctrinal questions.[43] He did not say who was to interpret the Bible.

Popular Bible-reading alarmed conservatives. St Thomas More in 1530 said that it was a 'pestilential heresy' to suppose that 'we should believe nothing but plain Scripture'.[44] Henry VIII complained to Parliament in 1546 that the Bible was 'disputed, rhymed, sung and jangled in every alehouse and tavern'.[45] Ivan Roots's epigram, that the Reformation started in the ale-houses of England, expresses a necessary truth.[46] Where else could ordinary people meet for discussion?

The printing explosion during the relative freedom from censorship of Edward VI's reign enabled protestantism and religious discussion to establish themselves in England. 'Printing put more and more people in direct contact with the Bible', Joseph Martin sums up. The Biblical sophistication of the lower-class Marian martyrs is one of the most remarkable things about them. They took on bishops and scholars, out-argued and out-texted them. The memory of this did not easily die. Martin has shown that under the brief Marian reaction Roman Catholic artisans published their views for others to read.[47] But, on the whole, defence of the old religion was left to the clergy, and in Mary's reign to suppression. It then perhaps still seemed possible that printing might be rooted out in England. John Standish's *Discourse where it is debated whether it be expedient that the Scriptures should be in English for al men to read at wyll* (1554) emphasized the *social* consequences of uncontrolled Bible-reading. Lay preachers 'in corners and

41. Jewel, *A Defence of the Apology of the Church of England* (1567), in *Works* (Parker Soc., 1848), III, p. 122.
42. *MCPW*, II, p. 527.
43. Jewel, *Works*, III, pp. 93, 173.
44. More, *Dialogue against Luther and Tyndale*, quoted in *Thought and Culture of the English Renaissance*, p. 441.
45. Quoted by H. Wheeler Robinson, *The Bible in its Ancient and English Versions* (Oxford U.P., 1940), p. 180.
46. I was unable to trace this reference. Nor could Professor Roots help me, though he accepted the attribution.
47. Martin, op. cit., pp. 4–5, 112–13; cf. his 'Miles Hogarth: Artisan and Aspiring Author in Sixteenth-Century England', *Renaissance Quarterly*, XXXIV (1981), *passim*.

conventicles' would set man against wife, master against servant and vice versa. Women 'have taken upon them the office of teaching'; servants have become 'stubborn, froward, and disobedient to their masters and mistresses'.[48] Now soldiers and serving-men can talk so much of Scripture, complained a character in the protestant Anthony Gilby's *Pleasant Dialogue* (1566), that they are no longer respectful to their betters.[49]

Objections to popular Bible-reading long survived. The Tudor church strove hard to build up a nation-wide network of parish ministers capable of meeting the new demand for preaching. Their existence would also serve a police purpose, since through them the authorities 'might truly know within a short time by name who and how many enemies there are . . . to religion and the commonwealth'. The Puritan Laurence Chaderton, preaching on Romans XII, stressed the espionage potential of a clergy loyal to the government.[50]

The Bible in English could not be abolished; but for the century after the Reformation, the Anglican church did its best to smother the revolutionary message which some English men and women read into it. Elizabeth's Archbishop Whitgift did not conceal his dislike of the practice of reading and expounding the Bible in the home, especially when outsiders were present, with no university-trained divine handy to interpret 'difficult' passages.[51] Sir John Coke in Charles I's reign declared frankly that 'the chief use' of the clergy 'is now the defence of our Church, and therein of our state'.[52] After censorship had broken down in 1640, the author of *Macaria* hoped that 'the art of printing will so spread knowledge that the common people, knowing their own rights and liberties, will not be governed by way of oppression'.[53] It was a hope that seemed on the way to fulfilment. When civil war came, Henry Oxinden urged the gentry to stand together to maintain episcopal government; presbyterianism would 'equalize men of mean condition with the gentry', and 'set up a teacher greater than a bishop in every parish'.[54] As late as 1672 Andrew Marvell

---

48. Quoted by Martin, *Religious Radicals*, p. 115.
49. Quoted by David Norbrook, *Poetry and Politics in the English Renaissance* (1984), pp. 63–4.
50. Martin, op. cit., pp. 73, 222.
51. Ed. H. Gee and W. J. Hardy, *Documents Illustrative of English Church History* (1896), p. 481.
52. *MSS. of the Earl Cowper* (Historical Manuscripts Commission), I, p. 90.
53. Ed. C. Webster, *Utopian Planning and the Puritan Revolution: Gabriel Plattes, Samuel Hartlib and Macaria* (Wellcome Unit for the History of Medicine Research Publications, No. 11, Oxford, 1979), pp. 72–3.
54. Ed. D. Gardiner, *Oxinden and Peyton Letters, 1642–1670* (1937), pp. 36–7.

pilloried Bishop Samuel Parker for complaining that 'unqualified people should have promiscuous licence to read the Scriptures'.[55]

The Anglican hierarchy wished to ensure that there was an educated clergyman in every parish, who would interpret the Scriptures for his flock, solve their problems and check their heretical thoughts; because he had been educated at Oxford or Cambridge such a clergyman was not expected to harbour dangerous ideas himself. As an additional aid to orthodoxy, catechizing became the approved method of spreading approved truths to the ignorant: the sixteenth and early seventeenth centuries saw a proliferation of catechisms. All this proved inadequate. The educational standard of the clergy improved significantly under Elizabeth and the first two Stuarts, but it still left much to be desired. Lay patronage prevented most parishioners having any say in selecting their ministers. There were still 'dumb dogs' – a Scriptural expression, we note (Isaiah LVI.10). Poor livings and the greed of parsons led to pluralism; some parishes lacked a resident clergyman, or were fobbed off with a miserably paid curate. The inadequacies of the clergy reinforced Puritan emphasis on household religion, Bible-reading and discussion presided over by the head of the household.

Worst of all, university education proved to be an insufficient safeguard. In the newly competitive world around them, young men at universities discovered in the Bible alternatives to a hierarchical society and a hierarchical church. The clerisy produced traitors from its midst. Once the Scriptures had been translated into the vernacular and printed, Pandora's box was opened. The mediaeval church had found it difficult enough to contain heresy; but now the unity of the church seemed gone for ever. The Bible proved divisive in a society where social tensions were accumulating. Despite repression under Mary and lack of encouragement from Elizabeth, the popular tradition continued to flourish. The witty and irreverent pamphlets of Martin Marprelate (1588–9) quoted Wyclif, and cited Judas and Simon Magus to the prelates as examples of non-residence.[56] Marprelate could be suppressed, but he was not forgotten. In 1641 pamphlets of his were reprinted, and many fresh tracts based on them were published, some by the future Leveller Richard Overton. They were popular in the Army.[57]

55. Marvell, *The Rehearsal Transpros'd*, pp. 15–16, 19.
56. Marprelate, *An Epitome* (1588), sig. D 4v, F 3v; *Hay any worke for Cooper?* (1589), p. 5.
57. Marie Gimelfarb-Brack, *Liberté, Egalité, Fraternité, Justice! La Vie et l'œuvre de Richard Overton, Niveleur* (Berne, 1979), Part III, Chapter 3; *Reliquae Baxterianae* (1696), p. 53.

Radical protestants made a special point of publishing cheap editions of the Bible. In Edward VI's reign the Bible and the Apocrypha were issued in six octavo parts.[58] The Geneva Bible was usually printed in italic, not old-style black letter. It was cheap, relatively small and pocketable; failure to produce cheap editions of the Bishops' Bible of 1568 helped to make the Geneva Bible the Bible of the people.[59] Monopoly kept the price of Bibles too high for the poor to buy, although cheaper copies were bootlegged over from The Netherlands. But monopolies collapsed after 1640, and cheaper Bibles circulated freely.[60] In the 1640s octavo bibles sold at 2s. 8d. with marginal notes, less in duodecimo without notes.[61] In 1650 the Army in Scotland was able to purchase Bibles at 1s. 8d. apiece, but 2s. to 2s. 4d. seems to have been the standard price in the 1650s.[62] All East India vessels carried the Bible as reading matter, together with Foxe's *Book of Martyrs* and Hakluyt's *Voyages*. The number of Bibles and New Testaments published in England between the Reformation and 1640 has been estimated at over a million.[63]

So by the mid-seventeenth century English men and women had experienced a quarter of a millennium of emphasis on the sovereignty of the Scriptures as the unique source of divine wisdom on all subjects, including politics, and a source which must be open to everybody. Henry VIII had rightly foreseen the dangers of allowing the lower orders to discuss the political affairs of their betters. Elizabeth's Secretary of State, Sir Thomas Smith, thought that the majority of Englishmen (and of course all English women) existed only to be ruled. In 1628 Charles I was outraged when the Commons called for the Petition of Right – the first significant modification of the royal prerogative – to be printed, because he did not want ordinary people to read or discuss it. In 1641 a proposal to print the Grand Remonstrance, a list of the Commons' grievances against Charles I's government, led to uproar in the House, in which swords were drawn for

---

58. J. N. King, *English Reformation Literature: The Tudor Origins of the Protestant Tradition* (Princeton U.P., 1982), p. 129.
59. Pollard, op. cit., p. 32. The Bishops' Bible was selling at 27s. 8d. in 1571. For the Geneva Bible see pp. 56–7 below.
60. *The Diary of Ralph Josselin, 1616–1683* (ed. A. Macfarlane, Oxford U.P., 1976), p. 173; cf. *Collectanea Curiosa* (ed. J. Gutch, 1781), I, pp. 275–6.
61. R. Baillie, *Letters and Journals* (Edinburgh, 1775), II, p. 174.
62. W. M. Clyde, *The Struggle for the Freedom of the Press: from Caxton to Cromwell* (Oxford U.P., 1934), pp. 225, 281–2.
63. L. B. Wright, *Religion and Empire* (North Carolina U.P., 1943), p. 53; C. J. Sommerville, 'On the Distribution of Religious and Occult Literature in Seventeenth-Century England', *The Library*, 5th Series, XXIX, 1974.

the only recorded time in its history. It presaged civil war, in which Parliament *had* to appeal to the common people if Charles was to be defeated.

The decisive moment had come in 1640, when censorship and church courts collapsed, and with them restrictions on free discussion of the Bible – or indeed of anything else. Groups of men and women could now assemble to listen to any 'mechanic preacher' who had a talent and thought he had a message. There was no possibility of controlling the heresies which might be preached: originality was one way in which a self-appointed preacher might win a following. In the 1650s the Cromwellian state church restored some sort of order and control; but it was far from complete: the church which Bunyan joined in the 1650s was effectively a 'gathered' church, but its minister held what was technically a living in the national church. This congregation, like any other, played an active part in politics.

The door which had been opened could never be shut again. 'In vain have English Parliaments permitted English Bibles in the poorest English houses, and the simplest man and woman to search the Scriptures', wrote Roger Williams in 1644, if they 'should be forced to believe as the church believes'.[64] After 1660 the existence of nonconformity had to be recognized, however reluctantly, as never before 1640. But the day of the self-selected 'mechanic preacher', with his often transient audiences, was over; Charles II's government insisted in 1672 that churches to which 'indulgence' was granted had to be registered and licensed. Thus some control was established: dissenting ministers could be held responsible for their congregations. Only in 1689 did Parliament pass the Toleration Act.

Francis Bacon thought that three great inventions had ushered in the new world in which he lived – gunpowder, the mariner's compass and printing. Gunpowder contributed to the establishment of centralized national states in Europe, and to warfare between them; gunpowder and the mariner's compass between them made possible the extension of European domination and plunder over the whole world, and so the enrichment of Europe. Printing extended knowledge. But its political consequences were ambivalent. On the one hand it created the possibility of more people receiving education, and so of extending the political nation; on the other, it offered new possibilities of manipulation and control of public opinion. In both processes the Bible was central. It also contributed to modes of thought justifying European expansion and supremacy.[65]

64. Williams, *The Bloudy Tenent of Persecution* (Hanserd Knollys Soc., 1848), p. 9.
65. See Chapter 5 below.

IV

The Bible was central to all intellectual as well as moral life in the sixteenth and seventeenth centuries. Controversies between Presbyterians and Episcopalians from Elizabeth's reign onwards turned on arguments about Biblical texts. For Walter Travers, for instance, the relationship of church and state was determined by the fact that Old Testament prophets had found it necessary to admonish even godly rulers like David and Hezekiah.[66] But it was not only in religious matters that the Bible was regarded as authoritative. The great Puritan oracle, William Perkins, declared that Scripture 'comprehendeth many holy sciences', including ethics, economics, politics, academy ('the doctrine of governing schools well').[67] Take the apparently secular sphere of political theory. Thomas Hobbes was denounced by his contemporaries as an atheist, a charge which he emphatically denied. He claimed that his *Leviathan* was derived from 'Principles of Reason': even if he had failed in that, he was 'sure they are Principles from the Authority of Scripture', and that he had demonstrated them in Parts III and IV of *Leviathan* – half the book – which deal with 'A Christian Commonwealth' and 'The Kingdom of Darkness'. In both of these the argument is preponderantly Biblical. 'There ought to be no power over the consciences of men', Hobbes declared, 'but of the Word itself'.[68] It has been calculated that there are 657 citations of Biblical texts in *Leviathan*, and that there are in all 1,327 Biblical quotations in his six major political works.[69]

Hobbes is of course not exceptional in his use of the Bible, though the extent of it is at first sight surprising. The whole argument of Sir Robert Filmer's posthumous *Patriarcha*, and of his works published earlier in the 1640s and 1650s, is based on Old Testament history from Genesis onwards. Filmer thought that the Bible should be given precedence over any other authority. Locke in his reply to Filmer did not challenge this assumption even in 1690, but concentrated on showing that Filmer's argument goes 'against the express words of Scripture'. For Locke too 'the Bible was the

66. P. Lake, *Anglicans and Puritans? Presbyterianism and English Conformist Thought from Whitgift to Hooker* (1988), pp. 15, 74, 217; cf. pp. 93–7.
67. Perkins, *Workes* (1616–18), I, pp. 10–11.
68. Hobbes, *Leviathan* (ed. C. B. Macpherson, Penguin ed.), pp. 378, 711.
69. This is the estimate of Wolfgang Palaver, of the Institut für Moraltheologie und Gesellschaftslehre, in *International Hobbes Association Newsletter*, new series, 10 (November, 1989), pp. 24–31.

primary historical source for any endeavour to supply a "historical" account of man's existence'.[70] Algernon Sidney, in his *Discourses Concerning Government* (1698), also controverted Filmer on his own ground, not by rejecting the Bible as authoritative.

James Harrington, like Hobbes, is thought of as a secular political theorist, but he quotes the Bible more often and more extensively than any other single source; the Bible and the history of Israel loom large in all his writings.[71] Milton in 1642 spoke of the Bible as 'that book within whose sacred context all wisdom is enfolded'.[72] His own political writings, notably *The Tenure of Kings and Magistrates* (1648) and the *Ready and Easy Way to establish a free Commonwealth* (1660), are Biblical through and through. J. H. Sims, *à propos* the epics, speaks of 'the Biblical saturation of Milton's mind'.[73] Scarcely less Biblical are the writings of Levellers, notably Lilburne, of Gerrard Winstanley, of Ranters and especially of Fifth Monarchists. Sexby's *Killing Noe Murder* (1657) has epigraphs from II Chronicles, describing respectively the murders of Athaliah and Amaziah. Both had the approval of the Geneva marginal notes.[74] Political practice preceded political theory. When the Parliaments of England and Scotland made their historic alliance against Charles I in 1643, it took the Old Testament form of a Solemn League and Covenant – harking back to Scotland's earlier national covenants. God's people were a covenanted people.[75]

For most scientists too the Bible was central. Richard Hakluyt is said to have been brought to cosmology by reading the 107th Psalm.[76] A main obstacle to acceptance of the heliocentric theory was the description in Genesis I.16 of the sun and the moon as 'two great lights', and Joshua's successful command to the sun to stand still, in Joshua X.12, on which the Geneva Bible did not think it necessary to comment. Calvin's principle of accommodation, that the Bible was written to the understanding of its readers, was the way round this and similar passages when they seemed to be contradicted by scientific observation. It gained force from traditional

70. Richard Ashcraft, *Locke's Two Treatises of Government* (1987), pp. 63–6, 147, 150.
71. C. Blitzer, *An Immortal Commonwealth* (Yale U.P., 1960), pp. 278–80. For Hobbes and Harrington see Chapter 7 below.
72. *MCPW*, I, p. 747. Cf. T.S., *A Divine Dictionarie. Or, The Bible abreviated* (1615), sig. ¶2v.
73. J. H. Sims, *The Bible in Milton's Epics* (Florida U.P., 1962), p. 250.
74. See p. 190 below. The attribution to Sexby is not certain.
75. See Chapter 11 below.
76. Ed. E. G. R. Taylor, *Original Writings . . . of the two Richard Hakluyts* (Hakluyt Soc., 2nd series, LXXVI, 1935), II, pp. 396–7.

scholarly contempt for the ignorance of the vulgar, now able to read writings hitherto limited to the educated. Moses, Calvin tells us, 'was not ignorant of geometry', but he described the building of the ark 'in a homely style, to suit the capacity of the people'.[77] Galileo had been warned that the Copernican theory could be maintained only on the assumption that the Bible speaks 'in accordance with the language of ordinary people'. Galileo agreed that 'the shallow minds of the common people' must be protected from the truth about the universe lest they 'should become confused, obstinate and contumacious' in yielding assent to 'the principal articles that are absolutely matters of faith'. 'Wise expositors' must 'seek out the true sense of Scripture texts', leaving the commonplace language of the Bible intact for 'the all-too-numerous vulgar'.[78]

Edward Wright, prefacing William Gilbert's pioneering work *Of the Loadstone* (1600), declared that the Copernican system could be reconciled with Scripture. 'It does not seem to have been the intention of Moses or the prophets to promulgate nice mathematical or physical distinctions; they rather adapt themselves to the understandings of the common people and to the current fashion of speech'.[79] 'The Bible speaks the language of everyman', said Kepler.[80] John Wilkins, future bishop, used similar arguments in defending the Copernican system. He said briskly that the 'penmen of Scripture' might be grossly ignorant, but that nevertheless 'astronomy proves God and a Providence', and confirms the truth of the Bible.[81] The mathematician Thomas Hood agreed that, after the Bible, 'the art of astronomy doth chiefly breed the knowledge of God'.[82] Sir Isaac Newton thought that Moses 'accommodated his words to the gross conceptions of the vulgar', translating astronomical concepts into everyday language.[83]

77. Calvin, *A Commentary on Genesis* (trans. and ed. J. King, 1965), I, pp. 85–7, 256. First published 1534.
78. Galileo, quoted by Margaret Jacob, *The Cultural Meaning of the Scientific Revolution* (New York, 1988), pp. 21–3.
79. Gilbert, op. cit., p. xlii.
80. Kepler, *Nova Astronomia*, quoted by F. E. Manuel, *The Religion of Isaac Newton* (Oxford U.P., 1974), p. 36.
81. Wilkins, *A Discourse Concerning a New Planet* (1640), pp. 10–14, 171–2; Arnold Williams, *The Common Expositor: An Account of Commentaries on Genesis, 1527–1633* (North Carolina U.P., 1948), pp. 176–7. Wilkins was not always so sure of the literal truth of the Bible; see p. 225 below.
82. Hood, quoted by Margot Heinemann, 'Rebel Lords, Popular Playwrights and Political Culture: Notes on the Jacobean Patronage of the Earl of Southampton', in *The Yearbook of English Studies*, 21 (1991), p. 81.
83. Newton, *Correspondence* (ed. W. H. Turnbull, Cambridge U.P., 1959–77), II, pp. 329–34.

In 1646 John Hall of Durham asked Benjamin Worsley 'whether the Scriptures be an adequate judge in physical controversies or not?' Worsley was against building 'an axiom in physics' upon a 'probable phrase of Scripture', preferring the 'evidence of reason or demonstration from experience'.[84] Both Napier of Merchiston at the beginning of the century, and Isaac Newton towards its end, were preoccupied with calculations relating to the end of the world, based on Biblical texts. Newton's *Chronology of the ancient nations amended* was an attempt to refute rational criticisms of the Bible and to unite profane history 'with the course of nature, with astronomy, with sacred history'.[85] Francis Bacon protested against making Genesis the sole basis for astronomy; but millenarian considerations motivated his own approach to science.[86]

We should not think only of what we consider 'science' today. Alchemy, the predecessor of our chemistry, was deeply Biblical. Donne in *The First Anniversary* wrote of 'a true religious alchemy'; and in a sermon of 1622 he quoted Isaiah to make the point that 'God can work in all metals and transmute all metals'.[87] Robert Fludd in his *Mosaicall Philosophy* relied on 'the axioms and testimonies of Scripture . . . to prove and maintain his philosophy'. For him the Bible is 'the ground of all arts' — astronomy, meteorology, magnetism, physic, music, arithmetic, geometry, rhetoric, mechanic arts, moral philosophy and politics.[88] Newton thought it an 'admirable and new paradox that alchemy should have a concurrence with antiquity and theology'.[89] Lyndy Abraham has recently richly illustrated Marvell's Christianized alchemy.[90]

Astrology, astronomy's predecessor, was less easy to reconcile with the Bible, since some of its claims seemed to rival rather than to complement

84. Stephen Clucas, 'Samuel Hartlib's *Ephemerides*', *The Seventeenth Century*, VI (1991), p. 42.
85. M. Hodgen, *Early Anthropology in the 16th and 17th centuries* (Pennsylvania U.P., 1964), p. 319.
86. Arnold Williams, *The Common Expositor*, p. 176.
87. Eugene R. Cunnar, 'Donne's "Valediction forbidding mourning" and the golden compasses of alchemical creation', in *Literature and the Occult: Essays in Comparative Literature* (ed. Luanne Frank, Texas U.P., 1977), pp. 74, 72.
88. Fludd, op. cit., To the Judicious and Discreet Reader, and pp. 17–25. First published in Latin in 1638. I cite from the English translation of 1659.
89. Newton, quoted by C. Webster, *From Paracelsus to Newton: Magic and the Making of Modern Science* (Cambridge U.P., 1982), p. 10.
90. Abraham, *Marvell and Alchemy* (1990); cf. Davenant, *Gondibert* (ed. D. E. Gladish, Oxford U.P., 1971), p. x.

Christianity. There was a particular antipathy between predestinarian Calvinism and an astrology which appeared equally determinist. Calvin in his *Commentary upon . . . Isaiah*, whilst insisting that 'men's actions are not governed by the stars', did not condemn 'that astrology which contemplates the course of the stars', and was prepared to admit that 'a man may at some time come to the discovery of certain things' by astrology/astronomy, and be able to predict famine, pestilence, fruitful and unfruitful years, 'and such like'.[91] The Calvinist theologians John Preston, Joseph Caryl, William Greenhill and Bishop Robert Sanderson were all interested in astrology.

Wither cheerfully had it both ways:

> For both by reason and by common sense
> We know, and often feel, that from above
> The planets have on us an influence
> And that our bodies vary as they move.
> Moreover, holy writ infers that these
> Have some such power.[92]

Bishop Carleton in 1624 published *Astrologomania*, a thoroughgoing refutation. During the Revolution Thomas Gataker, John Goodwin, John Owen, William Bridge, Philip Nye and many lesser divines attacked astrology. Milton depicted Satan as an astrologer in *Paradise Regained* (IV. 382–93), though he was prepared to concede that 'there is some astrology which is neither useless nor unlawful'.[93] In the 1640s and 1650s hostility between Presbyterians and astrologers was manifest, as well as the anti-clericalism of many almanac-writers.[94] Nicholas Fiske referred in 1650 to 'the malice of the clergy' which had prevented astrological books being published 'until of late years'.[95] Next year it was being said in Leiden that 'you are great astrologers in England'.[96] In February 1653 Thomas Scott, in a report to Parliament from the Committee for the Propagation of the Gospel, urged the utter suppression 'of the abominable cheat of judicial astrology, whereby

---

91. Calvin, op. cit. (translated Clement Cotton, 1609), pp. 191–2 (commenting on Isaiah XIX.12) and 473 (Isaiah XLVII.12–13).
92. Wither, *Fair Virtue: The Mistress of Phil'arete*, selections from *A Collection of Emblems* (1634, second pagination), p. 177.
93. Milton, *Of Christian Doctrine, MCPW*, VI, p. 696.
94. Capp, *Astrology and the Popular Press: English Almanacs, 1500–1800* (1979), pp. 32, 143, 153–6. See esp. pp. 164–79 for astrology and millenarianism.
95. Fiske, *An Astrological Discourse With Mathematical Demonstrations*, Preface.
96. *Mercurius Politicus*, 33, 16–23 January 1651, p. 545.

the minds of multitudes are corrupted and turned aside from dependency upon the providence of God'.[97]

Bernard Capp has produced many examples of sixteenth- and seventeenth-century attempts to reconcile astrology with Christianity, especially with millenarianism.[98] Miles Coverdale, whose translation of the Bible into English appeared in 1535, apparently published a *Spiritual Almanack* in the following year, which offered 'a theological astronomy'. A century later Archbishop Laud was noting astrological data in his Diary; in a sermon preached to Parliament in 1628 he referred to the conjunction of Saturn and Mars. The Rev. John Swan, the Laudian author of *Speculum Mundi* (1635), later published almanacs and defended astrology.[99] Elizabeth and her two successors consulted astrologers. Royal favourites like Elizabeth's Earl of Essex and the first Duke of Buckingham kept their own astrologers. Responsible politicians like Denzil Holles, Oliver Cromwell, John Lambert, Bulstrode Whitelocke, Lord Treasurer Clifford and Antony Ashley-Cooper believed in, or at least consulted, astrologers. President Reagan would have been intellectually respectable 350 years ago.

Radicals too. Gerrard Winstanley and John Webster recommended that astrology be taught, and astrological medicine was one of the many occupations to which Laurence Clarkson turned his hand: he noted George Fox's interest in the subject. After the restoration the Earl of Clarendon quoted astrologers in a speech to Charles II's first Parliament; the merrie monarch is said to have taken an astrologer to Newmarket to spot winners. Robert Boyle and John Locke used astrological reckonings to find a time favourable for planting peonies. There was a Society of Astrologers holding annual feasts in London before there was a Royal Society. A sermon prepared for them in August 1651 gave elaborate Scriptural references sanctioning astrology. Apparent expressions of disapproval of astrology in the Bible, the preacher suggested, were due to words being incorrectly translated. More remarkably, he claimed that Christ was now in his saints here on earth.[100] Was this a personal belief, or did many astrologers share that subversive

97. C. H. Simpkinson, *Thomas Harrison, Regicide and Major-General* (1905), p. 151.

98. Capp, op. cit., *passim*; cf. his *Cromwell's Navy: The Fleet and the English Revolution, 1648–1660* (Oxford U.P., 1989), pp. vii, 327–8. See pp. 300–301 below.

99. Capp, *Astrology and the Popular Press*, pp. 140, 143, 333; cf. *TRDM*, pp. 283–385.

100. [Anon.], *The New Jerusalem* (1652), sig. A 4v, and *passim*; Robert Gell, *Stella Nova, . . . Or A Sermon Preached to the learned Society of Astrologers*, 1 August 1649; *A Sermon Touching Gods Government of the World by Angels. Preached before the learned Societie of Artists or Astrologers*, 8 August 1650. See *TRDM*, pp. 304–5.

view? If so, combined with their many millenarian predictions, it would seem to align them with Fifth Monarchist advocates of a dictatorship of the saints, and would help to explain the rapid decline of astrology in respectable circles in the late seventeenth century.[101]

Capp cites the most popular texts: Genesis I.14 ('let them ["lights in the heavens"] be for signs and for seasons'); Judges V.20 ('the stars in their courses fought against Sisera'), and Job XXXVIII.31, 33 ('Canst thou bind the sweet influences of Pleiades, or loose the bands of Orion?' 'Knowest thou the course of heaven, or canst thou set the rule thereof in the earth?'). David was said to be the author of 'astrological hymns'.[102] The star which led the three magi to Bethlehem indicated that they were 'no other than plain astrologers'. The Rev. John Vaux quoted Christ, 'In my Father's house are many mansions', in refutation of those who denied the existence of the houses or mansions of the zodiac.[103] William Lilly, most famous of astrologers, published *Christian Astrology* in 1647. This was regarded as the classic statement of the case: Lilly claimed that it was well received in Oxford and Cambridge. Astrology was for Lilly the 'alphabet of divinity', essential to clerical learning.[104]

Medicine too sought Biblical authority. When Peter Chamberlen in the 1630s proposed the regulation of midwives (under his supervision) he summed up his ideas under the title *A Voice in Ramah*, basing himself on Genesis XXXV.16–20, Jeremiah XXXI.15 and Matthew II.18.[105] The object of George Hakewill's *An Apologie or Defence of the Power and Providence of God in the Government of the World* was to proclaim, paradox-

101. See pp. 300–301 below. Patrick Curry, in *Prophecy and Power: Astrology in Early Modern England* (Princeton U.P., 1989), traces this decline, which he attributes mainly to the undefined 'radicalism' of some astrologers during the revolutionary decades, as well as to their inability to meet the Royal Society's standards as 'scientists'. Whilst agreeing with him that the Royal Society played a conservative political and social role which is frequently underestimated, it is I think carrying relativism too far not to distinguish between the methods of Boyle and Hooke on the one hand and Lilly and Ashmole on the other (though Boyle was interested in astrology). Did astrology contribute anything to human welfare? Sir Keith Thomas and Capp seem to me to strike a better balance (*TRDM*, Chapters 10–12; Capp, *Astrology and the Popular Press, passim*).
102. On the other hand, Isaiah XLVII.13–15 is hostile to 'the astrologers, the stargazers and prognosticators'; and Daniel's magic was vastly superior to that of all the enchanters, astrologers and soothsayers in Nebuchadnezzar's realm (Daniel, I.20, II.27, V.7–8, 11; cf. Micah V.12 and Zechariah X.2).
103. Capp, *Astrology and the Popular Press*, pp. 133–4; cf. p. 164.
104. Ibid., pp. 142, 182, 187–9.
105. Chamberlen, op. cit. (1640); cf. Joyce Rushen, 'The Secret "Iron Tongs" of Midwifery', *The Historian*, 30 (1991), p. 13.

ically, that the world had got better, not worse. Hakewill's main disagreement was with defenders of the superiority of classical Greece and Rome. But he had to deal with many problems arising from the Bible. There were giants in those days, and are not now; the patriarchs lived longer than we do. Specific texts had to be discussed and explained away. In all Hakewill cites the Bible some 500 times, mostly the Old Testament.[106]

A great part of Ralegh's *History of the World* (1614) was written within the framework of the Mosaic chronology. Indeed, all ancient historians assumed the Bible as their basic text, into whose narrative the history of Egypt, Babylon and Greece had to be fitted. But Ralegh used his experience as navigator and colonizer to turn a sceptical eye on accounts of the Flood and of migrations of the Israelites. Ralegh's interest in the construction and tonnage of the ark is easily explained, as is that of John Wilkins. More surprising at first sight is Bunyan's interest in the same subject.[107] But it was natural for serious Bible-readers to ask questions about the how and why of the facts they assimilated; and in between Ralegh and Bunyan had come the widespread discussion of Biblical matters during the freedom of the 1640s and 1650s. In 1624 Richard Eburne in *A plain Pathway to Plantations* took his 'proofs and examples . . . most out of the Bible, . . . because the practice thereof was very much in those times', so precepts and precedents abound, starting with 'God's express commandment to Adam that he should "fill the earth and subdue it"'.[108] The future Archbishop, George Abbot, published a geographical textbook in 1605 in which he was agreeably sceptical of travellers' tales from South America and elsewhere about strangely-shaped men; but he had no doubts about Jonah's experiences in the whale's belly.[109] Another Archbishop, James Ussher, in addition to his famous work on Hebrew history and chronology, published *A Geographical and Historical Disquisition touching the Asia properly so-called*. John Swan's *Speculum Mundi* assumed the absolute truth of the Biblical stories of the Creation and the Flood.

Thomas Burnet's *Theory of the Earth* (Latin edition 1681, English translation 1689), the first serious treatise on geology in the English language, still wrestled with the problem of accommodating the physical evidence with

---

106. See pp. 76–7 below.
107. I owe Wilkins to Professor S. F. Mason's 1991 Wilkins Lecture, printed in *Notes and Records of the Royal Society*, 46 (1992), pp. 1–21; Offor, II, p. 464.
108. Eburne, op. cit. (ed. L. B. Wright, Cornell U.P., 1962), pp. 9, 41.
109. Abbot, *A Brief Description of the Whole World* (1605); *An Exposition upon the Prophet Jonas* (1613), pp. 219–20. This 600-page folio tome, first published in 1600, deals with one of the shortest books in the Old Testament.

Noah's Flood. John Ray's *Three Physio-Theological Discourses* argued that the Flood changed either the atmosphere or human diet and so shortened men's lives from the hundreds of years for which the patriarchs had lived.[110]

The common law itself was prepared to learn from the Bible. Sir Edward Coke quoted Acts XXV.27 to establish the unreasonableness of sending a man to prison without cause. His dictum that it is not lawful to predict the date of the end of the world, or even to announce that it is imminent, appears to be supported only by Biblical texts.[111] The Bible was a model for legal writers: 'The reporting of particular cases or examples is the most perspicuous course of teaching the right rule and reason of the law, for so did almighty God himself when he delivered by Moses his judicial laws'.[112] Sir Henry Finch, an enthusiastic millenarian lawyer, thought that the laws of England retained 'the substance and equity, as it were the marrow' of the Mosaic law, and urged reform to bring English law into fuller accord with the law of God. This would be a further move away from 'the general corruption of the religion of God under the popish and antichristian tyranny'. In particular, it meant removing many moral offences from the jurisdiction of church courts to that of the common law.[113] Despite attempts by Puritan reformers in the 1640s and 1650s, English law was never brought into full accord with the Bible: the lawyers were powerful enough to prevent that. But in the New World parsons were stronger than lawyers. Rhode Island introduced Old Testament style judges, and John Cotton advocated (unsuccessfully) a governmental structure based on the Old Testament.

Writers on farming and gardening looked back to Adam; Noah was the first cultivator of vines, the first vintner. Scholars were concerned to conflate classical and Biblical chronology, classical and Biblical myths. Deucalion was Noah.[114] The crafts, rather unexpectedly, appeared to have been invented by the descendants of Cain. The Canto of Sylvester's translation of Du Bartas's *Divine Weekes and Workes* which deals with Cain and his descendants is called *The Handie-Crafts*.[115] Margaret Hodgen's *Early*

110. Ray, op. cit. (2nd ed., 1693), p. 126. The Flood also shortened the lives of animals.
111. Catherine Drinker Bowen, *The Lion and the Throne: The Life and Times of Sir Edward Coke, 1552–1634* (1957), p. 417; Coke, *III Institutes*, pp. 120–29.
112. Coke, *La Size Part des Reports* (1607), sig. vi.
113. W. R. Prest, 'The Art of Law and the Law of God: Sir Henry Finch (1558–1625)', in *Puritans and Revolutionaries: Essays in Seventeenth-Century History* (ed. D. Pennington and K. Thomas, Oxford U.P., 1978), pp. 98–102.
114. Arnold Williams, op. cit., pp. 4, 110, 213–14.
115. Joshuah Sylvester, *Complete Works* (ed. A. B. Grosart, 1880), I, pp. 122–9; Arnold Williams, op. cit., pp. 144–5.

Anthropology in the 16th and 17th centuries is dominated by the Bible.[116] Men searched for the lost tribes of Israel in Central Asia, in Africa and in America; Africans were held to be the descendants of Ham and consequently rightly punished by slavery. The former Royalist Captain Matthias Prideaux, who died in 1646 leaving behind him papers full of very sceptical questions, asked whether the ten tribes of Israel 'peopled Tartary and the West Indies?'[117] Warner in *Albion's England* (1602), Camden and many others, assumed that Britons were descended from Adam through Noah, Japheth (father of the Gentiles) and the Trojans.[118] Linguists started from the Tower of Babel, and argued about whether Hebrew was the only language spoken before Babel's confusion. Richard Verstegan thought that Adam and Eve spoke Low Dutch.[119] Stonehenge had somehow to be accommodated within the Biblical chronology.

Milton's divorce pamphlets (1642–3) hinged on texts from the Old and New Testaments. His *Of Christian Doctrine* was a *summa theologica* based entirely on analysis, interpretation and collation of over 8,000 Biblical texts. Discussions of the position of women, not only for Milton, started from Eve's sin, supported by many other Biblical passages and stories which emphasized women's inferiority.[120] The Ranters Abiezer Coppe and Lawrence Clarkson based their libertarian sexual ethic on Biblical texts as well as on direct communications from God.[121]

Richard Hooker concluded judiciously that there is 'no part of true philosophy, no art of account, no kind of science rightly so called, but the Scripture must contain it'.[122] Samuel Hieron in *The Dignitie of the Scripture* (1607) declared that it taught magistrates how to govern, ministers how to

116. Hodgen, op. cit., esp. Chapters 6–8; cf. S. Piggott, *Ancient Britain and the Antiquaries* (1989).
117. Prideaux, *An Easy and Compendious Introduction For Reading all Sorts of Histories* (1648), p. 33. This book, which ran to six editions by 1682, was edited by Matthias's father, John Prideaux, Bishop of Worcester (1578–1650). The Bishop was an anti-Arminian pluralist, author of *The doctrine of the Sabbath* (1634). He was appointed to Worcester in 1641, when Charles I was trying to appease Puritans. He was nominated to the Westminster Assembly of Divines, but did not sit. We do not know how much editing he did. I shall cite Matthias Prideaux frequently.
118. Arnold Williams, op. cit., pp. 140, 155.
119. Prideaux, op. cit., p. 10; Verstegan, *A Restitution of Decayed Intelligence* (Antwerp, 1605), pp. 190–91. They spoke High Dutch, said Sir Epicure Mammon, up-to-date but wrong, in Jonson's *The Alchemist* (1610 – Act II, sc. i).
120. *MCPW*, VI, p. 106. Cf. pp. 401–9 below.
121. See pp. 180–83 below.
122. Hooker, *Laws of Ecclesiastical Polity*, Book I, xiv, 1.

teach, instructed masters of families in their duties. It gave a head of a household 'direction for his apparel, his speech, his diet, his company, his disports, his labour, his buying and selling, yea and for his very sleep, and for those things which may be thought most arbitrary and indifferent'. The Church of Rome is quite wrong to think that its traditions can rightfully add anything.[123]

In a Fast Sermon of 27 September 1643 Anthony Burges assured the House of Commons that 'all reason severed from God's Word is corrupt and carnal'.[124] Some Puritans would accept only those religious ceremonies and practices which are specifically mentioned in the Bible, because it was 'unlawful and sinful to do anything according to any other law'. Hooker cited this as an error, 'a snare and a torment to weak consciences'. 'In every action of common life to find out some sentence clearly and infallibly setting before our eyes what we ought to do' would be intolerable for normal Christians. For some matters, he concluded, we must rely on the strength of authority.[125] Chillingworth, another conformist Anglican, argued that the Bible was the sole authority in religion, but that each individual should be free to interpret it as his reason dictated.[126] This was to open a very wide door indeed, through which Ranters and others, including Milton, would pass.

It is not fortuitous that Queen Elizabeth in her first procession through London in 1558 is said to have pressed to her bosom the English Bible which the Lord Mayor presented to her; nor that this scene was reproduced at the conclusion of Thomas Heywood's *If you know not me, you know nobody; or, the Troubles of Queen Elizabeth* (1605), and in the first scene of Dekker's *The Whore of Babylon*.[127] Just over a century later Charles II, equally unexpectedly elevated to the English throne, was at pains to tell the mayor of Dover that he valued above all things the Bible which had just been presented to him. When London ministers made a similar presentation the King said that he would make the Bible the rule both of his life and government.[128] Untrue, but politically sensible. Bulstrode Whitelocke, Cromwell's ambassador to Sweden, presented

---

123. *Sermons of Master Samuel Hieron* (1624), pp. 72–3. Posthumously published: Hieron died in 1617.
124. *FS*, VIII, p. 205; cf. XX, pp. 202–3; XXX, pp. 197–202.
125. Hooker, *The Laws of Ecclesiastical Polity*, Preface, paragraph vii; Book II, viii. 6.
126. William Chillingworth, *The Religion of Protestants* (1637), *passim*.
127. J. D. Spikes, 'The Jacobean History Play and the Myth of the Elect Nation', *Renaissance Drama*, New Series, VIII (1971), pp. 136–9.
128. G. Davies, *The Restoration of Charles II, 1658–1660* (San Marino, 1955), p. 353.

Queen Christina with a copy of the English Bible, since *'rien ne vous manque que l'estude du principal Livre, que je me suis enhardi de présenter en Anglais a vostre majesté'*.[129] As late as 1689, in the Toleration Act, Parliament prescribed an oath to be taken by dissenters, in which they acknowledged 'the Holy Scriptures of the Old and New Testaments to be given by divine inspiration'.

V

The Bible then was central to all arts, sciences and literature. The radical separatist Robert Browne put it perhaps a trifle strongly when in 1590 he told his kinsman Lord Burghley that 'the Word of God doth expressly set down all necessary and general rules of the arts and all learning'.[130] But many would have agreed with him. There remained however problems of interpretation. The Scriptures, said Thomas Taylor, unlike any other writings, 'cannot err or speak anything contrary to the truth or to themselves'. But they were not necessarily easy to interpret. 'No man by his own quickness or apprehension can find out the true sense of the Scriptures', Taylor added. 'Bring prayer with thee', not learning, for proper understanding.[131] The Bible was nevertheless accepted as the ultimate authority on economics and politics no less than on religion and morals. The literature of the age is crammed with allusions to the Old and New Testaments, many of which we now miss.

The words and themes of the Bible were familiar in popular usage, to an extent which demands an effort from us to understand. Men faced with problems turned the pages of the Bible at random to find a text which would offer guidance.[132] During the civil war, it was believed, many Parliamentarians 'had their lives saved by bullets hitting upon the little pocket-bibles they carried'.[133] The godless Cavaliers lacked this protection.

---

129. Ruth Spalding, *Contemporaries of Bulstrode Whitelocke, 1605–1675* (Oxford U.P., 1990), p. 39.
130. Ed. A. Peel and L. H. Carlson, *The Writings of Robert Harrison and Robert Browne* (1953), p. 530.
131. Taylor, *A Commentarie upon the Epistle of St. Paul to Titus* (1619), sig. ¶¶.
132. *TRDM*, pp. 45–6, 118, 214. Cf. *Mercurius Politicus*, 24 February to 3 March 1653, p. 2262: a prayer meeting aboard the *Triumph* asked where the Dutch fleet was, 'and the answer was made out of II Chronicles XX.16'.
133. Ed. W. H. D. Longstaffe, *Memoirs of the Life of Mr. Ambrose Barnes* (Surtees Soc., L, 1866), p. 107.

It was a common belief that God (and the devil) might intervene in daily life. It is easier for us to assume a law-abiding universe now that 'acts of God' are rare. It was different when people lived in timber and thatched houses, highly inflammable, and there was no insurance: there were no anaesthetics, but there were regular outbreaks of plague and of famine, medical services were mediocre – and anyway beyond the pockets of the poor. Pain, starvation, sudden and premature death were normal occurrences. When the elderly wore no spectacles and there was no artificial lighting by night, it was easy to see ghosts and prodigies. If someone in your family died unexpectedly or was afflicted with a mysterious illness, you were as likely as not to look for the witch who had caused it. If you wanted to recover lost or stolen property you sought advice from a 'cunning' man or woman. Only in the course of the seventeenth century did the laws of nature harden: meanwhile scientists were of all men the most anxious to show that science proves the existence of God and is compatible with the Bible. Only from our modern vantage point do we distinguish between what is 'rational' in seventeenth-century science and what is not. Boyle and Newton were on both sides of the line.

The Bible was present in everyday speech. The old lady of Kingston who called out to the assassin of the Duke of Buckingham as he was being taken to the Tower 'God bless thee, little David' was hailing the slayer of the Goliath of her time. Goliath was a Philistine, one of the foreign rulers over Israel. In *Samson Agonistes* Milton used 'the Philistian Yoke' to convey 'the Norman Yoke': alien tyrants.[134] Among the charges in Strafford's impeachment in 1641 was that he had repeated to the King the advice given to the idolatrous Rehoboam, in consequence of which 'the King's little finger should be thicker than the loins of the law'. There was no need to recall the response of the people: 'to your tents, O Israel'; 'and Israel rebelled against the house of David unto this day'.[135] *To your tents O Israel* was the title of a pamphlet against which the King protested in 1642, and the cry was frequently echoed during the Revolution – e.g. as the conclusion of the near-Digger pamphlet *Light Shining in Buckinghamshire* (December 1648).[136]

134. S. R. Gardiner, *History of England from the Accession of James I to the Outbreak of the Civil War* (1883–4), VI, p. 354. See pp. 40–41 below.
135. I Kings XII.10–19; see also II Chronicles X.16, and cf. II Samuel XX.1. Cf. C. Russell, 'The Theory of Treason in the Trial of Strafford', *EHR*, LXXX (1965), pp. 41–2.
136. Sabine, p. 623.

In 1648 Oliver Cromwell, urging the severance of relations with Charles I, told MPs, 'It is written, "Thou shalt not suffer an hypocrite to reign."' Cromwell assumed his audience would need no more precise reference, even though his (or his reporter's) recollection of Job XXXIV.30 was inaccurate.[137] When Bulstrode Whitelocke in January 1650 proposed to a widow, she rejected him with a reference to I Timothy V.11: 'when they have begun to wax wanton against Christ, [widows] will marry'.[138] The charges against Bunyan in 1661 described him as 'a pestilent fellow' (Acts XXIV.5). The Rev. Edward Fowler, later Bishop of Gloucester, also used Biblical language when he described Bunyan as 'a turbulent spirit', 'a natural brute beast', who should be 'taken and destroyed' (II Peter II.12).[139] Biblical texts audibly forced themselves upon Bunyan during his desperate dialogue with Satan recorded in *Grace Abounding*.[140]

Henry Marten, not the most godly of MPs, enjoyed quoting the Bible against the godly. When the Assembly of Divines claimed *jure divino* rights for the clergy, Marten compared them to the sons of Zebedee, who had wanted no more than to sit on either side of Christ in heaven. The Divines, less modestly, 'would fain take Christ out of his throne, that themselves might sit in it, and place the House of Lords on their right hand, and the House of Commons on the left'.[141] In his draft of a bill for the abolition of monarchy, Marten declared that the nation would be 'restored to its ancient government of a commonwealth'. When rebuked for the 'notorious lie' contained in the word 'restored', Marten meekly replied 'there was a text had much troubled his spirit for several days and nights of the man that was blind from his mother's womb and whose sight was restored at last' (John IX.1).[142]

I have quoted the Biblicism mainly of writers on the Parliamentarian or Puritan side. Many Puritans, for instance, thought that the Book of

137. Abbott, *Writings and Speeches of Oliver Cromwell* (Harvard U.P., 1937–47), I, p. 576. Cromwell probably recalled the Geneva marginal note on Job's 'The hypocrite doth reign' – tyrants are hypocrites.

138. Ed. R. Spalding, *Diary of Bulstrode Whitelocke, 1605–1675* (Oxford U.P., 1990), p. 252. There could be even stronger arguments for not wishing to marry Whitelocke.

139. 'A Relation of my Imprisonment', in *Grace Abounding* (ed. R. Sharrock, Oxford U.P., 1962), p. 127; [Fowler], *Dirt wipt off . . .* [against] *John Bunyan, lay-preacher in Bedford* (1672), pp. 40, 70 and *passim*.

140. *Grace Abounding*, pp. 30–31, 52–3, 59–60, 64–5, 72, 80, 82.

141. C. M. Williams, 'The Anatomy of a Radical Gentleman, Henry Marten', in Thomas and Pennington, *Puritans and Revolutionaries*, pp. 123–4.

142. Aubrey, *Brief Lives* (ed. A. Clark, Oxford U.P., 1898), II, p. 47.

Sports was an invitation to break the Fourth Commandment. But Anglican royalist attitudes were equally Bible-based. In 1633 Scottish Presbyterian worship had offended the King by its lack of decency: Conrad Russell plausibly suggests that he thought it conflicted with I Corinthians XIV.40, 'Let all things be done decently and in order'. Lord Herbert of Cherbury, briefing Charles on the royal supremacy, drew all his arguments from the Bible, none from English statutes.[143] So did the author of *Eikon Basilike*.

We must beware of anachronism here. To say that politics and economics were discussed by reference to the Bible may lead us to suppose that men and women were influenced by 'religion' as men and women are not in the twentieth century. The nineteenth-century idea that the seventeenth-century English Revolution was a 'Puritan' revolution, and the modern version that it was 'the last of the religious wars', illustrate this point. The execution of Charles I was defended in religious terms, but we should hardly regard it as a religious act today. Milton thought it a religious duty to hate God's enemies, who were mostly also his political opponents. We must differentiate between the Biblical idiom in which men expressed themselves, and their actions which we should today describe in secular terms. But at the same time we must avoid the opposite trap of supposing that 'religion' was used as a 'cloak' to cover 'real' secular motives. This may have been the case with a few individuals; but for most men and women the Bible was their point of reference in all their thinking. So when scholars laboriously demonstrate that Levellers or Milton or Winstanley were 'primarily motivated by religion', they have proved no more than that these thinkers lived in the seventeenth century. Then the Bible was the source of virtually all ideas; it supplied the idiom in which men and women discussed them. Hobbes and Filmer used the language of the Bible no less than Levellers or Milton or Winstanley. Jesuits and radical Parliamentarians alike defended their causes with Biblical arguments. To say that the English Revolution was about religion is tautologous; it took place in the seventeenth century.

Conrad Russell, following Ivan Roots, has recently, very rightly, emphasized the British context of the English Revolution.[144] But contemporaries saw their situation in a wider context still, an international context.

143. Russell, *The Fall of the British Monarchies, 1637–1642* (Oxford U.P., 1991), pp. 41, 46, 106. For other examples see Lois Potter, *Secret Rites and secret writing: Royalist literature, 1641–1660* (Cambridge U.P., 1989), *passim*; Derek Hirst, 'The Politics of Literature and the English Republic', *The Seventeenth Century*, V, esp. pp. 139–50.
144. See '*Into Another Mould*' (ed. Roots, Exeter U.P., 1981), pp. 5–23.

From John Foxe to John Cotton they visualized the historical crisis in which they were aware of participating as 'the last times' of the world, the approach of the millennium. They were conscious of England's failure to fulfil her responsibilities as a chosen nation, as a great European power which had not come to the rescue of protestants in the Thirty Years War; as a potentially great naval power which was permitting Antichristians to monopolize the Americas. When we ask whether those who advocated war with Spain were motivated by religious or economic considerations, our question is unanswerable. Contemporaries could not have answered it, would not indeed have asked it. It is an anachronistic question.

Another form of anachronism is to push later denominational labels back to too early a date. Men spoke of Presbyterians, Independents, Baptists and Quakers in the 1640s and 1650s; but there were no organized sects which accepted these names then. Some who were called 'Presbyterians' went to churches which we should call 'Independent'; some 'Independents' were elders of the Presbyterian state church.[145] People called 'Baptists' disagreed about the correct mode of adult baptism, as well as about predestination. Most Quakers in the 1650s were not pacifists: Fox urged Cromwell to lead his armies to sack Rome.[146] If we ask what religious denomination such well-documented characters as Oliver Cromwell, Milton, Gerrard Winstanley or Marvell belonged to, we have no answer. It is not a very meaningful question. The word 'sect' should be prohibited for the period before 1660. Professor Davis proved to his own satisfaction that the Ranters were not a sect (correct), and drew the incorrect conclusion that they were a figment of the imagination of their contemporaries and of later historians. By the same logic we could prove that Baptists, Independents and Quakers did not exist.[147] This would be a little drastic in view of the usage of contemporaries and of long-established conventions of historical writing. But the labels should be used with extreme caution; we must never forget the fluidity of religious groupings before persecution forced organization upon what we may begin to call 'sects' after 1660. In the forties and fifties you did not find buildings marked 'Baptist chapel', 'Congregational chapel' or 'Quaker meeting-house' as you walked down the street: you found

145. See J. H. Hexter's justly famous article demonstrating that the names 'Presbyterian' and 'Independent' were applied to political and religious groupings which by no means necessarily coincided (reprinted in *Reappraisals in History: New Views on History and Society in Early Modern England*, Chicago U.P., 1979).
146. B. Reay, *The Quakers and the English Revolution* (1985), *passim*.
147. See Chapter 9 in my *A Nation of Change and Novelty*.

congregations of like-minded believers meeting where they could find a room – in pubs or in private houses. They would have regarded themselves as part of the church of Christ, and would have resisted any sectarian labelling. Their congregations included sermon-tasters, Seekers, attaching themselves to no fixed congregation.

Such labelling was done by enemies: 'the Quakers so-called' long resisted their nickname, which was not given them in any friendly spirit. But after 1660 congregations had to come together to defend themselves against persecution; and organization of the many meant exclusion of the few, the drawing of lines and defining of frontiers between sects. When Charles II offered 'indulgence' to dissenters in 1672 congregations had to register under a denominational name in order to qualify. Bunyan's church registered as Congregational, though Bunyan is often thought of as a Baptist. The choice in 1672 might have been fairly haphazard. John Gibbs, who wrote a Preface for Bunyan's *A Few Sighs from Hell* (1658), was licensed in 1672 as pastor to a Presbyterian church in one place and a Congregationalist church in another. In the next decade he was also pastor to a Baptist congregation.[148] It does not make much sense to ask what his denomination was. Historians, seeing individuals and churches labelled 'Presbyterian' or 'Baptist' in the forties and fifties, have too easily attributed to them characteristics and a specificity which the labels acquired only much later.

More important in our period are different lines of division – the opposition of protestants to catholics, acceptance or rejection of a state church and of tithes as a means of financing that church, of ordination by an ecclesiastical hierarchy as against lay preaching, of university training for ministers. Some historians have rebuked defenders of religious toleration like Milton and Locke for 'failing to understand' their own principles. The failure is in the historians' lack of understanding of the historical situation in which Milton and Locke found themselves.[149] Similarly there were millenarians inside and outside the Church of England, passive and active. There are still millenarians with us today, but the sort of active millenarianism which impelled men to take revolutionary political action had died by the end of the seventeenth century. Bishops and Sir Isaac Newton still retained an academic interest in dating the millennium, but when John Mason in 1694

---

148. Ed. R. L. Greaves and R. Zaller, *Biographical Dictionary of British Radicals in the 17th Century* (Brighton, 1982–4), II, s.v. Gibbs; Anne Laurence, *Parliamentary Army Chaplains, 1642–1651*, p. 128.
149. See pp. 409–12 below.

announced that Christ was coming to Water Stratford next Whitsunday and crowds assembled to welcome him, sharing their property in common, Mason was not arrested and imprisoned as a dangerous agitator: he was advised to take physic. Things had changed in forty years.[150]

Attitudes towards Catholics varied in like manner, as we shall see. Some millenarian protestants thought they were engaged in a life-and-death struggle with Antichrist; others had a less black/white view of the historical situation in which they found themselves.[151] Similarly with the distinction between Calvinists and Arminians, which turned on the future state of most human beings. There were predestinarian Calvinists within the Church of England and among Presbyterians and Particular Baptists outside it. There were Laudian Arminians and Arminian sectaries; the 'Arminianism' of the latter was poles apart from that of the catholicizing Laudians. The Great Tew circle before 1640 and Cambridge Platonists after 1660 wished to reconcile reason and religion but remained within the established church; men like Clement Writer, Milton and Samuel Fisher pursued their speculations outside the church. There were chasms in the ideology of the period between conservatives and radicals which sectarian labels are inadequate to distinguish. As we study the use made of the Bible in seventeenth-century controversies we shall find divergences of interpretation which transcend denominations.[152]

VI

We must not attribute too much to printing. Mediaeval sermons and miracle plays had drawn on the Bible to inculcate political and social lessons. But now the printed word could be pondered over and re-read, both privately and in group discussions. Preaching of course ante-dated printing. In the sixteenth and seventeenth centuries it was both an aid to and a rival of printing. In extending protestantism to the dark corners of the land the spoken word was more important than print: though the translation of the Bible into Welsh in Elizabeth's reign was a momentous event.[153] Vernacular printing, which Bacon had seen as an example of a

150. See 'John Mason and the End of the World', in my *Puritanism and Revolution* (1958).
151. See Part III below.
152. See Chapters 7 and 8 below.
153. See my 'Puritans and "the Dark Corners of the Land"', in *Change and Continuity in 17th-century England* (1974). See also pp. 439–40 below.

discovery made by accident, by industrial craftsmen rather than by learned academics, had transformed communication between men and men. The sixteenth-century German radical theologian Thomas Müntzer anticipated Wesley in seeing the whole world as his parish; printing knew no parochial boundaries.[154] As Defoe put it, 'preaching of sermons is speaking to a few of mankind; printing of books is talking to the whole world'.[155] Vernacular printing aided indoctrination and counter-indoctrination: it helped to diversify culture. Governments and ecclesiastical censors tried to keep this under control, but the break-up of the international church, and the establishment of protestant national churches, meant that heresies could be imported in print from outside England. And when the censorship collapsed in England after 1640 . . . !

We should not think of the Bible just as a book to be read, or to listen to. It was everywhere in the lives of men, women and children. Not only in the church services they had to attend, but in the ballads they bought and sang,[156] and in their daily surroundings. Where today we should expect wallpaper, almost all houses had hangings to keep out draughts and to cover the rough walls. These often took the form of 'painted cloths', 'the real poor man's pictures', among which Biblical scenes seem to have preponderated. In accordance with Deuteronomy XI.20, Biblical texts were very often painted on walls or posts in houses, 'probably representing the first and most common form in which an "illiterate" would encounter the written word'. In addition, walls were covered with printed matter – almanacs, illustrated ballads and broadsides, again often on Biblical subjects. More elusive, 'godly tables', specially printed for decorating walls and 'most fit to be set up in every house', often contained texts from the Bible (Psalms especially) as well as prayers, instructions for godly householders, medical information and advice. Such tables were for use and for reference: they may have been known by heart. It is likely that most of the population became acquainted with print and with the Bible through such decorations. The artefacts have perished; but enough has survived for Dr Tessa Watt to reconstruct the argument which I have summarized in this and the following paragraphs.[157]

154. Peter Matheson, 'Thomas Müntzer's Idea of an Audience', *History*, 267 (1991), p. 186.
155. Quoted by Ian Watt, *The Rise of the Novel* (1963), p. 107.
156. See Chapter 16 below.
157. T. Watt, *Cheap Print and Popular Piety, 1550–1640* (Cambridge U.P., 1991), esp. Chapters 5 and 6. The passages I have quoted will be found on pp. 220 and 223.

The Bible was thus omnipresent in houses. But houses include ale-houses, which with churches were the main centres of community life. Their walls and posts too had painted cloths and painted texts, and were covered with ballads and broadsides, 'godly tables'. Falstaff's chamber at The Garter was 'painted about with the story of the prodigal'.[158] Men and women who had never opened a Bible would be well acquainted with many of its best stories, with the commandments and the beatitudes, and with moral exhortations based on the Bible. Several generations of children grew up – unlike earlier and later generations – in an environment suffused with the new print culture and the vernacular Bible.

The printed vernacular Bible was an important literary discovery, especially for those who learned to read via the Scriptures. There are good stories in the Bible as well as models of conduct, good and bad. We take knowledge of the Biblical myths for granted now: they have been absorbed into our culture – and are now being forgotten. Some myths were well known before the advent of print; but the printing press enabled diverse interpretations to circulate, as we shall see when we come to look at the stories of Adam and Eve, Cain and Abel, Esau and Jacob.[159]

Now that print culture is in decline, it is perhaps easier not to exaggerate its importance. The Bible was no longer the secret sacred book of the educated élite. Most boys and girls learnt to read via the Bible. It was no longer a mystery accessible only to university-educated Latin speakers; for two centuries or so its stories were an essential component of light popular reading. The novel had not yet been invented to compete with exciting narratives like Noah and the Ark, Joseph and his brethren, Jonah and the whale, Samson and the Philistines, David and Goliath. Mediaeval miracle plays had made many of these stories familiar in highly popularized versions; now they could also be studied seriously and at leisure.[160]

I speak of 'the Biblical Revolution' in two senses. First to emphasize that the language of the Bible was used to express political and ultimately revolutionary opposition to Charles I's government, and to maintain morale during the civil war; and secondly because the political revolution and its consequences shattered the universal acceptance of the Bible as an infallible text whose pronouncements were to be followed implicitly. In so far as the

---

158. Shakespeare, *The Merry Wives of Windsor*, IV. v. Cf. Wye Saltonstall, 'A Country Alehouse', in *Picturae Loquentes* (Luttrell Soc. reprint, 1946), p. 50. First published 1631–5. For religious disputes in ale-houses, see p. 15 above.
159. See Chapter 8 below.
160. See Chapter 16 below.

Biblical Revolution was defeated, the Bible shared this defeat. It was only after I had completed this book that I recalled Marx's words: 'Cromwell and the English people had borrowed speech, passions and illusions from the Old Testament . . . When the bourgeois transformation had been accomplished, Locke supplanted Habakkuk.'[161]

VII

My discussion so far has been mostly about relatively sophisticated readers of the Bible. It is easier to find evidence about them, but they were probably not the majority. More typical perhaps was Arise Evans, a Welshman who tells us that before he came to London in 1629 'I looked upon the Scripture as a history of things that passed in other countries, pertaining to other persons; but now I looked upon it as a mystery to be opened at this time, belonging also to us'.[162] He thought that Revelation VIII and XI gave an account of the English civil war, and that Amos VIII and IX set down all that came to pass since the beginning of the Long Parliament, including the division between Presbyterians and Independents.[163] The Rump of the Long Parliament was the Beast in Revelation XIII.[164] Evans was – to say the least – eccentric in his interpretations. But the distinction between 'the history' and 'the mystery' was frequently made by radicals.[165]

So it was important that ordinary people should have the right to read and discuss the Bible: to decide for themselves, not 'to believe as the church believes'.[166] Milton's *Areopagitica* summed up a radical trend of thought which by 1644 was free to express itself. A non-Biblical legend of almost equal power was that of the Norman Yoke, looking back to the days of the free Anglo-Saxons before the Conquest of 1066 established the rule of alien kings and landlords. The agrarian changes of the sixteenth and early

161. Karl Marx, *The 18th Brumaire of Louis Bonaparte*, in *Selected Works of Marx and Engels* (1935), II, p. 317. Marx's literary sense got the better of him here. Habakkuk is not one of the prophets most quoted by Puritans.
162. Evans, *An Eccho to the Voice from Heaven* (1653), p. 17.
163. Evans, *A Voice From Heaven to the Common-Wealth of England* (1652), pp. 26–7, 33, 45, 74–5.
164. Ibid., pp. 63–70; Evans, *The Bloudy Vision of John Farley* (1653), title page and p. 21.
165. See pp. 237–8 below.
166. Roger Williams, *The Bloudy Tenent Yet More Bloudy*, address to the Reader.

seventeenth centuries, enclosure and evictions, the revolts of 1536, 1549, 1607 (in which the names of Digger and Leveller were used), 1628–31 – all these and many lesser disturbances witnessed to social tensions that expressed themselves in class theories of politics of which the Norman Yoke was one variant. 'When Adam delved and Eve span/Who was then the gentleman?' was a Biblical version.[167] The Bible gave confidence and reassurance to men and women who badly needed it. Their times were out of joint; unprecedented things were happening to their world and their lives, apparently beyond human control. Some of the more daring of them came to conceive of solutions which were so novel that they could only be contemplated if they were envisaged as a return to purer Biblical days. God was at work in the world, overturning in order to transform; where but in his Word should we look for explanations of his mysterious actions and intentions, and guidance as to his wishes?

The Bible was of especial use as a yardstick by which to measure and criticize existing institutions and practices. If they could not be found in the Bible they were suspect. The silences of the Bible became almost as weighty as its text. Both John Knox and Henry Barrow thought that ceremonies not authorized by Scripture were sinful, and Barrow added fasting in Lent, a state clergy and lay patronage.[168] The antinomian separatist John Traske came to require express instructions from the Bible for everything that was done.[169] In the revolutionary decades William Dell found no Scriptural authorization for a national church.[170] William Erbery and many others, try as they would, could not find the Trinity in the Bible.[171] Quakers, like Barrow, found nothing there to justify the clergy's 'call to the ministry by their human learning', nor their 'making bargains with the people for so much a year', nor for 'sprinkling water in baptism'.[172] Thomas Edwards in 1646 tells us of sectaries who point out that 'the Scriptures nowhere speak of sacraments, name or thing'.[173] Colonel Rainborough revealed in the

167. See Chapter 8 below.
168. J. Ridley, *John Knox* (Oxford U.P., 1968), pp. 58, 95, 97; Barrow, *A Plaine Refutation of Mr George Giffardes Reprochful Booke* (Dort, 1590–91), in *The Writings of Henry Barrow, 1587–90* (ed. L. H. Carlson, 1962), pp. 241–2, 558; *1590–1591*, p. 68; cf. Hooker, quoted on p. 29 above.
169. B. R. White, 'John Traske (1585–1636) and London Puritanism', *Trans. Congregational Historical Soc.*, XX (1968), p. 225.
170. Dell, *The Tryal of Spirits* (1666), in *Several Sermons and Discourses* (1709 reprint), pp. 493–509.
171. *The Testimony of William Erbery* (1658), pp. 264, 278–9.
172. *The Faithful Testimony of William Dewsbery* (1689), pp. 105, 291–2.
173. Edwards, *Gangraena* (1646), I, p. 28.

Putney Debates of 1647 that he found nothing in the Bible to justify the existing Parliamentary franchise;[174] William Aspinwall noted that there was no mention of juries in the Bible. Ergo . . . .[175]

On the crucial issue of tithes, the 10 per cent levy on the incomes of all Englishmen to maintain the parish priesthood, Lilburne thought they had been a Jewish ceremony, abolished by the Gospel.[176] Winstanley believed that tithes had been bestowed upon priests by William the Conqueror in order to keep the poor in submission, and so should be abolished in consequence of Parliament's victory in the civil war.[177] The Presbyterian (later bishop) John Gauden, on the other hand, argued that since the New Testament did not mention tithes, this must mean that they had not been abrogated.[178]

To question tithes was to question the existence of a state church, since without them there could be no regular maintenance for parochial clergy. But tithes also involved lay property rights. 'Impropriated' tithes were collected by laymen whose ancestors had been in a position to grab or buy monastic lands at the Reformation. This affected preaching, another crucial issue. Where tithes were impropriated, the impropriator might maintain a curate on a derisory stipend, insufficient to attract an educated preacher. There were many impropriations in the North and West: the Sidney family, for instance, held many in Wales. So the extension of preaching to 'the dark corners of the land' conflicted with the property rights of the well-to-do. More preaching seemed necessary to complete the protestantization of England – necessary for national security in a world where militant Catholicism was on the offensive. There were paradoxes here. Owners of impropriations formed a valuable protestant vested interest, since restoration of popery would force a disgorgement of impropriations; yet the most ardent protestants wanted more preaching – and the abolition of impropriations.

As the example of Gauden shows, arguments could be used more than one way. Hooker pointed out that neither the Trinity nor infant baptism was directly authorized by Scripture; nor were marrying with a ring, fasting, the churching of women, university degrees and nearly all church

174. Ed. A. S. P. Woodhouse, *Puritanism and Liberty* (1938), p. 56.
175. Aspinwall, *The Legislative Power is Christs Peculiar Prerogative* (1656), sig. A 2.
176. Lilburne, *Englands Birth-Right* (1645), p. 13, in Haller, *Tracts on Liberty*, III. Lilburne cited Hebrews VII and other New Testament texts.
177. Winstanley, *The Law of Freedom* (1652), in Sabine, pp. 520–25.
178. Gauden, *The Case of Ministers Maintenance by Tithes* (1653), pp. 13–17.

offices, dignities and callings. He was not disturbed.[179] John Udall, with more hostile intent, had pointed out that the office of Archbishop was unlawful because unknown to Scripture; so was ordination except to the cure of a particular church.[180] Archbishop Bancroft countered by asking whether it was unlawful to have Christian magistrates, since there were none in the Apostles' times.[181] Bishop Sanderson, more dangerously, added to the list of absences from Scripture kneeling at communion, the surplice, lord bishops, a liturgy, holy days. He tried to reduce the arguments of the church's critics to absurdity by telling them that if we 'seek direct warrant from the written Word of God' for every action, 'all human authority will soon be despised' – the authority of princes no less than of parents and masters.[182] Laud also warned against 'the neglect and contempt' of the authority of the church which would result from excessive exaltation of Scripture.[183] 'If we must admit nothing but what we read in the Bible', mocked Selden, 'what will become of the Parliament?'[184] George Fox asked Dr Cradock, who came to visit him in jail in Scarborough, where he read in the Bible 'that ever any priest did marry any?' He did not record Cradock's answer.[185] 'It is no hard thing', said the ever-memorable John Hales, 'for a man that hath wit, and is strongly possessed of an opinion, and resolute to maintain it, to find some place of Scripture which by good handling will be wooed to cast a favourable countenance upon it'.[186]

So political commands could be drawn both from the Bible's texts and from its silences. 'Let them chant what they will of prerogatives', said Milton in 1641, 'we shall tell them of Scripture; of custom, we of Scripture; of acts and statutes, still of Scripture, till ... the mighty weakness of the Gospel throw down the weak mightiness of man's reasoning', and puts an end to 'tyranny and superstition'.[187] Others found nothing in the Bible to justify differences of rank and wealth. Peerage and gentry are 'ethnical and

179. Hooker, *The Laws of Ecclesiastical Polity*, Book I, xiv. 2; Book III, v. 1.
180. Udall, *A Demonstration of Discipline* (ed. E. Arber, 1880), pp. 21–3, 33–50: first published 1588. On the tricky question of whether bishops are to be found in the Bible, see P. Lake, *Anglicans and Puritans?*, pp. 94–7.
181. Ed. A. Peel, *Tracts ascribed to Richard Bancroft* (Cambridge U.P., 1953), pp. 165–6. The editor dates this to 1583–5.
182. Sanderson, *XXI Sermons* (1681), sig. a: first published 1656; *XXXV Sermons* (7th ed., 1681), pp. 61, 65; sig. a–av: first published 1657. See also p. 419 below.
183. Laud, *Works* (Oxford, 1847–60), II, pp. xv–xvi.
184. Selden, *Table-Talk* (1847), p. 92.
185. Fox, *Journal*, II (8th ed., 1902), p. 65.
186. John Hales, *Golden Remains* (1659), p. 4.
187. *MCPW*, I, pp. 700, 747, 827; *Of Christian Doctrine*, ibid., VI, p. 118.

heathenish distinctions'.[188] Samuel Butler mocked what by his time had become an accepted argument:

> The word 'bear-baiting'
> Is carnal, and of man's creating;
> For certainly there's no such word
> In all the Scripture on record.
> Therefore unlawful and a sin.[189]

Henry Barrow spoke of 'that old popish term of laymen', and Scottish Presbyterians did not find the distinction between clergy and laity in the New Testament. They objected to elders being called 'lay elders': they too had a vocation, just as pastors and doctors did.[190] Oliver Cromwell in January 1650 told the Irish that the distinction between clergy and laity was 'unknown to any save to the Antichristian Church, and such as derive themselves from her, *ab initio non fuit sic*'.[191]

But we have overshot the chronological limits of this chapter. Let us return to the years before 1640.

188. [Bruno Ryves], *Angliae Ruina* (1647), pp. 22, 27; views attributed to 'the Brownists and Anabaptists of Colchester'.
189. Butler, *Hudibras*, Part I, Canto 1, lines 799–803. Wilders's note cites a passage showing that Butler was hardly caricaturing (Butler, *Hudibras*, ed. J. Wilders, Oxford U.P., 1967). Cf. John Hall of Richmond, *Government and Obedience* (1654), pp. 433–4, and H. C. Porter, 'The Nose of Wax: Scripture and the Spirit from Erasmus to Milton', *TRHS* (1964), pp. 161–4, 170–71, and *passim*.
190. F. J. Powicke, *Henry Barrow* (1900), p. 99; J. N. Buchanan, *Marginal Scotland* (New York, 1989), I, p. 269.
191. Abbott, *Writings and Speeches of Oliver Cromwell*, II, p. 197.

II. THE REVOLUTIONARY BIBLE

2. Before 1640

[English Puritans] maintain that the Word of God contained in the writings of the Prophets and Apostles is . . . the sole canon and rule of all matters of religion and the worship and service of God whatsoever. . . . And therefore that it is a sin to force any Christian to do any act of religion or divine service that cannot evidently be warranted by the same.
William Bradshaw, *English Puritanisme* (1605), Chapter 1. Republished 1640 and 1641.

When they and their Bibles were alone together, what strange fantastical opinion soever at any time entered into their heads, their use was to think the Spirit taught it them.
Richard Hooker, *Of the Laws of Ecclesiastical Polity*, Preface, VIII. 7.

The Bible in English under every weaver's and chambermaid's arm hath done much harm... For controversy is a civil war with the pen which pulls out the sword soon afterwards.
The Duke of Newcastle, quoted in A. S. Turberville, *A History of Welbeck Abbey and its owners* (1938–9), I, pp. 173–4. Disputations, the Duke added, ought to be confined to the schools, and books on controversial opinions should be written only in Latin, so as to prevent ordinary people from being heated by altercation.

I

There was a period a few years ago in which a number of historians reacted against what they believed to be Whig legends of a two-party struggle carried on in Parliament between government and opposition. This, they rightly suggested, is anachronistic. But some went to the opposite extreme of stressing above all consensus, basic agreement among members of the political nation on major constitutional and religious issues; they virtually ignored the vast majority of men and women who were not included in 'the political nation'. There were squabbles, 'revisionist' historians suggested, but they were not about constitutional or religious matters of principle; rather they were between court factions motivated by self-interest and careerism. It was a belated application of the Namier method, which produced useful results in interpreting mid-eighteenth-century politics, and demolished the Whig interpretation. But the applicability of the Namier method to the early seventeenth century has never been convincingly established. There is a circular ring of assumptions. First you assume that there are no quarrels of principle in that period; then you Namierize politics and politicians; then you claim that this shows there were no issues of principle. Q.E.D.

There is superficial evidence to back the 'revisionist' view. If you look at what men said in print, in Parliament and on other public occasions, consensus prevails in church and state. The simple social explanation for this was given by James I: 'If there were not a King, they [the gentry] would be less cared for than other men'.[1] 'Revisionists' ignore the tensions which rent this society. Sir Robert Cotton, like James, had them in mind when in 1628 he urged that MPs of the Parliament then assembling should continue to oppose the royal favourite, the Duke of Buckingham, but should be very careful not to go too far, lest a popular uprising should be triggered off.[2] That such a revolt was on the cards was asserted by several foreign ambassadors in the 1620s; it was 'hoped for' by Sir Simonds D'Ewes in 1622.[3] But he kept his diary in cypher. The private thoughts of MPs are more important than their public words on formal occasions.

Once we get behind the screen of loyal verbiage, it becomes clear that there were fundamental disagreements of principle at stake, among the rulers as well as between rulers and ruled. Books like Peter Lake's *Moderate Puritans and the Elizabethan Church: Presbyterianism and English Conformist Thought from Whitgift to Hooker* (1988) have made the point about religion. Richard Cust's *The Forced Loan and English Politics, 1626–1628* (Oxford U.P., 1987) has done the same for Parliamentary politics. The seminal collective volume edited in 1989 by Richard Cust and Ann Hughes, *Conflict in Early Stuart England: Studies in Religion and Politics*, has finally exposed the inadequacy of revisionism in the eyes of the younger generation of historians. Johann Sommerville in *Politics and Ideology in England, 1603–1640*

1. Ed. C. H. McIlwain, *The Political Works of James I* (1918), p. 340. This reprints the edition of 1616.
2. Cotton, *The Dangers Wherein the Kingdome now Standeth*. I owe this reference to the kindness of Simon Adams.
3. Ed. E. Bourcier, *The Diary of Sir Simonds D'Ewes, 1622–4* (Paris, n.d., ?1974), p. 58; cf. pp. 64–5, 83, 130, 145.

(1986) has restored issues of ideological principle to the centre of the picture. James Holstun is much to be congratulated for looking at the evidence of popular Biblically-based poetry, which Gardiner knew about but which revisionists have ignored. Holstun has revealed 'collective, rationally motivated political opposition' beneath the apparently arbitrary assassination of the Duke of Buckingham by John Felton. He cites a poem saying that many people call Buckingham the 'Achan of our English Israel', and another which makes Felton quote Ehud who slew Eglon, King of Moab (Judges II.15–21) and Phineas who stood in the gap – an oft-quoted folk hero comparable to Horatius who kept the bridge.[4] We must distinguish between the way in which men felt able to express themselves, their conventionally loyal language, on the one hand, and their actions on the other. Their language was often Aesopian, conveying messages different from what appears on the surface. To convince oneself of this possibility does not call for great intellectual or imaginative effort. A glance at the history of eastern Europe over the past decade might help.

The Bible facilitated this double-talk. Men knew their Bible very well in the seventeenth century, and could convey messages through allusions to it which are lost on a godless age. The Romanian priest László Tokes was able under Ceauşescu to get political messages across to his congregation by preaching on Nebuchadnezzar and other wicked rulers. Since most Bibles had been pulped in Romania, it is likely that informers in the congregation might miss some of his subtler points.[5] Similar tricks were used in seventeenth-century England.

The English protestant tradition, firmly based on the Bible, looked back to Edward VI ('good King Josiah') and to Elizabeth as types of godly rulers, to the Emperor Constantine as the type of Christian monarch. But even towards the end of Elizabeth's reign there were divisions in her Council, doubts about the Queen's whole-hearted dedication to the sort of protestantism that some of her subjects professed. Elizabeth had to be coerced into allowing Mary Queen of Scots to be executed; she tried very hard to avoid fighting Spain; the defeat of the Spanish Armada owed at least as much to private enterprise as to government preparation.

Under James I the godliness of the monarch came under more telling

4. Holstun, '"God bless thee, little David": John Felton as a Protestant Tyrannicide', in *Puritanism in Old and New England*, Millersville. Holstun quotes F. W. Fairholt, *Poems and Songs Relating to George Villiers, Duke of Buckingham and his Assassination by John Felton* (Percy Soc., 1850).
5. John Sweeney, *The Life and Evil Times of Ceauşescu* (1991), pp. 196–7.

criticism as the King manifestly failed to give a lead to European protestants in the hour of their need. But at least men could be confident of James's protestantism: he had denounced the Pope as Antichrist. Charles no longer gave even that assurance. The influence first of Buckingham then of Queen Henrietta Maria and Archbishop Laud seemed ominous, as did the King's behaviour towards Scotland, where he resumed confiscated church property as well as increasing the power of bishops and imposing a prayer book which appeared to make concessions to popery. The Bible taught obedience to godly princes. But the Old Testament at least had no doubts about the treatment which wicked kings deserved. What was the criterion of wickedness? Those sins which the marginal notes to the Geneva Bible especially emphasized were idolatry and persecution. Popery was by definition idolatrous, and papists were expected to persecute. So Charles's leanings, or alleged leanings, towards popery laid him wide open to criticism.

James's critics had been able to concentrate on attacking his ministers and favourites, especially Buckingham and his papist relatives. Parliamentarians tried to observe the same convention under Charles. But the King called their bluff. He closely associated himself with Buckingham, and personally protected and promoted high-flying clerics like Montagu and Manwaring. After the dissolution of Parliament in 1629 he took full responsibility for government policy. Critics, in England or in Scotland, still tried to preserve the distinction between the King and his evil councillors. But in Scotland this wore very thin as Charles again took personal responsibility for government decisions; and English politicians were watching Scotland closely.

The Scottish Presbyterians were diligent students of the Bible: their National Covenant was profoundly Biblical.[6] Knox had set a precedent of denouncing ungodly Kings and especially Queens; and in England during the eleven years of Charles's personal government men were reading their Bibles as well as watching Scotland. They found support for godly kings in the Bible; but they also found a disconcerting black/white, either/or emphasis. He who is not for me is against me. Men had to contemplate the possibility that it was not just the King's evil councillors who were to blame – though clearly they must go first of all. Was it just possible that Charles himself was so much under the influence of his Jezebel that he too was reprehensible?

In the censored society of sixteenth- and seventeenth-century England those who most wished to communicate, to discuss, were those who knew

6. See Chapter 11 below.

their Bible best. The Bible was what they wanted to discuss, for its guidance on the form of worship most pleasing to God in a society which had cast off one form and – some thought – not yet finally settled into a better one. Because church and state were one, religion became politics, with the Bible as text book for both. The words of the Bible limited the way in which men thought about society and its institutions. Hence the fierce quarrels during the Reformation about whether 'church' meant a national or international organization, or a local congregation. In 1633 two Somerset boys who were in trouble for breaking church windows by playing ball defended themselves by asking 'where is the church? The church is where the congregation is assembled, though it be at the beacon at the top of the hill of Quantock'.[7] That theological remark may have been no more than a ploy to get themselves out of a difficulty; but its sophistication suggests that they moved in circles where such ideas were familiar. A decade later Roger Williams similarly contrasted 'a church of dead stones, the parish church' with 'any true church of God, consisting of living and believing stones'. Quakers picked up a radical tradition when they insisted on speaking of 'the steeple-house' or 'stone-house', to distinguish it from 'any true church of God'.[8] If concepts changed, the Bible's words could not be replaced: their meaning had to be altered.

Similar problems arose from the word which the Authorized Version translated 'ordain' in Acts XIV.23. The Scot George Gillespie caused consternation in the Westminster Assembly of Divines when in 1644 he said that the word translated 'ordaining' by 'the Episcopal translators . . . was truly "choosing", importing the people's suffrages in electing their officers'.[9] This would have opened the door to congregational independency, and might have been difficult to reconcile with a national church.

Things had been relatively easy when the church exercised effective control, and heretics could be kept under, by violence if necessary. Heretics had always appealed to the Bible; with the Bible available in English the maintenance of one-mindedness became increasingly difficult. There was a battle in the sixteenth and seventeenth centuries to retain some authority in

7. H. A. Wyndham, *A Family History, 1410–1688: The Wyndhams of Norfolk and Somerset* (Oxford U.P., 1939), p. 168.
8. Roger Williams, *The Bloudy Tenent of Persecution*, pp. 286–7. First published 1644. Cf. Roger Crab, *The English Hermite* (1655) (ed. A. Hopton, 1990), pp. 30–36. Crab uses 'stone-house' and 'steeple-house' interchangeably.
9. R. Baillie, *Letters and Journals*, I, pp. 419–20. The Geneva Bible had it both ways, translating 'ordained them elders by election in every church'. The margin added 'chose and placed them by the voice of the congregation'.

interpreting the Scriptures. For if there was no recognized official interpretation, no 'Authorized Version', the appeal to the Bible became in effect an appeal to individual readers of God's Word. John Davies of Hereford criticized what he saw as presumption in interpreting the Scriptures:

> Sith they will learn but of themselves and pride,
> So not thy Word, but they are erring so.[10]

Unofficial guides to interpretation of the Bible, Biblical dictionaries and concordances, versifications of Scripture, were published in significant numbers in the early seventeenth century: they were clearly in demand, especially by the 'middle sort'.[11]

So the Bible became a battle-field. For those who knew it well, judicious selection could turn up the desired answers to most problems. You could find defences of the *status quo* – 'the powers that be are ordained of God' (Romans XIII.1); but you could also find severe criticism of kings, defences of the rights of the poor, attacks on usury.[12] You could find authorization for wholesale massacres of the heathen and idolaters: for a few examples see Joshua VI.20–21, VIII.21–6, X.28–41, XII *passim*. Bad kings in the Old Testament were usually those who spared idolaters. In the Middle Ages the church found justification alike of holy poverty and of crusades against the infidel. 'Thou shalt not suffer a witch to live' was a much-quoted text in the seventeenth century, when scepticism of witchcraft and of persecution of witches was already being expressed.[13]

The Bible could offer codes by which novel or unpopular ideas might be communicated with less risk. For Norwich Lollards in the early fifteenth century Caiaphas had been a useful shorthand expression for bishops; Abraham Fraunce in 1596 wrote that 'Caiaphas gan to be hot and took on like to a prelate.' 'The virtuous Josiah' was a model for kings, as he long continued to be.[14] In 1648 the author of *Persecutio Undecima* wrote of Puritans 'They took up a canting language to themselves . . . abusing

10. Davies, *The Muses Sacrifice* (1612), p. 37, in *Complete Works* (ed. A. B. Grosart, 1878).
11. L. B. Wright, *Middle-Class Culture in Elizabethan England,* Chapter VIII *passim.* See also p. 347 below.
12. See pp. 67–70 and Chapter 6 below.
13. See pp. 402–3 below.
14. Ed. N. P. Tanner, *Heresy Trials in the Diocese of Norwich, 1428–31* (Camden 4th Series, 20, 1977), pp. 18, 46–7, 147; Fraunce, *The Countess of Pembroke's Emanuell* (ed. Grosart, 1871), p. 49; A. G. Dickens, *Lollards and Protestants in the Diocese of York, 1509–1558* (Oxford U.P., 1959), p. 129.

phrases of Scripture, thereby to understand one another'.[15] New allegorical significance could be given familiar stories. As we shall see, Cain and Abel, Antichrist and Samson, could convey very different meanings to different people, different groups. Some nonconformists had agreed alternative meanings to those accepted by the state church; others were more certain of their disagreement with the establishment than of alternatives.

An apparently innocuous factual statement could convey much more than the words said. 'Judas was the first bishop', wrote Lord Brooke with deceptive simplicity.[16] Hobbes repeated this, carefully giving his reference to Acts I.20.[17] He also wrote 'of the maintenance of our Saviour and his Apostles, we read only that they had a purse (which was carried by Judas Iscariot); and that of the Apostles, such as were fishermen did sometimes use their trade'.[18] His historical accuracy cannot be faulted. But what he means is that the clergy should work for their living and not extract tithes from their parishioners. A parson who read Hobbes might find it a little less easy to claim a divine right to tithes. Bunyan tells us that Christ's 'little ones . . . are not gentlemen; . . . they cannot with Pontius Pilate speak Hebrew, Greek and Latin'.[19] Again the statement is accurate, if we accept 'Christ's little ones' as a description of Bunyan's church members. Yet the intention was to convey a contemptuous dismissal of the gentry, of parsons of the Church of England and of the universities which trained them, together with the classical curriculum whose only virtue was to distinguish them from the vulgar. George Wither delicately hinted at his disapproval of the hierarchy's suppression of lectureships by describing Jesus in Jerusalem:

> Possession of his house he got,
> The merchants thence expelled;
> And though the priests were mad thereat,
> His lectures there he held.[20]

Much could be conveyed by denial. Take for instance Charles Herle's dedication to the impeccably Anglican Thomas Fuller of *Ahab's Fall by his*

15. [R. Chestlin], op. cit. (1681), p. 28. First published 1648.
16. Brooke, *A Discourse . . . of that Episcopacie which is exercised in England* (1641), p. 75, in Haller, *Tracts on Liberty*, II.
17. Hobbes, *Leviathan*, p. 557. The Geneva Bible, unexpectedly, has 'charge' for the A.V.'s 'bishopric'.
18. Ibid., p. 564.
19. *BMW*, I, p. 304.
20. Wither, *Hymns and Songs of the Church* (ed. E. Farr, 1856), pp. 193–4. First published 1623.

Prophets Flatteries (1644). 'If any should construe what is (in pursuance of the text) spoken of King Ahab and Jezebel, any way to be meant of our dread Sovereign and his Consort . . . it was far from his purpose'. He has raised the possibility by denying it.[21]

Conrad Russell quotes an agreeable story of Dr Robert Jenison, who had been required to preach a sermon on obedience because of his suspected Puritanism. He took the traditional text, Romans XII.1 – 'the powers that be are ordained of God'; but he strayed into King Asa's victory over the Ethiopians because he had cut down idols, and to Psalm XXXIII.16: 'there is no king saved by the multitude of an host'. He said he was only talking of man's weakness without God.[22]

When Milton wrote 'Hail wedded love . . . as saints and patriarchs used' (*PL*, IV. 750–62), the word 'patriarchs' transformed this from praise of the matrimony acceptable in England to a furtive defence of polygamy. Milton had concluded his *Readie and Easie Way to Establish a Free Commonwealth*, his last desperate attempt to prevent a restoration of monarchy in 1660, with a reference to Coniah: 'though I have none to cry to but with the prophet, O earth, earth, earth; to tell the very soil itself what God hath determined of Coniah and his seed for ever'. His meaning would be clear to those who knew their Bibles and the Geneva annotations. 'Coniah' is a contemptuous nickname for Jehoiachin, the idolatrous King of Judah who (in the words of the Geneva margin) 'was justly deprived of his kingdom' when he was exiled to Babylon (Jeremiah XXII.24–9). Milton's Coniah is Charles I, 'a despised and broken idol'. 'He and his seed' had been 'cast out into a land that they know not'. 'There shall be no man of his seed that shall prosper and sit upon the throne of David'. Milton may have recalled hearing his former parish minister Richard Stock declare that 'exile and banishment . . . is a sign and a proof . . . of the anger and hatred of God'.[23]

As we read the words on the page of seventeenth-century literature we may miss a great deal if we are not always on the look-out for Biblical

21. Fuller, op. cit., sig. A 2v.

22. Russell, *The Fall of the British Monarchies*, p. 87, quoting *CSPD, 1638–9*. Jenison is said to have written a book 'concerning the idolatry of the Israelites', which does not appear to have survived.

23. *MCPW*, VII, p. 388; Stock, *An Exposition upon the whole book of the Prophecy of Malachi* (ed. Grosart, Edinburgh, 1865), p. 22. First published 1641, fifteen years after Stock's death. Was the delay in publishing due to considerations of censorship? William Greenhill included Coniah among kings whose 'memory stinks, their names rot. . . . for their idolatry and oppression' (*An Exposition of the five first Chapters of the Prophet Ezekiel*, 1645, pp. 41–2).

shorthand and codes. Michael Wilding, more alert than most critics to the political circumstances in which Milton had to write, has recently pointed out that 'yet once more' at the beginning of *Lycidas* does not mean that 'this is not the first time he has come forward with an immature perform-ance'. Milton was alluding to the 'very specific revolutionary implications of Hebrews XII.25–7: "Yet once more I shake not the earth only, but also heaven". And this word, "Yet once more" signifies the removing of those things that are shaken'. The words 'yet once more' were attributed to 'him that speaketh from heaven', apparently in reference to Haggai II.7. Wilding insists that 'this was the opening clue on how to read Milton's indictment of the corrupt clergy and academy of the 1630s'.[24] Close reading of this historically informed kind transforms our understanding of the poem.

Most preachers, Professor Cope reminds us, 'treated politics metaphori-cally if at all, so that the authorities would have scant evidence upon which to prosecute'.[25] They could rely upon their readers' knowledge of the Scriptures, or on the availability of open Bibles to members of godly congregations. Tricky issues were social and political as well as theological. Lollards had found profoundly subversive messages in the Bible.[26] Robert Crowley in 1550 published a tract against peasants who had revolted in the preceding year; but in it he reminded his readers that God had punished Pharaoh and Nebuchadnezzar for their tyranny.[27] As men and women outside the political nation came to study the Scriptures, it became increas-ingly difficult to maintain a single official interpretation.

The Elizabethan Homilies, which non-preaching parsons were intended to read regularly to their congregations, made full use of the Bible to teach passive obedience. The *Homily against Disobedience and Wilfull Rebellion* insisted that all kings, queens and other governors are specially appointed by God's ordinance; a rebel is worse than the worst prince. It cited the example of David to make the point that neither exceptional virtue, high rank nor the favour of God could justify rebellion even against the manifestly wicked King Saul. David was 'so good a subject that he obeyed so evil a king'.[28] Acts V.29 tells us that 'we ought to obey God rather than man'; the *Homily of Obedience* permits us to disobey kings or magistrates

24. Wilding, *Dragon's Teeth* (1987), pp. 11–13; 'Milton and the English Revolution', in *Revolution as History* (ed. S. N. Mukherjee and J. O. Ward, Sydney, 1989), pp. 40–41.
25. E. S. Cope, *Politics without Parliaments, 1629–1640* (1987), p. 217.
26. See pp. 9–11 above.
27. Crowley, *The Way to Wealth*, sig. A 3. quoted by Martin, *Religious Radicals*, p. 156.
28. *Sermons or Homilies* (Oxford U.P., 1802), pp. 471–3, 479–83.

only 'if they would command us to do anything contrary to God's commandments'. But even then we must not resist but 'patiently suffer all
wrongs and injuries, referring the judgment of our cause only to God'.[29]

II

After 1560 the marginal notes of the Geneva Bible offered interpretations
different from those of the Homilies, and the Geneva Bible was sup-
plemented by translations of Calvin's innumerable commentaries and
sermons on books of the Bible. Since Calvin lived in a republic he was free
to express more seditious sentiments than English divines could do. There
is, Calvin wrote, 'nothing more pernicious than a corrupt and wicked
prince, who spreadeth abroad his corruptions over all the body'.[30] His
Commentary on Daniel made much of the necessary subordination of
'earthly princes' to God.[31] In his Commentary on the Psalms Calvin was
very severe on kings (Psalm LXXXII), and on tyrants and wicked judges
when he discussed Psalm XCIV.[32]

The Bible had been a political creation from the beginning. Christians
rearranged the Hebrew Scriptures in the second century AD to produce 'the
Old Testament'. Gnostic texts were excluded from the New Testament,
the epistle of James and the Book of Revelation were admitted to the
canon very late. Translations into the vernacular were – and were
recognized to be – political constructions. Luther's German version was
directed against radical sectaries as well as against papists. The Bishops'
Bible of 1568 was intended to replace the Geneva Bible.

An English version of the New Testament had been published in Geneva
in 1557, while Mary was still on the English throne. It was the work of
exiles. The full Bible was published in England in 1560, dedicated to Queen
Elizabeth. The translation appears to have been mainly the work of William
Whittingham, with assistance from Anthony Gilby and Thomas Sampson.
In exile during Mary's reign Whittingham and Gilby had sided with Knox
in 'the troubles of Frankfort', against Richard Cox and other supporters of

29. Ibid., p. 93; cf. pp. 501–3, citing Romans XIII.
30. Calvin, *A Commentary upon the Prophecie of Isaiah* (translated by Clement Cotton,
1609), p. 17.
31. *Commentaries of that divine John Calvin upon the Prophet Daniell* (trans. Arthur
Golding, 1570), fol. 111v–112.
32. *The Psalmes of David and others. With M. John Calvins Commentaries* (trans. Golding,
1571).

the English prayer book. They later removed to the more congenial climate of Geneva. Changes in doctrine in the notes of successive editions of the Geneva Bible have been attributed to ideas put forward by Knox in books and pamphlets published in 1558, and to political developments in France and Scotland between 1557 and 1560.[33] The 1576 edition, edited by Laurence Tomson, included some of Béza's ideas. Whittingham contributed a dedicatory epistle to Christopher Goodman's *How Superior Powers ought to be obeyed* (Geneva, 1558) – a defence of Wyatt's rebellion against Mary, and a fierce attack on her and on the government of women in general. Sampson is believed to have been a part-author in 1572 of the Puritan *Admonition to Parliament*; Gilby published *A View of Antichrist, his Laws and Ceremonies in our English Church, unreformed*, six years later. He also translated Béza's *Psalms of David* in 1581 (reprinted 1590). Whittingham became a protégé of the Dudleys, Earls of Warwick and Leicester. The Geneva Bible came from a closely knit group of Marian exiles, including Laurence Tomson, who were prominent in the radical wing of the Puritan movement under Elizabeth, and who nevertheless had powerful protectors in the aristocracy. As late as 1604 William Covel, ex-Puritan, speaks of 'those bitter invectives' of Whittingham and Gilby in the same breath with Goodman, Knox, Buchanan, Martin Marprelate and Penry.[34]

The Preface to the Geneva Bible deplored the 'errors, sects and heresies' which 'grow daily for lack of the true knowledge' of the Bible. These heresies no doubt included many beliefs favoured by the bishops, such as Gilby was later to denounce in his *View of Antichrist*. The Geneva Bible aimed deliberately at a wide circulation, at helping men and women to be their own interpreters of the sacred text. It was published in handy quarto editions, with maps and concordances. Chapters were for the first time divided into verses, and were given much fuller headings summarizing the contents. The marginal notes, in addition to conveying Genevan views, helped the unsophisticated reader to find his or her way about.

In 1566 Archbishop Parker and Edmund Grindal, Bishop of London, wrote to Cecil asking for a twelve-year extension of the privileges of the printers of the Geneva Bible. Rather surprisingly, they remarked that 'It shall nothing hinder, but rather do much good, to have diversity of translations and readings'.[35] The Geneva version flourished under Grindal's

33. Ridley, *John Knox*, p. 288.
34. Covel, *A Modest and Reasonable Examination of Some Things in Use in the Church of England* (1604), p. 28.
35. *Correspondence of Matthew Parker* (Parker Soc., 1853), pp. 261–2.

archbishopric, and between 1560 and 1603 some ninety editions were printed. When Silver-tongued Smith told his congregation that 'this note is in the margin of your Bibles', he must have assumed that all of them used the Geneva version.[36] But after about 1616 it had to be smuggled in from The Netherlands. In 1632 a man was imprisoned for importing Geneva Bibles.[37] A year later Sir William Boswell, ambassador to The Netherlands, reported to Secretary Coke that among other seditious books secretly shipped from Amsterdam to London were 'two impressions lately of the Bible with Genevan notes', one with a false title-page. This report – one of many – was passed to and endorsed by Archbishop Laud.[38] At his trial Laud admitted suppressing the Geneva Bible, but claimed to have done so in the interests of English printers as well as because of the notes. He did not explain why it could not be printed in England.[39]

The Geneva translation remained popular. Among those who used it we may list Sir Walter Ralegh,[40] Sir Philip Sidney, Thomas Whythorne, Richard Hooker, Henry Vaughan, George Fox, Marvell: Shakespeare, Massinger, Dryden and Shadwell (and no doubt many more dramatists) refer to it. Lancelot Andrewes, a divine-right theorist who echoed James I in saying kings were gods, nevertheless normally took his texts for sermons from the Geneva version. Milton and Bunyan cite both the A.V. and Geneva. Milton seems to have preferred the latter, notably in *Samson Agonistes*; but some of his amanuenses used the A.V. The translators' Preface to the A.V. quotes Scripture fourteen times, each time from the Geneva Bible.[41]

Some of its marginal notes were thought to have political implications. The egregious Peter Heylyn tells us that the Geneva Bible's notes 'in many places savour of sedition, and in some of faction, destructive of the persons and powers of kings, and of all civil intercourse and human society'.[42] For

36. Henry Smith, *Sermons* (1631), p. 497. This was the 14th edition: it was first published in 1592, a year after Smith's death.
37. Ed. S. R. Gardiner, *Reports of Cases in the courts of Star Chamber and High Commission* (Camden Soc., new series, 1886), p. 274.
38. *CSPD, 1633–4*, p. 213; cf. *1634–5*, p. 116.
39. Laud, *History of the Troubles and Trial*, in *Works*, IV, pp. 262–3.
40. Ralegh occasionally quarrels with the Geneva marginal notes – e.g. *History of the World* (Edinburgh, 1820), I, pp. 152, 255–6; II, pp. 4, 10, 371.
41. P. A. Welsby, *Lancelot Andrewes, 1555–1626* (1958), pp. 193, 207; *MER*, p. 395. Cf. *The Writings of John Greenwood, 1587–1590* (ed. L. H. Carlson, 1962), p. 158, for Andrewes's scornful dismissal of the Geneva Bible. I owe the last point to David Daniell.
42. Heylyn, *Aerius Redivivus: Or, The History of the Presbyterians* (1670), p. 247. Heylyn is echoing King James, quoted on p. 64 below.

instance: 'The Lord took the defence of this poor stranger [Abraham] against a mighty king' (Genesis XII.17). Pharaoh, Saul (I Samuel XIX.15, XXIII.27), Ahab (I Kings XVI–XXI) and Nahash the Ammonite (I Samuel XI.2) are all described as tyrants. (Tyndale had thought that the 'giants in those days' of Genesis VI.4 referred to tyrants.) 'The more cruelly tyrants rage, the nearer is God's help' (note of Exodus, I.22, V.9, etc.). Tyranny is associated with idolatry (Exodus III.19), as Milton associated it; and with persecution (I Samuel XXIII.24), as Bunyan associated it. 'God . . . taketh vengeance on tyrants even in this life' (Judges IX.54, *à propos* Abimelech: cf. II Kings IX.33–7: Jezebel's death was 'a spectacle and example of God's judgments to all tyrants'). The note on I Samuel XXVI.19 said approvingly that 'Jehu slew two kings at God's appointment'.

The radical émigré Thomas Scott in 1620 concluded his pamphlet, *The Belgique Pismire*, with the last words of the 20th Psalm: 'Save, Lord; let the King hear us when we call him. Amen'. The Geneva margin glossed these words, lest too much be attributed to kings: 'Let the King be able to deliver us by thy strength, when we seek unto him for succour'. Sir Robert Filmer noted with approval that, although the word 'tyrant' appeared frequently in the Geneva Bible, it was never used in the Authorized Version.[43]

When Daniel disobeyed a decree of King Darius forbidding petitioning any God or man but the King, he was cast into the lions' den. He emerged unscathed, and explained the miracle by saying 'unto thee, O King, I have done no hurt'. The Geneva margin glosses this: 'he did disobey the King's wicked commandment [in order] to obey God, and so did no injustice to the King, who ought to command nothing whereby God should be dishonoured'. Unless we know that Daniel was in direct communication with God, that sounds rather like a sophistry: many seventeenth-century Englishmen thought they were in such direct communication with God whom the authorities in church and state would have totally rejected. Calvin's comment on the passage reads 'the fear of God must go before, that kings may obtain their authority. . . . Earthly princes deprive themselves of all authority when they rise up against God, yea, they are unworthy to be counted amongst the company of men. We ought rather to spit in their faces than to obey them when they . . . spoil God of his right'.[44] But then Calvin did not live under a monarchy. The Geneva margin raised the question of who should decide: the individual conscience or authority in church and state? What was to happen when they came in conflict?

43. Filmer, *The Anarchy of a Limited or Mixed Monarchy* (1648), in *Patriarcha and Other Political Works* (ed. P. Laslett, Oxford 1949), p. 292.
44. Daniel VI; Calvin, *Commentaries . . . upon the Prophet Daniell*, folio 111v–112.

Elizabeth had warned James VI of the dangers inherent in Puritan Biblicism, a warning which was unnecessary in view of his own experience with Scottish Presbyterians. James thoroughly disapproved of Puritans who set what they held to be God's commands against those of 'God's silly vassal', the King; they had been anticipated by Bonner, the great persecutor of Mary's reign, who under Elizabeth declared that he could observe the Injunctions and Homilies prescribed by authority only 'if they be not contrary and repugnant to God's law and the statutes and ordinances of the Church'.[45] When Isaiah XXX.33 said 'Tophet is prepared of old . . . even for the King', the Geneva margin hammered the point home: 'so that their estate or degree cannot exempt the wicked'.[46]

King James came to think the Geneva Bible the worst translation. He described the marginal note on Exodus I.19 as seditious for saying that when Hebrew midwives disobeyed an Egyptian order to kill all male Hebrew children, 'their disobedience herein was lawful'. Bishop Babington, publishing in 1604, thought that the midwives were right to obey God rather than man. Milton used the midwives' behaviour as one of many examples of lying 'approved by God himself'.[47] More reasonably, James was unhappy about the marginal note on II Chronicles XV.16: Asa 'gave place to foolish pity' and lack of zeal when he only deposed his mother for idolatry and did not have her killed. The King was perhaps sensitive on the subject of the deposition and execution of queens, his mother having suffered that fate. But James accepted that the example of 'that paction which God made with Noah after the deluge' meant that 'a king governing in a settled kingdom' must 'rule according to his laws'.[48]

Scholarly Biblical criticism, supported by the Geneva margin, made inroads into the doctrine of the Divine Right of Kings. In 1512 the words of Psalm CV.14–15, 'touch not mine anointed', were taken by the Abbot of Winchcombe to apply to the clergy, who should be exempt from secular criminal jurisdiction.[49] After the Reformation the phrase came to be applied to kings, who had been anointed at their coronation. 'The good old Archbishop of Dublin, Dr Buckley', was unkindly said to have had only one sermon, on this text, 'touch not mine anointed', which he *read out*

45. Quoted by Susan Brigden, *London and the Reformation* (Oxford U.P., 1989), p. 433.
46. *OED* defines 'Tophet' as 'a place for the deposit of refuse', hence 'the place of punishment for the wicked after death'.
47. Babington, *Comfortable Notes Upon the books of Exodus and Leviticus*, pp. 11–14; *MCPW*, VI, p. 763.
48. James I, *Works*, pp. 530–31.
49. G. R. Elton, *Reform and Reformation in England, 1529–1558* (1977), p. 54.

in his cathedral every year.[50] But the Geneva margin explained that this text referred to 'those whom I have sanctified to be my people'. This makes better sense in context: God suffered no man to harm the seed of Abraham, warning kings 'touch not mine anointed'. It was, as Coppe, Milton and Ludlow remarked, 'spoken to reprove kings', at a time when there were no kings in Israel.[51] The phrase was a matter of controversy at the beginning of the civil war, as we see from an anonymous royalist pamphlet of 1642: *The Soveraignty of Kings: Or An Absolute Answer and Confutation* (of schismatics who claim that Psalm C V refers to 'inferior subjects'). This 'dangerous tenet', the author added, will 'turn a monarchy into a democracy'. It 'hath been buzzed into the ears of the people, as if they only were anointed, none but they'.[52] Wither defiantly repeated the Geneva margin's version in the dark days of 1660: 'There be among those who are now despised some of those Anointed-ones of the Lord, who he will not permit to be harmfully touched without vengeance. For he hath other Anointed-ones beside kings, whom he reproves for their sakes'.[53]

Sometimes the Geneva Bible's comments were social. 'Oftentimes they which are despised of men are favoured of God' (Genesis XXIX.31 – the fruitful Leah as opposed to the barren Rachel). 'Godly counsel ought ever to be obeyed, though it come from our inferiors, for to such God oftentimes giveth wisdom to humble them that are exalted, and to declare that one member hath need of another' (Exodus XVIII.24). 'None should be preferred to honour that have not the gifts of God meet for the same' (Genesis XVI.38 – *à propos* Joseph in Egypt). 'When they linger which ought to be the chiefest preachers', God 'will raise up other extraordinarily, in despite of them' (Luke XIX.39). If 'they', Pharisees, were interpreted as bishops, then 'other' would be unlicensed preachers. There are limits on the

---

50. A. Clogie, *Speculum Episcoporum, The Life and Death of . . . Dr William Bedell*, in *Two Biographies of William Bedell* (ed. E. S. Shuckburgh, Cambridge U.P., 1902), p. 146. The reference is to Archbishop Bulkeley.
51. *MCPW*, VII, pp. 475–6; Edmund Ludlow, *A Voyce from the Watch Tower* (ed. A. B. Worden, Camden 4th Series, 1978), pp. 139–40, 204, 210; Smith, *Ranter Writings*, p. 55. The one Shakespearean king who claims to be the Lord's anointed is Richard III, murderer and usurper (IV. 14. 149). In his Commonplace Book Milton rejected 'what people now think, namely that all kings are the anointed of God' (*MCPW*, I, p. 474; cf. III, pp. 586–7). Cf. *Prynne's Vindication of Psalm CV.15* (1643). See also pp. 183–7 below.
52. Op. cit., sig. A 1v, A3, 4; [Anon.], *A True State of the Case of the Commonwealth*, pp. 14–15.
53. Wither, *Fides Anglicana*, p. 22, in *Miscellaneous Works* (Spenser Soc.), V, 1877.

power of the magistrate: the command 'thou shalt not slay the innocent' is glossed 'whether thou be magistrate or commanded by the magistrate' (Exodus XXIII.7). 'By God's just judgments they are made slaves to infidels which neglect their vocation in defending the faithful' (Judges XVI.25). But God does not use the vulgar multitude for such purposes. 'Neither dignity nor multitude have authority to pass the bounds that God's word prescribeth' (Exodus XIX.24). 'Learn what it is to obey God only and to forsake the multitude', we are told in connection with the story of Noah (Genesis VI.23). The Geneva Bible was anxious to guard against social revolutionary interpretations of the millennium, recalling no doubt Luther's experience with Anabaptists. On Isaiah LXV.17–25, which describes 'new heavens and a new earth' as a society in which there shall be no exploitation, it cautiously comments that this will be 'in the *heavenly* Jerusalem'; the church '*shall seem* to dwell in a new world' (my italics).

The New Testament offered fewer occasions for political comment; but there were some. Thus the Geneva margin elaborated on the Apostle's 'We ought rather to obey God than men' by saying 'We ought to obey no man, but so far forth as obeying him we may obey God' (Acts V.29). When Paul in Romans XIII.5 tells us to 'be subject . . . for conscience sake', the margin expands, in a very carefully worded passage: 'We must obey the magistrate, not only for fear of punishment, but much more because that (although the magistrate have no power over the conscience of man, yet seeing he is God's minister) he cannot be resisted by any good conscience'. Submission for conscience sake means 'so far as lawfully we may: for if unlawful things be commanded, we must answer as Peter teacheth us, it is better to obey God than men'. Simple believers may be wiser than the ungodly learned: the Geneva marginal note to Revelation IX.3 equated doctors of divinity with locusts. (The first edition of the Puritan *Admonition to Parliament* of 1572 attacked doctors, though this disappeared in the second edition.)

I have picked out examples of marginal notes which have possible social or political significance: they are only a small part of the message of the Geneva translation. Its theology was what mattered, for its readers no less than for its compilers. Nevertheless, the 'seditious' notes were there to be seized on by students of the Scriptures who were looking for them; they had all the authority of the printed text, and of Geneva. The number of such students increased after 1640. Not all were as simple-minded in their application of Scripture as Arise Evans, who thought that 'the lintel of the door' in Amos IX.1 must refer to Speaker Lenthall.[54] But many of the Geneva glosses were appropriate to Calvinist doctrines authorizing limited resistance if led by the lesser magistrate when kings had been tyrannical or had failed to do their duty.

Opposition to royal government did not originate in Geneva. John Foxe in his *Book of Martyrs* had printed documents concerning protestants imprisoned in Mary's reign, in the hope of persuading his contemporaries to keep the faith against 'those idolatrous *Egyptians* here in England' (my italics). William Whittingham and Anthony Gilby similarly urged their fellow ministers to stand fast in the controversy over clerical vestments, citing various Biblical examples.[55] William Perkins insisted that 'Princes must be obeyed in so far as they command in Christ; but Christ must be obeyed without exception'.[56] 'Though he be never so great a monarch in the world, every natural man is out of God's kingdom'.[57] This is a rejection of divine-right absolutism, an adjuration to the magistrate to remember that he rules over a Christian society.[58] But it is at most a doctrine of passive resistance. We may compare Silver-tongued Smith: 'When Paul . . . saith Obey princes for conscience sake, he meaneth not that we should obey them against conscience'.[59] George Abbot, in his *Exposition upon the Prophet Jonas*, thought that kings and queens should listen to good advisers, as the King of Nineveh did: it 'belongeth only to absolute princes' to act otherwise[60] – the implication being that Elizabeth was not an absolute queen.

The decision to have an 'Authorized Version' was consciously political. At first Whitgift and Bancroft were said to be unenthusiastic about a new translation, 'lest the Bishops' Bible [of 1568] be brought into disrepute'. They anticipated derisive comments from papists on the instability of the English Bible and its doctrines.[61] This is no doubt one reason why the instructions to the translators insisted on preserving certain traditional forms

54. See my *Change and Continuity*, pp. 59–60.
55. Martin, *Religious Radicals*, pp. 131–2, 162.
56. Perkins, *Workes*, III, p. 223.
57. Ibid., III, p. 191.
58. Ibid., I, pp. 756–7, 775–6.
59. Henry Smith, *Three Sermons* (1632), p. 23.
60. Abbot, op. cit., pp. 407–24. First published 1600: I cite from the edition of 1613. Abbot's is an interesting early example of use of the word 'absolute' in this context: see my 'The Word "Revolution"' in *A Nation of Change and Novelty* (1990), pp. 84–5. See p. 80 below.
61. Ed. G. B. Harrison, *A Jacobean Journal: Being a Record of those things most talked of during the years 1603–1606* (1946), p. 108.

of words. Thus 'church' was not to be translated 'congregation' – a bone of contention since More's dispute with Tyndale. On less directly political matters the translators seem deliberately to have made their readings 'capable of embracing differing, even apparently incompatible, interpretations'.[62] But there was no ambiguity about their version of I Peter II.13. The Geneva Bible had 'submit yourselves unto all' human ordinances, 'whether it be unto the King, as unto the superior . . .'. The Bishops' Bible had 'unto the King, as having the pre-eminence', the Catholic Rheims translation 'as excelling'. The A.V. plumped for 'to the King, as supreme'.[63] No doubts about its loyalty!

Notes kept by a member of the panel which prepared the Authorized Version suggest that the translators were concerned 'to achieve as open a reading as possible'.[64] We do not know whether this stemmed from the fact that they represented a wide range of opinions, or from anxiety to avoid the charge of theological bias. The A.V.'s hedging made it acceptable as an English compromise: black is black and white is white, but both could also in certain circumstances be seen as diverse forms of grey. The translators rightly claimed not to have made a new version, but to have revised existing translations, which could be taken as a covert defence of the Geneva Bible against the King.[65] In non-contentious passages the translators very frequently echoed Geneva, which itself goes back to Tyndale's version. The A.V. is a great literary achievement, partly because of the translators' respect for the work of their predecessors, partly because it came at a time when the Elizabethan compromise in church and state, though badly strained, had not yet broken down.

The main offence of the Geneva Bible lay in its notes: the crucial decision was that notes 'were not admitted to the margin' of the A.V. Some Geneva notes were, in James's words 'very partial, untrue, seditious and savouring too much of dangerous and traitorous conceits',[66] doctrinally as well as politically unsound, even on the divinity of Christ. Anne Hutchinson, whose heresies threw New England into turmoil in the 1630s, used the Geneva Bible in preference to the A.V. favoured by the orthodox of Massachusetts. After 1611 notes were missed. 'The people complained

---

62. G. Hammond, 'English Translations of the Bible', in *The Literary Guide to the Bible* (ed. R. Alter and F. Kermode, 1987), pp. 660–63.
63. Ed. W. Allen, *Translating for King James* (1972), p. 22.
64. Hammond, loc. cit.
65. Hammond, *The Making of the English Bible* (Manchester U.P., 1982), p. 174.
66. Pollard, op. cit., p. 46.

that they could not see into the sense of the Scriptures' in a plain text 'so well as formerly they did by the Geneva Bible'. At least one preacher of Fast Sermons to the Long Parliament went out of his way to emphasize that he was quoting from the Geneva version. He cited Psalm CX.3 as 'Thy people shall come willingly at the time of assembling thine army'. The A.V. is much less useful as recruiting propaganda: 'Thy people shall be willing in the day of thy power'.[67]

After 1640 the monopoly of Bible-printing came under attack.[68] 'Divers stationers and printers of London' petitioned the relevant committee of the Commons for permission to print either the Geneva notes or new ones. A group of eight divines was constituted to review the Geneva notes. They consulted (among others) Diodati's *Annotations* and the Dutch *Annotations* of 1637 (translated by Milton's friend Theodore Haak, at the instance of both Houses of Parliament and the Assembly of Divines, and published in 1657).[69] The result of their labours could not be contained within the most ample of margins, running to two large folio volumes.[70] That effectively killed the Geneva marginalia. A bill for a new translation was before the Rump of the Long Parliament when it was dissolved in April 1653. In June of the same year John Canne petitioned the Council of State for authorization to print the Bible with his own notes, and was given an exclusive licence for seven years.[71] In the following month the Council of State, 'on the request of Mr Milton', ordered that all papers required for the translation of the Bible should be imported free of duty. In Cromwell's second Parliament the question of a new translation was referred to a committee of which Bulstrode Whitelocke was chairman, but nothing came of that either.[72]

With monopoly unenforceable, prices remained low, thanks especially to the importation of foreign duodecimo and vigesimo quarto editions, some

67. John Greene, *FS*, XI, p. 68; cf. pp. 69, 78.
68. See especially Lilburne's *Englands Birth-Right Justified* (1645), pp. 8–9, 42, in Haller, *Tracts on Liberty*, III.
69. For Haak's translation see Pamela R. Barnett, *Theodore Haak, F.R.S. (1605–1690): The First German Translator of Paradise Lost* ('s-Gravenhage, 1962), pp. 71–5, 114–19.
70. *Annotations Upon all the Books of the Old and New Testaments* (1657), I, Preface; cf. *Mercurius Politicus*, No. 382 (17–24 September 1657), p. 1644. See also T. H. Luxon, 'Calvin and Bunyan on Word and Image', *English Literary Renaissance*, 18 (1988), p. 458.
71. Anne Laurence, *Parliamentary Army Chaplains*, p. 109; *CSPD, 1652–3*, p. 395
72. F. A. Inderwick, *The Interregnum* (1891), p. 130. The committee was at work during the spring and summer of 1657 (Spalding, *Diary of Bulstrode Whitelocke*, pp. 456–7.).

of which were said to be very inaccurate. In the early 1650s prices for such editions ranged from 20d. to 2s. 4d.[73] In 1656 a Bible free from such errata was produced, which the Protector insisted was to sell at not more than 12s. duodecimo.[74] But at the restoration the King's printers recovered their monopoly, and prices shot up again, 'especially in all the most useful and portable volumes, which they sold at very unconscionable rates, whereby the poorer sort in the nation became utterly unfurnished with Bibles'. Folio Bibles printed at Oxford cost £6, quartos 13s. 4d.[75] In 1686 Philip Henry bought a small Bible for 2s. 10d. – 'cheap enough, but they are ill bound'.[76] But in the long run, when governments no longer attempted to prevent the wide dissemination of cheap Bibles, the Geneva Bible's elaborate notes and apparatus priced it out of the market, with the help of the rapid decline of theological politics. The last edition of the Geneva Bible appeared in 1644, though between 1611 and 1715 eight editions of the A.V. were printed with the Geneva notes.[77]

III

Good kings are rare in the Old Testament. God warned his people in Deuteronomy that if they insisted on a king they must impose very strict conditions on him (XVII.14–20). Samuel repeated the warning (I Samuel VIII.6–19), listing the awful things which kings would do to their subjects. James I, with remarkable insensitivity, cited these verses as evidence of the absolute obedience owed to 'that king which God was to give them'. But 'I gave thee a king in mine anger', God told Israel through Hosea (XIII.11). A pamphlet of 1643 was entitled *A Parallel between the Israelites and the English desiring a King*.[78] Thomas Beard, in *The Theatre of God's Judgments* (1597), observed that of forty kings of Judah and Israel only ten pleased God, and one of these was doubtful. 'How rare . . . good princes have been

73. W. M. Clyde, *The Struggle for the Freedom of the Press from Caxton to Cromwell* (Oxford U.P. 1934), pp. 224–5, 281–2.
74. Inderwick, *The Interregnum*, p. 130. See an interesting advertisement in *Mercurius Politicus*, No. 334, 29 October – 6 November 1656, p. 164.
75. Ed. J. Gutch, *Collectanea Curiosa* (Oxford U.P., 1781), I, pp. 275–7. But about 1674 prices fell to £1.10s for folios, 5s. 6d. for quartos.
76. Ed. M. H. Lee, *Diaries and Letters of Philip Henry . . . A.D. 1631–1696* (1882), p. 353.
77. I owe this point to David Daniell.
78. *Political Works of James I*, pp. 56–7. The tract is listed by Catharine Macaulay in the *Catalogue* of her *Tracts* (1790), in the Bodleian Library, p. 89. Cf. p. 189 below.

at all times,' he reflected, with innumerable Biblical illustrations. It is 'unlawful both by the law of God and of man' for kings to tax 'above measure'. 'If you be mighty, puissant and fearful, know that the Lord is greater than you'. He 'is able (when he please) to bring princes to nothing'.[79] The young Oliver Cromwell had sat in Beard's congregation.

Hugh Broughton in *Job. To the King* (1610) stated baldly that 'the rulers that prosper are wicked', and for good measure spoke of 'wicked archbishops over-ruling common laws', a clear reference to the anti-Puritan Richard Bancroft. God, Broughton thought, has 'taken reason from bishops, as from Pharaoh and his councillors'.[80] Broughton was one of the translators of the A.V. and a Fellow of Christ's, Milton's Cambridge college. If bishops are Pharaoh's councillors, who is Pharaoh? Miles Smith, a learned bishop so puritanical that James I later appointed Laud his dean, observed that Hezekiah was called a rebel because he would not pay tribute to Sennacherib, King of Assyria. Daringly, he compared Elizabeth to Hezekiah: 'the Lord that fought for Hezekiah and Jerusalem will also fight for her Majesty and this realm against Sennacherib and the Spaniard'.[81]

The text 'God is no respecter of persons' (Acts X.34–5) was frequently quoted – e.g. by Bishop Babington in 1604 to remind his readers that God is 'able to shiver in pieces the greatest that ever was'.[82] The near-separatist Richard Rogers gave a sweeping view of Old Testament history in 1615. 'There were few of the kings good men, in Israel not one'. The judges 'for the most part' had been better. On the other hand Rogers had heard 'prophane and irreligious gentlemen' use Samuel's rebuke to Saul to argue that it was not 'meet that a mere minister should . . . be so bold with great personages'.[83] David and Solomon were good kings, but they committed many evil actions. Jehu was a just and godly king, 'faithful and valiant in killing . . . tyrants'.[84] Milton used the fact that Jehu killed his rightful king

79. Beard, op. cit., pp. 13, 386, 405, 460–62, 471.
80. Broughton, op. cit., pp. 116–20.
81. M. Smith, *Sermons* (1632), pp. 108–11.
82. Babington, *Comfortable Notes Upon . . . Exodus and Leviticus*, p. 2: Leviticus, Chapter X; cf. p. 344 on Exodus XXII.22–5, against oppression. Babington was a protégé of the Earls of Pembroke, and had been suspected of sympathy for the Earl of Essex in 1601.
83. Rogers, *A Commentary Upon the Whole Book of Judges*, sig. B 4v; *Samuels Encounter with Saul* (1620), pp. 226–8, referring to I Samuel XV.13–30.
84. The words are Bullinger's quoted by Laura B. Kennelly, '"Had Zimri peace who slew his master?": The Role of Jehu (II Kings IX–X) in 17th-century Religious and Political Literature', in *Praise Disjoined: Changing Patterns of Salvation in 17th-century English Literature* (ed. W. P. Shaw, New York, 1991), pp. 37–8. In these paragraphs I have drawn on this useful article.

at the bidding of a prophet to argue that 'it was not permissible and good to put a tyrant to death because God commanded it, but rather God commanded it because it was permissible and good'.[85]

Warning examples from the Old Testament were regularly quoted as the powers and responsibilities of the monarchy came increasingly to be questioned. We may compare attitudes towards monarchy in Jacobean drama, repeatedly contrasting the respected function of the King with the inadequacy of the holders of the office who failed to live up to conventional expectations.[86] Dramatists similarly made generalized references to the wickedness of courts, usually Italian courts. George Wither applied the same strategy to the Bible in his 'Hymn for a Courtier', referring to 'chaste Joseph . . . in Pharaoh's house', 'Obadiah in wicked Ahab's court';

> Wise Daniel dared the truth to say
> Where flattery did abound;
> Within the breast of Mordecai
> An honest heart was found'.[87]

The advantage of quoting the Bible was that the preacher or the writer could rely on a name to remind his audience of parts of the story which he did not think it prudent to emphasize. Thomas Goodwin's *Exposition of the Book of Revelation* (sermons preached in Holland in 1639, published posthumously) furnishes some good examples of cautiously expressed political criticism.[88] Or take John Preston's *Sermon of Spirituall Life and Death* (1630), in which he discusses the dangerous situation in which England found herself during the Thirty Years War. He too quoted 'that excellent speech of Mordecai to Esther': 'If thou holdest thy tongue at this time, comfort and deliverance shall appear to the Jews out of another place, but thou and thy father's house shall perish' (Esther IV.24). (The Geneva note says 'all God's children ought to have' Mordecai's faith, 'which is that God will deliver them though all worldly means fail'). Preston − addressing Charles I at a time when 'the [Huguenot] Rochellers in distress accused us' − added 'for us that are subjects, let us be exhorted to do our parts to contend and wrestle with God by prayer, and not to let him rest, till he

85. *MCPW*, IV, p. 407 − *A Defence of the People of England* (1651).
86. For examples see D. Norbrook, *Poetry and Politics in the English Renaissance* and Jonathan Dollimore, *Radical Tragedy: Religion, Ideology and Power in the Drama of Shakespeare and his Contemporaries* (Brighton, 1984).
87. Wither, *Hallelujah* (1857), p. 290. First published 1641.
88. Goodwin, op. cit., in *Works* (Edinburgh, 1861–3), III, pp. 35, 90, 103, 131, 140, 174–9, 189–91, 204–5.

have given rest to his churches'. Preston commended Mordecai's speech to 'those who have greatest power and opportunity of doing good in this business.' Deliverance did appear to the continental protestants, and therefore to England, not from Charles I but from Gustavus Adolphus; and Charles if not his house did perish.[89]

The Bible has much to say against marrying alien queens, especially if they were of the wrong faith. The conversion to popery of James's queen, Anne of Denmark, does not seem to have been held against her: her country was protestant, and she herself was no propagandist. But Henrietta Maria was very different. She was the daughter of one of the two great (and threatening) Roman Catholic powers, provocatively chosen after popular delight at the failure of Spanish marriage negotiations for Prince Charles. It was suspected, rightly, that France would demand concessions for English papists, and Henrietta Maria turned out to be a keen and successful proselytizer for her faith. This at a time when continental protestantism was under dire threat in the Thirty Years War. The proposed marriage of Prince Charles to a Spanish Infanta in 1623 had roused great alarm. A lecturer preaching at St Michael's, London, on Solomon's marriage to an idolater, had to be interrupted because he 'proposed to make an application to the present times'. The service was hastily closed by singing a psalm.[90]

The otherwise unknown author of *Sacrae Heplades, or seaven problems concerning Antichrist*, published the work in Amsterdam in 1625. The treatise was dedicated 'especially to King Charles defender of the faith and to the king and queen of Bohemia [James's son-in-law and daughter] professing the faith and therefore persecuted'. The author was alarmed by Charles's marriage to Henrietta Maria. 'This Egyptian darkness, . . . proceeds from [Antichrist's] enchantments, to hold Pharaoh still in hardness of heart'. Henrietta Maria's 'father, Henry IV of renowned memory', the author recalled, had been assassinated by papists. 'It cannot be denied, but Jezebel was once young, and chaste, and fair; but this proves not that she is so now'. He hoped for 'some Jehu (zealous for his own interest if not for God's)' to cause her to be thrown out of her window, 'that he may tread her under his horse's feet'. The writer does not actually identify Charles I with Ahab

---

89. Preston, op. cit., p. 27. Calamy quoted the same text in his Fast Sermon of 22 December 1641 (*FS*, II.49).

90. *CSPD, 1619–23*, p. 551. Nehemiah XIII.26, presumably the preacher's text, said that 'strange women caused [Solomon] to sin'. 'Shall we then transgress against our God, even to marry strange wives?' See also pp. 245, 285, 291 below.

or his Queen with Jezebel; but the juxtapositions do their own work. Jezebel's death, the Geneva margin assures us, was 'a spectacle and example of God's judgments to all tyrants'. For God 'will ever stir up some to avenge his cause . . . God's judgments appear even in this world against them that suppress his Word and persecute his servants'.[91] The author of *Vox Coeli* (1624) cited no less than nine Biblical texts dealing with the dangers to be apprehended from foreign queens of a strange religion.[92]

The same point was made by Thomas Hooker in an assize sermon preached in Essex on Guy Fawkes Day, 1626. Before 'a vast congregation' he prayed that God would 'set on the heart of the King' the eleventh and twelfth verses of Malachi. He did not quote them, since he no doubt expected his congregation to know them or to have them readily accessible in their Bibles. They ran 'an abomination is committed: . . . Judah . . . hath married the daughter of a strange god. The Lord will cut off the man that doth this'.[93] It was an astonishingly explicit suggestion that the King should repudiate his new French bride.

Hugh Peter in the same year was in trouble for praying that God would enlighten the King in 'those things which were necessary for the government of the kingdom', and would convert the Queen from 'the idols of her father's house'. This was at a private fast on which the Bishop of London reported to the Duke of Buckingham. It was kept, he said, 'by the meaner sort of the people', though he suspected that 'the better − I mean the richer sort − were belike content they should break the ice'. Among the better sort involved were the Earl of Warwick and Sir Robert Harley, Master of the Mint.[94] Alexander Leighton described the Queen as a 'daughter of hell', a 'Canaanite and an idolater'.[95] In 1627 Charles was likened to Rehoboam, a King who levied arbitrary taxes. Thomas Scott, the Kentish MP, compared Charles to Saul and Buckingham to Agag, whom Samuel slew in defiance of the King's orders.[96] Felton assassinated Buckingham in 1628.

91. Op. cit., sig. x 2v, pp. 210–15, sig. x 3v; II Kings IX.27, 33, 37.
92. Op. cit., p. 51.
93. Quoted by W. Hunt, *The Puritan Moment: The Coming of Revolution in an English County* (Harvard U.P., 1983), p. 201. The reference is to Malachi, Chapter II. See pp. 245, 285, 291 below. Cf. Russell, *The Fall of the British Monarchies*, p. 258.
94. *CSPD, 1625–49*, p. 175. For criticism of Charles for his marriage to a 'Babylonish woman' see Hunt, op. cit., p. 277. There are many other examples in this important book.
95. *DNB*.
96. Quoted by J. Morrill, 'Rhetoric and Action: Charles I, Tyranny and the English Revolution', in *Religion, Resistance and Civil War* (ed. G. J. Schochet, Folger Shakespeare Library, 1990), p. 95.

One serious reason for emigration in the 1620s was the sense that 'God was leaving England', because the nation was no longer worthy of his confidence and support.[97] The Barrington correspondence is full of such forebodings.[98] It was the likes of Sir Francis Barrington who called for fasts in the House of Commons; we should not take the feeling behind such demands lightly. Fasts and Fast Sermons were, it is true, used to make political points and demands; but they sprang from real anxiety. Disappointment and suspicion drove many to emigrate to New England; they made others easy recipients of the idea of a Popish Plot to subvert England's national independence: that seemed the most rational explanation of God's apparent withdrawal of his favour.[99] This was the background to Parliament's insistence in the Nineteen Propositions of June 1642 that none of the King's children should be married to any foreign prince or princess without Parliament's agreement.

'God is angry', declared Preston: 'and he is never angry but for sin'. The sins were national, sins of the church, as well as individual. 'God is about a great work, yea, to make a great change in the world, except we do as it were hold his hand by seeking and turning unto him, and by removing the things that provoke him'. This means, Preston thought, taking drastic action against the popish and Arminian fifth column: 'We must do with heresies as men do with a fire in a town, leaving not a spark lest it stir up a new fire'.[100] 'You must be men of contention', Preston had insisted in 1625, in words that would have appealed to Milton. 'If we be new creatures, then pull down all that is old'. But 'if you mean to follow Christ, look for a rainy day. It may be a fair morning, but yet we know not what the evening will be'.[101] This was the atmosphere in which John Winthrop thought that New England could be 'a refuge for many' against the

---

97. See Chapter 12 below.

98. *Barrington Family Letters, 1628–1632* (ed. A. Searle, Camden 4th Series, 28, 1983), esp. pp. 29, 36–7, 56, 60, 77, 90, 92.

99. C. Hibbard, *Charles I and the Popish Plot* (North Carolina U.P., 1983), *passim*. I do not of course wish to suggest that fears of a Popish Plot were groundless.

100. Preston, *A Sermon of Spirituall Life and Death* (1630), pp. 55–7; *A Pattern of Wholesome Words* (1658), p. 278.

101. Preston, *The Breastplate of Faith and Love* (5th ed., 1634), pp. 236–9; *The New Covenant; or, A Treatise of Sanctification*, in *The Saints Qualification* (2nd. ed., 1634), p. 433; *The Doctrine of Selfe-Deniall*, in *Four Godly and learned Treatises* (3rd ed., 1633), p. 225. Cf. David Loewenstein, *Milton and the Drama of History: Historical Vision, Iconoclasm, and the Literary Imagination* (Cambridge U.P., 1990), esp. Chapters 3 and 6.

judgment that was coming upon England.[102] The experiences of 'the Bible Commonwealth' had their influence on the mother country. Only after 1640 did emigration to New England slow down, because (Winthrop says) all men 'stay in England in expectation of a New World'.[103]

IV

The Bible offered doctrines not always in full accord with established assumptions. Private property is sacred against kings, Beard – following the Geneva margin – assured his readers. Even Ahab would not 'take from another man his [property] right without full recompense (I Kings XXI.2)'. Thomas Taylor, whose *Second Part of the Theatre of Gods Judgments* was published posthumously in 1642, had written a treatise in which he explained that 'the sword of the Lord' knew 'no difference between prince and people, young nor old, poor nor rich, if they be in the same sin, in what hand soever he please to put' the sword. He argued from Galatians V.1 that we must maintain our own (Christian) liberties.[104] John Preston, preaching before the King in the 1620s, went perhaps a little further. Kings who are rebels against God, including even Solomon, may provoke rebellion against themselves.[105] This is comparable with Hobbes's assertion of the absolute duty of obeying Leviathan in all circumstances, combined with a recognition that if and when the sovereign fails to protect his subjects, they will in fact cease to obey him.

Richard Sibbes used II Corinthians I.21 to prepare his readers to face persecution: 'an honest man may die and suffer much for civil matters. . . . Could I be content to lose the favour of great ones? to die in the quarrel if need be? . . . These unsettled times moved me to speak a little

102. Quoted by E. S. Morgan, *The Puritan Dilemma: The Story of John Winthrop* (Boston, 1958), p. 40.
103. Quoted by D. Masson, *Life of Milton* (1859–80), II, p. 585.
104. Taylor, *The Famine of the Word*, in *Works* (1653), p. 275; *The Principles of Christian Practice*, ibid., p. 77. Taylor died in 1633; 'the iniquity of former times' did not permit publication in his lifetime.
105. Preston, *Sermons Preached before His Majestie* (4th impression, 1634), pp. 53–4. Preston preached a sermon on *The Christian Freedome: or The Charter of the Gospel, shewing the privilege and prerogative of the Saints by vertue of the covenant* (1641). 'Charter', 'privilege' and 'prerogative' were all politically loaded words. Perhaps that is why the treatise was not published until 1641, by which date 'Covenant' also had political overtones.

more than ordinary, that we might labour to have our hearts stablished, that whatsoever comes, we may have somewhat that is certain to stick to, ... whatsoever becomes of our state in the world other-wise'.[106]

Dod and Cleaver gave many Biblical texts to illustrate the duty of having a vocation, since idleness was a sin.[107] They used Proverbs to argue that 'a mean estate' was safest, 'without excess on either hand'. The godly, they thought, were drawn mainly from the lower classes because God preferred 'poor, despised industrious and laborious' people to 'titles, ... birth or parentage'.[108] 'Even with wealth a man may be godly', observed Babington in 1592, *à propos* Abraham. Trades and handicrafts, he added, were the works of God; if they were abused, that was the fault of men, not of the skills.[109] Monopolies are wrong, Nicholas Fuller and Sir Edward Coke argued, because they deprive men of liberty to labour at their own trade. For 'the ordinance of God is that every man should live by his labour'; otherwise he shall not eat.[110]

Milton's 'matchless Gideon' was a popular self-made man.[111] 'My father is poor', he protested when the Angel of the Lord called him to rescue Israel from the Midianites, 'and I am the least in my father's house' (Judges VI.15). For Ludlow, 'the Lord raised up the Parliament in the year 1640 as his Gideon for the relieving of them from the hands of their enemies'.[112] The fact that Samson came of the tribe of Dan led Richard Rogers to insist that 'ever out of the mean and middle sort of people the Lord chooseth many, yea most, to be heirs of salvation. ... In comparison of these, few great ones are called'. And discussing the imprisonment of the blinded Samson Rogers praised the care that the Philistines took to set their

---

106. Sibbes, *Works* (Edinburgh, 1862–4), III, pp. 437–42; cf. pp. 526–7. Published posthumously in 1655: preached at Gray's Inn some time before Sibbes's death in 1635.

107. John Dod and Robert Cleaver, *A plain and familiar Exposition of the Ten Commande-ments* (19th ed., 1662), pp. 93–4, 274–6; cf. *A Plaine and Familiar Exposition of the Proverbs of Salomon* (1612), XVII.10, pp. 10–11. John Pym had been a member of Dod's congregation in the 1630s.

108. Dod and Cleaver, *Proverbs*, X.15, XI.1, 19, XII.9, XIII.70–73, XIV.23, XVII.10.

109. Babington, *Certaine Plaine, briefe and comfortable Notes upon everie Chapter of Genesis* (1592), fol. 48. *Comfortable Notes Upon ... Exodus and Leviticus*, note on Exodus XXVIII.3. For Babington, see pp. 60, 67 above.

110. D. H. Sacks, 'Religion, Liberty and the Commonwealth', in *Parliament and Liberty* (ed. J. H. Hexter, Stanford U.P., 1992), pp. 98–108.

111. Milton, *Samson Agonistes*, line 280.

112. Ludlow, *A Voyce from the Watch Tower*, p. 301.

prisoners on work. The example was worth following by Christians: it would get rid of 'the idleness and mischief of most prisons'.[113]

Sebastian Benefield, Fellow of Corpus Christi College, Oxford, published in 1629 a Commentary upon Amos, in which he stressed that 'Amos, of a herdsman or a shepherd, became a blessed prophet to carry a terrible word and fearful message to the king, nobles, priests and people of Israel'. Here God used a 'vile and despised person' 'to confound the great and mighty'.[114] Glosses in the Geneva Bible had drawn attention to the fact that Amos prophesied 'against the rulers of Israel', calling 'the prince and governors . . . by the name of beasts and not of men' and threatening the wealthy in particular (Amos IV.I, VI.1, VIII.1).

There were many warning voices, coming mainly from outside the political nation. The 'one just man' who repeatedly saves society in Books XI and XII of *Paradise Lost* was rarely a ruler, though Exodus XXII originally applied the phrase to Moses. It was in answer to the plebeian prophets of the 1640s and 1650s that in 1652 a Presbyterian doctor of divinity found it necessary to stress that Amos offered 'no ground for any man to come from a trade to prophetical office of his own head, as too many do nowadays, to the disgrace of prophesyings and discouragement from learning'. 'The Lord-like' Laudians had discredited 'pontifical' government; but ordination of the clergy was still a social necessity.[115] Paul Baynes in his *Commentary on Ephesians* emphasized especially what he took to be the Apostle's stress on the bourgeois virtues. The luxurious spendthrift would end up a pauper. Productive labour was what mattered: neither usury nor astrology was productive. One object of the Presbyterian discipline was to promote productive labour: the idle rich disliked it. More interestingly Baynes reflected that the covenant between man and God in effect limited the latter's absolute sovereignty – just as, some of his readers may have reflected, the social contract limited the absolute power of monarchs.[116]

In this book I have cited the Old Testament much more frequently than the New. The Old Testament is harsher and more brutal than the New, concerned with the indiscriminate collective elimination of God's enemies,

113. Rogers, *Judges*, pp. 614, 769.
114. Benefield, *A Commentary and Exposition upon . . . Amos* (1629), pp. 8–9. Benefield also instanced Joseph, Moses, David, Peter, Andrew, James and John.
115. John Mayer, *A Commentary Upon all the Prophets*, sig. A 7–7v, p. 661.
116. Baynes, *Commentary upon the whole Epistle of St Paul to the Ephesians* (ed. Thomas Alexander, Edinburgh, 1866), pp. 51–7, 233, 293. Cf. Chapter 7 below.

and with the salvation of the Jewish people, rather than with individuals. Only Revelation in the New Testament shares the Old Testament enjoyment of massacring the ungodly. W. K. Jordan long ago pointed out that Calvinist arguments for persecution of dissent were based on the Old Testament.[117] The protestant doctrine of predestination arose from attempts to adapt the Old Testament's message to the world of the sixteenth century; the doctrine of the priesthood of all believers starts from the Old Testament concept of priesthood, which has not always been easy to find in the New Testament. Jeremy Taylor recommended use of the New Testament for 'devotions' rather than the Old Testament.[118] Walter Cradock in 1650 remarked that the Old Testament was full of terror, the New Testament of love. In the former the Lord dealt with people 'by cities and nations; but now every man . . . is respected in every nation and city whatsoever'.[119] As the Soviet historian M. A. Barg pointed out, radical sectaries put their main emphasis not on the wrath of God but on his love; and they tended to extend the possibility of salvation to all. William Walwyn rarely referred to the Old Testament, basing his arguments on the New Testament.[120] But the Leveller emphasis on birthright, inheritance – like Milton's defence of divorce – looks back to the patriarchal society of the Old Testament. Winstanley cites the Old Testament more frequently than the New.[121]

Roger Williams saw the Old Testament as a historical document, to be expounded 'typologically'.[122] Part of the object of typology, whether conscious or not, was to minimize the savagery of the Old Testament; Samson was transformed from a bloodthirsty bully to a type of Christ. Thomas Middleton's *God's Parliament-House: Or, the Marriage of the Old and New Testaments* (1627) dealt with the fulfilment of prophecies, attempting to demonstrate the coherence of the two Testaments. Typology was an

117. Jordan, *The Development of Religious Toleration in England . . . 1640–1660: The Revolutionary Experiments and Dominant Religious Thought* (1938), p. 276.
118. Taylor, *The Golden Grove* (1655), in *The Whole Works* (1836), III, p. 727.
119. Cradock, *Divine Drops Distilled from the Fountain of the Holy Scriptures*, pp. 189, 245–6.
120. M. A. Barg, *The English Revolution of the 17th Century, Through Portraits of Its Leading Figures* (Moscow, 1990, in English translation), p. 59; *Writings of William Walwyn* (ed. J. R. McMichael and B. Taft, Georgia U.P., 1989), p. 6.
121. Winstanley, *Il Piano della Legge della Libertà* (trans. and ed. D. Bianchi, Turin, 1992), pp. 242–8.
122. Perry Miller, *Roger Williams: His Contribution to the American Tradition* (New York, 1953), pp. 32, 38.

affair of intellectuals: the Biblical literature of humbler sectaries in the 1640s tended to pick up some of the Old Testament savagery – Coppe, for instance, and the early Quakers. Milton's emphasis on the religious duty of hating God's enemies was based on the Old Testament.[123] Bernard Mandeville, with cheerful cynicism, later observed that 'whenever pillage or shedding of blood are to be justified or encouraged by a sermon, or men are to be exhorted to battle, to the sacking of a city or the devastation of a country, by a pathetic discourse, the text is always taken from the Old Testament'.[124]

The Psalms are extremely bellicose against the wicked, and against the psalmists' enemies. The later prophets are obsessed with denouncing the wrath to come. If one reads the Bible straight through, the remarkable tolerance of the gospels comes as a shock. Suddenly the emphasis is on mercy rather than judgment: on the underdog rather than the embattled invaders; on forgiveness, on helping the unfortunate, saving sinners, not the righteous (Matthew V, IX.12–13). Even the Book of Job, which is in part a satire on the hypocritical self-righteousness of both Job and his comforters, ends with Job becoming richer than ever (Job XLII). 'Take heed that ye give not your alms before men, to be seen of them', Jesus said (Matthew VI.1). His gentle irony to the young man who had great possessions – 'if thou wouldst be perfect' – is part of his sceptical subversion of established orthodoxies. It must have greatly influenced seventeenth-century readers like Walwyn, Winstanley, Coppe and Milton.

MPs before 1640 managed by use of Biblical quotations to combine outspokenness and caution. Thomas Wentworth (not the later Earl of Strafford) in the short-lived Parliament of 1614 cited Daniel XI.20–21 in criticizing impositions, and observed that France's 'late most exacting kings died like calves upon the butcher's knife'. That reference to the assassination of Henri III and IV was daring enough. But the speaker continued 'Such princes might read their destiny in XLV Ezekiel 9 and Daniel XI.20'. The latter tells us that a king 'shall stand up that shall raise taxes: but after a few days he shall be destroyed, neither in wrath nor in battle'. (The Geneva margin says it must have been by treason.) 'And in his place shall stand up a vile person'. The passage from Ezekiel reads 'Thus saith the Lord God . . . O princes of Israel: leave off cruelty and oppression, and execute judgment and justice: take away your exactions from my people, saith the Lord

123. See p. 384 below.
124. Mandeville, *An Inquiry into the Origin of Honour and The Usefulness of Christianity in War* (2nd ed., 1971), p. 158. First published 1732.

God'.[125] A fortnight later Francis Ashley referred to I Samuel XIII.6: 'As David, . . . we are in a wonderful strait'. He did not quote the rest of the verse: 'the people hid themselves in caves, and in holds, and in rocks, and in towns, and in pits'; his audience would no doubt recall it. Some might also remember Samuel's verdict on Saul eight verses later: 'thy kingdom shall not continue' and David would replace him (I Samuel XIII.14, XVI).[126] John Pym in 1628 had to pick his words very carefully when arguing that the text 'render unto Caesar the things that are Caesar's' could not be relevant to England, since 'the Jews were at that time a conquered nation, . . . subject to the absolute power of the Romans, . . . whereby the case is far different from the case of this kingdom, which hath always been free and hereditary'.[127] This is one of many examples of Parliamentary discourse where we are left to speculate whether Pym was deliberately or only accidentally ironical.

Few historical sources are as rich as the Old Testament in undesirable kings who come to exemplary bad ends. The anonymous author of *Tyranipocrit Discovered* (1649) made a general anti-monarchical point from the fact that 'Amaziah the Arch-priest will tell the prophet Amos that he must not speak the truth here, because of the King's court', even to warn the King.[128] Sibbes illustrated from the example of King David that 'to a man that knows that this world is a workhouse, and his life a service to God, he thinks of no rest till he be in the grave'.[129] Quakers in 1661 reminded Charles II and Parliament that Abel, Moses, Jacob and David had all been keepers of sheep, the Apostles fishermen, Paul a tentmaker.[130]

Most of what I have cited from seventeenth-century writers is what could get into print. We can only speculate about what was thought and said before 1640 and after 1660 that could not be printed. Ludlow, for

---

125. Ed. Maija Jansson, *Proceedings in Parliament, 1614 (House of Commons)* (American Philosophical Soc., Vol. 172, 1988), pp. 313, 316–17; cf. *Letters of John Chamberlain* (ed. N. E. McClure, American Philosphical Soc., 1939), I, p. 533. Wentworth cited the Geneva translation. Bishop Neile of Lincoln described his quotations from Daniel and Ezekiel as 'ill-applied' (Jansson, op. cit., p. 389).
126. Jansson, op. cit., pp. 415, 421.
127. Quoted by Conrad Russell, 'The Parliamentary Career of John Pym, 1621–1629', in *The English Commonwealth, 1547–1640: Essays in Politics and Society Presented to Joel Hurstfield* (ed. P. Clark, A. G. R. Smith and N. Tyacke, Leicester U.P., 1979), p. 161.
128. Amos VII.10–14 and *Tyranipocrit Discovered* (ed. A. Hopton, n.d., ?1990), p. 13: first published in Rotterdam.
129. Sibbes, *Works*, VI, p. 511.
130. [Anon.], *For the King and both Houses of Parliament*, 13 March 1661[–2], in *Somers Tracts* (1748–51), X, p. 280.

instance, a godly republican who was unable to print his Memoirs, devoted many pages to the wickedness of Biblical kings, and their punishment.[131] At certain times and places it could be a test of the preacher's ingenuity to see how far he could go with the aid of allusions and hints, without overstepping the limits. Our limitation to the printed text means that we lack the emphases, the gestures, the sidelong glances, by which a good preacher could convey much to his congregation. Bunyan's *A Few Sighs from Hell* (1658), based on a sermon or sermons on the parable of Dives and Lazarus, is the only example we have of the preaching which had made him famous before 1660. It must have contributed greatly to the Bedfordshire gentry's determination to silence him as soon as they got the chance. The sermon is a savage attack on the rich, and some of its strictures, I am sure, were recognizably applicable to known individuals in the locality. But this is a guess which I cannot prove: one great advantage of quoting the Bible is to avoid responsibility for specific assertions and personal attitudes. For another example, see a spy's report on the Fifth Monarchist Christopher Feake's attempt to identify the sinister Little Horn on one of the four great beasts described in Daniel VII – a favourite object of millenarian speculation. ' "I will name nobody", said he, but he gave many desperate hints'. After an obvious application to Oliver Cromwell – 'he should subdue three kings or kingdoms', 'he had a look more stout than his fellows', ' "I know", said he, "some would have the late King Charles to be meant by the little horn, but . . . I'll name nobody" '.[132] By then he had no need to. Catharine Macaulay quotes a preacher who asked Elijah's question to Ahab in I Kings XXI.19: 'Hast thou killed and also taken possession?'[133] Again there was no need to mention Cromwell.

Late nineteenth-century and early twentieth-century Russian revolutionaries commonly used what they called Aesopian language, in order to say what they wanted to say without falling foul of the censor. 250 years earlier English dissidents may have been much less consciously aware of what they were doing, but they too had things to say to which the censor might well object.

We have shot far ahead again, and must return to the 1640s.

131. Ludlow, *A Voyce from the Watch Tower*, pp. 132 sqq.
132. *CSPD, 1653–4*, pp. 304–8.
133. C. Macaulay, *History of England*, V, p. 145.

3. Fast Sermons and Politics, 1640–1660

Is it such a fast that I have chosen, that a man should afflict his soul for a day? . . . Is not this the fasting that I have chosen, . . . to take off the heavy burdens, and to let the oppressed go free, and that ye break every yoke? Is it not to deal thy bread to the hungry, and that thou bring the poor that wander unto thine house? When thou seest the naked, that thou cover him?
Isaiah LVIII.5–7.

A religious fast means that a man abstains not so much from food and drink as from sin, and does so in order to concentrate more upon prayers, either to avert some evil or to secure some good from God.
Milton, *Of Christian Doctrine, MCPW*, VI, pp. 677–8.

A skilful preacher, whether it be a Fast or a Day of Rejoicing, always finds ways to pursue his end, instils into his hearers whatever he pleases, and never dismisses an audience before he has acquainted them with what he would have them know; let the subject or the occasion he preaches upon be what they will.
Bernard Mandeville, *An Enquiry into the Origin of Honour and The Usefulness of Christianity in War* (1732), pp. 213–14.

I. Fast Sermons

As early as the 1570s English Presbyterians were calling for national days of fasting and humiliation as a remedy against afflictions, whether individual or national, which appeared to have been called down by divine wrath.[1] As Thomas Cartwright put it, 'fasting . . . is an abstinence commanded of the Lord, thereby to make solemn profession of our repentance'. Cartwright quoted Joel II.12–13 as well as Leviticus XVI.29–34. He had to counter the

---

1. I am much indebted here to T. D. Bozeman's 'Covenant Theology and "National Covenant"', Millersville.

idea that fasting was popish, or that it was a Jewish ceremony abolished in the Christian dispensation; the fasts that he proposed were not routine ceremonies at stated times and seasons but reactions to specific calamities. 'All the terrible threatenings that ever in the holy Scripture threatened against great sinners are threatened conditionally. . . . If at the preaching, reading or hearing of God's holy Word' they 'do repent and return unto God', then they will be forgiven.[2]

There was much history behind the demands for fasts made by the House of Commons. Richard Cosin in 1592 had attacked unauthorized fasting by Puritans in his *Conspiracie for Pretended Reformation*.[3] George Abbot, future Archbishop of Canterbury, in his vast *Exposition upon the Prophet Jonah*, published in 1600, had insisted that fasts were permitted only when officially authorized – as in Nineveh in Jonah's time, when a fast was proclaimed 'by decree of the King and his nobles'.[4] The Canons of 1604 laid this down officially. On the other hand Arthur Hildersham thought that Christians might lawfully fast secretly when public fasting was prohibited, since 'these times may also be called times of persecution'.[5]

Fasts, accompanied by a sermon, did not become a regular feature of Parliaments until the end of James I's reign. The practice might suggest that all was not well in the country, and that God's forgiveness was necessary. It could be taken to imply criticism of the government. For this reason (presumably) Elizabeth had always refused to permit fasts and fast sermons. We should take very seriously the anxieties which led MPs in the 1620s to call for national fasts, when the future of protestantism on the continent seemed in grave danger, and England was doing nothing to help. Yet 'this Christian duty of public fasting . . . is not only not allowed but opposed and suppressed', complained Arthur Hildersham.[6] As John Preston put it, 'It is a common opinion, that if men have strong friends, strong towers, and a strong land that is well begirt with sea and cliffs, or great estates that will defend them, then they are safe. But if the Lord be thine enemy, none of all these will do thee any good'.[7] 'The Lord then calls to fasting when

2. *Cartwrightiana* (ed. A. Peel and L. H. Carlson, 1951), pp. 84, 127–36.

3. Cosin, op. cit., sig. K6v.

4. Abbot, op. cit., (2nd ed., 1613), pp. 401–3.

5. Hildersham, quoted by Stephen Foster, *The Long Argument: English Puritanism and the Shaping of New England Culture, 1570–1700* (North Carolina U.P., 1991), pp. 97–8; cf. pp. 136, 321.

6. Quoted by Stephen Foster, 'Not What but Where? The Locus of Puritanism', Millersville.

7. Preston, *Life Eternall*, pp. 175–6 (second pagination).

his vengeance is coming', warned John Brinsley. It is the duty of God's ministers to forewarn and call to fasting, or else the blood of all must be required at their hands.[8] At the personal level, Sir Simonds D'Ewes used fasting to reassure himself of his elect status. But the evidence comes from 1627, when national anxieties were coming to a peak.[9]

In the difficult year 1624 James agreed to a fast, and from then onwards the practice became routine. Laud detested fasts, and used Charles I's authority in a new attempt to suppress them unless expressly permitted by the King. Unauthorized public fasts were 'contrary to the rules of Christianity and the ancient canons of the church'.[10] Fasts and fast sermons witness to problems which a chosen nation had to face when the breakdown of traditional consensus began to give its people some freedom of choice. What if *vox populi* did not choose what *vox dei* wanted? The issue seemed important enough for Sir Richard Hutton, one of the Ship Money judges who spoke in Hampden's favour in the Ship Money Case, to collect in his commonplace book seven Biblical references (and one from the Apocrypha) justifying 'public fasts upon extraordinary causes'; and eleven others concerning 'private fasts'.[11]

In 1636 a correspondent of John Winthrop's complained bitterly that 'in all these calamities we never went to God publicly by fasting and prayer, which was deemed as hateful as conventicles'. Fasts had to be organized by private enterprise. Three days before the Short Parliament met in 1640 'a general fast was held . . . privately in England and Scotland' for the success of the Parliament. Those who pressed for fasts in the Long Parliament were those who had called for support for continental protestants in the twenties, who in the thirties had feared that God was leaving England and who by 1640 were strong enough to organize a general fast in England and Scotland 'privately'.[12] Bunyan looked back to those days in *The Holy War*: the citizens of Mansoul held a day of fasting and humiliation when Emanuel had left the town because of its sinfulness.[13]

Fast sermons were preached to the Short Parliament in 1640, starting with Stephen Marshall; they became institutionalized in the Long

8. Brinsley, *The Third Part of the True Watch* (1922), pp. 444–6. For Brinsley see Chapter 12 below.

9. D'Ewes, *Autobiography and Correspondence* (1845), I, pp. 353–4, 362–3.

10. *CSPD, 1635*, pp. 522.

11. Ed. W. R. Prest, *The Diary of Sir Richard Hutton, 1614–1639* (Selden Soc., 1991), pp. 123–5.

12. Cope, *Politics without Parliaments,* pp. 64, 187.

13. Bunyan, op. cit. (ed. R. Sharrock and J. F. Forrest, Oxford U.P., 1980), pp. 158–9.

Parliament. Serious study of Fast Sermons to Parliament dates from Professor Trevor-Roper's essay, published in 1964. This is written with all Trevor-Roper's flair and ingenuity, and has been very influential. If I have a criticism, it is that his explanation of the origins of particular sermons is sometimes a little too pat: it inclines to a conspiracy theory of revolutions still supported by some conservative historians.[14] Often Trevor-Roper is right: Pym and later leaders of the House of Commons certainly used Fast Sermons to prepare for political action, including notably the trials of the Earl of Strafford, of Archbishop Laud and of the King himself.

Thus Achan, who 'troubled Israel' through his transgressions and was stoned to death, prefigured Strafford (Joshua VI; I Chronicles II.7).[15] Just three months before the execution of Laud, Edmund Calamy told the House of Commons that they had failed to repent sufficiently of (among other things) 'all the guilty blood that God requires you in justice to shed and you spare'. God will require this blood at your hands.[16] Thomas Brooks's sermon of 27 December 1648 is an even clearer incitement to approve the trial and execution of Charles I.[17] These were special occasions. For the normal monthly fasts it was open to any MP or peer to propose preachers, who had to be approved by the House. Each house chose its own preachers, and the two houses were often in disagreement on political issues. That said, however, Trevor-Roper's chronological analysis remains invaluable: I shall not attempt to compete with it.

Regular monthly Fast Sermons were not established until November 1641, but *ad hoc* fast sermons started on 17 November 1640, a date no doubt carefully chosen as Queen Elizabeth's Accession Day. The sermons preached then did not fail to make odious comparisons. Monthly sermons for each House continued until their abolition in April 1649. Charles I had to accept this, and in a proclamation of 8 January 1642 he authorized national public fasts for the last Wednesday of each month. These also continued until April 1649. By then the House of Lords had been

14. Here I am in agreement with David Morse, *England's Time of Crisis: From Shakespeare to Milton* (1989), p. 119.
15. Samuel Fairclough, *The Troublers Troubled, or Achan Condemned and Executed*, preached on 4 April 1641. Not printed in *FS*. See Trevor-Roper, *Religion, Reformation and Social Change and Other Essays* (1967), pp. 302–3.
16. *FS*, XIII, pp. 121–71, esp. p. 153. Calamy quoted many texts in support of this proposition, for which see Chapter 15 below.
17. *FS*, XXXII, pp. 81–133.

abolished, but Fast Sermons continued to be preached to the single-chamber Parliament until the dissolution of the Rump of the Long Parliament in April 1653. Normally the preacher was thanked and invited to print his sermon; failure to issue such an invitation was a gesture of dissatisfaction. William Dell was neither thanked nor asked to publish his sermon of 25 November 1646. He offended the House of Commons by printing it with an aggressively polemical dedication to the House, in which he referred to the 'clergy-Antichristian power', sitting 'upon the power of the nation'. He hinted that the Westminster Assembly of Divines constituted the 'last prop of Antichrist in the kingdom'.[18] Dell was never asked to preach to the Commons again. A proposal to invite him was voted down by the Rump on 28 January 1653.[19]

Between 1640 and the end of 1644 there are only ten sermons of which printed copies have failed to survive. But after that the number of unprinted sermons rose sharply to thirty in 1645, fifty-one in 1648. It fell to sixteen in 1649, with another thirty in 1650–53. The decline in the proportion of sermons printed from the late forties presumably reflects growing disunity among supporters of Parliament. Many interesting conclusions could be drawn from a comparative study of the sermons as a whole. One is a shift in the source of texts for sermons. Of 240 sermons which got into print, the texts of 181 were drawn from the Old Testament, 59 from the New: a ratio of 3 to 1. Twelve of the New Testament texts came from Revelation, the most Old Testament of all the New Testament books. From November 1640 to October 1645, the preponderance of the Old Testament is even more remarkable: 123 texts to the New Testament's 26, a ratio of $4\frac{3}{4}$ to 1. Capp noted that the Commons seemed to have a penchant for sermons on apocalyptic themes.[20]

In Fast Sermons we find new conventions of discourse. The MPs who assembled in November 1640 were soon to be deeply divided; but in the early months most, even of those who were to be royalists in the civil war, recognized that great changes were needed in the English state and the English church. There was a short-lived consensus: the King was not only badly advised, some of his ministers were seen as dangerous to the protestant English nation. The King was still exempt from personal criticism; but his ministers were no longer seen just as wicked individuals. The Grand

18. *FS*, XXV, pp. 1, 6, 259–64.
19. Trevor-Roper, op. cit., p. 325.
20. Capp, 'The Political Dimension of Apocalyptic Thought', in *The Apocalypse in English Renaissance Thought and Literature*, p. 109.

Remonstrance of November 1641 was an indictment of the government and its policies as a whole. That finally split the House into two irreconcilable parties.

National fasts included abstention from labour and attendance at special church services. It is difficult to obtain accurate information, but such evidence as there is suggests that fasts were more honoured in the breach than in the observance. Royalists would object on principle to asking God to support Parliament in the civil war, or thanking him for victories. Aubrey, long after the event, tells us that 'some did observe in the late civil war that the Parliament, after a humiliation, did shortly obtain a victory'. But Providence could not be relied on. Average sensual men (and women) may well have resented giving up time for week-day fasts which might have been better spent. 'Alas', said William Spurstowe in July 1643, 'it is not a naked vote that passeth within your walls that can vote our churches full and the taverns empty'.[21]

Orders for separate royalist monthly fasts were published at Oxford in November 1643. We may suspect that royalist fasts were no more successful than Parliamentarian. One sermon preached in Oxford before 'the members of the honourable House of Commons' there, on Jeremiah XLIV.10, complained that men 'are not humbled even unto this day', despite the revelation of God's wrath upon the whole land. National distress suggested to the preacher that it was high time for humble repentance. A Parliamentarian supporter in his congregation, if there was one, would have found the message familiar.[22]

II

Cornelius Burges preached the first Fast Sermon on 17 November 1640, his text being drawn from Jeremiah L.5: 'let us join ourselves unto the Lord in an everlasting Covenant that shall not be forgotten' (p. 3). 'Upon any notable deliverance', he said, 'God's people . . . enter anew into solemn and strict covenant with God' – for instance after Moses had delivered them out of Egypt (Deuteronomy XXIX), after the occupation of Canaan (Joshua XXIV.25–6), 'upon the deliverance of Judah from the tyranny of

21. Aubrey, *Miscellanies* (1890), p. 163; cf. Evelyn, *Diary* (ed. E. S. De Beer, Oxford U.P., 1955), III, p. 312; *FS*, VII, p. 287; see p. 100 below.
22. R. Chalfont, *A Sermon Preached at the Publique Fast*, 10 May 1644 (Oxford U.P.), pp. 2, 29.

that bloody monster Athaliah' by Iehoiada (II Kings XI.17), after Asa's victory over Zerah the Cushite with his million-strong army (II Chronicles XIV), and especially after deliverance from Babylon. 'Babylon ... had always been the most insolent, heavy, bitter, bloody enemy, that ever the church felt. The violence of Babylon was unsupportable, her insolency intolerable, her blood-thirstiness insatiable'. To make the application to Laudian rule absolutely clear, Burges continued 'Babylon began to besiege Jerusalem, and Antichrist began to pull off his vizard ... even then, when pictures and images began first to be set up in churches'.[23]

Burges looked back to England's great deliverances from the Spanish Armada and Gunpowder Plot. Why, he asked, has God 'not yet given us so full a deliverance from Babylon', why have there been 'so many ebbings and flowings in matters of religion, yea more ebbings than flowings?' 'Albeit God hath moved the heart of the King to call Parliament after Parliament, yet by and by one spirit of division or another ... still ... blasteth all our hopes'. This recalled 'the evil spirit which God sent between Abimelech and the men of Shechem, to the ruin of both' – Judges IX.23–4. Abimelech was slain by a woman, to his disgust and shame; but the men of Shechem suffered too because of their wickedness in 'making a tyrant their King', the Geneva margin tells us. In England, Burges continued, we have prayed, we have fasted: 'why then is deliverance and reform so slow in coming?' It is because we have launched out into Babylon's 'deepest lakes of superstition and idolatry'. We must renew our covenant with God. Israel had 'covenant upon covenant, and yet can no man ... charge it with any Puritan humour, or anything superfluous or uncomely for the greatest on earth to submit unto'. 'Even the present mercy and opportunity of opening that ancient, regular and approved way' of public fasts pleads hard for a covenant. Remember Gunpower Plot. 'You know not what need you may have of [God] this present Parliament. You cannot be ignorant of ... the whisperings of some desperate and devilish' plots 'now in the womb of the Jesuitical faction'.[24]

Laudian discouragement of preaching has made many in the dark corners of the land incapable of covenant with God. 'What fearful trifling is this in a business of such high concernment! Good Jehoshaphat, when his heart was once lift up in the ways of the Lord, took other order': so, by implication, should Charles I. The essential thing is to 'purge and cast away ... all idols and idolatry'. Idolatry 'will certainly be the destruction of

23. *FS.*, I, pp. 3, 19, 24–33, 51, 54. Cf. Chapters 9 and 11 below.
24. Ibid., pp. 65, 70, 74–6.

King and people, wherever it is entertained, especially if again received in after it hath been once ejected'. The resumption of idols by succeeding monarchs after good King Josiah 'became the ruin of those kings, and kingdoms'.[25]

The second Fast Sermon was preached on the same day by Stephen Marshall, clearly in concert. Both stressed idolatry and lack of preaching. Marshall's text was II Chronicles XV.2. 'The Lord is with you, while you be with him . . . but if you forsake him, he will forsake you'. The reference, as Marshall emphasized, was to the apostasy and idolatry of Israel under Rehoboam and Abijah, and to Asa's restoration of purity of worship after calling 'all his nobles and princes and elders together', and after fighting off a terrible military threat from Zerah the Cushite. 'It is no question', Marshall reminded his congregation, 'but your enemies are mighty, malicious and cunning'. But 'are we an holy people?' 'Egypt was never more bespread with locusts and frogs, than our kingdom is with horrible profaneness, uncleanness, oppression, deceit.' 'We have been hitherto kept as a land of Goshen, where light hath still shined, when all others have been in darkness'. But God may leave England, and 'if he go, all goes. . . . . All your counsels and advising will be nothing if God say, I will stay no longer in England'. 'There hath not been in all the Christian world such high affronts offered to the Lord's day as of late hath been in England': violation of the Sabbath, idolatry, profanation of the Lord's supper by admitting all to it promiscuously. Which of you MPs is not to some extent guilty? Marshall asked.[26]

In one way the bleak international situation is encouraging, Marshall added, since 'Satan knows his time is short'. 'It may be not only our welfare and peace and religion', but that of 'all Christendom, under God, depends upon your meeting'. If you fail, you 'may be more guilty than the very authors of our mischiefs, who had been firm to their own principles in bringing of them in'. Marshall's one positive proposal was: imitate Jehoshaphat, 'who sent princes and Levites . . . about through all the cities and taught the people' (II Chronicles XVII.7). Has the lack of a preaching ministry been due to 'the negligence and corruption of our governors', or lack of adequate maintenance for preachers? Has neglect of preaching been 'one main cause of the ill success of so many former Parliaments?'[27]

25. Ibid., pp. 89–90, 83–4.
26. Ibid., I, pp. 104–5, 121–2, 132–7, 142.
27. Ibid., pp. 145–51.

John Gauden a fortnight later rammed the case against idolatry home.[28] Marshall (again) and Jeremiah Burroughs, preaching on 7 September 1641 to celebrate the peace signed between England and Scotland, also welcomed the changes in England 'this year wherein we looked to have been a wonder to all the world in our desolation, and God himself made us a wonder to the world in our preservation: giving us in one year a return of the prayers of forty and forty years' – an end to 'the yokes which lay upon our estates, liberties, religion and conscience' – Star Chamber, 'the terrible High Commission', lack of regular Parliaments, etc., etc.[29]

'That which now it hath had', said Burroughs in his Commentary on Hosea, was 'the greatest blow that ever was given to Antichristian government; . . . Babylon is fallen, is fallen'. This had frustrated the plans of those that 'made the King glad with their wickedness and the princes with their lies' (Hosea VII.3). This was rather near the knuckle, since the King in question was the idolater Jeroboam. What astonished Burroughs was 'that we should have had such a change, . . . so sudden, so great, in a peaceable way' yet with 'so little change of hearts'. 'Nothing but a miracle of providence could have prevented misery'. 'Antichrist shall never prevail again *as he hath done*' (my italics). 'Take courage, against the Antichristian party'. These early sermons give us a startling picture of fears and resentments which could not previously find public utterance.[30]

III

But the triumphal note soon ceased, and was followed by deeper political and social questioning. The Irish rebellion of November 1641 led remorselessly into civil war in England. La Rochelle, Bohemia, the Palatinate and other parts of Germany cry 'God will not always make you like Goshen, when we are plagued as Egypt: make you like Noah in the ark, when we are drowned with a flood of miseries'. 'It is certain', Calamy continued, 'that God hath begun to build and plant this nation, and he hath made you [MPs] his instruments'. 'We have been in danger of despair, and we bless God for that little crevice of light let in by your means'. But 'when the people of Israel were come out of Egypt and very near Canaan', they were set back for another 'forty years journey through the vast howling wilderness'. 'God's covenant with a nation is conditional'. God 'repented that he

28. Ibid., p. 189.
29. Ibid., pp. 248, 253.
30. Ibid., pp. 312–13, 325, 328. Cf. p. 263 and Chapter 14 below.

had made Saul King; and the next news we hear, is that he was rejected from being King'.[31]

Marshall preached on the same day about God's wrath, which could not be turned away from Judah even by the peerless Josiah, so greatly had God's anger been provoked by Manasseh (II Kings XXIII.25–6). Josiah 'consulted not with flesh and blood', and led the work of destroying images, bringing the whole nation with him, but all his efforts came to nothing because the people's hearts were not right (Jeremiah III.10); and with us, Marshall added, 'the *vox populi* is, that many of the nobles, magistrates, knights and gentlemen, and persons of great quality, are arrant traitors and rebels against God'.[32] Strong words!

By 23 February 1641–2 Calamy was more openly critical of Charles I's government. 'The ill-affected party had got a mighty faction, men in authority and power; pits were digged for the righteous, gallows provided for Mordecai, because he would not bow to Haman; dens of lions for Daniel, because he would not leave praying; fiery furnaces for the three children, because they would not worship the golden image; dungeons for Jeremy, because he would preach the truth with boldness'. 'God hath delivered us from civil yokes and from spiritual; from monopolies'; from 'the late canons mounted up against all good men, but now turned against themselves; from the Star Chamber and from the terrible High Commission, that rack and torture of conscience and conscientious men, . . . from those two terrible oaths, the oath *ex officio* and the oath of the late canons'. 'God hath whipped out the enemies of this church and state by whips of their own making. . . . The endeavours to divide the nations of England and Scotland have been the means of their farther union'.[33]

The indispensable Stephen Marshall's famous sermon, *Meroz Cursed*, was preached to the House of Commons on 23 February 1641–2, well before civil war started. But the text from Judges V.23 assumed that the divisions were irreconcilable. The Angel of the Lord called for the inhabitants of Meroz to be bitterly cursed 'because they came not to the help of the Lord . . . against the mighty'. 'The Lamb's followers and servants are often the poor and off-scouring of the world'. But 'God's meanest servants must not be afraid to oppose the mighty'. Marshall quoted Psalm CXXXVII: 'Blessed is the man that takes [Babylon's] little ones and dasheth them against the

---

31. *FS*, II, pp. 34, 51–2, 70–75. Calamy cited Mordecai's warning to Esther, quoted on p. 68 above.
32. Ibid., pp. 85, 89, 126, 129.
33. Ibid., pp. 147–8, 153.

stones'.[34] On this text Calvin had commented: 'though it seems a cruel thing, . . . as he speaketh not of his own head, but fetcheth his words at God's mouth, it is nothing else but a proclaiming of God's just judgment'.[35] Marshall appears equally complacent about the infallible authority of God as related in Scripture.[36]

Although civil war was still six months ahead, Marshall fiercely proclaimed that 'the Lord acknowledges no neuters'. All people are 'blessed or cursed according as they join with or oppose the cause of God'. Quoting Jesus's 'He that is not with me is against me' (Matthew XII.30) Marshall added 'It may be some of you may be called, as soldiers, to spend your blood in the church's cause'. He was scathing about those who 'love the church, they pity the miseries of the church, they are sorry for Germany, when they think on it, and that is but seldom'; but they do nothing. 'They have a bottomless gulf called "self"'.[37]

Preachers in 1641–2 and later insist on the need for repentance for national sins which have provoked the Lord. MPs are 'public persons that must . . . bear the sins of others whom you represent'. Some preachers even suggest that MPs may have been among the sinners. Simeon Ash, preaching from Psalm IX.9, 'The Lord also will be a refuge for the oppressed', brought the accusation home to his auditors. 'There are country gentlemen who cry out of heavy oppressions in Westminster Hall, and yet they themselves do grind the faces of their tenants, by racking rents and fines at home'. He linked economic oppression with persecution: 'our prelates have . . . been (of late especially) the grand oppressors of the kingdom' – both of rich and poor. When the Parliamentarian army marched against the King in August 1642, Marshall and Ash accompanied it, together with Obadiah Sedgwick.[38]

Much alarm was still expressed in these sermons about lack of preaching in the 'dark corners', which were left in popish and pagan ignorance. This had long been a concern of Puritans, more particularly since the suppression of the Feoffees for Impropriations by Archbishop Laud in 1633 had

34. Ibid., pp. 191, 206, 208–9. Trevor-Roper cites four later Fast Sermons which repeat the curse on neutrality (op. cit. p. 308n). For a royalist criticism of this sermon see p. 112 below.
35. Calvin, *The Psalmes of David and other Psalmes*, Psalm CXXXVII.
36. Cf. pp. 91–2 below.
37. *FS*, II, pp. 214, 220–21, 251, 248.
38. *FS*, II, pp. 295, 264 (Cornelius Burges), 454–8 (Joseph Caryl), 317, 344–8 (Ash); cf. Thomas Hill and Obadiah Sedgwick (*FS*, III, pp. 59–67, 126); Ann Hughes, *The Causes of the Civil War* (1991), p. 181.

removed the most effective means by which private enterprise could remedy the situation. This became of political importance in the months leading up to civil war: the dark corners of Wales, Cornwall and the North were in fact to provide the King with the bulk of his troops. A preaching clergy was likely to be a Puritan clergy. As in the days of Jehoshaphat, preaching 'will secure the land, as much as that posture of war you intend'.[39] Fast Sermons stressed the need for changes in the government of the church.[40]

William Sedgwick was forthright in his sermon of 29 June 1642, *Zions Deliverance and Her Friends Duty*. Citing Revelation XX.2–3, he declared 'Satan shall be bound, and cast into the bottomless pit; and with him this Antichristian malignity'. On 31 August 1642 William Carter took as his text Judges XX.26–8, where Phineas asked 'Shall I yet again go out to battle against the children of Benjamin my brother?' and the Lord said 'go up'. From whence we may observe, 'However war be a bloody work, a civil war especially, yet in some cases it is God's command'. And God promised victory. 'Do not the work of God negligently, or to halves' is the conclusion. War called for emergency measures. The main rivals to the pulpit had long been taverns and ale-houses, brothels and the theatre: now was the time to suppress them, Thomas Temple told the House of Commons on 26 October 1642.[41] Taverns and ale-houses had become discussion centres in the new freedom of the 1640s, when 'religion is now become the common discourse and table-talk'.[42] 'Ale-houses generally', Henry Wilkinson moaned nearly four years later, are 'the meeting-places of malignants and sectaries', royalists and radicals.[43]

'Purple prelates and their corrupt clergy hinder the passage of God's redeemed ones into Canaan', declared Thomas Wilson on 28 September 1642, 'as the troops of Trent fortified themselves and made a wall about popery'. But the walls shall fall down. 'It is the honour of all the saints to triumph over all contrary royalty and nobility, "to bind their kings in chains and nobles with fetters of iron"'. Where now is the prelates' strong wall 'made of canons, oaths, constitutions and superstitions?' But the walls

39. *FS*, II, p. 423 (T. Goodwin); cf. p. 192 (Calamy); III, pp. 99–100 (Obadiah Sedgwick); VI, p. 169 (Andrew Perne); p. 202 (Cheynell – 'Is there not a Babylon in the North, and another in the West?'); XI, p. 73 (John Greene), pp. 171, 176 (Henry Hall), p. 283 (Gaspar Hickes), and others.

40. E.g. Thomas Goodwin and Joseph Caryl, *FS*, II, pp. 383–508.

41. *FS*, III, p. 194 (Sedgwick); pp. 357, 363, 400 (Carter); IV, pp. 151–2 (Temple).

42. [Anon.], *Religions Enemies* (1641), p. 6. Attributed to John Taylor, the Water-Poet.

43. *FS*, XXIV (21 July 1646), p. 40. For alehouses see pp. 15, 39 above, 227 below.

of Jericho fell not when men expected them to fall, but 'in God's appointed time, in which everything is beautiful'.[44] Humphrey Hardwick, in the difficult days of late June 1644, quoted Christ: 'It is not for you to know the times and seasons', as Milton did in *Paradise Regained*. We must say with Job, 'all the days of my appointed time will I wait till my change come'.[45] The change came a week later, with the battle of Marston Moor. 'Providence doth interrupt probabilities to see whether we can trust in improbabilities', said Obadiah Sedgwick.[46]

Risky critical points previously hinted at by Biblical quotations or allusions could be made more directly after the outbreak of civil war. Even on 29 June 1642 William Gouge told the Commons that 'Ye are now the judges of this land'.[47] A blood-thirstiness recalling Marshall's *Meroz Cursed* becomes more frequent, preachers citing the many Old Testament texts which call for the destruction of God's enemies. We must beware of 'groundless pity, that is an enemy to justice', Edmund Staunton told the House of Lords on 30 October 1644, citing Isaiah I.24. 'Pity to one may be cruelty to thousands'. He concluded 'Could I lift up my voice as a trumpet, had I the shrill cry of an angel, . . . my note should be, execution of judgment, execution of judgment, execution of judgment'. His text was 'Then up stood Phineas and executed judgment, and so the plague was stayed' (Psalm CVI.30).[48]

Thomas Case in August 1645 cited God's instructions to Joshua: 'thou shalt smite them, and utterly destroy them; thou shalt make no covenant with them, nor show mercy unto them' (Deuteronomy VII.2); John Maynard in October 1646 quoted Jesus Christ himself: 'those mine enemies, which would not that I should reign over them, bring hither and slay them before me' (Luke XIX.27). Nicholas Lockyer in the same month repeated words which Ezekiel attributed to God: 'slay utterly old and young' (Ezekiel IX.2).[49]

During the civil war there was also greater outspokenness about the Roman Catholic danger, and more explicit attacks on Henrietta Maria.

44. Ibid., IV, pp. 67, 69–70, 84.

45. *FS*, XI, pp. 243–4.

46. Sedgwick, *The Doctrine of Providence*, p. 393. Bound with his *The Shepherd of Israel*, 1658. Cf. ibid., p. 407.

47. *FS*, III, p. 159. In 1628 Alexander Leighton had appealed to MPs as 'the children of Israel' (*An Appeal to the Parliament*.)

48. *FS*, XIII, pp. 258–9, 266, 275–6.

49. *FS*, XVIII, p. 210 (Case); XXV, p. 105 (Maynard), p. 142 (Lockyer). Cf. *FS*, IV, pp. 73, 177; V, pp. 73, 103; VII, pp. 89–90; IX, pp. 195–6; X, p. 38; XI, pp. 46, 250; XIII, p. 109.

'The church of God hath had . . . sad experience of this sad effect and consequence of marrying with idolators and those that are enemies to the Church' – not only in Solomon and Jehoram, but also 'in other of the Kings of Israel and Judah, but even in Christian kings and princes . . . when they have matched . . . with such as professed the Christian religion, only not in purity': thus Matthew Newcomen on the anniversary of Gunpowder Plot in 1642. Francis Cheynell on 31 May 1643, and Stephen Marshall a fortnight later, referred to royalists as 'the Antichristian faction'. 'The question in England', said Marshall on 18 January 1643–4, 'is whether Christ or Antichrist shall be lord or king?' Away with 'Antichrist's stuff, root and branch, head and tail, throw it out of the kingdom'. Earlier he had insisted that 'Time (one of the best interpreters of prophecies)' had made 'the whole army of protestant interpreters' agree 'in the general scope and meaning' of Revelation.[50]

From about the time of the victory at Naseby onwards the preponderance of Presbyterian divines and of members of the Westminster Assembly among preachers of Fast Sermons diminishes; men like Dury, Sterry, Hugh Peter and Jeremiah Burroughs were often invited. There was greater emphasis on England's participation in a cosmic struggle against Antichrist. Already on 29 June 1642 William Sedgwick had seen 'the beginnings of dissolution and breakings in the very kingdom of the Beast itself'. Now is the time to redouble our prayers. 'Difficulties are in the way'; but 'if we continue begging, God must yield; if we be not weary of praying, he must be weary of denying'.[51] The Irish, Matthew Newcomen had suggested on 5 November 1642, had been plotting rebellion for years after the failure of Gunpowder Plot in 1605. The dissolutions and intermissions of Parliament had been part of the same Roman Catholic plot. England's strength lay in her Parliaments, as Samson's in his hair.[52] In April 1643 Greenhill's *Axe at the Root* combined constitutional appeals to Magna Carta and the Petition of Right with Biblical arguments. 'You are a free Parliament, preserve your freedom, our laws and liberties'; 'let not England become a house of bondage, a second Egypt.'[53]

50. *FS*, IV, pp. 246–8 (Newcomen); VI, p. 95 (Cheynell); pp. 355, 351, IX, p. 253, VI, p. 351 (Marshall).
51. *FS*, III, pp. 204–6 (Sedgwick). Sedgwick later in his *Inquisition for the Blood of our late Soveraign* (1660) used arguments from Genesis to expose the hypocrisy of the 'Parliament-men' whom he had formerly supported; they 'made famous prayers and sermons, but *devoured*' (pp. 41–2).
52. *FS*, IV, p. 275. Cf. XVII, p. 282 (Richard Byfield).
53. *FS*, VI, pp. 38–9.

Christ wages war against kings in the latter days, said Lazarus Seaman on 25 September 1644, citing Revelation XXVII.14. 'The kingdom of Christ goes up by Antichrist's going down', Thomas Temple had told the Commons on 26 October 1642: 'beware then of connivance at popery'. The concept of an international struggle was always present.[54] 'The nation of England at this day is God's Sion', Richard Byfield told the Commons on 25 June 1645; 'the nation of Scotland is so' too. Preachers drew attention to the signs of the Second Coming, dating the end of the Fourth Monarchy to 1650, the destruction of Antichrist to 1656: Noah's Flood had occurred in Anno Mundi 1656 and 'as the days of Noah were, so shall also the coming of the Son of Man be' (Matthew XXXIV.37).[55] Ireland figured largely in this international perspective.[56] At least six sermons between July 1646 and September 1647 appealed for help for protestants in Ireland where the Irish rebels were under the command of a Papal Nuncio. Things had begun to look brighter by 29 August 1649 when William Cooper cried 'Send all the pack of Babylonish trash to Rome, after the Nuncio.'[57]

Walter Bridge in February 1643–4 applied II Samuel XIX.5–8 to Charles I, recalling that Joab had rebuked David: 'Thou hast shamed this day the faces of all thy servants', and warned him that his people would desert him if he did not change his ways. 'We dare not think his Sacred Majesty doth intentionally hate his friends and love his foes,' Bridge observed; but the King must be convinced if he was to repent and retract. The preacher imagined Joab addressing his King: 'Sir, . . . if the Queen of your bosom stand in competition with your kingdom, your people, you must not love her better than us' (II Samuel XIX). To those who knew the text, Bridge's reference to Jeremiah XLVIII.10 conveyed a much more explicit message: 'Cursed be he that doeth the work of the Lord negligently, and cursed be he that keepeth back his sword from blood'.[58] Thomas Coleman in August 1643 compared Charles with Jeroboam, who made 'the basest of the people' priests, who in many ways look like Laudians. 'Is it

---

54. Ibid., XIII, p. 109 (Seaman); IV, pp. 152–3 (Temple); cf. III, p. 44 (R. Harris, 25 May 1642); pp. 204–5 (William Sedgwick, 29 June, 1642).
55. Ibid., XVII, p. 282 (Byfield); XXX, pp. 295–6 (Bridge, 17 May 1648); XII, pp. 11–12, 41–2 (Stanley Gower, 31 July 1644); XXXIV, p. 102 (Sterry, 5 November 1652); cf. XII, pp. 183–6 (William Reyner).
56. Ibid., III, pp. 94–5; VI, p. 355; VII, p. 332; XII, p. 91; XIII, pp. 23, 49; XIV, p. 136; XV, pp. 16, 288; XXIV, pp. 124–7; XXVI, pp. 59, 188; XXVIII, p. 181; XXX, p. 85; XXXIII, pp. 227–8, 275–8, 283.
57. Ibid., XXXIII, p. 52.
58. Ibid., V, pp. 209–31.

likely that Jeroboam will preserve religion, that persecutes away his faithful ministers?' Ironically, the author of *Eikon Basilike* was to make Charles I accuse the Parliamentarians of 'consecrating the meanest of the people to be priests in Israel'.[59] John Strickland on Guy Fawkes Day 1644 in effect equated royalists with idolaters, enemies of the Church of England.[60]

'The Philistines rejoice', Richard Byfield told the House of Commons on 25 June 1645, 'that they have our Samson, . . . our King, in their prison, and that they have put out his eyes, . . . shorn his locks where his strength lay, even the hearts of his faithful godly people and this his present Parliament, . . . his heart is from them, his hand is against them'. In these circumstances, breaking the law became 'a holy obstinacy'. On the other side, willingness to suffer death for a cause was no guarantee of the justice of that cause: there was no merit in the martyrdom of a heretic.[61] The ups and downs of war created a need for morale-boosting and emphasis on patience in adversity for which the Old Testament supplied a plentiful array of texts.

Charles Herle in *Ahab's Fall by his Prophets Flatteries* summed up the principles upon which Parliament had for some time been acting by saying specifically that the two Houses were 'not only requisite to the acting of this power of making laws, but co-ordinate with his Majesty in the very power of acting'. Historians of political and constitutional theory make much of the 'co-ordination principle', the sharing of sovereignty between the King and the other two estates, Lords and Commons.[62] It proved indeed very useful after 1660 as an argument for persuading royalists to abandon the idea that the King was sole sovereign and law-giver. But no one who has read the Fast Sermons of the 1640s can suppose that the niceties of constitutional theory were uppermost in MPs' minds. The question was rather Marshall's, 'whether Christ or Antichrist shall be lord or king?'

As Englishmen came to see their country as the centre of the international struggle, new prominence was given to the idea that she had been a chosen nation – at least since the beginning of Elizabeth's reign. Preachers of Fast

59. Ibid., VIII, pp. 62, 101–4 (Coleman); *Eikon Basilike: The Pourtraicture of His Sacred Majestie in his Solitudes and Sufferings* (1871 reprint), p. 97. First published 1649.
60. *FS*, XIV, p. 82 (Strickland); cf. XII, p. 66 (Palmer).
61. Ibid., XVII, p. 282 (Byfield); IV, pp. 399, 402 (Richard Vines, 30 November 1642).
62. Herle, op. cit., p. 42: three sermons upon I Kings XXII.22 (1644). For 'the co-ordination principle' see C. C. Weston and J. R. Greenberg, *Subjects and Sovereigns: The Grand Controversy over Legal Sovereignty in Stuart England* (Cambridge U.P., 1981), *passim*.

Sermons called for poems and histories to celebrate God's interest in England.[63] Thomas Goodwin put it forcibly on 25 February 1645: 'If we had stood at God's elbow when he bounded out the nations', and 'appointed the times and seasons that men should live in (as the Apostle speaketh)', we could have not chosen a better age or place 'in respect of the enjoyment of the gospel and the communion of saints' than England now. 'The God of heaven is the God of England', Hugh Peter assured both Houses of Parliament, the Lord Mayor and Aldermen of London and members of the Assembly of Divines on 2 April 1645. Herbert Palmer, five months later, spoke of 'our God, . . . not as engrossing him wholly to ourselves, but as challenging a special interest in him by his own grace.'[64]

Preachers began to stress England's indebtedness to the heretic tradition, especially the Lollard tradition, but also the Waldensians, Hus, Luther, Knox. Peter Sterry, on 5 November 1651, reminded his audience that 'the dispensations of God in spiritual privileges have been peculiar to this nation in many things' – the Emperor Constantine, Wyclif, Edward VI, and the recent revolution. So it was reasonable to expect Christ's Second Coming to occur first of all in England. John Owen, nearly a year later, agreed that 'God, secretly entwining the interest of Christ with you, wrapt up with you the whole generation of them that seek his face, and prospered your affairs on that account'.[65]

A new readiness slowly developed to challenge princes and rulers as such. Perhaps, in the words of Ezra summarized by John Ward, 'the hands of the princes and rulers hath been chief in the trespass'. We must search out 'the sins of the state, of our princes and nobles and judges, of our Parliament, former and later' (Ezra IX.2–3). On 14 January 1645–6 Jeremiah Whitaker recalled the surprise of historians at the number of successive kings of Judah who died violently: they attribute it, he said, 'next to the hand of God' to 'too much affecting an arbitrary government'.[66]

This emphasis naturally became more frequent. The day after the King's execution Owen contrasted the 'Antichristian tyranny' of monarchy with 'the interest of the many'. A year later Vavasor Powell claimed that God

63. *FS*, I, p. 338 (Burges); II, pp. 199–200 (Marshall); X, p. 229 (O. Sedgwick), XIV, p. 21 (W. Spurstowe); cf. B. Worden, 'Providence and Politics in Cromwellian England', *P. and P.*, 109 (1985), pp. 63–4.

64. *FS*, XI, p. 269 (Gaspar Hickes, 26 June 1644); XXII, p. 105 (Goodwin); XXIII, p. 106 (Peter); cf. ibid., pp. 182–3 (Owen); XXIV, p. 246 (Palmer).

65. *FS*, XXIV, p. 246 (Palmer); III, p. 311 (Hill); XXXIV, pp. 90–92, 102–3 (Sterry); p. 135 (Owen).

66. *FS*, XVI, p. 286 (Ward, 26 March 1645); XX, p. 313 (Whitaker).

opposes kings. John Maynard on 28 October 1646 had quoted Daniel II.35: the Lord 'will put down all rule, and all authority and power', though only Ranters went so far as to advocate that sort of anarchy.[67]

The peers too came under attack from Stephen Marshall and Francis Cheynell on 25 March 1645. Marshall told the Lords that they had 'no lordly rule' over religion. Cheynell and John Ward (preaching to the Lords on the same day) quoted Job: God 'striketh [the mighty] as wicked men' (Job XXXIV.24, 26). In November of the same year Jeremiah Burroughs was even more severe in his criticisms of the Upper House. Lords, Francis Taylor thought it necessary to remind them on 25 May 1646, are subject to the covenant no less than meaner men. Under the Commonwealth Vavasor Powell made claims for the right of the lower classes to rule, quoting Ezekiel XXI.26, Daniel IV.17 and Psalm CXIII.7–8. Moses, Joshua, Gideon, Jephtha, Saul, David and many others were originally 'mean men'. Psalms CX and CXLIX show that God intended kings to be opposed and destroyed. Marshall on 30 December 1646 had cited 'Moses, a shepherd', Gideon, 'it may be but a yeoman's son', Saul, 'a private gentleman's son', and Amos, 'a neatherd' as examples of God allowing careers to the talented, parallel to the 'tradesmen from their shops, and husbandmen from their ploughs' who had enabled the New Model Army to win the war for Parliament. In October 1651 Owen quoted Ezekiel: 'I the Lord have brought down the high tree, and have exalted the low tree' (Ezekiel XVIII.24).[68]

On 30 October 1644 Henry Scudder had suggested that English men and women had never sufficiently repented of the blood shed in Mary's reign: perhaps 'the guilt of that blood . . . doth lie upon the land and crieth for vengeance', so that 'God is punishing it this day'. He gave numerous Biblical references. In the recent civil war the land had been 'polluted with innocent blood': sooner or later God will avenge it (Deuteronomy XIX.13; II Kings XXIV.4). Even earlier, on 26 October 1642, Thomas Case had denounced failure to punish those guilty of bloodshed, citing I Kings XX.24. On 27 December 1643 the Scot Alexander Henderson observed that the King, 'when he sees so many poor people fall to the ground, so

67. *FS*, XXXII, pp. 330–58 (Owen); XXXIII, pp. 200–1 (Powell); XXV, p. 98 (Maynard). Maynard's reference to Daniel is wrongly extended to this passage, which is from I Corinthians XV.24.
68. *FS*, XVI, pp. 85–151 (Cheynell); 195 (Marshall); 250 (Ward); XX, pp. 81–130 (Burroughs); XXIII, p. 287 (Taylor); XXXIII, pp. 200–203 (Powell); XXVI, pp. 98–9 (Marshall); XXXIV, pp. 17, 21–4, 27–8 (Owen). Cf. Chapter 4 below.

much blood spilt, should be moved in his heart to say as David said, "I have sinned"'. On Guy Fawkes Day of the following year Charles Herle pushed this further to warn the House of Lords 'it is high time to look about you, lest your indulgence to any other men's sins multiply so much uncleanness as may both ruin your own houses and hazard the whole kingdom'.[69]

By the late 1640s this emerged as a full-blown theory that the Man of Blood, who had been responsible for two civil wars, must be called to account and punished, lest blood-guiltiness remained upon the whole people.[70] There are innumerable examples of Old Testament kings who were murdered and replaced because of their failure to proceed with sufficient severity against God's enemies. Often, by an irony not noticed in the seventeenth century, the supplanter was himself discarded once God's purposes had been achieved. Robert Heyricke in May 1646 declared that God, 'that pardons all other sins, will not pardon innocent blood . . . Reformation cannot hinder when God inquires for blood' (Ezra VII.26). Heyricke made his meaning clear by adding 'The highest court may reach the highest persons'. He cited Isaiah LX.14: 'All they that despised thee shall bow down themselves at the soles of thy feet', which he glossed as 'the greatest that have afflicted you and despised you shall lie at your feet'. Thomas Case on 26 October 1642 had quoted II Kings XX.24 to establish that those who failed to punish persons whom God held guilty would themselves be punished, 'your lives for their lives'. Bunyan's friend George Cockayne, preaching to the Commons a week before Pride's Purge in 1648, was much blunter: 'If God do not lead you to do justice upon those that have been the great actors in shedding innocent blood, never think to gain their love by sparing of them'. Thomas Brooks, a week later, took as his epigraph Numbers XXXV.33: 'Blood, it defileth the land, and the land cannot be cleansed of the blood that is shed therein, but by the blood of him that shed it'. He continued remorselessly: 'there is nothing of more power to divert the judgment of God from a nation than the execution of justice and judgment' (Jeremiah V.1, Psalm CVI.30–31). 'If thou be but a man that executes judgment and seeks truth, I will pardon you, saith God; I will turn away my wrath' (Ezekiel XXII.29–31). 'Neglect of justice and judgment will wrap you up in the guilt of other men's sins': and Brooks quoted the crucial Numbers XXXV.33–4. Those like Ahab and Saul who neglected the execution of justice perished basely and miserably (I Kings

---

69. Ibid., XIII, pp. 307, 311 (Scudder); IV, p. 182 (Case); IX, p. 162 (Henderson); XIV, p. 166 (Herle).
70. For what follows to the end of this section, cf. Chapter 15 below.

XXI, XXII.23–37, 40–41; I Samuel I.19; cf. Hosea I.4–5; II Kings X.30). 'It is cruelty to the good to spare the bad'.[71]

John Cardell took up this last point in his sermon of 31 January, the day after the King's execution. 'There is both a punishing mercy and a sparing cruelty' (I Kings XX.42). 'Hath not long experience taught some of you, how many decayed ceilings, and how many worm-eaten beams, and how many rotten posts and studs there are, . . . that must of necessity be removed?'[72]

IV

I quoted Capp's remark that the Commons seemed to appreciate sermons on apocalyptic themes.[73] On 25 February 1645–6 John Goodwin described the saints as God's Privy Councillors. 'God doth give these his saints a commission to set up and pull down by their prayers and intercessions'. Soon the saints' activities were not limited to prayer. Preaching to the Commons on 29 November 1648, just before Pride's Purge, Cockayne took as his text Isaiah LXV.16–18: 'Behold I create a new heaven and a new earth'. He announced that the saints 'are the men by whom God at last will judge all the causes of the sons of men' (I Corinthians VI.2). 'It may be God will pick out the meanest of his people in whom he will appear' – as he had appeared in Gideon (Judges VI.13, VII.18). But he made it clear that he was speaking to MPs when he added 'the Lord is risen in you and will judge the world by you'. In January 1649 John Cardell had insisted to Parliament that it must protect both the liberties of the people and the liberties of the saints. By February Vavasor Powell could assure Parliament that 'Jesus Christ accounts no men so . . . fit to rule his kingdom (under him) as his saints. . . . The saints should rule and govern the world'.[74] In September or October 1652 the Fifth Monarchist Christopher Feake was invited to preach a Fast Sermon, on the nomination of Major-General Harrison, millenarian Fifth Monarchist.

With this developed the doctrine of providences, so dear to Oliver

71. *FS*, XXIII, pp. 340–41, 349 (Heyricke); IV, p. 182 (Case); XXXII, p. 42 (Cockayne); pp. 81 (title-page), 101–5, 133 (Brooks).
72. *FS*, XXXII, pp. 172–5.
73. See p. 83 above.
74. *FS*, XXII, pp. 96–8 (John Goodwin); XXXII, pp. 33–4, 39 (Cockayne); 169–71 (Cardell); XXXIII, pp. 193–4, 197 (Powell). Cf. Chapter 13 below.

Cromwell. Vavasor Powell drew Parliament's attention to 'the concurrence of God's providence in effecting those great things which you have undertaken both in this land and in Ireland'. We must accept 'the divine sovereignty of God', and not grumble if God did not order things just as we would have them: that was 'flying in the face of God himself', said Cardell on the day after Charles I's execution. God's omnipotence is its own justification, John Warren argued on 19 April 1649 in *The Potent Potter:* 'it is not the goodness of a prevailing party among men that gives them power over others, but the iniquity of the falling side that makes them fall before the conquerors'.[75]

Owen, celebrating the crowning mercy of the battle of Worcester on 24 October 1651, told Parliament that men get set in their principles, 'wise principles forsooth, yea and very righteous too'; and they expect reality to conform to these principles: 'old bounds must not be broken up; order must not be disturbed.' But God is the spirit of revolution: his 'actings . . . are unsuited to the expectations of man'. 'The hardening of the late King's heart was an engine whereby he wrought mighty things and alterations'. 'The constant appearing of God against every party that under any colour or pretence whatever have lifted up themselves for the re-enforcement of things as in former days' proclaimed 'that the design which God had in hand is as yet marvellously above you. . . . We will not trust in Parliaments or armies, all flesh is grass' (Isaiah XL, XXIII.9; Psalms XX.6–7, XLVI.10.[76]

In such passages we can see how the doctrine of providences liberated the saints from laws, customs, habits and conventions, and gave them the revolutionary energy and freedom to bring about the unprecedented changes of the late 1640s and early 1650s. But the providences of God are a two-edged sword: they cut both ways. When Cromwell expelled the Rump of the Long Parliament in April 1653, the words of Isaiah XXIX.14–17 recurred to Henry Newcome: 'The wisdom of their wise men shall fail'. 'Shall the work say, He made me not? . . . Is it not yet but a little while, Lebanon shall be turned into Carmel?'[77]

75. Ibid., XXXII, pp. 227–8 (Powell); 157–9 (Cardell); 287, 303 (Warren, who cited Jeremiah XVII.6 and Job XXXVIII–XL).
76. *FS*, XXXIV, pp. 37–40, 45–6; cf. pp. 115–16 (Owen on Daniel VII.15–16).
77. N. H. Mayfield, *Puritans and Regicide: Presbyterian–Independent Differences over the Trial and Execution of Charles (I) Stuart* (Lanham, Maryland, 1988), *passim;* Newcome, *Autobiography* (ed. R. Parkinson, Chetham Soc., 1852), p. 44.

V

One reason for discontinuing Fast Sermons was radical opposition, expressed for instance in a pamphlet by T.W. in January 1648: *A Word to England Touching their Fastings.* Parliament would be much better employed, the author suggested, remedying social injustice and inequalities than in continuing with the ritual of public fasts. Quakers took up this theme with gusto. 'Hanging down the head for a day', said Fox in 1654, was hypocritical, popish and 'a burden to the Lord'.[78] Two years later he suggested that it would be far better to feed the starving poor than to 'fast like the Pharisees who sound the trumpet when entering the synagogue'.[79] National fasts interrupted the work of men and women in their callings. Walter Cradock thought it was a mockery to 'talk of humiliation and fasting' whilst keeping people 'from their trading; let us deal really with ourselves', he begged.[80]

After the expulsion of the Rump, later Parliaments continued to observe occasional days of fasting or of thanksgiving. John Owen preached two sermons on solemn occasions to Oliver Cromwell's Parliament of 1656. On 17 September, at the opening of Parliament, he preached on Isaiah XIV.32: 'What shall one then answer the messengers of the nation? That the Lord hath founded Zion, and the poor of his people shall trust in it'. The sermon dwells on the peace and freedom which England now enjoys, especially 'those who are very poor', and pleads for unity to preserve 'the Good Old Cause of England'.[81] Six weeks later, on a day of fasting and humiliation, he preached on II Chronicles XV.2. 'The Lord is with you, while ye be with him; and if ye seek him he will be found of you; but if ye forsake him, he will forsake you'. Again it is a plea for unity and trust in the government. Referring to those who would have preferred the rule of the saints to that of Oliver Cromwell, Owen cried 'If ever God cease to call saints – that is men interested personally in Christ – to places of chief authority in this nation ... there will be an end of England's glory and happiness'. The word 'cease' is curiously chosen. Since when did Owen

---

78. Fox, *A Warning from the Lord To all Such as hang down the head for a day*, esp. pp. 1, 3.
79. Fox, *A Declaration Concerning Fasting and Prayer* (1656), p. 2. Cf. the first epigraph to this chapter.
80. Walter Cradock, *Divine Drops Distilled from the Fountain of the Holy Scriptures* (1650). p. 12.
81. Owen, *God's Work in Founding Zion, and his People's Duty Thereupon, Works*, VIII, esp. pp. 406, 419–26.

suppose that 'those called to power' were saints? Owen touched on one
lasting problem of Parliamentarian politics: how to combine the rule of the
godly with the representative principle. 'My heart trembles at this thing –
namely that those who have, and it is fit should have, so great a share in the
government of this commonwealth, should have their rise from the body
of the people, that is dark and profane and full of enmity against the
remnant'. He put in a special plea for preaching in the dark corners of
Wales.[82]

In the following month John Rowe preached to Parliament on a day
of public thanksgiving for naval victory in the West Indies. Taking as his
text John XXVI.24–5, he proclaimed that Providence had declared for
Oliver's government. 'God worketh such great and eminent things in the
world that we might magnify his works (Psalm CXI.4)'. Rowe's main
question was the limits to be set to religious toleration; it was good in itself,
but not when it licensed preaching of 'that cursed doctrine of Socinianism'.[83] Owen had refuted Socinianism at the request of the Council of
State in 1654, in 750 pages. A fortnight after Rowe's sermon the Quaker
leader James Nayler's entry into Bristol in the manner of Christ's entry
into Jerusalem raised the issue of religious freedom in a new and sharper
form, leading to months of debate in Parliament culminating in the savage
punishment of Nayler. An echo of this occurred in the last weeks of
Richard Cromwell's Parliament (March–April 1659), when fierce
controversy was aroused by a proposal to hold a day of fasting and public
humiliation as a testimony against blasphemies and damnable heresies. This
was aimed against Quakers and their like, and against toleration in general.
The motion passed, but neither Richard Cromwell nor his Parliament
survived to see it implemented.[84]

Owen's last sermon to Parliament was delivered to the restored Rump
on 8 May 1659. The triumphalism of his and Rowe's earlier sermons has
gone. Preaching on Isaiah IV.5, 'Upon all the glory shall be a defence',
Owen was indeed on the defensive. His hope was that 'poor, unprofitable
unthankful creatures as we are, we may yet see the fruit of righteousness to
be peace, . . . quietness and assurance for evermore'. But 'God delights to
mix *a spirit of giddiness*, error and folly in the counsels of the wise men of
the world'. There are 'bitter divisions . . . among the people of God

---

82. Owen, *God's Presence with a People the Spring of their Prosperity, with their Special interest in abiding with him*, ibid., esp. pp. 445, 452.
83. Rowe, *Mans Duty to Magnify Gods Work*, 8 August 1656, esp. pp. 15–26.
84. Ed. J. T. Rutt, *Diary of Thomas Burton* (1828), IV, pp. 300, 328–45.

themselves', and 'in many places the very profession of religion is become a scorn'. 'Old forms and ways' are 'taken up with greediness'. Responding, I think, to criticisms of his sermon of September 1656, Owen explained that he was 'very far from thinking that a man may not be lawfully called to the magistracy if he be not a believer'. There are 'many false professors, hypocrites, that have thought gain to be godliness'.[85] We should not judge men by the denomination they profess. But the 'remnant of Christ' is to be found only 'amongst the professors of a nation.' On that he left the future to God.[86]

The restored Rump of the Long Parliament kept 3 August 1659 as a fast day, as Booth's rebellion loomed.[87] After its defeat Nathanael Homes preached a thanksgiving sermon for victory over the Cavaliers (*sic*) to Parliament and other notables on Psalm XXXIII.1: 'Rejoice in the Lord, O ye righteous!'[88] The restored monarchy tried to take over the practice, establishing the day of Charles I's execution (30 January) as a fast day and 29 May (Charles II's birthday and the day of his return to London) as a day of thanksgiving. But by May 1661 Pepys observed that 'in some churches there were hardly ten people in the whole church, and those poor people'.[89]

As an epilogue it is perhaps worth recording that in 1679, when relations between crown and Parliament were again strained, the Commons reverted to their old practice by appointing days of fasting and humiliation. Again the intention was to criticize the government. After 1688 such roundabout methods were superfluous.

---

85. This was a problem that worried Bunyan among many others; see my 'Bunyan, Professors and Sinners', in *Bunyan Studies*, II, pp. 7–25.
86. Owen, *The Glory and Interest of Nations Professing the Gospel, Works*, VIII, esp. pp. 461–70. For the date see G. Davies, *The Restoration of Charles II, 1658–1660* (San Marino, 1955), p. 95.
87. Spalding, *Diary of Bulstrode Whitelocke*, p. 525.
88. Homes, *A Sermon Preached before the Parliament and the Council of State, the Lord Mayor, Aldermen and Common Council of the City of London, and the Officers of the Army*. Unfortunately this sermon was not printed until 1660, when the righteous were no longer rejoicing.
89. Pepys, *Diary*, 29 May 1661.

VI. 1640–1660

From the revolutionary decades we get a rather different use of Old Testament sources. Freedom of discussion and free access by ordinary people to the printing press allowed views to be expressed which may or may not have been held before 1640, but which certainly could not have got into print, or into Parliamentary speeches. Pym in the Short Parliament compared the bishops to Jonah, who 'came into the ship by the master's command', but knew 'he was not doing *his* Master's command' and so 'was to be thrown overboard. . . . So these bishops, if they come in by Christ's command, as I conceive they did not, and not performing their Lord's commands, are to be extinguished'.[90]

'How often have they compared [Charles I] to Pharaoh, to Saul, to Ahab, yea to Manasseh', grumbled the Royalist Edward Symmons in 1644.[91] Levellers and others drew on these names, and added Biblical examples of bad kings and others who came to bad ends – Nebuchadnezzar, Absalom, Zephaniah, Hazael, Issachar, Omri, Ahaz, Herod. Egypt, Babylon and Antichrist were used as traditional symbols for evil régimes, Pharisees for inadequate priests or prelates: but now they are applied to the present. John Cook the regicide thought it an error to hold that the power of Antichrist must not be destroyed by the material sword.[92] Stephen Marshall, in a Fast Sermon of 1646, cited Moses, Gideon, Saul, David, Amos, as evidence that the Bible demonstrated the career open to the talents.[93] A new light-heartedness entered into the use of the Bible. A pamphlet of 1648 recalled that David's warriors were as wise as Levites: so were the preaching soldiers of the New Model Army.[94]

Herle in 1644, looking back 'almost twenty years since', thought it would have been 'no hard thing . . . to have prophesied what uses would in all likelihood be made by this time of those frequent prophesyings of these

90. Quoted in *Minutes of the Manchester Presbyterian Classis* (ed. W. A. Shaw, Chetham Soc., 1890), I, p. lxvii.
91. Edward Symmons, *Scripture Vindicated from the Misapprehensions, Misrepresentations and Misapplications of Mr Stephen Marshall* (1644), p. 84.
92. Cook, *Monarchy no Creature of Gods making* (1652), p. 144.
93. *FS*, XXVI, pp. 98–9.
94. [Anon.], *An Endeavor after the Reconciliation of the Long Debated and much Lamented Differences between the Godly Presbyterians & Independants about Church Government* (14 March 1648[–9]).

Court Prophets, viz. the immediate sole divinity, absolute domination, universal propriety, utter disobligedness towards all the human law, of monarchy. Doctrines so professedly and solemnly articled in the Court-creed, as they were, and so palpably preparatory no less to popery than tyranny. . . . Religion is contrived to make subjects slaves to kings, that thereby kings may be so much the greater slaves to the Pope'. That comes in a sermon entitled *Ahab's Fall by his Prophets Flatteries*.[95] Prynne, that indefatigable purveyor of precedents from English history, collected a vast number of Old Testament examples of deposition and regicide in *The Soveraign Power of Parliaments and Kingdoms* (1643). Even Clarendon gave examples of preachers of 'seditious sermons . . . profanely and blas-phemously' applying to 'their most gracious sovereign . . . whatsoever had been spoken . . . by God himself or the prophets against the most wicked and impious kings'.[96]

John Goodwin in *Anti-Cavalierisme* tried to spur on insufficiently active supporters of Parliament by quoting Genesis XIX.14 against Lot's sons, who mocked at their father's warning that 'the Lord would destroy the place and city where they were'. He cited Elisha's resistance to the house of Ahab, and David's resistance to Saul, as models to be followed; and he reminded his readers that 'the officers that obeyed King Nebuchadnezzar's command in casting those three innocent servants of God into the fiery furnace were suddenly consumed by the flame that came out of the furnace; whereas those that strained at the King's command' and obeyed God instead 'remained untouched of the fire'.[97] In November 1643, when things were looking so bad for Parliament that in London 'some are flying, others are preparing to fly', Joseph Caryl expressed himself cautiously but clearly in Biblical terms. 'God in justice hath put a sword into the hands of unjust men, men skilful to destroy. Moses, he thought, probably wrote the Book of Job before the deliverance of the Israelites out of Egypt.[98]

The Biblical commentaries of Jeremiah Burroughs and William Greenhill, published in the 1640s, were lengthy interpretations of and glosses

95. Herle, op. cit., pp. 30–32.
96. David Wootton, 'From Rebellion to Revolution: the crisis of the winter of 1642–3 and the origins of civil war radicalism', *EHR*, 416 (1990), p. 661; Clarendon, *History of the Rebellion* (ed. W. D. Macray, Oxford U.P., 1888), II, pp. 319–20.
97. Goodwin, op. cit. (1642), pp. 5, 13–16, 19–20, in Haller, *Tracts on Liberty*, II.
98. Caryl, *An Exposition . . . Upon the first three Chapters of the Book of Job*, sig. A 3v, Av, 6.

on current affairs.[99] Greenhill, for instance, describes Ezekiel's times in a way that would be familiar to his hearers and readers: 'There was then a malignant party which was active and at work, and did oppose and hinder the reformation. . . . The chief opposers then were the priests and false prophets'. 'Malignant' was almost a technical term for royalists: 'reformation' was a standard description of what Parliamentarians wanted. Greenhill continues by asking, even more explicitly, 'Was there ever any great disorder, corruption in the church, or any sedition, treason almost in the state, but some of the chief of the priests have had their hands in it? . . . God will overthrow even kings and their councils, kingdoms with their nobility and gentry'.[100]

Burroughs used his commentary on Hosea to make similar reflections on current affairs. *À propos* Chapter I.9 he asked his audience: 'what were your gentry in the kingdom but even slaves and vassals to every popish priest in the country, but especially unto prelates?' (Like Milton, Burroughs thought prelates were to be identified with Pharisees.) 'No evil', he continued, 'may be committed upon pretence of the commands of authority'. 'Where is the man that ever thought there would be such a party of the Lords and Commons, to join with a company of papists, atheists, malignants and Irish rebels against the cause of God and the Gospel' – *à propos* Hosea VI.4. 'By flattering [Jeroboam] in his wicked ways they did not only yield unto his unlawful edicts but commended them'. *À propos* X.2, 'we have no king', Burroughs asked 'whether it be better for a people to have no king or no protection from their king?' – though this was 'a question fitter to be discussed in a Parliament than in a pulpit'. 'Christ hath been but little

99. Burroughs, *An Exposition of the Prophecies of Hosea*, Chapters 1–3 (1643); Chapters 4–7 and 8–10 were published posthumously in two volumes (1650); Chapters 11–13 in 1651; Greenhill, *An Exposition of the five First Chapters of the Prophet Ezekiel* (1645); Chapters 6–13 followed in 1649, 14–19 in 1651, 20–29 in 1650. Burroughs and Greenhill were 'most intimate friends', who shared the patronage of Puritan magnates and had been involved in a Suffolk combination lecture which was suppressed by Bishop Wren. Greenhill had obtained a London lectureship through the Feofees for Impropriations before Laud suppressed them. Burroughs had been a chaplain in the household of the Earl of Warwick. I owe some of this information (and much more) to F. J. Bremer's forthcoming *The Congregational Connection: Friendship and Religion among 17th-century Puritan Clergy in the Atlantic Community*, which he kindly allowed me to read in typescript.
100. Greenhill, *Five First Chapters*, pp. 17–20; cf. p. 73. This volume was dedicated to Elizabeth, Queen of Bohemia, who had herself experienced the overthrow of her kingdom. Greenhill was an Independant, so there may have been a side-swipe against Presbyterians here.

beholding to . . . almost the most of our kings'. 'God can make a great change in the hearts of a people in reference to their king'. 'It is unlawful for any people to obey the unlawful commands of their governors', declared Burroughs forthrightly.[101] Joseph Caryl was less direct when in March 1643 he quoted Jeremiah XIII.18: 'Say unto the King and unto the Queen, "sit down, humble yourselves"'. 'I will not add that which follows', he continued, 'I have no commission for it'. In the printed version he then proceeded to add it, as he probably would not have done three years earlier: 'for your principalities shall come down, even the crown of your glory'.[102]

As we have abundantly seen, Jeroboam was a favourite bad king, a promoter of idol worship (I Kings XI), to whom the Stuart sovereigns were frequently delicately likened. 'He made Israel to sin', said Greenhill concisely.[103] Jeroboam reigned prosperously for forty-one years, during which period Hosea prophesied against him. But 'God came upon [his son] in six months' (II Kings XV.8–10). And Jeroboam had been defeated by an army half the size of his (II Chronicles XIII). Asa relied on God to rout an Abyssinian army more than three times the size of his (II Chronicles XIV.8–12). God also waited a long time before executing his threat to punish the brother of Jeroboam (1 Kings XIV.7–16). 'Our Parliament hath sat two years', Burroughs observed drily.[104] Burroughs set a high value on English freedom: 'every freeholder hath an influence into the making and consenting every law he is under', and he has the same right to his property as a peer. Burroughs's political egalitarianism looks forward to the Levellers. Edwards had his eye on him, and denounced Burroughs's principles as 'unsound and weak, fit to take women and weak people with, but not to satisfy any scholar'.[105]

In the radical pamphlet, *More Light Shining in Buckinghamshire* (1649), Jeroboam is described as 'the first [who] invented state worship', in the form of idolatry.[106] Four years later Captain John Williams in Radnorshire

101. Burroughs, *Chapters 1–3*, pp. 113, *Chapters 4–7*, pp. 580, 652–3; *Chapters 8–10*, pp. 331, 337, 339.

102. Caryl, *Davids Prayer for Solomon*, p. 37, quoted by D. Wootton, 'From Rebellion to Revolution', *EHR*, 416, p. 660.

103. Greenhill, *Five First Chapters* (1645), p. 41.

104. Burroughs, *Chapters 4–7*, pp. 464, 470, 652–3, *Chapters 1–3*, pp. 16–20, 45–6.

105. Edwards, *Gangraena*, p. 33. Burroughs retorted in *A Vindication of Mr Burroughs against Mr Edwards his foul Aspersions in his spreading Gangraena* (1646). One sees why universities were held in suspicion by radicals.

106. Sabine, p. 632; cf. p. 629.

compared the rulers of the Protectorate to Jeroboam, and their opponents to the prophet Amos. Citing Amos VIII.9, the informer tells us, Williams declared that 'in these days our sun was gone down at noon day and our light turned to darkness; and said there was a seed sowed in darkness which would spring in light; and he did believe this next spring . . .'.[107]

Solomon's son, Rehoboam, although continually at war with Jeroboam who had replaced him as King of Israel, was no less an idolater. His name was often used as a warning example. There was no need to cite the words, 'To your tents, O Israel', which presaged rebellion: the mention of Rehoboam's name was sufficient (I Kings XII.16–19, II Chronicles X.16). Similarly Milton in his ominous parallel between Charles II and 'Coniah and his seed' had no need to remind his readers of the circumstances in which Coniah was deprived of his throne and exiled.[108] The Duke of Newcastle had a point when he referred sourly to those who 'bring some example of a king with a hard name from the Old Testament. Thus one way you may have a civil war, the other a private treason'.[109] From Martin Marprelate to John Bunyan mention of Korah, Dathan and Abiram sufficed to recall the rebels against Moses and Aaron 'who presumed above [their] vocation', as the Geneva margin put it (Numbers XVI), and were swallowed up by the earth.[110] There was even less need for precision when reference was made to Pharaoh, Nebuchadnezzar, Belshazzar or Herod. The bishops who in 1587 were told to supply Biblical precedents for executing Mary Queen of Scots must have found their task easy.[111]

The royalist propagandist Bishop Griffith Williams was reduced in 1644 to citing Jeremiah XXVII.5–6 as 'a memorable place against resisting tyrants'. Here the prophet, speaking for the Lord of Hosts, told the people of Israel to 'put their necks under the yoke' of Nebuchadnezzar.[112] Matthias Prideaux asked 'whether the practice or prerogative of kings are set down in I Sam. 8?' That chapter contains Samuel's warning to the Israelites that if they choose a king he will be completely arbitrary, seizing their property and conscripting them to military and other service (cf. I Samuel VIII and XII). Although Prideaux had been a captain in the royalist army we may

---

107. *Thurloe State Papers* (1742), II. p. 46.
108. *MCPW*, VII, p. 388. Cf. Greenhill, *Ezekiel*, p. 41; cf. p. 54 above.
109. A. S. Turberville, *A History of Welbeck Abbey and its Owners* (1938–9), II, p. 60.
110. Marprelate, *An Epitome* (1588), sig. B 3; *BMW*, I, p. 270.
111. P. Collinson, *The English Captivity of Mary Queen of Scots* (Sheffield, 1987), p. 45.
112. Williams, *Jura Majestatis: The Rights of Kings Both in Church and State . . . and The Wickedness of this pretended Parliament*, p. 188.

suspect irony here.[113] If so, it was at the expense of King James, who quoted Samuel on behalf of kings.[114]

Amongst other useful examples we find Abimelech, killed by a woman ('Thus God by such miserable death taketh vengeance on tyrants even in this life' – Judges IX, Geneva margin; cf. II Samuel XI). James II was compared to Abimelech in 1689.[115] There was Omri, who walked in the idolatrous ways of Jeroboam, only more so (I Kings XVI); and his son Ahab, who 'did worse in the sight of the Lord than all that were before him' and married Jezebel, 'by whose means he fell to all wicked and strange idolatry and cruel persecution' (I Kings XVI, XXI – Geneva margin). Manasseh, King of Judah, restored idolatry and was slain by Pharaoh (II Kings XXI). Eliakim, son of Josiah, was made King by Pharaoh. He stood for James, Duke of York in Samuel Pordage's *Azariah and Hushai* (1682), a reply to Dryden's *Absalom and Achitophel*.

Greenhill added Ahaz to the list of kings whose names God makes to rot. 'God proceedeth against wicked kings to the third and fourth generation, for their idolatry and oppression'.[116] Other bad Biblical characters quoted in *Fast Sermons* include Haman, Joab son of Zeruiah and Absalom.[117] In January 1648, when the Commons were discussing the desirability of reopening discussions with King Charles, who had escaped from the Army's custody to the Isle of Wight, Sir Thomas Wroth observed that in the Bible only two places are named for frenetic persons – Bedlam for madmen and Tophet for kings. 'I desire any government rather than that of kings', he concluded.[118] Code had ceased to be necessary.[119]

113. Prideaux, op. cit., p. 19. Or the irony may be that of Prideaux's father. See p. 29 above. Cf. Prideaux, op. cit., p. 23: whether Joab might justify Absalom's killing, having a command from his sovereign (David) to the contrary?

114. See p. 66 above.

115. Matthew Meade, *The Vision of the Wheels seen by the Prophet Ezekiel*.

116. Greenhill, *First Five Chapters*, pp. 41–2.

117. *FS*, II, pp. 147–8, VII, p. 9, XXII, p. 39; V, p. 209; XIX, p. 151.

118. David Underdown, 'The Parliamentary Diary of John Boys, 1647–8', *Bulletin of the Institute of Historical Research*, XXXIX (November 1966), p. 155. For Tophet see p. 60n. above.

119. William Dowsing the image-breaker collected and carefully annotated 171 Fast Sermons – almost all preached (and printed) down to 1646 (J. Morrill, 'William Dowsing, the Bureaucratic Puritan', in *Public Duty and Private Conscience in Seventeenth-Century England: Essays in Honour of Gerald Aylmer*, (ed. J. Morrill, P. Slack and D. Woolf, Oxford U.P. 1992, pp. 181–2).

4. Metaphors and Programmes

Comfort ye, comfort ye, my people. .... Every valley shall be exalted, and every mountain and hill shall be made low; and the crooked shall be made straight, and the rough place plain.
Isaiah XL.1, 4.

And all the trees of the field shall know that I the Lord have brought down the high tree, and have exalted the low tree, have dried up the green tree, and have made the dry tree to flourish. I the Lord have spoken it and have done it.
Ezekiel XVII.24. This verse was used by John Owen as the text for his Fast Sermons of 24 October 1651, at a day of thanksgiving for Parliament's victory in the battle of Worcester (*The Advantage of the Kingdome of Christ in the Shaking of the Kingdomes of the World, FS, XXXIV*, pp. 13–50).

BABYLON MUST FALL WITH A GREAT NOISE.
Edward Burrough, *The Fourth General Epistle to all the Saints* (May 1660) in *The Memorable Works of a Son of Thunder and Consolation* (1672), pp. 665–6.

I

Because the Bible was deemed to be of contemporary relevance, certain assumptions were easily made. That the Pharisees in the New Testament corresponded to prelates of the Church of England came easily to radicals like Jeremiah Burroughs, Roger Williams, Walwyn and Milton. Some Biblical metaphors became very hackneyed: it is always worth suspecting an allusion when certain words are used. Even when writing under censorship, illicit meanings might be smuggled in. 'To liken Satan to the misty early morning or eclipsed sun', wrote Dr Keeble perceptively *à propos* Milton, 'is, overtly, no more than to imagine his impaired brightness; but since the sun was a traditional symbol of divine royalty, it may implicitly, as the licenser realized, associate evil with kings and Satan with Charles I.'[1]

1. N. H. Keeble, *The Literary Culture of Nonconformity in later Seventeenth-century England* (Leicester U.P., 1987), p. 119. The reference is to *PL*, I.594–9.

It had been pretty seditious in 1641 for an anonymous pamphleteer to hail Parliament as 'our bright English sun'.[2]

Certain Biblical metaphors seemed particularly appropriate to radical Puritans. Those who felt strongly that the Pope was Antichrist, and that the Laudians were moving in the direction of Rome, would find Egypt, Babylon, Sodom, natural code words to describe what they opposed. The Oxford preacher who in 1631 took as his text Numbers XIV.4, 'And they said to one another, Let us make us a captain and return to Egypt', was in fact attacking Laudian innovations. 'They pretended they were pulling down Babylon', said Samuel Bradley, chaplain of the *Gainsborough* in May 1654, speaking of the great Army officers, 'but behold they are setting it up'.[3] The advantage of such words lay in their imprecision. Everyone was against Egypt and Babylon in general; but what did the words signify in particular? Matthias Prideaux, in his sceptical *Essay and Compendious Introduction for Reading all sorts of Histories* (1648), thought that the Papacy had been occupied by 'Luxurious Sodomites' from AD 855 to 966, and by 'Incurable Babylonians' from 1503 to his own time.[4] In *The Whore of Babylon* (1603) Dekker had rather daringly anticipated Middleton's *A Game at Chess* of 1624 by putting on the stage the Kings of Spain and France, depicted as evil characters dependent on Rome.

In 1570 William Fulke preached *A Sermon* proving Babylon to be Rome. 'God first called his people out of Babylon by Luther's reformation', as Thomas Manton put it in 1658.[5] The author of *A Glimpse of Sions Glory* in 1641 was bellicose in denunciation of Babylon. But perhaps Babylon is Canterbury? 'Babylon's falling is Sion's raising', the author said. 'Babylon's destruction is Jerusalem's salvation. . . . It is the work of the day to cry down Babylon, that it may fall more and more; and it is the work of the day to give God no rest till he sets up Jerusalem as the praise of the whole world. Blessed is he that dasheth the brats of Babylon against the stones. Blessed is he that hath any hand in pulling Babylon down'.[6] Joseph Caryl, writing after civil war had started, was no less fierce. 'God hath made Babylonians the rod of his anger. . . . He hath given great commissions to

---

2. [Anon]., *Machiavel As He lately appeared to his deare Sons, the Moderne Projectors*, quoted by Gerald M. MacLean, *Time's Witness: Historical Representation in English poetry, 1603–1660* (Wisconsin U.P., 1990), p. 103.
3. Capp, *Cromwell's Navy*, p. 135.
4. Prideaux, op. cit., Section VIII.
5. Manton, *A Practical Commentary . . . On the Epistle of Jude*, sig. b 3.
6. Op. cit., in Woodhouse, *Puritanism and Liberty*, pp. 233–4.

Caldeans and Sabeans, who rob and spoil us'.[7] But are these continental papists, English papists, or royalists generally?

The first of all the Fast Sermons, preached by Cornelius Burges, was about 'the final subversion and ruin of Babylon and of that whole monarchy'.[8] Many other preachers referred to 'Babylonian government'. Francis Cheynell in May 1643 spoke of Elizabeth's 'Bishop Bancroft and the Babylonian faction', who suggested that 'this [Presbyterian] discipline of Sion would not only overthrow the Babylonish monarchy but the English monarchy also'.[9] 'Though we were not in Babylon', Thomas Case told the Commons a year later, 'yet Babylon was in the midst of us'.[10]

John Dury was famous for his efforts on behalf of protestant reunion. His Fast Sermon of 26 November 1645 must have been eagerly awaited, now that the war had been won. It was entitled *Israels Call to March out of Babylon into Jerusalem*, and he took as his text Isaiah LII.11: 'go out of the midst of her. . . . Be ye clean'. His assumption is that Babylon is in England. 'The main matter' of Dury's sermon was 'to know what the mystery of Babylon is'. 'You cannot possibly be reconciled unto Babylon, if you be faithful to your covenant'. (So the Solemn League and Covenant had been directed against Babylon?) 'If we make any stay in Babylon, we may be infected with her sins'. Even 'a slow departure' may be dangerous. We must resist 'the strong bent of our desires to remain in Babylon'. 'You should not take of Babylon any one stone for a corner, nor . . . for a foundation'. So what exactly is 'the mystery of Babylon'? 'The principle of the Babylonian government is that idol which politicians call the reason of state, or the interest of state' – safety, plenty and ease. 'All the states of this world are states of war'. Babylon seeks riches and strength, through violence. The methods 'which Babylon useth towards her subjects' are those 'which men use towards beasts: she rideth upon the beast'. 'With absolute power she doth bring her subjects into absolute obedience', to implicit faith. This is the way of all human government. Here we seem to be discussing something much wider than popery. But the alternative which Dury expects from 'the City of God' is less clear. He calls for better education to build up 'the spiritual Jerusalem', and for an end to 'the gibberish of the universities' and a settlement of courts of justice. This does

7. Caryl, *Exposition . . . Upon the first three chapters of the Book of Job*, sig. Av.
8. *FS*, I, p. 20.
9. Ibid., VI, p. 228.
10. Ibid., XVIII, p. 208.

not get us very far towards Jerusalem.[11] 'Under the notion of Babylon', snorted a royalist parson, are comprehended 'the King and his children, the nobility and gentry, the ministers of the Gospel of Jesus Christ, and Christians of all sorts'.[12]

In the Putney Debates of 1647 Oliver Cromwell took advantage of the ambiguities of the word Babylon when trying to restore unity in the Army. Sexby had said 'I think we have gone about to heal Babylon when she would not [be healed]' (Jeremiah LI.9), clearly referring to monarchy. Cromwell in reply rejected the implication that he and his fellow-generals 'would have gone about to heal Babylon'. But there is monarchy and monarchy: the word Babylon helped him to avoid precision.[13]

After the abolition of monarchy John Owen saw Babylon in international political terms. 'Antichristian tyranny draws to its period'. Do not bother about the interest of England, he told MPs, 'but look what suits the interest of Christ'. 'Babylon shall fall': that is his starting position. But again he is less specific about what exactly 'the interest of Christ' is.[14] In 1650 Isaac Penington depicted Babylon as a city much like London.[15] The more extreme radicals had a more precise emphasis. John Rogers linked 'the Babylonian and Norman Yokes', 'the Norman iron yoke of corrupt lawyers' and 'that Babylonian brazen yoke of tithes'.[16] William Erbery, who described himself as 'be-wildernessed', was also 'a man in Babylon', where 'there is no building of temples'.[17] Venner's manifesto of 1657, *A Standard Set Up*, promised that both saints as saints and men as men would benefit from 'the deliverance of the true church out of Babylon and all confusion'.[18] We still have to ask where and what was Babylon? There was a point behind Richard Blome's accusation in 1660: 'Babylon they would

11. Ibid., XX, pp. 11–12, 43–52, 60–61 and *passim*.

12. Edward Symmons, *Scripture Vindicated*, p. 53. Symmons referred to Marshall's Fast Sermon *Meroz Cursed* (see pp. 88–9 above).

13. Woodhouse, op. cit., p. 103.

14. Owen, *Works*, VIII, pp. 256–64, 278–9; *FS*, XXXII, pp. 328–39, 356–8.

15. Penington, *Babylon the Great Described: The City of Confusion. In every part whereof Antichrist Reigns*, *passim*.

16. Rogers, *Sagrir, or Dooms-day drawing nigh* (1654), title-page and sig. A 4; Rogers, Letter to Oliver Cromwell, in *Life and Opinions of a Fifth-Monarchy-Man* (ed. E. Rogers, 1867), p. 53.

17. *The Testimony of William Erbery*, pp. 11–12, 16–17, 237, 315.

18. My *The Experience of Defeat* (1984), p. 63. Cf. William Dewsbery: 'There is nothing but confusion in the kingdom of Babylon' (*The Discovery of Mystery Babylon*, 1665–?6, in *The Faithful Testimony of William Dewsbery*, p. 288).

overthrow; and within Babylon they included all magistracy and civil government, and all wealth and greatness. A great quarrel they had with the Babylonian gold'.[19]

The ambiguities of the words Antichrist, Babylon, Egypt, helped to preserve unity among supporters of Parliament in the early days of the civil war. But when it came to post-war settlement, the vulgar intruded with their own political and social ideas. The code words could no longer conceal wide disagreements. The near-Digger pamphlet *Light Shining in Buckinghamshire* (5 December 1648) forthrightly declared that 'kings are the only upholders of Babylon'. Rich men, lords, barons and priests, all 'cry for a king'. For 'the honest man that would have liberty' 'there is no way but to take down kingly power'; then the power of lords, lawyers, priests, monopolists and City corporations 'will down too'.[20]

Egypt similarly swings between being a religious and a political symbol. William Bridge, preaching to volunteer Parliamentarian soldiers at the beginning of the civil war, told them 'You are now again coming out of Egypt (for the Romish superstition and that party is called Egypt, Sodom, Babylon) . . . to the Promised Land'.[21] John Rogers in 1653 described Oliver Cromwell, rather prematurely, as a second Moses, 'that great deliverer of his people . . . out of the house of Egypt'.[22] In the same year a flag-captain recognized that victory over the Dutch showed how God 'will make a difference henceforth 'twixt Israel and Egyptians'.[23]

Egypt was an especially popular metaphor with radicals – Wither, William Sedgwick, Erbery, Feake, Winstanley. The Ranter Abiezer Coppe speaks of Egypt as 'the house of bondage' and Canaan as 'the land of liberty'.[24] Other Ranters – Jacob Bauthumley and Joseph Salmon – also equate England with Egypt, Salmon speaking of 'my late travels through Egypt-land'.[25] The Quaker Francis Howgil in 1655 told his readers to 'spare none; . . . bathe your sword in the blood of Amalek and all the

19. Blome, *The Fanatick History*, p. 19.
20. In Sabine, pp. 615–18.
21. *A Sermon Preached unto the Volunteers of the City of Norwich and also to the Volunteers of Great Yarmouth* (1642), quoted by Francis Bremer, '"To Live Exemplary Lives": Puritans and Puritan Communities', Millersville.
22. Rogers, *A Few Proposals Relating to Civil Government*, p. 5. Cf. p. 440 below.
23. Capp, *Cromwell's Navy*, pp. 130–31.
24. Ed. N. Smith, *A Collection of Ranter Writings* (1983), p. 42.
25. Ibid., p. 204.

Egyptians and Philistines'.[26] The more usual image was of the chosen people actually wishing to return to the slavery of Egypt. Burnet tells us of Cromwell speaking in 1648 of a few officers who seemed inclined to return to Egypt, and in 1656 of MPs who spoke against kingship for Oliver as going back to Egypt.[27] Robert South, in a post-restoration sermon, remarked ironically 'Israel was not to return to Egypt: Egypt was brought back to them by Jeroboam'. South thought Cromwell had been a lively copy of Jeroboam because he 'did authorize and encourage all the scum and refuse of the people to preach' (I Kings XIII.33–4).[28]

The usage was a favourite of Milton's. He had been sure in 1641 that God would not 'bring us thus far onward from Egypt to destroy us in this wilderness, though we deserve it'.[29] In the same year he spoke of the 'Egyptian tyranny' of bishops: 'no bishops, but Egyptian taskmasters'.[30] And in his *Defence of the People of England* (1651) he warned his countrymen lest, after becoming freed 'from the slavery of the kings of Egypt', they should hanker after their former captivity and 'be crushed under a heavier yoke'.[31] Booth's rising in 1659 he described as an attempt 'to call back again their Egyptian bondage'.[32] His derisive dismissal of agitation for a restoration of monarchy as 'choosing them a captain back for Egypt' was already a familiar phrase when he used it so effectively in April 1660. It had been anticipated, among others, by Wither in 1659:

> They now rebelliously a captain choose
> To lead them back to bondage, like the Jews.[33]

In *Of Christian Doctrine* Milton protested that if Sabbath observance were strictly enforced we should be 'brought out of one Egypt into another'.[34]

William Sedgwick in 1656 thought that 'we are escaped from an outward

26. In E. Burrough, *To the Camp of the Lord in England*, p. 17.

27. Burnet, *History of My Own Time* (ed. O. Airy, Oxford U.P., 1897), I, pp. 77, 123.

28. South, *Twelve Sermons Preached upon Several Occasions* (1692), pp. 158–9.

29. *MCPW*, I, p. 706.

30. Ibid., I, pp. 545, 793, 845; cf. *PL* XII. 348.

31. Ibid., IV, pp. 353, 532.

32. Ibid., VII, p. 325.

33. Ibid., VII, p. 463; Wither, *Epistolium-Vagum-Prosa-Metricum*, p. 24, in *Miscellaneous Works*, I (Spenser Soc., 1872). In *MER* I cite other examples from Thomas Taylor (1653, but posthumous, as Taylor died in 1633) and Moses Wall (1659) as well as from Ludlow again (1654).

34. *MCPW*, VI, p. 711.

Egypt', but that spiritually we were still in Sodom. Only the decimation tax reassured him that Cromwell was not looking back to Egypt, to alliance with Cavaliers.[35] In the deeper gloom of 1661 Sedgwick told Parliamentarians 'you have not led us out of Egypt into Canaan, but have been entangled and fettered in Egyptian darkness'.[36] Egypt thus became a code word for kings or institutions which one disliked: for Samuel Pordage in 1682 Egypt was France, and accordingly the Duchess of Portsmouth became 'the Egyptian concubine'.[37]

II

Isaac Newton believed that he had found a key to the Biblical prophecies in the writings of Joseph Mede. The heavens, the sun and moon, signify kings and rulers, the earth inferior people, hades or hell 'the lowest and most miserable of the people'. Newton worked out his own 'rules for interpreting the words and language in Scripture'. 'Frogs' for instance meant 'idolaters' (Revelation XVI.13; cf. Psalm CV.30).[38] Peter Sterry, preaching on Psalm XVIII, had drawn lessons for 1649: 'the earth often signifies the common people; the hills, the potentates of the earth'. 'The foundations, the greatness of the potentates, are moved and taken away by these shakings of the earth. . . . Those evil spirits which rule us as the gods of this world . . . clearly perceive the foundations of their kingdom to be shaken and almost overthrown'.[39] The giants of Genesis VI, Tyndale had thought, were 'mighty men and persecutors'.[40]

So they were for Bunyan over a century later. The waters of the Flood represent 'the great and mighty of the world', 'the flowing of them, their rage' – as transient as the waters of the Flood. Mountains are 'types of the high and mighty which God is used to stir up to deliver his church from the heat and rage of tyranny and persecution'. 'Persecution, . . . or the

35. Sedgwick, *Animadversions upon A Letter and Paper first sent to HH. by certain Gentlemen and others in Wales*, pp. 61, 64–6.
36. Sedgwick, *Animadversions Upon a Book Entitled Inquisition for the Blood of our late Soveraign*, p. 100; cf. p. 90.
37. Pordage, *Azariah and Hushai: A Poem*, p. 26.
38. H. McLachlan, *Sir Isaac Newton's Theological Manuscripts* (Liverpool, 1950), pp. 119–21; Newton, *Opera Quae Exstant Omnia* (ed. S. Horsley, 1775), V, pp. 306–10; F. Manuel, *The Religion of Isaac Newton*, pp. 96, 114–25.
39. *FS*, XXXII, p. 120, cf. p. 78 – Epistle Dedicatory.
40. Genesis VI.4. The Geneva Bible glossed 'giants' as 'tyrants'.

appearance of giants against the servants of God, is no new business'. Noah's ark signified 'a separation from the cursed children of Cain': the first gathered church. Bunyan concluded from this that we should not 'fear the faces of men, no not the faces of the mighty'. 'When the great ones of this world begin to discover themselves to the church by way of encouragement, it is a sign that the waters are now decreasing'. 'While we are in affliction' we should 'look this way and that, if it may be the tops of the mountains may be seen'. 'Men may be borne with, if they lie in their holes at the height of the tempest; but to do it when the tops of the mountains were seen, if then they shall forbear to open their windows, they are worthy of blame indeed'.[41] In the Preface to *Mr Badman* (1682) Bunyan declared that 'wickedness, like a flood, is like to drown our English world. . . . Could I but see the tops of the mountains above it, I should think that these waters were abating'.[42]

The metaphor was used by the Archdeacon of Coventry in 1661. 'All we lie in a low flat (as it were) but the gentry are the rising ground in a kingdom, and as it was in Noah's flood, so was it also in our late deluge, the very first sign of the abatement of those waters was when the tops of the mountains were seen, I mean when the gentry began to lift up their heads again'.[43] The raven which was sent out from the ark, Bunyan supposed, 'certainly . . . made a banquet of the carcases that were drowned by the flood'. The raven was a type of 'the worldly professor . . . who gets into the church in the time of her affliction', so that 'if time should serve, he might be made the Lord of his master's inheritance'. The dove is the type of 'another sort of professors in the church, that are of a more gentle nature; for all the saints are not . . . for feeding upon . . . the kingdoms of the Antichristian party'. But *both* are in the church.[44] Bunyan was no doubt thinking of the land-grabbers who had profited by the Reformation: he may have been thinking of James II who in 1688 was trying to cobble together an alliance between dissenters and catholics against the Church of England. Or he may have foreseen that the English aristocracy would be forced into

41. Offor, II, pp. 460–61, 467–8, 476–8.

42. Bunyan, *The Life and Death of Mr Badman* (ed. J. F. Forrest and R. Sharrock, Oxford U.P., 1988), p. 7.

43. John Riland, *Elias the Second, His Coming to Restore all Things* (Oxford, 1662), quoted by Ann Hughes, *Politics, Society and Civil War in Warwickshire, 1620–1660* (Cambridge U.P., 1987), p. 343.

44. Offor, II, pp. 278–9.

alliance with dissenters in order to defeat James's schemes for recatholiciza-
tion. Christ 'hath flesh to give them [the ravens], which the doves care
not for eating'.[45]

The Biblical symbolism of mountains and valleys, of great trees and little
shrubs, had long been familiar. I give a few random examples. The Geneva
marginal note on Jeremiah LI.25 explains that Babylon was called a
mountain 'because it was strong and seemed invincible'. William Reyner
on 28 August 1644 told the House of Commons that God warns us by
'Babylon's Ruining-Earthquake' to look for 'the restoration of Zion'.[46]
Zechariah IV.7 was a favourite text for preachers of Fast Sermons: 'Who
art thou, O great mountain? Before Zerubbabel thou shalt become a plain'.
Thomas Goodwin, preaching before the House of Commons on 27 April
1642 commented on this text: 'a mountain is a similitude frequent in
Scripture, to note out high and potent opposition lying in the way of
God's proceedings. (Every mountain shall be brought low, Luke II.5'.)
'There is no mention of opposition so great, that can stand before
Zerubbabel (or God's people)'. Thomas Wilson, five months later,
paraphrased Habbakuk III.6 (another favourite text) as 'Scatter the ever-
lasting mountains of firm settled Canaanites, make the perpetual hills
bow'.[47]

So a great deal could be said very economically by practised use of the
Bible. Marvell in *The First Anniversary of the Government under O. C.*
discreetly advised the Protector not to accept the crown by referring to the
parable in Judges IX: the trees offered the olive the chance of ruling over
them. He refused, saying 'should I leave my fatness, wherewith by me they
honour God and man, and go to advance me above the trees?'. The fig tree
and the vine in their turn refused the offer: only the bramble was prepared
to accept. Oliver, Marvell explained, had levelled 'every cedar's top' and
overawed 'ambitious shrubs' like the bramble.[48] What could be more
succinct than William Sedgwick's summing-up of the Parliamentarian
cause in 1660? 'We drove Pharaoh and the Egyptians out of Egypt, and
kept Egypt for ourselves'.[49] Sedgwick was busily accommodating himself
to the restoration by repudiating his former views and comrades. He used
Biblical arguments to demonstrate the necessity of a hierarchical society. In

45. Ibid., p. 479. For the sun as a metaphor for monarchy see p. 378 below.
46. *FS*, XII, p. 169 (title-page).
47. Ibid., II, pp. 392 and 406 (Goodwin); IV, p. 97 (Wilson). Cf. ibid., XVI, p. 220
(William Goode) and 303 (John Ward).
48. Marvell, op. cit., lines 257–64.
49. Sedgwick, *Animadversions Upon a Book*, p. 90.

the old world before the Flood, men might talk of levelling and common freedom. But now such ideas are 'ignorant, absurd and unrighteous'. The strictest reformed saints were no less guilty of Cain's sin than the bishops had been. 'The most ignorant and weak were Abel'. Society now was based on a three-fold division – Shem (the nobility), Japhet (freemen or gentlemen) and Ham (which, Sedgwick wrongly asserted, 'signifies black') – servants and peasants. 'This chain of reasoning leads us directly to his Majesty's late restoration'.[50]

William Greenhill in April 1643 preached to the Commons on Matthew III.10: 'Now also the axe is laid to the root of the tree'. 'An axe cuts, and cuts through; and God's judgments cut through the greatest and throws them down (Ezekiel XIV.21)'. Nebuchadnezzar, Herod, Pharaoh and Belshazzar were all cut off by the root. 'Great and small should now feel the strokes of God's hand'. God 'will deal severely with kingdoms and with particular persons'. Jeremiah V.1 reminded Greenhill that 'neither king, councillors, priests or prophets did execute judgment in England' against the Book of Sports; 'therefore he would not pardon'. 'Look at kings, they are tall cedars. Hew down the tree. (Dan. IV.14)'. 'God's axe neither fears nor spares the proudest'. 'All kingdoms have their periods', Greenhill concludes, 'few more than 500–600 years'. You all know 'how long we have been since the Conquest'. He did not want to prophesy, but observed that 'we are upon the tropic', 'if we be not ruined altogether there will be some great alteration in the kingdom.' 'The whole creation groans to be delivered from the bondage of corruption, and we groan to be delivered'. This, he suggested, offered a great opportunity to Parliament.[51] Calamy quoted Psalm XXIX: 'the voice of the Lord breaketh the cedars', continuing 'the higher the tree is, the more it is exposed to the thunder of heaven. So the greater any man is, the sooner God will punish him if he be a giant in iniquity. . . . If thou beest as a mountain in greatness, and thy sins as mountains in greatness, God will make thee smoke' (Psalm CIV.32).[52]

George Cockayne, preaching to the House of Commons at the end of November 1648, just before Pride's Purge set the stage for the trial and execution of the King, cited Psalm LXXXII.7: 'and fall like one of the princes', which he glossed as 'coming down from their great height': God puts down the mighty from their seats.[53] The Quaker W. T[omlinson] in

50. Sedgwick, *Inquisition for the Blood of our late Soveraign*, pp. 23–7, 58–63.
51. *FS*, VI, pp. 102–3, 120, 122–4, 147.
52. Ibid., p. 293.
53. *FS*, XXXII, pp. 21–7.

1657 asked 'the high and lofty in the earth . . . what do you think are those mountains and hills that are to be cast down, and those valleys that are to be borne up'?[54]

In 1648 a royalist pamphlet called *The Faerie Leveller* reprinted verses from Spenser's *The Faerie Queene*, in which a communist giant spoke:

> Therefore I will throw down those mountains high,
> And make them level with the lowly plain;
> These towering rocks, which reach unto the sky,
> I will thrust down into the deepest main,
> And as they were, them equalize again.

Artegall corrected him:

> The hills do not the lowly dales disdain,
> The dales do not the lofty hills envy,

for all are at God's disposal. This was reprinted as an anti-Leveller tract.[55]

The backward look in the Giant's last line is very Leveller. The Geneva marginal note to Isaiah II.14 explained that 'by high trees and mountains are meant them that are proud and lofty, and think themselves most strong in this world'. Verse 13 referred to 'cedars of Lebanon, oaks of Bashan'; the marginal note to 'cedars and oaks' in Zechariah XI.2 identifies them as 'strong men destroyed'. Greenhill referred to Pharaoh as 'a high tree, the highest in all Egypt'.[56] James Parnell prophesied that 'the high oaks and the tall cedars that oppress the little scrubs' would soon be brought low.[57]

The Geneva margin to Revelation XII.15 says 'it is an usual thing in Scripture, that the raging tumults of the nations should be compared unto waters'. John Owen confirmed that Scriptural waters 'are sometimes afflictions, sometimes people and nations. Be they seas (kings and princes) or be they rivers (inferior persons) they shall not be able to oppose'. That was in a sermon of October 1648 celebrating the fall of Colchester, which opened the way to the trial of Charles I.[58] In a sermon of April 1649, which is an

54. W. T., *Seven Particulars* (1657), pp. 20–22.
55. J. N. King, 'The Faerie Leveller: A 1648 Royalist Reading of *The Faerie Queene*, II.29–54', *Huntington Library Quarterly*, 48 (1985), pp. 297–308.
56. Greenhill, *Ezekiel*, Chapters 14–19 (1651), p. 445. Calvin in his *Commentary* on Isaiah XIV.13 remarks that cedars are the highest of trees, p. 31.
57. Parnell, *A Collection of Several Writings* (1675), pp. 33–5. Parnell died in prison in 1656.
58. Owen, *Works*, VIII, p. 110.

excellent summary of the Independent millenarian position, Owen explained that heaven and earth in Revelation XII–XV meant governments and peoples. 'The destruction of persecuting emperors and captains, with the transition of power and sovereignty from one sort to another, is here held out'. A new heaven and earth but no more sea (Revelation XXI.1) signified no more clergy. 'The whole present constitution of the governments of the nations is so cemented with antichristian mortar' that it must be thoroughly shaken to be cleaned.[59]

The height of the Amorite, Amos tells us, 'was like the height of the cedars, and he was strong as the oaks' (II.9).[60] The metaphor was frequently used. In January 1653–4 Stephen Marshall, preaching to both Houses of Parliament, the City of London and the Assembly of Divines, compared a bad king like Jeroboam to a great cedar, which when it falls breaks 'all the woods that are round about them'.[61] John Owen on 24 October 1651 preached on Ezekiel XVII.24: 'I the Lord have brought down the high tree and have exalted the low tree . . . . There are great and mighty works in hand in this nation, tyrants are punished, the jaws of oppressors are broke, bloody, revengeful persecutors disappointed and, we hope, governors set up that may be just'. 'He that thinks Babylon is confined to Rome and its open idolatry, knows nothing of Babylon nor of the new Jerusalem'. In England 'tall trees, green trees . . . this and that great lord, popular with the multitude' have failed us: 'low trees, dry trees, despised ones' did a better job. God has appeared against every party that aimed at 'the re-inforcement of things as in former days'.[62]

The anonymous *A Warning or Word of Advice to the City of London* (30 November 1648) announced that God 'is the great Leveller, and you [the City Fathers] are a mountain which resists him and which he will level'.[63] 'God is in these Levellers', William Sedgwick observed in 1648, 'casting the mountains into the depths of the sea.'[64] The Digger poet Robert Coster proclaimed in December 1649 that the gentry and clergy will

59. *FS*, XXXII, pp. 325–7, 333, 337, 351–2.
60. Sebastian Benefield, *A Commentary or Exposition upon the second Chapter of the Prophecie of Amos* (1620), p. 122.
61. *FS*, IX, p. 260; cf. ibid., XXXII, pp. 44–5 (Cockayne, 29 November 1648).
62. *FS*, XXXIV, pp. 21–2, 36.
63. Quoted by Elizabeth Tuttle, *Religion et Idéologie dans la Révolution Anglaise, 1647–1649* (Paris, 1989), p. 193. The reference is presumably to Jeremiah LI.25–6.
64. Sedgwick, *The Leaves of the Tree of Life for the breaking of the Nations*, pp. 101–2.

lie level with all.
They have corrupted our fountains;
And then we shall see
Brave community
When valleys lie level with mountains.

Coster too associated tyranny with the power of the gentry.[65] The prophetess Elizabeth Poole, at about the same time, announced God's intention to
'bring down the mountains and exalt the valleys; . . . all the high places of
the earth shall be brought down, not one left'.[66]

Gerrard Winstanley, in his last pamphlet, wrote 'a monarchical army
lifts up mountains and makes valleys, viz. advances tyrants and treads the
oppressed in the barren lanes of poverty. But a Commonwealth's army is
like John Baptist, who levels the mountains to the valleys, pulls down the
tyrant and lifts up the oppressed'.[67] Three years earlier Coppe had announced that God was 'coming (yea, even at the doors) . . . to level the
hills with the valleys'. 'High mountains! lofty cedars! it's high time for you
to enter into the rocks and to hide you in the dust'. 'Every one that is lifted
up . . . shall be brought low' – the cedars of Lebanon, the oaks of Bashan,
and all high mountains, hills, towers and fenced walls. The Lord will also
level 'your honour, riches etc.'[68] Calling on oaks and cedars to bow down
was a favourite metaphor with the early Quakers.[69]

For Bunyan heights included giants 'tall as the cedars and strong as
the oaks', 'the very dads and fathers of the monstrous brood of persecutors'; they could be mountains or 'walls as high as heaven . . . of purpose
to keep Israel out of his possession'.[70] Persecutors were likened to whales,
or lions in the wilderness.[71] 'The grace of God is compared to water',
Bunyan explained in the *The Water of Life* (1688). It 'naturally descends
to and abides in low places, in valleys and places which are undermost'.
It does not flow over 'steeples and hills', and so passes by the established
church and is in 'low esteem with the rich and the full;' 'it is . . . for the

65. In Sabine, pp. 659–60.
66. Poole, *An Alarum of War* (1649), p. 17. I owe this reference to the kindness of Dr
Valerie Taylor (formerly Valerie Drake).
67. Sabine, pp. 575–6.
68. Coppe, *A Fiery Flying Roll* (1649), in Smith, *Ranter Writings*, pp. 87–8, 90–92; cf.
Isaiah X.
69. E.g. Edward Billing, *An Alarm to All Flesh* (1660), p. 1; ed. H. Barbour and A. O.
Roberts, *Early Quaker Writings* (Grand Rapids, 1973), p. 81.
70. *BMW*, II, p. 8; cf. Offor, II, p. 460.
71. Offor, II, p. 422; Bunyan, *Grace Abounding*, p. 1; cf. p. 3 – Goliath.

poor and needy'. 'They that can drink wine in bowls . . . come not to this river to drink'.[72] In the millennium 'there shall be a smooth face upon the whole earth, all snugs and hubs and hills and dales shall now be took away.'[73] Sometimes Bunyan indulged in free association. Genesis VIII.1, 'and God made a wind to pass over the earth', reminded him of Isaiah XI.4, 'with the breath of his lips shall he slay the wicked'; 'it was a wind also that blew away the locusts of Egypt, Ex. X.19, which locusts were a type of our graceless clergy, that have covered the ground of our land'.[74]

Biblical winds were symbolic, especially the cold wind from the North (Job XXXVII.9), the whirlwind out of the North which stood for Nebuchadnezzar (Ezekiel I.4; Greenhill, *Ezekiel*, p. 67). At the end of time the King of the North shall come like a whirlwind (Daniel XI – a king whom the Geneva Bible identifies with Rome).[75] But earlier out of the North 'an evil shall break forth upon all the inhabitants of the land [of Israel], . . . and a great destruction' (Jeremiah I.14, IV.6, VI.1, 22–5, X.22, XLVI.20, XLVII.2; cf. Isaiah XIV.131). Babylon was in the north. Ultimately armies from still further North will conquer Babylon and deliver the captive Israelites (Jeremiah L.3, 9, 41–6: the Geneva Bible identifies these with the Medes and Persians).

There are Babylons in the dark corners of the land, Francis Cheynell told the Commons on 31 May 1643 – in the North, in the West, and even nearer home. 'Come forth and flee from the land of the north, saith the Lord' (meaning Babylon – Zechariah II.6).[76] John Ward, preaching to the Lords on 22 July 1645, also located evil in the land of the North, though now evil equals specifically popery.[77] In April 1648 the anonymous *Englands Alarm from the North* was a Baptist warning against collaboration with royalists and Scots.[78] On Guy Fawkes Day 1651 Peter

72. Offor, III, pp. 541–5.

73. *BMW*, III, p. 118. Cf. *The House of Lebanon*: faithful men will 'bear up the truth above water all the time of Antichrist's reign and rage' (Offor, II, p. 518).

74. Offor, II, p. 475. Cf. H. Schulz, *Milton and Forbidden Knowledge* (New York, 1955), pp. 186–7.

75. John Cotton quaintly takes the North wind in the Song of Songs, which was to 'blow on my garden, that the spices thereof may flow out' (IV.16), for Constantine, born in York, who would take the empire and drive away persecution (*A Brief Exposition Of the whole Book of Canticles*, 1642, p. 135). A more normal usage was the 'tyrannous' North wind in Shakespeare's *Cymbeline*, which 'shakes all our buds from growing' (I.iii.37–8).

76. *FS*, VI, pp. 202, 208.

77. Ibid., XVII, pp. 341–2.

78. Tuttle, op. cit., pp. 119–20.

Sterry, preaching from Jeremiah XVI.14–15, thought that England, the most northerly Christian nation, might be the country from which the Lord Jesus would return to lead his people.[79] But his title was *Englands Deliverance from the Northern Presbytery*. Barbarians came from the North in *Paradise Lost*.[80]

Greenhill seems to have conflated passages from Ezekiel with others from Jeremiah: 'Behold, a people cometh from the north country. . . . They are cruel and have no mercy. . . . The sword of the enemy and fear is on every side'. He must surely have been thinking of our brethren the Scots when he commented: 'God . . . can make use of a lusty, bitter and merciless nation, and that suddenly, to awaken a secure people, to correct his own servants, and to plague his enemies'. (The 'secure people' would be the English, 'his own servants' the Parliamentarians, and 'his enemies' the Cavaliers.)[81] In 1589 the anonymous *Martins Months Mind*, an anti-Marprelate tract, had said *'ab aquilone omne malum'* – presumably to associate Marprelate with the Presbyterian Scots.[82]

This symbolism was easily applied to the events of the 1640s and 1650s – to the Scottish invasions of 1639, 1644, 1648 and 1651, or to Monck's march to restore Charles II in 1660 – according to taste. When the preacher of a funeral sermon for Daniel Featley in 1645 referred to 'the storms of adversity caused by the north wind of affliction' this may have referred to the Scottish presence in the North of England.[83] Vane in 1655 referred to the King of Babylon in Ezekiel as King of the North, 'head of those heathenish nations'.[84] Herrick was certainly making a political allusion in 'Farewell Frost, or welcome the Spring' when he wrote

> As if here
> Never had been the *Northern Plunderer*
> To strip the trees and fields, to their distress,
> Leaving them to a pitied nakedness.[85]

Charles Cotton made a similar point in his 'Winter'.

79. *FS*, XXXIV, pp. 59–60.
80. *PL*, I. 351–5.
81. Greenhill, *Five First Chapters*, p. 73. Cf. Daniel XI.13, 43; Joel II.20.
82. Quoted by W. C. Hazlitt, *Faiths and Folklore of the British Isles: A Descriptive and Historical Dictionary* (1905), I, p. 286.
83. W. Leo, *A Sermon Preached . . . at the Funerall of . . . Daniel Featley*, p. 4. His reference was to Daniel VII.2.
84. Vane, *The Retired Mans Meditations*, p. 372.
85. Herrick, *Poetical Works* (ed. L. C. Martin, Oxford U.P., 1956), p. 224.

All the roarers of the North
Can neither storm nor starve us forth.

Let Winter Scotland take, and there
Confine the plotting Presbyter.[86]

Milton's reference to 'the false North' in his sonnet XIV to Fairfax could apply to the Scottish invasion of 1648, or to the Scots generally. The rebel angels in *Paradise Lost* were compared to

A multitude like which the populous North
Poured never from her frozen loins (I. 351–5).

Satan raised his standard in the North, as Charles I had done in 1642, as Diabolus was to do in Bunyan's *The Holy War*. Satan came out of the North for the final temptation in *Paradise Regained* (IV.448–9), as Bunyan's Doubters came from the land 'furthest remote to the North'.[87]

The North was not only the source of military invasion. It could also threaten social revolution. Isaiah XLI.25 tells us that the Lord has 'raised up one from the North, and he shall come . . . upon princes as upon clay, and as the potter treadeth mire under the foot'. In 1652 George Fox's eye was directed northward, and within a couple of years 'the Northern Quakers' were notorious all over southern England, 'the whirlwind from the North'.[88] 'O thou North of England', Edward Burrough apostrophized, 'who art counted as desolate and barren'.[89] When Samuel Highland in 1656 said 'those that come out of the North are the greatest pests of the nation' he was thinking of the Lancastrian Gerrard Winstanley as well as of the Quakers.[90] It was difficult to decide whether they were worse than the Scots – just different.

Another Biblical metaphor frequently used is that of the yoke. The yoke could be that of foreign enemies (Deuteronomy XXVIII.48: 'he shall put a yoke of iron upon thy neck until he have destroyed thee'; Jeremiah XXVIII.14: 'I have put a yoke of iron upon the necks of all these nations,

86. *Poems of Charles Cotton, 1630–1687* (ed. J. Beresford, 1923), pp. 65–8; cf. Earl Miner, *The Cavalier Mode from Jonson to Cotton* (Princeton U.P., 1971), p. 186; Robert Wild, *Iter Boreale* (1660).
87. Bunyan, *The Holy War*, pp. 189, 227.
88. Fox, *Journal* (8th ed., 1902), I, p. xlv; Erbery, *Testimony*, pp. 126, 135–7, 180; [Anon.], *A Brief Narrative of the Irreligion of the Northern Quakers* (1653); E. Pagitt, *Heresiography* (5th ed., 1654), p. 136; G. Fox, *Newes Coming up out of the North* (1654), title-page.
89. Burrough, *The Camp of the Lord in England* (1655), p. 6.
90. *Diary of Thomas Burton*, I, p. 155.

that they may serve Nebuchadnezzar, King of Babylon'. Cf. Isaiah X.27). This sense could be put to immediate political use. 'The Norman Yoke' was a traditional phrase, which could be used against monarchy or aristocracy;[91] Milton's 'Philistian Yoke' in *Samson Agonistes* deliberately echoed it. Henry Stubbe in 1659 compared the Norman Yoke with the bondage of the children of Israel in Egypt.[92] But the yoke could also be that of an individual tyrant – Rehoboam's, for instance (I Kings XII.4). Cf. Isaiah IX.4: 'thou hast broken the yoke of his burden'; Isaiah X.27: 'His burden shall be taken away from off thy shoulder, and his yoke from off thy neck'. Lamentations I.14 spoke of 'the yoke of my transgressions'. In the New Testament the metaphor is reversed. 'Take my yoke upon you ("all ye that labour and are heavy laden"); for my yoke is easy, and my burden light' (Matthew XI.28–30). 'Stand fast in the liberty wherewith Christ hath made us free, and be not entangled with the yoke of bondage' (Galatians V.1; cf. II Corinthians VI.14; but see also Acts XV.10: 'Why tempt ye God, to put a yoke upon the neck of the disciples?').

A Biblical metaphor is a programme in shorthand. Egypt is a place to escape from, never to return. Babylon is more than a place: it is an all-pervasive evil influence, corrupting rulers and prelates. Giants are tyrants and persecutors. Tall trees are for hewing down. As we shall see in Chapter 8 radicals thought that Abel's blood still cried out for political action – now. This was a new and highly contentious interpretation of the story of Cain and Abel, which for Winstanley became an emblem of all exploitation. But in principle, Biblical metaphor, provided we interpret it correctly, both states a problem and provides a programme for solving it. New England antinomians had begun to call William III 'the King of Babylon' in the early eighteenth century.[93]

The metaphor of the wilderness and the garden, to which we now turn, suggests solutions for a variety of problems.

---

91. See my 'The Norman Yoke', in *Society and Puritanism* (1964).
92. Stubbe, *An Essay in Defence of the Good Old Cause*, sig ˣ7*v*. Cf. pp. 40–41, 112 above.
93. M. Rediker and P. Linebaugh, 'The Many-Headed Hydra: Sailors, Slaves and the Atlantic Working Class in the Eighteenth Century', in *People and Power: Rights, Citizenship and Violence* (ed. Loretta V. Mannucci, Milan, 1990), p. 194.

5. The Wilderness, the Garden and the Hedge

═══

The land is as the Garden of Eden before him, and behind him a desolate wilderness.
Joel II.3.

When God redeems his people out of Babylon, he brings them not merely unto Sion ... but into the wilderness where the church lies unbuilt. ... There is a long travel from Babylon to Sion.
Isaac Penington, *Some Considerations Concerning the State of Things*, in *Works* (3rd ed., 1784), I, pp. 453–7.

True religion and undefiled is to let everyone quietly have earth to manure, that they may live in freedom by their labours.
Gerrard Winstanley, *An Humble Request to the Ministers of both Universities and to all Lawyers in every Inns-a-Court* (1650), Sabine, p. 428.

We are all wilderness brats by nature.
John Collinges, *The Spouses Hidden Glory* (1646), pp. 24–5, referring to Ephesians II.3. (Sermons on The Song of Songs.)

I

'The desolate land shall be tilled', said the prophet, 'whereas it lay waste in the sight of all that passed by'. The Lord 'will multiply the fruit of the trees, and the increase of the field, that ye shall bear no more the reproach of famine among the heathen' (Ezekiel XXXVI.34, 30). 'For they said, the people is hungry and weary, and thirsty in the wilderness' (II Samuel XVII.29). In the poetic juxtaposition of the wilderness and the garden, metaphor becomes argument. Nathanael Homes defined a garden as 'a place taken and separated from the field and guarded with a fence'.[1] For

1. Homes, *Commentary . . . on . . . Canticles*, in *Works* (1652), p. 309.

him, as for Paul Hobson, for John Bunyan, and for many others, the church (in the sense of congregation) was a garden, rescued from the waste land, the wilderness; the saints had separated themselves from the world by the hedge of discipline. The vineyard, the garden, had to be cultivated by labour. 'The barren fig-tree in the vineyard', 'the fruitless professor', was 'prepared for the fire'.[2] In the Bible gardens are everywhere, from Eden to Gethsemane. Christ's passion took place in a garden, Lewis Bayly explained, 'because that in a garden thy [i.e. man's] sin took first beginning'.[3]

'God Almighty first planted a garden', said Bacon. 'It is the greatest refreshment of the spirits of man'.[4] Biblical history began in the Garden of Eden. God only 'planted' it, a word which Bacon chose with some delicacy. To be cultivated it needed labourers, whom God presumably had in mind when he first planted the garden. Gardening was the pleasant work of Adam and Eve before they were turned out into 'the world's wilderness', where 'long-wandered man' remained, trying to recapture 'that happy garden-state'.[5] The Old Testament wilderness stretches from Egypt to the Promised Land, from Babylon to Jerusalem. There was no resting place short of the Promised Land; but *en route* the wilderness, with all its dangers and privations, is preferable to the slavery of Egypt or Babylon. The classic works on the subject of this chapter are G. H. Williams's *Wilderness and Paradise in Christian Thought* (New York, 1962), and Perry Miller's *Errand into the Wilderness* (Harvard U.P., 1956). It is difficult for us to envisage the extent of wilderness in England in the seventeenth century, before fens and marshes had been drained, before forests had been cut down, before the accelerated enclosures of the eighteenth century. From Robin Hood to Dick Turpin outlaws and highwaymen were relatively secure in this wilderness.[6]

Gardens and vineyards are hewn out of the wilderness, fenced off, irrigated and cultivated. The Lord's protection, Isaiah promised, would 'satisfy thy soul in drought, . . . and thou shalt be like a watered garden' (LVIII.11). But there is no cultivation without a fence, without water, any more than there is without labour. This had its immediate analogy for

2. *BMW*, V, p. 9.
3. Bayly, *The Practice of Piety* (55th ed., 1723), p. 451.
4. Bacon, Essay XLVI, 'Of Gardens'.
5. *PL*, XII.314–15; Marvell, 'The Garden'.
6. See Appendix A below.

English Bible readers in the sixteenth and seventeenth centuries: the equivalent of walling off the vineyard was enclosing land from the waste, in order to bring it under cultivation. Enclosure is the first step to agricultural improvement, labour the next. We start from 'an untilled place, . . . not yet manured'.[7]

Historically agriculture had at first no doubt been communal, collective. Private gardens are associated in the Song of Songs, as in the mediaeval literature of courtly love and in Spenser's Bower of Bliss, with sheltered and opulent luxury. Monasteries had gardens. But by the sixteenth and seventeenth centuries enclosure from the waste was being undertaken by individuals, marking off an area for cultivation for the market, or for privacy. The garden was associated with private property, with the family home, with individualism. Those excluded disliked enclosure. Formal gardens, made possible by the Tudor peace, were something new in sixteenth- and seventeenth-century England, as Bacon's Essay on Gardens shows. William Harrison believed that the art of gardening had been reinvented in Tudor England.[8] From the mid-seventeenth century market-gardening spread from London through the Home Counties and beyond. Sir Keith Thomas speaks of a 'gardening revolution' in the sixteenth and seventeenth centuries – both in market-gardening and nursery-gardening. Sir William Temple added that gardening had been 'mightily improved' in Charles II's reign.[9]

'The Lord . . . shall make her desert like Eden and the wilderness like the garden of the Lord' (Isaiah LI.3). Puttenham compared the poet to a gardener who improves on nature.[10] In the seventeenth century formal gardens had a space called 'the wilderness', a labyrinth of hedges designed as a maze.[11] But the process could be reversed. The wild growth of the wilderness continually presses in on the fragile gardens and vineyards, ready to take over, just as the jungle today presses on the outskirts of Singapore.

7. Collinges, *The Spouses Hidden Glory*, p. 23.

8. Harrison, *Elizabethan England* (ed. F. J. Furnivall, 1876), pp. 24–33.

9. Thomas, *Man and the Natural World: Changing Attitudes in England, 1500–1800* (1983), pp. 224–6; J. Thirsk, *Agricultural change: policy and practice* (Cambridge U.P., 1990), pp. 1, 9–10, 239, 300; Temple, *Selected Essays* (ed. J. A. Nicklin, Red Letter Library, n.d.), pp. 42, 45, 27–9.

10. George Puttenham, *The Art of English Poesie* (1589). For gardens see Thirsk, *Agricultural change*, chapter IA and *passim*; and *English rural society, 1500–1800: Essays in honour of Joan Thirsk* (ed. J. Chartres and D. Hey, Cambridge U.P., 1990), esp. pp. 12, 32–8, 49, 290–94.

11. G. H. Williams, *Wilderness and Paradise in Christian Thought*, p. 74n.

Maren-Sofie Røstvig's *The Happy Man* suggests that emphasis on rural retreat in England dates from the political crisis of the 1620s and 1630s. Gardens were no longer the perquisite of princes, but were becoming an essential feature of any gentleman's mansion. Oliver Cromwell 'lived reserved and austere' in his private garden, cultivating his flowers before his country's need called him forth to action; and Marvell also wrote of the garden of Cromwell's commanding officer, Fairfax, at Nunappleton. The garden – *hortus inclusus* – was shut off from the waste and from natural man – the sweaty vulgar – outside. Marvell's Mower is 'against gardens'. He threatens the garden as Death the Mower and Leveller threatens the ivory tower.

So the hedge is an ambiguous symbol. In the Old Testament it signifies property. Satan sneers that God had 'made a hedge about Job' and all his property. Take it away, he suggested, and see how he behaves (Job I.10; cf. III.10). In fact Job was soon wailing. Why, the psalmist asked, had God broken down the hedges of the vineyard which he had planted after bringing Israel out of Egypt, 'so that all they which pass by the way have plucked her? The wild boar out of the wood hath destroyed it, and the wild beasts of the field have eaten it up' (Psalm LXXX.8–16; cf. Isaiah V.1–8). John Brinsley in James I's reign lamented the 'unfruitfulness' of the Lord's vineyard in England, which brought forth only wild grapes. The wall had been taken away, and 'wild boars' rooted up the vineyard.[12]

Psalm LXXX was one of those translated by Milton as well as by George Sandys:

> Oh why hast thou her fences raz'd?
> Whilst every straggler pulls her fruit . . .
> And savage boors plough up her root.[13]

William Barton in 1644 asked, less elegantly,

> Why hast thou then broke down of hers
> The quick-set hedges so?

The vineyard is 'all wasted by the woodland boar'. His marginal note speaks of 'the poor people whom thou didst fence and favour'.[14] George

---

12. Brinsley, *The Third Part of the True Watch* (1622 ed.), p. 576.
13. Sandys, *A Paraphrase upon the Psalms of David* (1636), with poems to Charles I and Henrietta Maria. The courtly Sandys no doubt intended the pun on 'boars/boors'.
14. W.B., *The Book of Psalms in Meter*. For Barton see pp. 352–3, 359–60 below.

Gillespie, defending Scottish presbytery in a Fast Sermon preached on 27 March 1644, spoke of the dangers of breaking down 'the hedges of the Lord's vineyard', also quoting Psalm LXXX.[15] A church without proper discipline, said Robert Cawdrey in 1600, is like an orchard without a fence, or a city without government.[16]

Paul Baynes, commenting on Ephesians II.15, perceptively pointed out that ceremonies were like a wall or hedge, as divisive between Catholics and protestants as circumcision, sacrifices and pork had been between Jews and Gentiles. 'If of God', ceremonies 'serve both to be bonds of unity, and walls of separation from those without; if of men, they do bind together such as receive them, and are a wall betwixt such and others who cannot yield to entertain them'. 'The form of God's worship . . . is as a wall about us, both guarding us lest we go out, and keeping others from having access to us'.[17] Thomas Hooker neatly summed up the analogies between religion and economics, and the distinction between congregations and a national church: congregations in the latter were 'like to open pastures that are common for every man's cattle'.[18]

Radicals opposed hedging out – in fields or in church. They preferred the idealized village community, with its open fields and common lands; and they disliked the Presbyterian discipline which excluded some parishioners from the communal sacrament. A hostile witness, claiming nearly sixty years after the event to have been an eye-witness of Kett's rebellion in Norfolk in 1549, attributed the following sentiments to the rebels: 'Shall they, as they have brought hedges about common pastures, enclose with their intolerable lusts also all the commodities and pleasures of this life, which Nature, the parent of us all, would have common? . . . Now that it is come to extremity, we will also prove extremity: rend down hedges, fill up ditches, make way for every man into the common pasture'.[19]

15. *FS*, X, p. 144.
16. Cawdrey, *A Treasurie of Similies*, pp. 220–21.
17. Baynes, *An entire Commentary upon the whole Epistle of St Paul to the Ephesians*, p. 161. 'Entire' and 'whole' because an exposition of Chapter 1 had been published in 1618, a year after the author's death. The 'entire commentary' was published in 1643. Tyacke attributes the delay in publishing the full text to fear of censorship, citing this passage in particular (N. Tyacke, *The Fortunes of English Puritanism, 1603–1640*, Williams Lecture, 1990, pp. 11–12).
18. Hooker, *The carnal hypocrite* (?1626), quoted by P. Collinson, *The Religion of Protestants: The Church and English Society, 1559–1625* (Oxford U.P., 1982), p. 277.
19. Richard Woods, *Norfolkes Furies or A View of Ketts Campe* (1615), quoted by Annabel Patterson, *Shakespeare and the Popular Voice* (Oxford U.P., 1989), pp. 42–3. Cf. Crowley, *Select Works*, pp. 122–3.

The hedge comes to stand for private as against communal property; for enclosure of wastes, commons, fens and forests – one of the bitterest sources of class hostility in seventeenth-century England. The rebels of 1607 announced that they were destroying the fences which had turned them into starving paupers.[20] In *The Pilgrim's Progress* Christian and Great-heart are persecuted by giants who enclose public lands and the king's highway: it is not until they reach Immanuel's Land and Beulah that land becomes common property.[21] For Locke, property in land arises when man 'by his labour does, as it were, enclose it from the common'.[22] 'Love your neighbour, yet pull not down your hedge' was one of the 'outlandish proverbs' collected by George Herbert in 1640.[23] 'There are fewest poor where there are fewest commons', observed the improving Samuel Hartlib. Increased agricultural production and profits for farmers depended on bringing the waste under cultivation; and this meant getting rid of what Bacon called 'housed beggars': cottagers and squatters. Enclosure, said Adam Moore in 1653, 'will give the poor an interest in toiling whom terror never yet could inure to travail'.[24] 'A hedge in the field is as necessary in its kind as government in the church or commonwealth', added the Rev. Joseph Lee in 1656.[25] The hedge became associated with orderly, stable, lawful government.

Hence the labour theory of the origin of property. For Locke all land belongs to God; but that which a man brings under cultivation (from the waste, the wilderness) becomes his property. This property came to include, in Locke's notorious phrase, 'the turfs which my servant has cut'. Enclosed land became the property of those who could pay others to enclose it for them. And so enclosure meant shutting others out of the waste on which they might depend for sustenance. We may compare Winstanley's solution to the problem of the transition to a communist society: abolish wage labour by a national strike of wage labourers, and landowners will be

20. Quoted by M. A. Barg, *The English Revolution of the 17th Century through Portraits of its Leading Figures* (Progress Publishers, Moscow, 1990), p. 32. In English.
21. This point is well made by James Turner, 'Bunyan's Sense of Place', in *The Pilgrim's Progress: Critical and Historical Views* (ed. V. Newey, Liverpool U.P., 1980), pp. 99–104. For hedges see also R. B. Manning, *Village Revolts: Social Protest and Popular Disturbances in England, 1509–1640* (Oxford U.P., 1988), pp. 30–31.
22. Locke, *Two Treatises* (ed. P. Laslett, New York, 1965), Second Treatise.
23. Herbert, *Works* (ed. F. E. Hutchinson, Oxford U.P., 1941), p. 325.
24. Hartlib, *Legacy of Husbandry* (1653), p. 43; Moore, *Bread for the Poor*, p. 39. Cf. pp. 133–4 below.
25. Lee, *A Vindication of a Regulated Enclosure*, p. 28.

brought to heel; there is no point in owning land if no one will labour on it for you. They will see there is no alternative to joining communes voluntarily.[26]

Land was crucial to seventeenth-century politics. 'Do not all strive to enjoy the land?' asked Winstanley. 'The gentry strive for land, the clergy strive for land, the common people strive for land; and buying and selling is an art, whereby people endeavour to cheat one another of the land'.[27] Winstanley combined economics with religion in the startling epigram which I have quoted as an epigraph to this chapter. It is a brief sermon in itself, and it summarizes Winstanley's alternative policy for the land. Winstanley was playing on a formulation in the Epistle of St James. 'Pure religion and undefiled', James had said, is 'to visit the fatherless and widows in their affliction' (I.27). Winstanley may also have been thinking of Isaiah, whose definition of true fasting I cited as an epigraph to Chapter 3. The verb 'to manure' was regularly used in the seventeenth century as a synonym for 'cultivate intensively': but Winstanley presumably chose the word in contrast with the Laudian emphasis on religious ritual, sacraments and ceremonies rather than on charity and social justice. He was, I am sure, being deliberately provocative: we recall his adjuration to 'proud priests' to 'stoop unto our God'.[28]

For Winstanley true religion was neither 'the beauty of holiness' nor the Presbyterian power of discipline; it was to give economic security to all, to enable men and women to live better lives on earth. One-third of the

26. Winstanley, *The Law of Freedom in a Platform*.
27. Sabine, pp. 373–4.
28. Sabine, op. cit., p. 145; cf. Collinges, quoted on p. 128 above. Here I reluctantly disagree with Stephen Greenblatt's interpretation in 'Filthy Rites' (*Learning to Curse: Essays in Early Modern Culture*, 1990, pp. 74–6). I think Professor Greenblatt too easily assumes that 'manure' and 'dung' can normally refer to human excrement. *OED* has no seventeenth-century example of 'manure' so used, and of the allied 'dung' says that it is rarely used of human beings. Greenblatt misses the ironical Biblical context in which Winstanley sets the word manure. Greenblatt unfortunately relied on the work of George Shulman, who applies Freud's nineteenth-century hypotheses to Winstanley in the seventeenth century. He interprets the activities of the Diggers as an illustration of the twentieth-century practice of potty-training: Winstanley is presenting Mother Earth with 'an offering of gratitude to an authority that wants [him] to learn self-control' (Shulman, *Radicalism and Reverence: The Political Thought of Gerrard Winstanley*, California U.P., 1989, pp. 26–7). I find this a little far-fetched as an explanation, either of Winstanley's position or of the activities of the Diggers. It confuses cow-dung with human excrement and the seventeenth with the twentieth century. More important, it completely misses Winstanley's wit, and his passionate feelings about the plight of the poor.

land of England is waste and barren, 'unmanured all the days of . . . kingly and lordly power over you'. But there is land enough in England to maintain ten times as many people as are in it.[29] England can be a far richer country if all its land is cultivated by the improved methods now available: and the English people can be far more prosperous if the land is fairly distributed. True religion means raising the status of the oppressed peasantry, not as an act of charity but as a matter of sound economics. Everybody can live a good life if they are prepared to dirty their hands with labour: and then England will become the strongest land in the world. 'Adam himself', said Winstanley, 'or that living flesh, mankind, is a garden which God hath made for his own delight to walk in'.[30]

The hedge shuts in as well as shutting out. It can be a protective barrier as well as an obstacle in the way, as in Proverbs XV.19, Lamentations III.7, Hosea II.6–7 and Ezekiel XIII.5. Cotton saw the true church as a garden enclosed not by the defence of the Christian magistrate but by the restraints of persecution, the necessity of worshipping in secret places – woods and dens – and by the true church's refusal to admit all promiscuously.[31] Similarly Peter Sterry: 'God is round about his own: a wall encompassing, enclosing them around, . . . a wall between us and a sea of blood'.[32]

In 1601 JPs were empowered to seize any person found breaking a hedge or fence: offenders were to be handed over to the constable and whipped.[33] Hedges were symbolically destroyed in anti-enclosure riots. Levelling hedges in 1607 and later was identified with political radicalism: hence the name Leveller, then first applied. The Earl of Salisbury in 1610, dangling before the Commons the possibility of an agreement with the King to abolish feudal tenures, remarked that MPs could then 'return into your countries and tell your neighbours that you have made a pretty hedge about them'.[34] When Parliament in fact abolished feudal tenures

29. Sabine, pp. 200, 304, 356, 373, 408, 414, 507; cf. my *The World Turned Upside Down*, pp. 128–9.

30. Winstanley, *The Mysterie of God concerning the whole Creation, Mankind* (1648), p. 2. Winstanley cited Canticles IV.12 and Isaiah LVIII.11.

31. John Cotton, *A Brief Exposition of Canticles* (1642), p. 131. Jeremiah Burroughs in 1643 saw afflictions as 'God's hedge' (*An Exposition of the Prophecie of Hosea*, first three chapters), p. 33.

32. Quoted by V. de Sola Pinto, *Peter Sterry: Platonist and Puritan* (Cambridge U.P., 1934), p. 82.

33. 43 Eliz. cap. 7.

34. Joel Hurstfield, *The Queen's Wards: Wardship and Marriage under Elizabeth I* (1958), p. 319.

in 1646, after it had won the civil war, this had the effect of giving tenants-in-chief absolute property rights in their estates, to their great economic advantage.[35] Even the republican Henry Marten in 1648 said that 'the keeping of hedges, boundaries and distinctions . . . is a surer way to preserve peace among neighbours than throwing all open'. In 1653 he spoke of 'the hedge of propriety'.[36] The symbol of the hedge was extended to the parish, the unit of ecclesiastical and civil local government.

By the same token, the peasantry saw hedges as disruptive of the communal village. Hedges and fences were 'the outward and visible signs of enclosure'. Hence anger was directed against them.[37] 'By reason of the new enclosures and multitude of hedges', the churchwardens of Netherbury, Dorset, complained in 1613, we cannot go on perambulation.[38] Down to the eighteenth century some parish perambulations carried with them the necessary implements for demolishing fences or buildings erected without permission on commons or wastes.[39]

Winstanley fused the images of the wilderness and the garden with the Norman Yoke. He saw the man 'that hedges himself into the earth, and hedges out his brother' as an enemy to Christ; those that 'give the earth to some and deny the earth to others' – all these are 'upholding the Conquest still'.[40] Winstanley thought that 'money must not any longer . . . be the great god that hedges in some and hedges out others'.[41] The Quaker Edward Burrough said that church pews are enclosed like fields: 'lined stalls for the rich, with a lock and key to keep the poor out'.[42] Traherne, who was always much obsessed by property relations, associated

> Cursed and devised proprieties
> Hedges, ditches, limits, bounds,

35. See my *People and Ideas in 17th-Century England*, pp. 100–101.
36. Marten, *The Independency of England Endeavoured to be maintained . . . against the . . . Scottish Commissioners* (1648), p. 27; Marten's letter to Oliver Cromwell of 1653, a reference I owe to the late Professor C. M. William's unpublished thesis on Marten.
37. Joan Thirsk, 'Farming Techniques, 1500–1640', in *Agricultural Change* (ed. Thirsk), p. 33.
38 David Underdown, *Revel, Riot and Rebellion: Popular Politics and Culture in England, 1603–1660* (Oxford U.P., 1985), p. 81.
39. E. P. Thompson, *Customs in Common* (1991), pp. 117–20.
40. Sabine, pp. 428, 473, 259–60; cf. pp. 307–8.
41. Ibid., p. 270; cf. p. 214.
42. W. Smith and E. Burrough, *The Reign of the Whore* (1659), p. 17, quoted by Reay, *The Quakers and the English Revolution*, p. 37.

with the Fall.[43] When pirates established a community on Madagascar (*The History of the Pyrates* tells us) they emphasized that 'no hedge bounded any particular man's property', so demonstrating their egalitarianism.[44]

II

Sir Walter Ralegh had seen colonies as a dumping-ground for surplus vagabonds and so as a solution for England's population problems, as well as for the problems of younger sons of the gentry: Hakluyt insisted on Biblical authority for colonization, and stressed the difference between virtuous English colonists and brutal Spanish conquerors.[45] Ireland, from Spenser onwards, had proved a testing-ground for the religious motive in colonization. The Irish were lacking in 'civility' as well as in true religion: they did not regularly cultivate the soil in a settled manner, and their sexual customs were abominable. 'They are so inhuman and unlike men that we are first to reconcile them to our natural humanity, and their own reason', before we can hope to convert them.[46] Owen Roe O'Neill himself said that the Irish people were 'little better in their ways than the most remote Indians'.[47] The symbolism of wilderness and garden became especially relevant in New England.[48] The analogy with the forty years which God's people had to spend in the wilderness is constantly stressed: 'we are brought out of a fat land into a wilderness'.[49] Pym spoke of those who had 'fled into the desert of another world' in search of religious liberty.[50] 'Is not the way to Canaan through the

43. Traherne, *Poems, Centuries and Three Thanksgivings* (ed. A. Ridler, Oxford U.P., 1966), p. 8. See Chapter 10 in my *Writing and Revolution in 17th-century England* (Brighton, 1985).
44. [Defoe], *A General History . . . of the Pyrates* (ed. M. Schonhorn, South Carolina U.P., 1972), p. 427. The attribution to Defoe has been queried.
45. Hakluyt, *Voyages* (Everyman ed.), VIII, pp. 123–4.
46. [Anon.], *A Discourse Concerning the Affairs of Ireland* (1652), p. 5, quoted by Norah Carlin, 'Extreme or Mainstream: the English Independents and the Cromwellian Reconquest of Ireland, 1649–51', in *Representing Ireland* (ed. R. Bradshaw, A. Hadfield and W. Morley, ?1991). Cf. Barnabe Rich, *A New Description of Ireland* (1610), p. 15.
47. B. Jennings, *Wild Geese in Spanish Flanders* (Dublin, 1964), pp. 507–8.
48. G. H. Williams, *Wilderness and Paradise*, esp. pp. 99–104.
49. Peter Bulkley, *Gospel-Covenant* (1651), p. 209. I owe this and the reference in note 51 to A. Delbanco, *The Puritan Ordeal* (Harvard U.P., 1989).
50. Ed. E. S. Cope and W. H. Coates, *Proceedings of the Short Parliament of 1640* (Camden 4th Series, Vol. 19), pp. 155–6.

wilderness?' Richard Mather asked in his farewell sermon.[51] But some saw New England as a potential Paradise.[52]

There was greater freedom in the wilderness than in Babylon or Egypt. But it was no abiding city. The task of cultivating the soil was part of the extension of God's kingdom. Winthrop cited Genesis to establish the right of those who will 'possess and improve' the land to supplant the Indians who 'enclose no land, neither have any settled habitation, nor any tame cattle to improve the land by, and so have no other but a natural right to those countries, so as if we leave them sufficient for their own use we may lawfully take the rest, there being more than enough for them, and us'.[53]

Professor Kupperman has demonstrated the importance of economics in motivating English men and women to emigrate, especially in the hard times of the 1620s and 1630s, and as a cohesive force among the settlers. Land of their own and means to protect it were more important than religion as an inducement, though the dichotomy is false. To be truly independent through land ownership and economic competency was the way to protect men's ability to worship as they wished. 'Nothing sorts better with piety than competency' said John White of Dorchester.[54] 'Religion and profit jump together', was Edward Winslow's rather different way of putting it.[55]

The elder Richard Hakluyt's reasons for colonizing Virginia had included 'the glory of God' by planting true religion, and an increase in England's revenues and power.[56] The Pilgrim Fathers intended to bring the heathen from their spiritual wilderness into the Christian civilization of hard work and respectable clothing; it was a parallel process to taming the waste, bringing it under cultivation by establishing new gardens and independent congregations. Professor Kupperman has suggested that the controversy

51. Mather, *A Farewell Exhortation* (Cambridge, Mass., 1657), p. 3.
52. C. Webster, *The Great Instauration: Science, Medicine and Reform, 1626–1660* (1975), p. 44.
53. Delbanco, *The Puritan Ordeal*, p. 91; G. E. Thomas, 'Puritans, Indians and the Concept of Race', *New England Quarterly*, 48 (March 1975), p. 10. Cf. Locke, quoted on p. 131 above. For the usefulness of this argument for colonizers, see E. P. Thompson, *Customs in Common*, pp. 164–75.
54. White, *The Planters Plea* (1630).
55. Winslow, *Good Newes from New England* (1624), pp. 52, 64. I owe this and the preceding quotation to Professor K. O. Kupperman's contribution to Millersville. See also her seminal article, 'Errand to the Indies: Puritan Colonization from Providence through the Western Design', *William and Mary Quarterly*, 3rd series, XLV (1988).
56. Taylor, *Writings . . . of the two Richard Hakluyts*, II, p. 327.

between Lord Saye and Sele and Lord Brooke on the one hand, and Massachusetts on the other, was over the danger of clerical intolerance, from which the peers anticipated an encroachment on the independence of the colonists. They foresaw that the clergy might aspire to control the state, by restricting political rights to members of congregations. The small gardens may be linked in friendly voluntary unions but the gardeners must not usurp a monopoly of power.[57] Roger Williams agreed that to combine political and ecclesiastical power is 'to turn the garden and paradise of the church and saints into the field of the civil state of the world'. God had promised that 'this garden' would be taken in, enclosed and separated, 'from the howling desert of the whole world'. Disaster occurred when people 'opened a gap in the hedge or wall of separation between the garden of the church and the wilderness of the world'.[58]

The importance attached to discipline, cohesion, explains some of the less attractive features of early New England history – the expulsion of Mrs Hutchinson to the wilderness as well as Roger Williams choosing it. Joseph Hall thought that use of force against native Indians was impermissible, even in the interests of converting them to Christianity; Richard Baxter, more conveniently, believed that 'the law of nature may bind a Christian nation in charity to rule some nations by force', and compel them to admit missionary preachers.[59] Knowing the ultimate outcome as we do, the confusion of economic arguments about the religious duty of bringing waste lands under cultivation with arguments about preparing for the Second Coming by extending protestant Christianity over all the world appear insufferably hypocritical;[60] but for men like John Eliot, the Apostle to the Indians, this was still a tremendously inspiring hope. But Eliot too saw the way forward only through introducing Indians to western civilization: they must transfer from the wilderness to the garden, must become 'securely enclosed to

57. Kupperman, 'Definitions of Liberty on the eve of civil war: Lord Saye and Sele, Lord Brooke and the American Puritan colonies', in *Historical Journal*, 32 (1989), *passim*.
58. Williams, *The Bloudy Tenent*, pp. 65–6, 74–5, 435; *George Fox Digg'd out of his Burrow* (1676), and *Mr Cottons Letter*, quoted by K. Stavely, 'Roger Williams and the Enclosed Gardens of New England', Millersville.
59. Hall, *Satans Fiery Darts Quenchd: or, Temptations Repelled* (1646), in *Works*, VII, pp. 446–51; Baxter, *A Holy Commonwealth*, p. 170.
60. Cf. Perry Miller, *Errand into the Wilderness*, pp. 136–40, for the transition 'from a holy experiment to a commercial plantation' in early Virginia.

one plot of ground'.[61] 'Civility may be a leading step to Christianity', even Roger Williams agreed.

Failing Winstanley's solution of the land problem, free land in the New World (as in Ireland) was a great lure for the landless and exploited in the mother country. It ultimately proved an illusion for all but a fortunate few, usually those who started with some capital. But others, we are now beginning to discover, preferred life in the wilderness with the wild Irish or Indians to English 'civilization'.[62] The Connecticut Assembly in 1642 admitted that 'divers persons depart from amongst us, and take up their abode with the Indians in a profane course of life'. The complaint was repeated eleven years later; it had been heard in Maryland in 1639.[63] 'Indian' became a synonym for barbarism, for paganism, and so by extension for Catholicism in the 'dark corners' of Great Britain. Robert Burton, like Owen Roe O'Neill, compared the Irish to Indians.[64] 'We have Indians . . . in Cornwall, Indians in Wales, Indians in Ireland', said Roger Williams in 1652.[65] Traherne thought that 'our land . . . might have been a wilderness,/A blind corner of brutish Americans' but for the fact that the Gospel 'is owned and fully received'.[66] Rather contradictorily he also declared that 'there is no savage nation under the cope of heaven that is more absurdly barbarous than the Christian world'. Indians 'are like Adam or angels in comparison of us'.[67] Whether consciously or not, Traherne echoed a poem in which Roger Williams speaks for the Indians against the English settlers:

> We wear no clothes, have many gods,
>   And yet our sins are less;
> You are barbarians, pagans wild;
>   *Your* land's the wilderness.[68]

George Herbert upset the censor by writing

61. Stavely, op. cit., p. 11.
62. Nicholas Canny, *The Elizabethan Conquest of Ireland: A Pattern Established, 1565–1576* (Hassocks, Sussex, 1976), Chapter 5; Kupperman, *Settling with the Indians: The Meeting of English and American Cultures in America, 1580–1640* (1980), Chapter 7.
63. Quoted by Alden Vaughan, 'Puritan Statutory Law and the Indians', Millersville.
64. Burton, *Anatomy of Melancholy* (Everyman ed.), I, p. 86.
65. Williams, *The Hireling Ministry None of Christs, or a Discourse touching the Propagating the Gospel of Christ Jesus*, quoted by Perry Miller, *Roger Williams*, p. 200.
66. Traherne, *Poems*, p. 415. 'Brutish Americans' I think refers to the Indian inhabitants.
67. Ibid., pp. 269–70.
68. Quoted by G. H. Williams, op. cit., p. 103.

Religion stands on tip-toe in our land,
Ready to pass to the American strand.

England has back-slidden so grossly that no one can predict

what sins next year
Shall both in France and England domineer:
Then shall religion to America flee.[69]

Herbert may have got the idea from Sibbes's *The Bruised Reed*: 'the gospel's course hath hitherto been as that of the sun, from east to west, and so in God's time may proceed yet further west'.[70]

This was of course an extrapolation from the New Testament. St Paul carried the Gospel to the Greek islands, to the Greek mainland, ultimately to Rome: from Rome it extended over western Europe with the Empire. Gaps in the story as it affected Britain were filled by myths – the Biblically-based myth of Joseph of Arimathea (Mark XV.43–7), by Brutus in the parallel myth of the westward course of empire, or by Lucius the mythical King of Britain, who was held out as a model to James I in 1604.[71]

Whatever the original source, the idea took on. Samuel Ward of Ipswich was charged in 1634 with preaching that true religion was travelling westwards, though he denied the accusation.[72] John Winthrop in his *Journal* for 1646 associated the notion with millenarianism when he speculated that God 'means to carry his Gospel westwards, in these latter times of the world'.[73] William Twisse accepted that many divines saw a westward movement, and he himself wondered whether New England might not become the New Jerusalem.[74] Trapp in his *Commentary on the New Testament* quoted both Herbert, and Baxter quoting Herbert.[75] Henry Vaughan

---

69. Herbert, 'The Church Militant', *Works*, pp. 190–98; Izaak Walton, *Lives* (World's Classics), p. 315. Cf. Marvell, 'The Character of Holland', lines 67–70.

70. Op. cit., in Sibbes, *Works*, I, p. 100. George Wither's *The Motto* (1621) is also a possible source. Cf. P. F. Gura, *A Glimpse of Sion's Glory: Puritan Radicalism in New England, 1620–1660* (Wesleyan U.P., 1984).

71. John Russell, *A Treatise of the Happie and Blessed Union* (1604).

72. *CSPD, 1634–5*, pp. 361–2.

73. Quoted by D. D. Hall, *Worlds of Wonder, Days of Judgment: Popular Religious Belief in early New England* (New York, 1989), p. 103.

74. D. H. Corkran, 'The New England Colonists' English Image, 1550–1714' (University of California at Berkeley Ph.D. Thesis, 1970), p. 36, quoted by F. J. Bremer, *The Congregational Connection*, forthcoming.

75. J. Trapp, *Commentaries upon the New Testament* (Evansville, 1958), pp. 232, 528. First published 1657.

also echoed Herbert in saying 'farewell to Christian religion', since 'the growth of sin' in England meant that 'westward hence thy course will hold'.[76] The much more radical Gerrard Winstanley thought he saw in 'the age which is now dawning . . . the expiring of the selfish power and the rising up of the blessing . . . now appearing like lightning from East to West'.[77]

Herbert's 'The Church Militant' is far from triumphalist about the settlement in New England. Religion has fled from Greece to Rome, to Germany, to England, always pursued by sin; sin will follow religion to America, as it had pursued the church from Babylon to the papacy.

> New and old Rome did one empire twist;
> So both together are one Antichrist.

But

> Gold and grace did never yet agree:
> Religion always sides with poverty.

It is ironical that Herbert's version of the westward course of religion so soon got transmuted into Bishop Berkeley's proud 'westward the course of empire'.[78]

III

The enclosed garden then became an emblem of the congregation. 'It is the duty of the church', wrote Nathanael Homes, 'to look well to her keeping of her vines: . . . it is the duty of the vines to keep . . . within the particular vineyard or church whereof he [sic] is a member'.[79] From Richard Sibbes to Homes, Paul Hobson and John Bunyan, those who used the garden symbol drew on the imagery of the Song of Songs.[80] The world, said Roger Williams, 'is like a wilderness, or a sea of wild beasts', in which Christ has sown the good seed. 'The garden of the churches of both Old and New Testament' is 'planted with an hedge or wall of separation from

76. Vaughan, *Works* (ed. L. C. Martin, Oxford U.P., 1914), II, pp. 654–5.
77. Sabine, p. 376.
78. Berkeley, 'Verses on the Prospect of Arts and Learning in . . . America' (1720).
79. Homes, *Commentary . . . on . . . Canticles*, pp. 98–9.
80. Sibbes, *Works*, II, esp. pp. 10–13; for Hobson and Bunyan see my *A Turbulent, Seditious and Factious People* (Oxford U.P., 1988), esp. pp. 53–5, 91–2.

the world. When God's people neglect to maintain that hedge, . . . God hath . . . made his garden a wilderness, as at this day. . . . If he will ever please to restore his garden and paradise again, it must of necessity be walled in peculiarly unto himself from the world, and that all that shall be saved out of the world are to be transplanted out of the wilderness of the world, and added unto his church or garden'.[81] On a lower key Joseph Hall called on Christ to 'implant me with grace, prune me with meet correction' in 'this selective enclosure of thy church'.[82] Discipline was the hedge which shut these gardens off from the wilderness of the unregenerate world. The symbol was most applicable to congregations whose theology was Calvinist – Presbyterians, Baptists – and who wished to cut themselves off from the wilderness which the national church embraced. But again the symbol offered various possibilities.

The wilderness in the Old Testament is a symbol of disorder, darkness, death. The Hebrew word is the same as that used in Genesis I.2, when the newly created earth was 'without form and void'. But the wilderness could also be a place of testing and tutelage, even of punishment; or a place of refuge, contemplation and, ultimately, redemption – a moral waste but a potential Paradise, as in Milton's *Paradise Regained*.[83] 'As I walked through the wilderness of this world', *The Pilgrim's Progress* begins. 'A wilderness state is a desolate, a tempted, an afflicted, a persecuted state', wrote Bunyan in one of his posthumous works. For him this is almost the normal state of the church. 'Before this house [the church] was built, there was a church in the wilderness, and again after this house was demolished'. 'The milk and honey is beyond this wilderness', Bunyan observed in *Grace Abounding*.[84]

The children of Israel escaped from Egypt into the wilderness through the Red Sea. 'They trotted up and down in the wilderness for 40 years', recalled William Attersoll in 1609.[85] The Biblical 'howling wilderness' was rather more formidable and terrifying than anything with which Englishmen were acquainted. Isaiah spoke of whirlwinds 'from the desert, from the terrible land' (XXI.1). It was fitting that Ishmael grew up in the wilderness, after Sarah had cast him out from Abraham's house (Genesis XXI.19–21). Joshua lured the men of Ai into the wilderness, ambushed

81. Williams, *The Bloudy Tenent*, pp. 74, 435.
82. Hall, *Contemplations*, in *Works*, II, pp. 610–11.
83. G. H. Williams, op. cit., pp. 14–15, 18, 78.
84. *PP*, p. 8; Offor, III, p. 513; *Grace Abounding*, p. 4; cf. p. 1.
85. Attersoll, *The Pathway to Canaan: or An Exposition upon the XX and XXI chapters of the Book of Numbers*, To the Christian Reader. The Hebrew title of the book which we call Numbers is 'In the Wilderness'.

them and burnt their city, leaving it 'a wilderness unto this day' (Joshua VIII.15–28). David fled from Saul to the wilderness (I Samuel XXIII–XXVI). The fact that Elijah took refuge from Jezebel in the wilderness tells us something about her (I Kings XIX.4, 15–16; cf. *PR*, II.312–16).

'Some that have set out as if they would drive all the world before them', Bunyan wrote, 'have in few days died as they in the wilderness, and so never got sight of the Promised Land'.[86] After being baptized by John the Baptist, Christ fasted forty days 'in the waste wilderness' (*PR*, I.1–10). John's preaching in the wilderness fulfilled the prophecy of Isaiah (Matthew III.2; Isaiah XXXV.1–6, XL–XLII): 'Prepare ye the way of the Lord, make straight in the dust a highway for our God' for the return from Babylon to Jerusalem. 'Every valley shall be exalted, and every mountain and hill shall be made low'. God 'bringeth the princes to nothing, . . . the whirlwind shall take them away as stubble'. 'I will make the wilderness as a pool of water . . . I will set in the wilderness the cedar'. The Israelites, Milton observed, founded their government and laws whilst 'in the wide wilderness'.[87]

The wilderness then was another ambiguous symbol. Job spoke of God making 'the chief of the people of the earth . . . to wander in the wilderness out of the way. They grope in the dark without light: and he maketh them to stagger like a drunken man' (Job XII.24–5). On the other hand the Rechabites and Jeremiah preferred the wilderness to the corruptions of civilization, crying 'Oh that I had in the wilderness a cottage of wayfaring men, that I might leave my people and go from them' (Jeremiah IX.2. The A.V. has 'lodging place' for cottage). 'Oh that I had wings like a dove', sang the Psalmist; 'then would I fly away and rest, and lodge in the wilderness' (Psalm LV.6–7). Vaughan echoed this:

> I'll to the wilderness and can
> Find beasts more merciful than man.[88]

In one of his early writings Winstanley said 'this wilderness spoke of is a very safe condition or a hiding place from the face of the Serpent, wherein the soul is fed and nourished by God and not by any creature': dead to all human wisdom, learning and suchlike.[89] In *Paradise Regained* the Son of

---

86. *PP*, p. 257.
87. *PL*, XII.214–35.
88. Vaughan, *Works*, II, p. 406.
89. Winstanley, *The Breaking of the Day of God* (1648), quoted by T. W. Hayes, *Winstanley the Digger: A Literary Analysis of Radical Ideas in the English Revolution* (Harvard U.P., 1979), p. 31. Hayes gives no page reference.

God used his stay in the wilderness for rethinking, casting the balance, preparing himself for action before rediscovering the lost garden. The way back to a better Paradise lies through mankind's experience of adversity, suffering, temptation.

IV

The prophecy of Isaiah includes 'a song of my beloved to his vineyard'. He hedged it from the wilderness, removed the stones, and planted it with the best vines. What more could he have done? Nevertheless, it produced only wild grapes. 'And now I will tell you what I will do to my vineyard: I will take away the hedge thereof, it shall be eaten up; I will break the wall thereof, and it shall be trodden down'. Briars and thorns will grow over it. 'The vineyard of the Lord of Hosts is the house of Israel'. Israel had offended by oppressing the poor, joining house to house and field to field, till there was no place for the poor. A vineyard cut down is the symbol of desolation, when there 'shall be no singing nor shouting for joy' (Isaiah V.1–8, XVI.8–10). But a later chapter ran 'In that day sing of the vineyard of red wine.[90] I the Lord do keep it: I will water it every moment. . . . Who will set the briars and the thorns against me in battle?' (XXVII.2–4). The contrast is between the dried-up wilderness from which whirlwinds come (XXI.1), in which there is no life, in which fortified cities crumble and decay (XXVII.10) and holy cities, Zion, Jerusalem, are a desert (LXIV.10); and on the other hand the wilderness where waters break out, which will become as a fruitful field, shall flourish as the rose (XXXII.15, XXV.1, 6).

The church in Germany and Switzerland in Luther's time, said John Cotton, was 'fenced in as with a hedge, pale or wall (Song of Songs VI. 1–2)'. Previously the church had been visible 'not in open congregations, as it were gardens', but in individuals, 'sweet spices of flowers growing here and there whom the Popes and their instruments like wild boars sought to root out; yet God preserved them'. The world is a wilderness, or at least a wide field, said Cotton; only the church is God's garden or orchard.[91] The wilderness signified a time of preparation for the reformed churches, Isaac Penington suggested. They must wait on the Lord.[92] In I Corinthians X, St

90. 'Red wine in the Scriptures signifies excellency' Calvin assures us (*Commentary upon . . . Isaiah*, 1609, p. 261).
91. Cotton, *Canticles*, pp. 165–80, 130, 246; cf. pp. 362–70 below.
92. Penington, *Works*, I, p. 457.

Paul describes how the people of Israel were 'overthrown in the wilderness', giving way to idolatry, fornication and murmuring (verses 5–14). In Revelation XII.14 the woman, whom the Geneva margin takes to be the church, fled into the wilderness where she was nourished for a time, times and half a time – the period of suffering indicated in Daniel VI.25. This was applied to the Waldensians, whom some thought to be the woman in the wilderness 'who kept thy faith so pure of old'.[93] Milton spoke of 'our fourscore years vexation of [God] in this our wilderness since Reformation began'.[94] Cromwell reminded his first Parliament of 'a people brought out of Egypt towards ... Canaan', who 'through unbelief, murmuring, repining' languished 'many years in the wilderness before they came to the place of rest'.[95]

Through Joshua God made a point to the people of Israel, that they had been given a land in which they ate and drank 'of the vineyards and olive trees which ye planted not' (Joshua XXIV.13). That opened up big questions. What right had men to consume the produce of others' labour? A Quaker pamphlet of 1655 referred to 'tithe-takers' who 'plants no vineyard, nor labours in the vineyard; for first they must plant a vineyard before they eat of it'.[96] The imagery of the wilderness, the garden and the hedge could be put to a wide and often conflicting variety of uses in seventeenth-century England.

Winstanley's question, 'Do not all strive for the land?' remains. His solution was 'to make restitution of the earth taken and held from the common people'.[97] The Diggers wanted to cultivate the waste land, the wilderness, without establishing private property in land; to keep the garden community, not to split it up either by private property or by the discipline of the severer sects. Early Quakers (relying on 'the sense of the meeting') were with them against the discipline of exclusion. The Diggers would have cultivated the waste as a community of households. But for this to be peaceably possible, to avoid private property and exclusive discipline, Christ must first rise in sons and daughters; Ranters and 'rude persons' must somehow be disciplined.

Christ did not rise, and men awoke from Winstanley's dreams to be

93. A. L. Morton, *The World of the Ranters* (1970), pp. 115–42; G. H. Williams, *Wilderness and Paradise*, pp. 62–3, 74.

94. *MCPW*, I, p. 703.

95. Cromwell, *Writings and Speeches* (ed. W. C. Abbott, Harvard U.P., 1937–47), III, p. 442.

96. George Whitehead and John Harwood, *The People of the Just Cleared*.

97. Sabine, p. 373.

faced with large-scale capitalist farming which gave employment as wage-labourers to the fortunate. The relative security of copyhold yielded place to the instability of the capitalist market. Agricultural propagandists justified enclosure because it gave employment to the poor, because it reduced the number of vagabonds, a reputed source of political and social unrest; and also because it increased food production for the market, to the profit of the enclosers. The middling sort were those who mostly embraced the Puritan culture of discipline and hard work. The ultimate aim was to bring the wilderness under cultivation all over the world, and with this to bring the heathen to Christianity.

'The most part of all uncircumcised, impertinent and ignorant people do dwell [in] the wilderness land', the founder of Familism, Hendrik Niclaes, had declared: 'Fly now', the Lord had told the prophet Zechariah, 'out of the North and out of all wildernessed lands'.[98] Milton and other radicals believed that the church had been in the wilderness since the Apostles' times. God's people had come out of Babylon but had not yet found Zion.[99] Sexby in 1647 told the Army Council at Putney 'You are in a wilderness condition'.[100] That, one would have supposed, was a secular occasion; and Sexby one of the least religious of the Levellers. Milton thought that the church had taken 'flight into the wilderness' because of 'the perverse iniquity of 1600 years'.[101] 'Many of the saints of God', wrote Winstanley, are 'at a stand in the wilderness and at a loss, and so waiting upon God to discover himself to them'.[102] But vineyards, if not properly cultivated, might be unfruitful;[103] some might indeed turn out to be false churches.[104] 'That which was planted as a vineyard is become a wilderness for barrenness . . . so that God walks not there; . . . and that is the cause of all your woe, even his absence': so James Nayler in 1655.[105] Marvell saw England as having suffered a second Fall in the civil war, and having become a waste wilderness.[106]

98. H.N., *Terra Pacis: A True Testification of The Spiritual Land of Peace* (1649), pp. 11, 21–2; first translated 1575.

99. Penington, *Works*, I, pp. 452–3.

100. Woodhouse, op. cit., p. 102.

101. *MCPW*, I, p. 827.

102. Winstanley, *The Mystery of God* (1648), p. 39. Sir Henry Vane discusses the church in the wilderness in his *Epistle to the Mystical Body of Christ* (1661).

103. John Brinsley, *The Third Part of the True Watch*, sig. ¶¶2v.

104. H. Ainsworth, *Solomons Song of Songs. In English Meter* (1623), sig. C2, commenting on Canticles, I.6.

105. Nayler, *Love to the Lost* (1655), p. 5.

106. Marvell, 'Upon Appleton House', XLI–XLII; cf. 'The Garden'.

William Erbery retired from his Army chaplaincy to the Isle of Ely, where he saw himself 'bewildernessed as a wayfaring man, seeing no way of man on earth, nor beaten path to lead him'. The 'highway is found in Christ in us, God in our flesh'. 'A wilderness condition . . . with God is the most comfortable state . . . in that apostasy we are now in'. Those in the wilderness had no need of 'a man in black clothes' to preach to them, for 'they were all taught of God'. Erbery, like Milton, joined no church. The English churches 'do live in Babylon'; and so did Erbery.[107] According to Thomas Edwards Mrs Attaway saw herself as 'in the wilderness, waiting for the pouring out of the spirit'.[108] The Duchess of Malfi went

> Into a wilderness
> Where I shall find no path, nor friendly clue,
> To be my guide (I.ii.278–80).

In a Fast Sermon of 25 May 1642 William Sedgwick described England as 'this wilderness', in which MPs are 'our watchmen'.[109] 'Israel in their wilderness condition are happy in the extraordinary presence of God', Richard Vines assured the Houses of Parliament on 12 March 1644.[110] In 1648 Sedgwick expected God to shine forth 'in those that are the lowest of the people', who 'are in a wilderness, in a desolate, barren estate'.[111] In 1656 he thought Oliver Cromwell's way was 'in the wilderness and 'tis crooked'. But 'hath not our course been so from the beginning?'[112] In the same year Isaac Penington believed that the true church had fled into the wilderness, and that its 'time of preparation in the wilderness' was not yet ended.[113] Ranters saw the wilderness as the nothingness of the moral law. Clarkson was travelling in the wilderness in the late 1650s, which he seems to identify with Egypt.[114] For Quakers

---

107. *The Testimony of William Erbery*, pp. 18, 22, 100, 218–38, 337–8; Edwards, *Gangraena*, I, p. 78, III, pp. 89–90. Cf. Roger Williams, John Saltmarsh, Sir Henry Vane, Isaac Penington, Edward Burrough and other Quakers, cited in my *The Experience of Defeat*, pp. 122–3, 153, 299–303.

108. *Gangraena*, I, p. 87.

109. *FS*, III, pp. 177, 230.

110. Ibid., XVI, pp. 54, 56.

111. Sedgwick, *Some Flashes of Lightnings of the Sonne of Man*, p. 66.

112. Sedgwick, *Animadversions upon A Letter*, pp. 21–2, 39.

113. Penington, *Works*, I, p. 453; cf. *The Consideration of a Point Concerning the Book of Common Prayer* (1660), pp. 21–2.

114. Clarkson, *The Lost sheep Found*, pp. 10, 24–5, 34, 38.

the world was a wilderness. Muggleton saw only three estates – Egypt, the wilderness and Canaan.[115]

Milton in *Eikonoklastes* quoted Psalm CVII.40 as a judgment on Charles I's surrender to the Scots in 1646: 'He poureth contempt upon princes, and causeth them to wander in the wilderness where there is no way'.[116] In Milton's epic, Paradise was cut off by 'a steep wilderness' (*PL*, IV.135–7). After the Fall, man wandered long 'through the world's wilderness' until 'our second Adam' raised Eden 'in the waste wilderness'. Only after his wanderings there had been repeatedly emphasized did he ultimately return 'safe to eternal Paradise of rest.' We may compare Herbert:

> I did towards Canaan draw; but now I am
> Brought back to the Red Sea, the sea of shame.[117]

Rejection of established churches is for Erbery equivalent to going into the wilderness, as for Mrs Attaway, Milton, Bunyan. This is only a realistic estimate of the evil present: the wilderness is not an ideal state, but as things stand the only hope of anything better is to enclose the garden of a separate church in the wilderness. Erbery and Milton lacked even that hope. And there is no prospect yet of the whole wilderness becoming one garden.[118] Roger Williams contrasted the garden of the church with the wilderness of the world – a metaphor especially telling for those who had undertaken the errand into the wilderness of New England.[119]

If we can fence off a garden, a vineyard, in the wilderness, that would be a start, the emblem of a Christian society; but only if the garden was left alone, to be cultivated by a gardener or gardeners on strictly New Testament lines. 'Fruitful fields are quiet', Bunyan wrote, 'because they are fenced, and so shall the church be in that day', after persecution has ended.[120] For Thomas Hooker excommunication was the hedge that shut some in and others out.[121] Perkins had rejected the doctrine of universal redemption which 'pulls down the pale of the church, and lays

115. Muggleton, *The Neck of the Quakers Broken* (1663), p. 27.

116. *MCPW*, III, p. 546.

117. G. Herbert, 'The Bunch of Grapes', in *Works*, p. 128. The reference is to Numbers XIII.23–4.

118. Cf. Jeremiah Burrough, *An Exposition of the Prophesie of Hosea*, p. 263, citing, rather strainedly, Hosea II.3–4.

119. Roger Williams, *The Bloudy Tenent, passim*. Andrew Delbanco, *The Puritan Ordeal*, has some interesting passages on the wilderness in New England (pp. 72, 87–93, 212).

120. *BMW*, VII, p. 170.

121. Hooker, *The carnal hypocrite*; see p. 130 above.

it waste as every common field'.[122] (The word 'pale' reminds us of the effective exclusion of Irish natives from landownership and political rights in the areas of their country dominated by the English.) England has 'become a wilderness', said William Sedgwick in 1649, 'the pale of civil power being broke down, and men let loose to furious and beastly lusts'.[123]

Wither's headnote to Psalm LXXX called on God to 'repair those decayed fences, through which any strange lust or swinish condition hath broken in upon us'.[124] Francis Quarles repeated Perkins when he said that Arminianism was

> So poor a fence, young swain, that 'tis supposed
> Ye feed in common, though ye seem enclosed.[125]

Cowley alleged that Parliamentarians believed

> No things or places sacred
> But with their God himself in common live.[126]

And the (later) Duke of Newcastle saw enclosure as a moral virtue, as against the man

> Whose giddy humour suffers no control;
> Whose mind yet hath no bounds settled at all,
> No pale about him, hedge or ditch or wall.[127]

Winstanley on the other hand saw kingly power also as a hedge, predestinating mankind to inequality 'from their birth to their death'. All hedges would be cut down by Christ the Head Leveller.[128]

Erbery preferred the wilderness state to being forced into conformity. But how will the art of gardening be learnt? The wilderness state is one in which the saints begin to think for themselves against *enforced* community, conformity. After 1660 the sects realized that they could not both cultivate their gardens and run the state. They were forced back on to the former,

122. Perkins, *Workes*, I, pp. 295–6.
123. Sedgwick, *A Second View of the Army Remonstrance*, p. 15.
124. Wither, *The Psalmes of David* (The Netherlands, 1632).
125. Quarles, *The Shepheards Oracles* (1646), in *Complete Works*, III, p. 217.
126. Cowley, *The Civil War* (ed. A. Pritchard, Toronto U.P., 1973), p. 110.
127. Ed. D. Grant, *The Phanseys of William Cavendish, Marquis of Newcastle* (1956), p. 47. I owe this and the preceding reference to James Turner's *The Politics of Landscape* (Oxford, 1979), p. 129.
128. Sabine, pp. 529–30.

into the provincial philistinism of eighteenth- and nineteenth-century nonconformity. In the church of Christ there should have been many gardens blooming; but instead there were many sects wrangling.

A cultivated garden or a vineyard is the antithesis of the wilderness, the habitat of free-growing weeds and of natural man with no rein to his lusts. The garden belongs to God; but it must have gardeners, cultivators of the vines, planners acting for the absentee owner, imposing discipline on growth which always tends to run wild: the job of Adam and Eve in Paradise had been to keep the garden under control. Christ rising was indeed a gardener, Lancelot Andrewes had said; he 'shall turn all grass into garden-plots'.[129] In the wilderness there can be no discipline, and no satisfactory discipline in a national church. Discipline is voluntarily accepted in the garden congregation, but it is discipline, control, none the less, dependent ultimately on the power of excommunication, shutting out.

The early Quakers disliked discipline, but some had to be imposed on the Society to enable it to survive after 1660. This was the subject of much controversy and many splits – the Proud Quakers, the Story-Wilkinson separation, Perrot and his followers. Religious groupings that had no (or minimal) discipline – Seekers, Ranters – did not survive. It is not without its symbolic significance that William Penn returned to the traditional use of the image of the hedge in opposition to the Story-Wilkinson separation. They 'tread down your hedge under the specious pretence of being left to the light within'.[130]

Discipline was male, imposed by male elders. Bunyan thought that separate women's meetings would subvert male *power* (his word) in the church.[131] For his Bedford congregation discipline was the hedge; in *The Pilgrim's Progress* false pilgrims tried to get into the way by climbing over the wall.[132] (In *Grace Abounding* Bunyan recorded dreaming of the congregation as a walled estate, into which he had to force his way.) A wall is for safety, Bunyan wrote in 1665. 'Art thou crossed . . . in all thy foolish ways and doings? A sign God waits to turn thee. Has he made a hedge and a wall to stop thee?'[133] Henry Danvers in his *Treatise of Baptism* (1674) stated that

---

129. Andrewes, *XCVI Sermons* (2nd ed., 1631), p. 53.
130. W. C. Braithwaite, *The Second Period of Quakerism* (1919), p. 307.
131. See my *A Turbulent, Seditious and Factious People*, Chapter 24. For the importance of discipline for radical Puritans and separatists see Brachlow, *The Communion of Saints: Radical Puritan and Separatist Ecclesiology, 1570–1625* (Oxford U.P., 1988), Chapter 3, *passim*.
132. *PP*, p. 25.
133. *BMW*, III, pp. 98–101; XI, p. 86 (1688).

'none were esteemed members [of his church], or did participate in its ordinances, before they were baptized, being God's hedge or boundary'.[134] Philip Henry complained that post-restoration Independents 'pluck up the hedge of parish order' by refusing to conform.[135] One argument in favour of occasional conformity was that it recognized the integrity of the parish community.[136]

Cutting land off from the waste increased productivity: grain and fruit are grown in place of grass and weeds. 'Scripture, reason and experience showeth how we may be restored to Paradise on earth', by mastering nature, said John Beale; 'if we can but bring ingenuity into fashion', Walter Blyth had insisted in 1650.[137] Increased agricultural productivity would lead to what Anthony Low has called 'a Georgic Revolution'. The agricultural revolution was also envisaged as a moral revolution. Scientific agriculture plus hard work would lead to profits for cultivators and prosperity for the nation. But tenants withdrawing their lands from the plough would be excluded from the kingdom. ('No man that putteth his hand to the plough and looketh back is apt to the kingdom of God', said Christ – Luke IX.62.)[138] Adam had been an industrious gardener.

Charles Webster has shown how Biblical texts were quoted in favour of the improvement of nature, the advancement of arts and crafts and an increase in trade.[139] Enclosers, assumed a poem attributed to Samuel Butler, were naturally Parliamentarians during the civil war.[140] Private enclosure monopolizes lands hitherto open to all, whose products were essential to the way of life of many inhabitants. Greater productivity comes at the price of greater inequality. Independent congregations separate the godly from the world, from the national church: for their members the image of the garden seems wholly appropriate. Christians, wrote Bunyan, 'are like the flowers in the garden that stand and grow where the gardener has planted them'. The flowers fertilize one another. They 'have upon each of

---

134. Danvers, op. cit., p. 20.

135. Henry, *Diaries and Letters*, p. 277.

136. See my 'Occasional Conformity', in *Religion and Politics in 17th-century England*, pp. 301–20.

137. Quoted by C. Webster, *The Great Instauration*, pp. 16, 86, 478–83.

138. John Worlidge, *Systema Agriculturae* (1672), sig. B 2, quoted by Anthony Low, *The Georgic Revolution* (Princeton U.P., 1985), pp. 235–6.

139. Webster, op. cit., pp. 367 (Hugh Peter), 466 (Ralph Austen, Sir John Pettus), 510–14 (Benjamin Worsley, Bacon).

140. *The Posthumous Works of Mr Samuel Butler* (6th ed., 1754), pp. 77–106. (There is no reason to suppose the attribution is correct.) Lawrence Stone made the same assumption about enclosures in 'The Bourgeois Revolution . . . Revisited', *P. and P.*, 109 (1985).

them the dew of heaven, which being shaken with the wind, they let fall the dew at each other's roots, whereby they are jointly nourished, and become nourishers of one another'.[141] The garden is orderly: 'the flowers are divers in stature, in quality, and colour, and smell, and virtue; . . . where the gardener has set them, there they stand, and quarrel not one with another'.[142] The garden is enclosed from the open fields, where 'wild ("counterfeit") faith . . . and other wild notions abound'.[143] 'Wild faith' had indeed abounded in the freedom of the 1640s and 1650s. But the self-isolation of the self-selected saints, whose ministers water the plants of the Lord, made visible the assumptions of predestinarian theology, and must have stimulated in others the hope that all men and women might be saved.

The image of the garden could be put to other uses. The preacher of a Fast Sermon in 1647 told of a Turk who 'resembled the diversity of religions in his empire to the diversity of flowers in a garden'. But the preacher disagreed. 'Christian magistrates must account' such diversity 'as weeds, which if not plucked up will soon overtop the flowers of orthodox doctrine'.[144] Enclosure meant shutting out as well as shutting in. 'Wild notions' were perhaps more acceptable among what Ezekiel called 'the wilderness of the people' (XX.35). Theirs is a 'squatter' view of the church, analogous to the attitude of non-freeholders who lost out at enclosure 'by agreement' among their betters. I cited earlier the Rev. Joseph Lee who said that 'a hedge in the field was as necessary . . . as government in the church or commonwealth'. He was defending enclosure, but he might equally well have been defending a congregation's right to exclude.[145] Bunyan found the 'closed communion' of some Baptist churches offensively exclusive, no less than the Laudian railing off of the altar seemed to Milton to set up 'a table of separation'. This brings us back to Baynes's point that ceremonies shut out as well as shutting in.[146]

The emblem of the garden thus contains many facets. England is also a garden: 'this other Eden, demi-Paradise';[147] 'that renowned isle/Which all

141. *BMW*, III, pp. 10, 54; cf. ibid., V, pp. 20, 64; Offor, II, pp. 425–6.
142. *PP*, p. 202. This is from Part II (1684), in which Bunyan especially stresses mutual help and encouragement.
143. *BMW*, XI, p. 67.
144. Nathaniel Hardy, *FS*, XXVII, p. 80.
145. See p. 131 above.
146. See p. 130 above.
147. John of Gaunt, in Shakespeare's *Richard II*, II. i. 42.

men Beauty's garden-plot enstyle';[148] 'the garden of the world',[149] 'God's garden' which Cromwell's sword did defend.[150] George Fox in 1659 envisaged a socially reformed England as a garden.[151] Evelyn, who started his *Elysium Britannicum* around 1653, compared England to the Garden of Eden, a chosen nation. In a rather different spirit, William Dewsbery wrote that 'the Lord will make the earth as the Garden of Eden, and hath begun his strange work in this nation'.[152] England was threatened across the pathless wastes of the sea by Egypt and Babylon, Spain and France. But there were also vast opportunities; there were new areas to be opened up to Christianity and civilization on the other side of the Atlantic, new peoples for conversion and trade in the Far East.

The King's enemies, Martin Lluellin argued, are enclosure breakers. They let in the madness of the people, the raging of their sea.[153] The chief stake in our hedge was cut up when our King of ever-glorious memory was cut off, Thomas Washbourne agreed. Tithes too, he thought, were a hedge going down apace, 'voted away from the church by the fanatic party'.[154] From the other side, the anonymous *Armies Vindication* of 1659 also insisted that 'the ancient hedge of civil power is broken down'. 'It is a time of breaking down all worldly constitutions'. The Army remains as the only bulwark.[155]

The hedge then was a protector. Ezekiel denounced the priests, princes, prophets and rich people of Israel for oppressing the poor and needy, and strangers. He 'sought for a man among them that should make up the hedge and stand in the gap' (XIII.5, XXII.30). The Geneva margin added: 'He speaketh to the governors and true ministers that should have resisted' false prophets. Stephen Marshall in December 1641 took this as a reference to Phineas, who turned away God's wrath by rising up and slaying an

148. Browne, *Britannia's Pastorals* (1613), in *Poems of William Browne* (ed. G. Goodwin, Muses Library, n.d.), I, p. 18.

149. Marvell, 'Upon Appleton House', in *Poems*, p. 69.

150. Thomas Sprat, 'To the happy Memory of the late Usurper' (1659), in *Poems on Affairs of State* (1703), p. 18. 'Usurper' is manifestly a post-restoration afterthought by the future bishop. 'Happy' perhaps got left by mistake.

151. Fox, *To the Parliament of the Common-wealth of England*, pp. 3–5.

152. *A True Prophecie of the Mighty Day of the Lord* (1655), in *The Faithful Testimony of William Dewsbery*, p. 111.

153. Lluellin, *Men-Miracles* (1646), p. 102, quoted by James Turner, *The Politics of Landscape*, p. 129.

154. Washbourne, *The Repair of the Breach: A Sermon Preached at the Cathedral Church of Gloucester, 29 May, 1661*, pp. 17–19.

155. Op. cit., pp. 94–5.

Israelite and the foreign woman whom he had married (Numbers XXV.7–11; Judges XXII.28; Psalm CVI.30). Marshall was thinking of 'magistrates and ministers' in England who had failed to stand up against idolatry under Laud.[156] A year earlier he had explained how God had made a 'hedge . . . about the second commandment'.[157]

In 1672 Bishop Samuel Parker was accused of 'breaking the hedge of what is sacred, laying open the enclosures of all morality and civility in making the worthy common and level with the infamous' by his attack on dissenters in *A Discourse of Ecclesiastical Polity* (1669).[158] A year later the author of *The Ladies Calling* observed that God 'seems in many particulars to have closelier fenced [women] in, and not let them to those wilder excesses, for which the customary liberty of the other sex afford a more open way'.[159] Vavasor Powell wrote of the advantages of suffering under persecution: 'the storm that tends to drive them into one accord' – 'this is the hedge and wall that keeps thy people from ranging'.[160]

In this divided society the hedge, like the wilderness, was an ambivalent symbol. It protected the rich by keeping the poor out of their property; or it safe-guarded the sacred by excluding the profane. Sometimes it did both. This may give us cause to reflect on the social role of the gathered churches as seen by the excluded poorer classes. It may even throw light on the readiness of 'the rabble' to welcome back bishops as a preferable alternative to the kind of parish discipline offered by Richard Baxter and the Presbyterians. It also links up with Erbery's rejection of all churches.[161] It was difficult to separate religious order from political and social order: king and bishops came back together in 1660.

The garden represents privacy, property, the family, civilization, growing luxury, all cut off from the vulgar by the hedge. It can stand for the chosen nation in a heathen world, the colonial errand into the wilderness. It also asserts the godly's control over their congregations, the encloser's status; the superiority of the colonizer over the 'natives'. By exclusion, power and wealth and godliness are justified. The *nation* as well as the Lord is glorified by colonization.

156. *FS*, II, p. 123.
157. Ibid., I, p. 142.
158. John Humfrey, *The Authority of the Magistrate about Religion Discussed* (1672), pp. 6–7, quoted by Richard Ashcraft, *Revolutionary Politics and Locke's Two Treatises of Government*, pp. 43–4.
159. Op. cit. (1673), Preface.
160. In [Anon.], *The Life and Death of Mr Vavasor Powell* (1671), p. 105.
161. See pp. 112, 146–7 above.

6. Poverty, Usury and Debt

Jesus's first recorded sermon: I should preach the Gospel to the poor, ... deliverance to the captives, ... the acceptable year of the Lord.
Luke IV.18–19. The last phrase 'alludeth to the year of Jubilee' (Geneva margin).

> But such Scriptures you could not brook
>   As bade you give ought to the poor;
> You wished them out of the book,
>   But you were sure to have in store
> Plenty of Scriptures, evermore
>   To prove that you might aye be bold
> With your own to do what you would.

Robert Crowley, *Pleasure and Payne, Heaven and Hell* (1551), in *Select Works* (ed. J. M. Cowper, Early English Text Soc., 1872), p. 115, citing Matthew VII, X. The words are attributed to Christ.

Religion is not a matter of words, nor stands upon words, as wood consists of trees ... Religion is a matter of power, it makes a man able. It is a matter of practice: and there is nothing so speculative in religion but it tends to practice. ... A trade is not learned by words, but by experience. ...
    Let us show our understandings by our practice.
Richard Sibbes, *The Art of Contentment* (1629), in *Works*, V, pp. 175, 183.

Their sin ... is not so much in that some men are too poor, as it is in that some are too rich. ... If you cannot make all the poor rich, yet you may make the rich poorer.
[Anon.], *Tyranipocrit, Discovered with his wiles, wherewith he vanquisheth* (Rotterdam, 1649) (ed. A. Hopton, n.d., ?1990), pp. 36, 51.

I

Seventeenth-century radicals could derive fighting creeds from the Old
Testament, for use both in opposition and after victory. Puritans
emphasized the Old Testament rather than the New. The New Testament stresses suffering under persecution, constancy to the end, as well
as scepticism about established practices. In both Testaments there is much
support for the poor against the rich, the younger against the elder brother;
there are demands for social justice and denunciations of arbitrary power,
of persecution and idolatry of golden calves, insistence on the impossibility
of serving both God and Mammon. 'Blessed be ye poor, for yours is the
kingdom of God'. 'Blessed are ye that hunger now: for ye shall be filled'
(Luke VI.20–21). 'He that is greatest among you, let him be your servant'
(Matthew XXIII.12; cf. Mark X.43). 'Whosoever will be chief of you, shall
be the servant of servants' (Mark X.44). 'If I then your Lord and Master
have washed your feet, ye also ought to wash one another's feet' (John
XIII.14). Christ Jesus, said St Paul, 'made himself of no reputation, and
took on him the form of a servant' (Philippians II.7). 'There is no respect of
persons with God' (Romans II.11; cf. James II.2–4: gold rings and goodly
apparel count for nothing). He who will not work, neither shall he eat
(II Thessalonians III.10–11). This last was a little too revolutionary for some
theologians; William Bradshaw for instance said that the main point was to
forbid giving bread to sturdy beggars; denunciations of idleness referred to
servants rather than to rentier landlords.[1]

The parable of the rich young man who claimed to have kept all the
commandments was aimed against just that sort of complacency: 'if thou
wilt be perfect, go, sell that thou hast and give it to the poor'. He went
away sorrowful (Matthew XIX.21–2. Cf. also the parable of Dives and
Lazarus). 'Woe be to you that are rich', warned Christ in Luke VI.24.
The Epistle of James was also rather strong meat: God hath chosen 'the
poor of this world' (II.5). 'Go to now, ye rich men; weep and howl for
your miseries that shall come upon you'. Particularly relevant to
seventeenth-century England was James's assertion that the cry of under-
paid agricultural labourers had reached God's ears (V.1–4). Coppe in *The
Fiery Flying Roll* made much of 'your gold and silver is cankered', and
Henry Vaughan spoke of the rich moneylender as 'Nimrod of acres'.[2]

1. Bradshaw, *A Plaine and Pithy Exposition of the Second Epistle to the Thessalonians*
(1620), pp. 190–91. Posthumously published by Thomas Gataker. Bradshaw died in
1618.
2. Vaughan, 'In Amicum foeneratorem', *Works*, p. 43.

In the Old Testament respect for the poor, the fatherless and the widow was strongly expressed, notably in the Psalms. The rich oppressor 'lieth in wait in the villages' like a lion; 'heaps of the poor do fall by his might' (Psalm X; cf. XII.5, and Amos VIII.6). But they will be avenged: God 'lifteth up the poor out of the dung, that he may set him with the princes' (Psalm CXIII.7–8; cf. LXXII.13; CXLVI.9; Job XXIX.11–12; XXXI. 16–22; Isaiah X.2, XI.4; Jeremiah VII.6, XXII.3). The Geneva Bible was not above reading social attitudes into the text. When Isaiah tells us that the Lord threatened not to spare Jerusalem because the hands of its inhabitants were full of blood, the Geneva margin glossed 'blood' as 'avarice, deceit, cruelty and extortion' (I.15).[3]

During the exile, insistence on revenge could give rise to utopian ideas which were potentially revolutionary. Zephaniah envisaged 'an humble and poor people' who 'shall trust in the name of the Lord' (III.2). The Lord 'will bring down them that dwell on high', promised Isaiah; 'the feet of the poor . . . shall tread [them] down' (XXVI.5–6). Exploitation will be ended. 'They shall not build, and another inhabit; they shall not plant, and another eat' (Isaiah LXV.22–3; cf. LXII.8–9). Isaiah XXIV speaks of turning the world upside down, a phrase picked up in Acts XVII.6, which came into familiar use in the seventeenth century.

But there were limits to the Old Testament's concern for social justice. Slaves received very different treatment from freemen. Exodus XXI.20 provided in the name of the Lord that 'if a man smite his servant or his maid with a rod, and he die under his hand, he shall be surely punished'. But if the servant survive 'a day, or two days, he shall not be punished: for he is his money'. The Geneva Bible, shocked by this, glossed 'he shall not be punished' with the words 'by the civil magistrate; but before God he is a murderer'. Sir Thomas Aston in 1641 cited 'the old seditious argument, that we are all the sons of Adam, born free: some of them say, the Gospel hath made them free. . . . They will plead Scripture for it, that we should all live by the sweat of our brows'.[4]

Although the New Testament is the main source for texts on Christian liberty, there was in the Old Testament much denunciation of oppression, and celebration of liberation from slavery at the hands of Egyptian taskmasters (Exodus II.7–9), from slavery and captivity in Babylon (Daniel

3. Cf. Chapter 15 below.
4. *MER*, p. 247, and references there cited; Aston, *A Remonstrance against Presbytery* (1641), sig. 1, 4b. That Aston regarded this as an argument against Presbyterianism is interesting evidence of royalist failure to distinguish at that date between Presbyterians and sectaries.

IX–XI). 'The prey of the tyrant shall be delivered', the Lord promised Isaiah (XLIX.25). The imagery of such passages appealed especially to Gerrard Winstanley. M. Marsin in the 1690s quoted I Samuel II.8: God 'raiseth up the poor out of the dust, and lifteth up the beggar from the dunghill, to set them among princes, and to make them inherit the throne of glory'. 'Though the Lord be high, yet hath he respect unto the lowly; but the proud he knoweth afar off' (Psalm CXXXVIII.6). 'Before destruction the heart of man is haughty, and before honour is humility' (Proverbs XVIII.12).[5] For those suffering persecution there were the words heard by St Paul: 'I am Jesus whom thou persecutest' (Acts IX.5) – and many more passages which made suffering the path to glory. For Latin American liberation theologians solidarity with the poor and oppressed against 'the pharaohs of this world' is a key theme. 'Jesus took on oppression to make us free'.[6]

Biblical texts advocating social reform were cited by radicals more than by rulers. Despite 'there is neither bond nor free' in Christ (Galatians III.28), both St Augustine and Gregory the Great defended slavery, and the latter purchased and owned slaves. The Church was the largest slave-owner in the early Middle Ages. Four abbeys ruled by Alcuin of York employed 20,000 slaves.[7] In England it was heretics, from John Ball and Lollards onwards, who recalled that there were no gentry in the Garden of Eden. Lollards refused to swear, appealing to the absolute prohibition in James V.17. Levellers and Quakers looked back to this heretical succession.

The Old Testament witnesses to the beginnings of a market economy, such as was developing rapidly in sixteenth- and early seventeenth-century England. 'Men come to the market, as they were wont to come to the games of running and wrestling'.[8] 'A true weight and balance are of the Lord', said Proverbs XVI.11; deceitful weights and balances are denounced in Ezekiel, Hosea, Amos and Micah. Such passages were often echoed in the century which separated John Hall's *The Court of Virtue* (1565) from Richard Farnsworth's *Discovery of Truth and Falsehood* (1653).[9] Warnings to

5. M. M[arsin], *Good News to the Good Women* (1701), *passim*. See pp. 245, 407–9 below.

6. Clodovis Boff, *Introducing Liberation Theology* (English translation, 1987), pp. 43, 50, 53. See Appendix B.

7. Pierre Bonnassie, *From Slavery to Feudalism in South-Western Europe* (trans. Jean Birrell, Cambridge U.P., 1991), pp. 2–3, 25–37, 51–6.

8. Dod and Cleaver, *Proverbs*, XX.14 – p. 131.

9. Hall, op. cit. (ed. R. A. Fraser, 1961), pp. 275–7; for Farnsworth see p. 243 below.

merchants to weep and wail (Revelation XVIII.11–18), to rich men to weep and howl (James V.1–6), were highly quotable for Coppe and other radicals.

Dod and Cleaver reminded their many readers that God 'hath instituted the use of negotiation, market and exchange for the mutual benefit of both sides'. 'The Lord doth take notice of all the behaviour of men in their trafficking one with another'. We should be good husbands for our estates: if we preserve our goods we retain our freedoms.[10] Villeinage is dead, but debtors are either imprisoned or become servants. George Herbert's Parson was to 'labour for wealth and maintenance', so as to 'have the wherewithal to serve God better, and to do good deeds'.[11] Hebrews XIII.5 led William Gouge to conclude that 'desire of riches is not simply covetousness, for a man may hopefully pray for them'.[12] Bunyan was soon to write *Mr. Badman* to teach the godly how to behave in this perplexing world of the capitalist market.

There are many ways to be rich, Bacon had observed, and most of them foul. But Joseph Hall apostrophized 'rich citizens', telling them that 'ye may be at once rich and holy'.[13] We please God, Dod and Cleaver reassured their readers, by accepting 'his gifts when his gracious hand doth reach them out unto us'.[14] 'Doth not God say, He is worse than an infidel that provideth not for his family?' (I Timothy V.8). On the preceding page the authors had denounced 'fantastical companions' who will make a jest of it 'if any place of Scripture serve their turn'.[15] *The Ladies Calling* in 1673 went so far as to say that 'charity to myself may exceed that to my neighbours'.[16] Milton said something not so very different.

Yet there is a logic behind the Biblical selectiveness of the commentators. There was fairly general agreement that the prospects for the English economy were good only if a great deal of hard work was put in. 'Do they dream that godliness is like an alley in a garden, or a gallery in a house, to walk forward and to return back in for pleasure, and not a voyage for

10. Dod and Cleaver, *Proverbs*, Chapters XI–XII, pp. 2–3; Chapter XX.14, pp. 129–31; XX.10, p. 120.

11. Herbert, *Works* (ed. F. E. Hutchinson, Oxford U.P., 1941), p. 248.

12. Gouge, *A Commentary on the Whole Epistle to the Hebrews* (1655) (ed. Grosart, Edinburgh, 1865–7), I, pp. 212, 379; II, pp. 93–108; III, p. 290.

13. Hall, *Works*, V, p. 107; cf. VIII, p. 46.

14. Dod and Cleaver, *Proverbs*, p. 68 (X.6).

15. Dod and Cleaver, *Ten Commandments*, pp. 93–4.

16. Op. cit., in *Works of the Author of the Whole Duty of Man*, p. 125.

travail to be proceeded in till they come to heaven?' Industry is what matters: 'wealth not well managed is subject to waste'.[17]

This was especially true of the 'dark corners of the land'. If the Welsh people worked as hard as those in other countries, Thomas Churchyard told them in 1587, they could be as well off: a start has been made, but it will take a long time to throw off old habits.[18] Robert Burton generalized this point in his *Anatomy of Melancholy*. England has ample raw materials: 'only industry is wanting'. Hence beggars and vagabonds, for whom he had no pity.[19] St Paul's advice to 'redeem the season, for the days are evil' was a commercial metaphor, the Geneva margin pointed out (Ephesians V.16, Colossians IV.5).[20] It is 'not civility only', Joseph Hall wrote, 'but religion bids us to good husbandry. . . . What account can be given to our maker, if we never look after our own estate?' *The Whole Duty of Man*, in the very different post-restoration atmosphere, made a similar appeal to *gentlemen* to recognize the *duty* of improving their estates.[21]

Here religion was a useful watch-dog. 'He that obeyeth God with a good conscience', said Dod and Cleaver, *à propos* the Fourth Commandment, 'will labour for his master with an upright heart', even in his absence.[22] George Herbert's priest esteemed 'the great and national sin of this land . . . to be idleness'.[23] Richard Baxter took up the tale in his *Christian Directory* (1673): 'idleness is a crime not to be tolerated in Christian societies'.[24] Sylvester in his translation of Du Bartas had been at considerable pains to explain that God was not idle before the Creation.[25] In *Of Christian Doctrine* Milton collected texts stressing the importance of labour.[26] So closely linked was protestantism with the work ethic that Richard Sibbes thought popery had been set up 'to maintain stately idleness'.[27] The point

17. Dod and Cleaver, *Proverbs*, pp. 114 (XX.7), 70–73 (XIII.23), 123 (XIV.23). The pun in 'travail' was no doubt intended.

18. Churchyard, *The Worthiness of Wales* (1776 reprint), pp. 51–2.

19. Burton, op. cit. (Everyman ed.), I, pp. 90–104.

20. The Scot Robert Pont cited these texts ('redeem the time' in the A.V.) to incite his readers to industry (*A New Treatise on the Right Reckoning of Years and ages of the World*, 1599, pp. 93–104)

21. Hall, *Works*, I, p. 274; cf. II, pp. 419–20; *The Whole Duty of Man* (1704), I, pp. 419, 425, II, p. 284.

22. Dod and Cleaver, *Ten Commandments*, p. 146; cf. *Proverbs*, XXVII.23–4.

23. Herbert, *Works*, p. 274.

24. Baxter, *Chapters from a Christian Directory* (ed. J. Tawney, 1925), pp. 23, 41, 64.

25. J. Sylvester, *The Complete Works*, I, p. 84.

26. *MCPW*, VI, Book II, Chapters VIII–XVII, esp. pp. 728–32.

27. Sibbes, *Works*, I, pp. 91, 88

was regularly made that saints' days deduct fifty-two working days from the year. Monks were parasitic rentiers.[28]

Insistence on the necessity of hard work for the good of the commonwealth helps us to understand the brutal callousness of men like William Perkins towards vagabonds and the poor generally. All of the poor must labour for the commonwealth, wrote Dod and Cleaver: the good of the community is their good. They must ask themselves whether their poverty is not their own fault.[29] Rogues and vagabonds must be punished. Servants should obey their masters as if they were the greatest princes in the world.[30] Even Fuller suggested that 'Edward VI was as truly charitable in granting Bridewell for the punishment of sturdy rogues as in giving St Thomas's Hospital for the relief of the poor'.[31] Sibbes was unusual in arguing that the poor have a *right* to alms.[32]

The Homily against Idleness was also unusual in making a point which would seem obvious to us in our very different social circumstances: it criticized idle gentry as well as vagabonds.[33] Perkins did so too, logically enough; and Dod and Cleaver pointed out that those who refuse either to cultivate their land themselves, or to let others cultivate it, dry up the springs of the market and so depopulate the countryside.[34] Such points were not often emphasized until the radicals took them up in the more appropriate atmosphere of the revolutionary forties and fifties.

The Puritan and separatist congregations perhaps played a more important part in humanizing and cherishing the work ethic than has been appreciated. 'Vicinity and neighbourhood will fail, and alliance and kindred will fail, but grace and religion will never fail.' 'If we adjoin ourselves unto [the godly] for their virtue and goodness, they will not separate themselves from us for our calamities and troubles'.[35] The congregation established trading connections in time of prosperity, and provided social assurance in bad times. Vagabonds 'commonly are of no civil society or corporation, nor of any particular church'. They were outside church and commonwealth unless and until they could be

28. See my *Puritanism and Revolution*, pp. 220–22, 230–33, quoting Perkins.

29. Dod and Cleaver, *Proverbs*, XVIII.10 – pp. 10–11; X.4 – p. 64.

30. Dod and Cleaver, *Ten Commandments*, pp. 218–21, 169–70

31. Fuller, *The Holy State* (1841), p. 144. First published 1642.

32. Sibbes, *Works*, IV, p. 518.

33. *Homilies*, pp. 438–45.

34. Dod and Cleaver, *Proverbs*, XI.26 – pp. 92–3. The point recurs in Locke. Cf. p. 166 below.

35. Dod and Cleaver, *Proverbs*, XIV.26.

restored by labour discipline and hard work.[36] Just like the Irish, or the American Indians.

Dod and Cleaver affirmed stoutly that God 'doth prefer the poor'; and they asked 'Why should we give titles to ruffians and roysterers and idle companions?'[37] There was indeed an unfortunate verse in Acts (IV.32–7) which described community of property in the early Christian church. It worried some of the first reformers, but little attention was paid to it in print except to ridicule the idea of communism. We may speculate about the way in which Spenser and Shakespeare approach this subject: they seem to take for granted that it was being talked about:[38] but the early Christian model of communism received little published backing until Diggers, the anonymous author of *Tyranipocrit*[39] and Ranters dragged it into the open.

Many preferred to emphasize Christ's words, 'Ye have the poor always with you' (Matthew XXVI.11). Sir Thomas Browne blamed those who dreamed of abolishing poverty for forgetting this prophecy of Christ's.[40] 'The poor' rather than 'poor people' is a 'gentry-made term.'[41] It seemed to countenance the institutionalization of poverty by the Elizabethan Poor Law, and so to accept its inevitability. Indiscriminate personal charity may have encouraged professional beggars to haunt rich men's gates. But nothing was so cold as parish charity, or so meanly calculating. Boyd Berry quotes Arthur Dent's *The plaine mans Path-way to Heaven* (1610) to illustrate complaints by parsons of the hard and distasteful work involved in teaching and caring for the ignorant poor: no job for a scholar. Berry suggests that many parsons shared the state's desire to bureaucratize charity, discouraging personal alms-giving and replacing it by 'poor relief', administered by deacons: such relief could be used discriminately to enforce social control over the feckless and idle unemployed.[42]

Latimer had preached in 1550 on that favourite Lollard subject, the parable of Dives and Lazarus, to which Bunyan was to return. In 1551 Lever also preached on behalf of the poor, this time from Psalm XII. The

---

36. Perkins, *Workes*, I, p. 755; cf. III, p. 191 (first pagination). See my 'The Poor and the People' in *People and Ideas*.

37. Dod and Cleaver, *Proverbs*, XII.9, p. 140.

38. See especially Spenser's *Mother Hubberd's Tale*, and *The Faerie Queene*, V.1; Shakespeare *II Henry VI*.

39. Op. cit., esp. pp. 17, 30–33, 36, 45–54.

40. Browne, *Religio Medici* (1643), in *Works* (Bohn ed., 1852), II, p. 449.

41. Thompson, *Customs in Common*, p. 17.

42. Berry, 'Elizabethan Progressives, Puritan Self-Definition and the Silencing of the Poor', Millersville.

cause of protestantism was still thought to be linked to the relief of the poor.[43] Edward Elton, in his *Exposition of Colossians* (1615), justified the existing class-divided society in words which throughout the ages the haves have used to console the have-nots: 'God . . . out of sundry orders and degrees of men doth gather a sweet harmony and agreement'. But men must nevertheless be 'held in with the bridle of some greater authority and power. . . . When in the place where there should be justice there is wormwood, and in the place of judgment wickedness, yet therein appears the providence of God, who doth wisely order and dispose things . . . to . . . the preservation of the society of mankind. . . . Better a tyranny than an anarchy. . . . This may settle and stay our minds . . . when . . . justice and equity is bought and sold'. Reflect that the guilty will be punished in the after life if not earlier. 'Such as be of poor and mean condition in the world are to be cheered up in this'. Colossians III, laying down the duties of magistrates and subjects, husbands and wives, masters and servants, serves to rebuke 'the Anabaptistical fancy that all difference and distinction of men among Christians is taken away'. The rich must not succumb to guilt-feelings, however: 'works of mercy please not God which . . . are forced out from the gripe of a galled conscience. . . . We are to put on a sweet affection of heart towards all'.[44]

Thomas Manton thirty-eight years later was almost equally smug in dealing with the prohibition of respect for persons (James II.1–4). 'There is a respect due to the rich, though wicked', Manton observed; 'great men in the world have respect due to their place'. He was less eloquent in dealing with James's 'Weep and howl, . . . ye rich men . . .' (James V.1).[45]

The Puritan Richard Bernard used his commentary on Ruth to speak up for the poor against idle gentry as well as against the law's delays.[46] Richard Stock's posthumous *Learned . . . Commentary upon . . . Malachy* (1641) made Chapter III.8–11 the basis for an attack on impropriators and impropriations whilst defending tithes except in cities. Stock – rector of Milton's parish church of All Hallows, Bread Street, London – was famous for criticizing the unequal assessment of poor rates. He condemned usury, racking of rents and the class bias of the legal system. Malachi IV.3 enabled

43. Brigden, op. cit., pp. 320, 408–9. For Bunyan see his *A Few Sighs from Hell* (1658).

44. Elton, *An Exposition of the Epistle of St Paul to the Colossians*, pp. 13–14, 954–6, 963, 987–8.

45. Manton, *A Practical Commentary . . . on the Epistle of James* (1653), pp. 229–65, 515.

46. Bernard, *Ruths Recompense: or, A Commentary upon the Book of Ruth* (1628) (ed. Grosart, Edinburgh, 1865), pp. 35–7, 56–8, 93–4.

him to declare that 'the Lord ofttimes destroys the wicked, enemies of him and his church, by the hands of his church', who will tread them down in the dust.[47] Milton said something very similar in his *Of Christian Doctrine*.[48]

William Walwyn, in the mock confession which he attributed to Thomas Edwards, made that great persecutor admit to 'base fear that plain unlearned men should seek for knowledge any other way than as they are directed by us that are learned'. For 'if they should fall to teach one another, ... we should lose our domination in being sole judges of doctrine and discipline'.[49] Radicals like Winstanley and Coppe did not fail to emphasize and enlarge on such texts.[50] 'I command thee, to let Israel go free'. 'As the Scriptures threaten misery to rich men ... surely all those threatenings shall be materially fulfilled, for they shall be turned out of all'. 'As when the sun riseth with heat, then the grass withereth, and his flower falleth away; ... even so shall the rich man wither away' (James I.9–11).[51]

An alchemist and Ranter sympathizer, Lionel Lockier, published in 1652 a ballad on behalf of the poor. In this he attacked the saints who count 'all that hold community' to be Ranters. But

> To feed the hungry and naked clothe
> It is a work they much do loathe.

The real 'ranting sin' is committed

> When one riotously hath spent
> That which his fellow creatures want.
> But this the saints are frequent in.[52]

Levellers and other radicals opposed 'servile tenures' like copyhold, which they tried to get abolished, and the custom of primogeniture, which led to consolidation of estates in the hands of a few at the expense of the many. The words 'birthright' and 'inheritance', which figure largely in the story

47. Stock, op. cit. (ed. Grosart, Edinburgh, 1865), pp. 77–80, 113, 165, 223–34, 254. Cf. *MER*, pp. 24–5.
48. *MCPW*, VI, pp. 615–20, 743.
49. Walwyn, *A Prediction of Mr. Edwards his Confession* (1646), p. 9, in Haller, *Tracts on Liberty*, III.
50. See Chapter 8.
51. Sabine, pp. 389, 265, 181; cf. p. 260.
52. In *Cavalier and Puritan: Ballads and Broadsides . . . 1640–1660* (ed. H. E. Rollins, New York U.P., 1923), pp. 320–24; J. A. Mendelsohn, 'Alchemy and Politics in England, 1649–1665', *P. and P.*, 135 (1992).

of Esau and Jacob, were associated in the seventeenth century with land. The Bunyans, like countless other peasant families, had been selling parcels of land for generations. In *The Pilgrim's Progress* Christian seeks 'an inheritance . . . laid up in heaven', hopes to inhabit 'a kingdom of great plenty', where he will have a house of his own and all his material needs will be met.[53]

II

In one of the last books Bunyan published, *The Advocateship of Jesus Christ* (1688), he wrote of 'the man in Israel' who through poverty was forced to sell his land. Yet the Lord 'reserved to himself a right in the land', and in the year of Jubilee it was redistributed.[54] In Leviticus, Jubilee is 'the day of reconciliation, . . . joyful tidings of liberty'. In Ezekiel XLVI it is 'the year of liberty'. When the Jubilee occurred — at fifty-year intervals — bond-servants and debt-slaves were set free, lands and houses which had been sold were restored to their original owners.[55] Gervase Babington in 1604 suggested that the Jubilee principle of redistribution should be applied in time of plague and dearth.[56] Richard Sibbes described the year of Jubilee as 'the day of recovering all' for 'those that had their possessions taken away'. 'It was a comfortable year to servants that were kept in and were much vexed with their bondage. When the year of Jubilee came they were all freed. . . . Freedom out of bondage is a sweet message, . . . as Christ makes us free'.[57] Barrow had wanted lay patronage to be abolished, without compensation, together with impropriated tithes. 'Oh what a joy, what a jubilee, what a happy day were this to the whole land!'[58]

The approach of the year 1600 prompted Robert Pont to denounce 'the counterfeited jubilee holden at Rome', and to contrast 'the true jubilee and spiritual liberty purchased unto us by our Saviour Christ' — 'remission from the spiritual debt of sin'. This redefinition of Jubilee had the double

53. *PP*, pp. 55, 119, 155, 176, 187, 237–8, 303.
54. *BMW*, XI, pp. 183–6: Leviticus XXV; cf. Perkins, *An Exposition of the Creed*, in *Workes*, I, p. 220.
55. Ainsworth, *Annotations Upon . . . Leviticus* (1618), Chapter XXV. Cf. Deuteronomy XV.1 and Jeremiah XXXIV.16. See Linebaugh, 'Jubilating' in *The New Enclosures* (New York, Fall 1990), pp. 84–97.
56. Babington, *Exodus and Leviticus*, pp. 200–203: upon Leviticus XXV.9.
57. Sibbes, *The Spiritual Jubilee* (1638), in *Works*, V, p. 446: posthumously published in 1639: cf. p. 236. See also Jeremiah Burroughs, *An Exposition of the Prophesie of Hosea* (1643), pp. 412–28.
58. *The Writings of Henry Barrow, 1587–1590* (ed. L. H. Carlson, 1962), pp. 237–9.

advantage of rejecting sordid popish money-raising indulgences, whilst not encouraging false hopes of land-redistribution. Pont believed 'the latter day' was approaching.[59] The author of a popularization of Napier's work on Revelation, published in 1641 as 'a subject very seasonable for these last times', declared that the four angels in Revelation XIV divided the last age by jubilees, appearing at intervals of forty-nine years.[60]

Preachers of Fast Sermons also accepted the connection of the Jubilee with the millennium. The Scot George Gillespie, preaching to the House of Commons on 27 March 1644, spoke of 'the acceptable year of Israel's jubilee, and the day of vengeance upon Antichrist', which was 'now coming and is not far off'.[61] William Reyner five months later, following Napier, quoted Revelation XI.15: 'the seventh angel sounds a Jubilee, and then there be great proclamations and acclamations in heaven, that the kingdoms of the world . . . are become Christ's kingdoms', as Antichrist is overthrown.[62] In February 1649–50 Vavasor Powell declared that 'this year 1650 . . . is to be the saints' year of jubilee', according to the interpretation of 'most godly writers upon Daniel'.[63] Bunyan appears to equate the Jubilee with the day of Judgment, which he expected in the near future.[64]

In what appears to be a rather liberal interpretation of Leviticus XXV, the near-Digger pamphlet *Light Shining in Buckinghamshire* (December 1648) declared that 'in Israel, if a man were poor, then a public maintenance and stock was to be provided to raise him again. So would all bishops' lands, forest lands and crown lands do in our land, which the apostate Parliament men give to one another, and to maintain the needless thing called a King. And every seven years the whole land was for the poor, the fatherless, widows and strangers, and at every crop a portion allowed them'.[65] William Aspinwall in 1656 called for the cancellation of debts after seven years, in accordance with Old Testament law, which would be the only authority in the millennium.[66] Harrington was careful to point out that his agrarian law was exactly modelled on the Biblical jubilee which preserved 'the proper balance' of property.[67] But the word came to be used in a looser

59. Pont, op. cit., pp. 2, 5, 22–33, 83–92.
60. [Anon.], *Napiers Narration: or, An Epitome of his Books on the Revelation*, sig. B 2–3.
61. *FS*, X, p. 152.
62. Ibid., XI, p. 184.
63. Ibid., XXXIII, p. 232.
64. *BMW*, XI, pp. 183–6. Cf. Hosea IX.5, Amos V.18–20; Zephaniah I.
65. In Sabine, p. 616.
66. Aspinwall, *The Legislative Power is Christs Peculiar Prerogative*, pp. 30–32.
67. See pp. 191–3 below.

sense to describe moments of emancipation. Milton called the dismissal of Archbishop Laud 'the very jubilee and resurrection of the state'.[68] William Chamberlayne gave the title of *Englands Jubilee* to a poem celebrating the restoration of Charles II.[69]

The underlying concept of the jubilee was that the land is God's, the Hebrew people merely his tenants: any sale of land was limited to the period ending with the next jubilee (Leviticus XXV.10–17). This prevented the accumulation of land into a few hands, rather as Harrington's agrarian law was intended to do. Locke retained the view that the land belonged to God; the legal owner had an obligation to maintain the needy from its proceeds. If an owner did not cultivate land he had occupied those in need had a right to seize it – a right which Diggers had exercised. Diodati's *Annotations* had declared that the land 'must always remain as by perpetual improvements unto those to whom God has given it'.[70] One can imagine the power of this idea for the English peasantry as their land was being taken away from them (cf. Chapter 5 above).

À propos the Jubilee, Matthew Henry observed in 1706 that 'never was any people so secured in their liberty and property (those glories of a people) as Israel was'. But he noted that the restoration of land in the year of jubilee would lead to discounts in the earlier selling price of land (Leviticus XXV).[71] We are in the world of eighteenth-century nonconformity. But the idea of the jubilee survived. 'Was not the Jewish Jubilee a Levelling scheme?' asked the Scottish radical supporter of the American Revolution, James Murray, in 1775.[72] The jubilee played a big part in the writings of Thomas Spence, who was 'the unfee'd advocate of the disinherited seed of Adam'. For him and his followers the jubilee had millenarian associations. Spence wrote in 1795 'A song to be sung at the end of oppression or the commencement of the political millennium, when there shall be neither Lord nor landlords, but God and man will be all in all'.

> Hark! how the trumpet's sound
> Proclaims the land around
> The jubilee. . . .

68. *MCPW*, I, p. 669. Cf. III, p. 348, VI, p. 884. Cf. Vaughan, *Poems*, II, p. 447.
69. Reprinted in Saintsbury, *Minor Poets of the Caroline Period* (Oxford U.P., 1905–21), I, pp. 297–303.
70. J. Diodati, *Pious and Learned Annotations upon the Holy Bible* (2nd ed., 1651), sig. M 3.
71. Henry, *An Exposition on the Old and New Testaments* (4th ed., 1737).
72. Quoted by Malcolm Chase, 'From Millennium to Anniversary: the Concept of Jubilee in late 18th- and 19th-century England', *P. and P.*, 129 (1990), p. 135.

> This jubilee
> Sets all at liberty. . . .
> Let us be glad.[73]

'Jubilee' was used by William Benbow for a national strike, 'a grand national holiday'.[74] 'Sir William Courtenay', leader of 'the last agricultural labourers' rising' in 1838, told his followers that 'the great jubilee was to come, and we must be with 'em'. 'I am going for a jubilee'. Courtenay was a millenarian of sorts.[75] There is still much research to be done on the underground flowing of this tradition from the seventeenth century to its reappearance in the late eighteenth and nineteenth centuries.[76] In our own day the Nicaraguan Minister of Culture, himself a priest, reports a discussion with peasants in which one of them said 'the holy or jubilee year now means that people go to Rome to pray in the churches and receive a papal blessing. But the holy year should be agrarian reform and the socialization of all means of production'. Another peasant added 'A holy year is what's been done in Cuba'.[77]

III

The Jubilee was seen as a remedy for those thousands of families which – like the Bunyans – were having to sell land to make ends meet.[78] A linked issue in the traditional society of seventeenth-century England was usury. There has been much discussion of usury in England by historians, starting from Weber, and Tawney's edition of Sir Thomas Wilson's *Discourse on Usury*: I shall not add to it. But the issues were linked in ancient Israel too. The same chapter of Leviticus which provided for the Jubilee also laid it

---

73. Sung to the tune of 'God Save the King'. *The Political Works of Thomas Spence* (ed. H. T. Dickinson, Newcastle upon Tyne, 1982), p. 38; T. R. Knox, 'Thomas Spence: The Trumpet of Jubilee', *P. and P.*, 76 (1977); Linebaugh, op. cit., p. 85.

74. Benbow, *Grand National Holiday* (1832). Cf. Peter Linebaugh, 'All the Atlantic Mountains Shook', in *Reviving the English Revolution* (ed. G. Eley and W. Hunt, 1988), p. 214.

75. B. Reay, 'The last rising of the agricultural labourers: the Battle of Bossenden Wood', *History Workshop Journal*, 26 (1988), pp. 87–8.

76. Cf. J. F. C. Harrison, *The Second Coming: Popular Millenarianism, 1780–1850* (1979).

77. Ernesto Cardenal, *Love in Practice: The Gospel in Solentinane* (English translation, 1977), pp. 128 sqq., quoted by Christopher Rowland, *Radical Christianity* (New York, 1988), pp. 132, 183.

78. See my *A Turbulent, Seditious and Factious People*, Chapter 4.

down that usury should not be taken from the poor (XXV.36), repeating God's prohibition in Exodus XXII.25. Usury was permissible only in dealings with strangers (Deuteronomy XXV.19–20). Ezekiel thought that usurers should die the death (XVIII.8, 13, 17; XXII.12). 'Forgive us our debts,' said Christ; 'even as we forgive our debtors' (Matthew VI.12). But the Geneva margin observed that the steward who wrote off half his master's debts was guilty of 'naughty dealing, . . . very theft'.

The New Testament did not forbid practices which arose some fifteen centuries later. In sixteenth- and seventeenth-century England loans were essential to smallholders to bridge the gap between harvests, for independent craftsmen and petty traders needing capital if they were to survive. This is the 'usury' which most concerned those preachers who discussed it,[79] rather than the needs of big merchant exporters which economists had in mind. It was a man of affairs like Bacon who pointed to the necessity of loan-capital for fen-drainage as well as for long-distance trade.

There was a great deal of opposition to usury, from Crowley,[80] theologians like John Udall, John Jewel,[81] Bishop Sanderson,[82] satirists like Joseph Hall,[83] economists like Sir Thomas Colpeper,[84] poets like John Marston and Henry Vaughan ('Guard the dirt, and that bright idol hold/ Close, and commit adultery with gold').[85] A great scandal arose about Matthew Hutton, Dean of York, who was alleged in the 1580s to be a noted usurer as well as a favourer of papists.[86] It is perhaps significant that a great increase in usury cases coming before the church courts in the diocese of York is reported from this time.[87]

---

79. H. C. White, *Social Criticism in Popular Religious Literature of the Sixteenth Century* (New York, 1944), pp. 198–212.

80. Crowley, *Select Works*, pp. 41–2, 49–51, 125, citing Psalm XV.

81. Jewel, *An Exposition upon the two Epistles of the Apostle Paul to the Thessalonians* in *Works*, II (Parker Soc., 1847), pp. 51–61, discussing I Thessalonians V. 6. Jewel deals especially with those who claimed a right to 'do with mine own goods what I will'.

82. Sanderson, *XXV Sermons* (1681), pp. 23–4.

83. Hall, *Virgidemiarum* (1599), Book IV. But Hall later described usury as a bad practice now tolerated (*Works*, VI, pp. 35–6; cf. VII, pp. 372–81).

84. Colpeper, *Tract against Usury* (1621).

85. Marston, *Poems* (ed. A. Davenport, Liverpool U.P., 1961), p. 74; Vaughan, 'To his friend . . .' in *Works*, I, p. 45; cf. 'In Amicum foeneratorem', ibid., pp. 43–4.

86. J. Strype, *Annals of the Reformation . . . during Queen Elizabeth's happy reign* (1824), III, Part I, pp. 469–72.

87. J. S. Purvis, *Tudor Parish Documents of the Diocese of York* (Cambridge U.P., 1948), p. 200.

Much causistry was used. Dod and Cleaver on the Eighth Commandment thought that the borrower ought to recompense the lender, and that the latter might receive interest 'as a gracious fruit of God's love'.[88] William Harrison in his *Description of England* (1587) had said that usury was so common that 'he is accounted but for a fool that doth lend his money for nothing'.[89] Thomas Adams in 1619 said of usury 'books have been written to justify it', though not to his satisfaction.[90] Usury 'must not now be called a sin', complained Thomas Scott satirically in 1623; 'it is justified out of the pulpit to be none'.[91] Richard Bernard four years later recognized that usury had been 'brought under opinion, as lawful some way'.[92] Robert Burton regarded usury as prevalent, and assumed that some kinds of it must be tolerated.[93] Paul Baynes, Perkins's successor at St Andrew's Church, Cambridge, pointed out in his *Commentary upon Ephesians* that usurers, like astrologers and alchemists, were not productive members of the commonwealth.[94] In 1634 John Blaxton summed up the Biblicists' case against usury, citing more than two score texts against it. 'The usurer sinneth by idolatry', since its root is covetousness (Ephesians V.5, Matthew VI.24, XIX.8). He quoted Wither's allegation that landlords were griping usurers.[95] Nathanael Homes in *Usury is Injury* (1640) rejected Ames's defence of some types of usury in his *Conscience with the power and cases thereof* (English translation 1639).[96]

Meanwhile the Old Testament prohibition of usury was further undermined by the protestant emphasis on the motives of the individual conscience, which Perkins declared that no law can bind.[97] He and Locke made the sin of usury an internal matter: it all depended on how the usurer felt about it. In the long run the pressures of society proved decisive. But the perplexity of the commentators, their desire to distinguish between

---

88. Dod and Cleaver, *Ten Commandments*, pp. 284–5.
89. Harrison, op. cit. (ed. F. J. Furnival, n.d.), p. 121.
90. Adams, *The Happiness of the Church*, pp. 117–18, 143–6.
91. Scott, *The High-Waies of God and the King* (1623), p. 75.
92. Bernard, *The Isle of Man* (1803 reprint), pp. 75–6; first published 1627.
93. Burton, *The Anatomy of Melancholy*, I, p. 106; cf. p. 55.
94. Baynes, *Commentary upon . . . Ephesians*, p. 293, discussing Ephesians IV.28: 'let him that stole steal no more: but let him rather labour and work with his hands'. (Published posthumously in 1642.)
95. Blaxton, *The English Usurer, or Usury Condemned* (Oxford U.P.), pp. 1, 26, 83 and *passim*.
96. Homes, op. cit., p. 52.
97. Perkins, *Workes*, II, p. 116; I, p. 63.

'biting' usury and the tolerable sort, relates not only to ambiguities in the Bible but also to the different social interests involved in England itself. Selden was caustic at the expense of preachers who denounced the usury which the law permitted.[98]

Two examples. Sir Simonds D'Ewes's father made money by lending at interest, but came bitterly to repent of it. Sir Simonds himself regarded usury as unlawful,[99] and in November 1641 insisted on the word 'damages' being used rather than interest when a loan was being raised for the reconquest of Ireland – a cause of which D'Ewes approved.[100] (The act of 1624 had side-stepped the Bible's prohibition by use of the word 'damages'.) John Milton was the son of a scrivener, whose profession included money-lending, and who seems to have done well enough out of it to finance his son in relative idleness for many years. John Milton thought money-lending was no more reprehensible in itself than any other kind of civil contract. But he recognized that it was a controversial subject. 'It is a violation of justice to charge excessive interest', he wrote; 'and if the loan is made to a poor man, any interest at all is excessive.'[101]

So for Milton, as for Perkins and Locke, usury from being central and contentious, became something morally neutral – bad if used against the poor or maliciously, but perhaps permissible in the interests of overseas trade or drainage schemes, both necessary for national prosperity. By Locke's time there was no longer any need to explain away the Bible on this subject:[102] it was just forgotten. But in consequence reform of the law of debt was always prominent in radical programmes, from Levellers to Fifth Monarchists and Quakers.[103]

98. Selden, *Table-Talk*, pp. 218–19; cf. Roger Williams, *The Bloudy Tenent*, pp. 139–40.
99. D'Ewes, *Autobiography and Correspondence*, I, pp. 43–4, 322.
100. Ed. W. H. Coates, *Journal of Sir Simonds D'Ewes* (Yale U.P., 1942), p. 63.
101. *MCPW*, VI, pp. 775–8.
102. See my 'Protestanism and the Rise of Capitalism' in *Change and Continuity*; cf. W. Letwin, *The Origins of Scientific Economics in English Economic Thought, 1660–1776* (1963), pp. 81–2.
103. I must make it clear that in discussing the jubilee and usury I rely on what seventeenth-century persons claim to have found in the Bible. I have no expertise on the realities of life in the relevant Old Testament period. For my purposes they do not matter.

7. Political Divisions and the Civil War; Liberty and Libertinism

=====

I gave them a king in my anger, and took him away in my wrath.
Hosea XIII.11. God is speaking.

> Not all the water in the rude rough sea
> Can wash the balm off an anointed king. . . .

> With mine own tears I wash away my balm.

Shakespeare, *The Tragedy of King Richard the Second*, Act III, sc. ii; Act IV, sc. i.

> Even kings are but more splendid servants.

Owen Feltham, *Resolves, Divine, Morall and Politicall* (Temple Classics, 1904), p. 15, reprinting the second (enlarged) edition of 1628.

I

It is not my concern to write an account of seventeenth-century political theory. Even to discuss the role of the Bible in such theories would be a vast subject. I can only touch on a few questions in which the role of the Bible seems to me especially important. There is a relation between the government of the congregation and the government of the state. Criticisms of the Church of England, made both by conforming Puritans and by separatists, turned largely on discipline. Discipline was not a 'thing indifferent', as defenders of the hierarchy claimed. If an 'exact pattern' of discipline was laid down in the New Testament, as Walter Travers believed,[1] it must be enforced, by the magistrate as well as by the church. This was of course practical politics as well as Biblicism: Elizabethan Puritans had no doubt

---

1. Brachlow, op. cit., pp. 21–2, 29–30. I have drawn heavily upon this valuable book for what follows.

that popular popery could not be crushed in England without the cooperation of the secular power. Separatists like Henry Barrow and John Robinson insisted that the magistrate's sword should root out idolatry and compel individuals to attend church where their consciences could be freely persuaded to *choose* the way of faith. How else? Robert Browne, Robert Harrison and Barrow all appear to have favoured capital punishment for idolaters. People must be forced to be free, forced to think for themselves, with the aid of godly preachers. So discipline came to be regarded as a mark of the true church, in addition to the traditional preaching of the Word and correct administration of the sacraments.[2]

Since the ecclesiastical ordinances believed to have been laid down in the New Testament were given the force of Biblical law, breach of them was regarded as idolatry, a violation of the Second Commandment. Barrow, Henry Jacob and Robinson can all be quoted to this effect. It was a main ground for separation from the state church.[3] For Robinson discipline was a fence protecting the saints from the spiritual wilderness of the world: the church is a 'walled orchard'. For him discipline was designed to ensure that the judgment of the congregation prevailed over that of the individual, so giving him a greater sense of spiritual security.[4]

But here we encounter problems. How far does the emphasis on the congregation outweigh the rights and duties of the individual conscience? The separatist congregations gave real power to the (male) lay members of congregations, but they also demanded a higher level of authority for the ministry, including elders. It was a mixed monarchy, combining the kingship of Christ with the aristocracy of elders and a democracy of lay members of the congregation. The idea of mixed monarchy emerged in political theory at about the same time.[5] The exact balance of the mixture was no easier to determine in the church than in the state. Brachlow has illustrated at length the evasions and tergiversations to which this led, and the shifts in emphasis dictated by controversial tactics. Popular sovereignty was emphasized when criticizing the Anglican hierachy; the role of elders was stressed when on the defensive against charges of 'anarchy' and 'confu-

2. Ibid., pp. 21–2, 265–6, 116–17.
3. Ibid., pp. 43, 52, 57, 66–7.
4. Ibid., pp. 147–9. Cf. pp. 140–41 above.
5. C. Russell, *The Fall of the British Monarchies*, pp. 121–2. Russell sees Lord Saye and Sele as developing a theory of the sovereignty of mixed monarchy in 1642.

sion'. In either case power flowed originally from God but mediately through the congregation, the community.[6]

Elders act with the knowledge and approval of the church. At elections, Travers suggested, the elders advise before the people elect. Discipline is also monarchical, aristocratic and democratic. The key text was Matthew XVIII.17, 'Tell it unto the church'. Does this refer to the elders, who, the Geneva margin tells us, 'in those days . . . had the judgment of church matters in their hands (John IX.22, XII.42 and XVI.2)'? Or does it refer to the people? Cartwright thought that I Corinthians V.4 gave 'the active judgment' in disciplinary matters to the whole congregation; but he was controverting Whitgift at the time. Democratic meanings could be found in the Bible; but we must not give *carte blanche* to democracy. As Travers put it, 'if all men were so taught of God that they could know and judge of these things', there would be no need of elders to 'govern and direct the judgments of the people' against 'confusion and uproars'. But as things are, he added, this was 'rather to be wished than hoped or looked for'.[7] So Puritan theory raised expectations which were dashed by ministerial practice.

Radical theologians wrestled with this problem. John Smyth the Se-Baptist thought that only spiritually gifted men could be lawfully elected to office in the church; Browne and Barrow agreed with him here. But who decided what was lawful? How were spiritually gifted men identified? Presumably by those 'men of best gifts' who had already been chosen by the congregation. All church actions, Francis Johnson declared, were to be done 'in order', with due respect for a ministerial or social hierarchy. Henry Ainsworth agreed that 'all church actions' must 'be orderly carried out, either by the officers if there be any, or by the fathers of families, or the most excellent in gifts requested thereunto by the congregation. . . . This we firmly maintain against all popular confusion and disorder whatsoever'. No chance there of a revolt by the younger members of the congregation, still less of a revolt by women. If a charge is brought against an elder, this 'ought chiefly to be done by elders of that church,' declared Barrow. Ainsworth thought that the people can dissent, but if 'in matter or manner they transgress' they are to bear the rebuke of the elders. It was not easy to draw theoretically satisfactory lines in these eminently practical problems.[8]

---

6. Brachlow, op. cit., pp. 152, 157, 160. See also R. Tuck, 'Power and Authority in 17th-century England', *Historical Journal*, 17 (1974), pp. 43–61.
7. Brachlow, op. cit., pp. 166–8.
8. Ibid., pp. 180–85.

Henry Parker, William Ames, Henry Ainsworth and Henry Jacob distinguished between *possessing* and *exercising* power. Elections were theoretically made, and discipline was theoretically administered, by the people; in fact by the ministry, including the elders. There was a danger that the congregation's 'free consent' might turn into a rubber stamp. Robinson followed the Geneva margin in interpreting Acts VI to mean that the people chose those whom the elders thought fit. In dealing with scandalous sins judgment would rest with the elders, the male members of the congregation 'manifesting their assent thereunto by some convenient word or sign, and the women by silence'. Even the congregation's hold on the church's purse-strings may not have been an effective check, since final control over voluntary contributions lay with the ruling group. The elders could never in theory establish permanent rule against the will of the people, who like a jury possessed an ultimate power of veto which the judge could not over-rule, says Professor Brachlow;[9] but many seventeenth-century judges managed it, and so one must suspect did many ruling groups in separatist congregations. The only real sanction was that all were free to leave the congregation if they so wished.

Such ideas had political analogies. If office in the church was due to 'spiritually-gifted men', so in the state 'the natural rulers' naturally ruled: the main difference was that JPs were not elected, and until well on into the seventeenth century Parliamentary elections were formal occasions, confirming decisions taken elsewhere by the gentry. A further analogy between church and state is that Calvinist − like Hobbist − doctrines of the depravity of natural man led logically to authoritarian theories, whether of sovereignty in the state or of discipline in the church. Clerically-imposed discipline, whether Anglican or Presbyterian, was assumed to be essential to social and political order. The evil majority must be controlled, kept in subordination, or anarchy would result. As Baxter put it, majority government would make 'the seed of the Serpent' 'sovereign rulers', who hate ministers and magistrates.[10] Hence too the idea − shared by Charles I and Oliver Cromwell − that any stable government needs a clergy dependent on it. So separatist sectarianism, or abolition of tithes, must be a recipe for anarchy.

The analogy with 'democratic centralism' in the Communist parties of eastern Europe comes to mind. But this also suggests that we should not be too hastily condemnatory. The congregations in the early seventeenth

---

9. Ibid., pp. 172, 178, 186−8, 190, 198, 201.
10. Baxter, *A Holy Commonwealth* (1659), pp. 92−4, 226−31.

century, like the Soviet C.P. in the 1920s, formed a minority in an unfriendly world, whose strength lay in its agreement and its solidarity. In such circumstances 'democratic centralism' was more likely to be acceptable than later, when the crisis had passed and the pressures of conformity had set in. It is easier for us to condemn the ultimate weakness of the system than to allow for its initial advantages. Political theorists in the seventeenth century had to work out how 'the people' were to be defined in practice. Could the vote safely be given to all men, when so many were dependent on landlords and employers and could hardly ignore their wishes when voting in open court? But on what rational grounds could one distinguish between 'all men' and 'all free men', all rational men, or men free to act on reason's dictates?

In the Putney Debates of 1647 Levellers disagreed with one another, publicly. Flourishes about the rights of 'every man', 'the poorest he' were balanced by suggestions that those economically dependent might not qualify for the vote – the poor, for instance, apprentices and living-in servants. Harrington speaks regularly of government being based on 'the people', but in his ideal commonwealth servants are not citizens, and only the yeomanry, not the peasantry in general, were part of the people.[11] Algernon Sidney, James Tyrrell and John Locke agreed.[12] In New England, where church and state had emigrated together, exclusion from church membership meant exclusion from the franchise. In the Parliamentary Ordinance of 1646 which set up a Presbyterian state church, elders were to be elected by members of congregations who were not 'servants that have no families'.[13] In 1650 John Price, separatist and one-time Leveller supporter, decided after some experience that the rule of the Great Turk would be better than that of 'the rabble rout'.[14]

Nathanael Homes in the same year shared this panic fear of 'popular parity' which Levellers, Diggers and Ranters had instilled into middle-of-the-road millenarians. 'My heart trembles to think of . . . a living anarchy to which these times . . . much incline among the multitude'. But he also disliked 'the Scotified party'. Safest, he thought, would be 'a regular democracy', with some aristocratic elements. What he meant by democracy

11. Harrington, *Political Works* (ed. J. G. A. Pocock, Cambridge U.P., 1977), pp. 436–7, 764, 786–8.
12. Sidney, *Discourses Concerning Government* (1698), p. 79; Tyrrell, *Patriarcha non monarcha* (1681), pp. 73–4, 83–4, 118; Locke, *Works* (1823), V, p. 71.
13. C. H. Firth and R. S. Rait, *Acts and Ordinances of the Interregnum* (1911), I, p. 749.
14. John Price, *The Cloudie Clergie*, p. 14.

is suggested by his argument that the 'superstructure' of English government already contained many democratic elements – juries, elected MPs; kings had been deposed by 'the people' before the Norman Conquest. God had settled his decree against monarchy by Daniel II, in which Nebuchadnezzar's dream was interpreted. 'The time is now at hand', Homes concluded, 'to dethrone monarchy and to raise democracy according to Psalm CXLIX' ('to bind their kings in chains and their nobles with fetters of iron. . . . This honour shall be to all his saints' – verses 8–9). Rule should henceforth be by 'the people of the saints', who would subdue kings, nobles and nations (Scotland and Ireland in this case). 'If the great Dons will not be fit for place of magistrates, a choosing from among the Holy people must'.[15] This offers a clue to what 'the people' could mean in loose phraseology. But there was (and is) a real dilemma for democrats here. Locke, who these days is sometimes linked more closely with the Levellers than he used to be, is perpetually ambiguous about who are and are not people. To be a 'person' 'belongs only to intelligent agents capable of a law and happiness and misery'. How are 'persons' to be defined for political purposes? Being a rational creature for Locke involves – among other things – belief in the existence of God. But Locke continually slides from 'the people' to the electorate, as when he says that William III's title to the throne was made good 'in the consent of the people', which is the only foundation for 'all lawful governments'.[16] The 'consent' to William's title was just as much rubber-stamped as anything that happened in sectarian congregations.

We can broaden our canvas. Shelley in 1817 admitted that 'the consequences of the immediate extension of the elective franchise to every male adult would be to place power in the hands of men who have been rendered brutal and torpid and ferocious by ages of slavery'.[17] A Leveller would have recognized that heart-felt cry. Those who discussed democracy in seventeenth-century congregations could usually assume that a sifting process had taken place by the establishment of their church; perhaps we may flatter ourselves that in our day education has reduced the numbers of brutal and torpid and ferocious men: not to mention the enfranchisement of women. But it is not totally absurd to suggest that the role of the elders who decide and whose decisions are taken over by 'the people' is performed

---

15. Homes, *A Sermon Preached before the . . . Lord Maior* (and other London dignitaries) on a day of thanksgiving for the victory of Dunbar (1650), pp. 32–42.
16. Ashcraft, *Locke's Two Treatises of Government*, pp. 37, 47.
17. Shelley, *A Proposal for Putting Reform to the Vote*, in *Prose Works* (1912), I, p. 365.

in our society by the media. The main difference is in the way in which spokesmen of the latter find their way to such powerful positions: unlike elders, they are not elected.

A different political theory point relates to the moral economy, about which Edward Thompson has written so authoritatively. 'There is a deeply-felt conviction', he tells us, 'that prices *ought*, in times of dearth, to be regulated, that the profiteer puts himself out of society'.[18] That idea can be found in Locke, but – like so much in Locke – it goes back ultimately to the Bible which helped to fortify the 'deeply-felt convictions' of pre-capitalist men and women.

In 1556 John Ponet objected that St Peter's 'servants obey your masters' cannot be applied to *free* subjects under a king.[19] The concept of freedom in the sixteenth and seventeenth centuries still had overtones of freedom from servile status. The summary sentence which we often meet in court records, 'No goods; to be whipped', signified two things. First, that the condemned person was not worth fining, since he had no property; secondly that he was an unfree person, who *could* be whipped. Gentlemen – like the Roman citizen St Paul – should not be whipped. Edward Floyd, who in 1621 had said rude things about the Elector Palatine and his wife the Princess Elizabeth, was sentenced by the House of Commons to be whipped at a cart's tail, but only after he had been degraded from his gentry and declared 'an ignominious and base fellow'.[20]

Hence Lilburne's insistence on being accepted as a gentleman by courts before which he appeared. It had added insult to injury that he had himself been flogged through the streets of London under Laud. Just as anyone who disliked bishops had come to be dubbed a 'Puritan', so anyone who opposed the government had to emphasize his 'free' status. Semantic usage had political consequences: class and political status were determined by words and names. Coke's 'Lo, I thou thee, thou traitor!' hissed at Ralegh during his trial was intended as a *social* insult. To be freeborn – a freeholder, or free of a corporation – was vital if you were to have any say in how the country was governed. Sir Thomas Smith had summed it up succinctly:

18. Thompson, 'The Moral Economy of the English Crowd in the Eighteenth Century', *P. and P.*, 50 (1971), pp. 112, 131–2. See now his *Customs in Common*, Chapters IV and V.
19. Ponet, *A Treatise of Politike Power* (1642 reprint), p. 23. The date of the reprint is interesting.
20. *The Diary of Sir Richard Hutton*, pp. 36–7. See George Whitehead, *The Path of the Just Cleared* (1655), p. 7; cf. Pierre Bonnassie, *From Slavery to Feudalism in South-Western Europe*, p. 334. For St Paul see Acts XXII.25.

'day labourers, poor husbandmen, yea merchants or retailers which have no free land, copyholders and all artificers . . . have no voice nor authority in our commonwealth, and no account is made of them, but only to be ruled'.[21] John Cotton compared the conditions attached to the covenant of grace to those of becoming 'a free man of a corporation', by apprenticeship.[22] 'Free' meant privileged; freedom went with property. What was novel in the 1640s was the fact that the unprivileged, men without the university degree which conferred gentility, now had access to the printing press. Peter Bulkley likened the Gospel covenant to that between king and people. God effectively allowed himself to become a constitutional monarch, so why not Charles? Perry Miller, in citing Bulkley, drew attention to the parallels between the covenant theology and contract theories of politics, whilst admitting the difficulty of saying which was cause and which effect.[23]

Hence the importance of the New Model Army's claim, on the eve of taking political action, to be 'no mere mercenary army'; they were volunteers not conscripts, free citizens in uniform. But semantic usage did not tell you where exactly boundary lines between the free and the unfree were to be drawn. We saw the Levellers getting into difficulties in the Putney Debates when they called for the vote for all free men.[24] Hence Sir Thomas Aston's sneer, 'some of them say, the Gospel hath made them free'.[25] Popular interpretations of the New Testament could overrule the conventionally accepted status and subordination of a hierarchical society. This was indeed revolutionary. As Winstanley put it, 'freedom is the man that will turn the world upside down; therefore no wonder he hath enemies'. 'Will you be beggars still and slaves when you may be freemen?' the Diggers asked.[26] Thomas Edwards had noted in 1646 that 'instead of legal rights and the laws and customs of this nation, the sectaries talk and plead for natural rights and liberties such as men have from their birth'.[27] That was a decisive break from the past, made with the help of the Bible. When we come to consider antinomianism, freedom from laws, we must

21. Smith, *The Commonwealth of England* (ed. L. Alston, 1906), Book I, Chapter 24.
22. Cotton, *The Covenant of Gods Free Grace* (1645), pp. 19–20.
23. Bulkley, *The Gospel-Covenant, or the Covenant of Grace* (1646), pp. 219–20; Perry Miller, *Errand into the Wilderness*, pp. 90–92; cf. pp. 38–40, 63–7, 85. See my *Puritanism and Revolution*, Chapter 7, and *People and Ideas in 17th-century England*, Chapter 14.
24. See p. 175 above.
25. Aston, *A Remonstrance against Presbytery*, sig. 1, 4v; cf. p. 156 above.
26. Sabine, pp. 316, 408.
27. Edwards, *Gangraena*, III, p. 20.

recall that for some this meant freedom from social and political laws as well as moral laws.[28] The Ranters Clarkson and Coppe claimed freedom from both.

John Hall of Richmond, writing well after the event, took a firmly Biblical stand. He declared flatly that 'unto my strictest enquiry, there could not be found one text in the Bible countenancing and maintaining any other form' of government than monarchy. That remarkable assertion would have surprised Harrington, who collected innumerable texts in favour of a commonwealth. No text in the Bible, Hall continued, defends the power of the people, or the nobility, Parliaments or Senators. Hall describes how, 'in the beginning of our unhappy troubles' he was 'tainted . . . with the Pharisaical humour of judging for myself'; he accepted 'all those fine maxims and rules of examination which . . . were set on foot for trial and control of the actions of princes'. 'A king beset with all these limitations did look like a duck in a garden, brought to eat up snails and worms, and then tied up by the leg, for fear of trampling over the flowers'.[29] The metaphor is even more disrespectful than Selden's 'A king is a thing men have made for their own sakes, for quietness-sake. Just as in a family one man is appointed to buy the meat'.[30] But Selden meant it.

Republicans, Hall tells us, said that if monarchy was plainly and clearly advocated in Scripture, it would 'have overthrown our liberty' – since there would be no choice – and 'endangered the loss of God's honour' by facilitating 'a kind of idolatry of princes.' Hall himself was in favour of accepting any *de facto* authority. On the other hand there must be no religious toleration, which he thought inevitably leads to civil war.[31] Unsophisticated Hobbism.

II

The New Testament is full of libertarian ideas which could make a great impression on people turning to it for guidance in time of political or social oppression. Whatever the meaning for the original readers, uneducated men and women studying the Bible for themselves for the first time could see an immediate political relevance in the following texts, abstracted from

28. See pp. 180–82 below.
29. Hall, *Of Government and Obedience*, sig. b; pp. 434–5.
30. Selden, *Table-Talk*, p. 97. Cf. Feltham, cited as epigraph to this chapter.
31. Hall, op. cit., pp. 391–2.

their historical context. 'In Christ there is neither bond nor free, neither male nor female', St Paul told the Galatians (III.28); 'stand fast in the liberty wherewith Christ hath made you free, and be not entangled again with the yoke of bondage' (V.1). 'Where the Spirit of the Lord is, there is liberty'. 'The truth shall make you free', said Jesus to the Pharisees (II Corinthians III.17).[32] 'Ye are a chosen generation, a royal priesthood, an holy nation, a people set at liberty', I Peter informed believers (I Peter II.9). The Apostles, elders and brethren of the church at Jerusalem wrote to Gentile converts: 'It seems good to the Holy Ghost and to us, to lay no more burden upon you than these necessary things', which they proceeded to list (Acts XV.28). The context was quarrels about circumcision, but the passage could be taken in isolation – as it appears to have been by Milton – as a general principle of liberation from whatever ceremonies and regulations the reader might think unnecessary.

The protestant doctrine of the priesthood of all believers, of the supremacy of the individual conscience, enabled some radicals to carry emphasis on liberty further than social conservatives liked. Perkins had propounded the wide-ranging principle that no man's law can bind conscience. We have seen how this facilitated acceptance of usury.[33] A very different approach to individual freedom came when Calvinist predestinarian doctrines were pushed to their logical extreme. If the elect cannot fall from grace, can one speak of them as committing sin? Does it matter whether they do good works or not? The antinomian divine, Tobias Crisp (1600–1643), was so anxious to play down the part of good works in salvation that he warned men and women not to 'idolize their own righteousness'. 'Righteousness is that which puts a man away from Christ'. His object was to protect the elect from preachers' emphasis on the terrors of the law, from anxiety about the wrath of God, damnation and hell fire. God is not moved by our prayers: he hears only Christ's. 'Suppose a believer commits adultery and murder', he can nevertheless be certain of forgiveness. So was there any point in repentance?[34]

From the high Calvinist point of view Crisp seemed to have forgotten

32. Coleridge enjoyed giving the source of this text when he was accused of sedition for citing it (R. Holmes, *Coleridge: Early Visions*, Penguin ed., p. 107).
33. See my 'William Perkins and the Poor', in *Puritanism and Revolution*, Chapter 7 *passim*. See also pp. 167–70 above.
34. Crisp, *Christ Alone Exalted*, III (1648), pp. 129–30, 136, 185; *Christ Alone Exalted . . . Fifty-Two Sermons* (ed. J. Gill, 1832), pp. 391, 409, 412, 446. The Muggletonians took over (perhaps via Clarkson) the idea that God takes no notice of our prayers. For righteousness as idolatry see Chapter 9 below.

that the mass of mankind were unregenerate, that they might abuse these doctrines. Sin is finished, Crisp told his congregation. For him the believer's conscience is Christ. 'To be called a libertine is the most glorious title under heaven; take it for one that is truly free by Christ'. 'If you be freemen of Christ, you may esteem all the curses of the law as no more concerning you than the laws of England concern Spain'. Crisp offered no safeguards against the assumption that God's grace might be offered to all. What had happened to the comfortable doctrine of original sin? Whatever reservations Crisp may himself have made, after his death in 1643 (just when it became possible to publish his writings) the free discussions of the forties revealed a popular antinomian libertinism which Crisp had always denied advocating.[35] Baillie recorded 'libertines' in London in 1645,[36] and Joseph Caryl in a Fast Sermon of that year distinguished between 'liberty' and 'libertinism'.[37] Thomas Taylor had warned that Anabaptists and libertines think Christians need no magistrate 'because they are the Lord's freemen'.[38] 'Sin is finished' was soon to become Ranter doctrine.[39] In *The Civil War* Cowley listed antinomians together with libertines and Arians as the most enthusiastic supporters of Parliament.[40] His is certainly not evidence to be relied on; but it is supported by the loud cries of alarm from conservative Calvinists, who foresaw the potential consequences of supposing that Christ's grace might be offered to all. It led to proclamations of human equality, demands for democracy and communism, for sexual licence.

Crisp was of course not alone.[41] Before 1640 ideas such as his could not get into print. But they seem to have been preached from the 1620s in the Yorkshire moorland village of Grindleton – at the foot of Pendle Hill, George Fox's Mountain of Vision. Roger Brearley, curate there from 1615 to 1622, was alleged to have said that it was 'a sin to believe the Word . . . without a motion of the Spirit'.[42] That was repeated almost verbatim by the Ranter Jacob Bauthumley: it is sinful to perform an action authorized by the Bible if 'the commanding power which is God in me' forbids it.[43]

35. Crisp, *Seventeene Sermons*, pp. 87, 156–9; *Fifty-Two Sermons*, pp. 10, 43, 122, 132. Cf. Robert Towne, *The Assertor of Grace* (1644), p. 73.
36. Baillie, *Letters and Journals*, II, pp. 109, 142, 170–71.
37. *FS*, XVII, p. 157.
38. Taylor, *Commentary upon . . . Titus* (1619), p. 545.
39. See Chapter 8 below.
40. Abraham Cowley, *The Civil War*, pp. 110–11.
41. See my *Religion and Politics*, pp. 149–51.
42. Theodor Sippell, *Zur Vorgeschichte des Quäkertums* (Giessen, 1920), p. 50.
43. Bauthumley, *The Light and Dark Sides of God* (1650), pp. 76–7.

Lawrence Clarkson listened to Crisp's sermons, read all his books and approved of his doctrines, which he was to carry to extremes of sexual licence that Crisp seems to have forgone.[44] Samuel Rutherford spoke of both Hendrik Niclaes and William Dell as libertines; Clement Walker in 1649 called Milton a libertine, and many repeated the charge. William Lilly the astrologer used the word as a synonym for 'free man'.[45] Most protestants rejected the ceremonial law of the Old Testament. Now the moral law came in question. Ranters were alleged to hold that 'all the Commandments of God, both in the Old and New Testaments', are abolished, since they were 'fruits of the curse'.[46] Milton believed that the entire Mosaic law was abolished.[47]

Coppe was no doubt aware that he was echoing Crisp when he proclaimed that he spoke for 'the Eternal God, who am Universal Love and whose service is perfect freedom and pure libertinism'.[48] The word 'libertinism' was no mere synonym for 'liberty', as Coppe's choice of the provocative adjective 'pure' suggests. 'Libertinism' had been associated with heresy and profaneness from the days of Wyclif onwards: Foxe, Gabriel Harvey, Nashe, Shakespeare and Massinger all used it in this sense (*OED*). Cotgrave's *Dictionary* in 1611 defined 'libertinism' as 'disregard of moral restraint', especially in sexual matters; sensuality, epicureanism and libertinism were synonyms. Richard Baxter in *The Saints Rest* (1650) linked libertinism and sensuality. Milton may have been ironically echoing this conservative use when he wrote 'Licence they mean when they cry liberty'. He was punning on the word 'licence', meaning here official authorization or permission, and so the opposite of the kind of liberty he wished to see; but his line recognizes the prevalence of the idea that radical Puritans were abusing liberty in order to license to themselves all sorts of 'immoral' actions and beliefs.

John Everard, a friend of Brearley's, was one of many radicals who

44. Clarkson, *A Single Eye* (1650); *The Lost sheep Found*, p. 9.
45. Rutherford, *Christ Dying and Drawing Sinners to Himself* (1647), pp. 358, 465; *A Free Disputation Against pretended Liberty of Conscience* (?1648), pp. 115, 261, 402; *A Survey of the Spirituall Antichrist* (1648), I, pp. 193–4, 238–9. See *MER*, p. 109; cf. pp. 314–15.
46. John Holland Porter, *The Smoke of the bottomless pit* (1651), p. 4. He is a less irresponsible critic of the Ranters than most.
47. *MCPW*, VI, pp. 526, 711, 368. Cf. p. 374 below.
48. Smith, *Ranter Writings*, pp. 86–7; cf. p. 106, where Coppe quotes 'whose service is perfect freedom' without adding libertinism.

appealed to Christ in believers as a check on 'the dead letter' of the Bible.[49] Where was that to stop? The radical appeal to the spirit against the letter provoked conservative insistence on the sanctity of the Biblical text, the impermissibility of arbitrary interpretations by uneducated individual consciences. In response some Ranters rejected the Bible and the Gospel narrative altogether. 'The Christ that died at Jerusalem' was inferior to Christ in the believer. The Scripture is a history, not relevant to us.[50] That comes from an unfriendly witness, but it is confirmed by Bauthumley, quoted on p. 234 below, and by Clarkson: 'No matter what Scripture, saints or churches say, if that within thee do not condemn thee, thou shalt not be condemned'. And Clarkson himself is echoed by Milton in his 'dearest and best possession': 'precise compliance with the commandments ... when my faith prompts me to do otherwise ... will be counted as sin'.[51]

III

When it came to choosing sides for civil war, the Bible played a relatively small part. George Wither in 1643 cited Revelation XIX.11 for the right and duty of Englishmen to rescue a king who had been

> by an ambuscado sent from Rome
> Surprised lately in a traitorous wise
> And ... imprisoned lies.[52]

But most Parliamentarians used secular arguments. For instance, Henry Parker, nephew and close associate of Lord Saye and Sele, possessed a remarkable knowledge of the Bible and was sharply anti-clerical.[53] But he insisted that God was not the author of any form of government; power was 'originally inherent in the people', who entrusted it to a king or any other form of government for their own good. Hence there is a right of

49. Everard, *The Gospel Treasury Opened* (2nd ed., 1659), II, pp. 103, 257; cf. *CSPD, 1648–9*, p. 176.
50. Porter, op. cit., p. 3.
51. Clarkson, *A Single Eye*, in Smith, *A Collection of Ranter Writings*, p. 171; *MCPW*, VI, p. 639.
52. J. W. Allen, *English Political Thought, 1603–1660*, I, *1603–1644* (1938), p. 457 and *passim*; Wither, *Campo-Musae*, pp. 64–7, in *Miscellaneous Works*, I.
53. W. K. Jordan, *Men of Substance: A Study of the Thought of Two English Revolutionaries, Henry Parker and Henry Robinson* (Chicago U.P., 1942), pp. 72, 77.

resistance if this trust is abused. In England Parliament 'is indeed the state itself'. Royalist propagandists cited a number of Biblical texts which, they argued (or assumed), insisted on absolute obedience to the powers that be. Most Parliamentarian propagandists attempted to refute them. But Parker's only reference to allegedly pro-monarchical texts was highly ironical: the good shepherd, he recalled, lays down his life for his sheep (John X.10–14).[54]

Romans XIII.1 was the favourite text: 'Let every soul be subject unto the higher powers. . . . The powers that be are ordained of God'. There were ready-made answers to this as a royalist argument. The Geneva margin had insisted that 'the powers that be' referred to lesser magistrates as well as to the King, and Stephen Marshall maintained that 'King and Parliament . . . are the higher powers ordained unto you by God'. 'Touch not mine anointed', equally frequently used by royalist propagandists, was even more easily refuted, since the Psalmist – as the Geneva margin, Milton and Coppe insist – clearly stated that 'those whom I have sanctified to be my people' are the 'anointed' and not kings at all.[55]

The most effective work of Parliamentarian propaganda was John Goodwin's *Anti-Cavalierisme* of 1642, written with devastatingly urbane logic. It may, he suggested, be the religious duty of the people to defend godly magistrates against a king.[56] Here Goodwin's main arguments are millenarian, *assuming* that evil councillors have misled the King to acquiesce in an Antichristian conspiracy. In the 1630s, he observed, 'the spirits and judgments and consciences of men' had been 'as it were cowed and marvellously imbased and kept under (and so prepared for Antichrist's lure) by doctrines and tenets excessively advancing the power of superiors over inferiors'. Goodwin saw England's struggle as part of an international conflict, 'of very remarkable concernment to all the Saints of God in all those other churches. . . . Your light . . . shall pierce through many kingdoms, . . . as France, Germany, Bohemia, Hungaria, Polonia, Denmark, Sweden', as well as to 'your brethren in their several plantations', and

---

54. [Parker], *Observations upon some of his Majesties late Answers and Expresses* (1642), pp. 1–2, 5, 13–15, 34–5, 45, in Haller, *Tracts on Liberty*, II. Cf. B. Taft, 'Return of a Regicide: Edmund Ludlow and the Glorious Revolution', *History*, No. 247, pp. 199–200.
55. Marshall, *A Copy of a Letter* (1643), p. 14; John Goodwin, *Anti-Cavalierisme* (1642), pp. 9–10, in Haller, op. cit., II; *MCPW*, III, pp. 586–7; Smith, *Ranter Writings*, p. 45.
56. Goodwin, op. cit., pp. 10, 26. Goodwin cited many Old Testament precedents for active resistance to kings, especially tyrants and idolaters (ibid., pp. 7–20. 'Idolatry' of course equals 'popery').

especially to those in Scotland and Ireland. In the early days of the Christian church, Goodwin reflected, Christians 'might well be ignorant of that liberty, the knowledge whereof would have kept [Antichrist] from his throne.' But now 'God's will and pleasure is that he shall be thrown down'. 'The Saints shall have . . . the honour . . . to execute the judgment that is written upon the Whore'.[57]

Philip Hunton's *Treatise of Monarchie* (1643) is intellectually less interesting than Goodwin and Parker, since his object was to find a compromise between the two rival parties. He refers rather perfunctorily to the traditional Biblical texts – Genesis III.16, Psalm LXXXIII.1, 6, Romans XIII.1, 5, I Peter II.13: these are 'truths against which there is no colour of opposition'. But he begged all the questions by interpreting the Bible to mean that God bound no people to monarchy until they had bound themselves. The consent of the people is the only source of sovereignty, the only way in which God's ordinance can be rightly invoked. Here Hunton followed Charles Herle's *A Fuller Answer to a Treatise Written by Doctor Ferne* (1642).[58] The point was put more succinctly by Edward Gee in 1658: 'God's ordinance is conveyed to the particular magistrate by the consent of the community'.[59]

The Scot, Samuel Rutherford, in *Lex, Rex* (1644) produced texts to answer those of the royalists. Kings were a consequence of the Fall. God had discouraged the Israelites from having a king in the first instance, and had encouraged them to impose conditions on him (Deuteronomy XVII.15, Joshua I.8–9, II Chronicles XXXI–II). Obedience was not due to the king only; there was no prerogative royal in the Scriptures (Deuteronomy I.15–17). Inferior magistrates act for the king, and have on occasion acted without kings or against them (II Chronicles XIX.6–7, Jeremiah V.10, XXXVIII.25, Psalm CXXII.2–3). The people might indeed be God's instruments to dethrone kings (Deuteronomy XVII.14–20).[60] The secularly-minded sceptic Selden could make endless fun out of attempts to solve political problems by quoting Biblical texts. 'When a man has no mind to

57. Ibid., pp. 31–2, 36.
58. Hunton, op. cit., pp. 2, 5, 23: Herle, op. cit., pp. 2–4, 8, 13–15, 17; cf. C. Weston and J. R. Greenberg, *Subjects and Sovereigns*, pp. 57–61.
59. Gee, *The Divine Right and Original of the Civil Magistrate from God*, pp. 136–43; cf. Baxter, *A Holy Commonwealth*, pp. 22, 124, 461 – both quoted by Weston and Greenberg, op. cit., pp. 176, 334. The relevant Biblical text is II Samuel V.
60. Rutherford, op. cit., pp. 106, 142, 161–3, 173, 192–3, 232, 406. *Lex, Rex* was reissued in 1648 with a new title: *The Pre-eminence of the Election of Kings*, and again in 1657.

do something he ought to do by his contract, then he gets a text and interprets it as he pleases, and so thinks to get loose'.[61] Selden's remarks were made in private conversation, not in speeches in the Commons or in print. Few shared his wit, but many may have shared his views.

Parliamentarian propagandists had no catch-all texts equivalent to 'the Lord's anointed', 'the powers that be', or I Peter II.13–14, which told men to submit themselves 'unto the king, as unto the superior, or unto governors sent of him'.[62] The Geneva margin pointed out here that Peter was discussing 'all manner ordinances of man' which were to be obeyed 'for the Lord's sake': God could over-rule human ordinances. The Parliamentarians' popular slogans were drawn from the Norman Yoke, from the Anglo-Saxon constitution, from Good Queen Bess, rather than from the Bible. Their Biblical equivalent was Antichrist and the whole myth of anti-Catholicism built up in a millenarian context.[63]

For royalists too the Bible, although useful for producing familiar popular slogans, was never of crucial importance: their serious claims were historical and constitutional.[64] This casts considerable doubt on the arguments of those who have revived the nineteenth-century idea that the civil war was about religion. W. J. Jones puts it well: 'in inception it was the anti-Catholic rather than the Puritan Revolution'.[65] As we shall see, anti-Catholicism was political at least as much as religious in its motivation, and was linked to the millenarian concept which was also political and social as well as religious.[66]

But there was much history behind the civil war divisions. The royal supremacy over the Church of England originated against papal claims to overlordship. It proclaimed England's national independence.[67] Henry VIII's propagandists – Starkey (*Exhortation to the People*, 1536), and Richard Morison (*An Exhortation to stir all Englishmen to the defence of their country*), both writing in English, preached absolute non-resistance to the King, with much reference to Biblical texts. Henry VIII was sent by God 'to toss this

61. Selden, *Table-Talk*, pp. 7–12; cf. pp. 190, 192.
62. See p. 64 above for differing translations of this text.
63. See Chapters 9 and 14 below.
64. Allen, op. cit., pp. 486–7, 514.
65. Jones, *Politics and the Bench: the Judges and the Origins of the English Civil War* (1971), p. 136, quoted with approval by Joyce L. Malcolm, *Caesar's Due: Loyalty and King Charles, 1642–1646* (1983), p. 12.
66. See Chapters 13–14 below.
67. Christopher Morris, *Political Thought in England: Tyndale to Hooker* (Oxford U.P., 1953), pp. 56–7.

wicked tyrant of Rome . . . out of all Christian regions. See ye not to what honour God calleth our nations?' Papists were simply traitors.[68]

Starkey sometimes substituted 'the King in Parliament' for 'the King'. In the next generation John Ponet insisted that kings were not always ordained by God. St Paul refers only to 'such power as is his ordinance and lawful' – not to tyranny and oppression (Romans XIII). 'Kings and princes', Ponet continued, 'have their authority of the people'. 'The country and commonwealth is a degree above the king.' He gave copious examples from the Bible of disobedience to kings, who may be removed 'by the body of the whole congregation or commonwealth', and may be resisted in defence of true religion and for the extirpation of heresy. But private individuals have no right to resist authority.[69] John Knox and Christopher Goodman agreed. Their ideas look forward to the doctrine of the French monarchomachi and to the Dutch revolt against Spain. Resistance is not a *right* of subjects; it is lawful only as a religious *duty*. By the seventeenth century there was a long tradition of protestant resistance theories on the continent. In England, if the sovereign was an ally against Rome, so much the better. If not, there were other authorities.

It is significant that the main advocates of divine-right monarchy in England are the high-flying clergy – Neile, Montagu, Manwaring. Exaggerated claims for the religious significance of monarchy reached their apogee in Caroline court masques. They treat seriously the sort of rhetoric which Shakespeare had put into the mouth of Richard II with heavy irony and which Dekker had attributed to the Whore of Babylon.[70] Under the primacy of Laud it seemed as though high-flying clergy were coming to rule the state. With Henrietta Maria the Popish plot against England's national independence seemed to become a reality.[71] The Scottish war pricked the bubble. England's unacknowledged defeat, rather like that of the USA in Vietnam, had traumatic effects on morale. Even courtiers had to do a great deal of rethinking which – as Martin Butler has shown – is evidenced in post-1640 plays where monarchs are anything but divine – Habington's *The Queen of Aragon*, Suckling's *Brennoralt*, Denham's *The Sophy*.[72]

68. Morison, op. cit., sig. Dvii–Dviii.
69. Ponet, op. cit., pp. 26–8, 30–36, 40–49, 52–8, 63. I quote from the 1642 reprint.
70. Dekker, *The Whore of Babylon* (1607). *Richard II* is dated 1595. Whenever Richard makes an eloquent speech about the balm on an anointed king, disaster is about to strike him. Cf. epigraph to this chapter and p. 61 above.
71. C. Hibbard, *Charles I and the Popish Plot*.
72. Butler, *Theatre and Crisis, 1632–1642* (Cambridge U.P., 1984), Chapter 4.

IV

In my first chapter I asked whether the Bible might not be the equivalent for the English Revolution of Rousseau for the French Revolution and Marx for the Russian: a source of intellectual stimulus, new ideas critical of existing institutions. But the Bible produced no agreed new political philosophy: it came to be used as a rag-bag of quotations which could justify whatever a given individual or group wanted to do. As with the practice of seeking guidance from the Lord by turning up a text at random, the Bible ultimately contributed to pragmatism, lack of theory, the rise of empiricism.

Early protestants perforce had relied on the monarchy to break the power of the Roman church. Tyndale, for instance, wrote that 'the king is in this world without law, and may at his lust do right or wrong and shall give accounts but to God only'. Henry VIII naturally thought Tyndale's *The Obedience of a Christian Man* a book fit 'for all kings to read'. But Tyndale, like Calvin and Becon, found in the Bible the command 'obey God rather than man'.[73] Things were different in Scotland, where the Francophile Queen Mary was opposed by a protestant nobility which listened to the revolutionary doctrines of John Knox. But in England Jeremy Taylor could plausibly claim that 'perfect submission to kings is the glory of the protestant cause'.[74] However, in the course of the sixteenth century protestantism established itself securely enough in England for other questions to be asked. Calvinism in the sixteenth-century Huguenot and Dutch revolts had produced a political theory justifying revolt if supported by the lesser magistrates – i.e. the magnates who controlled local affairs. 'Magistrates are named gods' said Calvin, 'and do altogether bear the person of God'.[75] William Baldwyn's dedication of *A Mirroure For Magistrates* (1559) to 'the nobility and all other in office' accepted that 'ye be all gods'. Other contributors agreed: some stressed the importance of the law as a check on absolutism, but insisted that even properly accepted law should not be kept if it breaks divine law.[76]

But before 1640 the censorship ensured that the emphasis lay on the

73. Tyndale, *Doctrinal Treatises*, pp. 178–80, 202–4; Calvin, *Commentary on Daniel* (trans. and ed. T. Meyer, 1946), I, p. 382: first published 1561, English translation 1570; Becon, *Prayers and other pieces* (Parker Soc., 1844), pp. 302–4.
74. Taylor, *The Whole Works*, II, p. 62.
75. Calvin, *Institution of Christian Religion* (English translation, 1561), fol. 161.
76. Op. cit. (ed. Lily Campbell, Cambridge U. P., 1938), pp. 65, 52, 77, 421, 198.

rights of kings. James VI and I expressed this in its greatest simplicity. 'Monarchy', he said, 'as resembling the divinity, approacheth nearest to perfection'. James cited Samuel's warning of the horrors threatened by royal absolutism – conscription, forced labour, insecurity of property, heavy taxation (I Samuel VIII.9–20) as if it were a statement of 'the due obedience' owed to 'that king which God was to give them'. He seemed to think that only 'Puritans, and rash-heady preachers' with a 'Puritanical itching after popularity' would 'contend' with this definition of kingship. Men must not 'complain in words against any magistrate', it was stated in Star Chamber in 1603, 'for they are gods'.[77] This position proved double-edged: lesser magistrates claimed to be gods too.

Divine-right theories of absolutism were mainly propounded by ambitious churchmen. But the lawyer Sir John Hayward put forward a proto-Hobbist view in 1624. 'Sovereign power must be absolute. . . . Affairs of religion are to be managed by those who bear the sovereignty'. He was mainly concerned to ward off papalist claims, and was alarmed to find his theories contradicted by a bishop of the Anglican church.[78] Bishop Griffith Williams in 1644 produced a Biblical defence of monarchy. He quoted Jeremiah XXVII.5–6, where God commanded obedience to Nebuchadnezzar, as 'a memorable place against resisting tyrants'. The commandment 'Honour thy father and thy mother, that thy days may be prolonged upon the land which the Lord thy God giveth thee' (which the Geneva margin glossed 'by the parents also is meant all that have authority over us') 'is the most obliging of all the commandments of the second table' because it is 'the first commandment with promises'.[79]

Samuel Hieron, in a series of lectures on the seven penitential psalms, argued that in obeying Caesar men must not disobey God. 'It may seem that by this there is some allowances of rebellion given to subjects in some case', he admitted.[80] Three years later an Oxford preacher was in trouble for suggesting that tyrannical kings may be corrected and brought into

---

77. James I, *The Trew Law of free monarchies*, in *The Political Works*, pp. 53, 56–7, 6, 337–40. See p. 66 above.

78. Sir John Hayward, Doctor of Law, *Of Supremacie in Affaires of Religion*, sig. A4, pp. 1–8, 87–8. Dedicated to Prince Charles.

79. Williams, *Jura Magistratis: The Rights of Kings Both in Church and State . . . and The Wickedness of the Faction of this pretended Parliament*, pp. 173, 188.

80. S. Hieron, *Penance for Sin*, pp. 437–8. Posthumously published 1619, with dedication to the Earl of Pembroke. Quoted by Margot Heinemann in *Puritanism and Theatre: Thomas Middleton and Opposition Drama under the Early Stuarts* (Cambridge U.P., 1980), p. 275.

order by their subjects. James I thought this was heretical.[81] As civil war approached, Henry Burton argued that when the king became a tyrant nobles and commoners could take up arms against him, as the Scots had done against Charles I. Because this was led by lesser magistrates, it was not rebellion. 'There is a necessity of duty lying upon all Christian magistrates to exterminate and extirpate the whole hierarchy and prelacy as Antichristian enemies of Jesus Christ'. If the lesser magistrates did not do their duty, the common people must act.[82] There was no right of revolt, but it might become a duty.

The Bible authorized not only collective political resistance to tyrants, but also individual action. Deborah – after whom Milton named his youngest daughter in 1652 – incited Barak to lead a revolt against Canaanite rule; and Jael was prompted by God to murder the Canaanites' chief captain, Sisera, when he sought refuge in her tent (Judges IV and V). There is little advocacy of tyrannicide in the English protestant tradition, despite this Biblical authorization. Samuel hewed Agag in pieces before the Lord (I Samuel XV.33). Jehoida the priest ordered Athaliah to be slain (II Kings XI.16, II Chronicles XXIII.15). Ponet used Jael and others to justify tyrannicide, and Caliban appears to cite Jael in the same context in *The Tempest* (III. ii. 61–2). Sexby (if it is he) advocated the assassination of Cromwell in his *Killing Noe Murder* of 1657, which carries two Biblical epigraphs.[83]

Revolt led by lesser magistrates then could turn into revolt by the common people. There was little theory behind such statements until the Army's incursion into politics in 1647. In the Putney Debates of that year natural rights theories were put forward. They were at once opposed by Ireton and other senior officers, and in the next few years they helped to reunite the propertied class to defeat the radicals. That reunion overwhelmed the radicals, who after defeat had to accept that Christ's kingdom would be found only in the next world. This mood of disillusion was expressed in Winstanley's last published words:

> Knowledge, why didst thou come, to wound and not to cure? . . .
> O power, where art thou, that must mend things amiss?

They ended a pamphlet dedicated to Cromwell in 1652, 'you have power

81. McClure, *Letters of John Chamberlain*, II, p. 434. Cf. ibid., p. 443: a Paul's Cross sermon preached against Paraeus, the supposed author of the 'heresy'.
82. Burton, *A replie to a relation of the conference between William Laude and Mr. Fisher the Jesuit* (1640), sig. B 2v, C 4v, pp. 86–7, 296, 302.
83. See p. 21 above.

in your hand . . . to act for common freedom if you will; I have no power'.[84]

William Chillingworth had said that 'the Bible only is the religion of protestants'.[85] But like 'the law of England' 'the ancient constitution', 'the fundamental laws', the Bible had to be interpreted. When Edmund Waller asked in Parliament what the fundamental laws of the kingdom were, the only answer that could be given was that a man who did not know the answer to that question had no business to be sitting in the House.[86] Who was to interpret the Bible? Arguments which had been used to demolish the authority of the Pope could be turned against the King: arguments against the clerical tyranny of the Laudians could be turned against the Presbyterians. What alternative court of appeal could be found short of the consciences of individual believers? And then one had to ask, How do we know who are true believers? Men reasoned high

> Of providence, foreknowledge, will and fate,
> Fixed fate, free will, foreknowledge absolute,
> And found no end, in wandering mazes lost.

That had been the fate of the fallen angels in *Paradise Lost* (II. 558–61).

I drew attention in Chapter 1 to Thomas Hobbes's reliance on arguments drawn from the Bible.[87] Some have thought that he deliberately used Biblical texts in order to destroy the authority of the Bible. For our purposes it does not matter whether Hobbes took his Biblical arguments seriously, or whether he thought them necessary to lend conviction to his case. His main concern seems to have been to undermine belief in rewards and punishments in the after life.[88] By 1651, when *Leviathan* was published, England had passed through the *de facto* controversy, in which many writers had argued that obedience was due to *any* authority securely established in power, regardless of its origin and credentials. This position may be seen as a natural reaction of exhaustion and cynicism after years of civil conflict and social turbulence, a desire for a quiet life by both former Cavaliers and defeated radicals. But it too was expressed in Biblical terms. John Dury in 1649 argued that 'submission and subjection . . . for conscience sake unto

84. Winstanley, *The Law of Freedom*, in Sabine, p. 510.
85. Chillingworth, *Works*, II, p. 410.
86. Gardiner, *History of England from the Accession of James I to the Outbreak of the Civil War*, IX, p. 336.
87. See p. 20 above.
88. Cf. David Johnston, *The Rhetoric of Leviathan: Thomas Hobbes and the Politics of Cultural Transformation* (Princeton U.P., 1986), p. 136.

superior powers' was commanded by Romans XIII.1–8, I Peter II.13–14, Titus III.1. This reading of the New Testament, Dury agreed, begs the question of how any ruler has gained his position. 'It cannot stand with sound reason and a good conscience in any private man to take upon him to be a judge of that matter'. 'If they resist the power which God hath set over them for the public good, and which is actually and fully possessed with all the places of public administration, they resist the Ordinance of God, and they that resist this Ordinance (saith the Apostle) shall receive to themselves damnation, Romans XIII.2'.[89] History is the working out of God's providence, and must be accepted – an argument which was to be used on the royalist side after 1660.

Dury's argument is merely an adaptation of the old royalist divine-right position, though a reference to 'the sword which God hath put into their hands' shows that times have changed. For good measure Dury quoted Isaiah's prophecy, now beginning 'to be fulfilled amongst us somewhat more remarkably than in other parts of the earth as yet': 'It shall come to pass in that day, that the Lord shall punish the host of the high ones that are on high, and the kings of the earth upon the earth; and they shall be gathered together as prisoners are gathered in the pit'.[90] There was something there for everybody – Old Testament and New Testament, prophet and apostle, England as a chosen nation, an end to strife. The Bible had it all. *Mercurius Politicus* in December 1650 had printed an elaborate historical article using Nimrod to suggest that 'the power of the sword' was 'the original of the first monarchy, and indeed of the first politic form of government that ever was'. Apart from the government of Israel, 'which was of an immediate divine institution', no subsequent government has had any other title. The writer used this to justify submission to any *de facto* power.[91] Dury did better than that.

Hobbes's theory attracted attention by its emphasis on the brutal facts of power – especially relevant after the Army's coup in the winter of 1648–9.[92] Harrington's subsequent criticism of Hobbes, that an army is a great beast which must be fed, focused attention on the brutal facts of property. But Harrington, like Hobbes, found it expedient (to say the least) to demonstrate that his argument had Biblical authority. In *Oceana* (1656)

89. Dury, *Considerations concerning the present Engagement, whether It may lawfully be entered into; Yea or Nay?*, pp. 13–14, 17.
90. Ibid., pp. 22–3, quoting Isaiah XXIV.21–2. Dury uses the A.V. Cf. Ezekiel XXI.26.
91. Op. cit., No. 26, 28 November 1650, pp. 423–5. For Nimrod see pp. 217–22 below.
92. Winstanley came to recognize the all-importance of power: see pp. 190–91 above.

Israel is mentioned only incidentally;[93] but then, one must presume, he grasped the possibilities. In his later works Harrington is at great pains to show that Israel was a *Commonwealth*, and that its history illustrated his doctrine of the balance. *Pian Piano* (1656–7) deals with this question.[94] *The Prerogative of Popular Government* (1658) demonstrates at greater length that *Oceana*'s balance was achieved by the Israelites. Nimrod's was a monarchical balance; Samuel warned his people against monarchy; Jethro got it about right.[95] In *The Stumbling Block of Disobedience and Rebellion* (1658) Harrington says flatly 'God founded the Israelite government upon a popular balance'. In *The Prerogative of Popular Government* he tells us that his agrarian law was exactly calculated on the model of the Biblical Jubilee, which was 'a law instituted for the preservation of the popular balance'. 'There is nothing more clear nor certain in Scripture than that the commonwealth of Israel was instituted by God: the judges and the kings no otherwise than through the imprudence and importunity of the people', who, 'making a king, displeased God'. 'No absolute king can be of divine right'.[96]

In *The Art of Lawgiving* (1659) Harrington was at pains to show that 'the principles of human prudence, being good without proof of Scripture, are nevertheless such as are provable out of Scripture'. Book II deals specifically with 'the Commonwealth of the Hebrews'. Chapter III of Book II shows 'the anarchy, or state of the Israelites under their judges'.[97] Chapter IV deals with Israel under the monarchy, illustrating 'those dreadful curses denounced by Moses', and God's terrible warnings in Deuteronomy XXVIII.[98] After the restoration, continuity of imperialist policies and the agricultural revolution led to increased prosperity, and gave fresh life to Harringtonianism. Locke provided a theory of apparent philosophical respectability. Simpler upwardly mobile characters accepted Defoe's maxim,

> There can be no pretence of government
> Till they that have the property consent.[99]

93. *The Political Works of James Harrington*, pp. 174–8, 209–10, 279.
94. Ibid., pp. 370–82.
95. Ibid., pp. 459, 461–4, 411, 485, 496–7; cf. pp. 389, 420–23, 473–7.
96. Ibid., pp. 572, 463, 575–7.
97. Ibid., pp. 601, 614–53; cf. pp. 673, 680–85.
98. Ibid., pp. 640–43; cf. 380–81 and *A Discourse upon this saying* . . . (1659), pp. 739–43; cf. *Valerius and Publicola* (1659), ibid., p. 790.
99. Defoe, *Jure Divino* (1706), Book II, p. 12.

Filmer's *Patriarcha* was not printed until 1680. In his lifetime he published *The Anarchy of a Limited or Mixed Monarchy* and *The Freeholders Grand Inquest*, both in 1648. It was perhaps from one of these that an otherwise undistinguished W.J. got the idea that absolute monarchy derives from Adam and the Patriarchs.[100] The Presbyterian Edward Gee refuted patriarchal theory in *The Divine Right and Originall of Civil Magistrates from God*. He denied that Adam had been a king, and argued that in Romans XIII only just and lawful powers were 'ordained of God'; 'the ordinary means [which God] useth ... is the vote, elective act or consent of the body politic or people to be ruled'.[101] Richard Baxter in *A Holy Commonwealth* insisted that a nation should 'preserve themselves, or their representative body, from the unjust endeavours of a king that would destroy them'.[102] Neither of these solved the problem of who 'the people', 'the nation', were, and what their relation was to 'the body politic', or 'their representative body'.

It requires an effort today to take Filmer's political theory seriously, deriving the authority of monarchs by descent from Adam. But Locke took it seriously, and in a society in which the household was the basic economic unit it made sense to think of the state as an extended family, even if the direct descent of the Stuarts from Adam was difficult to prove.[103] The strength of the theory lay in its claim to Biblical authority. Filmer did not invent patriarchal theory: the abortive canons of the Church of England of 1606 laid it down that political power descended from Adam through the patriarchs. It was a great error to suppose that it derived from the people. Consequently, there should be no resistance to kings: the Jews could not have left Egypt against Pharaoh's wishes without having had express warrant from God.[104] If this canon had been accepted it would have corrected the Old Testament on the power of kings. John Hall of Richmond in 1654 believed that the authority of the king was that of the head of a household.[105] Even Gerrard Winstanley accepted that the

---

100. W.J., *A Dissection of all Governments, or An Answer to a Pamphlet, entitled the Priviledges of the People* (1649), p. 5. Cf. Bishop Griffith Williams, quoted on p. 189 above.

101. Gee, op. cit. (1658), p. 138, quoted by P. Zagorin, *A History of Political Thought in the English Revolution* (1954), p. 76.

102. Baxter, op. cit., p. 417.

103. The best statement on this subject is still Peter Laslett's Introduction to his edition of Filmer's *Patriarcha and Other Political Works*.

104. *Bishop Overall's Convocation Book* (1690), pp. 2–4, 16, 25–8, 53–9.

105. Hall, *Of Government and Obedience*, sig. 3v, pp. 28–35, 39–110, 233.

patriarchical household should be the basic unit in his democratic com-monwealth, with the father at its head.[106] Filmer suited the intellectual climate after 1660. Dryden echoed him in his *Poem on the Coronation* and in *Annus Mirabilis*. Evelyn's vicar preached on Proverbs XV and Psalm CXLIV to demonstrate that monarchy descended from Adam. Even in 1694 a young man preached on the same theme on the anniversary of the execution of Charles I.[107]

106. Sabine, pp. 536–8.
107. Evelyn, *Diary*, IV, pp. 135 (29 May 1678), 336 (9 September 1683), V, pp. 165–6 (30 January 1694).

8. The Bible and Radical Politics

═══

The Knowledge of God within ourselves and in his other creatures, that is all in all to us [i.e. not the Bible].
[Anon.], *Tyranipocrit Discovered* (1649), p. 5 (ed. A. Hopton, n.d.).

The Papists keep off the people from reading the Scriptures ... And so not only our Prelates of late, but the Presbyterians are too rigid to keep off the poor people from the Scriptures, fearing they would excel their teachers and take their pulpits from them. To see such in their pulpits as had not hands upon them [i.e. who had not been ordained], O, how they screech for fear!
John Rogers, *Ohel or Bethshemesh* (1653), quoted by Edward Rogers, *Some Account of the Life and Opinions of a Fifth-Monarchy Man* (1867), pp. 70–71.

> The Book thus put in every vulgar hand,
> Which each presumed he best could understand,
> The common rule was made the common prey
> And at the mercy of the rabble lay.
> The tender page with horny fists was galled,
> And he was gifted most that loudest bawled.

John Dryden, *Religio Laici* (1682).

I fear it is necessary to start by explaining my use of the word 'radical', since some purists hold that it is wrong to use for descriptive and analytical purposes a word which contemporaries did not use. I find this unacceptable. Jonathan Dollimore pointed out that ideology existed long before the word that describes it.[1] So did pantheists and minorities, communists, anarchists and revolutionaries. I do not know how otherwise than as radicals to describe people who in the mid-seventeenth century (and earlier) held unorthodox views on religion and politics which set them beyond the pale of the respectable groups which we call Anglicans, Presbyterians or

1. Dollimore, *Radical Tragedy*, p. 18.

Independents. This is the usage of Professors R. L. Greaves and R. Zaller in their admirable *Biographical Dictionary of British Radicals in the Seventeenth Century*.[2] Contemporaries might lump all my 'radicals' together as 'sectaries', and indeed most sectaries were likely to be 'radicals', most 'radicals' sectaries. But the word 'sect' did not imply in the mid-seventeenth century the degree of organization and ideological agreement that it does today: there were radicals whom contemporaries called Levellers and Ranters, but there was no Leveller or Ranter sect. I use 'radical' to describe those who held unorthodox opinions, not adherents of any religious or political group. Not all Levellers were sectaries: the very radical William Walwyn remained a member of the national church. The even more radical Gerrard Winstanley was a member of the Church of England after the restoration. Other 'radicals' – Milton, Colonel Hutchinson – were not committed to any church at all. Calling people 'radicals' implies no more and no less than that they rejected root and branch some established orthodoxies. Not all would reject the same orthodoxies, and they might disagree profoundly. But until somebody comes up with a better word to describe the people whom I discuss in this chapter, I shall continue to call them radicals.[3]

I

I called my first chapter 'A Biblical Culture'. But I take note of Edward Thompson's remark that 'the very term "culture", with its cosy invocation of consensus, may serve to distract attention from social and cultural contradictions, from the fractions and oppositions within the whole'.[4] The revolutionary Bible of the radicals is only one version of the Biblical culture. The Bible had long been adapted to the needs of an unequal society, and could be re-adapted to the rather different unequal society which established itself after the crisis of the forties and fifties – all the more decisively because of the millenarian aspirations of the radicals. But in this chapter I discuss the Biblical radicalism of these frightening decades.

What we do not know, and probably never shall know fully, is how much continuity of underground radical use of the Bible there was from Lollards through Foxe's martyrs down to the apparently sudden appearance

2. Op. cit., esp. I, pp. vii–xii.
3. See my 'The Word "Revolution"' in *A Nation of Change and Novelty*.
4. Thompson, *Customs in Common*, p. 6.

of Biblical radicalism in the 1640s. I gave some evidence in 'From Lollards to Levellers' for continuity in certain geographical areas, and in certain subjects – use of the Bible to criticize the sacraments and ceremonies of the church, denunciations of idolatry and encouragement of iconoclasm, millenarianism, the saints to judge the world, perfection in this life, the idea that all men and women may be saved, lay mechanic preaching, Biblical criticism; and for recurrent heresies – mortalism, anti-Trinitarianism, scepticism about the existence of heaven, hell, the devil and sin, rejection of church marriage. Thomas Nashe speaks of a variety of sects already existing in the 1590s, with their own 'mechanic preachers'.[5]

Whether there was continuity of radical ideas or not, there can be no doubt about the wealth of unorthodox theories, some of them fairly sophisticated, which surfaced after the breakdown of censorship. This aspect of the printing explosion of the 1640s is not always sufficiently emphasized. For the first time in English history anyone could get into print who could persuade a printer that there was money in his or her idea. Significant numbers of persons (including women) who had had no university education, often no grammar school education even, found no obstacles to publication.

So political advice was no longer supplied only by people who shared a classical education and assumed that discussion must be conducted according to established formal rules, starting from a syllogism. What became the radicals' manifesto was a sermon entitled *The Sufficiency of the Spirits Teaching without Humane-Learning*, published by Cobbler How in 1640. He argued that while learning might be useful to scholars, lawyers and gentlemen, uneducated persons were preferable to scholars in the pulpit, since the Spirit's teaching was all that mattered for understanding 'the mind of God'. All men should read the Bible and decide for themselves, not as the learned told them. How died a few months after his sermon appeared, but it attracted much attention. Of the vast number of books and pamphlets published between 1640 and 1660, a great many were by authors who were 'illiterate' in the eyes of academics. They knew as little Latin or Greek as Shakespeare. So in the interregnum discussions there was no longer a shared background of classical scholarship; the rules of logic which structured academic controversy were ignored. University scholars treated the newcomers with contempt, and this in its turn fuelled opposition to the universities as such. The whole classical curriculum and the conventions of

---

5. See my *Religion and Politics in 17th-century England*, pp. 89–116; Nashe, *Pierce Penilesse, his Supplication to the Divell* (1592) (ed. G. B. Harrison, 1924), pp. 27, 57.

academic argument were called in question. Indeed, were universities of any use at all? The Biblical culture fragmented.

Self-taught men like Gerrard Winstanley stressed proudly that they got their ideas not from books, or from other men, but either direct from God, or from the Bible, or from common sense. Writers of the calibre of the Leveller leaders John Lilburne, William Walwyn and John Wildman, the Ranters Clarkson, Coppin and Salmon, the Quakers Fox, Nayler, Isaac Penington and Arthur Pearson, the Muggletonians John Reeve and Lodowick Muggleton, the Biblical critic Clement Writer, the opponent of witch persecution John Webster, a religious writer like William Erbery, wholly secular writers like Walter Blyth the agricultural reformer, William Lilly the astrologer and Francis Osborn the essayist – all these could beat academics at their own games. Many of those I have named were important opinion-formers. They were supported by university men like William Dell who joined in the attack on academic education. 'Antichrist chose his ministers only out of the universities', remarked Dell. John Bunyan was deeply hurt by academic sneers at him for daring to preach and write without a proper education. He consoled himself with the reflection that God's own were not gentlemen, could not with Pontius Pilate speak Hebrew, Greek and Latin.[6]

So in the forties uneducated men and women read back into the Bible themselves and their problems, and the problems of their communities, and found Biblical answers there, which they could discuss with others who shared the same problems. It was a great period for public disputation. Jordan noted at least seventy-eight *recorded* meetings of this type in which Baptists were involved.[7] The conclusions emerging from these Biblical discussions were many and varied, not all popular with educated Parliamentarians. Radicals in Chelmsford were said to think that the relation of master and servant had no ground in Scripture; that peerage and gentry were 'ethnical and heathenish distinctions'. They found no ground in nature or Scripture why one man should have £1,000 a year, and another not £1. Universities should be abolished. Baxter noted that 'the antinomian doctrine is the very same in almost every point which I find naturally

6. *BMW*, I, p. 304, quoted on p. 53 above. The joke had been made in 1655, three years earlier, by two Quaker women, Priscilla Cotton and Mary Cole, *To the Priests and People of England*. But Bunyan, who prided himself on not taking his ideas from other people, would hardly have consciously cribbed from Quaker women.

7. W. K. Jordan, op. cit., pp. 454–5. See Ann Hughes, 'The Meaning of Religious Polemic: Oral Debate and Pamphlet Controversies in the sixteen-forties and fifties' – Millersville.

fastened in the hearts of the common profane multitude'.[8] That was a good reason for not tolerating it.

By 1644 Edmund Calamy in a Fast Sermon was complaining that 'the people of the City of London have almost disputed away their repentance'; in discussing 'this opinion or that opinion' about discipline they forget faith and repentance.[9] Liberty of discussion seemed to conservatives to be subverting the discipline whose establishment they saw as the only way to recover God's favour, to show that his chosen nation had indeed repented.[10] There was a profound difference of interest here, to which Walwyn himself had pointed when he complained of clerical attempts to restrict and control discussion of the Bible: 'What are you the better for having the Scripture in your own language? When it was locked up in the Latin tongue by the policy of Rome, you might have had a learned friar for your money at any time (to have interpreted the same); and though now you have it in your language, you are taught not to trust your own understanding (have a care of your purses!); you must have an university man to interpret the English. . . . Let me prevail with you to free yourselves from this bondage'.[11]

The Leveller leader, John Lilburne, was said to have the Bible in one hand and the writings of Sir Edward Coke in the other. He claimed that his attack on bishops 'could neither be factious nor seditious, unless the Book of God be faction and sedition, which were blasphemy once to think'.[12] 'God has revealed the way of eternal salvation only to the individual faith of each man, and demands of us that any man who wishes to be saved should work out his beliefs for himself': so Milton justified his religious creed, for which his only authority, he said, was 'God's self-revelation' in 'the Holy Scriptures'.[13]

The concept of social revolution also emerged in the forties and fifties, in Biblical phrases like 'the world turned upside down' and Ezekiel's 'overturn, overturn, overturn'.[14] Thomas Manton in 1648 recognized that 'the levelling humour is no new thing in the Church of God', instancing the rising of Korah, Dathan and Abiram against Moses (Numbers XVI.3).[15] 'Thus

8. [Anon.], *Angliae Ruina* (1647), p. 27; W. M. Lamont, *Richard Baxter and the Millennium* (1979), pp. 128, 143.

9. *FS*, XIII, pp. 124, 145.

10. See Chapter 12 below.

11. Walwyn, *The Power of Love* (1643), p. 47, in *Writings*, pp. 95–6.

12. Lilburne, *Come Out of her My People* (1639), p. 25.

13. *MCPW*, VI, pp. 118–21.

14. Psalm CXLVI.9, Isaiah XXIV.1–2, 20–21, Acts XVII.1–6, Ezekiel XXI.27.

15. Manton, *Commentary . . . On . . . Jude*, p. 406.

the wicked reason against God's ordinance', the Geneva margin commented on this passage. Quakers and William Aspinwall applied to their own activities the phrase 'the world turned upside down'.[16] Such phrases normally sounded hostile in the mouths of the respectable. James I, for instance, had used 'leveller' in the sense of 'anti-monarchist'.[17] Ballads on 'The World Turned Upside Down' depicted it as a nonsensical inversion of deferential normality. But George Wither saw Habakkuk and Ezekiel as predecessors of the Quakers.[18]

Adam is one of many Biblical figures who has a dual existence in seventeenth-century political mythology. In the covenant theology he is the representative of all humanity. All mankind are sinful not just because we are Adam's heirs, but because he was our representative, for whom we must take responsibility. Christ became our second representative person, and his righteousness was imputed us thanks to his victory over sin and death.[19] Robert Crowley in Edward VI's reign had claimed a natural right for all Adam's descendants 'to the riches and treasures of this world'.[20]

But for Winstanley Adam was more than our representative. He was not 'a single man . . . that killed us all by eating a single fruit called an apple . . . as the public preachers tell you'. Rather Adam symbolizes 'that covetous proud and imaginary power in flesh'.[21] Although, as Winstanley put it elsewhere, 'We may see Adam every day before our eyes walking up and down the street', he is not merely everyman: symbolically Adam 'sits down in the chair of magistracy, in some above others': hence tyranny and private property.[22] Winstanley had expressed this more poetically earlier in *The Saints Paradise*. God had placed 'glorious lights and sparks of glory, shining angels of light, . . . in the human nature, Adam, before his fall. [They] all lived in God, being alive within Adam, and Adam being alive within them'. But 'when Adam (or indeed any man or woman) doth give way to self and eat of that fruit, . . . then those glorious angels left God their habitation, and took up their glory within the circle of human defiled

16. W. Penn, Preface to Fox's *Journal*, I, p. xxxiv; Aspinwall, *The Legislative Power is Christ's Peculiar Prerogative*, p. 48.

17. J. Frank, *The Levellers* (Harvard U.P., 1955), p. 291.

18. Wither, *Parallelogrammaton* (Spenser Soc., 1882), p. 44. First published 1662.

19. For covenant theology see my *People and Ideas*, esp. Chapter 14.

20. Crowley, *An Informacion and Peticion agaynst the oppressours of the pore Commons of this Realme* (1548 or 1549), in *Select Works*.

21. Sabine, p. 203.

22. Ibid., pp. 120, 258.

flesh'. 'And now those glorious sparks which were angels of light while they lived in God and reflected upon him, are become angels of darkness'.[23]

Richard Coppin the Ranter thought that 'through the birth of Christ' men would 'return to a more excellent state' than the Paradise which Adam had lost.[24] This is Milton's 'Paradise within you, happier far'. Similar ideas were expressed by the Behmenist John Pordage, by Peter Sterry, as well as by George Fox and other Quakers,[25] and by Thomas Traherne, who inherited more from the radicals of the revolutionary decades than is usually recognized.[26] The almanac-writer John Gadbury, allegedly an ex-Ranter, said that in the Garden of Eden 'all men were Levellers'.[27] He might have been quoting the very respectable Puritan divine Richard Sibbes: 'If God be a Father, and we are brethren, it is a levelling word; it bringeth down mountains and filleth up valleys. All are brethren'.[28] As this demonstrates, dangers lurked in Puritan orthodoxy, to be exposed in the radical forties.

A second myth of Adam was perpetuated by the long-remembered rhyme of 1381, which Cleveland called this 'levelling lewd text':[29]

> When Adam delved and Eve span,
> Who was then the gentleman?

It was quoted under Edward VI, and as a 'common saying' by Bishop Pilkington in 1560–62. He added, remarkably. 'How true it is!'[30] A very different bishop, Bancroft, cited it in 1593 in order to associate Puritans with the rebels of 1381.[31] It reappeared in the same year in the play *The*

23. Winstanley, *The Saints Paradise*, pp. 68–70.

24. Coppin, *Crux Christi* (1657), p. 52. Cf. Samuel Pordage, 'Paradise doth open in the heart' (*Mundorum Explicatio*, 1661, p. 321. Pordage however thought that God created Adam as 'a King/And lord and ruler over everything', as well as a hermaphrodite – ibid., pp. 12, 60–63).

25. J. Pordage, *Innocencie Appearing Through the dark Mists of Pretended Guilt* (1655), p. 73; V. de Sola Pinto, *Peter Sterry, Platonist and Puritan, 1613–1672* (Cambridge U.P., 1934), p. 192; Fox, *Journal*, I. p. 28.

26. Traherne, *Poems*, pp. 35, 326. See my *Writing and Revolution*, Chapter 6.

27. Capp, *Astrology and the Popular Press*, p. 102.

28. Sibbes, *A Heavenly Conference between Christ and Mary*, in *Collected Works*, VI, p. 458; cf. p. 558. First published, posthumously, in 1654. For mountains and valleys see Chapter 4 above.

29. Cleveland, *The Rustick Rampant*, in *Works* (1687), p. 402.

30. James Pilkington, *Exposition upon the Prophet Aggeus*, in *Works* (Parker Soc., 1842), p. 125. 'Aggeus' is Haggai.

31. Richard Bancroft, *A Survey of the Pretended Holy Discipline* (1593), pp. 8–9. I owe this and the following reference to Annabel Patterson's *Shakespeare and the Popular Voice*, pp. 39, 46.

Life and Death of Jack Straw.[32] Jack Cade's remark in *2 Henry VI*, IV. ii, 'Adam was a gardener', which Shakespeare must have overheard someone saying, suggests a popular source. 'There are no ancient gentlemen but gardeners', declared the grave-digger in *Hamlet* (V. ii). The crowd in Marston's *Histriomastix* (1610) cries 'All shall be common, . . . wives and all'. 'We come all of our father Adam' (Act V). Milton in 1641 spoke of 'all men . . . since Adam being born free'.[33]

In the 1520s the extreme German radical Thomas Müntzer had declared that 'we [fleshly] earthly men shall become gods through the incarnation of Christ'.[34] Over a century later the Quaker William Dewsbery said 'The Lord will make the earth as the Garden of Eden', adding 'and hath begun his strange work in this nation', citing many texts.[35] Thomas Traherne proclaimed that

> every man
> Is like a God incarnate on the throne,
> Even like the first for whom the world began.

'An earthly man is a mortal God', he said in sober prose.[36]

So whilst covenant theology associated Adam with representation, the popular tradition associated him with human equality. Even after the restoration Traherne, who was always obsessed by property relations, described Adam in Paradise as having no gold, silver nor coin, no property nor trade.

> The trees, the free
> And fruitful fields his needful treasures were
> And nothing else he wanted there.[37]

II

One use which Puritan theologians made of the mixed heritage of the Bible was to illuminate the difficult doctrine of predestination, which

---

32. Quoted by R. B. Dobson, *The Peasants' Revolt of 1381* (1970), pp. 390–91.
33. *MCPW*, I, p. 624.
34. Quoted by G. Rupp, *Patterns of Reformation* (1969), p. 785; cf. p. 266.
35. Dewsbery, *A Faithful Testimony* (1689), p. 111. Cf. Dewsbery, *The Discovery of Mans return to his first Estate* (1665).
36. Traherne, *Poems*, pp. 35–6, 210, 348–50; *The Way to Blessedness* (the title which its editor, Margaret Bottrall, gave to Traherne's *Christian Ethicks*) (1962), p. 246; cf. p. 158. *Christian Ethicks* was first published posthumously in 1675.
37. Traherne, 'Adam', in *Poems*, pp. 82–3.

especially distinguished them from most Catholic theologians. Calvin preached thirteen sermons on grace and redemption, arising from the story of Jacob and Esau.[38] The 'comedy or interlude' upon *The Historie of Jacob and Esau*, dated between 1557–8 and 1568, showed Esau as a predestinate sinner from his youth, like Bunyan's Mr Badman. He was a noisy, rowdy, hunting type, greedy and selfish, who treated his servants badly. God loved Jacob and hated Esau: all Jacob's lies and deceit, amusingly depicted in *The Historie*, were irrelevant to that fact.[39] Humphrey Sydenham in 1626 used the same myth for a sermon concerned solely with election and reprobation. God hardens the heart of whom he will.[40] 'Cain was the elder, but Abel the better': so William Gouge explained God's disregard for the rights of primogeniture. Esau was 'an egregious fool ... to sell lands and inheritances for a bauble'. But he was also 'notoriously profane in lightly esteeming so holy and heavenly privileges' as his birthright implied.[41]

'It is not free will but free grace that puts the difference between Jacob and Esau', declared Calamy in a Fast Sermon preached on 23 February 1641–2. 'It is not of him that willeth, nor of him that runneth, but of God that showeth mercy'.[42] John Owen repeated the point in a Fast Sermon on 29 April 1646. Milton listed Cain and Esau along with Pharaoh, Saul, Ahab and Jeroboam among reprobates who vainly professed repentance, in order to expose the worthlessness of Charles I's 'good words and holy sayings in abundance'.[43] Could the elect ever fall from grace? Some of the acknowledged saints in the Bible had been notorious sinners – David, St Paul. Others, ear-marked as holy men, nevertheless backslid – Noah, Samson, St Peter. 'Though God suffered his [people] to run in blindness and error for a time', remarked the Geneva margin *à propos* Elijah, 'yet at

---

38. Arnold Williams, *The Common Expositor: An Account of the Commentaries on Genesis, 1527–1633* (North Carolina U.P., 1948), p. 172.

39. Cf. W. Sclater, *A Brief and Plain Commentary . . . upon the whole Prophecie of Malachy* (1650), pp. 13–16. (Published posthumously: probably preached some forty years earlier.) Many other examples could be given. Milton grappled with this aspect of the story in *Of Christian Doctrine* (*MCPW*, VI, pp. 196–8, 763; cf. p. 746).

40. Sydenham, *Jacob and Esau: Election and Reprobation opened and discussed*, p. 29, and *passim*.

41. Gouge, *A Commentary on the whole Epistle to the Hebrews* (Edinburgh, 1866–7), pp. 9, 218. Posthumously published in 1655. Described as 'the substance of thirty years' Wednesday lectures at Blackfriars church, London', where Gouge was minister from 1608 till his death in 1653.

42. *FS*, II, p. 162.

43. Ibid., XXIII, p. 182; Milton, *Eikonoklastes, passim.*

length he calleth them home to him by some notorious sign and work' (I Kings XVIII.37).

Old Testament stories were used to illustrate the apparent arbitrariness (to human judgment) of God's decrees. Why did God love Abel and hate Cain, love Jacob and hate Esau? Jacob, like so many Old Testament heroes, was not a spotless character wholly to be recommended as an example for the faithful. (The Geneva margin had difficulties here too.) Richard Bernard, the radical Puritan author of *The Isle of Man*, summarized laconically: 'Jacob lied three times to his father . . . and by deceit got the blessing from his brother; stayed twenty years from his father without visiting him, had two wives besides his wife's handmaid . . .'. Yet he was one of the elect.[44] Both Abraham and Isaac lied shamelessly in what they believed to be good causes. 'Such is man's frailty' was the Geneva marginal comment on Abraham. Bishop Babington in 1592 worried about Jacob's 'unlawful lie', which got him the birthright; but he sensibly concluded 'Let us leave it all to God, and make no doctrine either of rebuke or instruction to ourselves by extraordinary facts'.[45] Matthias Prideaux wondered whether Jacob's lying to get the birthright was 'fit for imitation?' Come to that, had Esau any legal right to sell his birthright, since it was not yet in his possession? Did Solomon repent before his death and receive forgiveness?[46]

Richard Stock hinted at a democratic meaning for the myth of Cain and Abel. To be out of favour with God is more dangerous than to be out of favour with a prince. It was Jacob's holiness and piety that mattered, not the birthright privileges of the flesh which Esau inherited.[47] Alexander Ross had shown unusual social consciousness in 1620 when he declared that the name Cain 'signifieth possession, a fit name to the wicked; for they seek nothing else but possessions and honour in this world; and therefore Cain built a city; so the wicked laboureth to be secure'. Four kinds of sin, he continued, are said in the Bible to cry out to God: (i) murder (Cain); (ii) sodomy (Lot and his daughters); (iii) 'the oppression of the poor' (the Israelites in Egypt under taskmasters); (iv) 'the keeping back of the

---

44. Bernard, *Thesaurus Biblicus* (1644), p. 68.
45. Babington, *Certaine Plaine, briefe and comfortable Notes upon everie Chapter of Genesis*, fol. 104–110.
46. Prideaux, op. cit., pp. 14, 23.
47. Stock, *An Exposition Upon the Whole Book of the Prophecy of Malachi* (first published in 1641, fifteen years after Stock's death. I cite from the reprint of 1865, ed. Grosart, Edinburgh), pp. 17, 21, 66, 88. Cf. Gouge, *Commentary on . . . Hebrews*, pp. 6–9, 226, 243–4.

labourer's hire' by fraud (James V – a favourite chapter with radicals from Lollards to Coppe). Cain, Ross added, was 'the first king and conqueror in the world': kings who 'delight in conquering kingdoms with blood' will be 'counted the successors of Cain and Nimrod'.[48]

William Perkins had taught that 'the way of Cain is the high and broad way of the world'. It was also the way of Papists (and Turks and Jews). 'However [Cain] was a prince, and mighty among men', yet he became 'a vagabond and runagate on the face of the earth'.[49] But if Cain represented the unacceptable face of capitalism for Alexander Ross, an MP in the Short Parliament claimed that 'Abel had property in goods', and so property was justified in Genesis.[50]

Thomas Scott gave a social turn to the myth when he said that an engrosser of farms was 'like another Cain' when he 'takes possession of all, and will not endure any man to thrive or live by him'.[51] The Marian martyr, John Philpot, traced two churches back to Cain and Abel.[52] Jean Paul Perrin of Lyon, in a book translated as *Luthers Fore-Runners* (1624), also distinguished between 'the church that began in Abel' and 'that which began in Cain'.[53] With the writings of Milton, Levellers, Diggers, Ranters, Muggletonians and Quakers, new interpretations began to be published which could never have got into print earlier. In William Gouge's posthumous *Commentary on Hebrews* Abel becomes the type of the victims of persecution, whose blood cried unto God from the earth (Genesis IV.10, Hebrews XI.4, XII.24).[54] Bunyan saw Cain as the type of all persecutors; so did Quakers.[55] Bulstode Whitelocke started his history of persecution with Cain and Abel.[56] Milton in *Of Reformation* (1641) had seen the war between England and Scotland as 'an abhorred, a cursed, a fratricidal war.

48. A. Ross, *The First Booke of Questions and Answers upon Genesis* (1620), pp. 74–80. For Cain and Nimrod see pp. 217–22 below.

49. Perkins, *Exposition upon the Epistle of Jude*, in *Workes*, III, p. 549.

50. Mr Peard on 30 April 1640, in *The Short Parliament (1640) Diary of Sir Thomas Aston* (ed. J. D. Maltby, Camden 4th Series, 535), p. 10.

51. [Scott], *The High-Waies of God and the King*, p. 75.

52. Quoted by Capp, 'The Political Dimension of Apocalyptic Thought', in *The Apocalypse in English Renaissance Thought and Literature*, p. 94.

53. I.P.P.L., op. cit. This is a history of the Waldensians and Albigensians, translated by Samson Leonard, formerly a follower of Sir Philip Sidney in The Netherlands. It was dedicated to the Earl of Pembroke.

54. Gouge, op. cit., III, pp. 243–4. Cf. pp. 245–6 below.

55. W. Y. Tindall, *John Bunyan, Mechanic Preacher* (New York, 1964), p. 266, and references there cited.

56. See p. 410 below.

England and Scotland, dearest brothers both in Nature and in Christ, . . . set to wade in one another's blood', to the advantage only of papist Ireland. It was 'fit for Cain to be the leader of' the war.[57] It would hardly escape notice that in fact Charles I was the leader. Jacob Boehme, not translated into English until 1649, had seen Cain and Esau, together with Ham and Ishmael, as 'types of the corrupt monarchy'; Abel, Jacob, Shem and Isaac were types of Christ.[58]

A rather different use of the analogy was made in a sermon preached in Edinburgh by 'a zealous brother of that nation', James Bonner, who told his flock that though Jacob was the younger brother, yet he had the blessing, and 'so it was with Scotland, both for the purity of the kirk and privileges of the civil state'. He added ('as our new pulpit-men are very full of such extravagances') that Jacob had not merely supplanted Esau by getting the birthright and blessing from him, but his posterity had rooted out Esau's and seized upon his large possessions.[59]

The fact that Jacob and Esau were twins could be put to many uses. In a brilliant article Thomas Cogswell has shown how Sir George More in 1621 spoke of grievances and supply 'as twins, as Jacob and Esau'. They 'should go hand in hand, for the grievances go first, yet the blessing may be upon subsidies'. After producing much more evidence, Cogswell concludes with justified irony at the expense of 'revisionists': 'Parliament can be held to be powerless and insignificant only if the definition of power does not include the ability to force the Crown to alter its foreign policy (1625) or to hamstring the war effort itself (1626)'.[60]

Walwyn in 1646 likened the imprisoned Lilburne to Abel persecuted by Cain: in 1648 he saw the Levellers collectively as Abel.[61] Even Lilburne,

---

57. *MCPW*, I, pp. 595–6. For England and Scotland see Chapter 11 below.

58. *Mercurius Teutonicus, or a Christian Information concerning the last Times . . . Gathered out of the Mysticall Writings of . . . Jacob Behmen* (1649), p. 34.

59. *Mercurius Aulicus*, 20–26 August 1643, p. 465. The report may be tendentious. Bonner (or Bonar) was minister of Maybole, Ayrshire, and a member of the Commission of the General Assembly of the Kirk in 1646. The comment in brackets is that of the editor, the royalist Peter Heylyn.

60. Cogswell, '"A Low Road to Extinction?" Supply and Redress of Grievances in the parliaments of the 1620s', *Historical Journal*, 33 (1990), pp. 283–303, quoting *Commons Debates in 1621* (ed. W. Notestein, F. H. Relf and H. Simpson, Yale U.P., 1935), II, p. 21. It is not given to many of us to put down Sir Geoffrey Elton and Earl Russell in one sentence.

61. Walwyn, *A Pearle in a Dunghill: or Lieu-Col. John Lilburne in New-gate* (1646); *The Bloody Project* (1648), both in *Freedom in Arms* (ed. A. L. Morton, 1975), pp. 80, 171. The editors of Walwyn's *Writings* think the first treatise is wrongly attributed to him.

the most secular-minded of the Leveller leaders, made extensive use of arguments and illustrations drawn from the Old Testament.[62] Winstanley had little to say about Cain and Abel, Esau and Jacob, in the pamphlets which he wrote before the digging started in April 1649. But from *The True Levellers Standard Advanced* (published in that month) the hostility of the elder to the younger brother becomes a regular symbol for class oppression in Winstanley's England. 'Cain lifted up himself and killed his brother Abel; and so one branch [of mankind] did kill and steal away the comfortable use of the earth from another, as it is now: the elder brother lives in a continual thievery, stealing the land from the younger brother. . . . The power of the sword over brethren in armies, in arrests, in prisons, in gallows, and in other inferior torments inflicted by some upon others, as the oppression of lords of manors hindering the poor from the use of the common land, is Adam fallen, or Cain killing Abel to this very day'. 'All kingly power (in one or many men's hands) reigning by the sword, giving the use of the earth to some of mankind (called by [the Conqueror] his gentry) and denying the free use of the earth to others, called the younger brothers or common people, is no other but Cain lifted up above Abel'.[63] Cain's 'cheating art of buying and selling, and of dividing the land into parcels, prevails amongst mankind' notwithstanding Moses's attempt to limit it.[64]

Cain becomes a symbol for all exploitation. 'Abel's industry made the earth more fruitful than Cain, thereupon Cain would take away Abel's labour from him by force (Gen. IV.3). These two brothers did type out, or fore-run, all the acting between man and man from that time to this'. 'All the great combustions that hath been, and yet is in the world, is but politic, covetous, murdering Cain holding Abel or the honest plain-dealing heart under him; or the son of bondage persecuting the son of freedom'.[65] 'But Abel shall not always be slain, nor always lie under the bondage of Cain's cursed property, for he must rise; and that Abel of old was but a type of Christ, that is now rising up to restore all things from bondage'. Men claim that their cause is justified by military victory. But 'victories that are got by the sword are but victories of the murderer, and the joy of those victories is but the joy of Cain when he had killed his brother Abel'.[66] The story of Esau and Jacob makes the same point. 'Esau, the man

62. As Dr Tuttle has shown, in *Religion et Idéologie dans la Révolution Anglaise*, Chapter V.
63. Sabine, pp. 323–4; cf. pp. 210, 215.
64. Ibid., pp. 490–92.
65. Ibid., pp. 425–6; cf. pp. 189–90, 228, 672.
66. Ibid., pp. 289–90, 297.

of flesh which is covetousness and pride, hath killed Jacob, the spirit of meekness and righteous government in the light of reason, and rules over him'. In consequence 'the earth hath been enclosed and given to the elder brother, Esau, . . . and hath been bought and sold one to another; and Jacob . . . is made a servant' to Lord Esau.

For Winstanley the myth of the two brothers blends with the myth of the Norman Yoke.[67] 'He lies hid in you, he is hated, persecuted and despised in you, he is Jacob in you, that is and hath been a servant to Esau a long time. . . . His time is now come'. 'Jacob now must have the blessing; . . . the poor shall inherit the earth'. It 'will be a great day of judgment' when Christ supplants Esau 'and takes the birthright and blessing from him (Isaiah XLIV.1 and chap. XLII.1)'.[68]

The near-Digger pamphlet *More Light Shining in Buckinghamshire* (March 1649) tells us that 'the rise of dukes was from wicked Esau'.[69] 'The earth', declared Winstanley, 'was never made by God that the younger brother should not live on the earth unless he would work for and pay his elder brother rent for the earth. . . . England cannot be a free commonwealth till this bondage be taken away'. Monarchy and the House of Lords have been abolished: 'now step two steps further, and take away the power of lords of manors and of tithing priests'.[70] Land is 'everyone's birthright' said Winstanley in *The Law of Freedom*; the land confiscated from King, church and royalists was 'the price of [the] labours, money, and blood' which Englishmen had expended in the civil war. 'Kingly government', under which the 'younger brother's creation birthright' is taken from him, 'may well be called the government of highwaymen'. It 'makes one brother a lord and another a servant while they are in their mother's womb'. The doctrine of rewards and punishments after death is a way of terrifying the younger brother into letting go 'his hold in the earth' and submitting 'to be a slave to his brother for fear of damnation in hell after death'. Those who preach such doctrines aim only 'to hinder Christ from rising, and to keep Jacob under to make him a slave to the man of the flesh'.[71]

All these myths, Winstanley argued, can be used to interpret contemporary political struggles: but they also describe conflicts within the heart of each one of us. 'Cain and Abel is to be seen within'. So are Esau

---

67. Ibid., pp. 253, 288–92, 323.
68. Ibid., pp. 309, 149, 178–9, 188, 209, 264–5 and *passim*.
69. Ibid., pp. 629; cf. pp. 637–5. See Genesis XXXVI.40 for 'the dukes that came of Esau' – even in the A.V. Cf. *BMW*, VII, p. 172.
70. Sabine, pp. 372–3; cf. pp. 480–86.
71. Ibid., pp. 528–31, 240–41; cf. pp. 288–9.

and Jacob, Abraham, Isaac, Moses, Israel, Judas, Demas, Simon Magus, scribes and Pharisees, Canaanites, Amalekites, Philistines. 'The land of Canaan, the habitation of rest', heaven and hell, Judas and Christ, are all to be seen within. Besides the Christ within 'there is no Saviour'.[72]

Winstanley's use of the Bible can be idiosyncratic. When he says 'I do walk in the daily practice of such ordinances of God as Reason and Scripture do warrant', we have to remember that in his view Reason and Scripture authorized neither prayer, preaching, holy communion, baptism, nor Sabbath observance.[73] Canaan, 'the land of rest and liberty', was divided by lots among the people of Israel. 'All that a man labours for, saith Solomon, is this, that he may enjoy the free use of the earth, with the fruits thereof. Eccles. II.24'.[74] More remarkably, 'that Scripture which saith, "the poor shall inherit the earth", is really and materially to be fulfilled'. All the prophecies concerning 'the restoration of the Jews' refer to the Diggers' 'work of making the earth a common treasury'. 'The time of Israel's restoration' is 'now beginning'. In consequence, 'Israel shall neither give hire nor take hire'.[75] Pharisees are the public preachers who try 'to hinder Christ from rising, or else to suppress and kill him again if they could after he is risen up in sons and daughters'. 'Priests and professors are . . . the successors of Judas'. 'Every treacherous and covetous heart is but the budding forth of Judas', who 'hath risen up to a mighty great tree'. 'University divinity . . . is Judas's ministry'. Babylon is 'that mighty city, divinity'.[76] The Beast of Revelation is 'kingly property'. Winstanley's references to 'plain-hearted Peter', 'single-eyed Nathanael . . . in whom there was no guile', 'Haman's proud heart', 'stout-hearted Pharaoh', and to 'meek-spirited Moses', 'a man that was mixed with flesh and spirit' – all these humanized Biblical characters. Men should be sceptical of clerical doctrine and 'become like wise-hearted Thomas, to believe nothing but what they see reason for'.[77]

'Cain is still alive in all great landlords', said a Digger broadside from Iver, Buckinghamshire, in May 1650. 'The Lord hath set Cain's mark upon lords of manors for their oppressions, cheating and robbery'. They must

---

72. Ibid., pp. 210, 214–15, 237–8; cf. pp. 99–102, 120–28.
73. Ibid., pp. 136–44. Cf. O. Lutaud, *Winstanley; Socialisme et Christianisme sous Cromwell* (Paris, 1977), esp. pp. 11–27, 80–82, 452–3.
74. Sabine, pp. 199, 520–21, 525, 413; cf. p. 215.
75. Ibid., pp. 389, 260–61, 190, 197.
76. Ibid., pp. 238, 436, 369, 237, 463, 479, 492, 570.
77. Ibid., pp. 160–63, 201, 207, 478–9, 483, 523.

'lie down and submit'.[78] When God's time is come, sang *The Diggers Mirth* in the same year,

> Then Esau's pottage shall be eat,
> For which he sold his right;
> The blessing Jacob shall obtain,
> Which Esau once did slight.

> And Jacob he shall then arise
> Although he be but small
> Which Esau once did much despise
> And Esau down must fall . . .

> But sing, O Jacob, for thy time
> Of freedom now is come;
> And thou thyself judge Esau,
> The which hath done thee wrong. . . .

> The time, I say, it is now come,
> In which the Lord will make
> All tyrants servants to the Son,
> And he the power will take.[79]

Loss of birthright freedom, and the struggle to recover it, became an issue for Levellers, Diggers, Army radicals and some early Quakers. In the background here is opposition to primogeniture, which was also a problem affecting sons of the gentry.[80] Harrington's agrarian law was intended to protect the interests of younger sons of gentry families. The radical Harringtonian William Sprigge in 1659 was still harping on Esau's sale of his birthright: he saw the Presbyterians selling their younger brother Independency. But with the failure of the Leveller campaign to win security of tenure for copyholders, with the progress of enclosure and consolidation of estates, accompanied by pauperization of those evicted, the issue of primogeniture may well have had wider repercussions.[81] 'Kingly

78. K. V. Thomas, 'Another Digger Broadside', *P. and P.*, 42 (1969), pp. 61–2.
79. In Sabine, pp. 673–5. The mess of pottage appears only in the Geneva version. Its survival in popular usage is testimony to that version's influence. Milton refers to 'Esau's red porrage' in *Animadversions upon The Remonstrants Defence against Smectymnuus* (1641), *MCPW*, I, p. 725; cf. III, p. 562.
80. Joan Thirsk, in her valuable article, 'Younger Sons in the Seventeenth Century' (*History*, 182, 1969), treats it as such. John Eliot, 'the Apostle to the Indians', thought Nimrod had tried to establish a new state composed of dissatisfied younger sons (J. Holstun, *A Rational Millennium, Puritan Utopias of Seventeenth-Century England*, Oxford U.P., 1987, pp. 107, 113).
81. Sprigge, *A Modest Plea for an Equal Commonwealth*, pp. 27, 44.

government', declared Winstanley, 'took his younger brother's creation birthright from him'. The manifestos of the Fifth Monarchist rebels in 1657 and 1661 promised to abolish primogeniture, so that 'the monopolies of elder brethren' would be destroyed.[82] The issue is everywhere in the literature of the time, from Shakespeare's *As You Like It* to Aphra Behn's *The Younger Brother*.

In the Old Testament, Ralegh pointed out, primogeniture seems not to be established.[83] Not only did Jacob supplant Esau but Reuben's birthright was given to Judah, Jacob's fourth son; and Jacob blessed Joseph's younger son despite his father's protests. David was Jesse's youngest son, and Solomon was David's ninth. When Jehoram, Jehoshaphat's eldest son, succeeded his father as King of Judah, 'he slew all his brethren with the sword' (II Chronicles XXI.3–4). Succession to the thrones of Israel and Judah by no means always went by heredity in the line of David. Jehu killed Jehoram King of Israel, son of Ahab and Jezebel, as well as Ahaziah King of Judah. Jehu demanded the heads of the seventy sons of Ahab; to make quite sure he 'slew all that remained of the house of Ahab in Israel'. In addition he slew all Baal's priests; God praised his diligence. He also slew all Ahaziah's brothers. Athaliah, Ahaziah's mother, destroyed all his seed (II Kings IX–XI).

For members of the English propertied class, however lowly, a gentleman's inheritance was his birthright, because he was freeborn, just as it was the birthright of the gentry 'to choose and be chosen commoners' (i.e. MPs).[84] For Winstanley the lower classes were the younger brother to whom the blessing should go. Esau sold his birthright, and all the perquisites belonging to it; he expected a *temporal* blessing, George Smith wrote in 1645: Jacob waited for a future happiness. This, Smith observed, often happens in families and kingdoms. There were always two sorts of men in the church of God, Cain and Abel, Esau as well as Jacob.[85]

Bunyan was much obsessed by Esau's sale of his birthright. Esau, like Cain, subsequently prospered, but to no avail.[86] Bunyan was naturally always on the side of the younger son, for Abel and Jacob against the older brother.[87] Bunyan's friend, John Owen, whose *Exposition of the Epistle to*

82. Sabine, p. 529; cf. the Digger's Song, ibid., pp. 673–5; [Anon.], *A Door of Hope*, p. 10; Capp, *The Fifth Monarchy Men*, pp. 105–7, 147, 176.
83. Ralegh, *History of the World*, II, p. 200. But cf. Deuteronomy XXI.15–17.
84. G. S[tarkey], *The Dignity of Kingship Asserted* (1660), p. 171.
85. Smith, *Englands Pressures, Or the Peoples Complaint*, pp. 4–5.
86. *BMW*, V, pp. 49–50.
87. Offor, II, p. 442.

the Hebrews was published from 1668 to 1684 (a year after his death) also stressed the uselessness of Esau's repentance.[88]

A century earlier, *The Historie of Jacob and Esau*, though sympathetic to Jacob, nevertheless allowed Isaac to state his position fairly. 'The title of birthright that cometh by descent', 'nature's law it is, the eldest son to [ac]knowledge' (lines 400–438). But in the 1640s and 1650s opposition to primogeniture was expressed by a broad spectrum of opinion, usually in Biblical language, by Levellers, Diggers, Fifth Monarchists, preachers of Fast Sermons,[89] law reformers,[90] Harringtonians and many other pamphleteers.[91] It was resented in New no less than in Old England.[92]

Others used Esau and Jacob to similar effect, though it seems impossible to determine who influenced whom. Boehme, many of whose works were translated into English in the revolutionary decades, had described the struggle between Esau and Jacob as one of good versus evil, of grace offered even to the wicked, but rejected by them.[93] Thomas Edwards attributed to Mrs Attaway 'and some of their tribe' the view that 'there was Esau's world and Jacob's world; this was Esau's world, but Jacob's world was coming shortly, wherein all creatures shall be saved'.[94] The anonymous *Certaine Queries Presented by many Christian People*, a millenarian pamphlet of 1649, proclaimed that 'Esau is the ending of the old world, and Jacob the beginning of the new. That is, the reign of the wicked Esau's progeny terminates the old world; and the reign of Jacob, of the saints (to whom the promise of dominion is made), begins the new world'.[95]

William Dell distinguished two seeds within the church, on grounds which were at once social and theological. One was 'dignified with degrees,

88. Owen, *Works*, VII, pp. 298–305.

89. Margaret James, *Social Problems and Policy during the Puritan Revolution, 1640–1660* (1930), pp. 26, 97–9 and references there cited; *FS*, XXVI, p. 326, where John Arrowsmith found 'a challenge of primogeniture' in Genesis XXXVIII.27–30.

90. Donald Veall, *The Popular Movement for Law Reform, 1640–1660* (Oxford U.P., 1970), pp. 217–19; William Sheppard, *Englands Balme* (1656), p. 214.

91. E.g. William Sprigge, *A Modest Plea for an Equal Commonwealth*, pp. 56–75; W. Covell, *A Declaration unto the Parliament* (1659), p. 17; cf. R. L. Greaves, *Saints and Rebels: Seven Nonconformists in Stuart England* (Mercer U.P., 1985), p. 204.

92. A. Delbanco, *The Puritan Ordeal*, pp. 47, 56.

93. Boehme, *The Signature of al things* (1621, trans. John Ellistone, 1651) (Everyman ed.), pp. 218–19; *Aurora* (1634, trans. J. Sparrow, 1656, reprinted 1960), pp. 7–9.

94. Edwards, *Gangraena*, Part III, pp. 26–7. The idea may derive from the Apocrypha, II Esdras VI.9.

95. Woodhouse, op. cit., p. 244.

names and titles, being exalted to great honour, authority and power'; the other lacked 'the titles and glory of the false teachers, which they utterly despise and refuse, and . . . all excellency of speech and wisdom and learning of this world'. The latter are acknowledged by 'all the true sheep of Christ'.[96] In 1653 G.W. (possibly George Wither) attacked the clergy who 'fish for honours, worldly power and riches'; 'the old itch of temporal lordship is wretchedly broke out upon you; your hands are the hands of Esau though your voice be the voice of Jacob'.[97]

Ranters made much less of Cain and Abel, Esau and Jacob, than the Diggers. In his Preface to Richard Coppin's *Divine Teachings* (1649), Abiezer Coppe contrasted the house of Esau – formal prayers and ordinances, fleshly righteousness, etc. – with Jacob's house ('that little spark that lies hid and buried under all your glorious formality'). The house of Esau 'is as stubble, and now as stubble fully dry'; Jacob's house will fall upon it like fire.[98]

Laud had observed that David speaks sometimes in his own person, sometimes in God's.[99] So did Coppe, in whose writings it is often unclear whether he or the deity is speaking. In *A Fiery Flying Roll*, published in 1650, he announced that 'Honour, nobility, gentility, property, superfluity' have been 'the cause of all the blood that ever hath been shed from the blood of the righteous Abel to the blood of the last Levellers that were shot to death' – presumably at Burford. Pointedly Coppe addressed Esau as 'Lord Esau'. Clarkson in his Ranter days used Cain as a symbol for the proud and rich.[100] Bauthumley too thought that 'the proud selfish being which is the Esau' was contrary to 'the sincere and pure divine being, which is the Jacob'; but both serve God's design. The Biblical stories of Cain and Abel, Esau and Jacob, good kings and bad, were for Bauthumley all allegories, not literal truths.[101] Erbery made the same point about Hagar and Ishmael, Sarah and Isaac, adding 'though such persons were'.[102] Winstanley had believed that the Spirit of universal love is the Lord of all the earth. 'His face is called the universal power of love; his back parts is called the selfish power'. Alternatively, they are

96. Dell, *Several Sermons and Discourses*, p. 542.
97. G.W., *The Modern States-man*, pp. 96–104, quoted by C. S. Hensley, *The Later Career of George Wither* (The Hague, 1969), p. 99.
98. In Smith, *Ranter Writings*, p. 78.
99. Lois Potter, *Secret Rites and secret writing*, p. 173.
100. Smith, *Ranter Writings*, pp. 174, 234, 262.
101. Bauthumley, *The Light and Dark Sides of God* (1650), in Smith, op. cit., p. 262.
102. Erbery, *The Mad Mans Plea* (1653), p. 1.

called the Son of Freedom and the Son of Bondage, Jacob and Esau, who 'strive in the womb of the earth, which shall come forth first, and which shall rule'.[103]

Richard Coppin had a similar idea: Jacob and Esau, a believer and an unbeliever, exist in all men. 'The beloved is elected and the hated is not'. God 'can save Jacob and destroy Esau, though they both remain in us'.[104] Roger Crab contrasted 'the law of the old man in my fleshly members' with 'the law of my mind'.[105] Coppin described the 'way of Cain' as 'looking for honour, acceptance and respect' for 'your works, religion, holy duties and so forth', and also for willingness 'to be promoted in the world, as to honour and greatness'.[106] He cited Cain's murder of Abel as one of many examples of the persecution of God's people.[107] He also uses the story of Jacob and Esau. 'By Esau is signified the greatness and honour of the world . . . for dukes, kings and nobles came from him'. But Jacob and Esau, believers and unbelievers, are to be found 'in each of us'.[108] In *Saul Smitten for Not Smiting Amalek* (1653) Coppin directly related Saul first to Charles I and then to the Long Parliament as exponents of Esau's principles. 'Jesus Christ is he that must recover . . . and restore into our hands again all our freedom, liberties and estates, both temporal and spiritual'.[109]

III

When Tawney tried to persuade the young Hugh Trevor-Roper that 'an erring colleague is not an Amalekite, to be hewn hip and thigh', he was both pleading for more civilized academic controversy and also implying that Trevor-Roper's methods were those appropriate to the barbarous tribes of the Old Testament, who had convinced themselves of their own righteousness and that their enemies were God's enemies. William Attersoll said that the Amalekites were 'discomfited more by the prayers of Moses

103. Sabine, p. 376.
104. Coppin, *The Exaltation of All things in Christ and of Christ in all things . . . Or, a Jacob and an Esau in one Rebecca* (1649) esp. pp. 4, 27–36, 46, 61; *Antichrist in Man*, pp. 56–7, and *passim*.
105. Crab, *The English Hermite and Dagons-Downfall* (1655) (ed. A. Hopton, 1990), p. 15.
106. Coppin, *Mans Righteousness Examined* (1652), pp. 25–7.
107. Coppin, *Crux Christi* (1657), p. 16.
108. Coppin, *Michael opposing the Dragon* (1659), pp. 83–9.
109. Coppin, op. cit., pp. 5–13, 29–30.

than by the sword of Joshua'.[110] *Mutatis mutandis*, his words apply to the outcome of the controversy between Tawney and Trevor-Roper. But in the seventeenth century the sword seemed the more appropriate weapon.

Amalek, 'the desperatest enemy that Israel ever had', was Esau's grandson (Genesis XVII.12, XXXVII.12). Milton described the prelates as 'beasts of Amalek'.[111] For Richard Coppin Amalek stood for kingly power, whether exercised by Charles I or by Parliament. The Amalekites include priests of the Church of England and their Presbyterian successors, as well as landowners. The Amalekites attacked the children of Israel in the days of Moses. and the 'Lord hath sworn that he will have war with Amalek from generation to generation' (Genesis XVII.16; Deuteronomy XXV). The sword of the Lord and of Gideon smote them (Judges VII), and Saul was commanded to finish them off. But he spared their King Agag, which made God repent that he had made Saul king. David did a better job, leaving not a man or a woman of the Amalekites alive (I Samuel XV, XXVII, XXX).[112]

Coppin saw Amalek as a symbol of the corruption of persecuting governments. 'Some all along in all ages have still appeared to war against Israel; ... papists, bishops, prelates and presbyters', and now probably Independents and Anabaptists, 'all like those oppressive Amalekites still acting against the appearance of the Lord Jesus in his people'. Amalek 'may relate to kings' houses and houses of former Parliaments', which 'tyrannized over my people'. As Saul was commanded to destroy Amalek, 'so the like command might come from the Lord to our general [Cromwell] to smite the late Parliament and to slay them of their oppressive power ... and to return all the rest, to wit, the people's interest, rights, privileges'. But, like Saul, Cromwell had not completed the job. 'Jesus Christ is he that must recover again ... and restore into our hands again all our freedoms, liberties and estates, both temporal and spiritual'.[113]

Joseph Salmon had argued on similar lines four years earlier. 'Time was when God dwelt amongst us in the darkness of absolute and arbitrary monarchy', veiling 'his beautiful presence with a thick cloud of darkness', a cloud of tyranny and persecution. Now he has 'come forth to rend this veil in pieces ... and clothe himself with another'. But 'the very soul of

---

110. Attersoll, *A Commentarie upon . . . Numbers*, p. 1095 (on Numbers XXV.17).
111. Gouge, *Commentary on . . . Hebrews*, III, pp. 217–18; *MCPW*, III, p. 435.
112. Coppin, *Saul Smitten for Not Smiting Amalek*, pp. 2, 5–6, 8–13, 29–30; cf. Gouge, *Commentary on . . . Hebrews*, III, p. 247.
113. Coppin, op. cit., pp. 56–7 and *passim*.

monarchy sunk into the Parliament'. 'It lost . . . its form, but not its power, they making themselves as absolute and tyrannical as ever the King in his reign'. Now the power has fallen to the Army. The generals are 'the rod of God'. 'You have a commission from the Lord to scourge England's oppressors'. But Salmon hoped that power would pass to 'the fellowship' of 'saints scattered' among common soldiers in the Army. He warned the generals that 'the same measure you mete, shall be met [sic] to you again, for the Lord will ere long cast his rod into the fire of burning and destruction. It will be a sweet destruction, wait for it'.[114] William Erbery, near-Ranter, used the familiar concept of Adam as a public person representing all mankind to argue that the New Model Army was 'the Army of God, as public persons', representing the people.[115]

Coppe used the Bible for his own purposes. Watching the extravagances of Nehemiah is preferable to hearing 'a zealous Presbyterian, Independent or spiritual notionist pray, preach or exercise'; he contrasted the 'mincing, nice, demure, barren Mical' with David's unseemly carriage, 'by skipping, leaping, . . . shamelessly, basely and uncovered too before handmaids'. Coppe spoke approvingly of the many 'pranks' of Ezekiel, son of Buzi (which being interpreted is the son of contempt) and of Hosea, 'who went in to a whore, etc.'[116]

Another legend full of possibilities was that of Nimrod, the first king, who built the Tower of Babel. He was the grandson of Ham, the accursed son of Noah (Genesis X.6–8). His tyranny 'came into a proverb', the Geneva margin declared. He appears as tyrant from Dante through Sir John Fortescue, Sir Walter Ralegh and many others down to *The Dutch Annotations Upon the Whole Bible* (1637 and later editions).[117] Foxe described the arch-persecutor Dr Edward Story as a 'Bloody Nimrod'.[118] Ralegh had seen Nimrod as a good colonizer, which perhaps tells us something

---

114. Salmon, *A Rout, A Rout,* (1649) in Smith, *Ranter Writings,* pp. 190–91, 193.

115. *The Testimony of William Erbery,* p. 25. Samson made the same claim in *Samson Agonistes*: 'I was no private, but a person raised/ With strength sufficient and command from heaven/ To free my country' (lines 1211–13).

116. Smith, *Ranter Writings,* pp. 42, 60, 63, 68, 70–71, 75, 77–8, 92–3, 100, 104, 107; cf. Salmon, ibid., p. 214, and Bauthumley, ibid., p. 236; Friedman, *Blasphemy, Immorality and Anarchy: The Ranters and the English Revolution* (Ohio U.P., 1987), pp. 33, 36–7 – Coppin. See also Smith, *Perfection Proclaimed: Language and Literature in English Radical Religion, 1640–1660* (Oxford U.P., 1989), p. 55.

117. T. R. Preston, 'Biblical Criticism, Literature and the 18th-century Reader', in *Books and their Readers in 18th-century England* (ed. I. Rivers, Leicester U.P., 1982), pp. 109–110.

118. Foxe, *Acts and Monuments,* VIII, p. 745.

about Sir Walter's colonizing methods.[119] The renegade Catholic archbishop, Mark Antony de Dominis, during his brief period in England, denounced the Pope as 'Nimrod, a tyrant, . . . yea even Antichrist himself'. This did not prevent him reverting to Rome when he failed to get what he regarded as adequate preferment in England.[120] In 1649 the King's prosecutor compared Charles I to 'Nimrod, . . . the first tyrant'; an anonymous Presbyterian writer accepted that Nimrod was a tyrant but argued that confusion was always worse than tyranny.[121]

Nimrod was of special significance for radicals, from Thomas Müntzer in 1525 and *Gods Promises* by John Bale[122] to the near-Digger pamphlets *Light Shining in Buckinghamshire* and *More Light Shining in Buckinghamshire* (1648 and 1649). The last-named generalized from Nimrod that 'the whole Scripture declares kings to be no better than tyrants and usurpers. . . . In that they were kings they were tyrants'. 'The titles of superiority, as king, lord, etc., are from the devil'.[123] Anabaptists were alleged – with considerable exaggeration – to have opposed all civil government because of Nimrod.[124] Matthias Prideaux described Popes between 608 and 855 as 'usurping Nimrods'.[125] Cornelius Burges in the first Fast Sermon (17 November 1640) complained that 'if but some of the Nimrods who have invaded their laws and liberties be pulled down (which is an act of justice) how do the many (who do nothing towards any reformation of themselves) rejoice!'[126] William Erbery in 1654, using Winstanley's pejorative phrase, spoke of 'Nimrod, that kingly power'. 'Kings with their nobles, lords and dukes all proceeded from a cursed pedigree'. They formed 'a race of oppression over the people of God'.[127]

Here, as with Cain and Abel, Esau and Jacob, the name of Nimrod is extended, to cover the tyranny of the upper class as well as of kings. Fulke Greville saw Nimrod, 'that man-hunting beast', as creator of 'the first God-

119. Ralegh, *History of the World*, II, pp. 119–35.
120. T. Fuller, *Church History of Britain* (1842), III, p. 298. First published 1655.
121. [Anon.], *The Lawfulness of obeying the Present Government and Acting under it* (1649), pp. 7–9.
122. *The Dramatic Works of John Bale*. Nimrod 'wrought abusion against God'.
123. In Sabine, pp. 612–13, 628–9, 632, 635.
124. Arnold Williams, op. cit., p. 222.
125. Prideaux, op. cit., Section VI.
126. *FS*, I, pp. 58–9.
127. Erbery, *The Man of Peace* (1654), pp. 5–6, in *The Testimony of William Erbery*, pp. 206–209. Former kings of England, including William the Conqueror and James I, had been just such oppressors.

scorning monarchy', which 'ended equality among men'.[128] Bishop
Babington in 1592 thought that 'a hard, a cruel, a greedy and covetous
man, that grindeth the face of his neighbours' was rightly called a
Nimrod.[129] Puritans saw Nimrod as an anti-Puritan. Robert Bolton
declared that 'every boisterous Nimrod, impure drunkard and self-guilty
wretch, is ready with great rage to fly in the face of every professor with
the imputation of Puritanism'.[130] Richard Stock, minister of the young
Milton's parish, wrote of 'men of riches, . . . honour and high places', who
'oppress others without fear; like mighty Nimrods, they tyrannize in peace
and war'.[131] Thomas Adams eloquently denounced 'cruel Nimrods, riding
over innocent heads, as they would over fallow lands'; 'the covetous
Nimrod, that rode on the black beast oppression'. He drew on other kings
from the Old Testament to describe landlords who 'have Rehoboam's
hand, a heavy hand on their tenants', usurers who 'have Ahab's hand, to
take the profit of the poor debtor's heritage', and parishioners who have
'Jeroboam's hand'.[132] Edward Benlowes too extended Nimrod to cover
the mighty hunting gentry

> Whose vast desires engross the boundless land
> By fraud or force.

But

> Nimrod's vulture talons pared shall be; . . .
> Their Bethsaida shall be turned to Bethany

– from the house of hunting to the house of mourning.[133]

Royalists were naturally on the defensive about Nimrod. Bishop Griffith
Williams in 1644 argued that Adam, not Nimrod, was the first king,
though he had to 'confess the first kingdom that is spoken of by that name
is the kingdom of Nimrod', and that monarchy had often been transferred
by conquest. But 'we are not to contest about words', he blustered; 'there

---

128. Greville, *A Treatie of Warres*, in *Poems and Dramas* (ed. G. Bullough, Edinburgh,
n.d., ?1939, I, p. 217).
129. Babington, *Notes upon everie Chapter of Genesis*, fol. 39v.
130. Bolton, *The Four Last Things* (1633), p. 169. (Posthumously published: Bolton
died in 1631.)
131. Stock, *Exposition Upon . . . Malachi*, p. 17. Stock had a reputation in the City for
social radicalism: see pp. 162–3 above.
132. Adams, *The Happiness of the Church* (1619), I, pp. 161, 175; II, p. 314.
133. Benlowes, *Theophila* (1652), Canto I, stanzas XXXVIII–XXXIX; H. Jenkins,
Edward Benlowes (1602–1676): Biography of a Minor Poet (London U.P., 1952), p. 97.

had been kings ever since Adam'.[134] Filmer is also a little hesitant about Nimrod, who 'against right did . . . enlarge his empire by seizing violently on the rights of other lords of families, and in this sense he may be said to be the author and first founder of monarchy'. But he derived his kingship originally, through Noah, from Adam.[135] Blair Worden cites a royalist newspaper, *The Man in the Moon* (26 December 1649 – 2 January 1649–50), as calling Oliver Cromwell 'proud Nimrod in Ireland'.[136]

The anonymous author of *Tyranipocrit Discovered* brought an additional charge against 'that proud Babylonian builder Nimrod'. Linguistic confusion dated from the building of Babel, so that now 'he that cannot speak strange languages [i.e. Latin and Greek] shall not be thought fit to preach, nor to teach Christians'. It had been another way of ending human equality.[137] Edmund Ludlow made an ingenious point when he said that it was 'the great design' of the post-restoration authorities 'to keep up their Nimrodian power by dividing the languages of the people of God': so opposition to Nimrod became a call to unity among the godly.[138]

Owen in 1652 spoke of 'great Nimrods and Oppressors'.[139] Three years later the Fifth Monarchist Christopher Feake cited 'the proud Nimrods of the world' in an attack on Oliver Cromwell and 'the new monarchical tyrants, who are but of yesterday'. He was defending the republican Good Old Cause.[140] John Rogers in 1657 distinguished two seeds since the Fall of Man. 'The governments of the world have been of the Serpent, and not of the Woman, to this day'. The time had come, he thought, when a period would be put to 'the Nimrodian dominions of the world'. 'Woe to you, tyrants and Nimrods of the earth, that do now rule over the

134. Griffith Williams, *Jura Majestatis: The Rights of Kings Both in Church and State*, pp. 14–15, 67.
135. Filmer, *Patriarcha and Other Political Works*, p. 59. Cf. Samuel Rutherford, *Lex, Rex*, p. 93, who accepts Nimrod as the founder of monarchy.
136. Worden, 'Andrew Marvell, Oliver Cromwell and the Horatian Ode', in *Politics of Discourse: The Literature and History of Seventeenth-century England* (ed. K. Sharpe and S. N. Zwicker, California U.P., 1987), p. 176. I find Worden's guess that Marvell's 'the English Hunter' in line 110 is Nimrod and therefore Oliver Cromwell far from convincing.
137. Op. cit., p. 26.
138. Ludlow, *A Voyce from the Watch Tower*, p. 309.
139. Owen, *Christ's Kingdom and the Magistrate's Power, Works*, VII, p. 373.
140. Feake, Preface to *Mr Tillinghasts 8 Last Sermons* (1655), sig. A 2v–8v.
141. Rogers, *A High-Witness, or a Heart Appeals*, pp. 67–9, bound with *Jegar-Sahadotha: An Oiled Pillar Set up for Posterity*; Rogers, Epistle before John Canne's *The Time of the End* (1657), sig. b 4–b 4v.

saints and make them to howl'.[141] The Fifth Monarchy manifesto, *A Door of Hope*, published in connection with the revolt of 1661, used Cain and Nimrod as symbols of oppressive rulers.[142] Nimrod, W. Y. Tindall tells us, was the usual name for the exiled Charles II among Baptists.[143] An Independent congregation, after his majesty's happy restoration, was reported as singing a hymn containing the line 'Let Nimrod end his reign'.[144]

From at least 1641 Milton had been denouncing bishops as 'cruel Nimrods'. Nimrod is 'said to have been the first tyrant'.[145] So there was no need for him to be named in *Paradise Lost*, any more than Milton named Cain in Book XI. Another 'rebel king', also unnamed, is Jeroboam (*PL*, I. 488), who introduced idolatry (*PR*, III. 414–32). Milton described mankind after the Flood as living 'in joy unblamed', 'in peace by families and tribes/Under paternal rule'. But Nimrod's 'proud ambitious heart' was 'not content/With fair equality, fraternal state', and arrogated to himself 'dominion undeserved/Over his brethren', 'from heaven claiming second sovereignty', which Joan Bennett interprets as a thrust at divine right theories.[146] Nimrod thus, Dr DiSalvo suggests, brought about 'a virtual second Fall'. She quotes Sebastian Franck, who saw the origins of private property in that second Fall, although 'God had made all things common'.[147]

Milton had often praised 'two things to [kings] so dreadful, liberty and equality'.[148] But the concept of 'fraternity' is not one that we often encounter in the seventeenth century, even among the revolutionaries: so it is interesting to see Milton picking up an earlier radical idea. He made the popular but erroneous assumption that Nimrod's very name derived from rebellion. After listening to Michael's account of human history, Adam concluded 'Man over man/[God] made not lord' – lines in which Professor

---

142. Op. cit., p. 1.

143. Tindall, *John Bunyan*, p. 266. Tindall cites many post-restoration references to Nimrod.

144. R. L. Greaves, in *Biographical Dictionary of British Radicals in the Seventeenth Century*, II, p. 215.

145. *MCPW*, I, p. 279; III, p. 598; IV, p. 473.

146. Bennett, *Reviving Liberty: Radical Harmonies in Milton's Great Poems* (Harvard U.P., 1989), p. 50.

147. Jackie DiSalvo, *War of Titans: Blake's Critique of Milton and the Politics of Religion* (Pittsburgh U.P., 1983), pp. 148, 192–3. Thomas Müntzer had also associated Nimrod with the origin of private property and inequality (N. Cohn, *The Pursuit of the Millennium*, 1957, pp. 267–8).

148. *MCPW*, III, p. 509. Cf. Fulke Greville, quoted on pp. 218–19 above.

Radzinowicz even sees Milton's republicanism.[149] The archangel agreed, but drew the sombre conclusion that

> Since thy original lapse, true liberty
> Is lost, which always with right reason dwells . . .
>   God in judgment just
> Subjects [man] from without to violent lords;
> Who oft as undeservedly enthrall
> His outward freedom: tyranny must be,
> Though to the tyrant thereby no excuse (XII.13–96).

The 'great laughter' in heaven which greeted the hubbub of Babel offends some of Milton's readers. For Milton it no doubt seemed the obvious reaction of omniscience to Nimrod.

So Nimrod could be a symbol for a bad king, of whom there were so many in the Old Testament. Or he could stand for all usurpers, and so cast no slur on legitimate kings. Milton is unusual in stressing that Nimrod's usurpation marked the origin of inequality as well as of kingship, the end of fraternity.

Bunyan is less specifically republican than Milton. But he too emphasizes that Nimrod was a rebel, who 'did scorn that others, or any, should be his equal', he and his like 'desiring mastership over their brethren'. Nimrod 'was the first that in this new [post-diluvian] world sought after absolute monarchy. . . . He therefore would needs be the author and master of what religion he pleased.' The Biblical description of him as 'a mighty hunter' meant that he was a great persecutor, in order to 'lord it over the sons of God and to enforce idolatry and superstition upon them'.[150] Absolute monarchy means tyranny, persecution and idolatry. Cain, Esau and Nimrod were captains of Diabolus's persecuting Bloodmen in *The Holy War*.[151] Bunyan's assumption seems to be that all Adam's seed were brethren, and presumably equal, before monarchy was established. He does not use the word 'fraternity', but he shares the concept with Milton. Filmer, appropriately, held that Nimrod was rightful lord or king over his family and thought none the worse of him for enlarging his empire by violence.[152]

149. M. A. Radzinowicz, 'The Politics of *Paradise Lost*', in *Politics of Discourse* (ed. K. Sharpe and S. N. Zwicker, California U.P., 1987), p. 213.
150. Offor, II, pp. 497–8.
151. Bunyan, *The Holy War*, pp. 228–9.
152. Filmer, *Patriarcha and Other Writings*, p. 8. See pp. 194–5 above, and cf. John Eliot on Nimrod, quoted on p. 211 n. above.

IV

The tendency to allegorize the Scriptures, and to stress the Spirit within believers rather than the letter of the Bible, undermined the authority of the sacred text for many of the radicals – Gerrard Winstanley, for instance. Before the digging on St George's Hill began, Winstanley had already rejected the Ten Commandments as 'the letter' to which the Spirit was superior. He suggested that the angels who visited Abraham, Lot and Samson's parents were material men: 'and their vanishing . . . is no other but their departure . . . when they had done the work they were sent about'.[153] In *Truth Lifting up its Head above Scandals* (1649) Winstanley had accepted that the text of the Bible was uncertain. 'There are many translations and interpretations which differ much from one another'. And he asked 'How can these Scriptures be called the everlasting Gospel, seeing it is torn in pieces daily amongst yourselves [the clergy] by various translations, inferences and conclusions'.[154] In *The New Law of Righteousness* (1649) he contrasted Cain's cry 'everyone that sees me will kill me' with the fact that, according to Genesis, Adam was the only other man then living in the world.[155] Winstanley rejected much Biblical history in favour of allegorical interpretations. The Fall of Man, the Virgin Birth, the resurrection, the 'ascension so-called', the Second Coming, are all allegories.[156] The War in Heaven, 'wherein Michael and the Dragon fight the great battle of God Almighty' takes place within 'the living soul'.[157] Winstanley's relaxed 'whether there was any such outward things or no [as the Genesis story of the Fall] it matters not much' sums up his attitude.[158]

Winstanley is I believe unique in asking the specific question, 'What use is to be made of the Scriptures?' And he replied that they are a record of experience, from which we can learn to wait upon the Father until he

153. Winstanley, *The Saints Paradise*, pp. 12, 36, 78.
154. Sabine, pp. 100, 128.
155. Ibid., p. 210.
156. Sabine, pp. 480–88; cf. ibid., pp. 113–16, 273; *The Saints Paradise*, pp. 82–8; *The Mysterie of God*, pp. 67–9. As Pocock put it, 'community of ownership of the earth and the resurrection of Christ are interchangeable concepts' for Winstanley (*Political Works of James Harrington*, p. 96; cf. p. 80).
157. Sabine, pp. 481, cf. *PL*, V. 474–6.
158. Sabine, p. 462; cf. pp. 153, 211, 216–19, 223, 226–7, 377, 409, 454, 463, 484, 495; *The Saints Paradise*, pp. 21–3. Winstanley had been anticipated by Henrik Niclaes: see Jean Dietz Moss, ' "Godded with God": Henrik Niklaes and His Family of Love', *Trans. American Philosophical Soc.*, 71 (1982), pp. 46–7.

teaches us. When Winstanley himself finds agreement between 'the feeling of light within my own soul' and the Biblical record of 'experimental testimony', his 'joy is fulfilled'. 'Every man and woman may declare what they have received, and so become preachers one to another.' We need no professional preachers.[159] Winstanley told Fairfax that the question of liberty for all men and women to cultivate the earth was 'not to be answered by any text of Scripture, or example since the Fall, but the answer is to be given in the light of itself, which is the law of righteousness, or that Word of God that was in the beginning, which dwells in every man's heart and by which he was made, even the pure law of the creation'. We must throw off the tyranny of the Bible.[160] But 'there are good rules in Scripture if they were obeyed and practised', Winstanley told Cromwell. One such good rule was Christ's instruction to soldiers 'be content with your wages (Luke III.14)'. Winstanley used this to warn officers against buying up debentures from their troops to enrich themselves with confiscated lands.[161]

Radicals were accused of using the Bible as a code which they understood among themselves but whose meaning was not immediately obvious to others. But conservatives could put the Bible to their uses too. John Trapp, commenting on the strait gate in Matthew VII.13, said that the moral was that we should not join 'the rude rabble ever running apace to the pit of perdition'. Christ's charity to blind men in Matthew XX.30–34 gave Trapp the chance to rail at vagabonds; Revelation XIV.3 made him pray for deliverance in England 'from the Antichristian rout and rabble'. Luke XIX.12–14 tells us that 'his citizens hated' the nobleman who 'went into a far country to receive for himself a kingdom'. Trapp's comment – not without its relevance to England in the 1640s – was 'such masterless monsters are rife everywhere'.[162]

As long ago as the fifteenth century Reginald Pocock had declared that the evident contradictions of Scripture meant that it must be submitted to human reason.[163] Protestant Bibliolatry temporarily pushed such ideas underground. There had of course been critics of the Bible, whose views before 1640 got into print only when the authors, or alleged authors, were

159. Sabine, p. 128.

160. Ibid., p. 289; cf. p. 569.

161. Ibid., pp. 509, 363. Cf. Milton's equally condescending attitude towards the decalogue, p. 374 below.

162. Trapp, *Commentary on the New Testament*, pp. 125, 226, 335, 766, 770.

163. Pocock, *The Repressor of over much blaming of the Clergy* (?c.1455), quoted by A. Hudson, *The Premature Reformation*, p. 441.

under attack. Fuller records the abjuration of the Rev. John Hilton in 1586. He had rejected the Trinity and had said that the Old and New Testaments were fables.[164] Christopher Marlowe was reported to have 'read the atheist lecture' to Ralegh and others. Marlowe discussed Biblical criticism, the contradictions of Scripture and comparative religion with Thomas Hariot, William Warner and Matthew Roydon, which scandalized the government's informers and helped to created the legend of Ralegh's 'school of atheism'.[165] Ralegh in his *History of the World*, though accepting the Biblical narrative as basic, saw Christianity as only one of many religions, and indulged in a good deal of textual criticism. He discussed the Flood and the location of the earthly Paradise in the light of his own experience in distant parts of the world.[166] Francis Osborn looked back to Ralegh as 'the first . . . to sail aloof from the beaten track of the Schools'; Osborn followed him.[167] Hariot was accused of denying the immortality of the soul and and of arguing that the world was eternal, not created by God[168] – a view later taken up by Ranters and repudiated by Bunyan. Hariot and Marlowe argued on Biblical evidence that there had been men before Adam – a view which Winstanley reproduced.[169]

The Copernican hypothesis put new strains on Biblical fundamentalism. Edward Wright, introducing Gilbert's *De Magnete* of 1600, refused to reject the theory of the earth's rotation on Scriptural evidence alone;[170] John Wilkins, future bishop, admitted that the 'penmen of Scriptures might be grossly ignorant', though he nevertheless claimed that astronomy confirms the truth of the Bible.[171] Many were the denunciations of sceptics. In Essex in 1575 there were 'divers that do not pass by the Word of God a whore's turd'.[172] There must have been a great deal of plebeian ribaldry

164. Fuller, *Church History*, III, p. 75–6.

165. My *Intellectual Origins of the English Revolution* (Oxford U.P., 1965), pp. 143, 172–3, and references there cited; *Works of Thomas Kyd* (ed. F. S. Boas, Oxford U.P., 1891), p. cxvi.

166. *Intellectual Origins*, pp. 185–91; Ralegh, *History of the World*, esp. I, pp. 63, 75–98, 138–40, 158, 223–50; II, pp. 8–16, 56, 223, 278–82, 369.

167. Osborn, *Essays*, p. 11, in *Miscellaneous Works* (11th ed., 1722), I.

168. Richard Harvey, *A Theologicall Discourse of the Lamb of God and his enemies* (1590); Thomas Nashe, *Pierce Penilesse* (1592).

169. Nashe, *Works* (ed. R. B. McKerrow, 1958), I, p. 171; C. Nicholl, *A Cup of News: The Life of Thomas Nashe* (1984), pp. 106–8.

170. Gilbert, op. cit., p. xli.

171. Wilkins, *Discourse concerning a new Planet*, pp. 10–14, 237–40.

172. F. G. Emmison, *Elizabethan Life: Morals and the Church Courts* (Chelmsford, 1973), p. 72.

about the Bible, very little of which got recorded. Thomas tells us of Essex parishioners who in 1630 asked where Adam and Eve got thread to sew their fig-leaves. 'When another contemporary preacher attempted to explain that heaven was so high that a millstone would take hundreds of years to come down from it, one of his hearers asked how long in that case it would take a man to get up there?'[173]

John Davies of Hereford confessed the difficulty of coming to knowledge of God's will by his Word, which can be so diversely interpreted, and 'many doctors so deceived have been'. Like the radicals of the 1640s, he relied on 'the inspiration of thy spirit of truth', not on the authority of 'great clerks' or anyone else. Like many others, he was shaken by Bartholomew Legate's public execution by burning at Smithfield in 1612, and depicted the heretic as saying

> Faith, though false it be
> Yet, if the soul persuaded be it's true,
> Upon the heart it worketh morally
> As faith doth which to heavenly truth is due.[174]

Lord Brooke subjected the Bible to searching textual criticism.[175] Francis Quarles believed that 'the Scripture lies open to the humble heart, but locked against the proud inquisitor'. We should not take our religion from our fathers, 'nor the Fathers, nor the church'. 'He that believes with an implicit faith is a mere empiric in religion'.[176] Sir Thomas Browne indulged in speculation about repeopling the world after the Flood, and about Babel, recognizing that 'there are in Scripture stories that do exceed the fables of poets'.[177] Joseph Hall in the same year 1646 published *Satans Fiery Darts Quenched: Temptations Repelled*, of which the first three decades deal with 'Temptations of Impiety'. Here there is much evidence of current criticism of Christianity.[178]

Controversies in James I's reign over exorcism had led to questions being asked about the reality both of diabolical possession and of miracles, which

173. *TRDM*, pp. 161 and 167–73.
174. Davies, *The Muses Sacrifice: or Divine Meditations* (1612), in *Complete Works*, II, p. 37; Appendix, p. 78.
175. Brooke, *A Discourse Opening the Nature of that Episcopacie, which is exercised in England*, esp. pp. 119–20.
176. Quarles, *Enchyridion* (1641), p. 47, in *Complete Works*, I.
177. Browne, *Pseudodoxia Epidemica* (1646), Book VI, Chapter 6.
178. Hall, *Works*, VII, pp. 285–314; cf. VIII, p. 9.

are reflected in Ben Johnson's *Volpone* and *The Devil is an Ass*.[179] Selden was criticized for the way in which, in his great *History of Tithes* (1618), he used the Bible as a historical source, to be treated with respect but to be interpreted in the light of other contemporary documents. He was a good deal more forthcoming in his *Table-Talk*, published posthumously.[180] Chillingworth's *The Religion of Protestants a Safe Way to Salvation* (1637) elevated the Bible above all human authority; but the Bible had to be interpreted by human reason. Lord Herbert of Cherbury believed that there was no way to prove that the Bible was the Word of God.[181] Edmund Waller thought that the Bible could be made to prove anything.[182]

James Cowderoy in 1608 quoted worldlings who said there were 'so many falsehoods and untruths, so many absurdities, in the Bible, that he is a senseless man that perceiveth it not, and a fool that believeth it'.[183] More moderately, Arthur Dent suggested that the Scriptures formed 'a devised or positive law, made for the civil government *only*, and authorized . . . lest man not being restrained . . . should not yield himself to necessary order'.[184] The word I have italicized is perhaps significant: the whole passage seems to look forward to Hobbes. In 1618 William Attersoll denounced atheists who deny the resurrection of the body and the immortality of the soul.[185] Jeremiah Lewis said a year later, in a sermon preached on Guy Fawkes Day, that profane atheists are 'in every ale-house'.[186]

What we do not know is how far the scepticism of the Ralegh circle extended. We hear echoes of it in Ralegh's Devon,[187] and when the Virginia Company drafted laws for its colony they thought it necessary to prescribe the death penalty for doing or saying anything that might 'tend to the derision' of the Bible.[188] In some circles, if not in every ale-house, the Bible had no doubt become the object of profane mockery. Richard Rogers in 1615 attacked those who laughed at Adam's sin: 'he did but eat

179. D. P. Walker, *Unclean Spirits: Possession and Exorcism in France and England in the Late 16th and Early 17th Centuries* (1980), p. 109 and *passim*.

180. Selden, op. cit., pp. 7–12.

181. Herbert, *De religione laici* (1645), pp. 308–13, 317.

182. Waller, *Speech . . . concerning episcopacie* (1641), p. 6.

183. Cowderoy, *A Warning for Worldlings*, pp. 202–3.

184. Dent, *The Opening of Heavens Gates* (1617), p. 6.

185. Attersoll, *A Commentarie upon . . . Numbers*, p. 933.

186. Lewis, *The Doctrine of Thankfulnesse: Or, Israels Triumph Occasioned by the destruction of Pharaoh and his hoste in the Red-Sea*, p. 45. Cf. pp. 15, 39, 90 above.

187. Pierre Lefranc, *Sir Walter Ralegh, Ecrivain: l'Oeuvre et les idées* (Paris, 1968), p. 381.

188. William Strachey, *For the Colony in Virginea Britannica: Lawes Divine, Morall and Martiall* (ed. D. H. Flaherty, Charlottesville, 1969), pp. 11–13.

an apple (a matter of nothing)'.[189] In 1656 John Reeve said that nobody who thought about it seriously 'could be so weak as to think that the Law of Eternal Life and Death depended upon the eating of an apple from a natural tree'.[190] Winstanley had anticipated him, and Milton's Satan was to make a jest of that apple.[191] Perkins had laboriously refuted 'atheists' who jeered at the idea that the roof of Dagon's temple, capable of accommodating 3,000 persons, could have been held up by the two pillars which Samson pulled down.[192]

But we should not think that use of the Bible in seventeenth-century controversy involved a 'holy pretence'. Most took it entirely seriously. When untraditional actions were being forced on men, they wished to find traditional authorities to justify them in a society where innovation was widely assumed to be wrong. Radicals who looked back to the heretic succession – the Waldensians, Wyclif, Hus – proclaimed the evolution of truth. 'The praise and glory of a church or Christian', declared William Bradshaw, 'doth not lie in this, being always the same, but in growing and proceeding from grace to grace'.[193]

Thomas Cartwright had advanced what proved to be the dangerous proposition, that 'the general tenor of the Bible's teaching' should be preferred to the letter.[194] This procedure enabled one to dismiss individual inconvenient texts, but it opened the door to completely subjective interpretations of 'the general tenor of the Scriptures'. As Anthony Ascham put it in 1649, speaking ostensibly of the Jews in the Old Testament: 'when they had a mind to change the government, to enter into civil war, to change a royal family, to reform religion and to dismember their kingdom, ... they presently had a voice from heaven to assure their actions and secure their courses'.[195] Some radicals developed the doctrine of 'continuous revelation' with similar effects. 'The believer', proclaimed William Dell, 'is the only book in which God now writes his New Testament'.[196] Thomas Goodwin made a similar point slightly differently, citing Ephesians II.6:

189. Rogers, *Commentary Upon . . . Judges*, p. 698.

190. Reeve, *A Divine Looking-Glasse*, p. 136. I cite from the edition of 1719. Cf. the Muggletonian Thomas Tomkinson, *Truth's Triumph: or, A Witness to the Two Witnesess* (1823), p. 107. First published 1676.

191. For Winstanley, see p. 201 above; *PL*, X. 485–90.

192. Perkins, *Cases of Conscience*, in *Workes*, II, pp. 59–60.

193. Bradshaw, *Exposition of the Second Epistle to the Thessalonians*, p. 18.

194. *Cartwrightiana*, pp. 17, 78–88.

195. Ascham, *Of the Confusions and Revolutions of Governments*, p. 109.

196. Dell, *The Tryal of the Spirits* (1653), in *Several Sermons and Discourses*, p. 419.

Christ 'hath raised us up together and made us sit together in the heavenly places in Christ Jesus'. He insisted that this occurred on earth, in this life. This concept of 'continuous revelation' fitted in with the millenarian idea that the last times were upon us, in which it was natural that the elect should have new insights.[197]

Radicals argued that 'the mystery' was more important than 'the history' for understanding the Bible. What objectivity remained in the text? Who was to decide between rival interpretations? That question had been put to the martyr John Philpot when he was on trial in 1555. He and the four bishops interrogating him were unable to agree,[198] and it was no easier a century later.

Arise Evans in his simple but shrewd way often expressed truths too obvious for cleverer men to state. The Bible, he said, used to be 'engrossed . . . in great men's hands, so that they might do as they pleased with the people that knew little or no Scripture'. But now, since the invention of printing and freedom to read the Bible, 'knowledge is increased among the people and shall increase; so that they will not be ruled by the kings set up after the manner of the Gentiles any more'. And he drew directly political conclusions: 'Here is the Good Old Cause that God raised our Army to stand for'.[199] Milton had asserted as early as 1641 that the Bible 'ought to be so in proportion as may be wielded and managed by the life of man, without penning him up from the duties of human society'.[200] Henry Parker said something very similar three years later: 'When we are treating of worldly affairs, we ought to be very tender how we seek to reconcile that to God's law which we cannot reconcile to man's equity; or how we make God the author of that constitution which man reaps inconvenience from'.[201] The heart of John Goodwin's argument for toleration, Ellen More tells us, was that Scripture must be read in the light of reason. Goodwin continued to believe in the divine authority of the Bible, but came to doubt whether agreement on the original, exact meaning could ever be arrived at by exegesis and debate.[202] But how then was one to

197. Goodwin, *An Exposition of the Second Chapter of the Epistle to the Ephesians*, in *Works*, II, pp. 243–4. Cf. p. 416 below.
198. Foxe, *Acts and Monuments*, VII, p. 619.
199. Arise Evans, *A Rule from Heaven* (1659), pp. 45–57.
200. *MCPW*, I, p. 699.
201. Parker, *Jus Populi* (1644), p. 57.
202. Ellen More, 'John Goodwin and the Origins of the New Arminianism', *Journal of British Studies*, XXII (1982), pp. 58, 63–6. She refers especially to Goodwin's *Redemption Redeemed* of 1651.

know who was right? The sceptical Leveller John Wildman could not 'think that anyone doth speak for God' merely because 'he says what he speaks is of God'. 'That only is of God', Wildman argued, 'that does appear to be like unto God – justice and mercy'.[203] But here again judgments could differ.

During the revolutionary decades bewildering novelties had appeared on the intellectual scene. Wide vistas of speculation were opened up by the anonymous author of *Tyranipocrit Discovered* in 1649, when he pointed out that 'hypocritical tyrants can alter and wrest the Scripture how they will have it'.[204] Milton licensed a translation of the Socinian catechism, and justified himself on the principles of *Areopagitica*. In 1649 a translation of the Koran was published. It led Bunyan to agonizing doubts about the authority of the Bible, asking with Samuel Fisher whether the Koran's traditional authority in Muslim countries might not be as good as that of the Bible in Christendom.[205] Boehme, also translated in 1649, had compared Turks favourably with many 'titular Christians'.[206]

Nearly a century earlier, in 1557, John Knox had observed that many Turks lived better lives than Christians; and he thought it necessary to add that this did not prove their religion true.[207] The opening up of trade to the eastern Mediterranean and to the Far East had brought merchants into contact with the great religions of Islam, Hinduism and Buddhism. George Sandys's *A Relation of a Journey* (1615), books like Henry Lord's *A Display of two Forraigne Sects in the East Indies* (1630), Sir Henry Blount's *A Voyage to the Levant* (1636),[208] showed that the newly-revealed religions could not be dismissed as mere 'heathenism'. The implications were open for discussion in the liberty of the 1640s. Wildman in the Putney Debates reflected that the sun or the moon might be God, for all we can tell by 'the light of nature'. He concluded that it was 'beyond the power of reason . . . to demonstrate the Scriptures to be . . . written by the Spirit of God'. More to the point, he added 'We cannot find anything in the Word of God what is fit to be done in civil matters'.[209] Francis Osborn wrote favourably of

203. Woodhouse, op. cit., p. 108.
204. Op. cit., p. 45.
205. Bunyan, *Grace Abounding*, p. 31; S. Fisher, *The Rustickes Alarm to the Rabbies* in *The Testimony of Truth Exalted* (1679), p. 388. See p. 235 below.
206. *Mercurius Teutonicus, or . . . Writings of . . . Jacob Behmen*, pp. 36–9, 51.
207. Knox, *Works* (ed. D. Laing, Edinburgh, 1846–64), IV, p. 264.
208. Cf. S. P. Chew, *The Crescent and the Rose: Islam and England during the Renaissance* (New York, 1937) esp. Part I, Chapter 3.
209. Woodhouse, op. cit., pp. 161, 108.

Mohammedanism and Turkish tolerance.[210] Henry Stubbe compiled a history of Islam, implying that it was in many respects preferable to Christianity: his book was unpublishable.[211] Henry Neville thought there was nothing to be said for the Bible which could not be said for the Koran.[212] Islam suggests monotheism. George Wither's Hymn for Ascension Day (1623) had stressed the humanity of Christ, in a way that looks forward to *Paradise Regained*. 'The human nature' is now above the angels; 'and at man's feet all angels bow'. Christ is 'our Lord and Brother'.[213]

William Erbery, Edwards tells us, questioned 'the certainty and sufficiency of the Scriptures', since the text varied in 'so many several copies'.[214] Edwards gives us a fascinating glimpse of a later occasion when Erbery, spending a night in Marlborough *en route* for Wales, spoke at an informal meeting there. He denied the divinity of Christ, and was taken up by a member of his audience who cited I John V.7 and other texts to the contrary. Erbery replied 'it was not so in the original; . . . those words were not in the Greek, but put in by some who were against the Arians'.[215] That sort of exchange, we must imagine, was going on all over the country in the mid-forties as self-educated men found themselves newly liberated to struggle with the fundamentals of theology, without inhibitions.

Winstanley noted contradictions in the Bible: it revealed the existence of men before Adam. To treat the Bible as a narrative of historical events is to make it an idol. Nor should we 'let the clergy be the keepers of [our] eyes and knowledge'.[216] 'Many thousands in these nations', wrote John Reeve in 1656, 'count the Scriptures mere inventions of wise men, to keep the simple in awe under their rulers'.[217] In the same year 'Jock of Broad Scotland', Alexander Agnew, was hanged for denying, among many other things, that the Scriptures are the Word of God.[218] Robert Gell, whom we have met in connection with astrology, accused the A.V. of mistranslating

210. Osborn, *Political Reflections upon the Government of the Turks* (1656), in *Miscellaneous Works*, II. See pp. 235, 257 below.

211. J. R. Jacob, *Henry Stubbe, Radical Protestantism and the Early Enlightenment* (Cambridge U.P., 1983), Chapters 5 and 8 and *passim*. Stubbe's *Account of the Rise and Progress of Mahometanism* was not published until 1911.

212. *Calendar of Clarendon State Papers* (ed. F. J. Routledge, Oxford U.P., 1872–1970), p. 161.

213. Wither, *Hymns and Songs of the Church*, pp. 206–7. 'Sing as the 117th Psalm'.

214. Edwards, *Gangraena*, I, p. 78.

215. Ibid., III, p. 90.

216. Sabine, p. 513. Cf. pp. 209–10 above.

217. Reeve, *A Divine Looking-Glasse*, p. 94.

218. *Mercurius Politicus*, 3 July 1656, No. 316, pp. 7064–6.

in order to avoid 'that (as too many esteem it) execrable error of inherent righteousness'. He claimed to have detected 676 pages of errors, mostly trivial, though he had 'wittingly passed by many oversights'. The translation of the New Testament is worse than that of the Old, the Apocrypha worst of all.[219]

In the early months of 1649 Ralph Josselin was busy collecting Biblical texts which appeared to contradict one another, with a view to reconciling them. His enthusiasm ceased after June, but we do not know whether this was because criticism of the Bible had become less vociferous in his locality, or because the task of reconciliation proved too much for him.[220] Walwyn, it is said, claimed that the clergy deliberately made the Bible difficult to understand in order to monopolize its interpretation. He used to annoy the orthodox by asking 'How can you prove the Scriptures to be the Word of God?' Allegedly he said that the Bible 'is so plainly and directly contradictory to itself' that it cannot be God's Word. Walwyn believed, nevertheless, that some passages did contain God's Word, but he was unenthusiastic about the Old Testament.[221] John Holland Porter accused Ranters of saying that the Bible was 'a bundle of contradictions, . . . the cause of all our misery and divisions, both in religion and civil affairs, . . . the cause of all the blood that hath been shed in the world. . . . There would never be peace in the world till all the Bibles were burned. . . The Scriptures belongs not to us, neither are they any rule for us to walk by'.[222]

This echoes the words of six Bible-burning soldiers at Walton-on-Thames in 1649: 'the Bible containeth beggarly rudiments, milk for babes', they said; but now 'Christ . . . imparts a fuller measure of his spirit to his saints than this [the Bible] can afford'. They had invaded the church of Walton-on-Thames, announcing that the Sabbath, tithes, ministers and the Bible were all abolished.[223] Possibly on the same Sunday in late March or early April the Diggers began work on the waste land at near-by St George's Hill: they too made demonstrations in Walton parish church, though there is no evidence to suggest that the two events were con-

219. R. Gell, *An Essay Toward the Amendment of the last English Translation of the Bible* (1659), sig. b 3–4, d 4v–e. See p. 25 n. above.

220. Josselin, *Diary*, pp. 155–69.

221. [Anon.], *Walwins Wiles*, in *The Leveller Tracts, 1647–1653* (ed. W. Haller and G. Davies, Columbia U.P., 1944), pp. 296–8.

222. Porter, *The Smoke of the bottomlesse pit* (1650[–1]), pp. 3–6.

223. Clement Walker, *Anarchia Anglicana, or, The History of Independency*, Part II (1649), pp. 152–3.

nected.[224] Five years later the goldsmith Thomas Tany, who called himself Theaureaujohn, publicly burnt the Bible as 'an idol' in St George's Fields, Lambeth, 'because the people say it is the Word of God, and it is not'. 'The Bible is letters, not life'.[225] He acted, he said, at God's command. Some supporters of the Quaker schismatic John Perrot in the 1660s are said to have burnt or torn up the Bible – 'The Pope's idol, the professors' idol, and the Quakers' idol'.[226] William Erbery helps us to understand the rationale behind these symbolic actions. He tells us of 'a chief one of the Army' who would 'usually say that the flesh of Christ and the letter of the Scriptures were the two great idols of Antichrist'.[227] Bible-burning is not something with which one can sympathize. But the violence of the language that accompanied it suggests that Bible-burning, like blasphemy, reveals very complex and mixed motives. It is perhaps possible to imagine the icono-clastic rage which lay behind it, as it lay behind Milton's *Eikonoklastes*.[228]

As early as 1646 Thomas Edwards had received a report from a London member of the Assembly of Divines about Thomas Webbe, later the Wiltshire Ranter, who was alleged to have said that the Bible was but a human invention, 'not fit for a rule of life and conversation for any to walk by'. 'The Scriptures were that golden Calf and brazen Serpent that set all at variance, King and Parliament, and kingdom against kingdom; . . . things would never be well until the golden Calf and brazen Serpent were broken to pieces'. To which end he had a book to come out shortly.[229]

There is a certain consistency in what we are told about the views of the Ranters. There is no God but nature only; matter is eternal. They call God 'Reason', as Winstanley did. Scripture is a tale, a history, a dead letter, not relevant to us, full anyway of contradictions. The Christ who died at Jerusalem does not matter: Christ is in believers. There is no hell, no day of judgment; they were invented just to keep men and women in awe. Monogamy is the curse: but we are freed from it. Ranters made much of the Song of Songs, as we shall see in Chapter 16.

Clarkson tells us that he had 'found so much contradiction (as then I

224. My *The World Turned Upside Down*, p. 110.
225. Burton, *Parliamentary Diary*, I, p. cxxvi; Arise Evans, *To the Most High and Mighty Prince Charles II, . . . An Epistle* (1660), p. 51; *The World Turned Upside Down*, p. 220.
226. K. L. Carroll, *John Perrot, Early Quaker Schismatic* (Friends' Historical Soc., 1971), p. 85.
227. *The Testament of William Erbery*, p. 84.
228. Cf. David Loewenstein, *Milton and the Drama of History: Historical Vision, Iconoclasm and the Literary Imagination* (Cambridge U.P., 1990).
229. Edwards, *Gangraena*, I, p. 54 (pagination repeated).

conceived)' in the Bible that he 'had no faith in it at all, no more than a history'. 'I really believed no Moses, prophets, Christ or Apostles, nor no resurrection at all'. He thought that there had been men before Adam and that the world was eternal.[230] There is no need to believe anything because Clarkson said it; but there is ample confirmation that such ideas were about in Ranter circles in the early fifties. Jacob Bauthumley denied that the Bible was the Word of God, and thought that 'Scripture as it is in the history' was no better 'than any other writings of good men'. 'The Bible without is but a shadow of that Bible which is within'. 'I do not expect to be taught by Bibles or books, but by God'. It was, he thought, sinful to perform an action authorized by the Bible if 'the commanding power which is God in me' forbids it.[231] The Ranter Andrew Wyke held that 'The Scriptures . . . were no more than a ballad'.[232] Lodowick Muggleton reported that in his Ranter phase many of his acquaintance 'did say in their hearts and tongues both, that there is no God but Nature only'.[233]

Muggletonians accepted that the text of the Bible was often corrupt: the spirit was superior to the letter. They gave no authority to the books attributed to Solomon.[234] James Nayler denied that the Bible was the Word of God.[235] 'Faith is the ground of the Scriptures, and not the Scriptures the ground of faith', declared the Quaker Richard Hubberthorne in 1657.[236] Edward Burrough thought that the Bible was not the most perfect rule of faith and life for the saints.[237] Milton agreed. Henry Oldenburg, soon to be Secretary of the Royal Society, reported many fundamental criticisms of the Bible circulating in England in 1656, such as that 'Moses concocted the whole story' of the creation, from motives of merely political prudence.[238] In the same year a Wiltshire man was saying

230. Clarkson, *The Lost sheep Found*, pp. 32–3

231. Bauthumley, *The Light and Dark Sides of God*, in Smith, *Ranter Writings*, pp. 257–64; cf. pp. 240–41, for examples of Biblical criticism. Roger Brearley and his Grindleton congregation had been charged with this last belief in 1617 (my *The World Turned Upside Down*, pp. 82–3).

232. *HMC Leybourne-Popham MSS.*, pp. 57, 59.

233. Muggleton, *The Acts of the Witnesses of the Spirit*, p. 18.

234. Reeve, *Joyfull News* (1706), pp. 11–14 (first published 1658); Muggleton, *A Looking Glasse for George Fox* (1668), p. 64; *The Acts of the Witnesses*, p. 62; Clarkson, *The Lost sheep Found*, pp. 26, 32.

235. Nayler, *A Publike Discovery of the Open Blindness of Babels Builders* (1656), pp. 9–10.

236. Hubberthorne, *Rebukes of a Reviler*, quoted by Elisabeth Brockbank, *Richard Hubberthorne of Yealand* (1929), p. 62.

237. Burrough, *Works*, p. 541.

238. Ed. A. R. and M. B. Hall, *Correspondence of Henry Oldenburg*, I, *1641–1662* (Wisconsin U.P., 1965), pp. 89–91.

that 'if the Scriptures were a-making again, then Tom Lampire of Melksham would make as good Scriptures as the Bible'.[239] But it was dangerous to proclaim such ideas too loudly, even in the 1650s. The Socinian John Bidle was lucky to escape the death penalty for denying that the Bible was the Word of God, thanks to the dissolution of Cromwell's first Parliament in 1655.[240]

After the restoration Samuel Butler also thought that the Bible was not the Word of God, using Writer's arguments; but he was more prudent than to publish his views.[241] Francis Osborn used the contradictions in the Genesis narrative to suggest that the story of the creation and Fall of Man might be 'an allegory or fable'. But he hastily covered up by saying he thought it 'as far from prudence as Christianity to oppose or in the least contradict' the church's traditional interpretation.[242] Bunyan heard Ranters and others casting doubts on the Bible's authority. They led him to ask 'How can you tell but that the Turks have as good Scripture to prove their Mahomet the Saviour, as we have to prove our Jesus is? . . . Everyone doth think his own religion rightest, both Jews and Moors and pagans. And how if all our faith, and Christ, and Scriptures, should be but a think-so too?' 'We made so great a matter of Paul, and of his words, . . . yet he, being a subtle and cunning man, might give himself up to deceive others with strong delusions'. The Scriptures might have been 'written by some politicians on purpose to make poor ignorant people to submit to some religion and government'. Bunyan for a time shared these doubts, and had many even worse thoughts which he dared not mention.[243] Bunyan is unique in having owned up to such subversive beliefs. We can only guess how many others of the godly and less godly had similar thoughts.

Quakers offered the authority of the inner light as an alternative to the Bible. 'None comes to the knowledge of the father by reading the Scriptures', declared the Yorkshire shepherd William Dewsbery in 1656. 'The Scripture is a true declaration of things believed among the saints,

239. Ed. B. H. Cunnington, *Extracts from the* [Wiltshire] *Quarter Sessions Great Rolls of the Seventeenth Century* (Devizes, 1932), p. 231.
240. Jordan, op. cit., pp. 113, 205; cf. p. 165.
241. Butler, *Prose Observations* (ed. H. de Quehen, Oxford U.P., 1979), p. 124. For Butler's scepticism about miracles see *Characters and Passages from Notebooks* (ed. A. R. Waller, Cambridge U.P., 1908), p. 355.
242. Osborn, *A Miscellany of Sundry Essays, Paradoxes and Problematical Discourses* (1659), pp. 40–44, in *Miscellaneous Works*, I.
243. Bunyan, *Grace Abounding*, p. 31; cf. *BMW*, I, p. 343; and *Poems, BMW*, VI, p. 44.

and a true testimony of Jesus Christ, but not many . . . can believe what is written therein only by the outward declaration and testimony of Scripture, but by word of faith, which is in the heart'.[244] But who decides when individual interpretations differ? It is only a small step, though a momentous one, from the Spirit, the Inner Light, to human reason.

By 1658 Thomas Manton was postulating the existence of a sect of Anti-Scripturists, alongside Quakers, Ranters, Familists, etc.[245] These I presume were those who accepted ideas like those of the Worcestershire clothier Clement Writer, who in 1657 summed up the new criticism in *Fides Divina.* 'How', Writer asked Richard Baxter, searchingly, 'can any history of words from men fallible and liable to error, without infallible evidence, be any sufficient ground for divine faith?' 'The Scripture reports the miracles; can the miracles reported by Scripture confirm that report?' Writer repeatedly claimed to be 'destitute of school learning and human arts and sciences': he intended his writings for 'the middle sort of plain-hearted people', who are 'not so engaged to any party or opinion, but that their minds lie open to the evidence of truth'. We must 'turn to the light and Word within'.[246]

The most impressive scholarly work on this subject was *The Rustickes Alarm to the Rabbies*, published by the ex-Baptist Quaker Samuel Fisher in 1660. Protestants, he said, had believed that 'all would be unity itself among them' once they had replaced the traditions of the church by the text of the Bible; but in fact 'dark minds diving into the Scripture divine lies enough out of it to set whole countries on fire'.[247] Fisher's book was published too late to be publicly discussed in England, where strict censorship of books like his was restored in 1660. But it was read by Spinoza, and through Spinoza the attitude towards the Bible of Fisher and his predecessors in England passed into the European Enlightenment.[248] These were the circumstances in which Hobbes had been able to say that the Bible derives its authority only from its allowance by the sovereign.[249]

244. In *The Faithful Testimony of . . . William Dewsbery*, pp. 119, 141.
245. See pp. 244, 424 below.
246. Writer, op. cit., and *An Apologetical Narration* (2nd ed., 1658), pp. 62, 78–80.
247. Fisher, op. cit., pp. 440–41.
248. R. H. Popkin, 'Spinoza, the Quakers and the Millenarians, 1656–1658', *Manuscrito*, VI (Brazil, 1982), p. 132; 'Spinoza and the Conversion of the Jews', in *Spinoza's Political and Theological Thought* (ed. C. De Deugd, Amsterdam, 1984), p. 174.
249. David Johnston, *The Rhetoric of Leviathan*, pp. 178–81.

It is difficult to be sure to what extent the absolute authority of the Bible had been accepted by ordinary people, and even more difficult to ascertain how far down the social scale doubts about its authority went in the 1640s. In 1642 John Dury had suggested that a popular lectureship should be set up in London to teach the common people 'how to make use of Scripture'.[250] Was he concerned because they did not use it enough, or because they misused it? Thomas Edwards, whose reporting is usually accurate though his comments may be biased, is interesting here. He had no doubt that Antiscripturists existed in 1646, who denied that the Bible was the Word of God or an infallible foundation of faith. The Biblical stories are allegories, not histories. At best, 'we are to believe the Scriptures . . . so far as we see them agreeable to reason, and no further'. He believed that such views were common among all sorts of sectaries.[251]

By 1650–53 we have the records of Fenstanton Baptist church in Huntingdonshire, which tell us of Mrs Robert Kent, Mrs Hare, Sister Pharepoint, and many, many others of both sexes who valued conscience or 'the Spirit' more than the Bible. Mrs William Austin looked upon the Scriptures as nothing, trampling them under her feet. Many emphasized 'the mystery' of the Scriptures whilst rejecting 'the history'. Some claimed direct revelations from God. These persons were being interviewed because they had lapsed from the Baptist congregation at Fenstanton, so they clearly belong to the category of sectaries identified by Edwards five or six years earlier. The Fenstanton church attributed these heretical doctrines to 'the errors of the times, viz. of . . . Diggers, Levellers and Ranters'; but Edwards's evidence shows that they were not novel. Some of Edwards's phrases are repeated verbatim, such as 'the Scripture is a dead letter'. The ideas recorded 'savoured of Rantism' rather than recalling Levellers and Diggers; Ranters are named more specifically as influences than any other group.[252] But two years later the Quaker James Parnell was corresponding with several Fenstanton Baptists who appear to have been interested in his teaching.[253]

Francis Osborn confirmed Arise Evans on the changed intellectual climate

---

250. Dury, *A Motion tending to the Publick Good of this Age and of Posteritie*, sig. C 3–3v.
251. Edwards, *Gangraena*, I, pp. 15–19. Cf. Erbery, quoted on p. 231 above.
252. Ed. E. B. Underhill, *Records of the Churches of Christ gathered at Fenstanton, Warboys and Hexham, 1644–1720* (Hanserd Knollys Soc., 1859), pp. 73–5, 88–93, 119–21, 198, 269–70.
253. Parnell, *A Watcher*, in *A Collection of Several Writings*, pp. 188–96.

when he wrote in 1656 'the liberty of these times hath afforded wisdom a larger passport to travel than was ever formerly to be obtained, when the world kept her fettered in an implicit obedience, by the three-fold cord of custom, education and ignorance'.[254] It is not surprising that in the 1950s Michael Wigglesworth, a sophisticated Harvard lecturer, came to doubt 'whether ever[y] word of the Scripture was infallible, because of the possibility of mistakes in the writings and of the points in the Hebrew and the various readings in the text and margin'.[255] Before Thomas Traherne went up to Oxford in 1653 he was a conscious sceptic, whose scepticism extended to the divine authority of the Bible.[256] Even Richard Baxter and his wife had their periods of doubt.[257]

V

After the suppression of the Ranters in 1650–51 their heritage seems to have been shared by the followers of John Reeve (later known as Muggletonians), Fifth Monarchists and Quakers. The Fifth Monarchist William Aspinwall thought that civil government as well as the government of the church belongs to Christ. Magistrates ought to be saints, but all the present governments in the world are Antichristian. Antichristian princes exercise their law-giving power only *de facto,* not *de jure.* Christ sometimes raises up better rulers – Edward VI and Elizabeth are examples – but even the best are broken reeds. Christians must be subject to this civil power so long as the Fourth Monarchy lasts. But 'in our days . . . we have nothing left but a stinking carcase': no wonder the saints are imprisoned, and are 'worse dealt with than in the days of the most wicked and profane persons'. Then, with a glance at Oliver Cromwell, would that 'God were pleased to give hearts unto men in chiefest place of power to set their hearts and hands to the work . . .'. Let us not forget that Pharaoh advanced Joseph, Nebuchadnezzar and Darius advanced Daniel, Ahasuerus Mordecai. When Israel groaned under Egyptian taxes, God heard them (Exodus II.24). Continued taxes and

254. Osborn, *Advice to a Son*, in *Miscellaneous Works*, I, sig. B 3. Cf. p. 229 above.
255. *The Diary of Michael Wigglesworth* (ed. E. S. Morgan, New York, 1965), pp. 49, 54, 59.
256. Gladys Wade, *Thomas Traherne* (Princeton U.P., 1944), pp. 43–6. Traherne was himself to produce a massive work of Biblical scholarship, *Roman Forgeries*, in 1673.
257. Ed. J. T. Wilkinson, *Richard Baxter and Margaret Charlton* (1928), p. 128; *Reliquiae Baxterianae* (ed. M. Sylvester, 1696), I, pp. 21–2.

burdens lost Rehoboam ten parts in twelve of his kingdom (I Kings XX.14–15). The imprisonment of the prophet Hanani cost King Asa dear (II Chronicles XVI.1–12). But, Aspinwall concluded, 'it is hard to speak without offence in these evil days. ... I shall forbear because I know God hath a purpose to destroy them. ... The Lord Jesus will shortly appear in his kingdom to rule with the saints.'[258]

Reeve, like the Diggers, saw Cain's seed as 'the lords of this world'. They are 'serpent-wise prudent men and women that mind earthly things. ... Their spirits lick up the gold and the silver, and put it into a bag, ... feeding upon riches and honours ...'[259] But the Muggletonians, thorough-going materialists, used the theory of the two seeds to explain the mysteries of predestination. Orthodox Calvinists had, rather unsatisfactorily, been able to say only that the division between sheep and goats, which God had foreseen from all eternity, rested on his inscrutable will: all humanity was worthy of damnation after Adam's sin, but some were saved thanks to God's mercy to them. Reeve – apparently following the Talmud, though presumably via intermediaries – Boehme, for instance[260] – thought that Cain and his offspring were the descendants not of Adam and Eve but of copulation between the serpent and Eve in Paradise.[261] So the distinction is not between Cain's seed and Abel's, but between Cain's and Adam's. Election and reprobation – 'blessed Israelites' and 'cursed Canaanites' – was 'by generation'. When the prophets Reeve and Muggleton told an individual that he was damned they were not pronouncing sentence; they were telling him or her that they were of the seed of Cain, and so ineluctably damned.

The fullest treatment of the two seeds by John Reeve comes in his *A Divine Looking-Glasse* of 1656, Chapter XXI. The 'curse denounced against Cain and his seed', Reeve explains, 'runs in the line of persons of maturity, not of minority'. Children of the seed of Cain dying young were not necessarily damned.[262] The two seeds conflict within each one of us, 'pure faith' against 'unclean reason'.[263] Unilluminated reason is covetousness, Dives the rich man. 'Woe unto all learned men', Reeve declared, 'especially

258. Aspinwall, *The Legislative Power*, pp. 7–8, 20–24, 29–42, 50–52, and *passim*.
259. Reeve, *A Transcendent Spiritual Treatise* (1711), pp. 34–5. First published 1652.
260. R. M. Jones, *Spiritual Reformers in the 16th and 17th Centuries* (1928), pp. 255–6.
261. The Quaker Edward Burrough shared this view of Cain's origin (*Works*, p. 39).
262. *A Divine Looking-Glasse*, pp. 152, 155.
263. B. Reay, 'The Muggletonians: An Introductory Survey' in *The World of the Muggletonians*, by B. Reay, W. Lamont and C. Hill (1983), p. 28.

if they be rich'.[264] Just as for Reeve Cain's seed were the lords of this world, so for Winstanley covetousness was the God of this world. But for Winstanley covetousness was unreasonable, and Reason was God. And of course for Winstanley 'the seed of Abraham' was not 'after the flesh'.[265]

Muggleton, who survived Reeve to experience post-restoration persecution, insisted that 'all persecuting men . . . have been [Cain's] children'. No one who persecuted those who seek liberty of worship for conscience sake 'will escape vengeance to come, no more than Cain did'.[266] 'The government of this world', Reeve had declared, 'belongs only to the wise and prudent heathen magistrates in this earth, who are the very sons of Cain'.[267] Politics was no business of the true seed: they cannot 'take upon them any place of honour from the lords of this world', since no magistrate will 'own any ministry, so long as the world endureth, but a ministry of his own setting up'. Hence Reeve, long before the Quakers, proclaimed absolute pacifism and abstention from politics. 'They cannot take the sword of steel to slay their brother, because they know that man is the image of God; neither can they go to law with their neighbours, whatever loss may come thereby'.[268]

So for the Muggletonians, as for the Quakers, the inner voice was decisive. 'If thou dost not obey my voice', God told Reeve, 'thy body shall be thy hell, and thy spirit shall be the devil that shall torment thee to eternity'.[269] This doctrine led Muggleton to declare 'I do well, . . . and I refrain from evil, not from fear God should see me . . . but . . . so that I might not be accused in my own conscience'.[270] The chief theologian of the Muggletonian second generation proclaimed that 'Antichrist was in Cain before Christ was in Abel'. 'There have been wrong principles ever since in Cain, therefore in matters of religion there is no pleading of antiquity, custom and tradition'.[271] It is the ultimate protestant liberation from the traditional church. Even the Bible, though the Muggletonian prophets quoted it frequently, was not the last word. It had to be interpreted. Where then could authoritative interpretation be found?

264. Reeve, *Of the Three Records* (1652), in *Sacred Remains* (1706), p. 76.
265. Reeve, *A Transcendent Spiritual Treatise*, p. 34; Sabine, pp. 149–53.
266. Muggleton, *A True Interpretation of All the Chief Texts . . . of the whole Book of the Revelation of St. John* (1665), pp. 66–7.
267. Reeve, *A Transcendent Spiritual Treatise*, p. 68.
268. Reeve, *Of the Three Records*, p. 83.
269. Reeve, *A Transcendent Spiritual Treatise*, p. 5.
270. Muggleton, *The Acts of the Witnesses*, p. 140.
271. Thomas Tomkinson, *A System of Religion* (posthumously published in 1729), p. 13.

Providentially, at the beginning of February 1651–2 God had given to John Reeve, tailor, understanding of the Scriptures 'above all men in the world'.[272] The Muggletonians claimed more specifically Biblical author- ity than any other sect. Reeve and Lodowick Muggleton were the two Last Witnesses foretold in Revelation XI. 'I will give power unto my Two Witnesses', the Lord had said, to prophesy for 1,260 days before they were slain and ascended to heaven. They also had power to pronounce any who refused to recognize their claims damned to all eternity. By virtue of their commission they silenced (among many others) a silk-weaver called Cooper, who could not see 'how a man may know the history of the Scriptures to be true, since they contradict themselves in many places'.[273] Muggleton aspired to leave behind him 'the third Testament of God', of which *The Acts of the Witnesses of the Spirit* and the various Epistles left by Reeve and Muggleton should be component parts.

Clarkson in his Muggletonian phase accepted Reeve's doctrine fully, contrasting 'the seed of Adam' with 'the seed of Reason'. Reason, Clarkson declared, 'hath erected magistrates, judges and lawyers to reconcile reason divided against itself, or else condemn it to be executed by the hangman'. 'Reason desires things impossible', such as calling on God to 'send fire from heaven, and blast the proceedings of its enemies'. 'If ye will not believe me, then believe the fruits of your own prayers, and much good may they do you:' for God takes no notice of men's prayers. Clarkson's *A Single Eye* (1650) was a sermon on Isaiah XLII.16. He saw Esau and Jacob, Pharaoh and Moses, Pilate and Christ, as powers all equally ordained by God. This world, he now told 'the children of Esau', 'is your inheritance by birthright, not the saints' at all'. So Clarkson came to the end of the radical road, accepting Muggletonian pacifism without attempting to penetrate the inscrutable workings of God's will. 'To our kingdom we must go, and without death we cannot go; but if ye ['the children of Esau'] be made instrumental to hasten our going, thereby ye hasten your misery'.[274]

The early Quakers were more radical socially than their successors. Parnell, who died in 1656, echoed Winstanley in denouncing the land-grabbing

---

272. Reeve, *A Transcendent Spiritual Treatise*, p. 4. Cf. John Harwood, *The Lying Prophet Discovered and Reproved* (1659), title-page and sig. A 2, p. 1.
273. Muggleton, *The Acts of the Witnesses*, pp. 62–4. After Reeve's death Clarkson aspired to usurp his place: see my *Religion and Politics*, pp. 257, 260–61.
274. Clarkson, in Smith, op. cit., pp. 167–8, 174; *The Lost sheep Found*, pp. 36, 55–9.

children of Cain and Esau. God had indeed made man lord over all creation, but not over his fellow men. Quakers preached the doctrine of the two seeds, but the seed was not physically inherited. Cain and Abel for Parnell represented the first and second birth. 'There is a time that Esau reigns over Jacob, and there is a time that the elder serves the younger'.[275] Priscilla Cotton and Mary Cole urged men and women 'to see what generation you are of, whether of Cain or Abel'.[276] The Lamb's war, Nayler pronounced, is against 'the seed of bondage', between 'the precious seed and the children of whoredom and deceit'. 'Though with Cain you sacrifice, or with Esau you pray with tears', God hates 'everyone that bears not the image of his Son in well-doing'.[277] 'Priests and curates and parsons and vicars', Fox told them in 1659, have 'sold your birthright for a mess of pottage, Esau-like, hunting up and down with his sword to kill and slay just Jacob and get great benefits. . . . But now the younger brother is risen, and the elder shall be servants'. (Note that Fox is concerned not only with the liberation of the oppressed but also with the punishment of the oppressors.) Dewsbery made the same point less abrasively when he said that Christ is the 'elder brother' of his people.[278] If you abuse your power, Dewsbery told the Northamptonshire justices, 'you will prove yourselves to be in the state of Cain, who was a vagabond'. The spirit of Cain and Esau is in all persecutors, Fox said later. 'Prophane Esau will lift up his sword and rough hands . . . and cry God hath fore-ordained a great number of men to reprobation'. But 'The spirit and nature of the prophane Esau', and of Cain, is within each one of us.[279]

When Fox discussed the two seeds in his *Journal*, he started with the seed of Abraham. Cain's way is easy, proclaimed the title-page of George Whitehead's *Cain's Generation Discovered* (1655).[280] An anonymous Quaker

275. Parnell, op. cit., pp. 28–9, 85, 87. My attention was drawn to Parnell's writings by Tatiana Pavlova's pioneering article, 'Radical-egalitarian ideas in the pamphlets of James Parnell', *The History of Socialist Doctrine* (Moscow, Academy of Sciences of the USSR, 1990 – in Russian).

276. Cotton and Cole, *To the Priests and People of England*.

277. Nayler, *The Lambs War against the Man of Sin* (1658), in *Early Quaker Writings* (ed. H. Barbour and A. Roberts, Grand Rapids, Michigan, 1973), pp. 113–16. Cf. Isaac Penington, *Concerning Persecution* (1661): the two seeds represent 'the spirit of God and the spirit of the world' (*Early Quaker Writings*, p. 376; cf. pp. 504–9: a sermon of 1680 by George Fox).

278. Fox, *The Lambs Officer* (1659), p. 19; Dewsbery, *Faithful Testimony*, p. 217.

279. Dewsbery, op. cit., p. 400 (probably *c*.1655); Fox, *Gospel Truth Demonstrated* (1706), pp. 675–9.

280. Fox, *Journal*, II, pp. 447–9; cf. Whitehead, op. cit., p. 9.

pamphlet of 1659 was entitled *Cain's Offspring demonstrated . . . in a bitter Persecution . . . at Newark.*[281] Five years later Cain again symbolized persecution in *Christian Information Concerning these Last times* (by F.E., 1664). Francis Howgil's *The Inheritance of Jacob* (1656) discussed 'Pharaoh the oppressor', arguing that the former victims of persecution have now become the persecutors.[282] Richard Farnsworth cited Moses and Jehoshaphat to demonstrate that righteousness should be the primary qualification sought when making judicial appointments.[283]

VI

In retrospect we can see January 1649 as the high point of radical millenarianism, and in a sense the high point of Biblical influence on English politics. Anti-climax came in the fifties, when the rule of the saints failed to arrive. 'Take heed of computations', said John Owen. 'How woefully and wretchedly have we been misled by this'. Bunyan too came to regret 'the forwardness of some . . . who have predicted concerning the time of the downfall of Antichrist, to the shame of them and their brethren'. William Sedgwick was unfortunate in setting a date for the end of the world: he found it hard to live down the name of 'Doomsday Sedgwick'.[284] Fifty years later, when the Rev. John Mason of Water Stratford made the same mistake, he was regarded as a medical case.[285]

Millenarian politics faded out in the futile insurrections of 1657 and 1661. Ranters continued after 1649 to threaten in the name of the Lord: they were suppressed or – better – they were made to recant publicly. Pseudo-Messiahs – John Robins, William Franklin – proliferated for a year or two and then disappeared. Muggletonians continued to pronounce their enemies damned to all eternity, but nobody bothered much. Theaureaujohn threatened MPs with a drawn sword but hurt no one; he symbolically

281. Op cit., p. 3.
282. In *Early Quaker Writings*, pp. 169, 176–9. The radical John Goodwin in 1653 treated Esau and Jacob simply as examples of the reprobate and the elect, with no suggestion of social overtones (*An Exposition of the Ninth Chapter of the Epistle to the Romans, passim*).
283. Farnsworth, *Discovery of Truth and Falsehood* (1653), quoted by R. Michael Rogers, 'Quakerism and the Law in Revolutionary England', *Canadian Journal of History*, XXII (1987), p. 163.
284. See my *Antichrist in 17th-century England* (Oxford U.P., 1971), pp. 104, 146–7.
285. See my *Puritanism and Revolution*, p. 322.

burnt the Bible, took ship for Jerusalem 'to call the Jews' and was drowned *en route*. Quakers heckled parsons in their own churches, and went naked for a sign. The tragi-farce of James Nayler's entry into Bristol, in imitation of Christ's entry into Jerusalem, with women strewing palms in his path, led to a concerted conservative attempt in Parliament to restrain religious toleration. Nayler was flogged ferociously (and died of it three years later). Oliver Cromwell – washing his hands, Pilate-like – used the occasion to consolidate his own position. Panic fear of Quakers contributed significantly to the restoration of Charles II in 1660, men of property preferring the traditional constitution and the old law to the anarchy of the inner light.[286]

As we move through the Protectorate towards the Restoration, conservative and middle-of-the-road Parliamentarians are looking for new lessons from the Bible. Nathaniel Hardy in 1656 noted 'the congruency' of the first Epistle of John 'to the age wherein we now live', beset by 'Antichristian heretics and carnal-gospellers'. He attacked 'our Levelling Quakers', who would not show proper respect to superiors, together with Socinians and Antinomians.[287] Thomas Manton, two years later, claimed to wish for a middle way when he wrote 'the people of God have ever been exercised with two sorts of enemies, persecutors and sectaries'. He denounced 'our modern Ranters, Familists, Quakers, libertines, Anti-Scripturists'.[288]

In 1660 William Sedgwick in his *Inquisition for the Blood of our late Soveraign* turned the tables on the radicals by using Genesis to criticize the Parliamentarian politicians whom he had supported until Providence declared against them. 'The strictest reformed saints' of the sects, he now thought, had been no less guilty of Cain's sin than the bishops. The saints, 'strong and high in gifts', had become 'enraged Cain, . . . children of pride and rebellion'. 'The most ignorant and weak are Abel'. The church having cast out these 'saints' for 'their pride and hatred of ordinances, they wandered like Cain from one religion to another, as vagabonds'.[289]

Gradually dissenters had to adapt themselves to the new régime. The garrulous Matthew Henry in 1706 saw Esau and Jacob not as representatives of two social classes but Esau as 'a man of the world', who 'never loved a

---

286. B. Reay, *The Quakers and the English Revolution*, esp. Chapter 5.
287. Hardy, *The first general Epistle of St. John,* Part I, pp. 2–3; Part II, sig A 2, pp. 613–14, 625–6, 688.
288. Manton, *A Practical Commentary . . . On the Epistle of Jude,* sig. b 2v, b 3v, pp. 403, 408. Manton was a protégé of the Earl of Bedford, and dedicated this Commentary to Lady Letitia Popham, wife of Colonel Alexander Popham.
289. Sedgwick, op. cit., pp. 23–7, 34–5, and *passim*. I discuss Sedgwick in my *The Experience of Defeat*, Chapter 4, section 2.

book', whilst Jacob was 'a man for the other world, a plain man dwelling in tents, . . . a student'. The moral was that plain and simple men often prove the wisest. 'Plain Jacob makes a fool of cunning Esau'.[290] Henry everywhere sought improving lessons for his own society. Cain and Abel both had callings: one was a keeper of sheep, the other a tiller of the ground, 'so that they might trade and exchange with one another' (Genesis IV.1). The omniscient God foresaw the advantages which would result from the market. If Cain had accepted God's verdict on his offering, he might still have ruled over Abel: dominion is not in grace, Henry concluded. So nonconformists offered no threat to the social order (Genesis IV.6).

Esau and Jacob, the elder and younger brothers, re-appear as 'the figures of the two worlds', or two sorts of people, in the pamphlets of M.M. (Marsin or Mercin) at the end of the century.[291] As late as 1704 White Kennett, in his notorious *Compassionate Enquiry into the Causes of the Civil War*, noted that 'Esau's taking to wife an alien' had been 'a grief of mind to Isaac and Rebecca', and the latter worried desperately lest Jacob should do the same. (See Deuteronomy VII.3–4.) The application was to Charles I and Henrietta Maria, whose marriage Kennett saw as a principal cause of the civil war, as well as to James II and Mary of Modena.[292]

VII

Radicalization of the Biblical myths – Cain and Abel, Esau and Jacob – is evidence that social groups with different social interests, aspirations and education are finding it possible to get their views into print. There was a similar shift in the social content of the myth of the Norman Yoke, also in the revolutionary decades.[293]

We must never forget that these myths do not express merely playful, poetic analogies. They are serious, because of their sacred origin. To say that Cain is in all great landlords is a declaration of war. To compare the

---

290. Henry, *An Exposition on the Old and New Testament*, note on Genesis XXV. Cf. William Gouge: Esau showed himself 'an egregious fool', quoted on p. 204 above.
291. M.M., *Good News to the Good Women* (1701), Advertisement and p. 10. See pp. 407–9 below.
292. Kennett, op. cit., pp. 10–11, 15. For alien wives see pp. 69–70 above, 285 and 291 below.
293. See my *Puritanism and Revolution*, Chapter 3. Cf. my *Antichrist in 17th-century England*, *passim*.

last Levellers shot (at Burford) with Abel amounts to saying that the generals are like Cain, beyond the pale of humanity. We should think rather of the black/white world of the Ayatollah Khomeini. Study of the Old Testament prophets would have the effect of polarizing, of excluding compromises and mediation. The Bible was not lacking in divine texts inciting to violent action: 'To your tents, O Israel!' 'Curse ye Meroz, said the angel of the Lord; curse the inhabitants thereof, because they came not ... to help the Lord against the mighty' (Judges V.23). That was the text of Stephen Marshall's famous sermon to the House of Commons on 23 February 1641–2.[294] Preached before the civil war began, it is a concentrated source for Biblical authorizations of violence against God's enemies. Whoever wields the weapon, it is God who smites kings and the mighty.

Such texts were useful for speeches in or before battle, especially no doubt in Ireland. It is the pleasant (or maybe even the painful) duty of God's servants to do the Lord's bidding, perhaps especially when flesh and blood are weak. Nor was such authorization to be found only in the Old Testament. 'He that is not with me is against me', Christ himself had said. Study of the Old Testament prophets might well lead men to be impatient with moderate counsels, for instance with conventional ideas of blaming the King's advisers or ministers in order to spare him. The Bible set the chosen people against the Amalekites, just as the myth of the Norman Yoke set free Anglo-Saxons against Norman invaders, and as believers in the myth of Antichrist saw highly placed enemies as doomed to destruction.

Before 1640 most MPs and Puritans had observed certain conventions of discourse. They attacked only the King's advisers or his bishops. Their care not to be too outspoken could sometimes be modified by using Biblical parallels to imply conclusions which were not drawn, but which would be recognized by those who knew their Bibles. No one could object to preachers and writers *quoting* the Good Book: danger lay only when precise conclusions were drawn, as they sometimes had been in the Geneva margin.

After 1640 the collapse of censorship and the incursion of 'illiterate' radicals into politics ensured a more direct approach, a sharper tone. Biblical myths were put to new uses. Cain and Abel, Esau and Jacob, no longer merely illustrated the workings of God's will in predestinating some to eternal life and others to reprobation. Abel and Jacob now represented the common people. Cain and Esau were their oppressors, here and now.

294. *FS*, II, pp. 195–253; see pp. 88–9 above.

Some radicals questioned all authority; kingly power is evil, whether wielded by a King or a Parliament. Idolatry is not limited to the worship of graven images: men may idolize money, social prestige, a king, the King's book.[295]

Sexby (if he is the author of *Killing Noe Murder*) was unusual in advocating tyrannicide under Cromwell, but he cited good Biblical authority. Starting with epigraphs from II Chronicles XXIII.21 and XXV.27, he quoted Moses, Ehud and Samson as well as Samuel who hewed Agag in pieces before the Lord (I Samuel XV.33) and Jehoida the priest who ordered the idolatrous usurper Athaliah to be slain (II Kings XI.16; II Chronicles XXIII.15). John Ponet, in exile under Mary, had cited Jael (Judges IV.21) and others to justify tyrannicide in his *Short Treatise of Politike Power* (1556). Caliban appears to refer to Jael in the same context in *The Tempest* (III. ii. 61–2). Ponet argued that tyrannicide was permissible, exceptionally, when 'the whole state' utterly neglected to punish 'tyrants, idolaters and traitorous governors'. A prince, Ponet held, may be a traitor to the commonwealth.[296]

But who is to decide? Who is to interpret the Bible? To these questions no acceptable answers were found. Milton's belief, proclaimed in *Areopagitica*, that free discussion would lead to the emergence of an agreed truth proved too optimistic. Some came to think that learning was an enemy to the Gospel as they wished it to be interpreted. Chelmsford radicals in 1643 were alleged to hold that 'it were a happy thing if there were no universities, and all books burnt except the Bible'.[297] Some Ranters later burnt the Bible as well. On the radical fringe some extremely eccentric Biblical views were held. In 1651, when repression of Ranters was at its height, Thomas Kirby was convicted for holding that Cain was the third person of the Trinity.[298] It was all too much. In this deeply divided society, radicals could retain power only with the support of the Army; conservatives needed a king to be able to disband the Army. So in 1660 Charles II, bishops, gentry and censorship came back: universities survived. Mechanic preachers were silenced, tithes were maintained in order to pay for a parochial ministry. Bunyan and Quakers, still squabbling fiercely with one another, were equally sent to jail. Soon Robert South was to dismiss the decades of freedom as a time when Cromwell, 'a lively copy of

295. See pp. 261–3 below.
296. Ponet, op. cit. (1642 ed.), p. 52. Cf. p. 187 above.
297. *Mercurius Rusticus*, III (3 June 1643), p. 22. See p. 199 above.
298. W. K. Jordan, op. cit., p. 136.

Jeroboam', did 'authorize and encourage all the scum and refuse of the people to preach (I Kings XIII.33–4)'.[299]

Already in the 1650s there was cause for social alarm. Some sectaries argued that each individual must interpret the Bible for himself; each man has his own God, Winstanley had said. We must not idolize the letter of the Bible, 'setting it up in the room of Christ', said Parnell, a Quaker whose ideas are very close to those of Winstanley. 'The light is above the Scripture'.[300] Some lower-class men and women found in the Bible such alarming doctrines as that sin was an invention of the ruling class, that provided you followed your own conscience you need not bother about social and moral norms. Others questioned the sanctity of the Bible itself, the sheet anchor of society. Some called on Biblical grounds for the rule of the saints; some saints expected this to give an opportunity for reversing the positions of rich and poor. The alarm of the rich was no doubt exaggerated; but it was not without foundation. The Diggers' demand for 'Glory here!', on earth, the Ranter and Quaker idea that we may be redeemed in this life – all these contain subversive secularist possibilities. It was time to call a halt.

VIII

There are two (at least) ways of using the Bible for political controversy, which are not easily separated. First, as code. When Thomas Goodwin in 1639 asked 'How, by degrees, do these Gentiles win ground upon the outward court in England?' he had already told us that Gentiles mean Papists. 'The outward court' continues a metaphor about the Jewish temple; but it was at Charles I's court that Papists were making headway. 'All carnal and corrupt worshippers or forms of worshipping', cleaving to popish ordinances which had survived 'the first reformation; . . . these are all comprehended under that expression of outward court'. A few pages later, lest we had failed to understand, Goodwin spoke of 'Papists overrunning their outward court' in 'the churches of the reformation in the West'.[301]

299. South, *Twelve Sermons Preached upon Several Occasions*, p. 160. 'Israel was not to return to Egypt; Egypt was brought back to them by Jeroboam' (ibid., pp. 158–9).
300. Sabine, p. 591; Parnell, op. cit., pp. 17, 24. For Parnell and Winstanley see pp. 241–2 above.
301. Goodwin, *An Exposition of the Revelation*, *Works*, III, pp. 131, 140.

Points can be made by reference to Cain and Abel, Esau and Jacob, Samson, Nimrod and Antichrist, bad kings and good kings, points which it might be dangerous to state directly. Messages can be conveyed by omission from the Biblical text, or by insertion into it, as Milton did in *Samson Agonistes*. A censor told Richard Baxter that nonconformists interpret 'all those passages of Scripture which speak of persecution and the sufferings of the godly' as 'against the times'. Baxter admitted that this was true. 'But I hoped Bibles should be licensed for all that'.[302]

After the restoration the codes had to be put to new uses to circumvent a new censorship. The fact that tyrants are persecutors and idolaters comes to be assumed; persecution can come from the gentry and lay ecclesiastical officials as well as, even more than, from the King and the bishops. Social issues loom large in the day-to-day struggle for the right to worship God in the way that dissenters believed that he wished to be worshipped. Christ's kingdom was not to be established in this world; but certain minimum standards of religious freedom were necessary for the very existence of organized dissent. There was no real possibility of suppressing dissent altogether, as the Laudians had tried to do before 1640: but survival still had to be struggled for, suffered for. Milton and Bunyan preach the heroism of standing fast, holding on, maintaining the faith in solidarity. The fact that resistance was passive, not aggressive, did not stop it being resistance.

Secondly, the symbols of the myth can be interpreted to taste. We have seen Cain pass from being all the reprobate to 'all great landlords', Nimrod from a tyrannical king to all kings, all persecutors; Samson from a type of Christ to a freedom fighter or a terrorist. There seemed to be no limits. Censorship had to be restored, mechanic preachers had to be silenced, tithes must be maintained in order to pay for an authorized interpreter of the Bible in every parish: on this Presbyterians now agreed with Anglicans.[303] Not until then was the *status quo* safe from the illiterate fantasies of 'the rude ignorant vulgar', who presumed to think that the Bible had been written for them too.

Some of the myths came to be put to secular uses. John Bull with his cudgel, the bully of the waves, the master slave-trader, becomes the symbol

302. *Reliquiae Baxterianae*, p. 123.
303. Cartwright had told Anne Stubbes in 1590 that amongst her separatist congregation 'there is not so much as one . . . that is fit for the function of the ministry' for lack of learning: so they were 'none of Christ's church' (*Cartwrightiana*, pp. 67–8); Peter Lake, *Moderate Puritans and the English Church*, Chapter 5.

of the chosen Anglo-Saxon people, of their manifest destiny to bring the world to protestant Christianity, to civilization, and in our century to 'democracy'. But long before then the Bible had lost its function as final arbiter.

III. INTERNATIONAL CATHOLICISM AND NATIONAL POLITICS

＝

9. The Decalogue and Idolatry

The human mind is, so to speak, a perpetual forge of idols.
Calvin, *Institutes of the Christian Religion*, Book 1, Chapter XI. 8.

All images ... set up publicly have been worshipped of the
unlearned and simple sort, shortly after they have been publicly
so set up. . . . Images in churches and idolatry go always together.
. . . The nature of man is none otherwise bent to worshipping of
images (if he may have them and see them) than it is bent to
whoredom and adultery in the company of harlots.
The Book of Homilies, pp. 186, 206.

> To worship an image.
> The Lord doth most abhor;
> But in our pilgrimage
> We honoured great store.
>
> That time I trust be past,
> For custom made us blind;
> And I am sore aghast
> Lest worse be left behind.
>
> Beware while you have space
> That idol of the heart:
> Lest at the last it chase
> Your souls in hell to smart.

John Hall, *The Court of Virtue* (1565) (ed. R. A. Frazer, 1961),
p. 206.

> But since of late Elizabeth
>   And later James came in
> They [the fairies] never danced on any heath
>   As when the time hath been.
>
> By which we note the fairies
>   Were of the old profession:
> Their songs were Ave Maries,
>   Their dances were procession.

But now alas they all are dead
Or gone beyond the sea,
Or farther for religion fled.

Richard Corbett, 'Farewell, Rewards and Fairies', in *Poems* (ed.
J. A. W. Bennett and H. R. Trevor-Roper, Oxford U.P., 1955),
pp. 49–51; cf. pp. 128–9.

As with other parts of the Bible, attitudes towards the Ten Commandments
were selective. The second table seems originally to have produced rules
for living together as nomadic tribal peoples adapted themselves to a
relatively settled existence in communities on the land. We may agree with
Milton that the Decalogue was not a perfect code, but the second table has
proved itself reasonably adaptable to different forms of society. The first
table is more problematical. Its object appears to have been to differentiate
God's people from the surrounding idolatrous heathen. Monotheism has
won out now, but the prohibition of idolatry led in the sixteenth and
seventeenth centuries to difficulties of interpretation; so did the commandment to keep holy the Sabbath day.

For protestants there was a sharp antithesis between observance of
saints' days, about which there was nothing in the Bible, and of the
Sabbath. The absence of saints' days from holy writ, historically easily
explicable, was used by protestants as an argument for abolishing them.
I have suggested elsewhere that another reason was the loss of labour
time for the working population, with disastrous consequences for
national production.[1] As the industrial and market sectors of the
economy become more important, so 'the protestant ethic' increasingly
insisted on the duty of labouring in one's calling. The seventh day's rest,
in addition to being commanded in the Bible, was also a necessary relaxa-
tion of the labour process. We move from the mediaeval agricultural
pattern of bouts of very intensive labour (seed-time, harvest), mitigated
by long periods of idleness, to the modern industrial pattern of six days'
labour and a regular weekly rest.

Protestant use of the Bible was thus not blind Bibliolatry but selective in
relation to the perceived needs of significant social groups. This is illustrated
by a dog that barked in the night, unavailingly. Arguments put forward by
Biblical literalists that Saturday should be observed as the (or a) Sabbath
day of rest failed to win acceptance. There was consensus for one day in

1. See Chapter V of my *Society and Puritanism*. As we have seen, fast days during the
Revolution were liable to the same objection (p. 100 above).

seven as a rest day, but no consensus for switching to Saturday. Here concern for what Milton called 'the duties of human society'[2] prevailed over the literal meaning of the Second Commandment; whilst for Sunday observance the absolute commandment of Exodus prevailed rather than Christ's more liberal teachings on the Sabbath.[3] Sabbatarian doctrines had been discussed by clerics and scholars throughout the Middle Ages. But now the Bible was being read by 'the industrious sort of people', and they helped to produce the Puritan Sabbatarianism which enjoyed a certain popularity in the late sixteenth and early seventeenth centuries.[4] Not everybody agreed with Thomas Collier, Milton and Ranters that 'the entire Mosaic law' had been abolished; or with Winstanley, who rejected the Ten Commandments as 'the letter' to which the spirit is superior.[5]

It is impossible to over-emphasize the importance given in the Old Testament to rejection of idolatry. God's covenant with the Israelites insisted on an end to idol worship (Leviticus X.1–3, Deuteronomy XXIX). The Geneva Bible thus explained the flight of the Israelites from Egypt: 'Because Egypt was full of idolatry, God would appoint those places where they should serve him purely' (Exodus III.18). Wicked kings were invariably those who countenanced idolatry and (as a necessary concomitant) persecuted God's people. The link remained strong in seventeenth-century expectations.

Gideon rescued Israel from the Midianites and destroyed the altars of Baal (Judges II.25–32). The history of Judah swings from Rehoboam (under whom idols were restored in 'groves on every hill, and under every green tree' – I Kings XIV.22–3),[6] to Asa and Jehoshaphat; between Joash and Hezekiah. In Israel idolatry flourished under Ahab, Jezebel and Ahaziah, until Jehu's massacres of the royal family and the priesthood 'destroyed Baal out of Israel'; though even Jehu had a weakness for golden calves (II Kings XX).[7] Under the captivity the pendulum swung from the idolaters

2. *MCPW*, I, p. 699.

3. For Saturday Sabbatarianism see D. S. Katz, *Philo-Semitism and the Readmission of the Jews to England, 1603–1655* (Oxford U.P., 1982), pp. 16–34.

4. K. L. Parker, *The English Sabbath: A Study of doctrine and discipline from the Reformation to the Civil War* (Cambridge U.P., 1988), pp. 17–23: my *Society and Puritanism*, p. 142; Brinsley, *The True Watch and Rule of Life* (9th ed., 1622), pp. 37–41, 47–51.

5. *MCPW*, VI, pp. 525–6, 531; cf. pp. 639–40; Woodhouse, op. cit., pp. 164–5; Winstanley, *The Saints Paradise*, pp. 12, 30, 78. See Edwards, *Gangraena*, I, p. 19 and p. 182 above.

6. For groves see pp. 391–3 below.

7. Jehu's arbitrariness displeased John Lilburne. See his *Legal Fundamental Liberties* (1648), in Haller and Davies, op. cit., pp. 443–4.

Manasseh and Amon to good King Josiah. The prophet Micah foretold the destruction of Israel and Judah 'chiefly for their idolatry'.[8] King Asa deposed Maachah his mother from her regency 'because she had made an idol in a grove: and Asa brake down her idol, and stamped it, and burnt it at the brook Kidron' (II Chronicles XV.16). But 'Asa lacked zeal', the Geneva margin comments; 'she ought to have died, but he gave way to foolish pity'. Hoshea – a better King of Israel than most in Milton's view – paid the penalty for his own idolatry and the sins of his ancestors with the loss of his kingdom.[9]

Idols were worshipped 'upon all the hills and under all green trees' (Jeremiah II.20), in groves 'under every green tree and every thick oak' (Ezekiel VI.13; Micah V.14). There seems to have been continuing pressure from below for idolatry, for the pagan magic of the Israelites' defeated predecessors in the Promised Land. The priesthood, or some priests, were liable to the same corruption. The prophets – or some of them – continually stress monotheism and individual hard work against the propitiatory communal ceremonies and sacrifices of the heathen. We can see, as contemporaries saw, analogies between this situation and that of post-Reformation England.

Lollards had attacked images in churches, and wished to replace them with the Ten Commandments in English on church walls. This became a common Anglican practice: Elizabethan bishops probably whitewashed more church walls than the seventeenth-century Puritans to whom this vandalism is often attributed. As images were destroyed, the Elizabethan church had to cater for a newly-literate public.[10] The Commandments painted on the walls were there to be read by any literate person who was bored by the sermon, and the Second Commandment was hard to miss. In the century before the Reformation men and women had often been accused of heresy on the strength of knowing the Commandments by heart, or of possessing copies of them in English.[11] The new idolatry of the printed word looks forward to the orgies of discussion and speculation released during the revolutionary decades, and to popular iconoclasm. This in its turn led to a decline in upper-class enthusiasm for uncontrolled popular education. Among other things, many iconoclasts wanted to

---

8. Headnote to Micah in Geneva Bible.
9. *MCPW*, VI, p. 386.
10. See pp. 14–15, 38–9 above.
11. M. Aston, *England's Iconoclasts: The Laws against Images* (Oxford U.P., 1988), pp. 105–7, 110–12; Foxe, *Acts and Monuments*, IV, pp. 239–40.

destroy family tombs, escutcheons and other symbols of gentry importance.

The prohibition of idolatry was not a separate commandment before the Reformation. It seems to have stirred strong feelings. Idolatry was associated with popery – with images, with the miracle of the mass. As Robert Burton recognized, worship of saints had incorporated much from pre-Christian worship;[12] this helps to account for its survival among the peasantry. It seemed to entitle educated protestants to treat papists and peasants with equal contempt. In Bishop Bale's play, *Three Laws, of Nature, Moses and Christ*, the character Idolatry, the child of Infidelity, was staged looking like an old witch, combining popery with peasant magic. In Bale's *God's Promises* God himself declared idolatry the worst of all sins.[13]

The Homily against Idolatry is by far the longest in the whole book, which may give some indication of the significance attached to its subject. It stresses not only the magical associations of image worship but also, as in the epigraph to this chapter, its popular appeal. The Homily even quoted Deuteronomy VII.12, which might sound like an incitement to popular action: 'Overturn their altars, and break them to pieces, cut down their groves, burn their images: for thou art an holy people unto the Lord'.[14] The temptation to idolatry must be removed, and preaching must be supplied to counter it: the latter point is strongly emphasized. Idolatry is spiritual fornication; an insult to God, said Dod and Cleaver, who agreed that 'man's nature is prone to idolatry'.[15] Richard Sibbes too assumed that 'naturally all men are idolaters before conversion'. All papists are idolaters, properly equated with heathen: they must not be tolerated.[16]

Protestantism, like Islam, witnessed to a re-assertion of monotheism though protestants were less tolerant than their Muslim contemporaries. The Presbyterian discipline was designed to counter back-sliding. Idolatry 'formerly destroyed, . . . they fell so generally to a liking of it, or to think it was not so bad as formerly they had conceived': Brinsley's words were intended to refer to England in his day as well as to Judah, whose idolatry, by angering the Lord, had hastened the captivity. Citing Jeremiah II.2–3 and XX.11, Brinsley emphasized that 'the Lord as much detests idolatry

12. Aston, op. cit., p. 368; Burton, *The Anatomy of Melancholy*, I, pp. 191–2.

13. Ed. J. S. Farmer, *Dramatic Works of John Bale*, pp. 35, 109–15.

14. *Homilies*, pp. 144–225, esp. pp. 152, 186, 206.

15. [Dod and Cleaver], *A plain and familiar Exposition of the Ten Commandments*, pp. 56–7.

16. Sibbes, *Complete Works*, I, pp. 288, 378, 386 and *passim*; T. Taylor, *Commentarie upon . . . Titus* (1619), pp. 719–20. Cf. *MCPW*, VIII, pp. 430–32, 439–40.

now as then'. But England was no more purged of idolatry than was Jerusalem before the captivity.[17] The ease with which many Englishmen 'went native' in Ireland and North America,[18] may indicate the popularity of pagan survivals, as well as of an undisciplined life (cf. fourth epigraph to this chapter).

The political consequences of the association of popery with idolatry were clear: any weakness or lenience towards popery must be hateful to God. It was right, Milton insisted, to hate the enemies of God and the church, and to strive against them. He explicitly compared Catholicism with Old Testament idolatry in his sonnet on the late massacre in Piedmont. The Vaudois kept their faith throughout the Middle Ages, 'when all our fathers worshipped stocks and stones'.[19] We must never forget the anxiety which most educated protestants felt before 1640 about the appeal of image and idol worship to the uneducated populace.

There were other anxieties. Towards the end of Elizabeth's reign Anthony Gilby feared that Englishmen had not truly repented of their relapse into popery under Mary: in consequence they were still liable to divine judgments. 'Our religion is not yet brought to full perfection in these 32 years'. 'Many do yet carry idols in their hearts'.[20] Gilby was echoing – almost certainly intentionally – Knox's *Brief Exhortation to England* of January 1559, in which he told Englishmen that all who did not unfeignedly repent their share of responsibility for the Marian persecutions were themselves idolaters and murderers. They should have 'resisted to the uttermost of your power that impiety in the beginning'. 'All have consented to cruel murder in so far as . . . none opened his mouth to complain of the injury, cruelty and murder'. That the people might be held responsible to God for the actions of their rulers had wide implications.[21]

In 1538 a London mercer hoped that Henry VIII would have 'the

17. Brinsley, *The Third Part of the True Watch* (1622 ed.), pp. 579, 357, 64, 70.
18. Nicholas Canny, 'The Ideology of English Colonization: From Ireland to America', *William and Mary Quarterly*, 3rd Series, XXX (1973), *passim*; Canny, *The Elizabethan Conquest of Ireland: A Pattern Established, 1565–1576* (Hassocks, Sussex, 1976), Chapters 6 and 8; Karen Ordahl Kupperman, *Settling with the Indians, passim*.
19. The phrase comes from Jeremiah II.27, though its apt alliteration is the A.V.'s not the Geneva Bible's. It is also echoed in Vaughan's 'In Amicum foeneratorem', though his reference is not specifically to Catholicism (*Works*, I, p. 43). This poem was published in 1651, four years before Milton's sonnet: Milton may have seen it.
20. Béza, *Psalms of David, translated by Anthonie Gilbie* (1590), Epistle Dedicatory. First published 1581.
21. Jasper Ridley, *John Knox*, pp. 304–5.

blessing that King Josiah had' for taking away all images.[22] More plausibly, Edward VI was often linked with Josiah. None of the many passages in the Old Testament which reported the slaughter of idolaters in any way disturbed the compilers of the Geneva marginal notes: all were approved. 'Where a tyrant and an idolater reigneth', said the note to II Chronicles XXIII.21, 'there can be no quietness'. Bishop Babington in his commentary on Exodus stressed the especial heinousness of idolatry, a 'grievous crime' and 'intolerable sin' which must be punished by death.[23] The best-selling Dod and Cleaver said revealingly that Jeroboam had set up 'infectious idols'.[24] Joseph Hall was slightly worried by Jehu's demand for the heads of the seventy sons of Ahab (II Kings X). 'Some carnal eye . . . would have melted into compassion'. But the future bishop consoled himself by reflecting that 'none of these died before they were seasoned with horrible idolatry'. It is 'our ignorance' that 'is ready to mistake . . . the holy severity of God in the revenge of sin . . . for cruelty'. Preston blamed 'superstition and idolatry of the people' for the plague of 1625.[25]

In 1628, as Catholics seemed to be winning the Thirty Years War, Sir Robert Harley moved in the Commons that the practice of idolatry should be added to the list of the ills of the kingdom to be presented to the King. Emulating the more famous iconoclasm of Henry Sherfield at Salisbury, in 1641 Harley broke the windows of the parish church of Leintwardine of which he was patron, 'and broke the glass small with a hammer, and threw it into the [river] Teme, in imitation of King Asa, II Chronicles XV.16'. He destroyed the cross at Wigmore, another parish of which he was patron.[26]

In 1639 a libeller had neatly summarized the unity of religious and constitutional opposition when he said that Ship Money was needed for setting up idolatry.[27] In January 1641, when the first draft of a bill for regulating bishops was discussed, it was proposed that the House of Commons should appoint commissioners to see that images and idols were

22. Brigden, *London after the Reformation*, p. 291.

23. Babington, op. cit., notes on XI.23–6, XXII.26, XXIII.30, XXXIV.12–13; cf. his comment on Leviticus XX: 'every worship not commanded of God is idolatry' (p. 178).

24. [Dod and Cleaver], *Ten Commandments*, p. 58.

25. Hall, *Contemplations* (1612), in *Works*, II, p. 145; for Preston see my *Puritanism and Revolution*, p. 251.

26. J. Eales, *Puritans and Roundheads: The Harleys of Brampton Bryan and the Outbreak of the English Civil War* (Cambridge U.P., 1990), pp. 115–16; cf. pp. 47, 107, and Eales, 'Sir Robert Harley K.B. and the "Character" of a Puritan', *British Library Journal*, XV (1989), p. 146.

27. Russell, *The Fall of the British Monarchies*, p. 14.

'utterly taken away'. Sir Simonds D'Ewes wanted 'a law to abolish all idolatry'.[28] The Grand Remonstrance, in November of the same year, condemned the bishops for having introduced idolatry: 'altar-worship is idolatry', said Pym in the debate. The first recommendation of the Westminster Assembly of Divines in its first session on 1 July 1643 was that 'all monuments of idolatry and superstition, but more especially the whole body and practice of popery', should be totally abolished.[29]

Denunciations of idolatry were particularly frequent in Fast Sermons in the years 1640–42. Stephen Marshall, listing the sins of the nation in December 1641, put idolatry first. 'God knows, and you [MPs] know, that we have not only abundance of idolatrous Papists, who are proud, insolent and daring, but abundance of Popish idolatrous spirits'. Magistrates 'dare not appear against idolatry'. He called on MPs to emulate Josiah.[30] Cornelius Burges on 30 March 1642 declared idolatry a 'special sin extraordinarily heinous'.[31] In June 1643 Herbert Palmer blamed the 'strange lukewarmness in us, to suffer such enemies to God' as 'idolatrous papists, traitors unto our kingdom' as well as to God. 'By compliances with idols and idolatry', John Strickland affirmed on Guy Fawkes Day, 1644, the Laudians 'went about to drive God away' from England.[32] John Cotton in 1642 had drawn sharp conclusions for Britain from the Song of Songs, Chapter I: 'if Solomon shall set up other gods, God will set up foreign princes in his kingdom'.[33] Roger Williams, in *The Bloudy Tenent of Persecution* (1644), thought that idolatry and superstition formed 'the first mountain of crying guilt lying heavy upon the backs of all Christians' in England.[34] Hence the burning of the Book of Common Prayer by Parliamentarian soldiers, because it had become 'the most abominable idol in the land'.[35] Baillie referred to 'that great idol of England, the Service-book'; James Parnell went one better by speaking of 'idolizing the letter of the Bible'.[36]

28. Ed. W. Notestein, *The Journal of Sir Simonds D'Ewes* (Yale U.P., 1923), pp. 270–71; ed. W. H. Coates, *The Journal of Sir Simonds D'Ewes* (Yale U.P., 1942), pp. 151–2; ed. J. Bruce, *Notes of Proceedings in the Long Parliament . . . by Sir Edmund Verney* (Camden Soc., 1845), p. 123.
29. Rushworth, *Historical Collections* (1659–1701), V, p. 339.
30. Marshall, *FS*, II, pp. 117, 128–9, 123, 135.
31. Burges, ibid., pp. 263–4.
32. Palmer, ibid., VII, pp. 49, 62; Strickland, ibid., XIV, pp. 82–4.
33. Cotton, *Canticles*, p. 31. See p. 368 below.
34. Roger Williams, op. cit., pp. 7–8; the second mountain was intolerance.
35. R. Ram, *The Souldiers Catechisme: Composed for the Parliamentary Army* (1645), pp. 20–22. Cf. pp. 232–3 above.
36. Baillie, *Letters and Journals*, I, p. 408. For Parnell see p. 248 above.

As actual physical worship of idols and images diminished, so the concept of metaphorical idolatry developed. Idolatry became an external symbol, like Antichrist or the Norman Yoke, applicable to varying modes of behaviour. Marshall demanded that idolatry should be punished together with 'heinous blasphemy' as a fundamental error.[37] Preston had equated covetousness with idolatry, as St Paul had done in Ephesians V.5 and Colossians III.5; and he added severely that 'enjoying pleasure, and mirth, and a high estate' was equivalent to committing idolatry.[38] 'Under idolatry and vain confidence in men all other sins are contained', Abdias Ashton had said towards the end of Elizabeth's reign.[39] The apocryphal Wisdom of Solomon tells us that 'the inventing of idols was the beginning, and the cause, and the end of all evil' (XIV.11, 26). Via covetousness, usury and rack-renting by landlords could be regarded as idolatry.[40] Sibbes thought that 'commonly the idol of the people is their king. . . . They fear him more than they do God'[41] – another theme that Milton was to develop in *Eikonoklastes*. In *Of Christian Doctrine* he wrote that idolatry was the only heresy which might be prohibited by the magistrate.[42] Fuller had agreed in 1655 that 'idolatry is not to be permitted a moment. . . . All that have power have right to destroy it'.[43] Joseph Salmon in 1649 referred to Parliament as an idol.[44] Human learning could be idolized, said both the Baptist Robert Purnell and the anti-Trinitarian John Fry in the same year, anticipating Milton in *Paradise Regained*. Thomas Tany thought the Bible had become an idol.[45]

Milton had already declared that idolatry was sufficient ground for divorce.[46] He hit more than one target when in *Paradise Lost* he said that

37. Marshall, *The power of the civil magistrate in matters of religion vindicated* (1651), pp. 5–9, 20.

38. Preston, *Sinnes Overthrow* (4th ed., 1641), pp. 59, 86; *The New Covenant* (5th ed., 1630), p. 156. Cf. *MCPW*, II, p. 241.

39. Ashton, quoted by Peter Lake, *Moderate Puritans and the Elizabethan Church* (Cambridge U.P., 1982), p. 148. 'There can be little doubt of the centrality of Ashton's position within Cambridge Puritanism', Lake adds (ibid., p. 117).

40. E.g. John Blaxton, *The English Usurer*, or *Usury Condemned* (Oxford U.P., 1934), p. 26, quoting Ephesians V.5, Matthew VI.24, XIX.8.

41. Sibbes, *Complete Works*, VII, p. 527: a sermon on Revelation XVII.17, preached on 5 November.

42. *MCPW*, VI, pp. 690–96.

43. Fuller, *Church History*, I, p. 438.

44. Salmon, *A Rout, A Rout*, in Smith, *Ranter Writings*, p. 193.

45. Purnell, *Good Tydings*, pp. 29–44; Fry, *The Accuser Sham'd*, *passim*. For Tany see pp. 232–3, 243–4 above.

46. *MCPW*, II, Chapter VIII, pp. 268–9.

Solomon was seduced into idolatry by his wife (I. 402, 444–6). There could
be idolatry in marriage: 'never was there a passion more ardent and less
idolatrous', wrote Lucy Hutchinson of her husband, with a side glance at
Charles and Henrietta Maria.[47] John Taylor the Water-Poet attacked the
idolatrous gallant, 'bare-headed on his knees', drinking a health 'unto an
absent whore'.[48] Such irony was wasted on the likes of Nicholas Hookes,
who sang

> I am a Papist, zealous, strict, precise,
> Amanda is the saint I idolize.[49]

Carew had declared honour to be an idol.[50]

The Philistine aristocrats in *Samson Agonistes* were 'drunk with idolatry'
as well as with wine.[51] In *Eikonoklastes* Milton spoke of 'a civil kind of
idolatry and idolizing their kings', to which 'the people . . . are prone
ofttimes'. In particular they 'are ready to fall flat and give adoration to the
image and memory of this man [Charles I], who hath offered at more
cunning fetches to undermine our liberties and put tyranny into an art than
any British king before him'. 'His idolized book', *Eikon Basilike*, had won
'the worthless approbation of an inconstant, irrational and image-doting
rabble'. Charles had not only compared himself to Job, Samson, David and
Solomon but even to Jesus Christ.[52] Milton felt it was essential to the
mental health of English men and women that they should see through the
shams of *Eikon Basilike*.[53] In 1656 the radical Fifth Monarchist William
Aspinwall thought that the death sentence should be introduced for idolatry,
blasphemy and profanation of the Sabbath; whipping was to be the penalty
for what he regarded as relatively minor offences such as rape.[54] In the
following year Roger Crab declared that the Sabbath had been turned into
an idol: so had 'stone-houses'.[55] George Wither after the restoration
conformed to the restored episcopal church. But he soon found that 'men

---

47. Ibid., p. 276; *Memoirs of the Life of Colonel Hutchinson* (ed. J. Sutherland, Oxford
U.P., 1973), pp. 32, 48–9.
48. Taylor, *All the Works*, II, p. 49.
49. Hookes, *Amanda* (1923 reprint), p. 41. First published 1653.
50. *Minor Poets of the 17th Century*, p. 103.
51. I collected some seventeenth-century uses of the word idolatry in *Milton and the
English Revolution*, pp. 64, 179–81, 379–80. See also D. Loewenstein, *Milton and the
Drama of History*, passim.
52. *MCPW*, III, pp. 343–4, 364, 417, 447, 567–8, 601.
53. Loewenstein, op. cit., esp. Chapter 3; *MCPW*, IV, pp. 369, 672.
54. Aspinwall, *The Legislative Power*, pp. 30–31.
55. Crab, *Dagons-Downfall*, pp. 28, 33–4, 37, 39, 46.

have made such idols of their discipline and formalities' that he could not confine his 'belief or practices' to any one society.[56] Milton and Colonel Hutchinson agreed with him. William Dewsbery consoled himself in the dark year 1660 with the reflection that God would soon destroy 'all idolatry out of the earth'.[57]

The importance of fear of idolatry in England before 1640 lay in its contribution to alarm about Laudian policies; after 1640 it made possible the dismissal of royalists as 'the antichristian army'. In the Old Testament atmosphere which prevailed, lack of confidence in popular commitment to protestantism led to an equation of idolatry with popular witchcraft and superstition as well as with popery. On the other hand, eloquent denunciations of Catholics in the House of Commons did not exclude friendly relations between MPs and their Roman Catholic neighbours. Anti-Catholicism was from one point of view related to fears of the populace; from another it was a question of foreign policy rather than of theology: court papists were the targets. Baroque high culture had its attractions not only for Charles I and the Earl of Arundel but also for Milton and other protestants who made the Italian tour – which many English gentlemen were now rich enough to afford. But Italy remained the home of Old Nick Machiavelli as well as of popish idolatry. This complex set of social factors makes it impossible to think of anti-Catholicism merely in religious terms.

John Morrill says of the pre-civil-war period, 'unless we grasp the bitterness of these years, and the sense that the protestant cause and therefore God were being betrayed, then the release of pent-up energy in the early forties cannot be understood.' He was discussing William Dowsing, who had a horror of idolatry long before he was appointed to demolish its monuments in Cambridgeshire and Suffolk. Dowsing was careful to act only in accordance with Biblical and Parliamentary injunctions.[58]

56. Wither, *Parallelogrammaton* (1662), pp. 108, 116–18; *Three Private Meditations* (1666), pp. 46–8.
57. *The Faithful Testimony of . . . William Dewsbery*, pp. 183–4.
58. Morrill, 'William Dowsing', pp. 201, 184, 188, 191.

10. *Chosen Nation, Chosen People*

===

O Lord God, save thy chosen people of England.
Prayer attributed to Edward VI in 1553, quoted by J. N. King, *English Reformation Literature: The Tudor Origins of the Protestant Tradition* (Princeton U.P., 1982), p. 410.

> Locrine. – For mighty Jove, the supreme king of heaven
> That guides the concourse of the meteors
> And rules the motion of the azure sky
> Fights always for the Britons' safety.

The Lamentable Tragedie of Locrine, the eldest son of King Brutus (1595), in *The Shakespeare Apocrypha* (ed. C. F. Tucker Brooke, Oxford U.P., 1908), Act V, sc. i.

The godly part of the nation are the national church.
Francis Cheynell to the House of Commons, 31 May 1643, *FS*, VI, p. 136.

I

We need not get involved in squabbles about whether England was thought to be 'the' or 'a' chosen nation. It seems to me a wrongly posed question. Men and women in our period did not think principally in terms of nation states. The chosen people of the Jews for much of their history comprised two kingdoms. England and Scotland were often compared to Israel and Judah. Protestants on the continent – whether in the republics of Switzerland or The Netherlands, in the kingdoms of Denmark and Sweden, or as minority groups in France or Germany – were more than political allies. They were our brethren, to whom duties of solidarity were owed. Writing for Englishmen, protestant writers made much of God's favour to their country. But their stress on such facts was usually not in pursuance of exclusive claims for England; it was rather part of a diatribe against Englishmen's failure to show proper gratitude for God's favours, their lack of deserts. Many protestants thought there were some chosen people within the inadequately protestantized English state church.[1]

Wyclif had been the Morning Star of the Reformation for Foxe and his successors, though Wyclif's followers had for long been a persecuted minority. Wyclif begat Hus who begat Luther. God had revealed things, in Milton's words, 'as his manner is, first to his Englishmen'.[2] Henry VIII was the first significant sovereign to break away from Rome, for his own not entirely theological reasons. Early protestant propagandists likened Henry VIII and Edward VI to good King Josiah who destroyed idols. When persecution followed under Mary the epic resistance of the martyrs, drawn overwhelmingly from the common people, created an unforgettable legend. The restoration of protestantism under Elizabeth was followed by other signs of divine favour like the defeat of the Spanish Armada, the unexpectedly peaceful succession of James I in 1603 and the union of the protestant crowns, the failure of Gunpowder Plot. The early separatist 'privy church' of Richard Fitz in 1567–8 had seen England as the Israel which God favoured.[3] The idea that England was *a* chosen nation came easily to Englishmen.

Under Elizabeth England was 'the beleaguered isle', holding on against fearful odds in face of a hostile Europe, and yet managing to extend the blessings of protestantism to Scotland, and to support Dutch protestant rebels and French Huguenots against Catholic monarchs. In the early seventeenth century England appeared to be the leading protestant nation, despite the failure of James and Charles to support our brother churches on the continent in the Thirty Years War, and the usurpation of the leadership of protestantism by Gustavus Adolphus of Sweden. Milton in 1641 assured God that he knew 'thou art with us'.[4] Yet he later wrote of the Vaudois as 'thy chosen saints' who had for so long preserved the faith. This was a reason for coming to their rescue when they were undergoing persecution. The 'chosen saints' were not restricted by nationality.

Similarly in New England, which still thought of itself as part of England. The Pilgrim Fathers were escaping from the wrath which they saw as

---

1. *MCPW*, II, p. 553; cf. ibid., I, pp. 526, 704.
2. See in this context Michael McGiffert, 'God's Controversy with Jacobean England', *American Historical Review*, 88 no. 5 (1983), pp. 1151–74; and a communication from him in ibid., 89 no. 4 (1984), pp. 1217–18.
3. C. Burrage, *Early English Dissenters (1550–1641)* (Cambridge U.P., 1912), I, Chapter II, pp. 13–18.
4. See Carol Z. Wiener, 'The Beleaguered Isle', *P. and P.*, No. 51 (1971); *MCPW*, I, pp. 615–16.

threatening England for its backsliding. The idea that they were establishing a model community for others to imitate came rather later, just as the revolution of the 1640s gave many Englishmen a new consciousness of a special role in world history for England (or England and Scotland). It was the failure of the godly revolution in England which gave the North American colonists a new sense of their special status. By 1702 Cotton Mather was speaking of New England as 'spied out' by God to be the New Jerusalem.[5]

So we need not waste printers' ink over the question who first thought of England as the (or a) chosen nation. Some have claimed this role for John Foxe, whom everybody read; but Foxe was at least as much an internationalist as a nationalist. Some have plumped for Thomas Brightman. But his writings were not easily available in England until the 1640s, when popularizations proliferated.[6] But by that time the idea was well established. Was it Joseph Mede, whose millenarian writings were also not published in English before 1640? The search for literary sources seems to me misguided. Once the Bible was available in English for ordinary people to read, they sought there for light on events in their own country. England should follow the example of the Hebrew people under godly rulers. This was not necessarily associated with a claim that the English were *the* chosen people.

When in 1559 John Aylmer's margin said 'God is English', he (or his printer) may or may not have been asserting an exclusive relationship. England was 'God's chosen nation' against Antichrist at one particular moment in time.[7] Aylmer was not denying that God might be Scottish, or Dutch. In 1579 John Stubb's *The Discovery of a Gaping Gulf* assumed that the English were a chosen people, and thought a marriage of Elizabeth to a popish prince would be like a Hebrew marrying a Canaanite.[8] Thomas Cartwright in the following year was grateful that God 'passing by many other nations . . . hast trusted our nation' with the Gospel: a great responsibility, he added, which we have not lived up to. John Lyly in the same year declared that 'the living God is only the English God'.[9] This, like the second epigraph to this chapter, was a literary flourish.

5. Mather, *Magnalia Christi Americana: Or the Ecclesiastical History of New England*, I, pp. 4–5.
6. For examples, see Joseph Frank, *Hobbled Pegasus: A Descriptive Bibliography of Minor English Poetry, 1641–60* (New Mexico U.P., 1968), pp. 49, 69, 92; K. R. Firth, *The Apocalyptic Tradition in Reformation Britain, 1530–1645* (Oxford U.P., 1979), p. 108.
7. Aylmer, *An Harborough for Faithfull and Trewe Subjects*, sig. P4v–Rv.
8. Stubb, op. cit. (ed. L. E. Berry, Charlottesville, 1964), p. 9.
9. Cartwright, *The Holy Exercise of a True Fast*, in *Cartwrightiana*, pp. 143–4; Lyly, *Euphues his England*, in *Works* (ed. R. W. Bond, 1902), II, p. 210.

Elizabethan Presbyterians had argued that the covenant of grace was applicable to the individual and the community. 'God hath given himself unto us', said John Field – to the English people, not only to the elect among them.[10] 'The Lord is in covenant with that people to whom he giveth the seals [i.e. sacraments] of his covenant', declared Cartwright, as 'he doth to our assemblies in England'.[11] 'God hath put his covenant of mercy in England', said George Gifford in 1591, since under Henry VIII 'the nation of England did profess Jesus Christ and were all sealed with the seal of the covenant'.[12] One professor can make a church; the elect within the nation can make a true national church.[13] This Presbyterian position was rejected by separatists; was indeed their reason for separating. Richard Hooker criticized Puritans for identifying themselves with 'God's own chosen people, the people of Israel'. They thought that 'they undoubtedly were themselves that New Jerusalem', and that God would work miracles for them.[14] In the English Revolution such men took the lead.

Hence the importance for the godly of *enforcing* morality on the unbelieving mass of the people, if God was not to lose patience with England. The failure of this policy in the revolutionary decades was the failure of the Presbyterian and Cromwellian concept of the nation's collective covenant with God. In New England the same assumption was made: deviants like Mrs Hutchinson, Samuel Gorton and the Quakers got short shrift.[15] The assumption had disastrous effects on relations with the Indians in the later seventeenth century: if they failed to shed their traditional cultural habits, to accept the standards of English settlers, their deviance threatened punishment on the whole community. They had to be forced to be freely Puritan.[16]

---

10. Field, *A godly Exhortation* (1583), sigs. A4–6. For this and what follows I depend upon T. D. Bozeman, 'Covenant Theology and "National Covenant"', Millersville. Cf. John Knewstub, *Lectures upon the Twelfth Chapter of Exodus* (1572), pp. 5–7, 318.
11. Cartwright, *An Answere unto a letter of Master Harrisons*, in *Cartwrightiana*, p. 52.
12. Gifford, *A Short Reply unto the Last Printed Books of Henry Barrow and John Greenwood*, pp. 39, 62.
13. Bozeman, loc. cit.
14. Hooker, *Of the Laws of Ecclesiastical Polity*, preface, VIII. 11. Philip Gura suggests that this belief, or illusion, lived on to create the concept of the manifest destiny of the United States (*A Glimpse of Sion's Glory*, esp. pp. 181–2, 215–34).
15. Bozeman, op. cit., *passim*.
16. Daniel Mandell, '"Changes in Latitude, Changes in Attitude": Indians and Puritans, 1640–1740', Millersville; Keith W. F. Stavely, 'Roger Williams and the Enclosed Gardens of New England', ibid.

In the Old Testament a distinction is regularly made between the nation of Israel and the chosen people within Israel.[17] In England too the chosen people became the elect to whom God's purposes were more especially revealed: they should take the lead because they understood something of God's plans. Isaac Penington referred to these especial people in 1650 when he said 'Israel is his first-born, whom he will not have any longer kept in bondage. . . . They are his anointed ones, who he will not have touched, but rebuketh kings and Parliaments, armies and Councils, for their sakes, saying Touch not mine anointed, and do my prophets no harm. . . . No strength nor counsel hath been able to prevail against them'.[18]

The millenarian Mary Cary in 1651 declared that England 'so far exceeds in glory and happiness all other nations because of those numbers of precious saints that are in it'. She quoted Thomas Goodwin's Fast Sermon of February 1645.[19] Obadiah Sedgwick declared that 'there is no people for whom [God] hath done as [much] for his church; he hath not done so for any nation'.[20] 'God hath special regard to England', wrote Arise Evans in 1653, 'even though Antichrist for the present plant his tabernacle there'. 'The elect are nowhere else but here in England'.[21] In Scotland too men distinguished between 'a faction, yea, the mixed multitude that came out of Egypt' and 'the dissenters from the Estates, the nation, the Israel of God'.[22]

John Vicars much earlier had seen England as Israel, protected by God against Gunpowder Plot.[23] Winstanley in 1649 proclaimed England to be 'a land wherein the most High hath greatly declared his power, both in casting down the pride of many men's hearts . . . and in casting down the bodies of some that were proud oppressors to be as dung to the earth, dashing one power against another, changing times and customs, and therein trying the sincerity of many that make a great show of love to

17. R. Davidson and A. R. C. Leaney, *Biblical Criticism* (Penguin ed.), p. 162.
18. Penington, *Babylon the Great Described: The City of Confusion. In every part whereof Antichrist Reigns*, p. 53 (not numbered). Cf. pp. 61, 184 above for 'the Lord's anointed'.
19. Cary, *The Little Horns Doom and Downfall*, sig. A 3v–A 4, citing Goodwin, *FS*, XXII, p. 105; cf. p. 95 above.
20. Sedgwick, *The Doctrine of Providence: Matthew X.29–31*, bound with *The Shepherd of Israel* (1658), p. 431.
21. Evans, *The Bloudy Vision of John Farley*, p. 38; *A Voice from Heaven to the Commonwealth of England* (1652), p. 19.
22. Quoted by J. N. Buchanan, *Marginal Scotland* (New York, 1989), II, p. 289.
23. Vicars, *November the 5, 1605: The Quintessence of Cruelty*, frontispiece. Quoted by G. M. MacLean, *Time's Witness*, pp. 112–13. Originally published in 1617, but Vicars was later refused licence to reprint under Laud 'because we are not so angry with the papists now as we were twenty years ago'.

him'.[24] In Marvell's *The First Anniversary of the Government under O.C.* England was hypothetically cast for the part of chosen people who would usher in the millennium: 'if these the times', then Cromwell 'must be the man'. But the English people rejected those who had regarded themselves as their elect leaders, and chose them 'a captain back for Egypt'.[25]

In 1615, preaching to the Lord Mayor, Aldermen and Sheriffs of the City of London, and the Commissioners for Plantations in Ireland and Virginia, Thomas Cooper saw the English people as chosen in a slightly different sense. 'Hath not God wonderfully preserved this little island, this angle of the world, that in former ages was not known or accounted to be any part of the world?' 'Can you do God better service than in promoting his kingdom and demolishing daily the power of Satan' by furthering 'this great and glorious work of the gathering in of the Gentiles' by colonizing Ireland and Virginia?[26] It was a note that was often to be struck in the future. In 1660 Joseph Blagrave cited Psalm XCI in support of the view that 'riches are tokens of God's love and favour unto his chosen people'.[27] In a proclamation of the same year Charles II complacently asserted that 'by ways and means no less miraculous than those by which [God] did heretofore preserve and restore his own chosen people . . . it hath pleased the Divine Providence . . . to restore Us and Our good subjects to each other'.[28] Clarendon told the Convention Parliament that 'God Almighty would not have been at the expense and charge of such a deliverance but in the behalf of a church very acceptable to him' – an argument from God's insistence on cost-effectiveness which must have been very acceptable to his audience.[29] The English are the chosen people throughout Dryden's *Annus Mirabilis*.

II

An alternative phrase to 'chosen people' is 'peculiar people'. This occurs four times in the Authorized Version, but only once in the Geneva Bible –

24. Sabine, pp. 296–7, 260–61; cf. p. 153.
25. Marvell, *Poems*, p. 106; *MCPW*, VII, p. 463.
26. T. Cooper, *The Blessing of Japheth, Proving the Gathering in of the Gentiles and Finall Conversion of the Jewes* (1615), sig. A 2–3, pp. 33–5.
27. Blagrave, *Ephimeris*, sig. A 3v, quoted by Capp, *Astrology and the Popular Press*, p. 150.
28. *A Proclamation against Vicious, Debauch'd, and Profane Persons*, 30 May 1660.
29. Quoted by R. W. Harris, *Clarendon and the English Revolution* (1983), p. 301.

Titus II.14. In the other cases the Geneva reading is 'a precious people unto himself, above all the people that are upon the earth' (Deuteronomy XIV.2), 'a precious people unto him' (Deuteronomy XXVI.18) and I Peter II.9, 'a people set at liberty'. In 1616 John Rolfe, Secretary to the Virginia Company, attributed to Sir Thomas Dale the view that the English were 'a peculiar people marked and chosen by the finger of God' to possess North America.[30] But the phrase soon ceased to be equivalent to 'the chosen people' and came to be restricted to descriptions of themselves by the saints. In 1659 Christopher Feake urged 'the real fifth-kingdom men' to 'become a peculiar people (or, as it were, a nation in the midst of the nation) waiting for the word of command from their leader [i.e. God] to execute the vengeance against Babylon'. Christ's cause will 'be amiable in the eyes of all the nations in due time'.[31] Quakers and Bunyan also used the phrase. It indicated a group conscious of its superiority but also aware that it was a minority.[32]

30. Rolfe, *A True Relation of the State of Virginia Left by Sir Thomas Dale Knight in May last 1616* (ed. H. C. Taylor, New Haven, 1951), pp. 33–41, quoted by A. Calder, *Revolutionary Empire: The Rise of the English-speaking Empires from the 15th Century to the 1780s* (1981), p. 241.
31. Feake, *A Beam of Light Shining In the midst of much Darkness and Confusion*, pp. 57–8.
32. Bunyan, *The Holy City* (1665), speaks of 'a people peculiarly fitted and qualified for this work of God', by contrast with the nobles of Israel who 'put not their hands to the work of the Lord' (*BMW*, III, pp. 84–5).

11. Covenanted Peoples: Scotland and England

These kingdoms [of England and Scotland] are guilty of many sins and provocations against God and his Son Jesus Christ, as is too manifest by our present distresses and dangers, the fruits thereof. . . .

We shall . . . endeavour the extirpation of Popery, prelacy, . . . superstition, heresy, schism, profaneness and whatsoever shall be found to be contrary to sound doctrine and the power of godliness, lest we partake in other men's sins, and thereby be in danger to receive of their plagues. . . .

Most humbly beseeching the Lord . . . to bless our desires and proceedings with such success as may be an . . . encouragement to the Christian churches groaning under or in danger of the yoke of Antichristian tyranny, to join in the same or like association and covenant.

The Solemn League and Covenant, taken by the House of Commons, 25 September 1643, in Gardiner, *Constitutional Documents of the Puritan Revolution*, pp. 267–71.

> It is not possible that any nation
> Should make a vow, upon consideration,
> To pin their faith upon another's sleeve;
> Things to profess which they cannot believe.

George Wither, *Prosopopoeia Britannica* (1648), in *Miscellaneous Works*, IV (Spenser Soc., 1875), p. 68; cf. pp. 91–3.

The matter of the Covenant was the freedom, peace and safety of the people of England, taking in all sorts of people.

Gerrard Winstanley, *An Appeal to the House of Commons* (1649), Sabine, p. 306.

I

The idea of covenant is central to the Old Testament. Moses called 'all Israel' together, and told them 'The Lord our God made a covenant with us in Horeb, . . . not with our fathers only but with us, even with us all here alive this day'. The prosperity of Israel depended on keeping this covenant (Deuteronomy V).[1] After the Flood God covenanted with Noah and his descendants that there should be no more such punishments: the rainbow was to be a perpetual reminder of this promise (Genesis VI.18, IX.8–17). The covenant which made the Jews the chosen people was made with Abraham, defining the territory of Israel. Male circumcision was the seal of this covenant (Genesis XV.18, XVII.2–14). It was confirmed to Isaac, Jacob and their descendants; to Moses, who wrote down 'the words of the covenant, even the ten commandments'; and to David. Hezekiah purposed 'to make a covenant with the Lord God, that he may turn away his fierce wrath from us'. The Geneva margin comments that 'there is no way to avoid [God's] plagues but by conforming themselves to his will' (II Chronicles XXIX.10; cf. Nehemiah IX and X). Asa's covenant, as the Geneva margin noted, was directed specifically against idolatry (II Chronicles XV.2–12). Milton saw here a possible subject for a tragedy.

Jeremiah gave what later seemed a revolutionary twist to the idea when he prophesied that God would make a new covenant with the houses of Israel and Judah, putting 'my law in their inward parts'. Then they will need no teachers, 'for they shall all know me, from the least of them unto the greatest of them' (XXXI.31–4; XXXII.40–42). The Geneva Bible glossed this as a prediction of the coming of Christ; but in sixteenth- and seventeenth-century England it might also give comfort to separatist sectaries who rejected any professional ministry. William Dewsbery turned to this passage when he languished in Northampton jail in February 1655–6.[2] The Geneva margin put rather radical words into God's mouth: 'I will give them faith and knowledge of God for remission of their sins . . . so that it shall *not seem to come so much by the preaching of my ministers* as by the instruction of my holy Spirit'; and 'the full accomplishing hereof is referred to the kingdom of Christ, where we shall be joined under one head' (Jeremiah XXXI.31–4, my italics. There is no authority in the text for the italicized words).

It was St Paul who used Jeremiah's prophecy to argue that the second

---

1. Davidson and Leaney, *Biblical Criticism*, pp. 143–4, 161.
2. Dewsbery, *The Mighty Day of the Lord is Coming* (1656), in *The Faithful Testimony of . . . William Dewsbery*, pp. 159–60. The Peruvian liberation theologian Gustavo Gutiérrez emphasizes this prophecy in *The Power of the Poor in History* (1979). I have used the English translation (New York, 1983), pp. 11–12. (See Appendix B.)

testament or covenant of Christ would abrogate the old; under the new covenant the laws would be put 'in their mind and in their heart'; teachers would no longer be necessary (Hebrews VIII.6–13). 'Ye are all the sons of God by faith in Christ Jesus . . . There is neither Jew nor Grecian, there is neither bond nor free, there is neither male nor female; for ye are all one in Christ Jesus'. 'And if ye be Christ's, then are ye Abraham's seed, and heirs by promise' (Galatians III, *passim*). The Geneva margin makes use of this chapter to argue at length for justification by faith.

The emphasis of the Old Testament covenant had been on the chosen people, on the sons of Abraham. The New Testament extends the covenant to the Gentiles, and includes women. In consequence the new covenant depended on individuals keeping the commandments rather than on the communal propitiation of the Old Testament. The covenant in this sense amounts to a bargain with God. It suggests a certain level of market development. There was something analogous in sixteenth- and seventeenth-century England, in the emphasis on the individual conscience rather than on ceremonies. The yearning to return to the old ways of communal propitiation may have been the basis for the popular popery which seventeenth-century preachers so much deplored, and saw as a sign that God was leaving his chosen English people.

Radical protestants in England proposed to replace ceremonial propitiation by 'the discipline', which monitored spiritual obedience to the laws implicit in the covenant. From the widespread belief that England qualified for succession to the Jews as a chosen people a whole series of conclusions could be drawn. God had favoured his people in the past, and would do so in the future – provided they remained steadfast in covenant. If God seemed to have withdrawn his favour, the reasons for this must be sought, and expiation made.[3] Under Elizabeth, Cartwright had postulated 'a virtual covenant being set up between God and England, whereby in return for the removal of the corrupt, popish government then in being, God would pour forth his spiritual graces in hitherto unprecedented profusion'.[4] The close mutual support of Scottish and English Presbyterians in the 1570s and 1580s foreshadows the alliance of the late 1630s and 1640s.[5]

3. See Chapters 10 and 12 above.
4. Lake, *Anglicans and Puritans?*, pp. 31–4.
5. Russell, *The Causes of the English Civil War*, Chapter 2, *passim*.

'The discipline', although it looks like a theocratic tyranny, contains democratic possibilities, as James I realized. Social rank counts for nothing in the congregation, and the authority of the kirk is superior even to that of 'God's silly vassal', the King. The Calvinist theory of revolt led by the magistrate assumes that lesser magistrates can represent 'the people' against the King.[6] 'There were religious assumptions and political attitudes inscribed within the Puritan attitude towards the godly community which predisposed Puritans (not only Presbyterians) to populist theories of power and a concomitant emphasis on the role of active consent in the practice of government'.[7] The even more radical concept of the inner light assumes that God is within each believer: he is no longer a distant feudal lord or employer to contract with.

II

Covenants played a bigger part in Scottish history than in English. Forming bands to achieve social or political objectives was an old Scottish custom. In December 1557 a group of nobles and gentlemen formed a band, known as the Lords of the Congregation. The signatories pledged themselves to defend the Gospel of Christ and his congregations against Satan and Antichrist.[8] By 1559 many similar bands had formed, obliging themselves to combine and defend one another.[9] Kirk and protestant nation were welded together in covenant. The proclaimed object was to have preaching and the sacraments truly ministered, to suppress superstition, tyranny and idolatry (note these three, associated so often later), and to secure 'the liberty of this our native country to remain free from the bondage and tyranny of [French] strangers.'[10] Knox claimed continuity in covenant for Scotland with Israel – from Abraham – Moses – David – to Christ.[11] In the process considerable radicalization took place. 'Who dare enterprise to put silence to the Spirit of God, which will not be subject to the appetites of wicked princes?' So Lord James Stewart, later Earl of Moray, wrote to Queen Mary and her husband, referring to 'us your poor subjects, God's

6. See pp. 174–5, 190 above.
7. Lake, op. cit., pp. 54–66, 127, 131.
8. John Knox, *The History of the Reformation*, p. 94. Jenny Wormald, *Court, Kirk and Covenant in Scotland, 1470–1625* (1984), p. 111; J. Ridley, *John Knox*, p. 252.
9. Knox, op. cit., pp. 123–4, 136, 138, 196, 342.
10. Ibid., p. 104; Ridley, *John Knox*, pp. 145–8, 158, 163.
11. Knox, *Works* (ed. D. Laing, Edinburgh, 1846–64), I, pp. 273–4, IV, p. 264.

chosen people'.[12] In 1581 the so-called 'King's covenant' united protestants against a confederacy of Catholic nobles again relying on foreign help, this time from Spain.

Scotland's covenants were almost unique in the history of the European Reformation, in that they united an aristocracy with its common people against foreign and Catholic rule. Something similar existed *de facto* in The Netherlands where some of the nobility allied with the common people against another alien rule, that of Spain; but it never took the form of a covenant uniting the whole people. The covenant gave the Scottish Reformation and the Scottish Presbyterian kirk a firmer and more unchallenged popular base than the Church of England ever had.

Projects for union of England and Scotland under Edward VI were frustrated by French influence, and Somerset's attempt to enforce union by war proved counter-productive. Under the rule of Mary Queen of Scots protestants in Scotland were the pro-English and anti-French party. The Scottish Reformation eliminated popery more completely than in England, and helped to establish friendly relations with the old English enemy, which had become the potential champion of European protestantism. When the succession of James VI to the English throne in 1603 re-opened the question of the union of the two nations, Biblical arguments played a considerable part. England and Scotland were depicted as Judah and Israel, originally one people, divided by idolatry.[13] In Ezekiel XXXVII.22 the Lord promised to 'make them one people in the land, . . . and one king shall be king of them all; and they shall be no more two people, neither divided any more henceforth in two kingdoms'.[14] The tract *Of the Union of Britayne* by Robert Pont, Bishop of Galloway, was 'trying to do for Britain what Foxe's *Book of Martyrs* did for Elizabethan England: create a belief among the inhabitants that they constitute an elect nation, singled out for great deeds and salvation', with a mission to restore religious purity and unity to Christendom.[15]

James's English succession was hailed as defeating idolatry, guaranteeing religious as well as political unity.[16] This was partly internal Scottish politics, since from the later sixteenth century the main threat to the kirk

12. Knox, *Reformation*, pp. 150, 140.
13. R. Pont, *Of the Union of Britayne* (1604), in *The Jacobean Union: Six tracts of 1604* (ed. B. R. Galloway and B. P. Levack, Edinburgh, 1985), pp. 25–6.
14. [Anon.]. *A treatise about the Union of England and Scotland* (1604), ibid., pp. 48, 132–3.
15. Ibid., pp. xxx, 242.
16. Ibid., p. xlviii.

seemed to come from Scottish sovereigns. The covenant, dating from 1580–81, 1590, 1596, was the symbol of popular national unity against this threat. The National Covenant of 1637–8 revived the union of aristocracy, kirk and people, against the monarchy and against innovations in religion. It gave new life to the idea that Scotland was a chosen nation, the new Israel. Archibald Johnston of Wariston in 1638 saw Psalms LXXXVIII and CVI, together with Nehemiah IX, as showing 'a very near parallel between Israel and this church, the only two sworn nations of the Lord'.[17] 'Now, O Scotland, God be thanked, thy name is in the Bible' as successor to Israel: so Samuel Rutherford.[18]

The Scots were more conscious of national and international obligations than the English. The *Remonstrance of the Nobility, Barons, Burgesses, Ministers and Commons within the Kingdom of Scotland* (1639) announced that 'so far as we can conceive and consider the course of divine providence in our present affairs, we begin to think that the Lord is about some great work upon the earth'. So the Scots were serious about their League and Covenant with England, whose last clause invited other Christian churches 'to join in the same or like association and covenant'. Robert Baillie in 1641, General Leslie in 1643, both envisaged an Anglo-Scottish protestant crusade in Europe. The English, from the Scottish point of view, not only betrayed the Covenant with their brethren of Scotland, but also reneged on their commitment to European protestantism.[19]

Milton noted Roger Ascham's remark in *Toxophilus, the Schole of Shootynge* (1545) that 'our league and union with the Scots, a thing most profitable and natural', was 'ever by the Pope sought to be hindered'.[20] In 1641, when his feelings towards Scotland were at their warmest, Milton wrote that 'Britain's God . . . hath yet ever had *this island* under the special indulgent eye of his providence'.[21] God, John Dury echoed in a Fast Sermon of 1645, 'is more interested in you [England] and in Scotland, than in any nation whatsoever'.[22] So when Conrad Russell says that the

17. Sir Archibald Johnston of Wariston, *Diary* (Scottish Hist. Soc., 1911–40), I, pp. 340–41; cf. p. 301.
18. S. A. Burrell, 'The Apocalyptic View of the Early Covenanters', *Scottish Historical Review*, 43 (1964), p. 6. In these paragraphs I have drawn heavily on this pioneering article.
19. Ibid., pp. 3, 19; ed. J. G. Fotheringham, *The Diplomatic Correspondence of Jean de Montereuil* (Scottish Hist. Soc., 1888–9), II, p. 550.
20. Milton, Commonplace Book, ?1639–41, *MCPW*, I, p. 502.
21. Ibid., I, p. 704. Italics mine.
22. Dury, *FS*, XX, p. 161.

Covenanters saw 'Charles I's attempt in 1639 to force his religion on Scotland' as an assault on their national independence,[23] he is right; but there is also an international dimension.

Robert Pont emphasized that union between England and Scotland would have the incidental advantage of bringing civility to 'the wild Irish of the English dominion', to Scottish Highlanders 'who for the most part are enemies also to tillage, and wear out their days in hunting and idleness after the manner of beasts', as well as to the thieves and assassins of the Anglo-Scottish pale. We noted the association of 'civility' with protestant Christianity in Chapter 5.[24]

III

Covenants were not part of the English political tradition until one was voted by Parliament in June 1643, at a time when Parliament's military fortunes were at a low ebb. Those who took this covenant engaged themselves to defend Parliament against 'the Papists now in open war against the Parliament'.[25] It is perhaps not unduly cynical to associate this Covenant – the sincerest form of flattery – with negotiations by Parliament later in the same month for a Scottish alliance against the King; and with the fact that on the same day that the covenant was voted Parliament agreed to the meeting of an Assembly of Divines; on the day that Parliament agreed to send a deputation to Scotland the Scots were asked to send ministers to sit in this Assembly.

It was natural for Scots to assume that England, which also had pretensions to be a chosen nation, would join fully with Scotland in religion. The claim to be God's chosen people had arisen in England, as in Scotland, in opposition to the monarchy and the government. But England's claims were not associated with the state church; the Laudians who had ruled the Church of England were now regarded as Antichristians. One powerful reason for opposing Laudianism had been its attempt to dominate the gentry and to subordinate local government to an Antichristian hierarchy. So there was intense hostility to clerical domination in any form. English Parliamentarians had no intention of reforming the Anglican church by

---

23. Russell, *The Causes of the English Civil War*, pp. 15, 50–52, 111, 115–18.
24. Galloway and Levack, pp. 21–2. Cf. esp. pp. 235–8 above, 398 below.
25. 'The Solemn League and Covenant', in Gardiner, *Constitutional Documents*, p. 270. See first epigraph to this chapter.

establishing a Scottish presbytery; even the so-called 'Presbyterians' drew the line at that. The English needed a political alliance because they needed the Scottish army; they did not want, as the Scots expected, reform according to the example of 'the best reformed churches', which for Scots meant the Scottish kirk. Sir Henry Vane played the Bible trick by insisting on inserting 'according to the Word of God and' before 'the example of the best reformed churches'. The Scots could hardly object, since they knew that Scotland was the best Biblically reformed church. The ambiguity of the phrase left England free to adopt 'a lame erastian presbytery'. Not for the first time, the appeal to the Bible failed to produce the unanimity which at least one side thought inescapable. If not exactly a sword to divide, it was a shield to cover up – or a fig-leaf. Yet in 1650 General Fairfax resigned rather than take command of the English army which was about to invade Scotland. Defensive war against a Scottish invasion in 1648 had been one thing; but Fairfax could not accept aggression against 'our brethren of Scotland, to whom we are engaged in a solemn League and Covenant'.[26]

IV

Changes in contract law in the sixteenth and early seventeenth centuries gave Englishmen a new freedom to regulate their business affairs according to their own wishes. Attitudes towards the Biblical covenant reflect this new outlook. The covenant was an agreement between equals, which established rights for both parties. So for God to contract with his people, his church, his chosen nation, put them on an equality with him: both sides undertook obligations. God of course retained the arbitrary powers of omnipotence, but graciously promised not to use them. It was a step towards a rational theology.[27] There were consequences also for political theory. If God was content to rule as a constitutional monarch, bound by his own laws, why should not the King of England do the same?[28] Robert Sanderson's argument that the Solemn League and Covenant was illegal

26. Abbott, *Writings and Speeches of Oliver Cromwell*, II, pp. 267–8.
27. Perry Miller, *Errand into the Wilderness*, esp. Chapter 3; D. Little, *Religion, Order and Law: A Study in Pre-Revolutionary England* (Oxford, 1969), pp. 204–5: R. Tuck, *Natural Rights Theories: Their origin and development* (Cambridge U.P., 1979), p. 30; Burrage, *Early English Dissenters*, I, p. 177; M. Walzer, *The Revolution of the Saints: A Study in the Origins of Radical Politics* (Harvard U.P., 1965), pp. 214–15.
28. See Chapter 7 above.

because contrary to the oath of allegiance ignores this equality of the contracting parties. He was appealing to feudal ideas in an increasingly capitalist society.[29]

But many supporters of Parliament nevertheless needed a lot of persuasion before they accepted the Solemn League and Covenant, which transferred the King's legal power to the King in Parliament. Interesting evidence for this comes from a sermon preached by John Shaw in York Minster on 20 September 1644, when Fairfax and others took the Covenant just after the Parliamentarian victory of Marston Moor. His text was II Chronicles XV.12: 'and they made a covenant to seek the Lord God of their fathers with all their heart and with all their soul'. Shaw did not quote the following verse, which said 'whosoever will not seek the Lord God of Israel shall be slain, whether he were small or great, man or woman'. Instead he argued that the Covenant was the way to turn away God's fierce wrath from the land, quoting II Chronicles XXIX.10. 'The King's legal power is in his courts. . . . How much more then is the King's legal power in his highest Court of Parliament? . . . The Covenant hath the authority of the King's legal power . . . though it may want his personal command'. Just to make sure by having it both ways, he also quoted Nehemiah IX and X, where the people made a covenant without the king.[30] Benlowes's jest that the Covenant contained 666 words may have appealed to anti-Scottish Parliamentarians as well as to royalists.[31]

After the failure of the Presbyterian movement in Elizabeth's reign, the covenants that mattered for active English Puritans were *church* covenants; in effect, if not in intention, such covenants *precluded* a national church, unless and until all God's children were saints. Wither's summary of Psalm LXVIII described it as a prayer 'that they who are, yet, without, may be received into the covenant'. The ungodly were outside the covenant until God had received them into 'his congregation, his church'.[32] Church covenants seem to go best with a Calvinist theology: the elect are to be separated from the rest of mankind, as the Hebrew people had been. 'Ye are a chosen generation, a royal priesthood, an holy nation, a people set at liberty' (I Peter II.9). Church covenants were favoured by the émigré

29. Bishop Sanderson, *Eight Cases of Conscience* (1674), pp. 111–12.

30. Shaw, *Brittans Remembrancer, or, the Nationall Covenant*, sig. B 1v–C 2. This title recalls Wither's long poem.

31. Edward Benlowes, *Theophila*, Canto III, stanza LXXVIII.

32. Wither, *The Psalms of David*. For church covenants, see K. L. Sprunger, *Dutch Puritanism: A History of English and Scottish Churches in the Netherlands in the 16th and 17th Centuries* (Leiden, 1982), esp. pp. 55–6, Chapter XII.

congregations in The Netherlands in the 1620s and 1630s.[33] The Arminian John Goodwin thought that the covenant of grace had been made with all mankind; he was seeking to 'redeem the power of the atonement from the encroachment of high Calvinist predestinarianism'.[34]

So when the Solemn League and Covenant was signed with Scotland in September/October 1643, it is not surprising that misunderstandings arose both over England's commitment to introduce a Presbyterian system and over her international obligations under the Covenant.[35] The Nineteen Propositions of June 1642 had demanded an alliance with The Netherlands and other protestant states 'against all designs of the Pope and his adherents' and for the recovery of the Palatinate.[36] That was perhaps intended rather to sever Charles from his popish allies than as a positive policy. The Scots however meant business.

V

In September and October 1643 two Fast Sermons celebrated the Solemn League and Covenant. They were preached by Thomas Coleman and Joseph Caryl (*FS*, VIII, pp. 221–311). The Covenant will 'separate the precious from the vile', Caryl declared (p. 259), quoting Ezekiel XX.37. He assumed without argument the Scottish interpretation of the Covenant, namely that it had committed England to introducing a Presbyterian system of government, despite the wily Vane's form of words which kept England's options open. But growing anxiety about the growth of separatism from 1644 onwards led conservative preachers again and again to stress England's obligations under the Covenant, which in time came to sound like a persecutors' charter.

The Scot Alexander Henderson raised the alarm on 18 July 1644. Preaching on Matthew XIV.21, Peter's failure to walk on the water, Henderson complained of sects which were splitting the English church (*FS*, XI, pp. 315–16). Herbert Palmer and Thomas Hill followed up in August. Palmer preached on Psalm XCIX.8, attacking Milton among others, citing

33. Sprunger, op. cit., pp. 165, 229, 333.
34. Goodwin, *The Saints Interest in God* (1640) and *Redemption Redeemed* (1651), quoted by Ellen More, 'John Goodwin and the Origins of the New Arminianism', *Journal of British Studies*, XXII (1982), pp. 54–5, 69.
35. Cf. Rutherford, *Lex, Rex*, pp. 381–3.
36. Gardiner, *Constitutional Documents*, pp. 253–4.

Hezekiah and quoting Thessalonians and Proverbs (*FS*, XII, esp. pp. 102–10); Hill preached on Haggai I.7–8, denouncing Roger Williams's *The Bloudy Tenent* (*FS*, XII, esp. pp. 123, 160). Matthew Newcomen on 12 September pleaded for discipline. The Assembly of Divines and reformation were despised: 'men wish themselves in Egypt again'. He picked out Walwyn's *The Compassionate Samaritan* for especial reprobation. A Presbyterian system, he thought, was the only alternative to leaving every man 'to the liberty of his own religion, . . . an opinion most pernicious and destructive, as to the souls of men, so to the Commonwealth' (*FS*, XII, pp. 302–7, 311–17). Stephen Marshall joined the chorus on 26 March 1645. Preaching on Psalm CII.16–17 he informed the Lords that they were not the church's masters but its servants (*FS*, XVI, pp. 195–6, quoting Hebrews III.1).

On 30 July of the same year the Scot Robert Baillie, also preaching to the House of Lords, used Isaiah LXIII.17 to thunder against sects (*FS*, XVIII, pp. 14–16). Cornelius Burges and Francis Taylor followed on in October. Burges stressed *The Necessity of Agreement with God*, citing Amos, 'Can two walk together, except they be agreed?' (Amos III.3); Taylor's *God's Covenant* drew on Psalm LXXIV.20. Both insisted that England was committed by the Covenant to a presbyterian disciplinary system and against toleration (*FS*, XIX, pp. 218–41, 247–75). Thomas Case on 19 February 1645–6 was almost hysterical in his denunciation of 'apostasy': 'this holy Covenant is become amongst many a brand of infamy, a Cain's mark almost' (*FS*, XXI, pp. 249–55). Case's language suggests the intensity of feeling on this issue. Scottish ministers, Trevor-Roper pointed out, preached to the Commons on the four successive fast days after their arrival in England. They lectured their captive audience so severely on their obligation to introduce a presbyterian disciplinary system that no Scot was asked to preach to the Commons again, with the sole exception of the celebration of the victory of Marston Moor, in which the Scottish army had played an important part. Scots did however preach to the Lords.[37]

A change of tone started towards the end of 1645, as preachers more favourable to the Army and Independency were invited to give sermons. The Erastian Thomas Coleman on 30 July 1645 urged Parliament to 'establish as few things *Jure Divino* as can well be'. He thought that Christian magistrates should be governors in the church (*FS*, XVIII, pp. 92–5). The Scot Gillespie, preaching to the House of Lords a month later, took

37. Trevor-Roper, op. cit., pp. 315–16. Cf. Baillie's sermon to the Lords in *FS*, XVIII, pp. 9–62.

particular exception to Coleman's sermon in a powerful diatribe (*FS*, XVIII, pp. 264–80). Jeremiah Burroughs and John Dury on 26 November 1645 resumed the argument for religious toleration. Dury denounced 'the Babylonian government' as opposed to that of Jerusalem (*FS*, XX, pp. 77–130, 171–6). Thomas Horton on 30 December 1646 attacked 'an hypocritical standing' upon Covenants, 'when we shall strive to draw that out of them which is not intended in them' (*FS*, XXVI, pp. 80–81).

Conservatives fought back. 'The violation of our Covenant', said John Lightfoot in February 1646–7, is 'one of the saddest stories . . . to be found in any record. . . . We vowed against error, heresy and schism . . .'. In March Richard Vines took as his text II Peter II.1: 'false prophets . . . among the people . . . shall bring in damnable heresies'. Thomas Hodges on 10 March of the same year preached on the following verse of II Peter II, continuing the denunciation of 'Familism, Antinomianism, Socinianism and many other desperate tenets' which prevailed so far amongst the people that they threatened the 'utter ruin of the nation . . . except some speedy course be taken to prevent their further spreading'. 'Arminianism, Socinianism, yea direct popery . . . was the milk they sucked at the university from ill tutors'. Even the Turks, expostulated John Bond on 19 June 1648, draw the line at covenant-breaking. Simeon Ash on 23 February 1647–8 had expressed outraged horror at a report 'that some great ones have said that the only end of our solemn National League and Covenant was to bring in the Scots, for our assistance in the time of our need. Oh tell it not in Gath, and publish it not in Ascalon!'[38] Sir William Mure's poem 'The Cry of Blood, and of a Broken Covenant' expresses a Scot's incredulous horror at the execution of Charles I.[39]

Some Scottish Presbyterians had seen the Solemn League and Covenant in millenarian terms, as the prelude to a crusade on the continent. They were disappointed to find themselves involved in the broils of internal English politics, in which the Covenant became the shibboleth which Presbyterians used against sectaries. Only after 1660, when the covenant was formally disavowed, did it come in some sense to symbolize the Good Old Cause.[40]

38. *FS*, XXVII, pp. 189–91, 203 (Vines); ibid., pp. 297, 335–6 (Hodges; cf. XXVIII, p. 30 – Robert Johnson); ibid., XXXI, pp. 97–8 (Bond); XXX, p. 155 (Ash).

39. In *The Penguin Book of Renaissance Verse, 1509–1659* (ed. D. Norbrook and H. R. Woudhuysen, 1992), p. 170.

40. See [Anon.], *The Phoenix of the Solemn League and Covenant* (1661). For the Covenant as a hedge or wall, see Chapter 5 above.

VI

Winstanley had his own ideas of what the Covenant meant, or should mean. By the Covenant, he declared, 'the powers of England' have committed themselves 'to make England a free people', in return for the sacrifices they had made in support of Parliament's cause. 'You and we took the National Covenant with that consent to endeavour the freedom, peace and safety of the people of England', 'everyone in his several place hath covenanted to preserve and seek the liberty each of other, without respect of persons'. It is difficult to find any such pledge in the text of the Covenant, which speaks vaguely of the 'religion and liberties of the kingdoms', and promises to 'assist and defend all those that enter into this league and covenant in the maintaining and pursuing thereof'.[41]

Winstanley continues, surely with tongue firmly in cheek: 'You swore in your National Covenant to endeavour a reformation according to the Word of God', which is true; and Winstanley glosses this as meaning 'to restore to us that primitive freedom in the earth'. The gentry have had their feudal tenures abolished; now 'let the common people have their commons and waste lands freed from entanglements of Norman lords of manors . . . and so keep your covenant, that you and all sorts of people may live in peace one among another'. It was 'a great breach of the National Covenant, to give two sorts of people their freedom, that is, gentry and clergy, and deny it to the rest'.[42]

Paying a fee to a lawyer, Winstanley even more remarkably argued, would be 'wilfully [to] break our National Covenant . . . by upholding the old Norman tyrannical and destructive laws'. The Diggers did not reject the law: they endeavoured 'a reformation in our place and calling according to that National Covenant'. Winstanley's textual accuracy in interpreting the Covenant is undoubtedly at fault, as he presumably knew; but no doubt there had been much loose propagandist talk about the cause of the covenanted Parliament which had given rise to hope of a social as well as a political transformation. What Winstanley read into the Covenant was strongly influenced by what he believed the Bible to say about 'equity', 'reason' and 'reformation'.[43] The more the Bible was discussed, the less agreement there seemed to be.

41. Sabine, pp. 275–6, 303–4. Cf. last epigraph to this chapter.
42. Ibid., pp. 305, 291.
43. Ibid., pp. 320–23.

12. God is Leaving England

===

The Lord hath a controversy with the inhabitants of the land, because there is no truth, nor mercy, nor knowledge of God in the land.
Hosea IX.1.

The withdrawing of the Lord's glorious presence from his church is both an evident sign of his displeasure and a manifest threatening of his departure.
John Brinsley, *The Third Part of the True Watch* (second ed., 1622), pp. 26–35.

As sure as God is God, God is going from England. . . . Stop him at the town's end, and let not thy God depart. . . . God makes account that New England shall be a refuge, . . . a rock and a shelter for his righteous ones to run unto.
Thomas Hooker, *The Danger of Desertion*, a sermon preached in 1631, in *The Puritans in America: A Narrative Anthology* (ed. A. Heimert and A. Delbanco, Harvard U.P., 1985), pp. 68–9.

I

The Preface to the Geneva Bible declared that 'after so horrible backsliding and falling away from Christ to Antichrist, from light to darkness, from the living God to dumb and dead idols', England under Elizabeth was fortunate to escape severe judgments from God. But the Queen and her bishops did not take the hint. During her reign Puritans had to walk a narrow tightrope. They praised 'the overthrow of idolatry', the establishment of preaching, the aid given to protestants in Scotland, The Netherlands and France. But true discipline had not yet been established, because of opposition from the bishops, and so what had been achieved was still threatened from external and internal papist enemies. God was angry with England for its lukewarmness.[1] By the end of the reign some had decided

---

1. P. Lake, *Anglicans and Puritans?*, pp. 78–84. Lake cites Cartwright, Chaderton, Travers, Fenner, Udall and the Marprelate Tracts.

to 'shake off the yoke of Antichristian bondage' without tarrying for the magistrate, and they went into exile. But many who remained in England were deeply uneasy. The failure of the Hampton Court Conference in 1604 and the subsequent harrying of Puritan ministers seems to have forced a degree of re-thinking about the status of the English people. The chosen Jews had been persecuted and exiled in punishment for their sins. Did a like fate await England? In 1608 John Downame asked this question in *Lectures upon the Four First Chapters of the Prophecy of Hosea*. It was followed by at least ten works on the same prophet in the next twenty-five years. The Israelites had broken their covenant with God, and had rightly been chastised. 'God punisheth national sins with national punishments', Downame concluded. His was a call to magistrates, ministers and people to reform before it was too late.[2]

Downame operated at a high theological level. A more popular work was *The True Watch and Rule of Life*, written by John Brinsley, best known as an educational writer. The first edition of this book was published in 1606. By 1622 it had reached its ninth edition, and a tenth appeared in 1632. A Second Part was published in 1607 (tenth edition by 1626) and a Third Part, which went into further editions in 1622 and 1623. In 1624 there was a Fourth Part. Parts 1 and 2 were progressively enlarged in later editions. What was the secret of the book's success?

First we must emphasize England's sense of isolation, surrounded by hostile and more powerful Catholic powers – Spain, France – as Israel had been isolated between Egypt, Babylon and Assyria.[3] As the Bible warned, there was continual temptation, in terms of human prudence, to ally with one of these great powers against another (cf. Isaiah VII.1–2). After exterminating most of the inhabitants of the Promised Land, Israel and Judah allied with Assyria or Babylon or Philistines against one another (e.g. II Chronicles XVI). The Babylonian captivity, the Geneva margin suggests, was the consequence of the inability of the two Jewish states to live peaceably with one another. 'It was baseness and madness of Israel', wrote Thomas Taylor, 'that being free from Pharaoh's oppressions they would run back into Egypt in all haste'.[4] Yet external pressures were strong; so

---

2. See M. McGiffert, 'God's Controversy with Jacobean England', quoted on p. 265 n. 2 above. Cf. the first epigraph to this chapter.
3. Carol Z. Wiener, 'The Beleaguered Isle', *P. and P.*, No. 51 (1971).
4. Taylor, *The Principles of Christian Practice*, in *Works* (1653), p. 77. First published posthumously in 1635, three years after Taylor's death. For heathen wives see pp. 69–70 and 245 above, 291 below.

was sheer fear. Solomon's 'outlandish wives' unduly influenced him towards tolerating heathenism and idolatry (I Kings XI.8). Similar causes produced similar effects in sixteenth- and seventeenth-century England. The ninth book of William Warner's *Albions England* (1592) deals with the wickedness of popery and the horrors of the Spanish Inquisition. Phineas Fletcher's *The Locusts, or Apollyonists* (1627) is a diatribe against popery, Jesuits and Spain – the Armada, Gunpowder Plot, ending with an appeal to Charles I to 'cast down this second Lucifer to hell'.[5]

From 1618 the Thirty Years War posed a great threat to European protestantism generally. England failed to respond to this threat, either by forming protestant alliances to check the Catholic advance before war broke out, or by giving effective support to protestantism on the continent once the war had started.[6] When Part 1 of Brinsley's work was published, the attempted Spanish invasion of 1588, worries about the succession to Elizabeth combined with revolt in Ireland in 1603, Gunpowder Plot in 1605, were all fresh in men's memories; and the hand of Catholic Spain was seen behind all of them. By the 1620s Catholic victories in Germany, persecution of protestants there and restoration of monastic lands confiscated at the Reformation, had roused general alarm among committed protestants and had raised the hopes of militant Catholics. James I and Charles I gave little comfort to our protestant brethren on the continent: Charles helped Louis XIII to suppress French Huguenots. This led to conflicts over taxation. A strongly protestant House of Commons would not vote taxes for war unless they were sure it was to be waged against the papist enemy.

Simultaneously the 'Arminian' faction in the Church of England was rising to positions of power; and 'Arminians' had long been suspect as favourers of the crown's right to tax without consent of Parliament, as well as being semi-papists. Questions affecting foreign policy and the constitution could not be separated from religious questions. Yet without agreement between crown and Parliament England could have no effective foreign policy, at a time when it was clearly unsafe to be weak. England was in a mess. No wonder the House of Commons called for days of humiliation and fasts, or that governments were unenthusiastic about agreeing to them. But from 1624 they could no longer be resisted.[7]

5. *Poetical Works of Giles Fletcher and Phineas Fletcher* (ed. F. S. Boas, Cambridge U.P., 1908–9), I, pp. 125–86.
6. Cf. T. Cogswell, 'War and the Liberty of the Subject', in Hexter, *Parliament and Liberty*.
7. See pp. 80–81 above.

The First Part of *The True Watch and Rule of Life* is a relatively conventional devotional handbook, commenting on the Ten Commandments and the Creed, with 'Special Preservatives against every sin'. Popery and idolatry are condemned as breaches of the First and Second Commandments. The author's strongly protestant position was proclaimed in his denunciation of 'hypocritical worship, as in outward ceremonies, or bare show of religion', and halting between two religions.[8] Parts 2 and 3, published within a year of Part 1, are more directly concerned with the international situation. Part 2 emphasizes the necessity of prayer, which 'will do more for turning away judgments from the church' and for 'overthrowing God's enemies'. Brinsley's object is to make his readers 'conscious of our unworthiness', aware 'of the main sins and wants of the land', and of the risks of 'the Lord's wrath due thereunto'. We are in perpetual danger, surrounded by a multitude of enemies. Brinsley prints 'a prayer for our realms and the churches in them', and calls on the Lord to 'fight thine own battles against that Roman Antichrist'.[9]

Part 3 is 'taken out of Ezekiel IX', which describes God's slaughter of the people of Jerusalem because of their idolatry and other abominations. Applying this to England, Brinsley declared 'Never nation had God's glory more apparent in protection. So never any from whom it was more nearly gone'. From Ezekiel IV and V Brinsley concluded that 'the Lord is most unwilling to depart from his church, so long as there is any other remedy'. It is up to us. But 'our devotion is waxen cold', we are torn by dissensions; even 'the name of Christian is reproachful to many'. 'God will not spare Jerusalem if it rebel against him'.[10] 'The sum of the whole book' is to show 'how the Lord did long forewarn his people of Judah, calling them to repentance sundry ways before he brought the 70 years captivity in Babylon'. 'And withal' to demonstrate 'the principal abominations which led him to this heavy judgment', all of which Brinsley clearly thought were present in the England of his day. Again and again he stresses, 'the manifold forewarnings which we have received, chiefly from Babylon, above all in the powder treason: showing evidently that the Lord is angry with us for our sins'. How can we 'appease the Lord' so as to prevent judgments and plagues falling upon us?[11]

What can we do 'to pacify his Majesty and to hold him still amongst

8. Brinsley, *The True Watch and Rule of Life* (9th ed., 1622), pp. 37–41, 153 sqq.
9. Brinsley, *The Second Part of the True Watch* (1607), pp. 16, 21, 91–3, 212–15.
10. Brinsley, *The Third Part of the True Watch*, pp. 35–51, 59, 504–5.
11. Ibid., p. xlv.

us?' God hath 'made this island the wonder of the world'. He protected us in 1588, at the death of Elizabeth, and in 1605; but we have still not sufficiently repented of the defilement of our land 'with the blood of God's servants in Queen Mary's days'. We suffer popery to revive and grow up amongst us. Remember Josiah. We are no more secure against idolatry than Jerusalem was in his days. A whole chapter lists the abominations of which the land is guilty, with a new emphasis on 'the horrible wickedness' and blindness of priests and prophets, magistrates and ministers. We must not rely on God's favour just because we have some worthy preachers and some good people. The sins of God's people may be so great that he will not spare them.[12]

In Chapter 9 we noticed that popery was more attractive to the populace than could be admitted. The point was picked up in 1644 by Roger Williams: 'a victorious sword and a Spanish inquisition will soon make millions face about as they were in their forefathers' time'.[13] In November 1659 Richard Baxter still gave as one of many reasons for refusing toleration to Catholics that 'their doctrine and worship is suited to the inclination of the ungodly multitude'.[14] That nagging anxiety was rarely openly discussed. Idolatry was not the only sin of the English people. Brinsley cited Amos VIII.6 on 'the general cry of the poor', who are likely to be brought to perpetual beggary by racking of rents and raising of prices. In England, as the rich grew richer and the poor poorer, soon all would be 'gentlemen or peasants (gentlemen or cormorants, peasants and slaves)'. Among the Jews covetousness causing oppression had hastened the captivity: what would it do in England?[15] 'Thou [God] didst never so long warn any of thy people but at length thou visitest indeed'. And Brinsley issued an earnest warning, desiring 'this favour for our dread sovereign, . . . that he should not only do himself but see all things done by us his subjects as thou hast enjoined'.[16]

In Part 4, dating from 1624, after the outbreak of the Thirty Years War, Brinsley's panic about the popish menace is even shriller. Addressing himself to 'all plain and simple-hearted people of our land' who have been seduced by popery, he cites Psalm L: 'what hast thou to do to . . . take my Covenant in thy mouth, seeing thou hatest to be reformed, and hast cast

12. Ibid., pp. 26–70, 127, 232–3, 276, 523, 588–91.
13. Roger Williams, *The Bloudy Tenent*, p. 280. Cf. p. 263 above.
14. Baxter, *An Answer to the Overturners and New Modelers of the Government* (1659), in R. B. Schlatter, *Richard Baxter and Puritan Politics* (Rutgers U.P., 1957), p. 134.
15. Brinsley, *The Third Part of the True Watch*, pp. 511–12, 612, 265, 295–6.
16. Ibid., pp. 569–79, 591.

my words behind thee?' (That is from the Geneva Bible. The Authorized Version substitutes 'hatest instruction' for 'hatest to be reformed', the latter presumably too Genevan an expression.)[17]

The horrors of the Thirty Years War are now always in Brinsley's mind. When we reflect on the sufferings of God's people under the popish yoke in Germany, we must 'think how near the like miseries may be unto ourselves', even though the Lord has 'hitherto preserved us by kings and princes'. 'The bloody enemies, executioners of [God's] vengeance' are 'on every side of us, and, as we may justly fear, . . . in the midst among us'. 'We are the men principally above all others devoted to destruction'. The knives are at our throats. Brinsley is silent here about what kings and princes are doing to protect us now. Nothing can give us 'any security but an unfeigned repentance'. Till then we can only expect 'some dreadful scourge'. Again and again he returns to the need for repentance for not doing enough to purge our land of popery.[18]

Brinsley's writings can perhaps be seen as a call for – among other things – a more rigid Presbyterian discipline, forcing goodness on a reluctant populace. Thomas Becon nearly a century earlier had insisted that failure to repent would mean that 'God will surely pour out his fierce plagues upon us, root us out of the earth and destroy us for evermore'.[19] Josias Nichols in 1602 expected divine punishment because of the popish remnants in Anglican worship and episcopal opposition to their removal.[20] Brinsley was far from being the first to sound so loud a note of alarm. But he was certainly the most persistent. Once we start to look there are many like him. Edward Elton, the conservative divine who wrote a Preface to *The Third Part of the True Watch*, declared that the increase of popery and profaneness in England was notorious to all. 'The Lord from heaven cries to us all to turn': his vineyard is unfruitful. But in 1607 the worst sign of God's wrath which he could report was 'the insurrection against enclosure', 'terrible to many in the area' (the Midlands). Everything pointed to the necessity of 'the renewing of our covenant'.[21] Sir Henry Finch in 1621 quoted Hosea on 'God's judgments against the people for their sins', blaming authority at least as much as the people. He attacked a king (Hebrew,

17. Brinsley, *The Fourth Part of the True Watch* (1624), sig. A 5, B 3–D 8.
18. Ibid., pp. 22–3, 27–8, 33–5, 330–90.
19. Becon, *The pathwaie unto Prayer* (1542), Preface, in *Early Works* (Parker Soc., 1843), p. 127.
20. Nichols, *The Plea of the Innocent*, pp. 38, 61, 225–9. I owe this reference to T. D. Bozeman's 'Covenant Theology and "National Covenant"', Millersville.
21. Brinsley, *The Third Part of the True Watch*, sig. ¶–¶¶¶2.

of course) who 'joineth hands with beastly drunkards', and does nothing 'to make clean the commonwealth . . . but sitteth still and letteth all alone'. But the Israelites, 'consociating with strangers and making a mixture of their religion with the superstitions of the Gentiles', framing to themselves 'a mingle-mangle out of both', sound very like the chosen people of England in the 1620s.[22] Sir Simonds D'Ewes in 1623 was preparing for 'worser times' which 'without God's admirable and infinite mercy we could not but shortly expect'.[23]

Even the Archbishop of York warned James I that by tolerating Catholics 'you labour to set up the most damnable and heretical doctrine of the Church of Rome, the Whore of Babylon'. And he ominously linked religious and constitutional grievances by adding 'It cannot be done without a Parliament, unless your Majesty will let your subjects see that you take unto yourself a liberty to throw down the laws of the land at your pleasure'.[24] The mistake appeared to be in letting his subjects see what he was doing even more than in doing it.

Jeremiah Lewis preached a sermon on Guy Fawkes Day, 1618, against 'the bloody Papist with whom peace is most dangerous'. He too emphasized the need to repent of England's sins.[25] So did William Attersoll in the same year.[26] John Preston's sermons in the 1620s repeatedly hammer away at the danger for England and its protestantism posed by the popish Antichrist: 'if the Lord be thine enemy' strong towers will not avail for defence.[27] By this time many were looking back nostalgically to the ideal-ized days of Good Queen Bess, despairing of James's failure to support God's cause in the Thirty Years War.[28] A protégé of the Earl of Warwick told his congregation that England was being punished for failing to come to the aid of 'God's people' in Germany. He ominously cited Manasseh in II Chronicles XXXIII, whose encouragement of idolatry led to disaster for

22. Quoted by W. R. Prest, 'The Art of Law and the Law of God: Sir Henry Finch (1558–1625)', in Pennington and Thomas, *Puritans and Revolutionaries*, pp. 112–14. See p. 28 above.

23. D'Ewes, *Diary 1622–1624*, p. 130; cf. p. 145.

24. [Anon.], *Cabala, Mysteries of State, in Letters of the great Ministers of King James and King Charles* (1654), p. 13.

25. Lewis, *The Doctrine of Thankfulnesse: Or Israels Triumph Occasioned by the Destruction of Pharaoh and his hoste in the Red-Sea* (1619), pp. 45–6.

26. Attersoll, *A Commentarie upon . . . Numbers, passim.*

27. Preston, *Life Eternall* (4th ed., 1634), pp. 175–6 (second pagination). See 'The Political Sermons of John Preston' in my *Puritanism and Revolution*, Chapter 8. Cf. Russell, *Causes of the Civil War*, pp. 74–82.

28. E.g. D'Ewes, *Autobiography and Correspondence*, I, p. 153.

Judah at the hands of the Babylonians.[29] Thomas Hooker's 5 November sermon in 1626 openly expressed fear lest the sins of England, including 'wickedness in high places', would cause God to withdraw his protection.[30]

Other preachers stressed, with copious Old Testament references, the
dangers to kings from marrying alien wives of strange religions. MPs
insisted that Laudian 'Arminianism' was either concealed popery or opening
the way to it. 'Idolatry' was a convenient blanket phrase to cover the
two.[31] Richard Sibbes faced these anxieties when he took as his text for a
sermon preached on Guy Fawkes Day 'If God be for us, who can be
against us?' (Romans VIII.31). He asked 'What course shall we take to keep
God comfortably with us?' He was with us in 1588, in 1605, and in the
great plague (of 1625 or 1630). God has defended our religion miraculously:
but we must bring our hearts to a more perfect hatred of popery. If
religion go, God will 'spue us out of his mouth'.[32] 'A more perfect hatred
of popery' was the essence of the matter.

Others felt the same anxieties, and had the same answers. In the 1620s,
David Cressy tells us, the tone of assize sermons on Guy Fawkes Day is
shifting from joy at deliverance to apprehension of a continuing Catholic
menace. Rous's *Diary*, Thomas Cogswell points out, reveals growing loss
of faith in Charles I in the late 1620s.[33] Private fasts to propitiate the
God who was angry with England's sins were complemented by calls in
Parliament for public fasts, since 'a land or nation . . . must be longer in
the fire than a particular person'. Laudians disliked fasts: this was one
expression of the cleavage between Laudians and Puritans.[34] Laud did
not preach on 5 November.[35] In the House of Commons in 1628 Sir
Robert Phelips recalled 'what misery befell the Jews when they broke
their peace with God. . . . I am afraid that God sitteth in the council of
our enemies against us. Doth not God plague us with enemies abroad

29. Hunt, *The Puritan Moment*, pp. 176–7. For a comparison of Charles I to Manasseh
in 1637 see ibid., p. 274.
30. *CSPD, 1625–49*, p. 175.
31. See pp. 69–70, 245, 285 above.
32. Sibbes, *Works*, VII, pp. 396–7.
33. Cogswell, 'The Politics of Propaganda: Charles I and the People in the 1620s',
Journal of British Studies, 29 (1990), pp. 187–9; cf. D. Hirst, *Authority and Conflict:
England 1603–1658* (1986), p. 158.
34. S. Foster, *Notes from the Caroline Underground* (Springfield, Ohio, 1978), pp. 17, 50;
S. Rutherford, *The Tryal & Triumph of Faith* (1645), p. 30. See p. 81 above.
35. D. Cressy, 'The Protestant Calendar and the Vocabulary of Celebration in Early
Modern England', *Journal of British Studies*, 29 (1990), pp. 43–5.

and destruction at home? We are become the most contemptible nation in the world'.[36]

John Randall in sermons on Romans VIII.38–9, published as *St. Pauls Triumph*, tells us that his text treats of 'the afflictions and dangers to which the faithful are, and may be, subject in this world'. 'In what time could the argument be more seasonable than now', when 'the church and people of God are in such distress, hazard and danger, and the destroying Angel of God is so abroad in many places of the world, and all places almost filled with wars, and who knoweth when these things shall end?' Randall, interestingly enough, gave the manuscript of these sermons to 'his loving friend Mr Edward Misselden, merchant', the famous economic writer, before he died in 1622. They were published seven years later.[37] In 1631 a further collection of Randall's lectures was printed as 'very necessary for the consolation and support of God's church, especially in these times'.[38]

The theme of God's abandonment of England became commonplace in the 1630s. A poem prefixed to Dod and Cleaver's *Ten Commandments* in 1630 told the Christian reader

> If in place thou have abode, where ignorance dark doth reign,
> I wish thee further seek forth truth, or there do not remain.[39]

The major literary achievement of the genre was George Wither's *Brittans Remembrancer* (1628), which chronicled at inordinate length England's failure to live up to her role as a land which God 'elected from among the heathen isles'. Cataloguing his compatriots' sins, Wither called for repentance and amendment if destruction was to be avoided. England has neglected favours, warnings and providences greater even than those vouchsafed to the Jewish people.[40] Again the background was the popish threat and England's failure to respond. Wither's *Hallelujah*, published in 1641, was subtitled *Brittans Second Remembrancer*. It contained over 200 hymns, some penitential, others warning of the wrath to come.

> Preserve this hopeless place
> And our disturbed state
> From those that have more wit than grace
> And prudent counsels hate.

36. *Cobbett's Parliamentary History*, II (1807), p. 447.
37. Randall, op. cit. (1629), sig. A3, A4v.
38. Randall, *Twenty-nine Lectures of the Church*.
39. Dod and Cleaver, *Ten Commandments*, sig. A 3v.
40. Wither, op. cit. (Spenser Soc., 1880), pp. 37–8, 46, 64–5, 314, 325–30.

That could hardly have been published before 1641. Wither hailed 'God that . . . is this island's guard' in a hymn for the 5th of November: he also wrote a hymn for 'troublesome and dangerous times' which summed up what many were thinking:

> For now they see Him drawing nigh
> And hastening to requite
> Their insolence and tyranny
> Who did in wrongs delight. . . .
>
> For though some have bewail'd the time,
> And reformation sought,
> But few do sorrow for their crimes
> Or mend themselves in aught. . . .
>
> And if I shall be one of those
> Who for example sake
> Must suffer for the public woes
> On me thy pleasure take.[41]

Thomas Hooker's famous sermon, *The Danger of Desertion* (1631), was specific about England's sins, and neglect of God's warnings. May not Germany's condition become that of England? 'The glory is departed from England . . . and the reward of sin is coming on apace'.[42] As early as 1629 John Winthrop told his wife he was persuaded that 'the increasing of our sins gives us . . . great cause to look for some heavy scourge and judgment to be coming upon us. The Lord hath admonished, threatened, corrected and astonished us, yet we grow worse and worse. . . . I am verily persuaded, God will bring some heavy affliction upon this land, and that speedily'.[43] He hoped that God would make New England 'a refuge for many whom he means to save out of the general destruction'.[44] Cotton thought the emigrants were 'forced to fly into the wilderness'. 'God hath provided this place to be a refuge'. The correspondence of the Barrington family is full of alarm about the dangers of the international situation and the possibility that God may be leaving England. 'God's heavy judgment – most likely to befall us'; 'those storms

41. Wither, *Hallelujah*, pp. 274, 269–71.
42. Hooker, op. cit., in Heimert and Delbanco, op. cit., pp. 66, 68–9. See third epigraph to this chapter.
43. *Winthrop Papers*, II, p. 91.
44. E. S. Morgan, *The Puritan Dilemma: The Story of John Winthrop* (Boston, 1958), p. 40.

which in the eye of reason this sinful nation is likely to endure'; 'these times wherein we so much increase in disobedience to [God], and wherein all sorts of sin so much aboundeth'.[45] No wonder Sir Francis Barrington and his like called for fasts in the House of Commons.[46]

Published in 1636, Henry Burton's *For God and the King* contained two sermons preached on 5 November, stressing that loyalty to God must come first. 'Divisions or heart-burnings between the King and his subjects are most perilous. . . . Can those be the King's friends, that go about to divide between him and his good subjects?'[47] Even grimmer were Thomas Goodwin's words in 1639. It would be 'happy for other states professing the Calvin religion if they could wash their hands of the blood of the churches . . . betrayed by them'. England was included in the 'other states'.[48]

Richard Mather, who left for New England in 1635, felt that he was exiled because of his devotion to purity in the church of Christ. In 1639 he too warned that the Lord was about to 'unchurch England'. When civil war came, he believed it marked the death throes of the Beast.[49] 'As long as Christ is here in England', said John Cotton, 'let us not go away'.[50] Stephen Marshall preached the second Fast Sermon to the House of Commons on Queen Elizabeth's Day, 17 November 1641. He warned that 'all your counsels and advising will be nothing if God say "I will stay no longer in England"'.[51] 'Oh that our heads were fountains of tears for the idolatry (that land-destroying sin) that reigns amongst us', cried Calamy in another Fast Sermon a month later.[52] Henrietta Maria's 'Popish Plot' and the Irish revolt of 1641 seemed to confirm the worst alarms.[53] When the King was so foolish as to allow his secret correspondence to be captured after the final defeat of Naseby, his

---

45. *Barrington Family Letters*, pp. 29, 60, 92; cf. pp. 36–7, 56, 77, 90. Cf. J. T. Cliffe, *The Puritan Gentry: The Great Puritan Families of Early Stuart England* (1984) esp. pp. 201–11.
46. See Chapter 3 above.
47. Burton, op. cit., pp. 56, 99–100.
48. Goodwin, *Exposition of Revelation*, in *Works*, III, p. 174.
49. Middlekauff, *The Mathers: Three Generations of Puritan Intellectuals, 1596–1728*, esp. pp. 31–2, 44.
50. Cotton, *Canticles* (1642), pp. 31, 127. In fact Cotton left England in 1633.
51. *FS*, I, p. 121.
52. Ibid., II, p. 49.
53. Caroline Hibbard, *Charles I and the Popish Plot, passim*. See also Robin Clifton, 'The Popular Fear of Catholics during the English Revolution', *P. and P.*, 52 (1971), *passim*.

enemies were horrified but not surprised by the extent of his concessions to international Catholicism. An analogy can be drawn between fear of Catholicism in the 1620s and 1630s and fear of fascism in England in the 1930s. In each case overwhelming force seemed to be accumulating in the hands of powers hostile to England's way of life, and governments seemed to be doing too little to oppose them. But Charles I found no Churchill.

Continuing fear of popery from the 1620s may explain why religion could seem the decisive reason for choosing sides in 1642. Tom May, the official Parliamentarian historian, thought that sins had caused the war.[54] Neither Fairfax nor Cromwell thought religion was the thing at first contested for.[55] The division in 1642 came between active millenarians, who chose Parliament, and on the other hand church-and-state Anglicans, with no urgent sense that they were living in the last times: they followed the court. But there were enduring issues at stake. Catholicism was to remain a divisive issue in foreign policy so long as the power of France seemed to threaten England: and the apparent acquiescence of Charles II and James II made this an issue of domestic politics too. On 23 April 1679 a prophetess warned that the Lord

> will kill and slay with his own hand
> When he lets the French into our land.[56]

The uproar over the Popish Plot released rather than created popular anti-Catholicism.[57] In a riot in Somerset in 1689, Monmouth was identified with Holland, protestantism and freedom, his opponents with France, popery and absolutism.[58]

A remarkable expression of the continuing power of anti-Catholicism as part of the English revolutionary heritage is given by Algernon Sidney and Lord William Russell, both relatively secular-minded politicians. As he faced execution in 1682 Sidney wrote an '*Apologie . . . on the Day of his Death*'. In this he said 'God will not suffer this land where the gospel

---

54. May, *History of the Parliament of England* (1647), p. 19: but he is perhaps not very good evidence on that subject.
55. *Fairfax Correspondence* (ed. G. W. Johnson, 1848–9), II, p. 40; Cromwell, *Writings and Speeches*, II, p. 587.
56. Anne Wentworth, *The Revelation of Jesus Christ* (1679), p. 12.
57. See for instance F. W. Fairholt, *The Civic Garland*, pp. 77–90; and T. Harris, *London Crowds in the Reign of Charles II* (Cambridge U.P., 1987), pp. 30–31, 73–4, 109–10.
58. R. Clifton, 'Lessons and Consequences of the Rebellion of 1685', in Schochet, *Religion, Resistance and Civil War*.

hath of late flourished more than in any part of the world; he will not suffer it to be made a land of graven images; he will stir up witnesses for the truth, and, in his own time, spirit his people to stand up for his cause and deliver them. I lived in this belief and am now about to die in it.'[59] Lord William Russell, executed in the following year, similarly rejected Catholicism in his speech on the scaffold: 'I look on it as an idolatrous and bloody religion, and therefore I thought myself bound in my station to do all I could against it'.[60] These statements express a sense of the English as a chosen people, whatever their failings, a horror of idolatry and a belief in the ultimate victory of the Good Old Cause because it was God's. In each of these respects they recall Milton, in *Areopagitica, Eikonoklastes*, the *Ready and Easy Way*, summed up in *Samson Agonistes*.

In the light of the foregoing, it is easier to understand why even some of the most tolerant of English protestants, including Richard Hooker, Ussher, Selden, Milton and Locke, were not prepared to tolerate Catholics. Henry Robinson's irenic *Liberty of Conscience* (1644) insisted that Catholics alone among Christians should not be tolerated — 'by reason of their idolatry'.[61] The Leveller Agreement of the People of May 1649 excluded Catholics from holding any state office. Roger Williams was exceptional in being prepared to extend toleration even to Catholics.[62] Walwyn may have shared this view, but it is perhaps significant that the pamphlets expressing it are of doubtful attribution.[63] Milton, like Samuel Butler, thought Catholicism was not a religion but a political organization owing allegiance to a hostile foreign power, which 'extirpates all religions and civil supremacies', 'a priestly despotism under the cloak of religion'.[64] Liberty of conscience might be permitted to Catholics, but — 'for just reason of state' — not 'the public and scandalous use of worship'.[65] William Erbery was prepared to extend toleration to Jews and Turks but not to papists 'till they can give assurance to the state of their peaceable subjection'. Then 'honest papists' could 'have private and public exercise of their religion', as protestants had in France.

---

59. In John Carswell, *The Porcupine: The Life of Algernon Sidney* (1989), p. 229.
60. Quoted by R. L. Greaves, 'The Radical Tradition, 1660–89', Millersville.
61. Robinson, op. cit., in *Tracts on Liberty* (ed. Haller), III, p. 114.
62. Williams, *The Bloudy Tenent*, pp. 149–52.
63. *Writings of William Walwyn*, pp. 56–9, 531–2.
64. Butler, *Prose Observations*, pp. 275–6; *MCPW*, II, p. 565 (*Areopagitica*); IV, p. 321 (*Defence of the People of England*).
65. *MCPW*, VII, pp. 254–5, 260–61, 268.

But this can be permitted only 'in due time . . . when our governors are good'.[66]

Fear of Catholicism reached a peak in the early 1640s, stimulated by the Irish rebellion of 1641, supported by the Pope. The preoccupation of France and Spain in the Thirty Years War prevented them from taking advantage of England's political turmoil to intervene; and in the fifties Cromwell's conquest of Ireland and Scotland, the Navigation Act, Blake's fleet, the Dutch and Spanish wars, removed all fear of foreign intervention with Catholic support. The Catholic threat became one exclusively of foreign policy, the dependence on France of Charles II and James II: the possibility of internal papist revolt disappeared. James II found dissenters more plausible allies than Anglican bishops. After 1688 it no longer seemed to occur to anyone that God might leave England. The word 'protestant' in this context came to have a political, or nationalist, significance. When Nell Gwynn was mistaken by a hostile crowd for the King's French mistress, she said, reassuringly, 'Be silent, good people, I am the *protestant* whore'. What mattered was her patriotism, not her theology.

66. *The Testimony of William Erbery*, pp. 333–4. Cf. S. L. Adams, 'Foreign Policy and the Parliaments of 1621 and 1624', in *Faction and Parliament: Essays on Early Stuart History* (ed. K. Sharpe, Oxford U.P., 1978), *passim*: M. Heinemann, 'Political Drama', in *The Cambridge Companion to English Renaissance Drama* (Cambridge U.P., 1990), pp. 198–202.

13. The Reign of the Saints

For behold, I will create Jerusalem as a rejoicing and her people
as a joy. . . . And the voice of weeping shall be no more heard in
her, nor the voice of crying.
Isaiah LXV.18–19.

God shall wipe away all tears from their eyes, and there shall be
no more death, neither sorrow nor crying, neither shall there be
any more pain: for the first things are past.
Revelation XXI.4.

You are the Rod of God. . . . You strike through King, gentry
and nobility; they all fall before you.
Joseph Salmon to the Army, *A Rout, A Rout* (1649), in Smith,
Ranter Writings, p. 190.

The last chapter considered English anxiety about possible loss of God's
favour, manifested by the Roman Catholic threat to her national religious
independence. But we must see this against a wider crisis of anxiety and
hope about the possibly approaching end of the world. For many centuries
millenarian ideas had tended to surface in times of social crisis. The subject
has been studied by Norman Cohn, who is not very sympathetic to millenarians.[1] But seventeenth-century millenarianism differed from earlier versions,
since it was based on new scholarly approaches to the Bible. The Reformation stimulated thought about the end of the world, not least because of the
protestant identification of the Pope with Antichrist, whose overthrow
would usher in the last times.[2] This led to closer study of the Biblical texts,
in an attempt to interpret the prophecies.

The Reformation and the vernacular Bible also stimulated millenarian
preaching.[3] Bishop Bale said of the Apocalypse that 'he that knoweth not
this book, knoweth not what the church is whereof he is a member'. 'Not

1. Cohn, *The Pursuit of the Millennium, passim.*
2. For what follows see my *Antichrist in 17th-century England, passim*; and my *Religion and Politics*, Chapter 13. See also Chapter 14 below.
3. Zaret, *The Heavenly Contract*, pp. 95–9.

one necessary point of belief is in all the other Scriptures that is not here also in one place or another'. It was an outrage that some had attempted to exclude this millenarian work from the canon.[4] Bale, Foxe's *Book of Martyrs*, Hall's *Court of Virtue* and the Geneva Bible with its notes, all helped to revive popular apocalyptic visions in England.[5]

Millenarian studies involved mathematical as well as historical and linguistic problems, for some of what were held to be the crucial texts included mysterious figures: 'a time, times and the dividing of time' (Daniel VII.25), 1,260, 1,290 and 1,335 days (Daniel XII.11–12 and Revelation XI.3); the thousand years during which the Dragon will be in the pit and the saints shall live and reign (Revelation XXI.1–7). More universally acceptable was Isaiah LXV.17, 'I will create new heavens and a new earth: and the former shall not be remembered' (echoed in II Peter III.13 and Revelation XXI.1). Others stressed texts which envisage a time when the exploitation of man by man shall cease (Isaiah LXII.8–9; Amos IX.13–15, Micah IV.3–4).

Many passages in the Bible prophesy good times for God's people, a material Land of Cockaigne. 'In that day shall thy cattle be fed in large pastures' (Isaiah XXX.23). 'They shall plant vineyards and drink the wine thereof; they shall also make gardens and eat the fruits of them' (Amos IX.13–14). 'In the last days . . . they shall sit every man under his vine, and under his fig tree' (Micah IV.1–3; cf. Zechariah VIII.12).

The poor especially will benefit. They shall not labour in vain and bring forth in fear.[6] 'The Lord . . . will make the meek glorious by deliverance' (Psalm CXLIX.4). Here to the consolation is added retributive justice: 'the kingdom, and dominion, . . . shall be given to the holy people of the Most High' (Daniel VII.27). 'Let the high acts of God be in their mouth, and a two-edged sword in their hands, to execute vengeance upon the heathen, and corrections among the people; to bind their kings in chains, and their nobles with fetters of iron' (Psalm CXLIX.6–8).

The expected cycle of events envisaged worsening conditions for the godly everywhere, wicked rulers; but then the overthrow of Antichrist,

---

4. Bale, *The Image of Both Churches*, pp. 251–3, 515. The Parker Society editor was uncomfortable with what *DNB* calls Bale's 'want of good taste and moderation'. He did not wish to be thought to approve all that the robustly outspoken bishop 'either said or did' (ibid., p. xi).

5. P. Christianson, *Reformers and Babylon: English apocalyptic visions from the reformation to the eve of the civil war* (Toronto U.P., 1978), pp. 36, 139. Cf. Hall, op. cit., p. 311: 'the last day is not far hence'.

6. Cf. epigraphs to this chapter.

the extension of Christianity over all the world and the conversion of the Jews (an argument for admitting them to England in the 1650s). Robert Eburne, in his *A Plain Pathway to Plantations* of 1624, argued that the Gospel must be preached throughout the whole world before the Second Coming (Mark XIII.10, Matthew XXIV.14) and therefore it was sinful for the English not to hurry up and colonize America.[7] Even a conservative theologian like Edward Elton believed in 1615 that we were living in the latter days.[8]

From Napier to Isaac Newton the greatest mathematicians of their time occupied themselves with the effort to make chronological sense out of the Bible's dark sayings. Slowly a consensus formed, which suggested that the cycle of events leading to the end of the world was likely to begin in the 1650s, or at latest during the 1690s. Noah's Flood was dated to Anno Mundi 1656, and Matthew's Gospel said 'as the days of Noah were, so shall the coming of the Son of Man be'. Taken in conjunction with the other pointers, this convinced many that AD 1656 or thereabouts would see the end of Antichrist's reign.[9] John Swan's *Speculum Mundi* (1635) soberly reviewed and then rejected evidence that the end of the world was due in 1657.[10] William Chillingworth defied accepted orthodoxy to say that 'the opinion of the millenaries is true', by which he referred to the thousand-years' rule of Christ.[11] John Cotton in 1640 told his congregation that 'the kingdom of heaven is at hand'.[12]

Bernard Capp has shown that astrological predictions frequently fused with millenarian calculations. Tycho Brahe had interpreted the new star which he discovered in 1572 as an omen of the Second Coming, a view which King James accepted. The astrologer Simon Forman indulged in Biblical exegesis, with special reference to the restoration of the Jews, Antichrist and the end of the world. Sir Christopher Heydon, author of *A Defence of Judicial Astrology* (1603), and a one-time follower of Elizabeth's Earl of Essex, also went in for astrological/millenarian speculations.[13] In

7. Eburne, op. cit. (ed. L. B. Wright, Cornell U.P., 1962), pp. 27–30.

8. Elton, *Colossians*, p. 649.

9. E.g. Thomas Goodwin, *Works*, III, p. 196; Peter Sterry, *Englands Deliverance from the Northern Presbytery* (1652), pp. 43–4; for other examples see my *Religion and Politics*, p. 272.

10. Swan, op. cit. (Cambridge U.P.), I, p. iii.

11. Chillingworth, *Works*, III, pp. 300, 369–80.

12. Cotton, quoted in F. W. Bremer's forthcoming *The Congregational Connection*.

13. Capp, *Astrology and the Popular Press*, Chapters 5 and 6 *passim* for what follows.

Sylvester's translation of Du Bartas's *Divine Weekes and Workes* (1603) 'judicial astrologers that presume to point the very time' of the end of the world were denounced.

> You have mis-cast in your arithmetics,
> Mislaid your counters, gropingly ye seek
> In night's black darkness for the secret things
> Seal'd in the casket of the King of kings.[14]

After 1640 it was 'an article of faith in the almanacs that the Pope was Antichrist, and that his fall was at hand'. Napier was described as 'a great lover of astrology'. His calculations of the date of the end of the world were especially popular in England in the 1640s. John Henry Alsted's *Beloved City: Or, The Saints Reign on Earth A Thousand Years*, translated into English in 1643, helped to focus expectations on a coming good society. He too combined Biblical with astrological data. Edwards reports Erbery as expecting new heavens and a new earth.[15] Nathanael Homes in 1650 said on a day of thanksgiving for the victory of Dunbar that he had been convinced for eight years 'that 1650 or thereabouts would be a time full of great and glorious works', citing Daniel XII and Revelation XIII.5. He still retained his conviction, but counselled patience to his congregation.[16] Such hopes were widespread; they were both contributory causes and consequences of the civil war. So it was natural that, in Capp's words, 'in England astrologers did much to keep alive a popular millenarian faith after the collapse of the hopes aroused by the civil war.' It may well be that astrological millenarianism survived better at the popular level after 1660 than Biblical millenarianism, whose dated prophecies had so frequently misfired.[17] It is almost certainly true that its association with popular millenarianism stood astrology in bad stead in the intellectual world of the restoration.[18]

The international situation contributed to the sense of impending crisis. George Wither believed in 1612 that 'the Lord's great day is near'; twenty years later he thought he was living in the worst age, and that the 'Second Coming . . . now draweth nigh'. In 1643 he accused Charles I of failing to protect England against the popish menace; and he saw the civil war as a

14. Sylvester, *Complete Works*, I, pp. 22–3.
15. Edwards, *Gangraena*, I, pp. 77–8.
16. Homes, *A Sermon Preached before the Right Honourable Thomas Foote, Lord Maior, and the Right Worshipfull the Aldermen, sheriffs . . . of London*, pp. 14–17.
17. Capp, op. cit., pp. 170, 178, 252.
18. See pp. 23–6 above.

battle against Antichrist.[19] Peter Lake has usefully distinguished in the late sixteenth and early seventeenth centuries between those on the one hand who accepted the equation of the Pope with Antichrist as little more than a part of the protestant case against Rome and those other millenarians whose opposition to Antichrist drove them into zealous political activity.[20] The correspondence of the Puritan Barrington family in the twenties and thirties shows how carefully men and women in the latter category were observing 'the foundations of the earth out of order'.[21] For the Barringtons this was cause for alarm; it encouraged many to flee to New England, from the wrath to come. But this changed after 1640, perhaps earlier. The Fifth Monarchist Christopher Feake tells us that he first became interested in the prophecies of Daniel and Revelation after hearing the news of anti-Prayer Book riots in Edinburgh in 1637.[22]

Activist belief in the approach of the millennium led not only to enhanced nationalism in England but also to protestant internationalism. English radical protestants were very conscious of a cosmic conflict between Christ and Antichrist, in which 'the churches abroad' were more actively involved. Spenser and Dekker both saw the Dutch revolt in apocalyptic terms.[23] Solidarity with foreign churches helped to unite English Puritans, for instance in collections for Palatinate exiles. Laud had Richard Sibbes, William Gouge, Thomas Taylor and John Davenport reprimanded by the High Commission for this.[24] Similarly support for preaching in 'the dark corners of the land', notably by the Feoffees for Impropriations, also brought activists together in an organized campaign of which the government and hierarchy disapproved. Preaching was a weapon against Antichrist, popery and ignorance within England. 'When the enemy is assaulting the churches afar off', declared Preston, 'he is even then striking at the root of this Church and Commonwealth. . . . Do we not see the whole body of those that profess the truth are

19. Wither, *Juvenilia* (Spenser Soc., 1870–72), II, p. 406; *Psalms of David*, II, pp. 184, 145; *Campo-Musae* (1643), pp. 53–4, 61–3; *Vox Pacifica* (1645), p. 68.
20. Lake, 'The Significance of the Elizabethan Identification of the Pope as Antichrist', *Journal of Ecclesiastical History*, 31 (1980), esp. pp. 175–8. Cf. Lake, 'William Bradshaw, Antichrist and the Community of the Godly', ibid., 36 (1985), *passim*. Cf. p. 295 above.
21. *Barrington Family Letters*, pp. 29, 36–7, 56, 60, 77, 90, 92, and *passim*.
22. In his Preface to John Tillinghast's *Eight Last Sermons* (1655).
23. Norbrook, *Poetry and Politics in the English Renaissance*, p. 136.
24. *CSPD, 1627–8*, p. 77.

besieged round about through Christendom?'[25] John Goodwin argued in 1642 that 'the action wherein the Church and people of God in the land are now engaged' was of great concern 'to all the Saints of God in all the reformed Churches. Victory in England will be the riches, strength and increase of them'.[26] The Stuart kings, Samuel Morland was to say, had 'most treacherously betrayed the protestant Cause'.[27] After the restoration Morland regretted and withdrew the book in which this phrase occurred: he got his knighthood.

Stephen Marshall, almost the official spokesman of the Parliamentarians, repeatedly in his Fast Sermons stressed England's role in the millenarian events which seemed to be opening up. 'The battle is not yours, but God's'.[28] In *The Song of Moses* he interpreted Revelation XV.3–4 to mean that 'the people of Italy, Germany, France, England, Scotland, Denmark, Sweden, Polonia, Hungaria . . . shall shake off the yoke of Antichrist'. 'In the end, all the kingdoms of the world shall be the kingdoms of our Lord and his saints, and they shall reign over them'.[29]

Hugh Peter told Parliament in December 1648 that the Army must root up monarchy also in France and other kingdoms round about.[30] Five years later John Rogers said we were 'bound by the law of God . . . to aid the subjects of other princes that are either persecuted for true religion or oppressed under tyranny'.[31] Cromwell, Marvell had prophesied, 'to all states not free/Shall climacteric be'. For Milton the Second Coming would bring 'an end to all earthly tyrannies', as well as throwing all bishops 'eternally into the darkest and deepest gulf of hell'.[32] In *Paradise Lost* he was still proclaiming to 'a world perverse' the

> odious truth, that God would come
> To judge them with his saints (*PL*, XI. 704–5).

25. Preston, *A Sensible Demonstration of the Deitie*, printed with *A Sermon of Spirituall Life and Death* (1630), pp. 52–3.

26. Goodwin, *Anti-Cavalierisme*, pp. 49–50, in Haller, *Tracts on Liberty*, II.

27. Morland, *The History of the Evangelical Churches of the Valleys of Piemont* (1658), sig. A 2v–3.

28. See especially *FS*, II, pp. 81–136, 241.

29. *FS*, VI, pp. 355, 393, 395.

30. Clement Walker, *The History of Independency*, Part II, pp. 49–50. Peter appears not to have published this sermon: Walker is not a very reliable witness.

31. J. Rogers, *Some Account of the Life and Opinions of a Fifth Monarchy Man*, pp. 84–6.

32. *MCPW*, I, pp. 616–17.

II

As soon as censorship broke down, popular pamphlets as well as serious theological tomes spread the views of Napier, Mede and Brightman. A translation of Mede's *The Key of the Revelation* was published in 1643 by order of a committee of the House of Commons, with Preface by William Twisse, Prolocutor of the Westminster Assembly of Divines. The translation was made by an MP. The publication could hardly have been more official.[33] Twisse had found the doctrine of the reign of the saints on earth repugnant when he first heard it. But he was convinced by reading Mede.[34] The intellectual crisis of the civil war thus suddenly brought new questions home to men and women, far beyond the scholarly circles in which they had hitherto been discussed. It has been calculated that nearly three-quarters of Presbyterian and Independent writings published between 1640 and 1653 expressed millenarian expectations.[35] This is confirmed by the alarmed Scot Robert Baillie, who reported in 1645 that 'the most of the chief divines' in London 'are express chiliasts'.[36]

Parliamentarian propagandists made the most of these exciting possibilities in urging support for their cause against royalists and their 'Antichristian army'. They met with a surprising response. Some troops in Wallingford in 1643 had heard rumours that the Earl of Essex, commanding the Parliamentarian armies, was John the Baptist, the precursor of Jesus Christ, and so of the Second Coming. Thomas Palmer, an Anglican chaplain, announced that God chose Essex 'to be his General and the champion of Jesus Christ to fight the great and last battle with Antichrist'.[37] Men and women were asking themselves what exactly the future held out. Would the last times start with the descent of Christ from heaven, to rule in person 'in and by his saints', as Thomas Collier put it in 1647, in a sermon preached to the New Model Army, and as Bunyan seems to have believed ten years later?[38] Or would the saints themselves rule alone for the thousand

33. See my *Antichrist in 17th-century England*, p. 28.

34. K. R. Firth, *The Apocalyptic Tradition*, p. 222.

35. F. D. Dow, *Radicalism in the English Revolution, 1640–1660* (Oxford U.P., 1985), p. 62.

36. Baillie, *Letters and Journals*, II, p. 156.

37. Ed. I. G. Philip, *The Journal of Sir Samuel Luke* (Oxfordshire Record Soc., 1950), I, p. 76; Palmer, *The Saints Support* (1644), sig. A 2, quoted by Capp, 'The Political Dimension of Apocalyptic Thought', p. 112.

38. Collier, *A Discovery of the New Creation*, in Woodhouse, op. cit. pp. 394–5; W. R. Owens, ' "Antichrist must be pulled down:" Bunyan and the Millennium', in *John*

years of the millennium, preparing for the final establishment of Christ's kingdom? George Fox in 1654 believed that 'the saints shall judge the world, ... whereof I am one'.[39] A dictatorship of the godly.

These were political questions. Who were the saints who should reign? Would existing magistrates be converted? Or would new men, with new policies – perhaps from new social classes – come to the helm? The answers to such questions tended to vary with social position. To those outside the political nation, who had hitherto existed only to be ruled, something like a political and social revolution appeared necessary before the saints could rule, whether this revolution was peaceful or violent.

A recently published book helps us to grasp the revolutionary significance of seventeenth-century millenarianism. Professor Mayfield has argued that belief in a temporal millennium at hand, in which the saints would rule whilst preparing for Christ's kingdom, made possible the unprecedented events of the execution of a King as a traitor to his people.[40] If the millennium is coming soon, there is no room for monarchy, least of all for antichristian monarchy. Kings had given their kingdoms to the Beast (Revelation XVII.17).[41] The New Model Army was seen (by Hugh Peter as early as 1645, by others later, including many of its own members) as the instrument for the downfall of Antichrist.

On 7 June 1646 William Dell preached a sermon to the Army in its camp outside Oxford. The Army had not yet intervened in politics, and its enemies in Parliament intended to disband it swiftly now that the war was won. Dell addressed himself directly to the Army's pride in its achievements, and to its solidarity, to its divine mission. His text was drawn from Isaiah LIV.11–17, which he said foretold 'the truly Christian and spiritual church'. He first praised the admirable unity of the Army, 'more the unity of Christians than of men'. 'The Lord hath ... knit them up in one bundle'. Thanks to their faith, 'the special presence of God' has been with them. 'Who is like unto thee, O people, saved by the Lord? ... Thou shalt tread upon' the 'high places [of] thine enemies'. 'God doth not now make any people, or kindred, or nation his church; but gathers his church out of

---

Bunyan and his England (ed. Anne Laurence, W. R. Owens and S. Sim, 1990), pp. 80–83.

39. G.F. and J. N[ayler], *Sauls Errand to Damascus*, pp. 10–11.
40. N. H. Mayfield, *Puritans and Regicides: Presbyterian-Independent Differences over the Trial and Execution of Charles (I) Stuart* (Lanham, Maryland, 1988), *passim*.
41. Sibbes, *The Beasts Dominion over Earthly Kings*, quoted by Mayfield, op. cit., p. 55. Cf. Revelation XIII–XVII *passim*.

every people, and kindred, and nation', and only from his elect. The intention was clearly to convince his audience that the Army still had a great role to play as the elect in arms, distinct from the nation.[42] 'All the weapons that are made against thee shall not prosper', Isaiah had said; for the righteousness of the Lord's servants 'is of me, saith the Lord' (Isaiah LIV.17). A year later, in the Putney Debates, Colonel Goffe envisaged a more positive millenarian role for the Army. To compromise with the King, he said, would be 'to set up that power which God has engaged us to destroy'.[43] For the Army to allow itself to be disbanded, argued John Cook in the same year, would be to retreat from its millenarian duty.[44]

This perception explains the regicides' ability to reject the formalities of traditional law in the name of a higher justice, and helps us to understand the sharp division between them and those whom we call Presbyterians. John Cook, prosecutor of the King at his trial, argued that 'When our law-books are silent, we must repair to the Law of Nature and Reason.' The 'holy and just' law of God is a 'fundamental law without which there can be no conservation of human society'; it is superior to the common law. The 'maxim in law that the King can do no wrong' is 'against reason, and therefore against law; the pronouncement of one thousand judges cannot make it law'.[45]

'Why hath Parliament abolished the kingly office?' Cook asked later 'Because God commanded them to. . . . There are no laws so righteous as those which it pleased him to give to his elect people'. Legal arguments were irrelevant. John Owen thought it stupid to espouse 'principles which are good in themselves' against 'the mind and providence of God' as they have been made clear to his elect. This vision gave those who shared it the moral strength and confidence to defy traditional laws and taboos.[46]

The years around 1647–50 saw the height of the radical movement. From its defeat emerged the organized group of Fifth Monarchists, who thought that Christ's kingdom must be expedited by military action to establish the rule of the saints. Quakers appeared at about the same time: they were not pacifists in the 1650s, calling for an aggressive foreign policy

42. Dell, *The Building, Beauty, Teaching and Establishment of the truly Christian Church*, in *Several Sermons and Discourses*, esp. pp. 72–6, 95; cf. N. T. Burns, 'William Dell's New Modelled Church Militant: Winning the Peace', Millersville.

43. Woodhouse, op. cit., p. 40.

44. Cook, *Redintegratio Amoris* (1647), p. 84; Mayfield, op. cit., pp. 165–6, 225–6, 235.

45. Mayfield, op. cit., pp. 165–8. Dr Mayfield denies that Cook's argument is tending towards secularism here.

46. Mayfield, op. cit., pp. 196, 203, 218, 221, 241, 243.

against the power of Antichrist as well as for immediate social reforms at home. In 1659 they offered their services to the republican government in order to keep out Charles II. 'We look for a new earth as well as for a new heaven', Edward Burrough told Parliament in early 1660; 'his people . . . shall be happy in this world, and for ever'.[47]

'That stupendous year' 1656 came and went. Even Ralph Josselin, who had not anticipated the end of the world, nevertheless had expected 'notable effects'.[48] But nothing in particular happened. Four years later Charles II was sitting on the throne, not King Jesus. The slow waning of millenarian enthusiasm in the later fifties led to recognition that Christ's kingdom was not of this world. Dissent succeeded insurrection. The desperately courageous revolts of the London Fifth Monarchists in 1657 and 1661 were the last fling of the military activists: Quakers adopted the peace principle and withdrew from political activity immediately after the defeat of Venner's revolt in 1661. The activist utopian millenarianism which flourished in the forties and early fifties had envisaged a better life on an earth where social relations and living conditions would be transformed. Similar utopian ideas arose in other periods of revolution or social crisis. In England, this seems to be a preponderantly lower-class millenarianism; women play a greater part, proportionately, in millenarian than in other forms of activity, including writing.[49]

Millenarianism easily took on social overtones. In 1646 Christopher Feake was said to have declared that there was 'an enmity against Christ' in monarchy and aristocracy. In the millennium, he predicted, there would be 'no difference betwixt high and low, the greatest and the poorest beggar';[50] John Tillinghast had thought in 1655 that 'the present work of God is to bring down lofty men'; John Rogers attacked 'corrupt and naughty nobles'.[51] The millenarian Baptist Thomas Collier, preaching to the New Model Army at Putney in 1647, on the favourite text 'Behold I create new heavens and a new earth', declared that the rule of the saints would mean the end of tithes, of free-quarter and of 'tyrannical and oppressing laws and courts of justice'; the laws would be in English.[52] George Cockayne, preaching on the same text to the House of Commons in November 1648,

---

47. Burrough, *Memorable Works*, p. 766; *To the Parliament of the Commonwealth of England* (March 1659–60), p. 3.

48. Josselin, *Diary*, p. 365.

49. Cf. pp. 406–9 below.

50. Edwards, *Gangraena*, III, p. 148; *Thurloe State Papers*, V, pp. 755–9.

51. *Mr. Tillinghast's Eight Last Sermons*, p. 219; Rogers, *Ohel* (1653), pp. 11, 22–3.

52. In Woodhouse, op. cit., pp. 390–96.

insisted that God will perhaps choose 'the meanest of the people' to 'judge all the causes of the sons of men'. The Welsh Fifth Monarchist Morgan Llwyd envisaged a redistribution of landed property to the advantage of the poor.[53]

Mary Cary, one of the most interesting and least studied of the Fifth Monarchists, in 1648 believed that the events of the preceding decade in England fulfilled the prophecies in Revelation. The King, being 'of one mind with the Beast', had made war against the saints. His time expired in 1645 with the 1,260 years of the Beast (Daniel XII.11–12). 5 April 1645 saw the resurrection of the Two Witnesses (prophesied in Revelation XI),[54] for that was when the New Model Army marched forth, standing for the defence of the saints against Antichrist.[55] The three and a half years which it took Parliament to win the war corresponded to the 'time, times and dividing of time' of Daniel (VII.25; cf. XII.7). 'Jesus Christ in the year 1645 began to take his kingdom'; the millennium would begin in 1701.[56]

Mary Cary looked forward to a time when men would not 'labour and toil day and night . . . to maintain other that live . . . in idleness'. They would 'comfortably enjoy the work of their hands'. She expected a material heaven on earth 'before twenty or ten or five years pass'. The saints would then join in judging 'all the workers of iniquity'. 'The time is coming when not only men but women shall prophesy; not only aged men but young men, not only superiors but inferiors; not only those who have university learning but those who have it not, even servants and handmaids'. The saints 'shall have abundance of gold and silver', and wear 'rich apparel'. It would approximate to a classless society.[57] In 1653 she urged Barebone's Parliament to abolish tithes, common law and lawyers, to eject drones from the church, pay ministers from the public treasury and reform universities and schools. Work should be provided for the poor, relief for the

53. Cokayne, *FS*, XXXII, pp. 33–4; R. T. Jones, in *Biographical Dictionary of British Radicals*, II, p. 194.
54. This appears to confuse the 1,290 days of the abomination of desolation in Daniel XII.11 with the 1,260 days for which the Two Witnesses were to prophesy.
55. Mary Cary, *The Resurrection of the Witnesses* (1648), pp. 82–100, 183; *The Little Horns Doom and Downfall* (1651), pp. 5–7, 118–19, 133, 207–9. *The Little Horn* had prefaces by Hugh Peter, Henry Jessey and Christopher Feake.
56. Mary Cary, *The Resurrection of the Witnesses*, pp. 82–9, 156–62, 183; *The Little Horns Doom and Downfall*, 208–9.
57. Mary Cary, *The Little Horns Doom and Downfall*, pp. 238, 282–317.

unemployed. No more confiscated lands should be sold. She supported the war against The Netherlands.[58]

Fifth Monarchist programmes were often remarkably secular. Peter Chamberlen, John Rogers and John Spittlehouse all called for judges to be elected; Spittlehouse, Aspinwall and Vavasor Powell promised that there would be no excise or customs 'in the days of the Messiah'.[59] *A Standard Set Up*, the programme of the Fifth Monarchist rebels of 1657, called (like Levellers) for abolition of tithes, copyhold, the excise and conscription, and for decentralized law courts. Complete equality before the law should be established. Venner's Fifth Monarchist manifesto of 1661, *A Door of Hope*, denounced the 'old, bloody, popish, wicked gentry of the nation'. It announced, disarmingly, that 'whatsoever can be named of a common or public good we mean by the kingdom of Christ', and insisted that thieves should not be executed but should be put to work until they had compensated their victims. The law of debt should be reformed, and town government and gilds should be democratized. Like the Levellers, *A Door of Hope* attacked primogeniture, because it increased inequality. The poor would be set to work, excise and customs abolished. An aggressive anti-Catholic policy in Europe was called for. The export of various industrial raw materials should be completely banned. This suggests the social groups to which this very earthly manifesto was intended to appeal. A pamphlet which assumed *The Coming of Christs Appearing in Glory, and its shortly breaking forth*, published in 1653, knew of 'nothing more important than matters of trade, as tending to strengthen the position against all eventualities'.[60] Fifth Monarchists then were relatively socially egalitarian; equality among saints. A sermon of 1663 declared that 'a nation is more beholden to the meanest kitchen maid in it that hath in her a spirit of prayer than to a thousand of her profane and swaggering gentry'.[61]

Gerrard Winstanley is not strictly a millenarian. He says nothing about the rule of the saints. He envisages social transformations resulting not from Christ descending from heaven to rule on earth but from Christ rising in sons and daughters. Winstanley preferred the word Reason to God, since

---

58. M.R., *Twelve Proposals to the Supreme Governours of the three Nations now assembled at Westminster* (1653), pp. 5–13. Mary Cary's married name was Rande. On the title-page of *The Resurrection of the Witnesses* she described herself as a minister.
59. Aspinwall, *The Legislative Power*, p. 12; Capp, *The Fifth Monarchy Men*, pp. 150, 160.
60. Quoted in H. A. Glass, *The Barbone Parliament* (1899), p. 52.
61. [Anon.], *The Failing and Perishing of Good Men* (1663), a funeral sermon for the Fifth Monarchist John Simpson.

he had been 'held under darkness' by the word God.[62] Christ rising signifies the triumph of reason in human beings. Reason teaches cooperation, do as you would be done by, not competition; and its rising would lead to a peaceful social revolution in which a communist society would be established. Winstanley expected no other Second Coming.

Quakers too in the 1650s expected Christ's kingdom on earth in the near future, and shared many Leveller and Fifth Monarchist views, including especially opposition to tithes. In 1659 Edward Burrough denounced 'all earthly lordship and tyranny and oppression, . . . by which creatures have been exalted and set up one above another, trampling underfoot and despising the poor'. Persecution, he added, 'must unavoidably tend to destroy and expel trading'.[63] It was difficult for contemporaries to differentiate between millenarian Quakers and millenarian Fifth Monarchists, whose social programmes and aggressive foreign policies were so similar. The opposite misunderstanding besets historians today. Looking through the wrong end of the telescope, we find it difficult to associate Quakers with active insurrectionists like Fifth Monarchists. But before 1661 this distinction did not exist. A government spy reported in 1657 'it is said that the Anabaptists and Quakers were chiefly active' in the Fifth Monarchist conspiracy of that year.[64]

In 1658–9 George Fox rebuked Cromwell's army for not having yet attacked Rome.[65] Many had seen the English Revolution as part of an international movement against Antichrist. Robert Leslie, commander of the Scottish army in England in 1643, was said to hope his troops would ultimately be used to 'go to Rome, drive out Antichrist and burn the town'.[66] The astrologer William Lilly in 1651 predicted that 'we Christians' would liberate Palestine from the Turks so that the Jews could return.[67] Blake's fleet would 'carry the Gospel with our navy up and down to the Gentiles', Feake was said to have proclaimed in 1653.[68] Thomas Cobbett, in a tract dedicated to Oliver Cromwell in the same year, foresaw the dethronement of Satan 'from his so large dominions'; and John Eliot told

62. Winstanley, *The Saints Paradise*, pp. 122–5; Sabine, pp. 114–15.
63. Burrough, *Works*, pp. 500, 771, 790–92, 818.
64. *CSPD, 1657*, p. 351.
65. Fox and Burrough, *Good Counsel and Advice Rejected* (1659), pp. 26–7, 37; G.F., *To the Councill of Officers* (1659), pp. 2, 8.
66. *Diplomatic Correspondence of Jean de Montereuil*, II, p. 550.
67. Lilly, *Monarchy or no Monarchy in England* (1651), p. 55.
68. Quoted by L. F. Brown, *The Political Activities of the Baptists and Fifth Monarchy Men in England during the Interregnum* (New York, 1911), p. 24.

Cromwell, also in 1653, that 'the Lord hath raised and improved you in an eminent manner to overthrow Antichrist'.[69] Other Fifth Monarchists promised that the army of the saints would overthrow Turks and the Pope.[70]

As American experience in the second half of the present century has taught us, solidarity with friends abroad and a determination to destroy evil powers can become a fig-leaf for imperialism. The Manifesto issued by Cromwell's government in defence of its invasion of the Spanish West Indies claimed that England's naval power was being used 'in avenging the blood . . . of the poor Indians . . . so unjustly, so cruelly and so often shed by the hands of the Spaniards. . . . All great and extraordinary wrongs done to particular persons ought to be considered as in a manner done to all the rest of the human race'.[71] Noble sentiments: but English practice in the fifties included the brutal conquest of Ireland, expropriation and transplantation of many thousands of its inhabitants, as well as trade wars against the protestant Netherlands and against Spain. 'The propagation of the Gospel was the thing principally aimed at and intended', Army officers in recently conquered Jamaica declared in 1655.[72] If it was the intention, it was not the result, as we know. When an opponent of slavery helped negroes on Providence Island to escape, he had been rebuked by the Providence Island Company: 'Religion consists not so much in an outward conformity of actions as in truth of the inward parts', he was told.[73] 'The Gospel in one hand and a sword in the other has made many slaves but I fear few Christians', said the author of *The Whole Duty of Man* later in the century.[74] Slaves were not allowed to convert to Christianity, but native Indians who did would naturally wish to wear Christian garments, and that was good for the English cloth trade, as Hakluyt and many others had foreseen.[75]

English radicals, including early Quakers, urged Cromwell to lead his armies to overthrow Antichrist. Few indeed of them opposed the conquest and subjugation of Ireland, though Walwyn was an honourable

69. Cobbett, *The Civil Magistrates Power in Matters of Religion Modestly Debated* (1653), to the Reader; Eliot, *Tears of Repentance*, dedicatory letter to Cromwell; both quoted by Francis J. Bremer in his forthcoming *Congregationalist Connection*.
70. Tillinghast, *Knowledge of the Times* (1654), p. 3; Capp, *The Fifth Monarchy Men*, p. 151.
71. *MCPW*, II, pp. 335–6.
72. *Thurloe State Papers*, III, p. 681.
73. A. P. Newton, *Colonizing Activities of the Early Puritans* (Yale U.P., 1914), p. 149.
74. *The Causes of the Decay of Christian Piety*, in *The Works of the Author of the Whole Duty of Man*, p. 302.
75. R. Hakluyt, *Principal Navigations* (Everyman ed.), VIII, pp. 110–20.

exception.[76] Millenarianism was well on the way to secularization in Marvell's *First Anniversary of the Government under O.C.* (1655). His vision of Oliver forwarding God's purposes depended on a powerful English navy commanding the seas. James Harrington also put forward a democratic sounding millenarian imperialism. The restoration seemed to some to open up new prospects for British supremacy.

> This is the time has been foretold so long,
> That England all her neighbours shall command;
> And on the continent obedience find.
> Nor must her empire be by seas confin'd.[77]

A poet in the following year had the same aspirations but was less self-confident. He wanted to see

> A fleet like that in fifty-three
> To re-assert our power at sea.[78]

Dryden in *Annus Mirabilis* (1666) depicted the English as God's chosen people, but with the emphasis on national power and national trade rather than on a protestant (or any other) crusade. In the *Horatian Ode* Marvell had recalled the Roman legend that a human head had been disinterred when the Capitol was founded.

> A bleeding head when they begun
> Did fright the architects to run;
> And yet in that the state
> Foresaw its happy fate.

Marvell was right to see that the British Empire was founded on a bleeding head.

A startling contrast with the radical millenarianism of the forties and fifties is Michael Wigglesworth's *The Day of Doom: Or, A Description Of the Great and Last Judgment* (1666). The New Englander, after the Restoration, has nothing to say about the rule of the saints on earth. His concern is to stress the torments to which the reprobate are condemned, including formal professors. The saints will observe all this with satisfaction.

---

76. See my 'Seventeenth-century English Radicals and Ireland', in *A Nation of Change and Novelty*.

77. Thomas Higgons, *A Panegyric to the King* (1660), in *Hobbled Pegasus*, p. 456.

78. *The Cavaliers Complaint* (1660), in *Political Ballads . . . during the Commonwealth* (Percy Soc., 1841), p. 264.

They're not dejected, nor aught affected
With all their misery.
Friends stand aloof and make no proof
What prayers or tears can do:
Your godly friends are now more friends
To Christ than unto you. . . .

One natural brother beholds another
In this astonied fit,
Yet sorrows not thereat a jot,
Nor pities him a whit.
The godly wife conceives no grief,
Nor can she shed a tear
For the sad fate of her dear mate
When she his doom doth hear . . .

The pious father . . .
Doth rejoice to hear Christ's voice
Adjudging his son to pain.[79]

The jolly jaunting metre of the poem makes its insensitive cruelty all the more appalling.

79. Wigglesworth, op. cit., esp. pp. 59–66. Two additional poems, *A Short Description of Eternity* and *A Postscript* ram the point home, rather superfluously.

14. Antichrist and his Armies

The spirits and judgments and consciences of men [had] been as
it were cowed and marvellously imbased and kept under (and so
prepared for Antichrist's lure) by doctrines and tenents excessively
advancing the power of superiors over inferiors, and binding
iron yokes and heavy burdens upon those that were in subjection.
John Goodwin, *Anti-Cavalierisme* (1642), in Haller, *Tracts on Liberty*,
II.

Prelates, . . . basking in the sunny warmth of wealth and promotion, . . . will hatch an Antichrist wheresoever.
Milton, *Of Reformation* (1641), *MCPW*, I, p. 590.

It is neither rebellion nor treason to fight for the King to recover
his power out of the hand of the Beast.
Francis Cheynell, *Sions Memento and Gods Alarum* (1643), *FS*, VI,
p. 208.

The way then to set up Christ's kingdom is to pull down
Antichrist's.
Thomas Temple, *Christs Government over his People* (1642), *FS*, IV,
pp. 151–3.

In the scenario for the last times which protestants found in the Bible,
Antichrist plays a leading part. His overthrow was an essential
preliminary to the Second Coming and the millennium.[1] Biblical author-
ity for Antichrist derives from I John II.18: 'Ere now there are many
Antichrists: whereby we know that it is the last time'. (Cf. II John 7).
Other names associated with Antichrist are 'the Mystery of Iniquity'
(II Thessalonians II.7–9; cf. Revelation XVII.5) and 'the Man of Sin' of
II Thessalonians II.3–6, who 'doth sit as God in the temple of God' and
who must be revealed before we can know that the day of Christ is at
hand. The Geneva Bible identified the Man of Sin with Antichrist, with

1. See my *Antichrist in 17th-century England*, *passim*.

the papacy and with the Beast in Revelation XIII. Genesis XLIX.17 was thought to predict Antichrist. Many were the computations of the time of Antichrist's overthrow.[2]

In June 1642 William Sedgwick thought he saw the first signs of Antichrist's fall.[3] From the days of Wyclif and the Lollards the doctrine that the Pope was Antichrist, and bishops his disciples, had been familiar among English radicals.[4] Langland had thought that the Pope and prelates side with Antichrist ('his temporalities to save') and that priests were prominent in Antichrist's army.[5] John Ponet had identified the Pope with Antichrist.[6] Thomas Cartwright derived Antichristianism from the human tendency to desire rule over one another, of which bishops and the Pope were the culmination. Martin Marprelate assumed that bishops were Antichristian.[7] So did Henry Barrow, speaking of the yoke of Antichrist in the Church of England, Antichristian bishops and Antichristian courts. The Archbishop of Canterbury was the second Beast in Revelation XIII.[8] Francis Johnson, preacher to English merchants at Middelburg in the 1590s, cited Wyclif and Lollards, Tyndale and the martyr John Frith, for the Antichristian nature of bishops.[9] The Se-Baptist John Smyth added that lay elders were Antichristian.[10]

That the Pope was Antichrist, and Rome Babylon, was established at some length by no less a person than King James VI and I. He called on protestants to prepare for the last battle against him.[11] A Hampshire recusant retorted the name of Antichrist back upon the King himself.[12]

2. See e.g. Thomas Goodwin, *FS*, II, pp. 438–9; Joseph Caryl, ibid., pp. 472–4; Stanley Gower, ibid., XII, pp. 11–12, 18, 39–42.
3. Sedgwick, *FS*, III, p. 204; cf. ibid., XII, pp. 171, 185, 198–217 (William Reyner); XXXIV, p. 102 (Samuel Bolton).
4. M. Aston, *Lollards and Reformers: Images and Literacy in Late Medieval Religion* (1984), *passim*; Anne Hudson, *The Premature Reformation, passim*. See also *Heresy Trials in the Diocese of Norwich, 1428–31* (ed. N. P. Tanner, Camden 4th Series, 20, 1977), pp. 11, 13 and *passim*.
5. Quoted by D. Aers, 'Reading Piers Plowman: Literature, History and Criticism', *Literature and History*, 2nd Series, I, pp. 15, 18.
6. Ponet, *A Short Treatise of Politike Power*, p. 19.
7. Lake, *Anglicans and Puritans?*, pp. 44, 83, 103.
8. *The Writings of Henry Barrow, 1587–1590*, pp. 57, 122, 139, 188; *1590–1591*, p. 257.
9. *The Writings of John Greenwood and Henry Barrow*, pp. 463–4.
10. Burrage, *The Early English Dissenters*, p. 135.
11. King James, *A Paraphrase upon the Revelation of the Apostle Saint John*, and *A Premonition to all most mighty monarchies*, both in *The Political Works of James I*, pp. 7–72, 128–50.
12. Capp, 'The Political Dimension', p. 103.

Thomas Beard, Oliver Cromwell's former minister, was only one of very many who published on *Antichrist the Pope of Rome* (1625). James did not argue that bishops were Antichristian, but many Puritans did.

William Bradford, future Governor of Plymouth, New England, spoke of 'religious people, near the joining border of Nottinghamshire, Lincolnshire and Yorkshire', who about the end of Elizabeth's reign shook off the 'yoke of Antichristian bondage' of the Church of England, 'and, as the Lord's free people', joined themselves 'by Covenant into a Church-state'.[13] William Ames, whose *Medulla* (1627, translated as *The Marrow of Sacred Divinity*, 1643) Nicholas Tyacke calls 'a handbook for Puritan revolutionaries', agreed with Cartwright (and Calvin) that bishops derive from 'the Roman Antichrist himself'.[14] John Lilburne described his flogging in 1638 as *A Worke of the Beast*. His *Come out of her my people* (1639) was a reply to a gentlewoman who was 'a professor in the Antichristian Church of England'. The prelates who had sentenced him, he told her, 'all of them are limbs of the Beast spoken of Rev. XIII.2'; and 'all those officers and ministers that are made by them . . . or by virtue of any of their muddy Antichristian laws . . . are all of them Antichristian'. In 1641 Lord Brooke proved 'that our episcopacy is the same really with Popery, taken properly'.[15]

The case against the bishops was strengthened by Archbishop Laud's equivocation on the subject. 'It is a great question even among learned protestants', he said, whether the Pope is Antichrist; 'the Church of England hath not positively resolved him to be so'. John Prideaux, future bishop, was profoundly shocked when he had to examine 'the first who publicly denied the Pope to be Antichrist' in Oxford. The Root and Branch Petition of December 1640 complained that 'the prelates here in England . . . plead and maintain that the Pope is not Antichrist'.[16]

It was a polarizing issue. Archbishop Ussher, who himself believed the Pope was Antichrist, nevertheless objected that 'nothing is so familiar nowadays . . . as to father upon Antichrist whatsoever in church matters

13. Bradford, *The New England Chronology*, in *An English Garner* (ed. E. Arber, 1896–7), II, p. 348.
14. Tyacke, *The Fortunes of English Puritanism*, pp. 12–13. Tyacke postulates 'a radical Puritan continuum from Elizabethan times to 1640' (ibid., p. 20).
15. Lilburne, op. cit. (Rota reprint, Exeter University, 1971), pp. 1, 3, 8; Brooke, *A Discourse opening the Nature of . . . Episcopacie*, in Haller, *Tracts on Liberty*, II.
16. W. Prynne, *Canterburies Doome* (1644), pp. 551–2; *The Genuine Remains of . . . Dr. Thomas Barlow* (1693), p. 192; Gardiner, *Constitutional Documents*, p. 140.

we do not find to sort with our own humours'. The point was made by Ralph Knevet:

> The purple Babylonian whore
>   Is spoken of no more;
>   Our reverend mitred priests
>   Are now termed Antichrists
> As if they were beasts more profane
> Than that upon the Vatican.[17]

Milton in 1641 declared the prelates to be 'more Antichristian than Antichrist himself'. John Owen in 1649 announced that 'the government of the nations . . . is purely framed for the interest of Antichrist'. But now 'the coming of the Lord Christ to recover his people from Antichristian idolatry and oppression' is 'in hand'.[18]

We are always in danger of under-estimating the strength of opposition to popery in the late sixteenth and early seventeenth centuries, and anxiety about its survival among the common people. Bishop Jewel in 1583 thought that many still bore affection to the papal Antichrist.[19] As late as 1640 Pym had to warn his fellow MPs that however nice Catholic gentry might appear in the localities, their church as an institution was dangerous to England's protestant independence.[20] And 'every papist is an Antichristian', declared the author of an anonymous pamphlet published in the mid-twenties.[21]

But – as the example of Jewel, that great defender of Anglicanism shows – passionate fears of popery were not confined to Puritans. Spenser was fiercely anti-Catholic, as were many other poets – the two Fletchers, Quarles, Henry Vaughan, Benlowes: the last three were royalists during the civil war. The election of James's son-in-law, the Elector Palatine, to

---

17. Ussher, *Works* (Dublin, 1847–64), VII, p. 45; Knevet, *Shorter Poems* (ed. A. M. Charles, Ohio State U.P., 1966), p. 334.
18. *MCPW*, I, p. 850; Owen, *FS*, XXXII, pp. 330–43, 351–8; cf. ibid., XXXIV, pp. 27–8 (1651), 145–6 (1652). Owen was still discussing the destruction of Antichrist in 1681 (*Works*, VIII, p. 618; though now Antichrist was located more especially in the Church of England).
19. Jewel, *An Exposition upon the two Epistles of the Apostle Paul to the Thessalonians* (1594), pp. 255–348. First published 1583: I cite from the third edition.
20. Quoted by W. Lamont, 'The Religious Origins of the English Civil War', in Schochet, *Religion, Resistance and Civil War*, p. 9. Cf. Hibbard, *Charles I and the Popish Plot*, passim. Cf. p. 263 above.
21. [Anon.], *Sacrae Heptades, or seaven problems concerning Antichrist*, quoted by Christianson, *Reformers and Babylon*, p. 114.

the Bohemian throne in 1619 seemed to many English protestants to be a call from God to which England should respond. Archbishop Abbot himself wrote to Secretary of State Naunton insisting on English support for the new king of Bohemia. He cited Revelation to argue that the kings of the earth were about to tear the Whore of Babylon and make her desolate.[22] Even Nicholas Ferrar, notorious for establishing a 'protestant nunnery', believed that the Pope was Antichrist.

The imagery of Antichrist, and its application to Laudianism, played a part in the line-up for the civil war. 'Were the press open to us', said Bastwick in the pillory in 1637, 'we would scatter [Antichrist's] kingdom'.[23] Lilburne from the same pulpit in 1638 called on the sympathetic crowd to study Revelation and continue the fight against Antichrist.[24] It was fear of a Roman Catholic plot that persuaded Richard Baxter to support Parliament – or so he tells us;[25] and many who fought for Charles in the civil war were worried about the presence of papist officers in his army, and the French connections of his Queen.[26] An anti-prelatical poem of 1642 was entitled *The Downfall of Antichrist*.[27]

Antichrist was no longer to be found only in Rome. He was among the supporters of King Charles in England. George Wither referred to royalists as 'bands and . . . confederates of Antichrist'.[28] 'The Antichristian party' was a familiar insulting nickname for them. Antichrist was also among the Irish, 'those sworn vassals of the Man of Sin', who have rendered themselves 'obnoxious unto vengeance'.[29] As with Cain and Abel, as with the Norman Yoke, the symbol of Antichrist lent itself to varying interpretations. Conversely, in a Paul's Cross sermon of 1618 Thomas Thompson had denounced 'Brownists and other schismatical heretics' because 'they have necessary dependance on Antichrist' (i.e. popery). They should be dealt with by the temporal sword.[30]

22. Gardiner, *History of England, 1603–1642*, III, p. 314.
23. Fuller, *The Church History of Britain*, III, p. 387.
24. Lilburne, *A Worke of the Beast* (Amsterdam, 1638), p. 18. Note that this tract had to be published abroad.
25. *Reliquiae Baxterianae*, pp. 39–40.
26. John Adair, *By the Sword Divided: Eyewitnesses of the English Civil War* (1983), pp. 37–8.
27. Frank, *Hobbled Pegasus*, p. 63; cf. p. 67.
28. Wither, *Campo-Musae* (1643), p. 64, in *Miscellaneous Works* (Spenser Soc., First Collection, 1872); *Vox Pacifica* (1645), p. 68, in ibid. (Second Collection).
29. Owen, *FS*, XXXIII, p. 283. Owen had just returned from Ireland.
30. Thompson, *Antichrist Arraigned*, pp. 209–15, 226. It must have been quite a long sermon.

In the 1630s Laud and the bishops were believed to be engaged in an international campaign to subvert the independence of protestant England. Queen Henrietta Maria seemed to be part of this plot: so did the Irish. When a papal Nuncio appeared in command of the rebel Irish army in the mid-forties the theory seemed to be confirmed.[31] Henry Burton thought that the civil war marked the beginning of Armageddon. He quoted Exodus XV.9, in which the Egyptians threatened to slaughter the Israelites: 'the very language of our Antichristian enemies at this time' he noted with some satisfaction, 'the Cavaliers at York'. In Exodus the Egyptians were just about to be swallowed up in the Red Sea.[32] 'Down go the Antichristians', said John Trapp, *à propos* Revelation XIV.19, 'by the power and prowess of the Christian armies, thus edged and eneagered [*sic*] by their preachers. This we have seen at Edgehill and Naseby'.[33] For Levellers, John Goodwin, John Canne, Milton, Colonel Goffe, John Spittlehouse and countless other radicals monarchy was Antichristian. 'The Lord', John Eliot told Cromwell in 1653, 'hath raised and improved you in an eminent manner to overthrow Antichrist'.[34]

A social twist was given to opposition to Antichrist. John Goodwin thought that Antichrist's rule was maintained 'by doctrines and tenets excessively advancing the power of superiors over inferiors'. Men 'of ordinary rank and quality' would execute God's judgments upon Antichrist.[35] For Winstanley the gentry were both Norman and Antichristian; Bunyan described Antichrist as a gentleman, the Whore of Babylon as 'this gentlewoman'.[36] The Fifth Monarchist John Tillinghast used Jeremiah LI.20–24 to argue (against Oliver Cromwell) that 'the present work of God is to bring down lofty men, and to throw down Antichrist'.[37] James Nayler put it simply: 'Saith God: Thou shalt not covet. . . . Saith Antichrist: Thou must live by thy wits that God hath given thee, and this is not covetousness, but a provident care; and he that

31. Hibbard, *Charles I and the Popish Plot*, *passim*; Francis Cheynell, *FS*, VI, p. 192; S. Marshall, ibid., p. 355; my *A Nation of Change and Novelty*, pp. 138–46.
32. *A narration of the life of Mr. Henry Burton* (1643), p. 27.
33. Trapp, *Commentary on the New Testament*, pp. 707–8.
34. My *A Turbulent, Seditious and Factious People*, p. 99. Eliot, *Tears of Repentance*, dedicatory letter to Oliver Cromwell.
35. *Anticavalierisme* (1642), p. 31, in Haller, *Tracts on Liberty*, II. See first epigraph to this chapter.
36. *BMW*, III, p. 169; my *A Turbulent, Seditious and Factious People*, p. 215.
37. Tillinghast, *Eight Last Sermons*, pp. 219, 230–31; *Generation-Work* (1653–4), sig. A 6–6v; *Knowledge of the Times* (1654), sig. A 5v.

will not provide for his family is worse than an infidel' (I Timothy V.8). 'If thou . . . do not help thyself by thy wits, both thou and thine may be poor enough'.[38] The Ranter Richard Coppin thought that Antichrist's was 'a kingdom of gain, hire and self-interest'. Milton called Antichrist 'Mammon's son'.[39]

Soon any persecutor, anyone who seemed to be thwarting the establishment of Christ's kingdom, could be described as Antichrist. Thomas Edwards reported Paul Hobson as saying that Presbyterianism was the Beast spoken of in Revelation. Richard Overton's Mr Persecution was 'a most dangerous, inveterate Antichrist'. Overton gave fourteen Biblical references for toleration of sects and different religions, including Samson among the Philistines, Lot in the land of Uz, and divers sects in the time of Christ.[40] Fifth Monarchists saw the clergy of the state church as 'ministers of Antichrist'. 'One of the most grievous errors that ever reigned under Antichrist', said William Dell in 1651, is 'to affirm that universities are the fountains of the ministers of the Gospel'. On the contrary, Antichrist 'chose his ministers only out of the universities'.[41] Those who scoff at hymn-singing, asserted John Cotton in 1647, are 'Cathedral priests of an Antichristian spirit'.[42] Persecution is a chief reason for calling the Pope Antichrist, Milton said; rulers who force consciences in matters of religion deserve the same appellation. He was thinking no doubt of Charles II among others. Bunyan agreed.[43] But the blame did not attach only to governments. 'The hot men at Blackfriars [Fifth Monarchist] meeting' were said in 1654 to have declared 'the whole majority of the nation Antichristian'.[44]

The application to foreign policy seemed as clear in the 1650s as it had been to Ponet a century earlier, when he affirmed flatly that Spaniards seek 'to destroy the liberty of the English nation'.[45] Spaniards were an

38. Nayler, The old Serpents Voice, or Antichrist described (n.d., ?1656), p. 6.
39. Coppin, Truths Testimony (1655), p. 15; MCPW, I, p. 590.
40. Edwards, Gangraena, I, p. 32; Overton, The Araignment of Mr. Persecution (1645), pp. 12–15, in Haller, Tracts on Liberty, III.
41. Dell, Several Sermons and Discourses, pp. 403, 246; cf. pp. 264, 297, 516, 600. First published 1652. Cf. Nayler, A Salutation to the Seed of God (3rd ed., 1656), p. 5; The old Serpents Voice, p. 5.
42. Cotton, Singing of Psalms A Gospel Ordinance, p. 61.
43. MCPW, VI, pp. 797–8; my A Turbulent, Seditious and Factious People, p. 99 and references there cited, and Chapter 25.
44. Thurloe State Papers.
45. Ponet, An Apologie fully aunsweringe by Scriptures . . . D. Stephen Gardiner (1555), sig. A3–3v.

'Antichristian brood whose fall draweth nigh', said Captain Robert Plumleigh, 'a known Anabaptist'. An *Elegie on the death of . . . Blake* in 1657 praised the Admiral as 'a zealous hater of the scarlet Whore'.[46]

Yet by the 1650s the international situation had become paradoxical, as John Owen realized: 'One Abel after another undertakes the quarrel against you, yea such Abels as Scotland and Holland', old allies against Antichrist.[47] Owen did not however conclude from this that the aggressive imperialist foreign policy which the English Commonwealth had adopted had transformed her into Cain. From a more radical point of view Erbery pointed out that 'the state of Holland and Commonwealth of Venice' are 'as much for Antichrist as the King of France or Spain'.[48] The implication was that the change from monarchy to republic in England had not made a significant change for the better. Winstanley would have agreed.

This may perhaps help to explain the otherwise perplexing fact that Bunyan in his later years revived an idea prevalent in the early seventeenth century, that it is kings who must cast out Antichrist. Charles II and James II as enemies of popery? It seems a little odd. But if we remember that Bunyan (and many others) thought persecution of the godly was Antichristian, it makes better sense. Both Charles and James after him, for their own reasons, were prepared to authorize toleration for protestant dissenters in order to secure toleration for Catholics. By the 1670s the menace of international popery seemed remote: Giant Pope in *The Pilgrim's Progress* 'is by reason of age, and also of the many shrewd brushes that he met with in his younger days, grown so crazy and stiff in his joints, that he can now do little more than sit in his cave's mouth, grinning at Pilgrims as they go by, and biting his nails because he cannot come at them'.[49] In Part II (1684) Giant Maul, though he has many characteristics attributed to Giant Pope, seems to represent persecution in general rather than Catholicism in particular. He is much more dangerous and threatening than Giant Pope in Part I.[50] We recall that the fiercely anti-clerical (as well as anti-Puritan) Samuel Butler thought that post-restoration bishops would gladly restore popery in order to retain their properties.[51] For Bunyan persecutors were the Church of England and the Anglican gentry, against both of whom Charles and especially James seemed possible allies: James

46. Capp, *Cromwell's Navy*, pp. 148, 300, 373.
47. Owen, *FS*, XXXIV, p. 137; cf. Capp, *Cromwell's Navy*, p. 131.
48. *The Testimony of William Erbery*, pp. 209–11.
49. *PP*, p. 65.
50. See my *A Turbulent, Seditious and Factious People*, p. 217.
51. Butler, *Prose Observations*, pp. 50, 53.

seems deliberately to have handed local government over from the traditional gentry to lower social types, nonconformists and supporters of toleration.

Edward Haughton in 1652 published *The Rise, Growth and Fall of Antichrist together with the Reign of Christ*, a compendious survey which is a convenient summing up. He assumed that the civil war had been fought between Christ and Antichrist. 'Christ hath lately trampled upon the royal glory of this nation'. 'When Christ is going in good earnest to set up his kingdom . . . there is very great hazard' of the 'downfall of kings'. 'God hath sometimes given men commissions that all the world knew not of nor any in the world besides themselves could read or understand': Pharaoh was a prominent example. Haughton cautiously refused to affirm or deny that God had given 'this kind of commission . . . to those men that are now in place and power'. But he seemed to think it likely.[52]

Biblical myths could be used for widely different purposes, because the symbols of the myth can be interpreted according to taste. Antichrist begins as the Pope in Rome; then he becomes the bishops, then the King who protects them; royalists who fight for church and king are 'the Antichristian party'. For Winstanley and other radicals the landed ruling class was Antichrist.[53] Ultimately Cromwell also became Antichrist. John Rogers, writing in 1657, the year in which the crown of England was offered to Cromwell, quoted Calvin to the effect that Antichrist 'shall come peaceably and obtain the kingdom by flatteries'. Rogers added, maliciously, that Antichrist will at first assume 'the name of a Protector or Preserver (so saith Mayor on Nehemiah)', only later taking the title of King.[54] John Hall of Richmond had argued provocatively in 1654, with many Scriptural references, that 'Antichristianism is opposed to Christian monarchs'. Those most guilty of it were sectaries and republicans. He was consciously fighting against the tide (as well as against the evidence) when he wrote that 'there could not be found one text' in the Bible 'countenancing and maintaining any other form of government than monarchy'.[55]

A sharp change came with the restoration. Biblical politics were deliberately linked with social radicalism; indiscriminating use of the concept of Antichrist made it unacceptable to the respectable classes, some of whose best friends were Catholics. Henry More noted the combination

---

52. Haughton, op. cit., pp. 76–88.
53. See Chapter 8.
54. Rogers, Preface to John Canne's *The Time of the End*, sig. A 2–2v.
55. Hall, *Government and Obedience*, sig. b, pp. 391–2, 473.

of radicalism and imprecision when he sneered at 'the rude and ignorant vulgar' who 'have so fouled' the words Antichrist and Antichristian that they are now 'unfit to pass the lips of any civil person'. In their 'mad mistaken zeal' the vulgar denounce not only 'every well-ordered church' as the Whore of Babylon but also 'every legitimate magistrate' as Antichrist.[56] So the name of Antichrist, a terrifying political symbol for two generations of English protestants, could now be dismissed as unsuitable for polite drawing-room conversation. The majority of mankind were perhaps no longer thought to be irretrievably damned, but they were silly and insignificant on earth. Academic discussions on the date of the end of the world continued, but now they were not associated with any political programme.

An unexpected by-product of seventeenth-century emphases on the legend of Antichrist was its contribution to the replacement of circular by linear history: the overthrow of Antichrist would be a point of no return. Simultaneously other radicals were ceasing to insist on a return to the liberties of the free Anglo-Saxons, to the procedures of the primitive Christian church, to the innocence of unfallen Adam and Eve. Instead they began to look forward to a new and better society to be established on earth. As we have seen, secularization of the idea of England as the chosen nation enabled John Bull to see the expansion of the British Empire as contributing to the overthrow of Antichrist and the establishment of Christ's kingdom on earth.[57]

---

56. More, *A Modest Enquiry into the Mystery of Iniquity* (1664), sig. A 3v, pp. 185–7. I owe this reference to the kindness of Dr W. R. Owens of the Open University. The same association with 'enthusiastic' radical politics led Swift in 1708 to say that astrology was now credited by 'none but the ignorant vulgar' (quoted by P. Curry, *Prophecy and Power: Astrology in Early Modern England*, Princeton U.P., 1989, p. 160).
57. See pp. 249–50 above

15. 'The Man of Blood'

═══

Blood defileth the land, and the land cannot be cleansed but by
the death of him who caused it to be shed.
Numbers XXXV.33.

Because the people consented with the King in shedding innocent blood, therefore God destroyeth both the one and the
other.
Judges IX.24.

But alas, the King's blood was not our burden, it was those
oppressing Norman laws, whereby he enslaved us, that we
groaned under.
Winstanley, in Sabine, p. 308.

An important article published by Patricia Crawford in 1977 stresses
the significance of calling Charles I 'The Man of Blood'.[1] I had thought
that this was just a term of abuse for a hate figure. But it was far more
than that. Numbers XXXV.33, the first epigraph to this chapter, was
cited by the prosecutor at the King's trial, when he called for the land
to be purified by the blood of him who had caused the bloodshed.
Many other Biblical texts support Numbers XXXV: Lilburne cited over
thirty.[2] If England was a chosen nation, it must not remain defiled by
blood.

The point was familiar enough. It had been made by Brinsley in 1622.
'Our land is fearfully defiled with the blood of God's servants in the days
of Queen Mary', as Jerusalem had been in the days of Manasseh. Shedding

---

1. Crawford, '"Charles Stuart, That Man of Blood"', *Journal of British Studies*, Spring
1977. See also Elizabeth Tuttle, *Religion et Idéologie dans la Révolution Anglaise*, Chapter
IX. Dr Tuttle was apparently not aware of Dr Crawford's article when she arrived at
similar conclusions. In my review of Dr Tuttle's book in *History Workshop Journal*
(No. 31, Spring 1991) I was seriously at fault in failing to recall the priority due to Dr
Crawford's pioneering article.
2. Crawford, op. cit., p. 52.

the blood of God's servants had hastened the Babylonian captivity of the Jews. The blood of all Englishmen would be required at the hands of ministers if they did not forewarn and call their countrymen to repentance.[3] If Catholics triumphed in the Thirty Years War, Babylonian captivity might well face Englishmen. How could the land be cleansed? Who was responsible? As early as January 1644–5 the Presbyterian Christopher Love, in attendance on the Parliamentary commissioners for negotiations with the royalists at Uxbridge, had preached a sermon in which he denounced Charles as a Man of Blood. This was premature, and he was imprisoned; but within a few weeks he was released.[4] The General Assembly of the Kirk of Scotland publicly warned the King in 1645 that he must repent of the blood-guiltiness 'which cleaveth fast to your throne'. The tone which the Kirk adopted, Patricia Crawford observes, 'showed the significance of blood guilt as a levelling idea', obliterating the expected reverence for the monarch. 'The discussion of the King's blood guilt undermined his divinity'.[5]

Once this question had been raised, an answer was urgently needed. Especially by rank-and-file soldiers. They searched their Bibles and their consciences. Until the guilty person was identified and punished, defilement would lie upon the whole land. 'Whoso sheddeth man's blood', God had told Noah, 'by man shall his blood be shed' (Genesis IX.6). Unless the guilt could be clearly brought home to someone, the stain would lie on those who fought for Parliament no less than on the King.

From 1647 the idea had wide currency. Henry Marten, not the godliest of MPs, cited many Biblical kings who had lost their power because they ignored God's commands. They thought that the 'laws would not allow kings to be punished'.[6] Pressure from below mounted on Army officers. A pamphlet of October 1647 deplored the generals' negotiations with the King. Why do they 'kneel, and kiss, and fawn upon . . . a man of blood?'[7] In the Putney Debates George Bishop, later a Quaker, referred to Charles as 'that man of blood', whose 'principles of tyranny'

---

3. Brinsley, *The Third Part of the True Watch*, pp. 209–10, 214, 444–6, 513, 523. For the importance of this work see Chapter 12 above.
4. Anne Laurence, *Parliamentary Army Chaplains*, p. 149. Ironically, Love was executed in 1651 for participating in a plot to restore the Man of Blood's son.
5. Crawford, op. cit., pp. 50, 61.
6. Marten, *The Parliaments Proceedings Justified* (7 February 1648), p. 8. It was dangerous to negotiate with a guilty king, Marten argued.
7. [Anon.], *A cal to all the Souldiers of the Armie*, p. 5. Attributed to Wildman.

God 'hath manifestly declared against'. Colonel Harrison distanced himself from Cromwell and Ireton, demanding that the Man of Blood be brought to trial.[8]

The outbreak of the second civil war in 1648 was the last straw. In April 1648 a meeting of officers decided to call 'Charles Stuart, that Man of Blood, to an account for the blood he has shed'. Pamphlets of 1648 recalled that God condemned Saul and Ahab to death for disobeying his orders to kill kings Agag and Ben-Hadad; God will mete out similar justice to those who, knowing the King's blood-guiltiness, wish to sign a treaty with him, contrary to the revealed will of God.[9] Regiments petitioned for the prosecution of the Man of Blood. To retain control of the Army the generals had to act. By November 1648 Edmund Ludlow, MP and general, 'was convinced by the express words of God's law' that they must not 'leave the guilt of so much blood upon the nation, and thereby . . . draw down the just vengeance of God upon us all'.[10] On the 16th of that month a General Council of officers called for 'the capital and grand author of all our troubles' to be brought to justice for 'the treason, blood and mischief' of which he had been guilty. Colonel Pride purged Parliament three weeks later, and Charles was brought to trial.

On 26 December 1648 Thomas Brooks, in a Fast Sermon to the House of Commons, recalled Phineas to stiffen their resolve. 'Consider this: your execution of justice and judgment will free you from the guilt of other men's sins'. 'When justice is not executed, a land is defiled'; and he cited Numbers XXXV. 'Those that have neglected the execution of justice . . . God hath left to perish basely and miserably'.[11] This was well calculated to counter fears some MPs may have entertained about what would happen to regicides in the event of a restoration of monarchy.

Patricia Crawford sums up. 'The legend of blood guilt offered a new set of arguments for dealing with the King and breaking the deadlock'. In fighting the second civil war 'the soldiers had struck a bargain with the Lord: if they were victorious, they would bring Charles to justice'. 'Blood

8. Woodhouse, op. cit., p. 107; ed. C. H. Firth, *Clarke Papers* (Camden Soc.), I (1891), pp. 417–18.

9. Crawford, op. cit., p. 54; Tuttle, op. cit., p. 175.

10. *Memoirs of Edmund Ludlow* (ed. C. H. Firth, Oxford U.P., 1894), I, p. 207; cf. Ludlow, *A Voyce from the Watch Tower*, pp. 130–38, 141–5.

11. Brooks, *FS*, XXXII, pp. 103–4, 132–3.

guilt for Ludlow was more than a moral justification for action. It was an incentive to action'. Colonel Hutchinson looked to the future as well as to the past. If justice was not executed upon Charles, 'all the blood and desolation which should ensue by their suffering him to escape when God had brought him into their hands' would fall on his captors. In 1650 the Army claimed that its victory was 'a second testimony given from heaven to justify the proceedings of his poor servants against that bloody Antichristian brood'.[12]

Nehemiah Wallington, a typical enough London artisan, recorded in his journal the murder of his brother-in-law by Irish rebels in October 1641. The brother's last words were said to predict that if the rebels, as they claimed, had the King's commission to kill all protestants, 'then surely the Lord will not suffer the King nor his posterity to reign'. And Wallington added later a terse note: 'January the 30, 1649 . . . was King Charles beheaded on a scaffold at Whitehall'.[13] A pamphlet of 1649 was entitled *Charles I No Man of Blood*, but the appellation was later extended to his son, 'the Young Pretender'.[14]

The rhetoric of 'the Man of Blood' had other political effects than regicide. The Army came to occupy a special place in what was increasingly represented as the working out of God's millenarian purposes for England. It had overridden traditional constitutional authority in the name of God, whose purposes the saints understood. The concept almost certainly had greater influence with those below the political nation than Leveller arguments for a democratic republic. Coppe, for instance, extended the blood-guiltiness from Charles I to 'all the honourable (both persons and things) upon the earth, Isaiah XXIII.9' which 'hath . . . been . . . the cause of all the blood that ever hath been shed' from the beginning of history. 'And now (as I live, saith the Lord) I am come to make inquisition for blood'.[15] But the millenarian emphasis worked to the great advantage of the generals, and helps to explain the eclipse of the Levellers. The alliance between Levellers and sectaries had been based on the demand for liberty of conscience. But now the generals, by purging conservatives from Parliament, not only ensured toleration for most sectaries: they also identified the Army with the saints in a millenarian

12. Crawford, op. cit., pp. 45, 54, 58–9, 56.
13. P. S. Seaver, *Wallington's World: A Puritan Artisan in Seventeenth-Century London* (1985), pp. 168–9; cf. p 83.
14. [Anon.], *A True State of the Case of the Commonwealth* (1654), p. 48.
15. Coppe, *A Fiery Flying Roll* (1649), in Smith, *Ranter Writings*, p. 88.

scenario which Cromwell found congenial and which marginalized Leveller democratic projects. Much was made in hostile propaganda of the alleged irreligion of the secularist Levellers. Opinion was polarized. Once the generals were sure of the backing of the sects, it was safe to provoke a break with the radicals, in and out of the Army. The Levellers lost their two main bases when the generals guaranteed toleration for the sects and wages for the Army. The sophisticated democratic and constitutional theories, which seem to us the most interesting part of the Leveller programme, perhaps counted for less with ordinary seventeenth-century people. The final bloodshed at Burford in May 1649, when leaders of rebellious regiments were shot, was the political outcome of the trial of the Man of Blood. 'It is the Calvinist conquerors of Burford', says Lamont, 'and not their Leveller victims, who were looking forward then to a "rule of the saints" '.[16]

On 12 August 1650 NCOs and soldiers of the Army which had invaded Scotland published a Declaration in which they asserted that 'we are persuaded we are poor unworthy instruments in God's hand', since 'the Lord's purpose was to deal with the late King as a Man of Blood'. Their task was 'to bring about . . . the destruction of Antichrist and the deliverance of [God's] Church and people'. It is Jesus Christ 'that leadeth us'.[17]

The trial and execution of the King were then a necessary first step against Antichrist, clearing the way for the rule of the saints. The regicides, freed from ordinary inhibitions, could reject the formalities of traditional legal procedure in the name of higher justice. Oliver Cromwell knew that the saints possessed 'the mind of Christ': legal arguments of men who were not saints were irrelevant.[18] The cataclysmic events of December 1648–January 1649 led many to expect King Jesus. The Fifth Monarchist Christopher Feake thought that before December 1648 the Good Old Cause had become 'a very pitiful, dull, dry, lean, barren, ill-favoured thing'. But after the execution of the King it suddenly became 'the most lovely, lively, growing, sparkling, prosperous Cause in all the earth'. 'The power and spirit of our Cause was great and high after the King's death, more than at any time before'.[19]

16. W. Lamont, 'Pamphleteering in the English Revolution', in Schochet, *Religion, Resistance, and Civil War*, p. 192.
17. Woodhouse, op. cit., pp. 475–7.
18. Ibid., pp. 101–7
19. Feake, *A Beam of Light Shining in the midst of much Darkness and Confusion* (1650), pp. 35–6.

John Cook, prosecutor at the King's trial, had argued that the court which sentenced him foreshadowed the Day of Judgment when the saints would judge the world. Milton, Hugh Peter, William Dell, Mary Cary and John Canne all agreed.[20] Many Fifth Monarchists accepted the view of the returned New Englander William Aspinwall, that Christ 'delegates his authority to the saints', who 'shall be his vice-gerents when he comes shortly to justice'.[21] Indeed the object of military intervention could only be to establish the rule of the saints as a preliminary to the reign of King Jesus; when the time came for that, the King of Glory would presumably not need military assistance.

If the saints were to take the initiative, then, as John Tillinghast put it, 'there must be civil and military power in the hands of the saints . . . before the day of Christ's appearance'.[22] This view gained strength when the execution of the King was not followed by any attempt to establish Christ's kingdom by either the Rump of the Long Parliament or Barebones Parliament. But it led only to the pathetic Fifth Monarchist revolts of 1657 and 1661; and that was the end.

Dr Crawford has given us new insights into the turning point of the English Revolution. We can now see that the Bible was primarily responsible for the execution of Charles I; and regicide may be held responsible for the ultimate failure of the radical revolution. Regicide split the Parliamentarians, aligning conservatives with royalists; and it split the radicals, dividing constitutional democrats like the Levellers and way-out communist Diggers from godly millenarians.

It had perhaps even more far-reaching consequences. The Bible had enabled men to conceive of the possibility of regicide. After 1660 regicide was condemned (by those whose opinions mattered) as the ultimate in social and political wickedness. But it was a wickedness at which most Englishmen had connived, actively or passively. There was a great revulsion from the 'enthusiasm' which had made regicide possible, a great sense of guilt; and this was one more reason for the dethronement of the Bible, whose absolute demands had led some men to imagine that regicide was pleasing to God, and for rejection of all manner of 'enthusiasm' by the respectable.

20. See my The Experience of Defeat, pp. 52–3, note 6.
21. W. Aspinwall, A Brief Description of the Fifth Monarchy (1653), pp. 4, 9–10; cf. W. A[spinwall], The Legislative Power, pp. 33–50.
22. Mr Tillinghasts Eight Last Sermons, pp. 60–68. Erbery added the point that the saints should judge the world 'not only in spiritual things, but in the civil state also' (The Testimony of William Erbery, pp. 207–8).

And what had regicide achieved? It did not usher in the millennium; it failed utterly to bring about the political and social aims of the radicals. The passage from Winstanley cited as epigraph to this chapter shows that the Diggers at least thought that regicide had made no great difference. It left the generals sitting on bayonets, supported otherwise mainly by sectaries, an insufficient base without military backing. Cromwell tried desperately to restore relations with conservative Parliamentarians after the regicide, a process which continued throughout the Protectorate; but he and his allies always had enemies on both flanks. The Army was purged and repurged till it became a professional force like any other. In the fifties its main function was to collect the taxes which paid for the Army which collected the taxes . . . When Army unity crumbled in 1659–60 the republican government collapsed as easily as that of Charles I in 1640.

As usual Winstanley drew different, more radical, conclusions from accepted premises. If Parliament maintained 'the old Norman laws, and this especially, that the lords of manors shall still be lords of the common land and the common people be still enslaved to them, then you pull the guilt of King Charles his blood upon our own heads . . . . Your aim was not to throw down tyranny, but the tyrant'.[23] From a very different angle anti-Catholic officers in Ireland in 1656 insisted on the duty of avenging protestant blood spilt in 1641 so as to 'free the English in this nation from those judgments which may otherwise fall on them'.[24]

So the duty of avenging bloodshed, and indeed millenarianism itself, came to mean different things to different people. John Reeve and Lodowick Muggleton believed that they were the two Last Witnesses referred to in Revelation XI, who foreshadowed the last days. Some thought of Christ's rule on earth as something totally different from existing worldly society: the Geneva Bible had pointed the way here. It glossed the words 'I will create new heavens and a new earth' as 'I will so alter and change the state of my church, that it shall seem to dwell in a new world' (Isaiah LXV.17). In this sense millenarianism had long been widely accepted; men hoped for great transformations, no doubt the product of long periods of struggle, to which the English Revolution was a prelude. Others, simpler folk, thought that in the thousand years' reign of the saints with Christ (Revelation XX.1–7) there would be more mundane changes which would improve the lot of ordinary people. They interpreted Isaiah LXV as

23. Sabine, p. 307.
24. *Mercurius Politicus*, 29 March – 5 April 1655, pp. 5236–8, quoted by T. C. Barnard, 'Crises of identity among Irish Protestants, 1640–1685', *P. and P.*, 127 (1990), p. 65.

foretelling the end of exploitation. 'They shall not build, and another inhabit; they shall not plant and another eat . . . . They shall not labour in vain, nor bring forth in fear'. The Geneva margin, dampingly, commented that 'under temporal things [the Lord] comprehendeth the spiritual promises': this will be 'in the *heavenly* Jerusalem' (verses 21–5; my italics). There was to be no commune of Münster in the Genevan millennium. In England the failure of Barebones Parliament showed that Army rule was not that of the saints ushering in the millennium; and after 1660 dissenters recognized that Christ's kingdom was not of this world.

But the concept of the Man of Blood lived on in popular parlance. Edward Thompson quotes 'a clergyman in the country' who in 1756 cited Ecclesiasticus XXXIV.22: 'The bread of the needy is their life: he that defraudeth them thereof is a Man of Blood'. 'Justly may such oppressors be called "Men of Blood"', the clergyman added; 'and surely will the blood of those who thus perish by their means be required at their hands'.[25]

---

25. [Anon.], *Artificial Dearth: or, the Iniquity of Withholding Corn*, pp. 20–21, quoted by Thompson, *Customs in Common*, pp. 254–5.

IV. THE BIBLE AND ENGLISH LITERATURE

16. Some Biblical Influences

Ye prostitute the Scriptures . . . as bawds do their harlots, to the ungodly, unlearned, rascal people, . . . prentices, light persons and the riff-raff of the people. . . . The unlearned people [before the Reformation] were kept from the reading of the Scriptures by the special providence of God, that precious stones should not be thrown before swine.

John Jewel, *A Defence of the Apologie of the Church of England* (1568), in *Works* (Parker Soc.), III, p. 122, quoting the papal defender Thomas Harding.

> Let foreign nations of their language boast,
> What fair varieties each tongue affords,
> I like our language, as our men and coast;
> Who cannot dress it well, want wit, not words.

George Herbert, 'The Sonne', in *Works*, pp. 167–8.

I

The century from the 1580s to the 1680s is the greatest age in English literature. There is far more to be said about the Bible's influence then than I can manage in a single chapter, even if I possessed the necessary expertise. I wish only to emphasize the part that the English Bible played in the transformation of English literature in this crucial period. I suggested in Chapter 1 that the vernacular Bible and English patriotism were closely interlocked, from Wyclif's days onwards. Richard Mulcaster saw use of the vernacular as an indication of England's emancipation from subservience to the papacy.[1] I am not entirely happy with the present fashion of attributing power to literature. If any book in sixteenth- and seventeenth-century England had power, it was the Bible; but this was because men and women believed in its truth. The belief was held most strongly by

---

1. Mulcaster, *The First Part of the Elementarie, which entreateth chefelie of the right Writing of our English Tung* (1582), pp. 259–64. For this chapter see J. N. King's bibliographical article, 'Recent Studies in Protestant Poetics', *English Literary Renaissance*, 21 (1991).

translators, who undertook enormous labours and ran great risks on behalf of the cause.

Richard Helgerson has long been stressing the sixteenth-century sense of England's *cultural* inferiority, and especially the inferiority of the English language. English men of letters longed to establish a native literature fit to rival the greatness of Greece or Rome, parallel to the emergence of England as a 'powerfully self-conscious realm'.[2] Englishmen of any literary pretensions had to be able to read Italian, Spanish and French; no continental need bother to learn English, since no English author except Sir Thomas More (who wrote in Latin) had any reputation on the continent. Hence the determination of Spenser and his circle to create an English literature of which account had to be taken. Ultimately this was successful. Milton proudly claimed in *Areopagitica* that England had been 'chosen before any other' to be the 'trumpet of reformation to all Europe'. England was by then a cultural centre for protestants: Transylvanians came to England to learn.[3] Comenius and Hartlib sought refuge there. By the eighteenth century the European intelligentsia had to read English.

But this is to look far ahead. The late sixteenth century was a time of experiment. The controversy between classical quantitative verse and rhyme was part of an ongoing battle. Thomas Wilson in 1560 suggested that rhyme was a popish invention.[4] Hexameters turned out to be a false start, but both Spenser and Sidney for a time thought that quantitative measures would enable the English language to escape from Gothic barbarism. Abraham Fraunce's *Emanuel together with Certaine Psalmes* (1591) was in hexameters, sometimes rhyming; William Loe wrote his *Songs of Sion* (1620) entirely in words of one syllable, because he believed the English language had originally been monosyllabic before it was 'blended and mingled with the commixture of exotic languages'. He instanced a translation of the Lord's Prayer made in the time of Wyclif.[5]

2. Helgerson, 'Barbarous Tongues: The Ideology of Poetic Form in Renaissance England', in *The Historical Renaissance: New Essays on Tudor and Stuart Literature* (ed. H. Dubrow and R. Strier, Chicago U.P., 1988), pp. 273–4, 286; expanded in Helgerson, *Forms of Nationhood: The Elizabethan Writing of England* (Chicago U.P., 1992). Cf. Katherine Duncan-Jones, *Sir Philip Sidney, Courtier Poet* (1991), pp. 210, 233.
3. *MCPW*, II, pp. 552–3; cf. ibid., I, p. 526.
4. Wilson, *The Art of Rhetorique*. Roger Ascham thought rhyme was Gothic (*The Scholemaster*, 1570, in *Elizabethan Critical Essays*, ed. G. G. Smith, Oxford U.P., 1904, I, pp. 29–33).
5. Loe, op. cit., pp. 29–30. I cite from the 1870 reprint edited by Grosart.

Samuel Daniel rejected the whole set of historical premises which the quantitative movement had defended. 'Gothic' was not identical with 'barbarous'. 'Let us go no further but look upon the wonderful architecture of this state of England and see whether they were deformed times that could give it such a form'. This was an act of political bravado, inventing a literary tradition to go with the radical political myth of the 'Norman Yoke'. It looked back to the good old days of the free Anglo-Saxons, which had been brutally interrupted by the Norman Conquest. 'England's verse is Gothic', said Daniel, 'and so is the English state'.[6] Quantitative measures went with classicism, with absolutism; Gothic rhyme, the poetry of the people, went with Gothic architecture, the immemorial common law and Parliamentary government.

This was part of a resurgence of English protestant nationalism after the defeat of the Spanish Armada in 1588, which embraces Shakespeare's history plays as well as *The Faerie Queene*. Michael Drayton followed Spenser in looking back to the Chaucerians – 'our own most excellent authors and most famous poets', though twenty years later he was complaining of the 'base balladry' which was still too popular, and of the 'blind Gothic barbarism' which was driving English poetry into the wilderness like the woman in Revelation.[7] Henry King in 1636 knew better:

> Now the language, like the church, hath won
> More lustre since the Reformation.[8]

Perhaps there are wider connections. The Bible could be set up against the Greek and Roman classics as a rival authority. When George Hakewill came to defend the Moderns against the Ancients, a great part of his *Apologie for the Providence of God* consisted of attacks on the classics.[9] This was expressed by John Collop in one of ten epigrams talking down the Greek and Latin classics:

> Can Egypt's garlic we, or onions, need?
> On th' milk of th' word can't our youth better feed?[10]

The Bible – only recently known in the vernacular – offered good stories, some already familiar from mediaeval miracle plays. These were

6. Helgerson, 'Barbarous Tongues', pp. 286–91, quoting Daniel's *Defence of Rhyme* (1602).
7. Joan Grundy, *The Spenserian Poets* (1969), p. 94.
8. *The Poetical Works of George Sandys* (ed. R. Hooper, 1872), I, pp. lxvi, xcii.
9. For Hakewill see pp. 349–50 below.
10. *The Poems of John Collop* (ed. C. Hilberry, Wisconsin U.P., 1962), pp. 108–11.

now rescued from ecclesiastical control. The Bible also provided much that appealed to the new middle-brow reading public which printing was creating. Paraphrases of the Psalms and other books of the Bible proliferated: would-be poets cut their teeth on paraphrasing the Psalms or the Song of Songs. Spenser and Sidney took their paraphrases very seriously, though Spenser's Canticles has not survived. Middleton served his apprenticeship with *The Wisdom of Solomon Paraphrased* in 1597 before going on to write the plays for which we remember him. Scores of lesser men whom we do not remember also started with Biblical verses. Ballads on Biblical themes enjoyed a remarkable vogue in the late sixteenth and early seventeenth centuries, as a glance at the standard collections will show. David and Bathsheba, Samson, Solomon, Job, Jonah, Tobias, Esau's birthright, the fall of Jerusalem, Doomsday and the resurrection,[11] were among the favourite themes: but there were many ballads on episodes from the life of Christ and other Biblical subjects. A ballad of 1569–70 on Manasseh, whose restoration of graven images brought destruction upon Jerusalem, had an immediate relevance to the revolt of the Northern Earls.[12]

Biblical themes seem to have declined slowly, and more sharply from about the beginning of Charles I's reign. There are hardly any in the *Pepys Ballads* or the *Bagford Ballads*, none in *Cavalier and Puritan*. In the mid-sixteenth century the stories had been novel, and the subjects chosen were relevant to the life of Elizabethan and Jacobean society – social mobility, proverbial wisdom, heroic sacrifice for the nation. Popular fiction was in short supply. Ballads and chapbook romances were the equivalent of today's pulp novel, just as speeches of condemned felons and accounts of the exploits of highwaymen corresponded in their appeal to the crime thriller. Exciting stories about Solomon, Joseph and Job had real popular appeal so long as the novelty lasted. The number of ballads published, as of almanacs, increased sharply in the 1640s.[13]

11. *Black-Letter Ballads and Broadsides* (ed. J. Lilley, 1867), pp. 103–4; *A Pepysian Garland* (ed. H. E. Rollins, Cambridge U.P., 1922), pp. 366, 350: *Old English Ballads, 1553–1625* (ed. Rollins, Cambridge U.P., 1920), pp. 209–12, 219; *Shirburn Ballads, 1585–1616* (ed. A. Clark, Oxford U.P., 1907), p. 31. 'The Great Assize', written by Mr Stevens, minister, dwelt upon the sins and punishment of the rich (*Roxburghe Ballads*, I, ed. W. Chappell, 1871, pp. 394–401). The ballad on Jonah was 'to the tune of Pagginton's round' – used by Ben Jonson for a ballad in *Bartholomew Fair*. 'The Judgment of Solomon' was to the tune of 'The Ladies Fall'. Rollins lists several other ballads about Jonah in *A Pepysian Garland*, p. 66.
12. Tessa Watt, *Cheap Print and Popular Piety, 1550–1640*, p. 117.
13. See my *Writing and Revolution*, pp. 39–40.

Ballads were intended to be sung, and singing was vastly more significant in ordinary life than today. It was not something done only in church, in pubs or at football matches. Street singers had to compete only with the relatively silent traffic; there was no TV to compete with in ale-houses, no radio or washing or washing-up machine or vacuum-cleaner to sing against in private houses. A similar pattern prevailed with madrigals and lute songs, which presumably were bought by a rather different section of the population. The third edition of E. H. Fellowes's collection of *English Madrigal Verse, 1588–1632*, covers almost exactly the period in which Biblical themes proliferate in ballads. Of ninety-eight items by Byrd printed in this volume, twenty-eight use Biblical texts, and many of the others are on Biblical themes. A similar proportion of Thomas Ravenscroft's madrigals start from Biblical texts. Other composers are less Biblical, but nearly all have some madrigals deriving from the Bible. Milton's father set texts from the Geneva Bible to polyphonic tunes.[14]

In her valuable book, *Cheap Print and Popular Piety, 1550–1640,* Dr Watt associates a decline in the popularity of ballads based on Biblical narrative with the rise of small, cheap 'godly' chapbooks in James I's reign. By this time the best Bible stories were well-known; and publishers – the same publishers – switched to 'penny godlies', 'appealing directly to an audience at the bottom levels of rural society'. Sermons by popular preachers like Henry Smith and William Perkins, and 'market-place theology' by John Andrewes and John Hart, proved to be best-sellers. Publishers followed the market, now composed of literate men and women who took their religion seriously. 'Book prices remained steady from 1560 to 1635, when other commodities more than doubled in price'.[15]

We may wonder how far the decline of household music-making and singing contributed to the end of the fashion of versifying Biblical songs. Private reading replaced community or family singing – a momentous change – just as it replaced reading aloud or repetition of sermons followed by family or group discussions – both frowned on by the ecclesiastical hierarchy. The freedom ultimately won by organized dissent made such exercises superfluous, or at any rate less in demand. Ballads and the ballad

14. Fellowes, op. cit. (revised and enlarged by F. W. Sternfeld and D. Greer, Oxford U.P., 1967), *passim*; E. Brennecke, *John Milton the Elder and his Music* (New York, 1938), p. 89.
15. Watt, op. cit., Chapters 7–8 and Conclusion. I have drawn heavily on Dr Watt's work in the preceding paragraphs. Her dating of publications is based on entries in the Stationers' Registers, and may not allow sufficiently for reprints of the most popular Biblical ballads.

quatrain fell out of fashion, partly because of their association with the 'enthusiastic' religion and politics of the radical sectaries during the revolutionary decades.

II

One advantage of the Bible is that, like history, it links everything with everything else: sometimes with the daring effects of metaphysical poetry. To compare the kingdom of heaven with a mustard seed, to refer the sluggard to the ant, to prefer the lilies of the field to Solomon in all his glory, to welcome home the prodigal son with a fatted calf, to declare that he that will save his life shall lose it; to him that hath shall be given; that more joy shall be in heaven over one sinner that repenteth than over ninety and nine just persons; that the poor shall inherit the earth, that wisdom is folly and folly wisdom – these paradoxes delighted those who eagerly read Donne and his followers:

> Nor ever chaste, except you ravish me

> Here in dust and dirt, oh here
> The lilies of his love appear.

Christ came

> Leaping upon the hills to be
> The humble King of you and me.[16]

Fulke Greville and Henry Vaughan sum up several Biblical themes which we have been considering. Man is

> created sick, commanded to be sound.

> Arks now we look for none, nor signs to part
> Egypt from Israel; all now rests in the heart.

> Heaven hath less beauty than the dust he spies,
> And money better music than the spheres.

> And in the desert grows the rose.[17]

---

16. Donne, *Complete Poetry and Selected Prose* (Nonesuch ed., 1929), p. 285; Vaughan, *Works*, II, p. 643; Crashawe, *Poems* (Muses Library, n.d.), p. 266.
17. Greville, *Poems and Dramas* (ed. G. Bullough, Edinburgh, ?1919), II, pp. 136–7; *Remains* (ed. G. A. Wilkes, Oxford U.P., 1965), p. 226; Vaughan, *Works*, II, pp. 461, 652. Cf. p. 143 above.

Job anticipates Donne: 'Lo, though he slay me, yet will I trust in him' (XIII.15). Hamlet recognized not only that the world was out of joint but that his 'own soul is at variance with himself', just as Troilus found that 'within my soul there doth conduce a fight' (V. ii).

When we try to account for the popularity of Psalms in this period, we should not forget the Psalmist's 'double heart' (Psalms XII.2: 'the ungodly speak with a double heart').[18] I have discussed elsewhere the importance of this concept in the literature.[19] To the authors whom I then cited, I might add *The Revenger's Tragedy*[20] and John Preston, who referred directly to the other source-text, James I.8: 'when the heart is divided, it is imperfect'; a 'double-minded man is unconstant in all his ways'.[21] Oliver Cromwell in the difficult days of decision just before the trial and execution of the King wrote to his cousin Robert Hammond: 'Our hearts are very deceitful, on the right and on the left'. But 'what think you of Providence disposing the hearts of so many of God's people this way, especially in this poor Army?'[22]

It would be difficult to answer the question of cause or effect: did the vernacular Bible prepare for and influence metaphysical poetry, or did the mood which produced that poetry open men's minds to this aspect of the Biblical message? The paradoxical element in the Bible, newly made available to non-academic readers, chimed with the conflicts and contradictions of a society in transition such as England was in the late sixteenth and early seventeenth century. The existence of the Bible in English helped a realization that parts of it were in fact poetry, songs. Versions of the Psalms and of the Song of Songs opened up a new genre of lyric, which looks forward to the sonnet sequence and to the poetry of meditation. Such lyrics were popular because they were intended to be sung, often to popular tunes. But the scope of the genre was soon exhausted. The triumph of Sternhold and Hopkins's version of the Psalms put all other competitors out of the race.

As the Bible became more familiar, straight paraphrase gave way to meditations on a verse or two from the Bible. George Herbert paraphrased only one psalm – the famous Psalm XXIII – but composed several meditations on a text, and two sonnets on the Bible as a source of meditative

18. The Geneva margin comments 'he meaneth the flatterers of the court'.
19. In my *Writing and Revolution*, Chapter 1. Sibbes speaks of 'a kind of doubleness of heart' in *The Soules Conflict* (1635), p. 469; cf. *Works*, VII, p. 411.
20. Jonathan Dollimore, *Radical Tragedy*, pp. 139–43.
21. Preston, *The New Covenant* (1630), pp. 224–8. James's Epistle was always a favourite with radicals. Cf. Hosea X.2: 'Their heart is divided'.
22. Abbott, *Cromwell's Writings and Speeches*, I, pp. 697–8.

poetry. Crashawe's version of the same Psalm is a meditation rather than a paraphrase. Quarles attached 'soliloquies' to each chapter of his paraphrase of Ecclesiastes: they seem to one reader better as poetry than the paraphrase. Herbert's imitator, Christopher Harvey, published in 1647 a book wholly composed of meditations on Biblical texts. 'Translations' and paraphrases had been mainly of Old Testament narrative: meditations drew more freely on the New Testament. The editor of *Parnassus Biceps* claimed in 1656 that Biblical meditative poems were a speciality of priestly royalist poets. Eldred Revett, who meditated on Genesis and on Psalm VI, may have been a royalist; Joseph Beaumont was ejected from his living for royalism: some of his best poems are Biblical meditations.[23]

III

Perhaps we should think more about the Bible and literary genres, or literary fashions. Professor King speaks of the Reformation as 'a time of unimpeded lay Biblical education', with reference especially to protestant nativity plays.[24] Traditional miracle plays on Biblical subjects provided models for proto-protestant propagandist drama. Bale wrote three plays specifically for a popular audience. Professor Lily Campbell regards them as harbingers of a new type of protestant Biblical play rather than as survivals of traditional plays with their Catholic associations. They made use of the interlude, coming into acceptance in secular drama. Foxe thought that 'players, printers and preachers' had all been 'set up of God' to bring the Pope down. Bale's plays, Latimer's sermons and Foxe's *Book of Martyrs* were *literary* events of national significance; so were versifications of the Psalms and other books of the Bible.[25]

Religious drama did not last. Initially protestant theories of comedy helped to elevate the status of the genre.[26] But the cult of the Word led to a reaction against Biblical drama as a profanation. *Sola Scriptura*: not the

---

23. Harvey, *Schola Cordis*, in *Complete Poems* (ed. Grosart, 1874), pp. 110–239: Abraham Wright, op. cit., sig. A 4–4v: I cite from the reprint of 1927 (ed. G. Thorn-Dury); Revett, *Selected Poems* (ed. D. M. Friedman, Liverpool U.P., 1966), pp. 56, 65–6. Originally published in 1657.
24. J. N. King, *English Reformation Literature*, p. 296.
25. L. B. Campbell, *Divine Poetry and Drama in 16th-century England* (California U.P., 1959), pp. 141–260; Foxe, *Acts and Monuments*, VI, p. 57; cf. L. Fairfield, *John Bale; Mythmaker for the English Reformation* (1976).
26. King, op. cit., Chapter 6; Norbrook, op. cit., Chapter 2.

imagery of the miracle of the mass, the elevation of the host, the worship of relics, the representation of saints and even the deity on a human stage.[27] Tyndale, Becon, Jewel and Foxe can all be quoted to this effect. Farce was an integral part of the interludes, and this displeased more austere protestants. A century later Bunyan was reproved by some of the godly for the frivolity of *The Pilgrim's Progress*. *Samson Agonistes*, Milton is careful to tell us, was not intended for the stage.

Plays came to be associated with the licentious suburbs, with immorality and profanation of the Sabbath. Government worries about public order complement protestant scruples. A proclamation of 1559 prohibited 'unlicensed interludes and plays especially on religion or policy' as 'not convenient in any good ordered Christian commonwealth to be suffered'.[28] But it took time for the prohibition to become effective. In Elizabeth's reign there were interludes or plays on Mary Magdalene, Jacob and Esau, David and Absalom, Esther, Susanna and the elders, Abraham and Lot, Nebuchadnezzar, Pontius Pilate, Jephtha, Tobias, Samson, Joshua, Jonah. Biblical plays were produced for the public theatre by Golding, Greene, Peele, Lodge, Dekker, Munday and Chettle. They appear to have ceased towards the end of the reign.[29] But they were followed by a group of 'Foxeian' plays, glorifying England's Biblical protestantism, in the first decade of the seventeenth century.[30] It must have seemed a curious throwback when in the 1670s Roger Boyle wrote *Herod the Great* and *King Saul*.[31] But for a vital period in the history of the theatre Biblical plays of one sort or another were crucially important. Market forces must have contributed greatly here to the opinion-forming role of the theatre.

The Bible lent itself less controversially to epic. Much of the Old Testament, and Revelation in the New, is in the epic vein. It has been argued that Revelation and other related Biblical texts provide the pattern and most of the imagery for Book I of *The Faerie Queene*. It is an allegory of the final battle against Antichrist. Duessa and Lucifer are the Great Whore, the Babylonian harlot. Una is the woman clothed with the sun, the Bride

---

27. Michael O'Connell, 'The Idolatrous Eye: Icons, Anti-Theatricalism and the Image of the Elizabethan Theatre', *English Literary History*, 52 (1985), pp. 279–89; cf. Thomas Barish, *The Anti-Theatrical Prejudice* (California U.P., 1981), esp. pp. 159–65.
28. *Tudor Royal Proclamations* (ed. P. L. Hughes and J. F. Larkin, 1964–9), II, no. 458.
29. Campbell, op. cit., pp. 141–260; Watt, *Cheap Print and Popular Piety*, p. 285.
30. M. Heinemann, 'Rebel Lords, Popular Playwrights and Political Culture', *Yearbook of English Studies*, 21 (1991), p. 75. She suggested that these plays had a political purpose, linked with the Southampton group.
31. *Dramatic Works of Roger Boyle* (ed. W. S. Clark, Harvard U.P., 1937), II.

of the Lamb, as well as the bride in the Song of Songs; by extension she is the Church of England and Queen Elizabeth. The Dragon (Leviathan) comes from Isaiah, Daniel and Job. The Red Cross Knight is Christ himself.[32]

Paraphrases of Scripture stories and hexameral epics were popular with poets of some calibre – Sylvester/Du Bartas, Quarles, Wither, Cowley's *Davideis*, Henry More. Again Milton is nearly the last good poet to try the genre. Biblical epics continued to be written later, but not by significant poets. The Earl of Surrey and Henry Lok both versified Ecclesiastes, though only the latter printed his version (in 1597).[33] Sternhold had paraphrased *Certayn chapters from Proverbs* in 1550. John Hall's seminal *The Court of Virtue* (1565) is almost entirely Biblical. Nearly 40 per cent of its pages contain paraphrases drawn from thirteen books of the Old Testament and two of the New Testament; another forty pages paraphrase Psalms.[34] William Kethe, famous as the translator of Psalm C, 'All people that on earth do dwell', and the largest single contributor to the Geneva Bible, also wrote *A Ballet, declaringe the fal of the Whore of Babylon, intytuled Tye thy Mare, Tom-boy*. *The wailings of the Prophet Hieremiah* were paraphrased in 1566 by Thomas Drant, together with two books of Horace's satires (*A Medicinable Morall*). William Forrest published a *History of Joseph* in 1569, and William Hunnis *The Life and Death of Joseph*, a versification of Genesis (1578), as well as other Biblical poems. Earlier he had published *Certayne Psalms* (1549); in between he took part in a plot to assassinate Queen Mary. John Merbecke published *The Holie Historie of King David* in 1579, and Thomas Hudson *The Historie of Judith* (Edinburgh 1584), with an introduction by James VI. Francis Sabie's short divine epic, *The Old Worlds Tragedie* and *David and Bathsheba*, appeared in 1596.[35]

Jeremiah proved popular. An anonymous version of the Lamentations was published in 1587; both George Wither and Francis Quarles wrote paraphrases. Donne paraphrased 'The Lamentations of Jeremy', admitting

32. John E. Hankins, 'Spenser and the Revelation of St John', *Proceedings of the Modern Language Association*, LX (1945), pp. 364–81; cf. Florence Sandler, 'The Faerie Queene: an Elizabethan Apocalypse', in *The Apocalypse in English Renaissance Thought and Literature*, pp. 148–74.

33. We know of Surrey's version because Archbishop Parker referred to it in his translation of the Psalms (Campbell, op. cit., to which I am indebted throughout these paragraphs). For Lok see L. B. Wright, *Middle-Class Culture*, p. 238n.

34. Hall, op. cit. I have used R. A. Fraser's edition of 1961, which contains 366 pages of text.

35. Campbell, op. cit., pp. 70–76, 93–4, 106, 114.

that he worked 'for the most part according to Tremellius', the Latin translator.[36] Spenser used unrhymed sonnets for his translations from Revelation (1569). Sidney translated part of Du Bartas's Biblical epic a generation before Joshuah Sylvester's best-selling *Divine Weekes and Workes* of 1605 – in which there are many political allusions.

A religious poem (or paraphrase) was a good way for a young poet to introduce himself to the public or a patron. Drayton's first publication was *The Harmonie of the Church* (1594), including 'Moses his birth and miracles', 'David and Goliath', 'Noah's Floud', ten songs from the Old Testament and eleven from the Apocrypha. Thomas Middleton too began with the Apocryphal Wisdom of Solomon, paraphrased in six-line stanzas and dedicated to the Earl of Essex in 1597. Even as late as 1627 Middleton published *Gods Parliament-House: Or, The Marriage of the Old and New Testaments*, a work designed to show the cohesion of the two Testaments and the fulfilment of prophecies. Around the turn of the century there were lachrymose poems about Mary Magdalene – by Gervase Markham and Nicholas Breton.[37] Dekker published *Fowre Birds of Noahs Arke* in 1609.

Francis Quarles was the most prolific of all writers of Biblical poems. *A Feast for Worms* (1620) was 'set forth in a poem of the history of Jonah'. There followed paraphrases on Esther (1621), Job (1624), Jeremiah (1624), the Song of Songs (1625), Samson (1631) and Ecclesiastes (1645). Esther led him to the topical conclusion that

> The strongest arteries that knit and tie
> The members of a mixed monarchy
> Are learned counsels, timely consultations,
> Ripened advice, and sage deliberations. . . .
>
> How many hopeful princes (ill advised
> By young and smooth-faced counsel) have despised
> The sacred oracles of riper years
> Till dear repentance wash the land with tears![38]

The brothers Fletcher each wrote a Biblical epic – Giles *Christs Victory and Triumph*, published in 1610, Phineas *The Locusts, or the Apollyonists* (1627), identifying the Jesuits as the locusts of Revelation IX.3–5.[39] Phineas also paraphrased Psalms.

36. Donne, *Complete Poetry and Selected Prose* (Nonesuch ed., 1929), pp. 307–20.
37. Campbell, op. cit., pp. 115, 120.
38. Quarles, *Hadassa: or, The History of Queen Ester, Complete Works*, II, p. 50.
39. Joan Grundy, op. cit., pp. 190–93.

George Wither's *Hymns and Songs of the Church* (1623) contains a versification of the Song of Songs, together with twenty-one hymns from the Old Testament and five from the New. Wither makes political points as he goes along. The Lamentations of Jeremiah 'are as useful as any part of the Old Testament for these times (nigh fallen asleep in security)'. Jeremiah's warnings are related to the fear of Catholicism and anxiety lest God be leaving England discussed in Chapter 12 above. If the commonwealth's prosperity 'go to ruin', Wither observed, 'the particular church there cherished must needs be affected also. . . . The overthrow of kingdoms and empires follows the abuse and neglect of religion'. The fifth chapter of Lamentations is especially appropriate for us to 'sing unto God in the behalf of many particular churches even in these times'. 'The Prayer of Daniel' 'may be sung whenever any of these judgments are poured out on the commonwealth, which the prophets have threatened for sin'.[40] Song LVII, for Ascension Day, treats Christ's ascension as the triumph of *mankind*. This emphasis on the Son of God's humanity anticipates Milton's *Paradise Regained*.

William Habington in the 1630s wrote ten paraphrases of verses from the Psalms, five from Job, and five from other books of the Bible. To these we may add Thomas Fuller's *David's Heinous Sin* (1631), Sir William Alexander's *Jonathan: An Heroic Poem Intended* (unfinished: in *Recreations with the Muses*, 1637), and George Sandys's *Paraphrases upon the Divine Poems*, which included Job: he had already paraphrased the Psalms (1636), and went on to the Song of Songs in 1641. William Knivett wrote poems upon Moses, David and Solomon, as well as paraphrasing a psalm. Cowley has an ode from 'The thirty-fourth chapter of Isaiah'.[41] Henry King's *The Woes of Esay* was not published until 1657: it envisages the end of the world.[42] Sir Francis Hubert returned to a familiar theme with *England's Favourite: The History of Joseph* (1651, though it was written much earlier: Hubert died in 1629). Sir Thomas Salisbury's *History of Joseph* appeared in 1656.

In view of the foregoing, Cowley's remark that before him 'none have attempted writing a divine poem in English' sounds a little presumptuous, Cowley spoke disparagingly of Quarles and of 'mr. Heywood of Angels' –

40. Wither, *Hymns and Songs of the Church*, pp. 92–3, 121, 125.
41. Habington, *Poems* (ed. K. Allott, Liverpool U.P., 1948); *The Shorter Poems of William Knivett*, pp. 279–80, 405; Cowley, *Poems* (ed. A. R. Waller, Cambridge U.P., 1905), pp. 211–14.
42. In *Minor Poets of the Caroline Period* (ed. Saintsbury), III, pp. 230–32.

each of which 'so far from elevating prose only debases devotion'.[43] Cowley was writing about his unfinished *Davideis* (1656), the most ambitious work in this genre. It shows considerable knowledge of Jewish history, and is accompanied by self-consciously careful classical annotations, which occupy more than half the poem's pages. The genre continued after 1660. Dryden's *Absalom and Achitophel* (1681) was a satirical mock-epic, a retort to Puritan versifications of the Bible; it led to a not very Puritan response from Samuel Pordage, *Azariah and Hushai*, in the following year.[44] Thomas Flatman's paraphrase of a chapter of Job was published in 1674 and had reached its fourth edition by 1686.[45] John Norris also paraphrased Psalms, the Song of Songs, and chapters from Job and Isaiah. Traherne's *Hexameron, or Meditations on the Six Days of the Creation*, in prose and verse, was not published until 1717.[46] I draw a veil over Sir Richard Blackmore.

L. B. Wright spotted the importance of verse paraphrases or summaries of the Bible. Henoch Clapham's *A briefe of the Bible* (Edinburgh, 1596) seems to have been one of the first, but it was rapidly followed by John Weever's rhyming life of Christ, *An Agnus Dei* (1606), dedicated to Prince Henry, by John Taylor's *Verbum Sempiternae* [*sic*] (a rhyming paraphrase of the Old Testament and the Apocrypha) and *Salvator Mundi*, which did the same for the New Testament. Both were published together in 1614, forming a cheap and fantastically popular volume. Known as 'the thumb Bible' because of its pocketable size, it was constantly reprinted throughout the following two centuries in England and America, and was even translated into French.[47] Wright, with his unfailing eye, also noted other aids to understanding the Bible published in the early years of the seventeenth century. Thomas Wilson's *A Christian Dictionarie: Or, The Bible abreviated* (1615) was a summary: Clement Cotton's *The Christians Concordance* was designed for 'simple and illiterate' readers like himself. It was followed by *A Complete Concordance to the Bible Of the Last Translation* in 1631. This was intended specifically 'not . . . for the most learned, or for the most unlearned, but for the middle sort'.[48]

Spiritual allegory had blossomed with Spenser's fervently protestant

43. Cowley, *Poems*, pp. 13–14, 266. Thomas Heywood's *The Hierarchy of the Blessed Angels* appeared in 1635.
44. For Pordage see my *The Experience of Defeat*, pp. 222–42.
45. Saintsbury, *Caroline Poets*, III, pp. 420–22.
46. Norris, *A Collection of Miscellanies* (6th ed., 1717); Traherne, *Poems*, pp. 148–54.
47. Wright, *Middle-class Culture*, pp. 238–9. Taylor's title was corrected to *Verbum Sempiternum* in later editions.
48. Wright, op. cit., p. 237.

Faerie Queene, and was continued by the Spenserian poets, partly because of the usefulness of allegory as a protection against the censor. But it lost its political point – for radicals, at least – with the liberation of the press in the 1640s. Early protestant reformers had reacted vigorously against allegorizations of the Bible by mediaeval scholars, and had insisted on returning to the literal text. Radicals in the 1640s argued that 'the mystery' was more important than 'the history' when reading Scripture. This was no mere retreat to what had been dismissed as the arbitrary fantasies of priestly academics. Prising out 'the mystery' enabled men and women to read into the Bible truths which the problems of their own society had brought home to them. The myths were there to be used for current political purposes. [49]

Gerrard Winstanley said of the Biblical narrative 'whether there was any such outward things or no, it matters not much'.[50] The insouciant post-scepticism of this remark may be related to the imaginative processes which were to lead to the emergence of the novel. Under renewed censorship Bunyan revived religious allegory with *The Pilgrim's Progress* and *The Holy War*, though criticisms of the former by the godly showed the marginality of the genre. The future lay rather with the novel, of which Joan Grundy sees *The Faerie Queene* as a precursor. It matters not much whether *Paradise Lost* is historically accurate. It matters not at all whether *The Pilgrim's Progress* and *Clarissa* are fact or fiction. The drawing of moral lessons was ceasing to be regarded as the main object of writing history: the novel had a more subtle moral purpose as well as offering the entertainment value of romances and epics. When the novel did emerge, it was (among other things) about social mobility (cf. Joseph, mobile upwards, and Job, mobile downwards), about love and marriage (cf. David and Bathsheba, Solomon), about heroism (Samson – one man's freedom fighter is another man's terrorist).[51]

On the way to the novel, the brief vogue in the early seventeenth century of the 'character' as a genre may owe something to the wisdom books of the Old Testament and the Apocrypha. Overbury showed that the 'character' offered a way of making political comment without falling foul of the censorship. Selden's *Table-Talk*, like Ben Jonson's conversations with Drummond, demonstrates how much freer with political and other

49. See pp. 40, 237–8 above, 364 and 416 below.
50. Sabine, p. 462.
51. Grundy, op. cit., p. 24; Michael McKeon, *The Origins of the English Novel, 1600–1740* (Johns Hopkins U.P., 1987), esp. Part II.

comment writers could be in conversation than in print. The woodcuts of early protestant literature, including the Geneva Bible, it has been suggested, may presage the popularity of the emblem.[52]

The influence of the Bible on English poetry, though intense, was relatively short-lived. The Biblical repertoire was limited. Biblical drama lacked sex-interest, though David and Bathsheba and the apocryphal Susanna and the elders did quite well. *Samson Agonistes* was the last of its genre to be written by a major poet, just as *Lycidas* was the last significant pastoral before Shelley, *Comus* very nearly the last masque, *Paradise Lost* and *Paradise Regained* very nearly the last epics to be written by a serious literary figure.

IV

George Hakewill's *An Apologie or Declaration of the Power and Providence of God in the Government of the World* (1627) fits into this picture of struggle for an independent English literature, a struggle which lasted throughout the seventeenth century as the battle of the books. Hakewill's main thrust, like that of the Elizabethan poets, was against the tyranny of the Greek and Roman classics. This occupies over one-third of his book (pp. 331–546).[53] The Bible, he argued, gave no justification for a theory of degeneration in the universe or in human beings (esp. pp. 53, 73–4, 83–7, 152–3). He cited thirty-four pages of Biblical texts and commentators on his side. But the commentators are almost all modern (and protestant) – Cartwright, Béza, Paraeus; they draw especially on the Old Testament (pp. 273–307). Hakewill has little use for the early Christian Fathers or for mediaeval scholasticism. Instead he relies on human reason. 'Though I am bound steadfastly to believe what St Paul affirms, yet am I not bound to believe your affirmation that St Paul affirms it, and for any such convincing infallible demonstration (as you speak of) that he so doth, I confess as yet I cannot find it' (p. 583 – replying to 'doubts presented me by a worthy friend', I.D.). The reason is that of the individual Bible reader; and reason changes over time.[54] Godfrey Goodman thought that such an appeal to human reason opened the door to atheism (Book V, pp. 81–2, second pagination). Goodman's arguments here illustrate the scholastic quagmire

---

52. J. N. King, op. cit., pp. 152, 462–4.
53. Hakewill, op. cit.
54. See my ' "Reason and reasonableness" ', in *Change and Continuity*.

from which Bacon and Hakewill extricated us, contrasting reason and experiment with 'the Logic rule which serves only for the framing of syllogisms'. 'I pray charge me not hereafter for leaving old philosophy, but if you can charge me for leaving the truth spare me not' (Book V, pp. 7, 57, 63–4). Many think Antichrist shall come towards the end of the world, which will then 'be filled with all kind of impiety, impurity and misery, the attendants of his coming, ... much beyond all former times'. But – Hakewill argues – Antichrist in the person of the Pope has already come, some centuries ago. From which we are to conclude 'that extreme prophaneness hath reigned in the world almost in all ages'; it is not peculiar to our age (pp. 552–9).

We can see Hakewill, helped by the stubborn Bishop Goodman, being pushed further down the road of reliance on his own reason, his own interpretation of the Bible (Book V, pp. 81–2). Hakewill distinguishes sharply between the authority of the infallible Bible and the right of the individual to interpret it for himself. It took the free discussion of the 1640s to bring to popular attention the contradictions and inconsistencies of the Bible, and then the courage of Walwyn, Winstanley, Writer and Fisher to draw the conclusion that it could not be the Word of God.

For Hakewill the Bible is all-important. His *Apologie* justifies the ways of God to man. It was written not like *Paradise Lost* in the darkness of defeat, but in an epoch of threatening danger when it was essential to have confidence that God was not deserting his people, and when humanism and protestantism were merging in a defence of reason and the possibility of progress – economic progress and intellectual progress. Hakewill noted with pride increased production by the lead mines of the Mendips (p. 163). Goodman was worried lest if we deprave the Ancients 'how apt shall we be for innovation, what danger of a mutiny; the country boors may rise in sedition' if 'all things may be improved'. Hakewill drily replied that Goodman need not worry about innovation and the peasantry ('who I think trouble themselves little with my book'). It was more likely that 'laziness and murmuring' would be caused by Goodman's doctrine that 'nothing can be improved by industry'. Hakewill was offering something approaching a theory of progress (Book V, p. 132; cf. p. 192). Goodman was pushed into popery to cover up his confusions under the authority of the Church. Hakewill was mildly appalled by the strange seas of rational thought into which he found himself sailing, alone; but he nevertheless accepted the modern world in which the individual captains his own soul.

VI. Psalms

The great literary resources of the Bible had suddenly become available to the English laity from the 1530s onwards, opening up a world hitherto known only to a few, and those few more interested in theology than in literary expression. Hence the exaggerated praise of the Psalms by Sidney and Milton: they offered new aesthetic experiences. Ben Jonson credited the origin of poetry to the Hebrews, but did not assert their authority. Translations and imitations of the Greek and Roman classics continued, but Hebrew poetry was *new*. The novelty lasted for a century and a half. Looking back in 1679 Samuel Woodford saw the Bible as far more than a source of inspiration rivalling the classics. The Hebrew language, he explained, had never been brought under 'those Greek and Latin laws'. The wit, the extremely bold metaphors, daring similes and rapid transitions of Hebrew poetry offered a new challenge.[55]

The Psalms often seemed topically relevant. They were useful if you wanted to attack persecutors. 'He will ordain his arrows for them that persecute me' (Psalm VII.13). 'Princes have persecuted me without cause' (Psalm CXIX.161). John Pullam used a jaunty rhythm when he translated Psalm CXLIX for the Sternhold and Hopkins version:

> To bind strange kings fast
> In chains that will last:
> Their nobles also
> In hard iron bands.

Oliver Cromwell cited Psalm CXIX to Speaker Lenthall when he called for social reform in July 1651. Bunyan quoted Psalm LVIII.10 in attacking persecutors: 'the righteous shall rather rejoice when he seeth the vengeance of God upon them'. As Professor Greaves notes, Bunyan prudently omitted the remainder of the verse: 'he shall wash his feet in the blood of the wicked'; but many of his hearers or among his readers would no doubt recall it.[56] Psalm LVIII was a favourite with critics of

55. Jonson, *Timber or Discoveries* (Temple Classics, 1941, p. 115. First published 1616). S. Woodford, *A Paraphrase upon the Canticles and Some Select Hymns of the New and Old Testaments*, sig. bv. Woodford had an ear. He pointed out that we should not notice anything odd if passages from Milton's controversial prose were printed as blank verse, or lines from *PL* as prose (sig. b 6v–7). See also pp. 361–2 below.
56. Abbott, *Writings and Speeches of Oliver Cromwell*, II, p. 433; Greaves, 'John Bunyan: Tercentenary Reflections', in *American Baptist Quarterly*, VII (1988), p. 523, quoting *A Few Sighs from Hell* (1658), *BMW*, I, p. 284.

monarchy. Sternhold and Hopkins, addressing 'ye readers', translated the passage on persecutors

> In them the poison and the breath
> Of serpents do appear. . . .
> O God, break thou their teeth at once . . .
> The just . . .
> Shall wash their feet in blood
> Of them that him forsake.

Béza's headnote to this Psalm ran 'There is no greater iniquity than that which doth oppress under the cloak of law'.[57] Calvin had recognized that washing one's feet in blood even of the ungodly 'seems to attribute to the righteous an affection far from godly meekness'. But 'it cannot but be a pleasure to them when wickedness is paid its rightful reward'. Thomas Wilcocks, one of the authors of the 1572 *Admonition to Parliament*, saw Psalm LVIII as aimed against 'Saul's court and council'. And he comments that, although 'there is mildness and gentleness in faithful men's hearts', still, 'being led with a true zeal, they take pleasure in the execution of God's judgment'. The righteous may wash his feet in the blood of the wicked 'by a manner of speech'.[58] William Barton in his translation says that Psalm LVIII is directed against 'ungodly governors and great ones, . . . showing their corrupt obstinacy and utter destruction'. Psalm LXIX is 'a prayer against persecutors' who are 'mighty men'.[59]

Catharine Macaulay spotted propagandist use of the Bible in the Cambridge edition of 1629. Here 'the explanatory title to Psalm CXLIX is altered from "To praise the Lord for his victory and conquests that he giveth his saints" to "The praises given to God for that power he hath given to the church to rule the consciences of men"'. The shift from the saints' opposing men's power to the church's power to rule men's consciences is striking: it survived, Catharine Macaulay tells us, in all editions of the Bible down to 1743.[60] This contrasts interestingly with the reading of Psalm CXLI by Thomas Wilcocks, who remarked in 1586 that

---

57. Sternhold and Hopkins (1566); Béza, *Psalms of David*.
58. Calvin, *Commentary on the Psalms of David* (Parker Soc., 1840); Wilcocks, *Works* (1629), pp. 128–51. Wilcocks also wrote *An Exposition upon the Book of Canticles* (1624).
59. W. Barton, *The Book of Psalms in Meter* (1644), p. 124.
60. C. Macaulay, *The History of England from the Accession of James I to the Elevation of the House of Hanover* (second ed., 1766–8), IV, pp. 8n, 151n. The Geneva headnote had been even more forthright: it read 'to praise the Lord for his victory and conquest that he giveth his saints against all man's power.'

the psalmist 'seemeth to lay the common people's fault . . . upon the rulers and judges themselves . . . in their own personal infamous examples . . . . When the great ones shall be discomfited and overthrown, the people shall be wise and come to amendment. This is good', but Wilcocks preferred an alternative reading.[61] Sternhold and Hopkins and the Geneva margin both comment on this Psalm that David prayed the Lord to bridle his affections 'till God take vengeance on his enemies'. Barton's marginal note in 1644 ran 'while these tyrants reign they chop the righteous as flesh to a pot'.

On Psalm CXLIX we may quote a witness against Hugh Peter, on trial as a regicide: 'I heard the prisoner at the bar preaching before Oliver Cromwell and Bradshaw, who was called Lord President of the High Court of Justice; and he took his text out of the Psalms. . . . "Bind your kings with chains, and your nobles with fetters of iron". . . . Says he in his sermon, "Beloved, it is the last psalm but one, and the next psalm hath six verses and twelve Hallelujahs, praise ye the Lord . . . and so on. For what?" says he. "Look into my text, there is the reason of it – that kings were bound in chains".'[62] Milton proclaimed that 'to bind their kings in chains and their nobles with links of iron' was 'an honour belonging to his saints' who must first overcome 'those European kings which receive their power not from God but from the Beast'.[63] George Wither was more cautious in a poem dedicated to Charles II in 1660. Although, he said,

> It to the saints pertains
> To bind in fetters and in chains
> Both kings and peers,

nevertheless they must not attempt this 'unseasonably'.

> With carnal weakness, in a carnal mode,
> Seeking their own ends when they [God's] pretend.

God will provide deliverance, but in his own good time.[64] Greaves quotes a metrical version of Psalm CXLIX 'with obvious militant overtones', which was said to have been sung by Newcastle dissenters in November 1668.[65]

61. Wilcocks, *Works*, pp. 423–6.
62. [Anon.], *Trial of the Regicides* (1713), pp. 183–4.
63. *Eikonoklastes, MCPW*, III, p. 598.
64. Wither, *Speculum Speculativum*, pp. 55–6; *Parallelogrammaton* (1662), pp. 46, 68–70, 74.
65. R. L. Greaves, *Enemies under his Feet: Radicals and Nonconformists in Britain, 1664–1677* (Stanford U.P., 1990), p. 149.

Early translations of the Psalms then were often political. The necessity of putting verse into a different language allowed the translator to insert phrases of his own in the interests of 'clarification'; such clarification might contain theological or political ideas. But the main place for commentary was the headnote. Wither's headnote to Psalm X said 'it may be used when we are oppressed by temporal or spiritual oppressors', 'poor men wronged by tyrants'. Béza's summary of the same Psalm reassured his readers that 'all the enterprise of . . . tyrants against the church shall come to nought'. In his commentary on this Psalm Calvin had put it more succinctly: 'the princes of this world . . . are but downright fools till they become the lowly scholars of Christ.' Béza's argument to Psalm XXVI commented that 'it is a hard thing in the court to retain true religion and true uprightness of life, . . . chiefly when wicked men . . . and . . . flatterers do reign'. The Geneva Bible's headnote to Psalm XCIV refers to the 'violence and arrogancy of tyrants'.

It became almost a convention in mid-sixteenth-century England to translate Psalms during political imprisonment or disgrace. Surrey translated Psalms LXXXVIII and LV in prison in 1547. His version of Psalm LXXIII ran

> So shall their glory fade; thy sword of vengeance shall
> Unto their drunken eyes in blood disclose their errors all.

During his final imprisonment he returned to paraphrasing the Psalms and Ecclesiastes. Sir Thomas Smith translated five psalms in prison in 1549–50, lamenting national catastrophes and civil dissension.[66] Sir Thomas Wyatt's version of the seven penitential psalms gave them a distinctly protestant slant. He added a disapproving comment on outward ceremonies in religious worship to his version of Psalm LI.[67] Two sons of the Duke of Northumberland – the later Earls of Warwick and Leicester – translated psalms during their imprisonment in 1553.

Matthew Parker, future Archbishop, translated the whole book of Psalms during Mary's reign. The Earl of Strafford quoted Psalm CXLVI.3 when he heard that Charles I had agreed to his execution: 'Put not your trust in princes'. Bulstrode Whitelocke, when it came to his turn to be discarded,

66. Rivkah Zim, *English Metrical Psalms: Poetry, Praise and Prayer, 1585–1601* (Cambridge U.P., 1987), pp. 88–98.
67. S. Greenblatt, *Renaissance Self-fashioning: From More to Shakespeare* (Chicago U.P., 1980), p. 115; for other examples of theological and political critical insertions see ibid., pp. 125, 127–8.

found reading the Psalms a consolation for disappointed hopes, especially Psalm CXII: 'He will not be afraid of evil tidings, for his heart is fixed and believeth in the Lord'.[68] Johnston of Wariston, on the other hand, in the blissful dawn of 1638, had discovered in Psalm CVII 'a perfect pattern of our cause, as the conclusion is of our duty'.[69] The psalm rejoices over Scotland's triumph in the Lord, who 'turneth the wilderness into pools of water, and the dry land into water springs. And there he placeth the hungry, and they build a city to dwell in. . . . He poureth contempt upon princes, and causeth them to err in desert places out of the way'. The conclusion was 'Who is wise, that he may observe these things? for they shall understand the loving kindness of the Lord'.

Robert Crowley's version of the whole psalter (1549) was perhaps intended as a protestant service book, and included some of his own radical theology.[70] He was the first to use the metre for translating psalms that was to become standard because of its adoption by Sternhold and Hopkins. Crowley rebuked social injustice, especially the rentier's sin of sloth. Calvin in his Commentary on Psalms IX and X had emphasized that God 'forgot not' the cry of the poor.

Thomas Sternhold had been imprisoned as a heretic in 1543. His version of Psalm CXX – 'prayers against the enemies of the church' and 'histories' of 'God's folk elect' – shows where he stood. Sternhold published thirty-seven Psalms in 1549, and a fuller edition in 1551, dedicated to Edward VI.[71] Sternhold was Groom of his Majesty's robes, and Edward had heard him sing some of his metrical versions.[72] English metrical psalms were no doubt sung to popular ballad tunes; hence their wide acceptance. Sternhold's original translations really were *songs*. There were twelve editions of his psalms in Edward VI's reign.[73] Sternhold died before the Sternhold and Hopkins collection was edited in Geneva during the Marian exile. One of the chief editors was William Whittingham, whom we met in connection with the Geneva Bible.[74] He himself versified many Psalms. The Geneva psalter (1559–62) went through nearly 300 editions before 1650, and it was used in parish churches until the end of the seventeenth century. Shakespeare's reference to weavers singing psalms suggests something of

68. Spalding, *Diary of Bulstrode Whitelocke*, p. 290.
69. *Diary of Sir Archibald Johnston of Wariston*, 1911, pp. 340–41.
70. Martin, *Religious Radicals*, p. 6.
71. Zim, op. cit., pp. 87–8, 104–7.
72. Sternhold, *The Psalmes of David in Meter* (1551), sig. A iii.
73. Zim, op. cit., pp. 152, 120–24, 144.
74. Ibid., pp. 125, 140–43. See p. 56–7, 63 above.

the popularity of the metrical version.[75] With his impeccable social discrimination, he depicted Falstaff and Sir Toby Belch as less sympathetic.

Saintsbury wondered how the magic of the quatrain which we find in Donne and Jonson got submerged by the jog-trot of Sternhold and Hopkins.[76] Donne emphasized the vast superiority of the translation by Sidney and his sister – and its greater suitability for singing in church.[77] 'Tom Sternhold's wretched pricksong for the people' was what Milton's nephew Edward Phillips was to call it. The social reputation of Sternhold and Hopkins fell too. The Prologue to Boyle's *The Tragedy of King Saul* (not by Boyle) sneers at them, and associates them with the defeated Parliamentarian cause.[78] Boyle himself had switched from royalism to staunch support for Oliver Cromwell, before hastening to contribute to the restoration of Charles II. Thomas Ward, who was incapable of literary appreciation, criticized Sternhold and Hopkins on social grounds for their excessive use of the word 'trade'.[79]

Community singing of psalms was used in churches as a protestant demonstration in 1560,[80] and by London Puritans in 1641 to drown Laudian services. The importance of psalm-singing for morale in the New Model Army is proverbial. Cromwell interrupted his pursuit of the defeated Scots after Dunbar to sing Psalm CXVII. Fortunately it is the shortest in the book.[81] Despite St Paul's authority for 'singing and making melody to the Lord' (Ephesians V.19; cf. Colossians III.16) and James's instruction to 'any among you afflicted . . . let him sing' (V.13), some Quakers were to object to psalm-singing because it meant repeating other men's words by rote: there was no evidence that the Apostles sang David's Psalms. They did sing, George Whitehead admitted, but according to the spirit. He was denouncing Jonathan Clapp, who had defended psalm-singing, as a 'Cain-like' blind guide.[82] George Fox had no objection to singing in meetings so

75. Shakespeare, *I Henry VI*, II. v.
76. Saintsbury, *Caroline Poets*, I, p. 488.
77. Donne, 'Upon the translation of the Psalmes by Sir Philip Sidney and his sister', *Complete Poems and Selected Prose*, p. 303.
78. *The Dramatic Works of Roger Boyle*, II, p. 706, 821.
79. Ward, *England's Reformation* (1715), Canto I, pp. 93–4.
80. G. Burnet, *History of the Reformation of the Church of England* (1825), V, pp. 349–50.
81. Abbott, *Writings and Speeches of Oliver Cromwell*, II, pp. 318–19.
82. Whitehead, *Cains Generation Discovered* (1655), pp. 6–9; cf. Christopher Atkinson and George Whitehead, *Davids Enemies Discovered, Who of him made Song but without the Spirit* (1658). Hymn-singing flourished during the revolutionary decades and was especially popular among the sects: cf. John Cotton's *Singing of Psalms a Gospel Ordinance* (1650) and Thomas Ford's *Singing of Psalms the Duty of Christians* (1653).

long as the Sternhold and Hopkins versions were not used, 'after the manner of the priests'.[83] In the mid-seventeenth century Ranters sang blasphemous songs to the well-known tunes of Sternhold and Hopkins.[84]

Zim lists ninety translations of (some) psalms between 1530 and 1601.[85] Coverdale's *Goostly psalmes and spirituall songs* (*c.*1535) was banned and burnt towards the end of Henry VIII's reign. John Hall (editor of *The Court of Virtue*) translated Psalms. So did the Catholic Richard Verstegan, and the Puritan William Bradshaw. Arthur Golding rather endearingly translated both Ovid's *Metamorphoses* and Calvin's *Commentaries* on the Psalms.[86] Some of Abraham Fraunce's *Psalmes* in English hexameters (1591) were surprisingly good.[87]

Wyatt pioneered the Psalms as poetry of meditation and introspection, followed by Surrey, who saw himself as the 'New David'.[88] Sir Philip Sidney and his sister the Countess of Pembroke were unusual in adopting sophisticated stanza forms rather than the popular ballad quatrains which Sternhold and Hopkins had made almost obligatory. Fulke Greville in his *Life* of Sidney stressed the political motivation behind his hero's translation of the psalms.[89] The Countess of Pembroke translated Psalms XLIV–CL. She was more dependent on Béza's prose paraphrases (translated by Gilby), on Calvin's *Commentaries* and on the Geneva Bible than her brother had been.[90] In some of her versions she used quantitative measures. Sidney thought the Psalms were 'the most excellent and very highest kind of poetry'.[91] He took immense trouble over his version, using a different stanza form for each of the Psalms which he paraphrased. Only two of the forty-three stanza forms were used in Sidney's other poems. Sometimes he achieves bold effects – e.g. Psalm XIII:

> How long, O Lord, shall I forgotten be?
> What? ever?

83. Fox, *Short Journal*, pp. 214–15; Zim, op. cit., p. 143. William Dewsbery gave reasons for not singing 'David's Psalms in metre' in *The Discovery of Mystery Babylon* (1665–6?), p. 294.

84. Anne Laurence, 'Two Ranter Poems', *Review of English Studies*, XXXI (1980), p. 58.

85. Zim, op. cit., pp. 57, 32, 213–59.

86. Ibid., pp. 112, 123–39, 5.

87. Esp. Psalms I, LXXIII and CIV.

88. Zim, op. cit., pp. 206–7.

89. Maureen Quilligan, 'Sidney and his Queen', in *The Historical Renaissance* (ed. H. Dubrow and R. Strier, Chicago U.P., 1988), p. 108.

90. Zim, op. cit., pp. 152, 156–7, 187–96.

91. Sidney, *Poems* (ed. W. A. Ringler, Oxford U.P., 1962), p. 505.

Sidney was apparently still working on his translations when he was killed in battle in 1586.

It is difficult to find a notable poet from Wyatt to Milton who did not try his hand at a version of the Psalms. We may list Bishop Bale, Archbishop Parker, Spenser (whose version of the seven penitential psalms has not survived, any more than his Song of Songs), Sir John Davies, John Davies of Hereford, Phineas Fletcher, Gervase Markham. George Wither, like Sidney and Milton, exalted the Psalms above all secular poetry.[92] His version, dedicated to Elizabeth of Bohemia, was so radical that it had to be published in The Netherlands in 1632: no English publisher would take it on. Wither's verse here seems to me of higher poetic quality than he is usually given credit for, but his object was political. 'There is nothing in the Psalms', he declared, 'written for its own sake; but all things there are types, figures, examples, prophecies or parables, to inform or figure out what should be fulfilled in the New Testament at the coming of the Messiah'. In his comment on Psalm LXVIII Wither prayed that 'heretics, hirelings and contentious persons may be reproved, or cut off'.[93] The dangerous word was 'hirelings', state clergy; but 'contentious persons' might well apply to Laudians like Richard Montagu – who I am sure equally thought Wither 'contentious'.

George Sandys's version of the Psalms (1636) – like Sidney's, in varying stanza forms – was dedicated to Charles I and Henrietta Maria, with an introduction by Falkland. Sandys prudently eschewed commentary to his verse. But he was perhaps the best craftsman among paraphrasers of the early seventeenth century. He also wrote paraphrases upon Job, Ecclesiastes, the Lamentations of Jeremiah (1638) and the Song of Songs (1641). Virtually the whole of his verse is Biblical. Sandys had a much wider knowledge of the world than most men of letters in his day. His early travels in the Turkish empire gave him a feeling for the orient. As Sidney Godolphin – himself no mean poet – put it

> Next you have known (besides all arts) their spring,
> The happy East; and from Judea bring
> Part of that power with which her airs you sing.[94]

Sandys's brother Sir Edwin had translated fifty Psalms in 1615.

Other poets included Joseph Hall (who was discouraged by the reception

92. Wither, *Hallelujah*, To the Reader.
93. Wither, *The Psalms of David*, II, p. 141.
94. Sandys, *Poems* (ed. R. Hooper, 1872), I, pp. 86, xcv.

of his versification of the first ten Psalms),[95] George Herbert (whose version of Psalm XXIII became justly popular as a hymn), Sidney Godolphin,[96] Henry Vaughan, Thomas Carew (nine psalms – rather unexpectedly), Richard Crashawe, Sir John Denham, Henry King, John White of Dorchester, Charles Cotton, Richard Baxter. The penitential psalms proved especially popular. William Hunnis's *Seven Sobs* ran to ten editions between 1583 and 1629.[97]. Samuel Hieron's *Penance for Sin* (1619) consisted of lectures on the seven penitential Psalms. William Byrd included ten Psalms in his *Sonets & Songs of Sadnes and Pietie* (1588).

Among those who versified the whole Psalter Henry Dod deserves special mention for his clumsy verse and word order. He also paraphrased a number of Biblical songs, and is (I hope) the only person ever to have versified an Act of Parliament – that of 3 Jac. cap. 1 for a public thanksgiving to be held every year to celebrate the failure of Gunpowder Plot.[98] Another is Henry Ainsworth, whose *Booke of Psalmes* appeared in 1612 at Amsterdam, followed by a version of the Song of Songs in 1623; his commentary on Psalms and the Song of Songs was not published until 1843. Thomas Ravenscroft paraphrased *The Whole book of Psalms* in 1621. The Parliamentarian general Sir Thomas Fairfax translated but did not publish the whole psalter. Among those not generally thought of as poets, we should not fail to record that Queen Elizabeth and King James I each translated a psalm, and Sir Francis Bacon seven – so well that more use might have been made of them by those anxious to prove that Bacon wrote Shakespeare. The Scot Robert Pont, whom I quoted on p. 165 above, translated several Psalms.

There were acrimonious disputes about translations in the 1640s and 1650s. Francis Rous's *Psalmes of David in English Meeter* (1643) had been approved by the Westminster Assembly of Divines and authorized by Parliament for general use. (Rous happened to be an MP at the time.) It looked as though his version might supplant Sternhold and Hopkins; but it came into general use only in Scotland. In 1655 William Barton complained, with copious examples, of errors and infelicities in the versions of others.

---

95. T. F. Kinloch, *The Life and Works of Joseph Hall, 1574–1656* (1951), p. 195.
96. Saintsbury, *Caroline Poets*, II, pp. 237, 241. The rather tough last verse of Psalm CXXXVII ('blessed shall he be that taketh and dasheth thy children against the stones') Godolphin rendered

> Thy children's cries will fill the air
> And none shall pity their despair.

97. Campbell, op. cit., pp. 43, 49. Hunnis also versified the first chapter of Genesis.
98. Dod, *Al the Psalmes of David* (1670), sig. S 3v–6.

The Assembly of Divines, he said, had made Rous's translation 'much more harsh and far less acceptable than it was before'. Two psalm books, he alleged, 'one published by the Scots, the other in the name of Mr White of Dorchester deceased', had been cribbed from his and Rous's versions. In compensation he printed four pages of poems praising his own version.[99] In January 1657 a committee of divines reported to Parliament that Rous's version of the Psalms was best fitted to be publicly used, with another version (probably Barton's) as runner-up. Both were preferred to Sternhold and Hopkins. Parliament resolved that the latter should no longer be printed with the Bible.[100] But that got overtaken by events.

A *New Version of the Psalms* was published by Nahum Tate and Nicholas Brady in 1696, and obtained a royal recommendation for use in churches. Tate had become Poet Laureate in 1692. Brady was chaplain to both William and Mary, and later to Queen Anne. Tate and Brady also produced a version of the Song of Songs in 1698, together with other Biblical paraphrases in verse. Their version made its way slowly as a 'Whig' psalter. Lines quoted from it in *DNB* suggest why:

> The prince who slights what God commands
> Exposed to scorn must leave his throne.

Propagandist use of the Psalms was not confined to Parliamentarians. Henry King's version, published in 1651, was decidedly political. He amended the text in order to minimize criticism of kings, and to attack those who took the Engagement to be faithful to the Commonwealth.[101] Clarendon's *Contemplations and Reflections upon the Psalms of David* was also not above tendentiousness. When it was published in 1727 it was dated 1647; but internal evidence makes it clear that it contains much post-1660 hindsight. The Contemplations on Psalms CXXIV, CXXVII and CXXIX use Charles's unexpected restoration to show that God can work political miracles. Psalm XX teaches that the Church is necessary to the state, and Psalms XXII, LXIX and LXXIII show that success and victory do not justify a cause – a view with which, for

---

99. W. B[arton], *The Book of Psalms in Meter*, To the Reader; *A View of many Errors and some gross Absurdities in the Old Testament and the Psalms in English Metre; as also in some other Translations lately published* (1655), To the Reader.
100. *Diary of Thomas Burton* (1828), I, pp. 349–50. Rous's version had no commentary.
101. D. Hirst, 'The Politics of Literature in the English Republic', *The Seventeenth Century*, V (1990), pp. 150, 155.

different reasons, Milton agreed. Psalm XLIV, Clarendon believed, demonstrated the necessity of studying history if we are to avoid revolution.[102]

William Nicholson, Bishop of Gloucester, published in 1662 *David's Harp Strung and Tuned: Or, an easie Analysis of the whole Book of Psalms*. It was dedicated to the Earl of Clarendon, to whom (Wood says) the Bishop had recently paid £1,000 for his promotion.[103] Nicholson had had to face 'sad and cloudy times' during the Revolution; but he had 'lived to see . . . the day of resurrection', in which he became no mean pluralist. He too made political use of the Psalms. On Psalm LXXXII, one of those which Milton translated, the Bishop wrote that the Psalmist 'saith not, "You that are oppressed, rise against your judges", but that they leave it to God'. The most that is admitted is 'a holy impatience' at the patient long-suffering of God. When he comes to Psalm CXLIX, with its notorious 'Bind their kings in chains, and their nobles with fetters of iron', Nicholson explains that 'the phrase is metaphorical'. Contrary to the dreams of a golden age when the saints shall execute vengeance on kings and nobles, the chains and fetters to which the Psalmist alludes are the law and precepts of the gospel, 'sharp rebukes by ministers of the Word to stubborn sinners. . . . The greatest princes have submitted their necks to the yoke and doctrine of Christ'. But that went a bit too far in putting down 'Anabaptists, Fifth Monarchy men and millenaries'; the Bishop added hastily, 'not that any of Christ's ministers usurp authority over kings and princes in temporal matters'.[104]

Samuel Woodford was highly praised for his paraphrases of the Psalms and of the Song of Songs by Thomas Flatman, who himself paraphrased Psalm XV and some verses of Psalm XXXIX.[105] Woodford managed in his version to make Psalm XXI refer to the restoration of Charles II, and Psalm LXVIII.31 to England's imperial policies. In the Geneva version this runs 'Then shall the princes come out of Egypt: Ethiopia shall hasten to stretch her hand unto God'. Woodford ignored Egypt – no colony – and expanded the rest to describe the British empire:

> Black Ethiopia at his feet shall bow
> His neck . . .

102. Clarendon, op. cit., pp. 427–32, 544–6, 556–60, 484–7.
103. Anthony Wood, *Athenae Oxonienses* (1813–20), IV, p. 825.
104. Nicholson, op. cit., sig. A 2v, pp. 124, 237–8, 532.
105. Flatman, *Poems and Songs* (1674), in Saintsbury, *Caroline Poets*, III, pp. 306–7, 317, 329, 366–7. Saintsbury quotes the edition of 1686.

The Western Continent and farthest isles
And both the Indies gifts shall bring . . .
To him they shall present the spoils
Of sea and land, as universal king.[106]

VII. The Song of Songs

In Hosea I the beloved is a garden, a vineyard enclosed from the wilderness. Isaiah has 'a song of my beloved his vineyard' (V.1–6)[107] which Wither paraphrased in his *Hymns and Songs of the Church* (1623). The most interesting evocation of the garden/vineyard is the Songs of Songs, or Canticles, attributed to Solomon. Here the well-beloved comes up out of the wilderness; in her vineyard she calls to her lover, 'thou that dwellest in the garden' (III.6, VIII.5, 13). 'My sister my spouse is as a garden enclosed' the lover says and she replies 'let my well-beloved come to his garden and his pleasant fruit' (IV.12, 16; V). Since this erotic poem got into the canon, it continued to be treated – as in the Middle Ages – as an allegory ('even in its jolliest expressions', as Milton put it).[108] The Geneva Bible tells us that the Song 'describeth the perfect love of Jesus Christ . . . and the faithful soul his church'. This assumes that the author knew there was going to be a Christ, and that he was going to have a church. Even if the author were Solomon, he must be thought more experienced in earthly than divine love. Such points were the sort that were being made by the profane in the 1640s, and which the new Biblical criticism had to face. It is perhaps significant that the Song of Songs is one of the few books of the Old Testament not quoted in the New Testament.[109]

The Geneva margin managed to remain poker-faced when commenting on the love affair. 'The King hath brought me into his chambers' is glossed 'meaning the secret joy that is not known to the world'. 'Let him kiss me with the kisses of his mouth' is spoken, we are told, 'in the person of . . . the faithful soul inflamed with the desire of Christ' (I.1). The simple request, 'Show me, O thou whom my soul loveth, . . . where thou liest at noon', is explained 'the spouse, seeing her fault, fleeth to her husband only

---

106. Woodford, *A Paraphrase of the Psalms of David* (1667), pp. 51, 196–9. 'Spoils' is perhaps rather an unfortunately accurate word.

107. See p. 143 above.

108. *MCPW*, II, p. 597.

109. R. Lane Fox, *The Unauthorized Version*, p. 122.

for succour' (I.6). 'My well-beloved ... shall lie between my breasts' means no more than 'he shall be most dear to me' (I.12). 'Thy two breasts are as two young roes' is glossed 'wherein are knowledge and zeal, two precious jewels' (IV.5). A reference to 'our bed' can only mean 'the heart of the faithful, wherein Christ dwelleth by his Spirit' (I.15). Just because the Song so manifestly is not about the love of Christ for his church, it gave rise to quarrels between literary appreciation and theological tradition.

Of the many translations of and commentaries on the Song of Songs written, a surprising number were not published in the author's lifetime, or at all. John Dod commended a sermon which Richard Sibbes had preached on the subject, but it was not published. John Davenport preached a series of sermons on the poem, which are said to have been prepared for the press, but again they never appeared.[110]

The best of the translations seems to me to be the first, William Baldwyn's of 1549. His title, *The Canticles or Balades of Solomon*, relates the work to English conditions.[111] His dedication to Edward VI hoped – alliteratively – that songs like his 'might once drive out of office the bawdy ballads of lecherous love that commonly are indicted and sung of idle courtiers in princes' and noblemen's houses'. Baldwyn wanted to counter the effect of 'the wanton words' which he agreed that the Song contained. The theme of his version is the conflict between true faith and false hypocrisy. Those who labour in the 'fields and vineyards' are the Lollards who defied persecution. Unlike later versifiers, Baldwyn eschewed commentary, restricting himself to translation and summaries of the argument. He uses various metres and at his best captures a light-hearted sensual happiness.

> Oh how fair, how fair art thou my joy.
> How lovely my Love, how lovely art thou alse;
> Oh my spouse, how wanton and how coy
> Thou art in delights when I do thee enhalse,
> O my darling.

110. *Massachusetts Historical Soc. Collections*, 2nd Series, 8, p. 345. I owe both these references to Professor Frank Bremer's forthcoming book, *The Congregational Connection*.

111. The Great Bible of 1539, of which Baldwyn was the printer, had called Canticles 'The Ballet of Ballettes of Solomon' (Lily B. Campbell, *Divine Poetry and Drama*, p. 57). Baldwyn's own *Balades* is said to have been the earliest printed book of original English poetry (G. L. Scheper, 'Reformation Attitudes towards Allegory and the Song of Songs', *Proceedings of the Modern Language Association*, 89, no. 3, 1974, p. 556).

> Like thou art in stature to the tree
> Of palms, for no wight can set thee for to grow;
> And thy breasts are syke as seemeth me
> To clusters of grapes, that ripe hang down below,
> O my darling.

But elsewhere he cheerfully inserts the proper phrases to show he knows it is really about Christ and his church; and the argument assumes this.

Baldwyn was no mere 'Puritan' in the later sense of that word. He wrote masques for Edward VI, and has been described as 'the pre-eminent imaginative author of the English Reformation', editor of *The Mirror for Magistrates*, author of the first printed English sonnet and of *Bell the Cat* (1570, written 1553), a satire which J. N. King calls 'arguably the first English novel, describing Reformation England as a world of cats, good and bad, tame and wild'.[112]

In 1575 Jud Smith published a paraphrase of Chapters V and VI of the Song of Songs.[113] Dudley Fenner, exiled as a young man for his Puritanism, became chaplain to the Merchant Adventurers at Middelburg, and published his verse translation of the Song of Songs there in 1587. 'It seemeth', he rather mysteriously told the Company in his dedication, 'to be prepared for your daily order and use'. His not very good translation is in poulter's measure. He repudiated the idea, which he attributed to Jesuits, that it is really a love-song of doubtful canonical authority – a view which he admits was shared by the more respectable Sebastian Castellio.[114] But Fenner himself has no doubts, as he explains in his commentary, which occupies more than twice the space of his translation. He smuggles in a fierce contribution to current theological disputes, consigning 'the ornaments of scarlet, fine linen, silk, gold, organs, copes, surplices, albs, crosses and all ceremonies ... to the Babylonian strumpet'. That passage alone explains why he published abroad, away from censorship by the minions of the Whore of Babylon. Fenner promised to translate the Lamentations of Jeremiah and 'all the other Psalms scatteringly inserted in the Scriptures';

---

112. Baldwyn, op. cit., *passim*; J. N. King, *English Reformation Literature*, pp. 225–6, 358–406.
113. Smith, *A Misticall Devise of the Spirituall and Godly Love between Christ, the Spouse, and the Church or Congregation*.
114. Grotius was said to agree in thinking it a carnal love-song (John Collinges, *The Intercourses of Divine Love betwixt Christ and the Church*, 1676, sig. a 3: sermons preached before 1662).

but if he did they were not published: his early death before reaching the age of thirty may be the explanation.[115]

Henry Barrow illustrated the behaviour of the true church by a controversial reference to the Song of Songs in *A Brief Summarie of the Causes of our Separation* (1591).[116] Another separatist, Henry Ainsworth, whom we have already met as a Bible commentator, was also a religious refugee in The Netherlands who paraphrased the Song of Songs. 'He had not the faintest breath of poetical inspiration', as *DNB* rightly observed; but he is (appropriately) the most garrulous of the annotators, giving his readers seventy-seven pages of comment to eleven pages of text. His version was published in 1623, a year after his death.[117] James Durham, a Scot (1622–58), also failed to publish his *Clavis Cantici* in his lifetime. He was chaplain to Charles II during the latter's brief reign in Scotland in 1650–51: though presumably the King did not choose him. We are told that Durham was seldom known to smile.[118] Arthur Hildersham (1563–1632) was another nonconformist, frequently in trouble with the ecclesiastical authorities. His translation was not published until 1672, and is notable only for the fact that the space given to commentary is more than three times that given to the verse.[119]

There was no nonsense about the church in Michael Drayton's version of the Song of Songs, also in poulter's measure, published in 1591. This was his earliest published work, and is frankly and luxuriantly erotic, despite being based on the Geneva Bible.[120] Gervase Markham also tried his prentice hand at a verse rendering in 1595.[121] The distinguished lawyer, Sir Henry Finch, wrote *An Exposition of the Song of Songs*. It was published anonymously, by William Gouge, in 1615: Finch's commentary amounted to five times the length of the text. Finch also wrote, and failed to publish, an exposition of Hosea.[122] George Wither regarded the song as a history of

---

115. Fenner, *The Song of Songs . . . translated out of the Hebrue into Englishe meeter* (Middelburgh, 1587), sig. A 2–3, A 4v–5, Chapter IV.
116. *The Writings of Henry Barrow, 1587–90* (1962), pp. 146–50.
117. Ainsworth, *Solomons Song of Songs*.
118. Durham, op. cit. (1668).
119. Hildersham, *The Canticles or Song of Songs Paraphrased*.
120. In *The Harmonie of the Church, Works of Michael Drayton* (Oxford U.P., 1941), V, pp. 1–2.
121. Markham, *Poem of Poems, or Sions Muse, conteyninge the Divine Song of Salomon in Eight Eclogues*.
122. Finch, op. cit., sig. A 6. For Hosea see p. 362 above. Cf. W. R. Prest, 'The Art of Law and the Law of God: Sir Henry Finch (1558–1625).

the church, 'from Abel to the last judgement', when the 'blessed marriage' (of Christ and his church) shall be fully consummated. His paraphrase treated the allegory seriously, though at one point he remarked 'the explanation of each several metaphor will be too large for this place'.[123]

In 1625 Francis Quarles published *Sions Sonets: Sung by Solomon the King*, with elaborate marginal notes pressing the allegory on the reader. In Chapter I, for instance, 'enforced to keep a stranger's vine' is glossed 'forced to idolatrous superstitions, . . . being seduced by false prophets'. 'Bowls of nectar' are 'the holy Scriptures'. 'To kiss the lips of so, so fair a bride' means 'to offer up the first fruits of obedience'. 'Thy curious tresses' are reduced to 'ornaments of *necessary* ceremonies' (my italics); 'thy ivory teeth' to 'sincere ministers'; and 'thy neck' to 'magistrates'. 'Thy snowy breasts' become the Old and New Testaments. The bridegroom's 'legs like purest marble' means 'his ways constant, firm and pure'.[124] There are echoes of the Song of Songs, appropriately enough, in Henry Constable's *Spirituall Sonnettes* (*c*.1590–1612) and in Benlowes's *Theophila, or Loves Sacrifice* (1652).[125]

Joseph Hall repeated the cliché that the two breasts on which the lover reposed are the two Testaments.[126] Joseph Beaumont wrote several poetical meditations on Canticles which were not published in his lifetime.[127] Thomas Valentine, preacher of a Fast Sermon to the House of Commons on 28 December 1642, encouraged his congregation by applying Chapters II–V. The Church was sick with love now too, he agreed, but becoming a little impatient. 'Leaving the particulars, I urge the main duty of waiting upon God'.[128] Thomas Washbourne composed an elaborate meditation on Canticles I.5 in a volume published in 1654.[129]

Ranters naturally enjoyed the Song of Songs. Clarkson, looking back from his Muggletonian days, believed 'Solomon's writings' had been 'the original of my filthy lust, supposing I might take the same liberty as he did, not then understanding his writings were no Scriptures'.[130] Muggleton –

---

123. Wither, Song of Songs, in *Hymns and Songs of the Church*, p. 39: twenty-three pages of text, twelve and a half of comment.

124. In Quarles, *Complete Works*, II, pp. 119–32.

125. Ed. Joan Grundy, *Poems of Henry Constable* (Liverpool U.P., 1960), p. 81: Benlowes, in Saintsbury, *Caroline Poets*, I, pp. 361–8, 459; cf. p. 328.

126. Hall, in *Works*, III, p. 293.

127. Beaumont, *Minor Poems* (ed. Eloisa Robinson, 1914), pp. 16, 19, 45.

128. *FS*, V, pp. 89–95.

129. Washbourne, *Poems*, pp. 109–11. See p. 152 above.

130. Clarkson, *The Lost sheep Found*, pp. 26, 32.

no doubt echoing Clarkson – agreed that 'the Ranters' practice was grounded upon Solomon's practice, who knew so many women'.[131] Abiezer Coppe, who associated the vineyard closely with the wilderness, used the Song of Songs in *Some Sweet Sips, of some Spirituall Wine* (1649) to justify libertinism.[132] This interpretation of the Song does not often get into print in the seventeenth century, though Owen Feltham spoke of Solomon being 'flamingly amorous in the Canticles'.[133] One wonders how widespread it was among unsophisticated readers.[134] Nevertheless Coppe, like John Reeve and Laurence Clarkson, thought that the Song of Songs should be excluded from the Biblical canon. One of the Ranter poems which Anne Laurence discovered also echoes the Song I.13.[135]

Commentaries upon the Song of Songs were written, among many others, by William Gouge (1615) and Richard Sibbes (*Bowels opened . . . sermons on the 4th, 5th and 6th chapters of the Canticles*, published 1648), and by many less famous persons. Sibbes emphasized Canticles as a song about marriage, following in this a tradition set by Bartimeus Andreas, *Sermons upon the Fifth Chapter of the Song of Songs* (1595), John Dove, *The Conversion of Salomon* (1613) and continued by Francis Rous, *The Mystical Marriage* (1635).[136] Wither had seen the Song of Songs as an allegorical account of the history of the church. This aspect was a special feature of the commentaries of Brightman and Cotton. The Introduction to the 1644 edition of Brightman's *Commentary on the Canticles* claimed that the author's interpretation had been (when he wrote it) different from all others. It treated the true church 'from the time of David till the end of time'.[137] Chapter V describes this church fighting back against Antichrist in the later Middle

---

131. Muggleton, *A Looking-Glass for George Fox* (1668), pp. 63–4: cf. Reeve, *Joyfull News from Heaven* (1706), pp. 11–14: first published 1658; *The Acts of the Witnesses*, p. 62. On Ranters and the Song of Songs, see Noam Flinker, 'Milton and the Ranters on Canticles', in *A Fine Tuning: Studies of the Religious Poetry of Herbert and Milton* (ed. M. A. Malaski, Binghamton, New York, 1989).

132. Coppe, op. cit., in Smith, *Ranter Writings*, pp. 42, 47, 51–7: *A Second Flying Fiery Roll*, ibid., p. 108.

133. Feltham, *Resolves*, p. 64. Second enlarged edition published in 1628.

134. Or indeed among the sophisticated. Giordano Bruno told his Inquisitors that reading the Song of Songs gave him an erection (J. Bossy, *Giordano Bruno and the Embassy Affair*, Oxford U.P., 1991, p. 176).

135. A. Laurence, 'Two Ranter Poems', pp. 58–9.

136. Scheper, op. cit., pp. 556–8.

137. Printed with Brightman's *The Revelation of St. John Illustrated*, sig. a.a.a.a.a.a. 3, sig. 3v. John Davenport's unpublished sermons on Canticles (see p. 363 above) apparently shared Brightman's historical interpretation.

Ages – Waldensians, Lollards, Hussites. Chapter VI deals with the Reformation. Among the virgins in verse 7 Brightman reckoned the Anabaptists, Libertines, Anti-Trinitarians, Arians, etc., who now waste and destroy Moravia, Poland, Hungaria, Transylvania and a great part of Denmark. The dove in verse 8 is the church of Geneva. In the last age of the world the church will be 'terrible as an army with banners' (VI.9). Chapter VII is about the Second Coming.

John Cotton's *A Brief Exposition Of the Whole Book of Canticles* was published in 1642, before Brightman's *Commentary*, which Cotton may or may not have read. Cotton put marriage at the centre of the Song of Songs. But for him the Song was equivalent to a divine abridged version of Foxe's *Acts and Monuments*, 'an historical prophecy or a prophetical history'. Cotton was anxious to draw conclusions for his own age. He interpreted IV.6 as meaning that a church may be beautiful, though consisting of 'mean persons, former notorious sinners'. 'Pastors and ministers of the primitive church did ... without help of universities' (IV.11). Like Brightman, Cotton saw Chapters V and VI as relating to mediaeval heretics and to the Reformation. VI.2–9 describes the church under Luther: 'to feed in the gardens' suggests the spread of the Reformation to Switzerland and to other parts of Germany, where lilies were gathered. 'Beautiful as Tirzah' refers to Henry VIII, 'comely as Jerusalem' to Edward VI, 'terrible as an army with banners' to Elizabeth (VI.4). 'Clusters of grapes' in VII.7 means 'full of strong liquor of sound doctrine'. Chapter VIII brings us down to the present: verse 3 ('his left hand shall be under mine head, and his right hand shall embrace me') can only refer to Christian magistrates and faithful ministers. The final verse, 'make haste my beloved', tells of the calling of the Gentiles.[138] Brightman and Cotton achieved masterpieces of scholastic ingenuity which may now seem misplaced. In Brightman's *Commentary* the text occupies less than ten pages out of a hundred; in Cotton's *Exposition*, twelve pages out of 233.

Nathanael Homes's *Commentary ... on ... Canticles* was not published until 1652. It ran to 471 pages. He treated the poem both as an allegory of the love of Christ for his church and as a history of the church from the beginning to the end of time, though his main emphasis was on 'the mystery' rather than on 'the history'. He explained the verbal repetitions in the poem by the re-occurrence of similar events in different historical periods. The over-riding theme of the poem, for him, was the super-

138. Cotton, op. cit., pp. 10, 32, 62, 112, 116, 180–81, 153–60, 227, 238.

eminence of love: 'the   life of love is beyond the love of life'.[139] For Homes the breasts are not only the usual two Testaments; they are also the ministry of the Word, and the Apostles and the seventy disciples. Our little sister who has no breasts is 'the people who have not yet ... God's two testaments to nourish their souls'. The bed was the 'place for the enlightenment of the daughters of Jerusalem' – i.e. the souls of the faithful. But it was also the Temple, and Christ in his human nature. There are indeed 'three sorts of metaphorical or figurative beds'.[140] The allegory led Homes into all sorts of scholastic absurdities. 'The Scripture speaks of five sorts of honest kisses'. Christ is like an apple tree 'in his humiliation in two particulars' and 'in his exaltation in two particulars'. Chapter V led Homes to six propositions touching the hair. He discusses 'the meaning of shoes spiritually applied'.[141] He side-stepped the ticklish problem of what the lover's right hand was doing whilst he demonstrated 'his handiness to help with his left hand under the head' of 'my sister, my spouse' (VIII.3). *Annotations upon All the Books of the Old and New Testaments* admitted that Chapter V verse 4 'is more apt to foment lewd and base lust than to present holy and divine notions'.[142] Despite all this, Leicester city corporation in 1651 recommended 'the Canticles for poetry' in its curriculum for schoolchildren, which suggests that teachers are better at drafting curricula than politicians.[143] The Jews, we are told, restrained those under the age of thirty from reading the poem.[144]

Homes was nothing if not thorough. 250 pages of his *Works* are devoted to a commentary on Psalm XLIII, and another twenty-eight to a single verse each from Psalms CVI and CXLIV.[145] The longest commentary I have encountered is that by John Collinges, published in 1676 and 1683 but almost certainly composed in the 1640s and 1650s. This runs to 1,439 pages on Chapters I and II.[146] Collinges had earlier published two sermons on

139. Homes, op. cit., in *Works*, sig. A2–A2v, pp. 11–30, 164, 168, 452–5.
140. Ibid., pp. 43, 142, 289, 72–3, 50–1, 254, 275, 256.
141. Ibid., pp. 4, 184–5, 372–6, 421.
142. Ibid., p. 204; *Annotations* (3rd ed., 1657), sig. 712, quoted by Scheper, op. cit.
143. Hirst, 'The Politics of Literature in England of the Republic', p. 145.
144. Durham, op. cit., p. 42. I cite from an edition published by the Banner of Truth Trust, undated but *c.*1982.
145. Homes, op. cit., pp. 312–562, 577–94, 625–36. This is beaten only by Thomas Manton's three huge volumes of sermons on Psalm CXIX – admittedly the longest – published posthumously in 1681.
146. Collinges, *The Intercourse of Divine Love* (1676), on Chapter II; ibid. (1683), on Chapter I.

Canticles VIII.5.[147] John Mason, whom we have met in another context, published a paraphrase of Canticles in 1683 together with some psalms.[148]

Samuel Woodford in his *Paraphrase*, dedicated to the Archbishop of Canterbury in 1679, considered carefully the possibility that the Song of Songs might be just a love poem, but concluded against, the Jews 'not allowing in the female sex . . . such open demonstrations of love'.[149] But Mrs Rowe in a paraphrase of Canticles V (1695) referred to the male lover as 'Son of Venus' and 'the God of love'.[150]

Biblical poems offered an alternative to the all-pervasive classics. The vernacular Bible had revealed a new non-pagan lyric poetry to ordinary readers – lyrics for common people as well as for kings, queens and heroes. Compared with the crude knockabout miracle and mystery plays, here was something for scholars and gentlemen which popish countries had not got. Men used the Bible to defend the humanizing virtues and educational powers of poetry and music, citing New Testament parables, David's and Solomon's Songs. From Sidney to Sir William Davenant the case was made out, though the latter used it not disinterestedly to support his project for a revived and purified theatre in the 1650s.[151] The Song of Songs – unlike the Psalms – lent itself to learned commentary, demonstrating that the poem was really about Christ and his church, not about a love affair at all. It offered a little titillation to the most determined allegorizers. And it was magnificent poetry, which for Milton described married love, 'stronger than death': 'many waters cannot quench it'.[152] In Milton's epic Eden was like Solomon's garden, enclosed from the wilderness.

---

147. Collinges, *The Spouses Hidden Glory* (1646).

148. Mason, *Spiritual Songs or Songs of Praise to Almighty God. . . . Together with the Song of Songs . . . First Turn'd then Paraphrased in English Verse*. For Mason see pp. 36–7, 243 above.

149. Woodford, op. cit., sig. b. 3.

150. Quoted in *Kissing the Rod: An Anthology of Seventeenth-Century Women's Verse* (ed. Germaine Greer and others, New York, 1988), pp. 384–6. Other versions by Anna Trapnel (1658) and Elizabeth Sym (1695) are cited.

151. J. R. Jacob and T. Raylor, 'Opera and Obedience: Thomas Hobbes and *A Proposition for Advancement of Moralitie by Sir William Davenant*', in *The Seventeenth Century*, VI, 1991, pp. 212, 230, 245.

152. *MCPW*, II, p. 251, quoting the Song of Songs VIII.6–7; cf. *PL*, V. 17–25.

17. Milton, Bunyan and Marvell

> Victorious deeds
> Flamed in my heart . . .
> To rescue Israel from the Roman yoke.
>
> Milton, *Paradise Regained*, I. 215–17. The Son of God is speaking.

> Promise was that I
> Should Israel from Philistian yoke deliver:
> Ask for this great deliverer now, and find him . . .
> Himself in bonds under Philistian yoke.
>
> Milton, *Samson Agonistes*, lines 38–42. Samson speaking.

> God's people are (as it hath always been, Ezra IV.12–16) looked
> upon to be a turbulent, seditious and factious people.
>
> Bunyan, *I Will Pray with the Spirit* (1662–3), *BMW*, II, p. 253.

> The Spirit of grace shall spring up in *some* that are great and
> mighty as well as in *many* that are poor and low.
>
> Bunyan, *PP*, Part II (1684), p. 231. Italics in the original.

I. Milton

Milton and Bunyan seem to me to be respectively the greatest poet and the
greatest prose writer of later seventeenth-century England, though Milton
was also a great prose writer, and Bunyan's verse, especially his satirical
verse, is better than is usually allowed.[1] Both were soaked in the Bible, and
both found their hopes of a Biblically just society dashed after 1660. To see
them in a Biblical context helps us to grasp their links with the radicals of
the 1640s and 1650s, whose political and social use of the myths of Cain
and Abel, Esau and Jacob, Adam and Nimrod we have been considering.
Milton and Bunyan shared the millenarian expectations of the radicals:
Milton in 1641 spoke of Christ as 'shortly-expected King', no doubt with

---

1. See Graham Midgley's Introduction to Bunyan's *Poems*, *BMW*, VI.
2. *MCPW*, I, p. 616.

the 1650s in mind;[2] Bunyan in 1658 thought that Christ's kingdom was 'at hand'.[3]

Paradise Lost and *The Pilgrim's Progress*, the two great epics of Biblical Puritanism in defeat, were published within eleven years of each other; parts of them at least were almost certainly written at the same time. The blind old Milton envisaged the quarrelsome couple Adam and Eve finally facing catastrophe and advancing slowly and alone but united through the uncharted wilderness. In Paradise they had enjoyed the company and conversation of God and angels; relations with animals were friendly. All was totally different in the howling wilderness. So far as we know Milton found no garden, joined no religious denomination. Bunyan had his congregation, but he was in jail when his Pilgrim, deserting wife and family, fled from the City of Destruction, not knowing whither.

Milton and Bunyan did not reproduce Biblical stories, as earlier verse paraphrases had done: they re-imagined the myths in the light of the problems of their own society. Gerrard Winstanley saw Adam every day walking up and down the street. He is every man, like Langland's Piers Plowman and Bunyan's Pilgrim: Christiana, heroine of Part II of *The Pilgrim's Progress*, is every woman; Wittreich saw Eve as the real hero of *Paradise Lost*.[4] Milton and Bunyan stand half-way between Biblical verse paraphrases and the novel.[5]

Milton from 1640 dedicated his life to the service of the Parliamentarian Cause. His anti-episcopal pamphlets of the early forties were followed by the triumphal utopianism of *Areopagitica*, the passionately anti-monarchical *Tenure of Kings and Magistrates* and *Eikonoklastes*, and by his two *Defences of the People of England*, written in Latin, which made him better known to the European intelligentsia than any English writer since the author of *Utopia*. On the eve of the restoration of Charles II Milton published a blistering attack on monarchy in general and Charles in particular: he was lucky to escape – very narrowly – the traitor's death by hanging, disembowelling and quartering which so many of his friends and colleagues suffered.

Milton had also won notoriety by defending in 1643–4 divorce in the event of married couples proving mutually incompatible; from the 1650s he was working on *Of Christian Doctrine*. Under the Presbyterian Blasphemy Ordinance of 1648 this treatise would have rendered him liable

3. *BMW*, I, pp. 84, 99.
4. Joseph Wittreich, *Feminist Milton* (Cornell U.P., 1987), pp. 94–109.
5. See p. 441 below.

to five death sentences and eight sentences of life imprisonment. He was not an orthodox reader of the Bible.[6]

Milton was more politically committed than Bunyan. The background for *Paradise Lost*, *Paradise Regained* and *Samson Agonistes* is the defeat of the cause in which Milton had believed so profoundly and to which he had sacrificed so much. In his Preface to *Of Christian Doctrine* he scarifies 'those two repulsive afflictions, tyranny and superstition', and insists on the right and duty to resist tyranny. He pleads for 'free discussion and inquiry', without which 'violence alone prevails; and it is disgraceful and disgusting that the Christian religion should be supported by violence'.[7] He cannot have had much hope for free discussion or religious freedom after 1660. His *Eikonoklastes* and *Defence of the People of England* were burnt by the public hangman, and *Of Christian Doctrine* was unprintable.

In this work it has been estimated that Milton cites over 8,000 proof texts.[8] This contrasts sharply with the Commonplace Book which he started to keep around 1630, in which there is virtually no mention of the Bible. Milton began his self-education by studying ancient history and philosophy together with the Christian Fathers. But he was brought up on the Bible; the outline for tragedies which he drew up, probably in the years immediately before the civil war, contains more themes from the Bible than from English history.[9] Biblical references are frequent in his early poems, still more so in his polemical tracts. In the first thirteen lines of *Paradise Lost*, in which Milton announces his theme, there are no less than fifteen Biblical quotations or echoes.[10] In *Prelaticall Episcopacy* (1641) he insists on 'the all-sufficiency' that Scripture 'hath to furnish us . . . with all . . . spiritual knowledge'.[11] In the following year he wrote of 'that book, within whose sacred context all wisdom is enfolded'.[12]

6. M. A. Larson, 'Milton and Servetus', *Philological Quarterly*, XLI (1926), p. 891.

7. *MCPW*, VI, pp. 118, 121–3. In the 1650s Milton regularly linked tyranny and superstition (ibid., IV, p. 535, VII, p. 421). In *Of Christian Doctrine* he added money to the violence with which the state church is supported – referring to tithes (ibid., VI, pp. 597–8). I have discussed the political background to *Of Christian Doctrine* more fully in *MER*, Chapter 18. See also W. Empson, *Milton's God* (1961), pp. 203–10.

8. *MCPW*, VI, p. 106; Roger Lejosne, *La Raison dans l'oeuvre de John Milton* (Paris, 1981), p. 63 and references there cited.

9. *MCPW*, I, pp. 344–528; VIII, pp. 539–85.

10. J. H. Simms, *The Bible in Milton's Epics*, pp. 10–11; cf. pp. 128–9 – Biblical echoes at the end of the poem.

11. *MCPW*, I, p. 625.

12. Ibid., I, p. 747.

It seems to have been the vigorous discussions and polemics of the forties and fifties that decided him to build up his own *summa* based on *sola Scriptura*. If *Of Christian Doctrine* had been published in the seventeenth century it might have expedited the decline in the authority of the Bible. Milton believed that 'the rule and canon of faith is Scripture alone'; but Scripture must be interpreted. He carried the protestant principle of the priesthood of all believers to its logical extreme. 'No one else can usefully interpret [the Bible] for him, unless that person's interpretation coincides with the one he makes for himself and his own conscience'. 'Each man is his own arbitrator'.[13]

Milton believed that parts of the Bible had been lost and that both testaments, especially the New Testament, were textually corrupt; this too meant that 'all things are eventually to be referred to the Spirit and the unwritten word'.[14] Some of Milton's interpretations are idiosyncratic. He persuaded himself, *à propos* divorce, 'that it is absolutely certain that the word 'fornication' means not so much adultery as *the wife's* constant contrariness, faithlessness and disobedience' (Deuteronomy XXIV.1, Judges XIX.2 – and other references cited in *Tetrachordon*).[15]

In a tantalizing phrase, Milton admitted that he was 'not one of those who consider the decalogue a faultless moral code'. He believed that 'we are released from the decalogue', and that 'the practice of the saints interprets the commandments'.[16] That opens wide doors. His verdict on the doctrine of transubstantiation was that it was 'practically turning the Lord's supper into a cannibal feast', which was 'utterly alien to reason, common sense and human behaviour'.[17]

Arguing that divine decrees are conditional, not absolute, Milton quotes God's words in Exodus VIII.17: 'I have come down . . . to liberate them . . . and to lead them out into a good land'. 'In fact', Milton added grimly, 'they perished in the desert' – because, like the people of England, they were incapable of profiting by the opportunity God gave them. Having established to his own satisfaction the conditionality of God's decrees, Milton felt himself entitled to say that 'Moses forgot' this when in Exodus XXXII.32–3 he quoted God as saying 'I shall blot out from my book the man that rises against me'.[18]

13. *MCPW*, VI, pp. 583–5.
14. Ibid., pp. 586–90.
15. Ibid., pp. 378–81. My italics.
16. Ibid., pp. 711, 526, 368.
17. Ibid., p. 554.
18. Ibid., pp. 83–6, 155–66, 173, 178.

From an early date Milton insisted that 'the general end of every [Biblical] ordinance . . . is the good of man, yea his temporal good not excluded'. 'It is not the stubborn letter must govern us'.[19] So he was able to explain away Christ's apparent prohibition of divorce except in case of adultery. The authority of the text was undermined by his insistence on human reason, on the spirit within believers; decisions were left to individual consciences, not to the pronouncements of a church. It was noble; but it destroyed the Bible's unique authority.

Nevertheless, the Bible remained of great significance. Milton cited Deuteronomy XXVIII: if you obey God's voice and observe his commandments, God will set you on high above all nations of the earth, and lead you to prosperity and power. But if not, you will be accursed, subject to poverty, powerlessness and failure. The Lord will scatter you among all people from one end of the world to the other. Milton called this 'a chapter which should be read again and again by those who have the direction of political affairs'.[20] In his other writings Milton quotes the New Testament more frequently than the Old: in *Of Christian Doctrine* the Old Testament predominates. Like John Owen preaching to Parliament in October 1652, Milton found the Old Testament especially useful in discussing kings and magistrates; though Milton laid more emphasis on justifying their election.[21]

There is no reason to suppose that Milton became any less radical as he grew older; there is much evidence to the contrary. He continued to work on *Of Christian Doctrine* whilst writing *Paradise Lost* and *Samson Agonistes*. It was necessary to justify the ways of God to his servants, since he appeared to have let them down after they had laboured and suffered so much. It was also necessary to puzzle out a way forward for the defeated remnant.[22] That is why Milton discreetly proclaimed his continuing loyalty (writing under censorship):

> I sing . . . unchanged,
>> . . . though fallen on evil days,
> On evil days though fallen and evil tongues.

Milton's reputation had not hitherto been that of a great poet, but of the

19. Ibid., II, pp. 623, 604.
20. Ibid., V, p. 151.
21. Fletcher, *Use of the Bible in Milton's Prose* (Illinois U.P., 1929), pp. 108–18; *MCPW*, VI, pp. 795–6, 805, *FS*, XXXIV, pp. 160–61.
22. For the sense that God was on trial after 1660, see 'God and the English Revolution' in my *Religion and Politics*, pp. 332–3.

defender of regicide and the English Revolution to a hostile Europe. His 'fit audience' would understand that it was in this respect that he was 'unchanged'. Stella Revard is quite right to argue that in *Paradise Lost* Milton expects us to see a reference to the English civil war in the 'particular tyrants, . . . now a Nimrod, now a Pharaoh, now a Charles', who all derive from Satan. *Paradise Lost* is thus, among other things, about the struggle between Charles I and 'the battling soldiers of the Commonwealth' and its aftermath.[23]

Milton inserts his political points when and as he can, unobtrusively. The conclusion that Adam draws from the Archangel Michael's gloomy preview of human history is that we should not be in too ambitious a hurry, but proceed

> by small
> Accomplishing great things, by things deemed weak
> Subverting worldly strong, and worldly wise
> By simply meek (*PL*, XII.566–9).

As soon as we ask ourselves why Adam – lord of the world, undisputed sovereign of his kingdom of two – should wish to subvert 'worldly strong', it is obvious that Adam is in fact addressing the supporters of the Good Old Cause in the England of the 1660s. The rebel angels who revolted against God were guilty of pride, ambition, self-interest, greed – the vices which Milton believed had led to the fall of the Commonwealth. But he does not fail to point out that the devils were more united among themselves than those who supported better causes. In *Paradise Regained* the Son of God faces and overcomes the temptations to which the English revolutionaries had succumbed. Why is the hero of *Paradise Regained* regularly referred to as 'the Son of God' rather than Jesus or Christ? Satan gives us the answer: 'all men are sons of God'. The hero of *Paradise Regained* represents humanity: Milton was always unsound on the Trinity. But putting the explanatory words into Satan's mouth absolves the poet of responsibility for the heresy. John the Baptist baptized the Son of God by total immersion, which Milton – following Servetus – believed to be the correct form of baptism:[24] but the scene is described by Satan.

23. Revard, *The War in Heaven*: Paradise Lost *and the Tradition of Satan's Rebellion* (Cornell U.P., 1980), pp. 292–8. Cf. Loewenstein, *Milton and the Drama of History*, pp. 96–7, 105.

24. Williams, *Wilderness and Paradise*, p. 71.

Milton's poetry was always political, from *Lycidas*[25] and *Comus*[26] onwards. He makes little reference to the traditional myths which radicals employed to make social points. Cain and Abel get thirty lines in Book II of *Paradise Lost*: Jacob's dream 'when he from Esau fled', and that only, is mentioned in Book II (510–22). In *Of Christian Doctrine* Esau and Jacob are used – paradoxically – against any defence of a decree of reprobation, whether Calvinist or Muggletonian. 'The promise . . . is not to the children of Abraham in a physical sense, but to the children of his faith who received Christ, . . . to believers'.[27] Milton cited Abraham to defend his belief in the lawfulness of polygamy and divorce, David, Gideon and Joash for polygamy. (Defoe's Roxana also quoted the patriarchs for polygamy, though Defoe – unlike Milton – was no supporter of polygamy.) Moses, Rahab, Ehud, Jael and David all lied in a way which Milton held to be justified.[28]

Noah is treated at length in Book XI of *Paradise Lost*, mainly to emphasize that

> The conquered also and enslaved by war
> Shall with their freedom lost all virtue lose (lines 796–7).

Noah was 'the one just man alive', who saved humanity from destruction though ignored by his compatriots (lines 712–901). Similarly when God was 'wearied' with the 'iniquities' of mankind he selected Abraham, 'one faithful man', who left 'his gods, his friends and native soil' to journey to Canaan (XII.113–54). Moses leads his people 'to the land/Promised to Abraham and his seed' (XII.259–60), despite the wish of some to choose 'rather/Inglorious life with servitude' and return to Egypt (XII.216–21).[29] The one just man who saves his people is rarely a ruler.

The Old Testament supplied evidence for attacks on monarchy and royal courts. Milton had once thought of writing tragedies on Ahab and Jezebel, as well as on Jeroboam (the 'rebel king', who 'made religion

25. D. S. Berkeley, *Inwrought with Figures Dim* (The Hague, 1974), *passim*; J. Martin Evans, *The Road from Horton: Looking Backwards in* Lycidas (Victoria U.P., 1983), *passim*.

26. See especially C. C. Brown, *John Milton's Aristocratic Entertainments* (Cambridge U.P., 1985); Michael Wilding, *Dragon's Teeth: Literature in the English Revolution*, esp. Chapter 3; Roger Lejosne, 'Le Personnage Muet dans *Comus*', in *John Milton: Comus or a Maske at Ludlow Castle* (ed. A. Himy, Paris, 1990), pp. 63–71.

27. *MCPW*, VI, p. 197.

28. Ibid., pp. 177, 196–7, 337, 366–7, 377, 386, 783–4, 795–7, 805.

29. Ibid., VII, p. 461. For other examples see *MER*, pp. 206–7.

conform to his politic interests'). 'The murderous king' Herod gets a brief mention, unnamed, in *Paradise Regained* (II.71). In *Eikonoklastes* Charles I is described as worse than Ahab, Jeroboam, Rehoboam or Saul, comparable with the wilful apostate Ahaz, with Nimrod, Balak and Agag. Milton noted that 'the cowardly and idolatrous King Amaziah' was put to death by his own people, and that his own subjects drove out Nebuchadnezzar. Belial,

> than whom a spirit more lewd
> Fell not from heaven, or more gross to love
> Vice for itself,

is often found 'in temples and at altars'. 'In courts and palaces he also *reigns*' (my italics). In the *Of Christian Doctrine* Milton gave many Biblical references for 'the immorality of royal courts'.[30]

The sun was an accepted metaphor for monarchy. It was pretty seditious for the anonymous author of *Machiavel: As He lately appeared to his deare Sons, the Modern Projectors*, to refer in 1641 to Parliament as 'our bright English sun'.[31] In *Paradise Lost* Milton described Satan in hell:

> as when the sun new risen
> Looks through the horizontal misty air
> Shorn of his beams, or from behind the moon
> In dim eclipse disastrous twilight sheds
> On half the nations, and with fear of change
> Perplexes monarchs (I.594–9).

This passage is said to have alarmed the censor: the king/sun is not only being eclipsed, it is also associated with Satan.[32] (John Booker's almanac had been censored in 1639 for referring to an eclipse.)[33] Preston had compared good kings to brightly shining comets; those who suffered idolatry and superstition at home, or allied with Assyria and Egypt abroad, fell to the earth and vanished.[34] It was not difficult to imagine who Assyria and Egypt might be.

30. Ibid., I, p. 574; III, pp. 208–9, 213–16, 234, 365, 393–4, 534–5, 554, 569–70, 600; IV, pp. 201, 335, 370–71, 403–8, 435; VI, pp. 177, 367, 796–7; VII, p. 266; *PL*, I. 470–76, 484–5, 490–520, XII. 173, 214; *PR*, I. 372–6, II. 71, III. 242.
31. Op. cit., quoted by Gerald MacLean, *Time's Witness*, p. 103.
32. N. H. Keeble, *The Literary Culture of Nonconformity*, p. 119.
33. [Booker], *Mercurius Coelicus* (1644), pp. 1–2. Booker had to wait till then to be able to publish such a fact.
34. Preston, *Sermons Preached before his Majestie* (4th impression, 1634), p. 55.

Good kings are rarer than bad in Milton, but there are a few. 'Good Josiah' destroyed idols:[35] and there are Hezekiah, Asa, Nehemiah and Jehoshaphat. David and Solomon were a little ambiguous.[36] In *The Tenure of Kings and Magistrates* Milton praised David's sanctified prudence, and used him as a foil to Charles I in *Eikonoklastes* and the *Defence of the People of England*.[37] But he reserved his highest praise for 'the matchless Gideon', 'greater than a king', who overthrew the altars of Baal, smote the Midianites and Amalekites, and refused a crown when it was offered to him.[38] Similarly Marvell pointedly expressed his disapproval of the possibility of Oliver Cromwell becoming king by comparing him in *The First Anniversary* (1655) not with the obvious David but with Noah, Gideon and Elijah.[39] Anna Trapnel had seen Oliver Cromwell as Gideon.[40] Those good republicans Sir Henry Vane and Edmund Ludlow both spoke up for Gideon.[41] As against kings and empire builders, the Son of God in *Paradise Regained* praised men who

> have oft attained
> In lowest poverty to highest deeds;
> Gideon and Jephtha and the shepherd lad,

David (II.436–42). Job was

> Made famous in a land and time obscure, . . .
>
> Without ambition, war or violence;
> By deeds of peace, by wisdom eminent,
> By patience, temperance (*PR*, III.88–114.)

Howard Schulz argued persuasively that the temptation of learning in *Paradise Regained* is a rejection of 'the abuses of universities, academic

---

35. *PL*, I. 416–18; *MCPW*, VIII, pp. 251, 266; *PL*, I. 487.
36. Ibid., VIII, p. 556 – tragedies; II, p. 623; IV, pp. 371–3, 403–4; VI, pp. 333, 343–4, 367, 469, 761, 779–80; cf. Stock, op. cit., p. 72. Milton had projected a tragedy on Hezekiah (*MCPW*, VIII, p. 557).
37. *MCPW*, III, pp. 240, 547, 571; IV, p. 408.
38. Ibid., IV, p. 370; *PR*, II. 439; *Samson Agonistes*, lines 279–80; *MCPW*, VIII, p. 556 – two projected plays, one significantly entitled *Gideon Idoloclastes*.
39. S. Zwicker, 'Models of Government in Marvell's "The First Anniversary"', *Criticism*, XVI (1974), pp. 8–10.
40. Trapnel, *The Cry of a Stone* (1650), pp. 6, 30, 35, 52.
41. Vane, *The Retired Mans Meditations* (1655), pp. 381–2; Ludlow, *A Voyce from the Watch Tower*, pp. 135–6, 301.

appointments and hirelings' divinity'.[42] 'Learned Mr Milton' was not opposed to learning as such. But the learning of the universities seemed to him Antichristian, part of a system of exploitation and oppression. University learning was attacked on these grounds by most radicals, from Cobbler How to William Dell, Master of Gonville and Caius College – and Bunyan. University learning leads to contempt for the vulgar and to social recognition. It was Satan who asked the Son of God

> Without their learning, how wilt thou with them
> Or they with thee hold conversation meet? (*PR*, IV.231–2).[43]

Milton saw bishops as agents through whom Charles had proposed to force Antichristian tyranny upon England, a nation of prophets.[44] So when in 1673, in his (necessarily) very carefully worded *Of True Religion, Heresie, Schism, Toleration*, Milton rejoiced that England had 'shaken off [the Pope's] Babylonish yoke', we may easily guess who as well as papists were included among the 'spies and agents' with which the Babylonians were still trying to 'seduce, corrupt and pervert as many as they can of the people'.[45] Thanks to the 'lavish superstition' of the Emperor Constantine, bishops had set up 'Mammon and their belly' as gods. Against the 'great riches' which Constantine had given to the clergy, against the 'deluge of ceremonies' which Laud called 'the beauty of holiness', Milton set 'the beauty of inward sanctity', preferring 'a homely and yeomanly religion' to the 'gorgeous solemnities of paganism' which the Roman church had inherited.[46]

Professor Radzinowicz suggested that Milton may have had political objectives in mind when he translated a number of Psalms in 1648 and 1653.[47] It may be worth adding a few words to her study of the context. Looking back, it is certainly true that Milton's paraphrase of Psalm CXLVI in 1623–4 had political overtones. It was the Psalm sung in St Paul's Cathedral in October 1623 when Prince Charles returned from Spain

---

42. Schultz, *Milton and Forbidden Knowledge* (New York, 1955), pp. 226–7.

43. See *MER*, pp. 423–6.

44. *MCPW*, II, pp. 442, 510, 536–7; cf. Numbers XXII–III. Charles I had previously waged 'Antichristian war against the poor protestants of [La] Rochelle' (*MCPW*, III, pp. 436–7).

45. Ibid., VIII, p. 430.

46. Ibid., I, pp. 551–60, 576–9. Marvell too saw Constantine as the villain of the early history of Christianity (*The Rehearsal Transpros'd*, p. 237).

47. M. A. Radzinowicz, *Toward Samson Agonistes: The Growth of Milton's Mind* (Princeton U.P., 1978), pp. 198–208, and references there cited.

without the Popish Infanta whom he had gone to woo: 'When Israel came out of Egypt and the house of Jacob from among the barbarous people'. Milton made this

> When the blest seed of Terah's faithful son
> After long toil their liberty had won.

In July 1647 the Westminster Assembly of Divines appointed a committee to review Rous's translation of the Psalms. The Committee divided the Psalms into four groups, the third of which began with Psalm LXXX. In April 1648 Milton translated Psalms LXXX–LXXXVIII. The situation then must have looked grim to radical supporters of Parliament. Victory in the civil war had been followed by disagreements among the victors about how to deal with the captured King, between conservative 'Presbyterians' and the Army and Parliamentary 'Independents'. Quarrels between generals and rank and file had very nearly split the Army. A Presbyterian–royalist rising was being planned. The former Parliamentarian Colonel John Poyer seized Pembroke in South Wales on 23 March. Four days later, the anniversary of the King's accession, more bonfires were lighted in London than at any time since his return – unmarried – from Spain twenty-five years earlier. The overwhelming preponderance of City opinion seems to have been in favour of his restoration to power. A formidable riot on 9–10 April had to be suppressed by the Army. Prince Charles announced his readiness to return to England.

Fortified by these events, the King refused to accept the terms which had been offered to him, and on 6 April attempted to escape. Meanwhile in Ireland the English commander, the Earl of Inchiquin, had declared for the King (3 April). On 28–9 April Scottish forces seized Berwick and Carlisle. There were supporting movements in South Wales, in Kent and the eastern counties of England. The Second Civil War had begun.

Royalist victory would mean the end of all Milton's hopes. The Geneva Bible's introductory Argument to the Psalms summarized: 'the wicked and the persecutors of the children of God shall see how the hand of God is ever against them, . . . though he suffer them to prosper for a while'. Here are some of the Geneva version's embattled notes to Psalms LXXX to LXXXVIII, which must have seemed relevant to these events. Psalm LXXX is described as 'a lamentable prayer to God to help the miseries of his church', which seems to have lost the favour which the Lord originally showed to it. 'Declare again thy love', the Psalmist implores, 'and finish the work that thou hast begun'. 'If the Israelites had not broken covenant with God', the margin to Psalm LXXXI tells us, 'he would have given them victory over their enemies'.[48] 'If princes and judges do not their duty', says the comment on Psalm LXXXII, 'God will take vengeance on them'. 'No title of honour shall excuse you' – which in April 1648 might have seemed to imply a threat to Parliament from the Army.

Calvin was very severe on kings and rulers in his commentary on Psalm LXXXII. Béza's argument ran: 'faults of magistrates' are 'to be called to account'. 'You shall die, O ye kings, and you shall stand at my judgment seat'. Wither insisted that this Psalm was to be 'sung before those who advise in the great affairs of Church or Commonwealth, to remind them of their duties', for it 'instructs and reproves princes, pastors and magistrates abusing their authority'. Wither prayed 'Grant, almighty God, that they to whom thou committest the government of thy churches and commonweals may not (as it often happeneth) be their greatest oppressors'. 'God condemneth wicked governors' was William Barton's simpler comment.[49]

'The people of Israel', said the Geneva Bible's headnote to Psalm LXXXIII, 'pray unto the Lord to deliver them from their enemies both at home and far off, which imagined nothing but their destruction'. 'God is glorified in the destruction of persecutors', Barton commented on this Psalm. 'There can be no moderation nor equity where proud tyrants reign' (Psalm LXXXVI). The faithful, 'sore afflicted by sickness, persecutions and adversity', said his comment on Psalm LXXXVIII, are 'as it were left of God without any consolation'. Yet the Psalmist 'calleth on God by faith and striveth against desperation'.

Milton's translation of Psalms II to VIII he dates precisely 8 to 14 August 1653. (Psalm I is dated only 1653.) This too was a crucial moment in the history of the Revolution. The Rump of the Long Parliament had been dissolved and replaced by the nominated Barebones assembly. That had meant a breach with the republican Independents, and inevitably led to a revival of royalist hopes. On 10 August the Council of State proposed to set up a High Court of Justice to try royalist plotters *without a jury*. The new assembly divided into radical and conservative wings, of which the latter ultimately proved the stronger. On 15 July a

---

48. These phrases from the Geneva Bible's chapter headings are repeated verbatim in the headnotes to the Sternhold and Hopkins psalter of 1566. This is the case with many psalms.
49. His *Book of Psalms in Meter* was first published in 1644. A revised edition appeared in 1645, and many later.

motion to abolish tithes – whose abolition Milton held to be essential to religious freedom – was only just defeated. The Leveller John Lilburne, returned from the exile to which the Long Parliament had condemned him, was at once arrested, and his trial was ordered. Petitioners supporting him were also arrested. The dissolution of the Rump did not seem likely to forward the radical causes in which Milton believed. He had recently become completely blind.

Again the Geneva margin fitted Milton's defensive mood. 'Though the wicked seem to bear the swinge[50] in this world, yet the Lord driveth them down' (Psalm I). David 'exhorteth kings and rulers that . . . it is vain to resist God' (Psalm II). 'Be the dangers never so great, yet hath God every means to deliver his' (Psalm III). God is 'the defender of my just cause' (Psalm IV). 'When the wicked think that the godly shall perish, God delivereth them suddenly, and destroyeth their enemies' (Psalm VI). Psalm II was addressed to kings. Sternhold's 1551 translation read

> Now ye, O kings, and rulers all
> Be wise therefore and learned. . . .
> Lest in his wrath you perish all.

Wither had

> Kiss the Son, lest wroth he turn
> And overthrow you in your way.

God's grisly jokes, as Empson called them, and his mockery of human weakness, which some have found offensive in *Paradise Lost*, derive from the authority of the psalms. Milton's version of Psalm II ran:

> He who in heaven doth dwell
> Shall laugh, the Lord shall scoff them;

– 'them' are 'the kings of the earth and princes'. Psalm LII.6 says that 'the righteous . . . shall laugh at . . . the man [of power] . . . that trusted unto the multitude of his riches'. Psalms XXXVII and LIX also depict God laughing at the wicked and the heathen, upon whom retribution will shortly fall. In *Paradise Lost* God is rather more intellectual: he found amusing men's attempts to explain the workings of the heavenly bodies, 'their quaint opinions wide'. He laughed at Nimrod (*PL*, XII. 52, 59–62).

---

50. Obsolete, meaning sway, authority, influence (*OED*).

Professor Radzinowicz argues persuasively for the influence of Psalms on *Samson Agonistes*.[51] I have discussed the poem elsewhere. But one or two points are relevant here. First, those critics who find Samson's blood-thirstiness shocking must be very ignorant of Old Testament history, where God repeatedly calls for the extirpation of whole tribes and peoples, women and children included, who have incurred his enmity. In Bale's play, *Gods Promises*, God himself is made to boast of how he slew 50,000 men in a day

> For the wicked sin of filthy idolatry;
> In the time of Ahaz, an hundred thousand and twenty
> Were slain at one time, for their idolatry.
> Two hundred thousand from thence were captive led.[52]

'Where God condemneth, beware of pity', Bishop Babington said à propos Exodus XXXIV.12–13.[53] 'If God so rejoice in the execution of his wrath upon wicked men', Jeremiah Burroughs reasonably observed, 'then the saints also may rejoice'.[54] Milton agreed that we were not to argue with God, and in *Of Christian Doctrine* cited many texts – including Psalms XXXI.7 and CXXXIX.21 – to demonstrate that it was a religious duty to hate the enemies of God or the church. 'We are even commanded to curse, in public prayer, the enemies of God and the church'.[55] We may compare the gentle Traherne, who laid it down that 'in strict justice we must render hatred to whom hatred is due'.[56] To whom more than the enemies of God? In Milton's case, as in the Psalmist's, the enemies of God turn out to be the enemies of the writer (Psalms XVIII.40, XL.14–17, XLI.5–11).

Samson is only one of many elect persons who fell into sin and recovered grace by repentance. I cited above Richard Bernard's sardonic comments on Jacob.[57] He was equally forthright about Samson. 'Samson kept company with a whore . . . to whom he revealed where his strength lay, whereby the vow of a Nazarite . . . was broken. Such was yet God's mercy

51. Radzinowicz, op. cit., pp. 204–60.
52. Bale, *Dramatic Works*, pp. 109–15.
53. Babington, *Comfortable Notes Upon . . . Exodus and Leviticus*, p. 344.
54. Burroughs, *Hosea*, Chapters 8–10 (1650), p. 175, Chapter IX.5. The reference is to Psalm LVIII.10.
55. *MCPW*, VI, pp. 675 and 743, the latter quoting Psalm CXXXIX.21 and Luke XIV.26.
56. Traherne, *The Way to Blessedness*, p. 108.
57. See p. 205 above.

to him . . . as that he heard his prayers and increased his strength, so as he pulled down the house on the Philistines his enemies'.[58] It is necessary to make these points because Professor Wittreich has argued recently that Milton did not intend Samson to be a type of Christ or hero, but a damned soul. There were those who held such a view of Samson in the seventeenth century, but they were people of a very different political outlook from Milton.[59] In Fast Sermons Samson is always treated as a Christian hero. Milton is quite specific that 'Scripture everywhere declares that . . . reprobation is rescinded by repentance'.[60]

There are many Biblical precedents for the 'rousing motions' which Samson often received, one of which led to his final act of strength. Jehu was inspired 'by the motion of the spirit of God' to have Jezebel killed.[61] For a useful corrective to 'commentators who wish to see Milton as a more temperate thinker and writer in his later works', see David Loewenstein, *Milton and the Drama of History*.[62]

II. Bunyan

Unlike Milton, Bunyan was not primarily a politician. Twenty years younger, Bunyan came to take for granted the religious liberty for which Milton had to fight. Unlike Milton, Bunyan went to no grammar school, so far as we know, certainly to no university. He was never, like Milton, maintained 'out of the sweat of other men'.[63] Bunyan's education came from his two and a half years in the Parliamentarian army from 1644 to 1647. These must have been traumatic for the country yokel, coming from what he with some exaggeration called one of the 'meanest and most despised of all the families of the land'.[64] The war ended when he had been in the army for six months; for the next two years, at the susceptible age of sixteen and a half to eighteen and a half, he had little

---

58. Bernard, *Thesaurus Biblicum*, p. 71.
59. I have argued this case in 'Samson Agonistes again', *Literature and History*, 2nd series, I, 1990.
60. *MCPW*, VI, p. 191.
61. II Kings IX.33, Geneva margin. Cf. the Duke of Newcastle on men who say the Old Testament authorized them to commit treason, quoted on p. 107 above.
62. Loewenstein, op. cit. (Cambridge U.P., 1990), esp. pp. 150–51. The operative words are 'wish to see'.
63. *MCPW*, I, p. 804.
64. *Grace Abounding*, p. 5.

to do but talk and listen. *Grace Abounding* tells us that he became well acquainted with radical doctrines, especially those of the Ranters; we know from the agitated correspondence of the commander of Bunyan's garrison town, Newport Pagnell, that just such talk went on there.[65] Bunyan found the sexual libertinism and sceptical questioning of the Bible that he listened to quite attractive, 'I being but a young man and my nature in its prime'.[66] When he was demobilized he took the lead of a group of wide boys in his village. He no doubt later exaggerated their drunkenness and sexual activities; but there is no escaping the libertine ideas which he records in *Grace Abounding*, and which he continued to struggle with for the rest of his life.[67]

The Army seized power in 1647, Charles I was tried and executed in January 1649. But the radical moment soon passed, and Bunyan experienced a profound spiritual crisis. He was overwhelmed by the recollection of Esau who sold his birthright; and 'afterwards, when he would have inherited the blessing, he was rejected, for he found no place of repentance, though he sought it carefully with tears' (Hebrews XII.16–17). For two years Bunyan was haunted by fear that he had sold his birthright. 'What have I disinherited my soul of?' he cried. He returned again and again to this threatening text.[68] In *The Pilgrim's Progress* there was a 'byway to hell, a way that hypocrites go in at' for 'such as sell their birthright with Esau'.[69]

The crisis was resolved, Bunyan tells us, when he overheard two or three poor women sitting in the sun talking about the things of God 'as if joy did make them speak'.[70] Bunyan joined them, then joined their Bedford congregation, and soon discovered his true vocation as a preacher. The scene is emblematic. The wide boy found assurance from the poor old women, who knew so much more about the things of God than the clever 'intellectuals' whose ideas had tempted Bunyan. He never forgot his humble origins. Although no politician, he was always, on all issues, staunchly and theologically on the side of the poor and unprivileged against their betters. One of his most successful early sermons was on the parable of Dives and Lazarus – the rich man who goes to hell, and there is granted a glimpse in heaven of the 'poor scabbed creep-hedge' whom he had spurned as he sat

65. Ed. H. G. Tibbutt, *The Letter-Books 1644–1645 of Sir Samuel Luke* (1963), *passim*.
66. *Grace Abounding*, p. 17.
67. Ibid., pp. 7–17.
68. Ibid., pp. 45–72. Bunyan compared himself to Cain (ibid., p. 50).
69. *PP*, pp. 11, 122, 127–8.
70. *Grace Abounding*, pp. 14–15.

at the rich man's gate hoping for alms. But Lazarus cannot help him. It is too late, as it had been too late for Esau to repent. Bunyan's sermon was a fierce and Biblically supported attack on the rich generally, spiced with what I suspect were colourful references to local Bedford gentry. 'The great ones of the world . . . will build houses for their dogs, when the saints must be glad to wander and lodge in dens and caves of the earth'. (The dreamer of *The Pilgrim's Progress* was sleeping in a den.) Rich landlords eject their godly tenants or 'pull down the house over their heads'. Bunyan included the clergy in the denunciation: they preach 'for filthy lucre's sake'.[71]

The gentry got their revenge after 1660. Bunyan was arrested for preaching without being ordained, and ordered to give an undertaking to stop. He refused, claiming preaching as his divine vocation. His vocation was that of a tinker, he was told: and he went to prison for what turned out to be twelve years, longer than any but the most notorious political leaders. In prison he wrote *The Pilgrim's Progress*. When he was released, Bunyan started to break the law again. He insisted steadily on the right and duty of God's servants to worship him in the way they thought he wished, and for that cause he was prepared to undergo any suffering.

The radicals of the revolutionary decades help us to understand Bunyan. He is close to Winstanley, the Ranters and the Muggletonians in his social use of the legends of Cain and Abel, Esau and Jacob. In *The Holy War* only the inhabitants of Mansoul can be saved, as for Reeve and Muggleton it was only the spiritual descendants of Abel. This fuses with the radical theory of the Norman Yoke. Natives of Mansoul were distinguished from Diabolonians who 'came with the tyrant when he invaded', and used an 'outlandish' speech.[72] For Winstanley and other radicals the Normans were the gentry and nobility.

For Bunyan the struggle between good and evil began in the first week of creation: light against darkness, the waters above the firmament against those below. Humanity became involved in this cosmic conflict, first with the sin of Adam and Eve, then with Cain's murder of Abel. This is treated as a symbolic political act. After murdering his brother, Cain 'seeks to be a head or monarch'. He is a tyrant: 'tyrants matter nothing, neither nearness of kin, nor how much they destroy'. 'If tyrants should have their will, even to the destroying all the remnant of God,

71. Bunyan, *A Few Sighs from Hell* (1658), *BMW*, I, pp. 252, 257, 314.
72. Bunyan, *The Holy War*, pp. 8, 119–23, 138, 149, 161, and *passim*.

their sacrifice and worship would be yet before God as abominable as they were before'. Cain endeavours 'the extirpating of all true religion out of the world'.[73] (Here we must remember that Bunyan, unlike Winstanley, Coppe and Reeve, wrote under a strict censorship, and with the reputation of a man who had served a prison sentence for breaking the law of the land.)

'The proper voice of all the blood of the godly', Bunyan wrote, 'is to call for vengeance on the persecutors, even from the blood of Abel to the blood of Zacharias that was slain between the altar and the temple'. The words recall Coppe. 'To maintain God's truth', Bunyan recognized, 'cannot be done but with great hazard so long as Cain or his offspring remain'. But the godly must learn 'to be quiet and patient under the hand of wicked bloodthirsty men', to suffer passively. 'Let Cain and God alone, and do you mind faith and patience; suffer with Abel until your righteous blood be spilt'. 'When men persecute the worship and people of God, as Cain did his blessed and religious brother', they are 'beyond grace and forgiveness'. Yet God forbade men to take vengeance on Cain. By becoming a persecutor, he had set himself against God. 'Such an one the Christian must let alone and stand off from, that God may have his full blow at him in his time'. Those last words were written in 1684, at the height of persecution. It was a neat way, under censorship, of proclaiming Bunyan's doctrine of non-resistance whilst threatening a worse fate to persecutors. Bunyan managed simultaneously to get in a blow at social climbers within his own congregation when he added that Cain had been 'a professor' – i.e. a member of the church, and he 'had yet a notable share' of the blessings of this world.[74]

In a tract published in 1665, whilst Bunyan was still in prison, he attributed to persecutors 'the very heart of Cain the murderer, of Judas the traitor'. But eventually hypocritical traitors will be judged, 'be thou King or Keser'.[75] In a later pamphlet he spoke again of the 'greatness' of 'men of a persecuting spirit'. By such means he made his points without running foul of the censorship. In addition to associating the first murderer with monarchy and persecution, Bunyan stresses the social moral of the story. Originally, he tells us, 'Cain was the man in favour, even he that should . . . have enjoyed the inheritance; . . . but Abel was set in the lower rank'.

73. Offor, II, pp. 419, 445–7.
74. *BMW*, X, p. 100: Offor, II, pp. 447–54; *BMW*, V, p. 47; cf. Smith, *Ranter Writings*, p. 88.
75. *BMW*, III, pp. 261, 275.

Yet 'the blessing of grace is not led by outward order'. 'It is the lot of Cain's brood to be lords and rulers first, while Abel and his generation have their necks under persecution.'[76]

From the example of Cain, Bunyan suggested that persecutors put themselves 'beyond the reach of God's mercy'. And he quoted Ezekiel XXXV.6: 'sith thou hast not hated blood, even blood shall pursue thee.' Noah's was the first gathered church, maintaining 'a separation from the accursed children of Cain'. Noah's separation teaches us 'not to fear the faces of men, no not the faces of the mighty'. Bunyan's reference to the Church of England here was made explicit by making 'the locusts of Egypt' a type of 'our graceless clergy' of the state church.[77] The parable of the unjust judge and the poor widow in St Luke's Gospel was designed, he said, 'for the relief of those that are under the hand of cruel tyrants'.[78] Bunyan gives a social twist to Nehemiah III.5 about the building of Jerusalem after the captivity: 'their nobles put not their hands to the work of the Lord' (cf. Geneva margin: 'the rich and mighty'). 'All their princes shall be nothing, saith the prophet, and when they call their nobles to the kingdom, none shall be there'.[79] Few peers and gentlemen had supported Parliament, Calamy reminded the House of Lords in June 1643.[80] Richard Bernard, whose *Isle of Man* (1627) Bunyan had almost certainly read, had used his *Commentary on Ruth* to mount a fierce attack on idle rentiers, 'who brag of their gentry'. Moses 'pleaded not his birth, his gentry: he lived in a calling'.[81] Noah, Daniel, Jeremiah and Paul were all open to charges of treason or sedition, said Bunyan; but 'a man is not to be counted an offender how contrary soever he lieth, in doctrine or practice, to men etc., if both have the command of God and are surely grounded upon the words of his mouth'. 'What God hath said in his Word, how offensive soever it be to ungodly men, that we that are Christians ought to observe'.[82]

Bunyan is one of the most class-conscious writers in English literature. In *The Pilgrim's Progress* and *The Holy War* undesirable characters are almost

76. Offor, II, pp. 442, 445.
77. Ibid., II, pp. 445–50, 460, 475. Bunyan here uses the A.V. The Geneva version differs.
78. *BMW*, X, pp. 113–18, 196–7.
79. Ibid., III, pp. 85, 138; cf. pp. 165–9.
80. *FS*, VI, p. 282.
81. Bernard, *Ruth's Repentance*. I cite from the reprint of 1865 (ed. Grosart), pp. 37, 56–8. Cf. my *A Turbulent, Seditious and Factious People*, pp. 87–9 and Chapter 12 *passim*.
82. Offor, II, pp. 465–6. The 'etc.' was useful.

obsessively labelled as lords and ladies, gentlemen and gentlewomen; the hero of *The Pilgrim's Progress* is a man in rags, a poor itinerant with a burden on his back. The enclosing landlords who warn him off their property address him as 'thou' and expect the deferential 'you' in return. Giant Despair has the jurisdictional rights and the lock-up of a JP.[83] But in the Celestial City all material needs are met, and the inhabitants are in continual and familiar contact with the king. It recalls the millenarian utopias of the forties and fifties: but now we get there only after crossing the River of Death.

The ex-Parliamentarian soldier Bunyan was always cautious in his published writings not to appear to be inciting his readers to sedition. But in one work which he did not publish he came very near to it. He was as usual telling his people to be patient under persecution, not trouble-makers. But then, referring to Psalm LXXX, he continues: 'Suppose they were the truly godly that made the first assault, can they be blamed? For who can endure a boar in a vineyard? [i.e. a persecutor of the Christian church] . . . Why did the boar come here? What had he to do in God's house?' God will 'return the evil that its enemies do to his church . . . when his time is come . . . even in this world'. 'The Medes and Persians', he added, 'helped to deliver the church from the clutches . . . of the King of Babylon'[84] — as Dutch William was shortly to deliver England.

Bunyan's use of the Bible serves different purposes from that of Milton, but both were defending a defeated cause against powerful tyrants and persecutors. In the Bible they found rich resources, including an insistence on the duty of standing fast. The rebel angels and Adam and Eve in *Paradise Lost*, the Son of God in *Paradise Regained*, Samson in *Samson Agonistes*, were all free to stand or free to fall — like the English people during their Revolution. Samson, like the English people, sinned and fell; but he repented and remained true to God's cause; when he was given the opportunity to wreak vengeance on the Philistine aristocracy and priests he seized it and opened up the possibility of liberation for his people,

> let but them
> Find courage to lay hold on this occasion (lines 1715–16).

Historically they didn't, as Milton very well knew. But the opportunity

---

83. J. G. Turner, 'Bunyan's Sense of Place' in *The Pilgrim's Progress: Critical and Historical Views* (ed. V. Newey, Liverpool U.P., 1980).
84. Offor., III, pp. 512–37.

might offer itself to others. The names of Bunyan's Mr Great-heart, Mr Standfast, Mr Valiant-for-the-truth, describe this determination. Even Mr Fearing 'never looked back'. Indeed the pilgrims were issued with armour which defended them only from frontal attack.

The important thing is to testify, to do what one can when one can, 'by small/Accomplishing great things'. The Son of God, after the miracle of the pinnacle in *Paradise Regained*, goes back to his mother's house to resume his daily round of preaching. Standing fast became an end in itself for embattled dissenters after 1660. Bunyan tells us that some of the godly became impatient because after doing great things in less than forty years on earth, Christ has now been in heaven for above 1600 years 'and yet has not done'. But the good Christian should not 'faint at seeming delays'.[85] 'We dare not despair', said the Lord Mayor of Mansoul in the town's darkest hour, 'but will look for, wait for and hope for deliverance still.'[86]

III. A note on Marvell's 'great prelate of the grove'

I have written elsewhere about Marvell and the double heart, Marvell and gardens,[87] Milton and Marvell,[88] and Marvell's millenarianism.[89] This is a brief note on some lines in 'Upon Appleton House' which may relate to my earlier remarks about groves and idolatry.

Groves were traditionally associated with worship. Abraham planted a grove in Beersheba, and called there on the everlasting God (Genesis XXI.33). But Deuteronomy XVI.21 was explicit: 'Thou shalt plant no grove of any tree near unto the altar of the Lord thy God'. The Israelites nevertheless repeatedly provoked God to anger by making groves (e.g. I Kings XIV.15). Even Gideon had to be ordered to cut down and burn the grove near the altar of Baal which his father had built; not until that had been done could he undertake the deliverance of the Israelites (Judges VI.25). (In Judges III.7, where the Geneva translation has 'served Baalim and Asheroth', the A.V. translated 'served Baalim and the groves'.) King

---

85. Offor, III, p. 507; *BMW*, X, p. 114.
86. Bunyan, *The Holy War*, p. 211.
87. My *Puritanism and Revolution*, Chapter 13.
88. My *Writing and Revolution*, Chapter 7.
89. Ibid., pp. 174–5; my *Religion and Politics*, Chapter 13. See now Margarita Stocker, *Apocalyptic Marvell: The Second Coming in Seventeenth-Century Poetry* (Brighton, 1986), *passim.* Cf. p. 256 above.

Asa, in Cowley's words, 'cut solemn groves where idols stood', even the 'idol in a grove' which his mother had made (I Kings XV.13). 'This superstition of consecrating groves to idols', Cowley added in a note, 'grew so frequent that there was scarce any fair green tree that was not dedicated to some idol'.[90] Ahab made a grove, and provoked the Lord 'more than all the kings of Israel that were before him' (I Kings XVI.32-3); and Manasseh too restored idolatry and made a grove (II Kings XXI.3). Under Hoshea the Israelites 'left all the commandments of the Lord their God ... and made a grove' (I Kings XVII.16). Hoshea was the last of the kings of Israel. Good King Josiah of Judah burnt the groves (II Kings XXXIII.4-7; cf. Isaiah XXVII.9). Faustus in Marlowe's play was urged by Valdes to 'haste thee to some solitary grove' in order to be initiated into the mysteries of 'magic and concealed arts'. In the grove Faustus raises Mephistophilis; later he works effective magic against Benvolio in another grove.[91]

The radical pamphleteer Thomas Scott (if it was he) spoke in 1624 of 'our Roman Catholics ... already preparing to erect their groves and altars, to set up their idols and images'.[92] Benlowes addressed 'ye sirens of the grove'.[93] Oliver Cromwell when Lord Protector was criticized for having statues of classical gods in his garden, 'for whilst the groves and altars of the idols remained untaken away in Jerusalem, the wrath of God continued against Israel'.[94]

In the light of this let us read again Marvell's lines in 'Upon Appleton House', whose full resonance we easily overlook.

> And see how chance's better wit
> Could with a masque my studies hit!
> The oak-leaves me embroider all,
> Between which caterpillars crawl:
> And ivy, with familiar trails,
> Me licks, and clasps, and curls, and hales.
> Under this *antic cope* I move
> Like some great *Prelate of the Grove*.

'Prelate' warns us that the image is unfriendly, suggesting the bad old days

---

90. Cowley, *Poems*, pp. 298, 315.
91. Cf. Roger Sales, *Christopher Marlowe* (1991), Chapter 7.
92. [Anon.], *Vox Coeli* (printed in Elisium, 1624), sig. A 3v.
93. Benlowes, *Theophila*, Canto III, stanza xxxiii.
94. Quoted by Derek Hirst, 'The Politics of Literature in the English Republic', *The Seventeenth Century*, V (1990), p. 153.

of Laudianism;[95] and the suspicion is enhanced by the caterpillars which crawl between the leaves that form the 'antic cope', the fool's vestment. But 'of the grove' is the severest cut of all. Marvell is not only linking prelates and Laudians with the foolishness of jesters, but also deliberately associating them with paganism. A poem attributed to Richard Corbett ironically made a Puritan confronted with a maypole protest that

> Baal's worshipp'd in the groves again.[96]

Samuel Pordage picked up the metaphor in his *Azariah and Hushai* (1682), a retort to Dryden's *Absalom and Achitophel*. Pordage's name for Charles II is 'Azariah', who

> though he God did love
> Had not cast down Baal's priests, and cut down every grove.[97]

Not a Josiah, to say no more.

95. Cf. 'Scaevola Scoto-Brittannicus: 'insons si praesul quilibet esse potest' – 'if any prelate could be innocent' (Marvell, *Poems*, p. 196).
96. 'To Mr Hammon Parson of Beudly. For pulling down the May-pole', in *Parnassus Biceps* (1971 reprint), p. 19. Corbett died in 1635.
97. Pordage, op. cit., p. 1.

V. THE END OF THE REVOLUTIONARY BIBLE

===

18. *The Bible and an Unequal Society*

====

When the Lord God shall bring thee into the land whither thou
goest to possess it, . . . then thou shalt utterly destroy them: thou
shalt make no covenant with them, nor have compassion on
them . . . . For . . . the Lord thy God hath chosen thee to be a
precious people unto himself, above all people that are upon the
earth.
Deuteronomy VII.1–6. See pp. 269–70 above.

I will therefore that the men pray . . . . Let the woman learn in
silence with all subjection. I permit not a woman to teach,
neither to usurp authority over the man, but to be in silence.
St Paul, First Epistle to Timothy II.8–12. For women to 'be placed
above men . . . is against God's ordinance', the Geneva margin
comments.

I

The canon of the Bible is the product of a series of historical compromises.
In consequence those who look hard enough can find texts to support very
different points of view. So far I have been discussing mainly radical uses of
the Bible during the revolutionary decades. But there had always been
more conservative readings, and from the late 1650s many found them
more appropriate. Even earlier the Bible must take some responsibility for
the continuance of practices which were already beginning to disturb more
intelligent English men and women.

I argued earlier that the concept of the chosen people and of the struggle
against Antichrist could be adapted to purposes like colonization and imperial expansion, which seem alien to the concerns of the Bible.[1] Colonial
conquest was justified, among other things, by desire to spread the truth of
Christianity and the rule of the chosen people. God's commandment to the
Jews was clear: there was to be no false pity.[2] Wars of extermination, or
for domination and enslavement, were justified by God's command.

1. See Part III above.
2. See first epigraph to this chapter.

Columbus, we are told, got from the Bible his attitude towards the Indians whom he met in America. The consequences could hardly have been worse, or more lasting. English settlers who sometimes started with benevolent ideas about the Irish or the Indians soon came to see in their lack of civility as well as of religion a justification for the use of force. And this reacted back upon England. Popery was equated with heathenism. The anonymous *Paganopapismus* described papism as flat paganism.[3] There were 'Indians', uncivilized heathens, in the North and West of England as well as in America.[4]

> As savage slaves be in Great Britain here
> As any one that you can show me there

wrote the poet Drayton to the poet George Sandys in Virginia.[5]

There is less opposition to slavery as an institution than one might have expected, even among Quakers. This is no doubt in part because the Old Testament seemed to take slavery for granted; but also because the full horrors of plantation slavery were not appreciated until late in the century. The occasional African who was to be seen in England was a curiosity, not part of a system of exploitation. The anonymous author of *Tyranipocrit Discovered* is one of the few who denounced slavery (and war).[6] Aphra Behn's *Oroonoko* was not published until 1698, though probably written much earlier. Richard Baxter admitted that slaves were equal with their masters and should not be treated like animals. No man might be enslaved except as a just punishment for crimes: the slave trade was 'one of the worst kinds of thieving in the world', unworthy of Christians.[7]

Anti-semitism was justified by the Jews' rejection of Christ and by I Thessalonians II.14–16. Bishop Nicholson's comment on Psalm CIX, which calls for protection from the vengeance of the psalmist's enemies, was 'a Jew will ever be a Jew'.[8] Ham (the name was thought to mean black) was held to be the ancestor of negroes. Noah cursed Ham's posterity because of Ham's disrespect for his father's drunken nakedness. 'A servant of servants shall he be unto his brethren' (Genesis II.22–5), which the Geneva margin glosses as 'a most vile slave' (Cf. I Chronicles I.8). George

3. Cited in Trapp, *Commentary on the New Testament*, p. 779.
4. See p. 277 above.
5. Sandys, *Poems*, I, p. lxvii. For 'civility', see pp. 135, 138, 159, 277 above.
6. Op. cit., p. 21. For Ham and slavery see pp. 29, 118 above.
7. Baxter, *Chapters from A Christian Directory* (ed. J. Tawney, 1925), pp. 26–35.
8. Nicholson, *David's Harp*, p. 355.

Hakewill, preaching before the Privy Council on Psalm CI, took the opportunity to call for reform, denouncing 'monopolies and impositions, . . . projects and perquisites', but he accepted that servitude derived from 'the ungraciousness of Ham'.[9] Not till much later could the anti-slavery movement and foreign missionaries free themselves from the Bible sufficiently to proclaim the possibility of real human equality. The Old Testament seemed to justify the use of force against the recalcitrant heathen, though that should perhaps be attributed to religion rather than to racism. The two are not always easily distinguishable.

II

Mankind's superiority over animals was justified by Genesis I.26–8, confirmed by the eighth Psalm. God gave man 'dominion over the fish of the sea, and over the fowl of the air, and over every living thing that moveth upon the earth'. God presumably first slaughtered the animals with whose skins he clothed the nakedness of Adam and Eve (Genesis III.21). God's blessing to Noah after the Flood confirmed that 'everything that moveth and liveth shall be meat for you' (Genesis IX.2–3). On this the Geneva margin commented, possibly with premature defenders of animal rights in mind: 'by this permission man may with a good conscience use the creatures of God for his necessity' – i.e. eat them. The millenarian Mary Cary saw no objection to killing animals for food. Adam was a vegetarian, but Abel kept sheep – presumably not only for their fleeces.[10] Locke still spoke of mankind's God-given power over animals. The severity of this denial of animal rights was modified a little by Proverbs XII.10: 'a righteous man regardeth the life of his beast', and by Exodus XXIII and Deuteronomy XXII.3–4, 6–7: though here the concern may be to protect property in the asses, oxen and birds which are to be preserved. Milton cited these texts to show that 'a pitiful person is not cruel even to animals'.[11]

Many protestants accepted that, while man might domesticate animals

---

9. Hakewill, *King Davids Vow for Reform* (1621), pp. 221, 262–3.
10. Cary, *A new and more exact mappe or Description of New Jerusalems Glory*, printed with *The Little Horns Doom and Downfall* (1651), pp. 315–16.
11. Locke, *Two Treatises of Government* (ed. P. Laslett, Cambridge U.P., 1960), pp. 170–71, 185–6, 222–4; *MCPW*, VI, p. 747. Cf. also Numbers XXII, Isaiah I.11, Jonah IV.

and kill them for food and clothing, they should not be caused unnecessary suffering.[12] Wither wrote a hymn for 'When we ride for pleasure':

> He that wilfully shall dare
> That creature to oppress or grieve
> Which God to serve him doth prepare
> Himself of mercy doth deprive.
>
> And he, or his, unless in time
> They do repent of that abuse
> Shall one day suffer for his crime,
> And want such creatures for their use.[13]

'Neither Christianity nor humanity abideth a needless tormenting of the creatures', declared Thomas Taylor.[14] Here Taylor found himself in the unlikely company of the Duchess of Newcastle, whose two poems 'The Hunting of the Hare' and 'The Hunting of the Stag' were published when she was still 'the Lady Newcastle'. Her vivid description of the suffering of hunted animals leads up to theological conclusions. Man is so proud that he thinks.

> that all creatures for his sake alone
> Was made for him to tyrannize upon.

And of the stag: 'men for love of mischief dig his grave'.[15] The author of *Tyranipocrit Discovered* pointed out that the law of Moses 'condemned him that did not help the burdened ass': how much more would the law of Christ condemn him that took no care for the soul of his neighbour?[16]

Lamont has drawn attention to the heresy of supposing that animals will participate in the final resurrection, based on Romans VIII.19–22 and Acts III.21. The martyr John Bradford accepted it.[17] Among those who supported the idea were Nicholas Bownde, George Abbot, Nathanael Homes, Richard Overton, Ralph Josselin and Henry Vaughan.[18] John Reeve

12. See Thomas, *Man and the Natural World: Changing Attitudes in England, 1500–1800* (1983), pp. 151–5, for the best treatment of this subject.

13. Wither, *Hallelujah*, p. 28.

14. Taylor, *Works* (1653), p. 113.

15. Margaret Cavendish, *Poems and Fancies* (1653), pp. 110–16.

16. Op. cit., p. 4.

17. W. Lamont, 'Muggletonians versus Millenarians', Millersville; G. H. Williams, *Wilderness and Paradise in Christian Thought*, pp. 83–4.

18. Thomas, *Man and the Natural World*, pp. 138–9; Bownde, *The Unbelief of St. Thomas the Apostle* (1817), pp. iv, 127 (first published 1608); Abbot, *An Exposition upon the Prophet Jonas*; Nathanael Homes, *The Resurrection Revealed* (1661), pp. 250–52;

rejected it, but his disciple Thomas Tompkinson insisted on it.[19] The idea had in fact been prevalent in radical circles at least since the 1640s.[20] Most interesting of all is the propagandist vegetarian Thomas Tryon (1634–1723). In 1657 Tryon gave up eating meat and fish or wearing leather, and rejected tobacco and alcohol. He was also one of the first to attack negro slavery. There is something very remarkable about a teetotal vegetarian who could convince Aphra Behn; and his longevity should interest modern vegetarians. Tryon thought that consumption of animals as food after the Fall had contributed to bellicosity among men. He deserves a full-dress modern study.[21]

III

What may seem to us the most outstanding constraint on seventeenth-century radicals is the Bible's attitude towards women. Other factors were working against women – the household economy, the long tradition of their exclusion from public and professional life, and from higher education. But it is unfortunate that the three major religions of the Mediterranean world – Judaism, Christianity and Islam – took their final form at a time when patriarchy was very much in the ascendant. Most specific statements about women in the Bible as we have it assume male supremacy. There are surviving traces of pre-patriarchal women military leaders and prophetesses in the Old Testament, the former recalling Boadicea in pre-Roman Britain. Some early Hebrew inscriptions and papyri suggest that God had a female consort. But the patriarchs came to dominate. The original stories showed Rebecca outwitting her husband Isaac and her elder son Esau on behalf of her younger son, Jacob; and Rachel, who had been swindled by her father,

---

Overton, *Mans Mortallitie* (ed. H. Fisch, Liverpool U.P., 1968), pp. 68–70; Josselin, *Diary*, p. 342; Vaughan, *Works*, II, p. 540; Alan Rudrum, 'Henry Vaughan, the Liberation of the Creatures and Seventeenth-Century English Calvinism', *The Seventeenth Century*, IV (1989), pp. 33–4.

19. Lamont, op. cit., quoting Tompkinson, *Truths Triumph* (1676).
20. Edwards, *Gangraena*, I, p. 27, II, p. 36.
21. Thomas deals with Tryon, op. cit., esp. pp. 155, 170, 291–2, 298. He has many other examples of writers giving Biblical references for not ill-treating animals. For Tryon see also Serge Hutin, *Les Disciples anglais de Jacob Boehme* (Paris 1960), pp. 71–3, 229–30.

out-swindled him on behalf of her husband, Jacob the trickster. These stories were considerably modified in later redactions of the Torah.[22]

The printed Bible in English has been blamed for promoting witch-hunting.[23] 'Thou shalt not suffer a witch to live', the Lord told his people through Moses (Exodus XXII.18). That sealed the fate of many a poor old woman. Six years before Oliver Cromwell's birth his grandmother was believed to have been killed by witchcraft: a woman was hanged in consequence. Oliver's grandfather endowed an annual sermon to be preached in Huntingdon on the subject: the future Lord Protector must have heard many of them. In *Macbeth* and Middleton's *The Witch* the authors look back to an earlier stage of society; but witches have a serious political role. Accusations of witchcraft could be politically useful. James VI of Scotland apparently genuinely believed that the Earl of Bothwell had used witchcraft in an attempt to murder him. James's stoutly Biblical *Daemonologie* (1597) considers, among many other subjects, the devilish device of using witchcraft to cause impotence. In the Essex divorce case Lady Essex, with the King's support, alleged that her husband had been bewitched and so was unable to consummate their marriage. Middleton's *The Witch* (1614) may relate to this case.[24]

In 1660, John Ray tells us, some 120 women were 'burnt for witches' in Scotland, where witchcraft beliefs died hard.[25] In England some Fellows of the Royal Society defended belief in witches by the authority of the Bible. 'No spirit, no God', declared Henry More, later F.R.S., just as Wesley was to say that giving up witches meant 'in effect giving up the Bible'.[26] The radical reformer John Webster suggested that the Bible had been deliberately mistranslated in order to maintain belief in witchcraft.[27] But sceptical voices were heard. In 1652 *Mercurius Politicus* reported from Scotland on a pauper condemned as a male witch: he was unable to get work, and was so poor 'that he confessed, or rather said, anything that was put into his head' by his accusers. To this remark, all too familiar in our own day, the journalist added: 'By this means you may guess upon what

22. Lane Fox, op. cit., pp. 243, 409; D. Rosenberg and H. Bloom, *The Book of J* (1991), pp. 263–5.
23. R. Holmes, *Witchcraft in British History* (1974), p. 213; cf. Jewel, *Works*, II, pp. 1027–8.
24. A. A. Bromham and Zara Bruzzi, *The Changeling and the Years of Crisis, 1619–1624* (1990), pp. 24–6.
25. C. E. Raven, *John Ray: naturalist* (Cambridge U.P., 1950), p. 119.
26. More, *An Antidote to Atheism* (1653), p. 164; cf. Joseph Glanvill, F.R.S., *Sadducismus Triumphatus* (1666), *passim*; *TRDM*, p. 570.
27. Webster, *The Displaying of Supposed Witchcraft* (1677), Chapter VI.

grounds many hundreds have heretofore been burnt in this country for witches'.[28]

'Thou shalt not covet thy neighbour's wife, nor his ox, nor his ass, . . . nor anything that is his' ran the Tenth Commandment. In Shakespeare's early problem-play on the relation of the sexes, *The Taming of the Shrew*, Petruchio says that a wife

> is my goods, my chattels. She is . . .
> My house, my ox, my ass, my anything (III. iii).

Hebrew wives could be repudiated. This was more difficult for the unpropertied in seventeenth-century England, for whom the only conventionally accepted form of divorce was 'wife-sale' – leading a wife by a halter to the market and there offering her to the highest bidder.[29] The patriarchs did not limit themselves to monogamy. Nothing is said in Exodus, or anywhere else in the Bible, about women coveting their neighbours' husbands: husbands were not property to be owned or stolen. (This proved convenient for Milton's arguments in favour of divorce for incompatibility of temperament: although in theory open to both parties, in fact he is thinking primarily of husbands who do not find their wives compatible.)

The Bible represents the position of women as having been permanently affected by Eve's sin in Paradise, which caused the fall of all mankind. God punished Eve by subjecting all women henceforth to the rule of their husbands (Genesis III.16). But there appears to be a theological contradiction here. Eve is also taken to be inferior *before* the Fall. She was created after Adam, and she was made from Adam's rib, in order, William Whately explained, that 'she should acknowledge her subjection'.[30] This point was emphasized forcibly by Filmer. 'The woman for the man was made/And not the man for her', sang Wither.[31] Whichever explanation we choose, women are inferior.

The Old Testament is not sentimental about women. Moses after a military victory over the Midianites instructed his troops to kill all the

---

28. *Mercurius Politicus*, no. 127, 4–11 November 1652, p. 1994.

29. But wife-sale was often an *agreed* form of divorce, the purchaser having already been chosen by the wife. It remained a humiliating ceremony. See Edward Thompson's classic chapter on the subject in *Customs in Common*.

30. Whately, *Prototypes, Or The Primarie Precedent Presidents out of the Book of Genesis* (1640), pp. 3–4. Whately speaks of the *joint* sin of Adam and Eve (ibid., p. 13).

31. Sir Robert Filmer, *Patriarcha and Other Political Works*, pp. 283–90; Wither, *Hallelujah*, p. 319. The lines were part of a hymn 'For a Wife'.

women and children except virgins, whom they might 'keep alive for yourselves'.[32] The Geneva margin expressed no surprise at this, even though a propagandist in 1670 described the Geneva Bible as the 'women's Bible'.[33] The patriarch Judah sentenced his daughter-in-law Thamar to death by burning for committing adultery (Genesis XXXVIII.24). The Geneva margin noted this with approval, and Filmer with some relish.[34] Esther became Queen of the Medes because her predecessor had been put away for disobedience; a special law had been promulgated that all women should honour their husbands and that every man should bear rule in his own house (Esther I). 'That women should obey their husbands', declared Thomas Taylor, 'none are so rude as not *in general* to acknowledge'. Much may be read into the words which I have italicized. 'But to come to particulars . . .' Taylor continued.[35]

In the New Testament St Paul told wives to submit themselves to their husbands (Colossians III.18) and to keep silence in church. If they had problems, they must ask their husbands in the privacy of their homes (I Corinthians XIV.34; cf. the second epigraph to this chapter). (But it is to Paul's credit that he favoured marriage for bishops and priests: he is not to blame for the church's doctrine of celibacy.)[36] The woman taken in adultery was told – by a male – to go and sin no more, and so escaped being stoned. We do not hear of husbands being stoned for adultery, though Leviticus XX.10 and Deuteronomy XXII.22 suggest that they should have been. Joseph Hall was shocked both by Christ's lenience, and by his interference in a matter where he had no jurisdiction. We must not argue from his exceptional behaviour, the bishop insisted, that adultery was not rightly punishable by death.[37] For the patriarchs and Hebrew kings, having additional wives and concubines was a form of conspicuous consumption, indulged in even by godly kings like David. Solomon had 700 wives and

---

32. Numbers XXXI.14–18. Not a text often used for sermons today, I believe. Marlowe's Tamburlaine similarly divided up 'Turkish concubines' amongst his common soldiers (Part II, Act iv). No doubt such things occurred during the Thirty Years War.

33. [Dr T. Pittis], *A Private Conference, between A Rich Alderman and A Poor City Vicar*, p. 87.

34. Filmer, op. cit., p. 58; cf. Lane Fox, op. cit., pp. 357–8, 407.

35. Taylor, *A Commentarie upon the Epistle of St. Paul to Titus* (1619), pp. 391–3. The dedication is dated 1612.

36. Nor indeed is his authorship of I Timothy now generally accepted (Lane Fox, op. cit., p. 136).

37. Hall, *Contemplations*, in *Works*, II, p. 492.

300 concubines (I Kings XI.3), Rehoboam a mere eighteen wives and sixty concubines (II Chronicles XI.21).

Theology is often linked with sex. In Galatians V and VI, Paul had to claim direct inspiration to overrule the Apostles on the subject of circumcision, now replaced by baptism. Circumcision of male children had been the sign of the covenant between God and the Jews (Genesis XVII; cf. *MCPW*, VI, pp. 548–9). But now women could be baptized: a woman was the first to be baptized at Philippi. There is neither male nor female in Christ; 'neither circumcision availeth anything nor uncircumcision' (Galatians III.28, VI.15). Galatians is more heavily annotated than any other book in the Geneva Bible.

In a remarkable poem published in 1611 Emilia Lanier argued that Adam was more to blame for the Fall than Eve:

> He never sought her weakness to reprove
> With those sharp words, which he of God did hear.

Women had no share in the far greater crime of betraying and crucifying Christ.

> Your fault being greater, why should you disdain
> Our being your equal, free from tyranny?[38]

Quaker women got round Paul's prohibition of women's preaching by saying that Christ in either sex is to be heard; so women may speak in church when it is Christ that speaks in them. George Fox took over this argument, and expanded it by saying that man's dominion belonged to sin; in the new life man and wife are equal.[39] Very early in his career Fox had come to the support of a woman whom a clergyman had forbidden to speak in church.[40]

---

38. Emilia Lanier, *Salve Deus Rex Judaeorum* (ed. A. L. Rowse, 1978), pp. 104–5; cf. pp. 77–8.
39. Fox, *The Great Mistery of the Great Whore* (1659), p. 286. The point was made in 1655 by Mary Cole and Priscilla Cotton, *To the Priests and People of England*, pp. 3, 6–8, and by Ann Audland, *A True Declaration of the Suffering of the Innocent*, p. 5; cf. Cotton, *As I was in the Prison House* (1656). I owe all these references to Dr Valerie Drake's important Oxford Polytechnic D.Phil. Thesis, '*I matter not how I appear to men': A View of Women's Lives, Concentrating on the Writings of non-élite Women, 1640–63* (1988). Cf. Emilia Fogelklou, *James Nayler, the Rebel Saint, 1618–1660* (1931), p. 140.
40. Martyn Grubb, 'George Fox and Social Justice', a paper delivered at the George Fox Commemoration Conference, Lancaster, 26 March 1991. The woman became a Quaker. I am grateful to Martyn Grubb for this information.

There had been women preachers among the Lollards, but not all early protestant reformers wished to encourage women even to read the Bible. An act of Parliament in 1543 forbade anyone below the rank of gentlewoman to read or discuss it. There was renewed liberty for women in the congregations which sprang up in the revolutionary decades – liberty to participate in church government and even to preach.[41] Quakers were especially notorious for this: the opportunity which they offered women to roam the country – and indeed the world – unchaperoned must have seemed an intoxicating liberation for unmarried Quaker women missionaries – unless it ended in execution, as in New England. William Gouge in his *Commentary on the Whole Epistle to the Hebrews* (1655) attacked 'such women as presume to preach publicly', together with preaching apprentices and young men.[42]

When John Bunyan cracked down on an attempt of the women in his Bedford congregation to establish separate women's meetings, he based his opposition largely on an array of Biblical texts; but he also frankly stated that this was a question of *power*, which belonged to men. If he agreed to it he would be 'a Ranter or a Quaker'. The Ranter Abiezer Coppe rebuked a correspondent who had spoken of women as 'weaker vessels'. 'I know that male and female are all one in Christ, and they are all one to me. I had as lief hear a daughter as a son prophesy'.[43] In New England 'men contend about male and female in point of ruling and not ruling, speaking or not speaking in the church', said Samuel Gorton; but such notions are 'impotent and beggarly rudiments . . . by which men are under the bondage of the Law'. Women could pray – i.e. prophesy – if Christ came into their hearts.[44]

Leveller women were very active politically – lobbying, leafleting, petitioning – on behalf of the vote for their menfolk, never for themselves. Among Fifth Monarchists 'the sisters' seem to have been active in conspiracy. In April 1657 'the declarations' were to be 'left with the sisters that meet together, to be sent into the countries [counties] to be delivered to the churches and meetings' in London; the pistols were to be left at sister Kerwit's house.[45]

41. Aston, *Lollards and Reformers*, p. 52; cf. Edwards, *Gangraena*, I, p. 30.
42. Gouge, op. cit., I, pp. 212, 379; II, pp. 93–108; III, p. 290.
43. Bunyan, in Offor, II, p. 664; 'power' is Bunyan's word; Coppe, *Some Sweet Sips, of some Spirituall Wine* (1649), in Smith, *Ranter Writings*, p. 66.
44. Gorton, quoted by P. Gura, 'Another Visit with An Old Friend, so setting an Agenda for the Study of Radical Religion in New England', Millersville.
45. *Thurloe State Papers*, VII, pp. 186–8. 'A Psalm of Mercy', dated 26 January 1660, is

The sexism of St Paul is modified by the example of female disciples in the New Testament, and Eve is counter-balanced by the Virgin Mary. In a curious passage Thomas Goodwin suggested that Eve was the first believer. 'We have a warrant that she believed; we have not a certain ground that Adam did, for the covenant is made with her ... She first trusted in Christ'.[46] Goodwin did not work out the full implications of this idea, which could play havoc with traditional male supremacy.

There are heroic women in the Old Testament, and Judith in the Apocrypha, as well as faithful disciples in the New Testament. Ponet cited Jael (among others) to justify tyrannicide. Stephen Marshall, with a certain relish, asked 'What made Jael such a blessed woman?' and he replied 'Even this, "she put her hand to the nail, and her right hand to the workman's hammer, and with the hammer she smote Sisera; she smote off his head when she had pierced and smitten through his temple"'.[47] The relish is for a craftsman's job well done, as well as for the fact that another of God's enemies had perished. A Women's Petition to the House of Commons in February 1642 noted that Esther the Queen petitioned the King on behalf of the church, 'with the hazard of her own life, it being contrary to the law to appear before the King before she were sent for'.[48] Mary Pope in 1647 observed that David, though a king, listened to and took the advice of a woman, and that Josiah consulted Huldah the prophetess.[49] Deborah had been a radical heroine since Lollard times.[50] The phrase 'Curse ye Meroz', made famous by Marshall's sermons, came from Deborah's song in Judges V. Biblical hymns like Deborah's were often translated with the Psalms.[51]

The unknown M.M. published pamphlets between 1696 and 1701 warning about the approaching end of the world. She believed that she had discovered how to reconcile the contradictions within the Bible, and so could interpret it better than anyone before her. And she believed that this

---

satirical about Fifth Monarchist 'sisters' (in *Rump: or an Exact Collection of the Choycest Poems and Songs relating to the Late Times*, 1662, II, pp. 193–5).
46. T. Goodwin, *Works*, I, p. 222; cf. II, p. 244.
47. Marshall, *FS*, II, p. 207. The reference is to Judges V.24–6, 31.
48. *A True Copy of the Petition of the Gentlewomen and Tradesmens Wives in and about the City of London*, in *Harleian Miscellany* (1746), VII, p. 569. I owe this reference, and that in the following note, to Dr Valerie Drake's thesis, quoted on p. 405 above.
49. Pope, *A Treatise on the Power of the Magistrate* (1647), sig. A2, B4-Cv, p. 108.
50. Aston, *Lollards and Reformers*, pp. 55–6.
51. E.g. Béza, *Psalms of David*.

had been vouchsafed to her because she was a woman. 'As there was a Virgin to conceive, given as a sign of the Messiah's first coming', so the good tidings of the second coming 'shall be declared by a woman'. 'Woman was to bring to light that truth which man had declined'. Her theory was that some Biblical texts contain eternal truths, instructions about belief and conduct which are valid for all time; other passages are merely historical, recording events and instructions valid only in the particular circumstances then prevailing.[52]

Eve was held responsible for the fall of all mankind; God condemned women to bring forth children in sorrow and to submit to male rule 'in church and state and in their own family' (Genesis III.16). At the Second Coming, M.M. continued, 'women will be delivered from that bondage, which some has found intolerable'. Strong words, which come near to questioning the justice of God. Did M.M. mean to do that? There is an extraordinary juxtapostion of ideas at the end of one of her latest pamphlets. When St Paul in I Corinthians XIV.34 said 'Let your women keep silence in the church', she argued that these words were spoken *ad hoc*: they have no general reference. St Paul had just lost his temper with some women in Corinth; if we compare what he said then in his tantrum with what he says elsewhere, and with the message of the Gospels generally, we can only conclude 'that he might not understand the Scriptures as to the mind of the Lord herein'.

This is cool enough. But M.M. goes straight on to discuss God's reaction to Eve's transgression in Paradise. She does not proclaim an analogy, but the train of thought seems to suggest one. God laid all women for all time under subjection because of Eve's mistake, though she could have had no idea of what would be the consequences of eating the apple. M.M. does not say that God over-reacted: but she hints at it (as Harold Bloom suggests that the (female) author of *The Book of J* did).[53] And how successful had men been? They alone are responsible for everything that has gone wrong in the fallen world. 'Entrusted with the Word, for themselves and their posterities, they made pretence of being teachers of the Gospel', but they

52. M.M., *Two Remarkable Females of Womankind* (1701), pp. 4, 12–15, 20, 24. The two females are the Virgin Mary and M.M. Milton had said something not totally dissimilar fifty years earlier in his *Doctrine and Discipline of Divorce*: 'all places of Scripture wherein just reason of doubt arises from the letter are to be expounded by considering upon what occasion everything is set down and by comparing other texts' (*MCPW*, II, p. 282). I am deeply indebted to Tim Hitchcock of the Polytechnic of North London for introducing me to M.M., on whom I hope he will soon be publishing.
53. Rosenberg and Bloom, op. cit., pp. 151–4.

have 'laid the world in darkness'. 'Women . . . have had no hand in overturning the Bible, for that had been done by the wise and learned of this world' – men by definition. So 'God saw good that . . . a woman should conceive aright how to bring the true knowledge again to light'. Whether or not God is now correcting his too hasty action, he 'is near at the door to call men to an account how they have ruled in church and state, and in their own families, and what good example they have showed'. Women must rally round M.M. and help to spread her message.[54] It would be interesting to study the women who spoke up for their sex in the 1690s and early years of the eighteenth century. Mary Astell, for instance, bases her case in *Reflections upon Marriage* (1706) very largely upon the Bible.[55]

IV

Religious toleration became a burning issue in the late 1640s, and naturally men turned to the Bible for guidance. But Scripture gave no very clear lead. Walwyn was unusual in declaring that 'the Word of God is express for toleration'.[56] There is much intolerance in the Old Testament: Roger Williams observed that 'persecutors seldom plead Christ, but Moses'.[57] In the Whitehall Debates of December 1648, when Commissary-General Ireton and Philip Nye argued that the state had a duty to curb sectarianism, they based their arguments mainly on the Old Testament.[58]

Before 1640 those who advocated toleration in England wanted it not on abstract general principles but as a means of establishing unity against an enemy. For radical protestants that enemy was international Catholicism, against which all who rejected the Pope could be united, even if they did not accept the national church; but for many members of that church

54. M.M., *Good News to the Good Women* (1701), pp. 4, 13–16; *Two Remarkable Females*, p. 21; *The Woman's Advocate* (1697), p. 1. Note the word 'conceive' – continuing the parallel between M.M. and the Virgin Mary.

55. See Bridget Hill, *The First English Feminist: Reflections on Marriage and other writings by Mary Astell* (1986), *passim*.

56. Walwyn, *Toleration Justified and Persecution Condemned* (1646), in *Writings of William Walwyn*, p. 170.

57. Quoted by D. M. Wolfe, *Milton in the Puritan Revolution* (1941), p. 33. See e.g. Deuteronomy XVII.2–7 and XVIII.20 – those who serve strange gods or prophesy falsely are to be stoned to death.

58. Woodhouse, op. cit., esp. pp. 146, 155–6, 162–3, 165.

peaceful papists were harmless and should be left alone.[59] Toleration was from one point of view an aspect of foreign policy; much turned on one's assessment of the international situation. So long as the Thirty Years War continued, and a papist invasion of England (or Ireland) seemed a real possibility, radical protestants strongly opposed toleration for papists. But after the defeat of Spain by an alliance of protestant powers with Catholic France (which tolerated its Huguenots) fear of an international Catholic crusade against England diminished; and then the Cromwellian conquest of Ireland closed that back-door to invasion.[60]

After 1660 Quakers accepted the peace principle, and dissenters in general accommodated themselves to the status of second-class citizens, abandoning the bellicosity of the forties and fifties. At the same time, the restored Stuart monarchs were uncomfortably pro-French; the revocation of the Edict of Nantes in 1685 rang alarm bells, and contributed significantly to the expulsion of James II, which finally made possible the Toleration Act of 1689. Until then, as we have seen,[61] even generous defenders of religious toleration for protestants would have refused to tolerate Catholics.

But of course there was more to it than foreign policy. All persecution is antichristian, Overton, Walwyn, Fifth Monarchists, Milton and Bunyan agreed.[62] For Bunyan, Muggletonians and Quakers Cain was the type of all persecutors.[63] When Bulstrode Whitelocke after 1670 settled down to write a history of persecution, he began with Cain.[64] But such men were thinking of persecution of the godly by the ungodly, of protestants by papists, of sectaries by Anglican bishops. It was unusual when the author of *Tyranipocrit Discovered* in 1649 thought that the intolerance of Catholics in France and Spain, of the English in Ireland, and of English Presbyterians, were all equally bad: all aimed to establish tyranny: the names do not matter.[65] Turks are more tolerant than most Christians, Francis Osborn complained.[66]

Political and social issues became clear in the fascinating Whitehall

---

59. For example Sir Thomas Browne and the Great Tew circle.
60. See Clifton, 'Popular Fear of Catholics', pp. 53–5.
61. See pp. 296–7 above.
62. Overton, *The Araignment of Mr. Persecution*, pp. 12–15, in Haller, *Tracts on Liberty*, III; Capp, *The Fifth Monarchy Men*, pp. 183–4; *MCPW*, VI, pp. 797–8; my *A Turbulent, Seditious and Factious People*, p. 99 and references there cited.
63. See Chapter 8 *passim*.
64. Spalding, *Diary of Bulstrode Whitelocke*, p. 762.
65. Op. cit., p. 32.
66. See pp. 230–31 above.

Debates of December 1648. Discussion turned on the limits to the power of the magistrate. There was pretty general agreement with Ireton that anyone 'submitting to the civil government of the nation should have liberty to serve God according to his conscience'. But should this cover 'anything that any man will call religion'? – idolatry or atheism, for instance? If not, who was to decide? Radicals found Ireton's questions difficult to answer. They accepted that there was a 'law written in men's hearts, and a testimony left in man by nature', which will tell men's consciences that there is only one God, and that human life and property are sacred. But on many lesser matters even the self-selected few gathered at Whitehall could not agree. What about swearing? Sabbath observance? adultery? Wildman found it 'an hard thing' to conceive by the light of nature 'how there can be any sin committed'. Ireton was convinced that 'the light of nature' supported all the assumptions of the existing class-divided society.[67]

Those whom we call Congregationalists – men like Thomas Goodwin, Jeremiah Burroughs, Joseph Caryl, John Owen, John Cotton – found themselves caught between Presbyterian severity and sectarian tolerance to the left. But even radicals in the Whitehall Debates – like Wildman, Overton, John Goodwin, Joshua Sprigge and Thomas Collier – found it hard to distinguish between toleration for the saints and 'the exorbitant liberty which those that are not religious, but would pretend to be so, would take'.[68] They fell back upon the Bible. Texts can be found in the New Testament calling for patient and sympathetic treatment of believers; but the only sanction available to the church of the New Testament was excommunication. Was that enough in a society where Christians ruled?

Throughout the period one group remained beyond the pale of toleration: those who denied the existence of God. This was thought to preclude a recognition of rewards and punishments in the after life, regarded as a necessary prop of the unequal social order. This consideration should be borne in mind when we comment – as we must – on the absence of evidence for open atheism in the seventeenth century. The Bible then gave no lead here. Tolerance of sceptics and unbelievers came only when the authority of the Bible had lapsed.

The Quaker Edward Burrough observed in 1661 that persecution 'must unavoidably tend to destroy and expel trading'.[69] He was arguing for toleration because of the strength of the dissenting interest among

---

67. Woodhouse, op. cit., pp. 142–4, 156, 161.
68. Ibid., p. 149. The speaker was the Fifth Monarchist Colonel Nathaniel Rich.
69. Burrough, *Works*, p. 818; cf. p. 310 above.

merchants, artisans and yeomen; but he was in fact envisaging a different sort of social order. Burrough did not reveal his attitude towards toleration of unbelievers: the idea probably never occurred to him. But foreign trade, as Defoe noted in *Robinson Crusoe*, necessitated tolerance not only of Catholics but also of Muslims and adherents of even more alien faiths. The descent of the slippery slope started slowly, but accelerated with its own momentum, leaving the Bible behind.[70]

Selected use of the Bible had helped radicals to plead several forward-looking causes in the revolutionary decades; but the Bible's ambivalence rendered it difficult to convince their conservative opponents. Nor should we underestimate the effect of courtly mockery of vulgar enthusiasm. What was so funny about Puritans in Ben Jonson's *The Alchemist* and *Bartholomew Fair* was that they took the Bible seriously. Cowley used 'The Plagues of Egypt' to make royalist political points in the 1650s. The Israelites were beginning to 'curse their new-gotten liberty' (as, he implies, were the people of England under the Commonwealth) when God to their astonishment divided the Red Sea for them to pass through.[71] After 1660 awareness of multiple possible interpretations was largely responsible for declining belief in the universality of Biblical authority. Biblical texts were again used to defend an unequal society, as the millennium was postponed till kingdom come.

70. See my 'Daniel Defoe (1660–1731) and Robinson Crusoe' in *Writing and Revolution*, pp. 111–14, 126.
71. Cowley, *Poems*, pp. 219–31.

19. The Bible Dethroned

=====

'Tis madness to resist or blame
The force of angry heaven's flame.
Marvell, *Horatian Ode upon Cromwel's Return From Ireland.*

The seeming desertion of Providence at a time when, to the eye
of the enthusiast, matters were tending to the establishment of a
new Jerusalem on earth . . . gave a considerable shock to religious
confidence, and enlarged the narrow limits into which scepticism
had hitherto ranged.
Catharine Macaulay, *History of England from the Accession of James I to
the Elevation of the House of Hanover* (1763–83), VIII, p. 68.

I

With the restoration of monarchy, Church of England and censorship in
1660 the intellectual climate changed. The otherwise sceptical Charles II,
who proclaimed his devotion to the Bible, nevertheless made Isaac
Vossius Canon of Windsor who – the King said – would believe anything
if only it was not in the Bible. Charles claimed no Biblical divine right:
Parliamentarians no longer expected the millennium in the near future.
Antichrist had become a vulgar word.[1] Before 1660 the Bible was
everywhere – in ballads and madrigals, in sermons and in literary allusions. But acceptance of the Bible was based on cultural assumptions
which rapidly broke down in the free-for-all discussions which erupted
after censorship and ecclesiastical controls collapsed. Laymen preached as
well as clerics, and sermons and Biblical commentaries with rival theologies were published in great profusion. Everywhere political and social
controversy turned on rival interpretations of the Bible, on what was
read into it. No longer could opposition be silenced merely by saying
'The Bible says so'. The Bible continued to be quoted; but it was ceasing to
be exclusively authoritative.

The total collapse of government in 1640 seemed to suggest that God

1. See p. 323 above.

favoured the cause of Parliament. But the infinity of reversals and changes after the civil war showed that a providential theory of history was an uncertain way of interpreting God's purposes. The equivalent collapse of Army rule in 1659–60, despite frantic efforts of Quakers and other radicals to save it, seemed at least to suggest that divine Providence now favoured monarchy. 'The Lord raised up the Parliament in the year 1640 (as his Gideon for the relieving of them from the hands of their enemies)' was Ludlow's way of putting it. In 1660 'this great change was brought about by the immediate hand of God', who as in 1649 appeared to work against human organization, whether of the Army or of the religious radicals. The providential theory seemed to make purposeful human activity irrelevant. 'The Lord had . . . spit in their faces', wailed Major-General Fleetwood of his republican friends. After 1660 'the Lord is pleased for the present to make them the tail who before were the head', Ludlow concluded. 'It's the Lord's pleasure [his people] should take this turn in the wilderness, and that man may not have whereof to boast'.[2] This was one reason for nonconformist quietism after 1660, with the Quaker peace principle of 1661 as its most conspicuous example. That Christ's kingdom was not to be of this world seemed a rational conclusion to draw.

But this recognition should not lead us to underestimate the long-term intellectual consequences of the upheaval of the 1640s and 1650s. Milton and other radical protestants had believed that when the Bible was available in the vernacular to all men and women it would become the basis for informed critical discussion of society and its institutions, its customs and demands. The doctrine of the priesthood of all believers, implying that all believers might interpret the Bible for themselves, could lead to relatively democratic notions, countering the traditional view that politics was a matter for the élite, the aristocracy and clergy, only. Tyndale thought a ploughman could understand the Scriptures as well as (or better than) many learned clerics. Was the implication that ploughmen might be better at running the state than some prelates? Shakespeare's plebeians drew this horrific conclusion in *Henry VI*, Part 2, and in *Hamlet*; King Lear seemed to agree with them. Such heresies were normally expressed only by madmen or vulgar people; but even to hear it proclaimed from the stage that 'Adam was a gardener' could provoke thoughts subversive of degree and hierarchy.

2. Ludlow, *A Voyce from the Watch Tower*, pp. 301, 119, 149–50; cf. pp. 200, 248, 309–10.

But the priesthood of all believers could be no more than relatively democratic. It was a way of identifying the saints, those who by understanding God's will and God's Word through his Spirit must become the vanguard who will bring about God's kingdom on earth. In appropriate political circumstances their self-recognition gave cohesion, solidarity, comradeship, and a sense of purpose and unity, which could weld them into a powerful revolutionary force – the New Model Army, for instance, or on a pitifully smaller scale the Fifth Monarchist artisans who terrorized London in 1657 and 1661.

But after 1660 the hedge that united the saints could become a wall of separation between them and the rest of society, now divided into two nations. Study of the Bible could, at the right time, encourage resistance to constituted authority, whether passive or active, as a religious duty. The true church is always liable to be persecuted: that is how its members know they are God's people. But the Bible also showed that persecuting kings came to bad ends; ultimately God will vindicate his own. We must hold on, stand fast. Victory is certain, but it is not for us to say when it will come.

Bible-reading, especially of the Old Testament, had led many to identify the English people, or some of them, as a chosen people. This might necessitate resistance to a régime believed to be Antichristian, in order by the rule of the saints to prepare for the millennium. Yet should, ultimately, the saints fail to agree in interpreting the Bible, should their rule fail, the New Testament had a solution for that too. Christ's kingdom was not of this world. The consolatory passages in the Bible, used as a call to action in the forties and fifties, were now taken to refer to the after life:[3] *Because* the Bible could be all things to all men, a book for all seasons, it ultimately lost its usefulness as a guide to political action.

What for our purposes is important in this period of English history is the emergence of radical/critical social attitudes. All serious English political theory dates from this period – Hobbes and Harrington, Levellers, Milton and Winstanley. To explain this we must study the society rather than – as well as – the Bible. The legend of the younger brother, which we found illustrated from the stories of Cain and Abel, Esau and Jacob, derived its significance from tensions in the society. What matters is the locomotive, not the steam which appears to drive it. But if there were no steam there would be no motion.

What men and women found in the Bible depended on the questions

---

3. See 'God and the English Revolution' in my *Religion and Politics*.

they asked of it: and these questions derived from problems of the society in which they lived. *New* uses of the Bible show either that new problems have arisen or that social groups previously silent are now able to present their views – or both. The concept of progressive revelation allowed the possibility of new insights, new interpretations. Emphasis on the spirit rather than the letter of the Bible, on 'the mystery' rather than 'the history', is a way of wringing new answers to new problems from the familiar text.[4]

The protestant doctrine of the priesthood of all believers opened doors to innovation, because it was ultimately an appeal to individual interpretation of the Bible, to the consciences of (some) individual lay men and women. William Perkins had stated that the master of a family may with a good conscience seek that measure of wealth which is sufficient to maintain himself and his family in convenient style. To the question, how are we to assess what is sufficient, Perkins replied: 'not by the affection of covetous men,' but by 'the common judgment and practice of the most godly, frugal and wise men with whom we live'.[5] Frugal lay consciences set the standard.

Milton advanced this a good deal further when he wrote that 'the preeminent and supreme authority . . . is the authority of the Spirit, which is internal and the individual possession of each man'. We ought 'to believe what in our conscience we apprehend the Scripture to say, though the visible church with all her doctors gainsay'. That still retained the ultimate authority of the Bible, however much it might be interpreted. But the Bible is subject to the over-riding good of man in society.[6] Clarkson pushed this attitude one stage further when he wrote 'no matter what Scripture, saints or churches say, if that within thee do not condemn thee, thou shalt not be condemned'.[7] For him conscience interpreting Scripture is replaced by conscience alone, just as Milton had substituted 'men' for 'believers'. In either case the effect of the appeal to lay consciences was to admit the possibility that standards are not eternal. Conscience changes with social attitudes and pressures when faced with new facts and problems. Individual consciences may change at different speeds in different social groups – sometimes in different or indeed opposite directions. The appeal

4. See pp. 229, 237–8 above, and my 'Protestantism and the Rise of Capitalism', in *Change and Continuity*.
5. Perkins, *Workes*, I, p. 769.
6. *MCPW*, VI, pp. 121, 368, 537–41, 585–90; cf. pp. 558, 640, 652; VII, pp. 239–72, *passim*: *A Treatise of Civil Power in Ecclesiastical causes* (1659); *MER*, Chapter 19.
7. Clarkson, *A Single Eye*, p. 16.

to conscience against authority is an appeal to the present against the past. Sir Philip Sidney's Muse told him to 'look in thy heart and write', and Winstanley's very different conscience advised 'read in your own book, your heart'.[8] The possibilities were infinite. As Fulke Greville's priests in *Mustapha* admitted,

> when each of us in his own heart looks
> He finds the God there far unlike his books.[9]

The revolutionary decades produced momentous changes. Sir Thomas Browne's timid armchair criticisms of the Bible were compatible with his cautiously royalist stance.[10] But, as Francis Osborn put it in 1656, 'the liberty of these times hath afforded wisdom a larger passport to travel than was ever able formerly to be obtained, when the world kept her fettered in an implicit obedience, by the three-fold cord of custom, education and ignorance'.[11] Yet as late as May 1648 a Parliamentary Ordinance had threatened with imprisonment any who should teach 'that man is bound to believe no more than by his reason he can comprehend'.[12] So rapidly did the climate change that by 1662 we find a bishop saying 'Nothing is by Scripture imposed upon us to be believed which is flatly contradictory to right reason and the suffrage of all our senses'. That was John Gauden, author of *Eikon Basilike*.[13] In May of the previous year Samuel Pepys was listening to a mathematician who did not so much 'prove the Scripture false as that the time therein is not well computed nor understood'.[14]

When Hobbes wrote that the disciples' purse 'was carried by Judas Iscariot',[15] he was superficially just being naughty, *pour épater les croyants*. But his point is very serious. His objection was less to tithes claimed by the law of the land, than to *jure divino* claims to them. Yet in mocking divine right Hobbes also discredited the Bible. Once given the freedom of discussion which Milton praised in *Areopagitica*, it is impossible to force men to revere the Bible as the Church or the sovereign tell us to interpret it.

I cited above the strictures on the gross ignorance of the 'penmen of

---

8. Sidney, *Astrophel and Stella* (1591), stanza 1; Sabine, p. 213.
9. Greville, op. cit., Act V, Chorus of Priests.
10. Browne, *Religio Medici* (1642), in *Works* (Bohn ed. 1852), II, pp. 365–73.
11. Osborn, *Advice to a Son*, in *Miscellaneous Works*, I, sig. B3.
12. Firth and Rait, *Acts and Ordinances of the Interregnum* (1911), I, pp. 1133–6.
13. Quoted by Susan Staves, *Players' Scepters: Fictions of Authority in the Restoration* (Nebraska U.P., 1979), p. xii.
14. Pepys, *Diary* (ed. H. B. Wheatley, 1946), II, p. 38.
15. Cf. p. 53 above.

Scripture' made by John Wilkins, future bishop and President of the Royal Society.[16] The linguist Christian Ravis, friend of Selden, declared in print in 1650 that the Authorized Version was 'very full of non-sense, almost in every chapter some falsehood', and thought that Parliament ought to consider an improved translation.[17] John Owen, when Vice-Chancellor of Oxford University, wrote a Prefatory Note to William Twisse's *The Riches of Gods Love* (Oxford U.P., 1653), a defence of the absolute decree of reprobation. Owen admitted, rather uneasily, that 'the Scripture doth not so much abound in the delivery of this doctrine [reprobation] as of some others', though the saints 'who have learned to captivate their understandings to the obedience of faith' could find it there.

> Their Bibles cannot reconcile
> Parsons themselves when once in broil . . .
> For everyone has leave to cite
> Texts to his fancy, wrong or right,
> And put what sense he pleases on 'em.

So Thomas Ward's vulgar Hudibrastics summed up, in a poem published posthumously in 1710.[18] Ward, Roman Catholic convert, thought himself something of a Biblical expert, having published in 1688 *Errata to the Protestant Bible, or the Truth of the English translations examined*. In *Englands Reformation* he gave examples of the Authorized Version returning to traditional phrases from earlier versions.

By the 1650s reaction had set in against extreme sectarian demonstrations. Going naked for a sign (on the authority of Isaiah XX.2–4), Bible-burning, and Milton's *Eikonoklastes* had been furious manifestations of frustration at the refusal of other people either to see what God wanted (and had imparted to his elect) or to perceive the truth which is written in every man's heart.[19] As early as 1646, when William Franklin, rope-maker, proclaimed himself to be Jesus Christ, a sceptical physician recommended bleeding. But it did not effect a cure: it may indeed have strengthened his conviction.[20] Monck's word 'fanatic' proved very useful in 1660 in putting radicals beyond the pale; so did the post-restoration pejorative 'enthusiasm'.

16. See p. 22 above.
17. Ravis, *A Generall Grammar . . . of the Orientall Tongues*, p. 197.
18. Ward, *Englands Reformation* (1715), Canto III, p. 15. This is the first English edition. First published in Hamburg.
19. See Lowenstein, *Milton and the Drama of History*, passim.
20. Humphrey Ellis, *Pseudochristus* (1650), p. 6.

Divisions among the sects increased rather than diminished during the 1650s, each group claiming Biblical authority for its position. This consolidated conservatives against them. Peter Lake has shown how the anti-Puritan Calvinist Robert Sanderson argued that the Presbyterians' own principles led to Anabaptism and Quakerism, rather as – though with very different objectives – Milton in *The Tenure of Kings and Magistrates* (1649) had explained that justification of regicide originated in traditional Calvinist doctrines. Sanderson employed the dialect of radical sectaries to ask 'Where are your lay presbyters, your classes etc., to be found in Scripture? where are your steeple-houses, your national church? your infant sprinklings? Nay, your metrical psalms, your two sacraments? Your observing a weekly Sabbath?'[21] His object was to reunite Presbyterians and Episcopalians around a state church against the competing sectaries.

The horrendous consequences of religious toleration, as they seemed to conservatives, led to a closing of the ranks. When Parliament debated the Nayler case, all the arguments against toleration were rehearsed. The Biblical extremes of Quakerism – going naked for a sign, refusal to take oaths, the Fifth Monarchist attempt to establish the rule of the saints by military violence, stories of 'arming the Quakers' in 1659–60, all contributed to the panic which precipitated the unconditional return of Charles II in 1660.

II

The consensus which brought about the restoration of monarchy and Church of England was socially restricted. As Professor Greaves has amply shown, seditious use of the Bible continued after 1660, though now it was more circumspect. In the 1660s men were imprisoned for preaching on Hebrews XII.4 ('Ye have not resisted unto blood, striving against sin'), on Judges III.7 ('The children of Israel did wickedly in the sight of the Lord, and forgate the Lord their God, and served Baalim and Asheroth') and on Isaiah LII.2 ('Shake thyself from the dust; arise, and sit down, O Jerusalem; loose thyself from the bands of thy neck', which the preacher was alleged to have interpreted to mean 'Arise, O Jerusalem, and obey neither prince

21. Preface to the 1657 edition of Sanderson's *Thirty Four Sermons*, and a letter of 1649 from Sanderson printed in his *Works* (ed. W. Jacobson, Oxford U.P., 1854), VI, pp. 368–71, quoted by P. Lake, 'Serving God and the Times: The Calvinist Conformity of Robert Sanderson', *Journal of British Studies*, 27 (1988), pp. 110–11. Cf. pp. 41–3 above.

nor prelate'). A Durham dissident said that study of Esther had convinced him that 'the people of God had no peace until Haman's ten sons were destroyed'; 'the application', the informer said, 'is obvious'. Charles II was discreetly compared to Nimrod, Nebuchadnezzar, Darius, Nero and Ahab. Some dissenters who had been permitted to preach 'do use before they begin their sermons to lecture upon part of scripture', which enabled them to criticize contemporary ecclesiastical and political practices. The Council prohibited this habit in January 1670. Bibles printed abroad – presumably with the Genevan notes – circulated illegally.[22]

Translation of the Bible into English had led from the start to problems and controversies about the precise meaning of words. Did 'ecclesia' mean 'the congregation' or 'the church'? – international, national or local? The Westminster Assembly in 1644 had a long and 'tough dispute' on whether the word which the A.V. translated as 'ordain' should not more properly be rendered 'choosing' – 'importing the people's suffrage in electing their officers'.[23] How completely reliable was the text of the Vulgate compiled in times of popery? Scribes and copyists make mistakes: so do printers. Some books of the Bible have been lost. Manuscripts have different readings. So the quest for the true Bible led to scholarly Biblical criticism. Jewel, Hooker, Thomas James, William Crashawe, Chillingworth – all these strengthened the protestant position by exposing papal forgeries. But in the end such work led to questioning the attribution of books of the Bible to named authors[24] and then to questioning the authority of the Bible itself.

In the freedom of the forties men searched the Scriptures for solutions to current problems, and in the search they found other exciting matter. So long as it was assumed that the apparent contradictions and inconsistencies of the Bible must be more apparent than real, there was scope for reconcilers. More fundamental scholarly criticism started from questions which had been raised by sceptics like Ralegh, Marlowe and Hariot. When it was possible to discuss such matters in print it rapidly led to pious Christians like Clement Writer and Samuel Fisher convincing themselves that the Bible could not be God's infallible Word because the contradictions and inconsistencies were real.

There were many reasons for the cooling of the temperature of debate

22. R. L. Greaves, *Enemies under his Feet*, pp. 156, 258, 171, 91, 172.
23. Baillie, *Letters and Journals*, I pp. 419–20. The reference was to Acts XIV.23, where the Geneva Bible also has 'ordain'. Cf. I Timothy V.7 and Titus I.5. See p. 51 above.
24. Cf. Caryl, *An Exposition . . . Upon the First three Chapters of the Book of Job* (1643), p. 6 (dating); Manton, *Commentary . . . On the Epistle of James*, sig. Av–3v (authorship).

after 1660. Twenty years of frenzied discussion had shown that text-swapping and text-distortion solved nothing: agreement was not to be reached even among the godly on what exactly the Bible said and meant. Antinomians and others had insisted with Milton that each individual must decide for himself. Winstanley implies that each of us has his own God.[25] Confident predictions of the coming of the millennium had failed, leaving scepticism and lassitude even among fervent believers. By the late fifties many politicians were suffering from a surfeit of Biblical advice, which did not always seem to be either useful or constructive. In 1657 MPs actually laughed at a member who incessantly and boringly quoted the Scriptures. In June 1659 Johnston of Wariston noted in his diary that 'Sir Henry Vane debated for the Senate from Scripture, and Henry Neville against it without Scripture'.[26] Within a year the House of Lords was back, and constitution-making was over.

Not everybody accepted the scepticism of *Leviathan*, even after 1660, and few indeed of those who did dared to admit it; but the Bible lost its ascendancy as the prime source of political ideas. The balance of property which Harrington praised survived against all attempts to subvert it by military coup. Social helplessness forced both the Quaker James Nayler and Fifth Monarchist conspirators into desperate attempts: God *must* help his people before it was too late. Their failure seemed to justify upper-class cynicism about enthusiasm.

Quakers decided to abandon political activity and use of the carnal sword – ten days after the collapse of a violent Fifth Monarchist revolt in London. This was only an extreme form of the reaction of all sectaries. (It was not a sudden panic decision by the Quakers: the thought of some of them had been moving in that direction ever since the restoration.) There had always been individuals who lacked the convictions of extremists on either side; and a 'couldn't-care-less' attitude flourished under the Merrie Monarch and his sceptical libertine court.

When in 1698 Toland published Ludlow's *Memoirs*, an important document for the history of the English Revolution, he thought it necessary to eliminate a great deal of Biblical millenarianism. By that date it would have been an obstacle to the reception of Ludlow's political message; for Ludlow it had been an essential part of that message. George Fox's *Journal*

25. *MCPW*, VI, pp. 587–9; Sabine, p. 591.
26. Johnston of Wariston, *Diary*, III, pp. 71, 120. Cf. John H. F. Hughes, 'The Commonwealthmen Divided: Edmund Ludlow, Sir Henry Vane and the Good Old Cause, 1653–1659', *The Seventeenth Century*, V (1990), p. 62.

was similarly edited for publication, first by Fox himself, then by Thomas Ellwood, so that 'nothing may be omitted fit to be inserted, nor anything inserted fit to be left out'. What was fit in 1694 was very different from the revolutionary fifties, before Quakers were pacifists. Nothing remains in the *Journal* about Fox's millenarian expectations, his Cromwellian sympathies, his advocacy of an international anti-Catholic military crusade, his lending of a meeting-house to soldiers, his claims to be the Son of God or Moses, or his miracles.

Quakers ultimately succeeded in convincing their contemporaries that fixed prices were more rational (and ultimately more profitable) than the traditional haggling of the market, and that an honest man's word did not need to be confirmed by an oath (Matthew V.34–7). They underwent savage persecution on behalf of these principles, and on behalf of what is now seen as their main historical significance – their assertion of the peace principle. There had been individual pacifists before them, including the Muggletonian John Reeve and the ex-Leveller John Lilburne. But the Society of Friends was the first organized body to proclaim pacifism and abstention from politics *as a principle*. It is as relevant in the age of nuclear armaments as it was in the seventeenth century.

III

The end of Biblical literalism and certainty was a European phenomenon: Pascal's sceptical reference to truth on one side of the Pyrenees being a lie on the other witnesses to this. What was unique about the English experience was, first, that the translation of the Bible into printed English at the Reformation drew on a century of underground experience with the heretical Lollard manuscript version; secondly, that discussions of the Bible had initially been encouraged by protestant propagandists if not by governments, so that they later became very difficult to control. Thirdly, that during periods of reaction and censorship (some years of Henry VIII's reign, the whole of Mary's) emigration was possible to other protestant countries – first Switzerland and Germany, then The Netherlands – where a dialogue with representatives of different traditions facing different problems produced new and more sophisticated ideas. Fourthly, that the ferment of virtually uncontrolled discussion during the Revolution led to the flourishing of radical theologies like those of Fifth Monarchists and Quakers, and to secularizing ideas like those of Levellers and Diggers. We look forward to the Royal Society, Newton and Locke. Finally, the intermittent flirtation by Charles II and James II with a policy of tolerating Roman Catholics as a balance against the power of the Anglican church and the Anglican gentry confirmed the impossibility of eradicating dissent.

A key word was law. Jeremy Taylor in a sermon preached at the opening of the Cavalier Parliament in 1661 remarked that 'both sides pretended Scripture; but one side only can pretend to the laws'.[27] Law had been defined by the ruling landed class: it was safely predictable. The Bible was not. Parsons came to find it wiser to base their claim to tithes on the law of the land rather than on Scripture. It was difficult to get back to the pre-1640 world, when Hooker had argued that we could take the Bible to be the Word of God on the authority of the church. Hobbes and the discussions of the forties and fifties had made that an untenable position. The Bible had produced no universally acceptable solutions even on questions of church government where earlier protestants had most confidently expected it – bishops or presbyters, state church or voluntary congregations, ordination or lay preaching, tithes or voluntary maintenance. . . . What authority was there? As late as 1706 Matthew Henry still held that 'if the Scriptures be not the Word of God, there is . . . no discovering at all God's mind concerning our duty and happiness'.[28] This seemed to him to leave mankind rudderless on a stormy sea.

When we speak of the decline of the Bible's influence, we must not think that England suddenly became a pagan country. But Stillingfleet spoke in 1662 of 'the affronts and indignities which have been cast on religion by such who account it a matter of judgment to disbelieve the Scriptures'.[29] The author of *The Whole Duty of Man* felt it necessary to call the faithful to the defence of Holy Writ's authority against the fashionable cavil and prejudice of its atheist detractors.[30]

Richard Baxter captured the spirit in which conservative Parliamentarians welcomed the restoration of Charles II and the Church of England. He was an old opponent of bishops, but in his *Sermon of Repentance*, a Fast Day Sermon preached to the Convention Parliament on 30 April 1660, Baxter had no doubt that now 'the question is not whether bishops or no,

---

27. Taylor, *The Whole Works*, II, p. 47.
28. Henry, *An Exposition of All the Books of the Old and New Testaments* (1867 reprint), I, p. 2, Preface.
29. Stillingfleet, *Origines Sacrae*, Preface to Reader.
30. *The Lively Oracles Given to Us, or the Christians Birthright And Duty in the custody and use of the Holy Scripture*, pp. 260–65, in *The Works of the Author of the Whole Duty of Man* (1704). First published 1677.

but whether discipline or none'.[31] He had made his social anxiety clear in *A Holy Commonwealth*, published the previous year. 'All this stir of the republicans is but to make the seed of the serpent to be the sovereign rulers of the earth . . . . Were not this multitude restrained they would presently have the blood of the godly . . . . That the major vote of the people should ordinarily be just and good is next to an impossibility . . . The rabble hate both magistrates and ministers . . . . Many a time have I heard them say, "It will never be a good world, while knights and gentlemen make us laws, that are chosen for fear and do but oppress us, and do not know the people's sores. It will never be well with us till we have Parliaments of countrymen like ourselves, that know our wants"'.[32]

An ex-royalist like Samuel Butler, hostile as he was to radical religious views, did not think the Bible was the Word of God.[33] Anti-Scripturism, said Boyle in 1663, 'grows . . . rife, and spreads fast'.[34] John Crowne's *Calisto* (1675), performed at court, was ostensibly mocking the gods of classical antiquity: but some of its shafts struck home at Christian theology.[35] The anonymous *The Country-Gentleman's Vade Mecum* of 1699 noted that procuresses at playhouses attracted the attention of young men by combining quotation of Scripture with bawdy talk.[36]

The most effective argument against irreligion was believed to be exposure of its licentious social consequences. An anonymous interregnum pamphlet, *A Memento*, had believed that 'those that say in their heart, "there is no God", they'll yet allow the political convenience of persuading the people otherwise'; and that meant restricting freedom of religious discussion.[37] Francis Osborn had noted that 'the exploding of . . . belief [in heaven and hell] would be of no less diminution to the reverence of the civil magistrate than the profit of the priesthood'. But he saw an interconnection of dangerous ideas here. 'Since so considerable a falsehood is thought to be discovered by our governors in the clergy's tenet for the impunity of kings, why may not their poor subjects be unsatisfied' about the existence

31. Baxter, op. cit., p. 43.

32. Baxter, op. cit., pp. 92–4, 226–31.

33. Butler, *Characters*, p. 466; *Observations*, p. 124.

34. Robert Boyle, *Some Considerations Touching the Style of the Scriptures*, in *Works* (ed. J. Birch, 1772), II, p. 295.

35. *The Dramatic Works of John Crowne* (1873–4), I, esp. pp. 264–5, 285. Crowne was a protégé of Rochester's.

36. Op. cit., pp. 43–4, quoted by D. Roberts, *The Ladies: Female Patronage of Restoration Drama, 1660–1700* (Oxford U.P., 1989), p. 90.

37. Op. cit. (n.d.), p. 206.

of heaven and hell?[38] The Earl of Rochester stressed the contradictions of the Bible even to Burnet on his death-bed; he still thought that all came by nature, and that the stories of the Creation and Fall were parables. He had doubts about rewards and punishments after death, and rejected monogamy. But Burnet was able to persuade him (or so he tells us) of the social usefulness of a religion in which he did not believe.[39] Burnet himself wrote a treatise, *De Statu Mortuorum*, in which he cited the view of the Fathers that 'the received doctrine and words must be used ... when preaching to the populace, which is inclined to vice and can be deterred from evil only by the fear of punishment'.[40]

Thomas Hobbes had wanted to get rid of belief in posthumous rewards and punishments because he held that hope of eternal bliss gave courage and tenacity to revolutionaries and heretics. Effective belief in rewards in the after life did in fact diminish as moral behaviour came to seem more important than bringing about an earthly millennium. In the Bible God appears to threaten sinners with eternal torment (Matthew XII.42, 50; XV.8; Revelation XIV, XX). But the attribution of deliberate cruelty to God, and the justice of punishing those who might have sinned out of ignorance, raised difficult questions. Tillotson in 1690 argued that God would not be breaking his word if he did not carry out his threat of eternal punishment of the wicked; but he did not wish this idea to be generally preached. Hell still had its social uses.[41]

If no hell, no law and order: that other consequence of the Fall, private property, would be endangered. But a noble lie like Tillotson's could hardly satisfy honest Christians, least of all if it confronted a theology which asserted that the wicked were predestined to hell from all eternity and that there was nothing they could do about it. Arminianism and the decline of hell must have gone together. Dr John North, an Arminian by conviction, justified Calvinism as 'more politic, and thereby in some respects, fitter to maintain religion' in 'ignorant men ... because more suited to their capacity'. 'But that', he concluded, 'is referred to art, and not to truth, and ought to be ranked with the *piae fraudes*, or holy cheats'.[42] By contrast, Latitudinarian Arminianism might seem an intellectually respectable creed.

38. Osborn, *Advice to a Son*, in *Miscellaneous Works*, I, p. 99.
39. Burnet, *The Lives of Sir Matthew Hale, . . . Wilmot Earl of Rochester; and Queen Mary* (1774), esp. pp. 18, 44, 58, 76–9.
40. Burnet, op. cit., p. 309, quoted by D. P. Walker, *The Decline of Hell* (Chicago U.P., 1964), p. 159.
41. John Tillotson, *A Sermon Preached before the Queen at White-Hall, March 7th, 1689–90*.
42. Roger North, *Lives of the Norths*, III, p. 344.

Opinion in the seventeenth century regarding the burning of heretics and use of torture in legal processes was changing. As fewer and fewer men and women were prepared to die for their beliefs, so they became less tolerant of the execution of those holding unorthodox ideas. As early as 1612 it had been recognized that the public burning of heretics was counter-productive. Inspired no doubt by stories of the heroism of Foxe's martyrs, the victims of early seventeenth-century burnings won the sympathy of the crowds which were supposed to applaud their punishment. Public executions were not cost-effective. In 1639 the Archbishop of York wanted to revive the practice, which he thought had done the church much good; and after 1660 Hobbes believed that the bishops would like to burn him. No doubt they would: but it was too late. Henry IV's statute *De haeretico comburendo* was repealed in 1677. Experience of Laudian intolerance in the 1630s, and of Presbyterian intolerance in the 1640s, followed by the relative tolerance of the 1650s, had left its mark. England did not suddenly become a tolerant country – far from it. But the fact that the dissenting interest was also the interest of rich London merchants financially useful to the government helped to change the intellectual climate.

The cooled temperature was demonstrated by the 'reasonableness' of Latitudinarian theologians, separating ethics from religion and so – for some – from the Bible. The Latitudinarians were closely associated with the Royal Society, whose first Secretary was John Wilkins, symbolically both brother-in-law to Oliver Cromwell and a future bishop. Wilkins explained Biblical miracles by natural causes, and spent much time and energy in trying to create a universal language. One of its objects was to end religious controversies by producing agreement on the meaning of words. This programme was supported by the Royal Society.[43] Locke, in *The Reasonableness of Christianity*, was concerned to end citation of 'scattered sentences in Scripture-language, accommodated to our notions and prejudices'.[44] John Toland insisted that 'to believe the divinity of Scripture or the sense of any passage thereof, without rational proof and an evident consistency, is a blamable credulity and a temerarious opinion, ordinarily maintained out of a gainful prospect'.[45] We have come a long way.

But the prophets of the age of reason fell short of modern standards of

43. I am indebted here to the John Wilkins Lecture of Professor S. F. Mason, delivered in Oxford on 2 May 1991: 'Analogies of Thought-Style in the Protestant Reformation and Early Modern Science'.
44. Locke, op. cit. (1695), pp. 291–5.
45. Toland, *Christianity not Mysterious* (1696), pp. 31–6.

rationality. Locke believed that kidney pains could be cured by burying the patient's urine in a stone jug. He made computations from Daniel with a view to dating the end of the world.[46] Newton spent as much time on millenarian studies as on astronomy. William Whiston used Newton's physics to explain Noah's Flood, the elliptical orbit of the earth and the final conflagration which would lead to the millennium.[47]

Between 1669 and 1678 Theophilus Gale published four parts of a massive work, *The Court of the Gentiles*, in which he argued that all arts and sciences came from the Jewish people – from Adam, Moses (skilled historian and philosopher), Seth and Enoch (astronomy), Noah (navigation), Solomon (architecture) and Job (a great philosopher). Geometry derived from the division of the land of Canaan among the chosen people. Gale's work was taken very seriously – published by the Oxford University Press even though Gale was a dissenter. Traherne was so impressed that he copied out long extracts into his commonplace book.[48]

Gale's idea was not novel: Ralegh had thought that Homer stole from Moses.[49] The novelty lay in Gale's thoroughness. But he was still hedged in by the Bible. Roger Williams had seen virtues even in the culture of the American Indians; Gale could see only inferiority in pagan Greece and Rome. Gale knew enough to have been a Vico. But he failed to profit by the intellectual experiences of the interregnum. We may contrast Samuel Fisher's *The Rustickes Alarm to the Rabbies*, which does mark the transition to a new intellectual epoch. Fisher summed up the insights of Walwyn, Winstanley, Writer, Ranters. His title suggests a populist appeal from priests and universities to peasants, and his work contrasts in all respects with Gale. The latter, steeped in classical learning, popular among dons, meticulously mapped a blind alley.

Or consider the controversial works of Prynne, Herle, Brady and others on the mythical history of Parliament in Anglo-Saxon and early Norman times. Their disputes played a significant part in seventeenth-century politics, but were left behind by the pragmatism of Hobbes and the Harringtonians. The radical theory of the Norman Yoke survived until

46. K. Dewhurst, *John Locke (1632–1704), Physician and Philosopher* (1963), p. 204. The computations I owe to Professor Frank Manuel.

47. Perry Miller, *Errand into the Wilderness*, pp. 229–33.

48. Wade, *Thomas Traherne*, pp. 67, 102, 250–56. For Gale I am indebted to D. W. Wallace's 'Puritanism and the Hermetic Tradition: Revolution and the Ancient Theology in Theophilus Gale', Millersville.

49. Ralegh, *History of the World*, I, p. 195. For many other examples of cultural derivation from the Jews see ibid., I, pp. 167–227, IV, pp. 572–3.

nineteenth-century Chartism because it continued to correspond to the observed fact of the dominance of the gentry, just as the New Testament's egalitarian pronouncements always retained their relevance.

Milton's *Of Christian Doctrine*, with its criticism and manipulation of the Bible, had the misfortune of being by-passed by history. When it finally appeared in 1825 it had lost the revolutionary significance which Milton as well as his government had attributed to it. It was as irrelevant as Newton's researches into the date of the end of the world.[50] Gale, Milton, Fisher: each of their books testifies to the vast labours of a lifetime. But only Fisher's contributed to the mainstream of European intellectual life. If Milton's *Of Christian Doctrine* had been published in the seventeenth century it might have had a comparable liberating effect. The same is true of Henry Stubbe's *History of the Rise and Progress of Mahometanism*, not printed until 1911.[51] Gerrard Winstanley, who had one of the most powerful minds of his age, never worked out his ideas systematically. He was too busy – digging, herding cows, warding off attacks on his commune, defending the Digger experiment in court or in pamphlets. He left no system, but threw off aphorisms summing up aspects of his thought. His answer to the question, How should the Bible be used?[52] is relevant to posterity.

IV

The Bible lost its universal power once it had been demonstrated that you could prove anything from it, and that there was no means of deciding once the authority of the church could not be enforced. (How right Rome had been!) Hobbes's attempt to substitute secular authority failed. Fragmentation – both intellectual and of congregations – was one of the most important consequences of religious toleration. Many still continued to believe that truth could and should be found in the Bible but could not agree on what it was. (We may compare the devastating consequences of the abolition of the authoritative position of the Communist Party and its ideology in eastern Europe in 1989–90.) The Bible became a historical document, to be interpreted like any other. Today its old authority exists only in dark corners like Northern Ireland or the Bible Belt of the USA.

50. See pp. 32–3 above.
51. J. R. Jacob, *Henry Stubbe*, Chapter 4.
52. See p. 223 above.

When Lady Brute in Vanbrugh's *The Provok'd Wife* (1697) was reminded that the Bible told us to return good for evil, she replied without hesitation 'That may be a mistake in the translation'.[53] Mary Astell, more pious than Lady Brute, but a fierce defender of women against men, was faced with what had always been the knock-down argument that men must be superior because God created Adam before he created Eve. She replied that God had created the animals before he created Adam. What should one conclude from that?[54] It was devastatingly simple; and the fact that such an argument could be put forward in print by a good Anglican tells us much about the changed status of the Bible. The question was asked before 1612, when Thomas Taylor answered it; but then it was printed only in order to be refuted. Taylor's rather feeble retort was that in I Timothy II.13 'the Apostle proveth not Adam's superiority so much from the order as from the end of the creation of woman' – as helpmeet. Soon Lady Bradshaigh was to snap back at Samuel Richardson, 'What do I care for the patriarchs?'[55]

Arnold Williams points out that 'the Renaissance commentary on Genesis' ceased to exist in the second half of the seventeenth century. The last examples he cites are John Pearson's *Critici Sacri* (1660) and Matthew Poole's *Synopsis Criticismi* (1669). *Paradise Lost* is the last of the hexameral epics. Edward Eccleston's opera, *Noah's Flood: the Destruction of the World* (1679), seems to have been the last of its kind. Dryden's *State of Innocence* (1677) was a dramatization of *Paradise Lost*.[56] Archaeology and geology slowly liberated themselves from the Genesis narrative. Not only witchcraft but also suicide ceased to be regarded as a diabolical crime.[57]

In 1684 a nonconformist preacher was charged with treason for comparing the King to Jeroboam.[58] Next year Richard Baxter was jailed for a publication which was held to be libellous of the Church of England. But after 1689 the *fact* that men could not be compelled to attend their parish churches every Sunday was recognized by the cessation of proceedings in the ecclesiastical courts against non-attenders. It was also a recognition of the courts' decline as effective instruments of control. Much deist material was published in England in the 1690s, based on comparative religion,

---

53. Vanbrugh, op. cit., Act I, scene i.

54. M. Astell, *Reflections upon Marriage* (3rd. ed., 1706), sig. a2. First published 1700.

55. Taylor, *A Commentarie upon the Epistle of St. Paul the Apostle to Timothy* (1619), p. 391; Richardson, *Correspondence* (ed. A. L. Barbauld, 1804), VI, p. 194.

56. A. Williams, op. cit., pp. 238, 259; ibid., pp. 264–7.

57. See Michael MacDonald and Terence R. Murphy, *Sleepless Souls: Suicide in Early Modern England* (Oxford U.P., 1990), esp. pp. 214–15.

58. D. Ogg, *England in the Reign of Charles II* (Oxford U.P., 1934), II, p. 514.

together with Locke's *The Reasonableness of Christianity* and Toland's *Christianity not Mysterious* in 1695–6. In 1695 an Oxford M.A. published a letter to a nobleman in London concerning 'some errors about the creation, general flood and the peopling of the world'. 'The most rational way to examine these problems', he insisted, 'is by the laws of gravity, or by the hydrostatics'. The Biblical accounts are unacceptable: 'the present age will not endure empty notions and vain speculations. . . . We presently call for clear proof or ocular demonstration'. 'The universal disposition of this age is bent upon a rational religion'.[59]

The breaking of the absolute authority of the Bible in all spheres is one of the many triumphs of the human spirit, parallel to (and connected with) the decline of hell in the seventeenth century which D. P. Walker has documented.[60] Only re-established political consensus in the later seventeenth century, and publishers' readiness to exercise self-censorship on the basis of this consensus after the lapse of the Licensing Act in 1695, prevented 'the rude ignorant vulgar' from enjoying the freedom of sceptical discussion and printing that had prevailed between 1640 and 1660, and which their betters continued to enjoy. Societies for the Propagation of the Gospel and for Promoting Christian Knowledge helped to preserve traditional respect for the Bible among the lower orders.

For practical purposes the Bible had turned out to be as ambiguous as the ancient oracles. No acceptable interpreter was found. The Pope had proved unsatisfactory to national sovereigns since they could not be sure of controlling him all the time: he was most likely to fail when most needed. The Two Last Witnesses, Reeve and Muggleton, did not win the universal acceptance they expected. *Leviathan* was theoretically attractive, especially to governments; but Hobbes's assumption that the sovereign and he alone may demand acceptance of his version of the Scriptures fell foul of the intellectual individualism inherent in protestantism: *quis custodiet ipsum custodem?* The fear of anarchy on which Hobbes relied was not a sufficient counter-balance.

The Church of England's solution had been ecclesiastical control of the censorship, plus an authorized interpreter of the Bible in every parish: not rigorously supervised, but educated and conditioned in ways that made it unlikely that he would deviate too far from the accepted norm. Robert South in the early months of 1660 told the lawyers of Lincoln's Inn that 'if there were not a minister in every parish you would quickly find cause to

---

59. L.P., Master of Arts, 'Two Essays', in *Somers Tracts* (1748–51), XI, pp. 291–308.
60. Cf. Joseph Frank, *Hobbled Pegasus*, pp. 26–7.

increase the number of constables'.[61] But too many protestant consciences had called a state-authorized priesthood in question. Complete censorship had proved impossible to enforce. The assumptions on which the age-old intellectual edifice had stood crumbled. What took their place?

The Bible itself was revealed as the greatest idol of all. It was not overthrown, like Stalin's statues in eastern Europe: it was still honoured as a venerable antique, like the gods of classical Greece and Rome; but it had lost its political power. Divine Right of Kings and the clergy's divine right to tithes ceased with this Biblical authority — which did not mean that kings ceased to rule or tithes to be collected: it meant that different arguments had to be found to defend them. And in the long run these arguments were open to rational criticism. Kings as 'the Lord's anointed' were a joke for *The Vicar of Bray*.

Discussion of the Bible had been the crucial issue. Lollards were forbidden it; Henry VIII first authorized the Bible in English and then tried to prevent the lower classes from discussing it. Edward VI went too far in one direction, Mary in the other. Elizabeth tried to prevent 'prophesyings', discussion classes after sermons; Archbishops Whitgift, Bancroft and Laud all wanted to discourage too much preaching. After the breakdown of controls in the 1640s, 'mechanic preachers' were self-selected, popularly accepted chairmen, presiding over *novel* discussions. When the Earl of Leicester read the House of Commons' Declaration of 31 December 1645 against preaching by unordained persons, he exclaimed that 'by this Declaration it is made dangerous to read the Bible', since there was no point in Bible-reading unless the Bible was expounded and discussed.[62] The strength of dissent after 1660 was such that the Anglican church could not recover its monopoly position. The next best thing was to license nonconformist ministers so as to retain some control, to guard against too much democracy. Ministers who could be held responsible for their flocks, and so would control them, gave stability and continuity. This was aided by nonconformist exhaustion after two decades of conflict and failure to agree, by the need for consolidation under the persecution of the reigns of Charles II and James II, and by recognition that the world was not to be changed by the efforts of even the most dedicated saints. So Puritans rejected politics and declined into dissent.

One conclusion may be that the Bible can serve any social/political

61. Quoted by Irène Simon, *Three Restoration Divines: Barrow, South, Tillotson* (Bibliothèque de la Faculté de Philosophie et Lettres de l'Université de Liège, Fascicule CLXXXI, 1967–76), II, p. 60.
62. Ed. R. W. Blencowe, *Sydney Papers* (1825), p. 2.

purpose. It and the Christian religion have evolved over centuries and have had to incorporate many divergent social interests. The seeds of all heresies are to be found in the Bible, and most of them were cultivated and flowered during the Revolution. The glory of that Revolution, as Milton grasped, was the discussion, the ferment: truth may have more shapes than one[63] – the principle of dissent, the contempt for established authority shown by those ordinary people who could not, in Bunyan's immortal phrase, with Pontius Pilate speak Hebrew, Greek and Latin.[64] Failure to prevent continuing discussion by the middling and lower classes, to which the survival of dissent testified, was perhaps as important in preparing the intellectual climate for the Industrial Revolution as the political changes and liberation of the revolutionary decades.[65]

V

The vexed questions of predestination and free will, infant or adult baptism, state church or independent congregations, were still unresolved when the restoration abruptly terminated much of the debate. The hope that free discussion of the Bible would soon lead to agreement on such matters proved hopelessly wrong. It was perhaps not surprising that the royalist Sir John Denham thought that printing was 'the devil's most pernicious instrument'.[66] But in 1643 the Laudian John Jegon, an Essex parson, was also alleged to have said ''Twas pity that ever the Bible was translated into English, for now every woman and beggarly fellow think themselves able to dispute with reverend divines'.[67] A few years later the sceptical layman, Matthias Prideaux, was asking 'whether the invention of printing and gunpowder have done more harm than good?'[68] The juxtaposition suggested the answer. Popular diffusion and discussion of the Bible led, ironically, to a lessening of its authority.

63. *MCPW*, II, p. 563.

64. *BMW*, I, p. 304. Cf. p. 199 above.

65. I owe this idea to discussions with Jack Goldstone of the University College of California, Davis; see also M. C. Jacob, *The Cultural Meaning of the Scientific Revolution*, p. 245.

66. Denham, *The Progress of Learning*, in *Poems and Translations* (7th ed., n.d.), p. 96.

67. Quoted in W. Davids, *Annals of Evangelical Nonconformity in . . . Essex* (1863), p. 236; cf. Hobbes, *Behemoth*, in *English Works* (ed. Sir W. Molesworth, 1839–45), VI, pp. 190–91. Jegon nevertheless managed to cling on to his living, through all vicissitudes, until he died after the restoration.

68. Prideaux, *An Essay and Compendious Introduction*, p. 141.

It was fair game when the Catholic Patrick Carey, Falkland's brother, used the analogy of the Bible to object to the laws being translated into English:

> Our Church still flourishing we had seen
> If the holy-writ had ever been
>   Kept out of laymen's reach;
> But, when 'twas English'd, men half-witted,
> Nay women too, would be permitted
>   T' expound all texts, and preach.
>
> Then what confusion did arise!
> Cobblers divines 'gan to despise,
>   So that they could but spell:
> Their ministers to scorn did bring:
> Preaching was held an easy thing,
>   Each one might do't as well.[69]

We saw above how millenarian/disciplinarian Puritanism could prove in many respects congruent with the interests of parish élites, improving yeomen and industrious artisans who wished to impose order on their families and on the landless poor as well as to cultivate acres enclosed from the waste. It also proved acceptable to settlers in the American wilderness.[70] I suspect that those who stress that in 1642 individuals chose sides in the civil war for religious reasons neglect this congruence between ideology and economic interests. As Conrad Russell wisely remarks, 'to say the parties were divided by religion is not the same thing as to say that religion caused the civil war'.[71] Active millenarian Puritanism fitted economic expansion and colonization better than did traditional religion. Anti-clericalism demonstrated, among other things, a wish to liberate lay consciences. As the millenarian impetus failed, this ideology turned into one of self- and class-interests, utility, decked out with selected Biblical texts. In time the texts came to count for less and less, and the authentic English ideology of pragmatic empiricism emerged like a butterfly from the chrysalis – the least theoretical of all ruling ideologies because its Biblical basis had been abandoned. The ideology was spiced with proverbial wisdom which sometimes took Biblical forms, but more often than not it was pure peasant or artisan lore drawn from practical experience. Bacon

---

69. Carey, *Trivial Poems and Triolets* (1651), in Saintsbury, *Caroline Poets*, II, p. 461.
70. See Chapter 5 above.
71. Russell, *The Causes of the Civil War* (Oxford U.P., 1990), p. 59.

had taught English intellectuals to learn from craftsmen; Sprat eulogized their plain style of writing in his *History*, which was sanctioned by the Royal Society patronized by the Head of the Church of England.

The English pride themselves on 'muddling through', 'conquering an Empire in a fit of absence of mind', 'the English genius for compromise'. These apparent failings of which we boast with mock humility are perhaps vestigial remains of the Calvinist conviction that God will help his elect, regardless of their merits. The fact that England became for two and a half centuries the world's strongest power in economic and military/naval terms permitted the survival of the attitude. The English were no longer the people of the Book but they seemed to have been selected; and England was succeeded by the manifest destiny of the USA. The gift for holy humbug among Anglo-Saxons allows them still to believe that their use of power is different from, and nicer than, that of lesser breeds. It is so much second nature that it is difficult to know in any given instance whether the hypocrisy is conscious or unconscious.

We are looking at a much bigger process than the decline of Bibliolatry. Antichrist, after a century and a half in which he was central to English politics, sank into vulgarity as millenarianism was secularized.[72] Hell declined too: so did executions for witchcraft. Calvinism lost the ascendancy it had long held in English intellectual life, though it continued to thrive in the sub-culture of dissent. Providential history, God working out his purposes for mankind, yielded place to a more secular history to which Machiavelli, Hobbes and Harrington were more relevant than the Bible. Preachers always condemn the exceptional ungodliness of their times, but the sophisticated and hard-headed John Owen thought that 'no age can parallel that wherein we live' for atheism, 'an abomination that these parts of the world were unacquainted withal until these latter ages'.[73] Yet 'atheism' was still an attitude, a rejection, rather than a philosophy. Francis Osborn was one of many to argue its impossibility: there must be a first cause.[74] The Earl of Rochester told Burnet that he had never met an entire atheist.[75] Until a scientific

72. See p. 323 above.
73. Owen, *Works*, XIII, p. 364 (1669), VIII, pp. 612–16 (1681); cf. IX, p. 345 (1672). Cf. *The Travels of Cosmo III, Grand Duke of Tuscany, through England* in 1669 (written in fact by Lorenzo Magalotti): 'atheism has many followers in England' (English translation, 1821, p. 468).
74. Osborn, *Miscellaneous Works*, I, p. 28.
75. Burnet, *Life . . . Of . . . Rochester*, p. 12. A century later John Wesley said he had encountered only two atheists in fifty years (Rivers, *Reason, Grace and Sentiment*, p. 230).

theory of evolution emerged it was indeed difficult to conceive of a universe without a creator. Ranters insisted on the eternity of matter: but where did matter come from?

One unexpected consequence of the failure of the radical revolution was that the A.V. replaced the Geneva Bible: the last edition of the Geneva version was published in 1644. For this I think market forces must have been mainly responsible. Once there was no longer governmental opposition to popular editions of the Bible, the A.V. was far cheaper to produce than the Geneva Bible with its copious notes, illustrations and other accessories. The attempt to produce a revised annotated edition in the 1650s came to nothing. The decline of theological politics, consequent on Parliament's victory in the civil war, failure to reach agreed solutions and the fading of the millenarian hope, all contributed to Geneva's marginal notes losing the immediate relevance which they appeared to have before 1645.[76] The anti-Puritan intellectual climate which became respectable after 1660 led to denigration of the Geneva Bible as of Sternhold and Hopkins's Psalms. James I's desire to produce an uncontroversial Bible came to fruition a generation and one revolution after the publication of the A.V. Not for the last time in English history, 'uncontroversial' meant conservative.

76. But see p. 66 above. Editions of the A.V. with Genevan notes continued to be published.

20. Unfinished Business

Can these [dry] bones live?
Ezekiel, XXXVII.1–14.

Accident is but a term invented to relieve ignorance of causes, as physicians use to call the strange operations of plants and minerals 'occult qualities', not that they are without their causes, but that their causes are unknown. And indeed there is not any thing in nature or event that has not a pedigree of causes which – though obscure to us – cannot be so to God, who is the first Cause of all things.
Samuel Butler, *Characters and Passages from Note-Books*, p. 300.[1]

All you which have cast out any old tyrants, consider seriously what you have yet to do, and so near as you can make and maintain an equality of all goods and lands; . . . which if you will not perform, you are worse than the old tyrants, because you did pretend a bettering, which they did not.
[Anon.], *Tyranipocrit, Discovered with his wiles, wherewith he vanquisheth* (Rotterdam, 1649) (ed. A. Hopton, n.d.), p. 33.

The civil war of the seventeenth century . . . has never been concluded.
T. S. Eliot, *Milton* (1947).

I

One long-standing conviction of mine that struggling to write this book has confirmed is that we impoverish our understanding of the past if we chop it up into little bits labelled 'constitutional history', 'economic history', 'literary history', 'political history' and so on, no less than if we allow the statistics of demographers to conceal the human lives behind unreliable records of births, marriages and deaths.

1. Sir Thomas Browne had said something similar, though less concisely, in *Religio Medici* (1642), *Works* (Bohn ed., 1852), II, pp. 344–6.

I remember being very struck when I first read, at an impressionable age, T. S. Eliot on the art of the poet. 'A poet's mind ... is constantly amalgamating disparate experience. The ordinary man ... falls in love, or reads Spinoza, and these two experiences have nothing to do with each other, or with the noise of the typewriter or the smell of cooking: in the mind of the poet these experiences are always forming new wholes'.[2] Without wishing to claim too much for history, still less to distinguish historians from 'ordinary men' and women, I think there is force in Sidney's statement of a familiar trope: 'the best of the historian is subject to the poet'.[3] Writing to his brother Robert in 1580, Sidney described the poet's art in words which fit the historian. 'A poet, in painting forth the effects, the motions, the whisperings of the people, which though in disputation one might say was true, yet who will mark them well shall find them taste of a poetical vein, ... for though they were not so, yet it is enough that they might be so'.[4]

There are analogies between the interpretative task of the historian and Sidney's and Eliot's description of the poet's practice. The historian should not stay on the surface of events; his interest should not be limited to State Papers, Parliamentary debates, acts and ordinances, decisions of judges and local magistrates, still less to battles and the amours of kings. He should listen – carefully and critically – to ballads,[5] plays, pamphlets, newspapers, tracts, 'the whisperings of the people', the cypher diaries and private correspondence of MPs, spiritual autobiographies – to every source that can help him or her to get the feel of how people lived and in what ways their sensitivity differed from ours. He or she must try to understand why even the most democratic of seventeenth-century reformers apparently never thought of giving a share in the political or professional life of the country to the 50 per cent of the population who were women. Nor do women seem to have asked for such things. The historian must listen to alchemists and astrologers no less than to bishops, to demands of London crowds; and he or she must try to understand the motivation of rioters, whether they are labelled anti-Catholic or anti-enclosure rioters or simply food rioters. A good deal of valuable work has been done here, not least by literary

---

2. Eliot, *Selected Essays* (1932), p. 287.
3. Sidney, *Apologie for Poetrie* (ed. J. Churton Collins, Oxford U.P., 1907), p. 22.
4. Quoted by Katherine Duncan-Jones, *Sir Philip Sidney*, p. 170.
5. Including political ballads of the type collected by Fairholt (see e.g. pp. 49 n., 295 n. above) but not limited to them.

historians and literary critics, which is still not incorporated into mainstream history.

Good – imaginative – history is akin to retrospective poetry. It is about life as lived – as much of it as we can recapture. In the seventeenth century the Bible was central to emotional as well as intellectual life. The majestic prose of Tyndale, the Geneva and Authorized Versions, transformed English ways of thinking as well as the English language – not only ways of thinking about theology. Considering the Song of Songs led us into millenarianism as well as into the wilderness. The linked symbols of the wilderness, the garden and the hedge relate to the rise of the congregational churches as well as to agriculture; and in both connections they lead us across the Atlantic – where anti-Catholicism also takes us. Cain and Abel, Esau and Jacob, help us to understand theological controversies about predestination and free will; but they also tell us about the economic problems of younger sons, and illuminate the political ideas of Levellers and Diggers, memories of which remain with us till the nineteenth century. The millennium disappointingly failed to arrive; but revolutionary millenarianism tells us much about the need for social reform, and secularized millenarianism helped Britain to become a world empire. The Biblical concept of idolatry was put to political uses against Charles I: ultimately the Bible itself was condemned as an idol. Psalms raise questions about politics and literary genres as well as about theology. They lead us to Milton, as the garden leads us to Marvell and metaphysical poetry. The Bible links Hakewill with Samuel Fisher and Spinoza, the battle of the books with the battle over the Book.[6]

Men and women used Biblical idiom and Biblical stories to discuss religious, political, moral and social questions which it might have been dangerous to approach directly. The concept of the chosen people helped to express England's emergent nationalism as well as giving Gerrard Winstanley and the Diggers confidence that their communist colonies were realizing the truth of Biblical prophecy; it ultimately helped to establish dissent as a lasting feature in English society. The idea that God was deserting his chosen Englishmen led some to emigrate to America, others to fight for a more godly society at home, and for a society more conscious of international obligations.

If we are to understand mentalities in seventeenth-century England we could do worse than follow Jack Fisher's recommendation, to start from the Bible. The Bible in English helped men and women to think about

6. See p. 236 above.

their society, to criticize its institutions, to question some of its values. It enjoyed an authority to which no other book could aspire: kings and their opponents appealed to the Bible in the great conflicts of the revolutionary decades. At least one commentator pointed out that the Jesuit Robert Parsons, the regicide John Bradshaw and the Whig republican Algernon Sidney all cited the same Biblical texts in support of their diverse political objectives.[7]

Those who founded congregational churches were often those younger brothers and sisters who knew land hunger and social oppression. Bunyan tells us of his temptations to sell his birthright in Christ, like Esau; he cited with approval the Hebrew Jubilee. 'For the land shall not be sold for ever, for the land is mine, said God. Levit. XXV.23'.[8] So the land sales to which poverty had driven Bunyan's ancestors got mixed up with the state of his soul. The land question was still unresolved when the Spenceans took up the Jubilee. The wrath of God from which some nonconformists decided to flee was demonstrated in the injustice of English society. The millennium, the reign of the saints and the promised land were the names they gave to their hopes for a better society, whether in New or old England. In addition to threats of retribution the Bible offers hope – the prophets of return from exile, the good tidings of the Gospels, Revelation. The end of all three of Milton's last great poems gave hope, after and through defeat, in a cause greater than individual life. Idolatry was the word that Milton and Theaureaujohn used for false values.

When we say, rightly, that the English became the people of the Book, we must not suppose that theology or the after life were all that they studied in that Book. The after life indeed has no place in the Old Testament.[9] They found lessons and consolations for living on earth as well as the path to heaven. Some Englishmen also found confirmation and justification of their worst vices – sexism, patriarchalism, racialism, social hierarchy, national arrogance. Nor did the pious monopolize the idiom of the Bible. In the late eighteenth century popular songs celebrated the Biblical virtues of highwaymen.[10] The Bible has established cultural norms which survived religious beliefs.

I have said nothing in this book about the Bible in Wales, though it had lasting consequences for that country's cultural history. The epistles and

---

7. William Assheton, quoted by John Carswell, *The Porcupine*, p. 232.
8. Bunyan, *Grace Abounding*, pp. 42–5.
9. Lane Fox, op. cit., p. 98.
10. See Appendix A below.

gospels were translated in 1551, all of the New Testament in 1567, the whole Bible into more popular Welsh in 1588. A relatively cheap translation, selling at 5s., appeared in 1630. A comparative study of the influence of the vernacular Bible on national and cultural developments in protestant countries would be useful; but it is beyond the scope of this volume, and beyond my capacities. Protestant English Biblicism was in many ways unique. But in the eighteenth and nineteenth centuries some of it was exported. Professor Valentine Boss has argued convincingly that Milton's *Paradise Lost* was a best-seller in pre-revolutionary Russia *before* the Bible was available in the vernacular. It had great influence as a Bible-substitute.[11] In China missionaries had Bunyan's great Biblical allegory translated, and when the Taiping rebels in the middle of the nineteenth century roused millions of peasants in revolt, coming nearer to overthrowing the Emperor than any other movement before 1948, the Bible and *The Pilgrim's Progress* were the favourite books of their leader.[12]

II

This book has turned out to be almost exclusively concerned with the Old Testament, apart from Revelation in the New Testament. That was not my intention when I started to think about the subject, but it is the way the material seemed to point. The Old Testament describes the journey to the Promised Land. Oliver Cromwell is I believe the last English politician to be hailed seriously as Moses. This occurred just after his forcible dissolution of the Rump of the Long Parliament. George Fox was perhaps the last religious leader to be likened to Moses.[13] But old England was not transformed into Israel: New England turned out not to be a land flowing with milk and honey, but to be a useful market for manufactured goods and for slaves. Edwards listed, as one of the sectaries' errors, that the Old Testament does 'not concern nor bind Christians now under the New

11. See Professor Boss's forthcoming book, *Russian Popular Culture and John Milton*, which I was privileged to be allowed to read.
12. G. Wagner, *Re-enacting the Heavenly Vision: the Role of Religion in the Taiping Rebellion* (Institute of East Asian Studies, University of California, Berkeley, 1982), pp. 16, 59–60, 102, 109.
13. [Anon.], *The Humble Petition of the Church of Christ* (1653), quoted by I. Gentles, *The New Model Army: In England, Ireland and Scotland, 1645–1653* (Oxford, 1992), p. 434; *The Short Journal and Itinerary Journals of George Fox* (ed. N. Penney, Cambridge U.P., 1925), pp. 243, 366. See p. 113 above.

Testament'. The memory of Babylon and the fear of Antichrist receded into the background as the Navigation Act and the new imperial policy gave Englishmen new wealth and greater confidence in themselves. The favourite texts of the Latitude Men came almost exclusively from the New Testament.[14]

The great protestant doctrine of predestination attempted to adapt the Old Testament's message to the world of the sixteenth and seventeenth centuries; the doctrine of the priesthood of all believers starts from the Old Testament concept of priesthood, which has not always been easy to find in the New Testament. The ideas of birthright, inheritance, go back to the patriarchal society of the Old Testament. Monarchy was a problem for the children of Israel, as it was for men and women of sixteenth- and seventeenth-century England – and as it was not for the men and women of the New Testament, helplessly subordinated to the Roman Empire. The virtues of the Old Testament were the unsophisticated, 'heroic' military virtues which Samuel Butler rejected when Hudibras tried to

> Prove his doctrine orthodox
> By apostolic blows and knocks

– but of course they were not apostolic but rather prophetical. Milton . rejected the 'chivalrous' military virtues; his better fortitude is to be found in the Old Testament, but it is perhaps more specifically a New Testament virtue. But Milton is the last great writer of Biblical epic: the Augustan age lost interest in the tribal society of ancient Israel. By the end of the seventeenth century England's cultural self-confidence and English literature were established. Defoe, whose ideology marks the climax of anti-popery, also helped to create the new bourgeois novel, in which England led the world.

On balance I think the Bible in English did far more good than harm; we must be grateful that critics were at work on it, undermining its super-rational authority and dethroning it after its period of absolute sovereignty. Someone said that 'the world the Bible made dethroned the Bible'. It was the radical godly whose passionate desire to make sense of the Bible led them into the critical activity which ultimately dethroned it. Let us pay tribute to the scholarly labours of Tyndale, Thomas James, William Crashawe, Perkins, Preston and Chillingworth as well as lesser luminaries like Greenhill and Burroughs; the greater Milton and Owen, the radicals Walwyn, Winstanley, Writer and Fisher. They read their present back into

14. Edwards, *Gangraena*, I, p. 19; Rivers, op. cit., pp. 72–3.

the Bible, as Hobbes read it into the state of nature. They found the Bible a guide to action, as they eagerly strove to comprehend the relevance of the barbarous stories in Judges, Kings and Chronicles to their own rather more sophisticated society. The actual achievements of their vast exegetical tomes may seem inadequate to the effort put in; but the effect of their scholarship in giving authority to their sermons and books should not be under-estimated. To the extent that England ultimately became a democracy it owes much to the discussions initiated by these scholars – discussions whose ironical effect was in the long run to force men and women to rely on their own intelligence rather than on citations from a holy text. They cut off the branch on which they sat, letting in more light, to the great advantage of those who followed them.[15]

15. A book which appeared too late for me to make proper use of it is David Harris Sack's *The Widening Gate: Bristol and the Atlantic Economy, 1450–1700* (California U.P., 1992). Sacks shows in convincing detail how religion is mixed up with economics, foreign trade with sectarian religion, local with international politics. When we have more studies like his and David Underdown's *Fire from Heaven* we shall begin to understand the complexities of capitalism's triumph in England. I am very grateful to Professor Sacks for sending me a copy of this important book.

Appendix A. God the Highwayman

I read Peter Linebaugh's *The London Hanged: Crime and Civil Society in the Eighteenth Century* (1991) only after I had finished writing this book. He quotes a ballad about Dick Turpin in which that successful highwayman claims

> the Scriptures I fulfilled
> Though I this life did lead,
> For when the naked I beheld
> I clothed them with speed. . . .
> The poor I fed, the rich likewise
> I empty sent away.[1]

This recalls Abiezer Coppe, who in 1649 depicted God as a highwayman, warning the rich man 'Thou has many bags of money, and behold, now I come as a thief in the night, with my sword drawn in my hand, and like a thief as I am – I say "deliver your purse, deliver sirrah! Deliver or I'll cut thy throat"'.[2] Another Ranter, Laurence Clarkson, 'apprehended there was no such thing as theft . . . but as man made it so'.[3] It was right to expropriate the expropriators.

Between the time of the Ranters and of William Blake the law had expropriated many Englishmen and robbed them of rights recognized as customary by Deuteronomy XXIV – by enclosure and eviction, prohibition of gleaning and collection of fuel and fruits. In industry too traditional perquisites had been stopped, without compensation. The law, backed up by the whip, the branding iron, transportation and the gallows, enforced new absolute rights of property against those from whom had been taken even what they thought they had.[4] Bunyan, we recall, was always whole-heartedly on the side of the poor. Defoe put it strongly:

1. 'Turpin's Appeal to the Judge', quoted in Linebaugh, op. cit., pp. 203–4. In this Appendix I have incorporated some phrases from my review of Linebaugh's book in *Tribune*, 27 March 1992.
2. Coppe, *A Second Fiery Flying Roule* (1649), in Smith, *Ranter Writings*, p. 100.
3. Clarkson, *The Lost sheep Found*, in Smith, op. cit., pp. 181–2.
4. Linebaugh, op. cit., Chapters 11 and 12.

> The very lands we all along enjoyed
> They ravaged from the people they destroyed. . . .
>
> 'Tis all invasion, usurpation all . . .
>
> 'Tis all by fraud and force that we possess
> And length of time can make no crime the less. . . .
>
> Religion's always on the strongest side.

A poor woman who was hanged in 1739 for stealing coals thought it was 'no sin in the poor to rob the rich', and anyway Christ had died to procure the pardon of such sinners.[5]

The dangerous words of the Bible remained familiar to men and women even when they had lost faith in the God of the church. 'Christ died as an unbeliever', declared Blake. Blake himself said that all he knew was in the Bible. But 'to defend the Bible in this year 1798 would cost a man his life'. 'The Beast and the Whore rule without control'. Like Ranters, Blake rejected Scriptural literalism: he understood the Bible in the spiritual sense: 'as to the natural sense, that Voltaire was commissioned by God to expose'. His 'The Everlasting Gospel' invokes a seventeenth-century revolutionary theme. Blake contrasts true Christianity with formal orthodoxy:

> Both read the Bible day and night,
> But thou read'st black where I read white.[6]

As in the seventeenth century, the question was how to interpret the Bible.

For Coppe God had been 'that mighty Leveller' as well as a highwayman. God had told Clarkson to break all the Ten Commandments except 'Thou shalt do no murder' (and Clarkson contemplated the possibility of that being included at some future date). Like Coppe, Clarkson believed that acting out 'sin' with a pure mind was the way to true purity. That wise historian, A. L. Morton, speculated about the possibility that Blake had read pamphlets by Coppe and other Ranters, but decided that it was more

5. Daniel Defoe, *Jure Divino* (1706), pp. 206–17; Linebaugh, op. cit., p. 307–8.
6. A. L. Morton, 'The Everlasting Gospel', in *The Matter of Britain* (1966), reprinted in *History and the Imagination: Selected Writings of A. L. Morton* (ed. M. Heinemann and W. Thompson, 1990), pp. 113, 109, 122; Morton, *The World of the Ranters* (1970), pp. 82–3. I have drawn heavily on these two seminal works.

likely that ideas had been transmitted verbally, stripped of their millenarian associations. *The Beggar's Opera* perhaps gives evidence of verbal transmission of ideas and attitudes: so do the writings of Defoe. Mandeville uncovers some of the harsh and brutal realities hidden by the politeness of Augustan society. Blake took over the use of words like Jerusalem and Babylon as social and political symbols. He is, in Morton's phrase, 'the greatest English antinomian but also the last'.[7]

Peter Linebaugh suggests that memories of seventeenth-century radicalism survived among the marginal outcasts of the ruthlessly acquisitive eighteenth-century society – among pirates[8] and highwaymen, though we may doubt whether Dick Turpin expressed his sentiments in the Biblical language of the ballad quoted above. In the eighteenth century men were still asking 'When Adam delved and Eve span/Who was then the gentleman?' There were reprints of *The History of Wat Tyler and Jack Straw* in 1750 and later.[9] If I had read Linebaugh's important book earlier I should have laid more stress on this radical antinomian tradition, on aggressive lower-class Robin Hoodery. Striking Chatham workers described themselves as 'free-born subjects' in 1768; the attack on Lord Chief Justice Mansfield's house in 1780 recalled to contemporaries the 'levelling spirit' of the English Revolution, its rejection of the rights of property.[10] I should not have emphasized so exclusively the quietist, pietist other-worldly Biblicism of official dissent.

Continuities are difficult to establish. Naturally aggressive lower-class antinomianism could not get into print after 1660. But the records of the Fenstanton Baptist congregation in the 1650s reveal a radical rejection of 'the Christ who died at Jerusalem' by a lady who 'trampled [the Scriptures] under her feet'.[11] Richard Baxter had said in 1654 that antinomianism came naturally to the lower classes,[12] and Wesley pays frequent tribute to its survival in the mid-eighteenth century. The ethos of robbing the rich to

7. Morton, *History and the Imagination*, 134–5, 138, 124.
8. Cf. 'Radical Pirates?', reprinted in my *History and Ideas*, Chapter 8. 'They rob the rich under cover of law forsooth', as one pirate captain put it, 'and we plunder the rich under the protection of our own courage', quoted from *The History of the Pyrates* (1724), ibid., p. 165.
9. Linebaugh, op. cit., p. 347.
10. Ibid., pp. 381, 358.
11. *Records of the Churches of Christ gathered at Fenstanton, Warboys and Hexham* (ed. E. B. Underhill, Hanserd Knollys Soc., 1854), p. 90. See p. 237 above.
12. *Richard Baxters Confutation of a Dissertation for the Justification of Infidels* (1654), p. 288.

give to the poor has a long popular history, going back at least to the Robin Hood ballads. But in the eighteenth century the state was more ruthlessly enforcing the rights of property against the unpropertied: we cannot visualize Sir Robert Walpole or the Duke of Newcastle fraternizing with Dick Turpin as the ballads make the King fraternize with Robin Hood and his men, or as Shakespeare's Prince Hal enjoyed the company of Falstaff and his cronies.

As Linebaugh and his colleague Marcus Rediker[13] emphasize, far more Englishmen in the eighteenth century became acquainted at first hand with waste wildernesses across the Atlantic, through piracy, service in army, navy or mercantile marine, through emigration or transportation. Simultaneously they experienced the violence associated with imperial conquest, and got to know victims of imperialism and slavery who came to London in large numbers. The latter contributed significantly to the revival of political radicalism at the end of the century. But by then Paine had succeeded the Bible as their handbook.

13. See his *Between the Devil and the Deep Blue Sea: Merchant Seamen, Pirates and the Anglo-American Maritime World, 1700–1750* (Cambridge U.P., 1987), *passim*.

Appendix B. A Note on Liberation Theology[1]

―――

Our reading of the Bible will be a *militant* reading. . . .
Those who change the course of history are usually those who pose a new set of questions rather than those who offer solutions. . . .
History must be turned upside-down from the bottom, not from the top.
Gustavo Gutiérrez, *The Power of the Poor* (1979), English translation by R. R. Barr, 1983, pp. 4, 35, 21.

We Latin Americans talk of liberation and Europe talks about freedom, a freedom paid for by others sacrificing their freedoms.
Leonardo Boff, 'The Originality of the Theology of Liberation', in *The Future of Liberation Theology: Essays in Honor of Gustavo Gutiérrez* (ed. M. H. Ellis and O. Maduro, New York, 1989), p. 47.

I have made no serious study of twentieth-century liberation theology in Latin America. But even a cursory reading of the secondary material suggests interesting analogies between it and radical religion in seventeenth-century England. Liberation theology is 'mainly a product of the laity', and emphasizes lay Bible-reading.[2] Like seventeenth-century radicals, Gustavo Gutiérrez, the leading liberation theologian, pays special attention to the sufferings and needs of the poor, relying on the same Biblical texts.[3]

Gutiérrez is able to draw on the memory of Bartholomé de Las Casas, the sixteenth-century spokesman for American Indians against the Spanish conquistadores. In the Indies Las Casas had seen 'Jesus Christ, our God,

1. I am greatly indebted to Marcus Rediker for drawing my attention to the relevance of liberation theology, and for guidance with reading matter.
2. Ellis and Maduro, op. cit., esp. pp. 20, 79–80, 314, 413–14, 426, 506.
3. E.g. Luke VI.20–22; Psalm CXCVI.9; Isaiah I.17; Jeremiah VII.6, XXII.3; Job XXXI.16.

scourged and afflicted and crucified, not once, but millions of times'.[4] In Latin America today 'where to be a true Christian is to risk one's life', Gutiérrez said, 'we speak of social revolution, not reform; of liberation, not development; of socialism, not modernization of the prevailing system'.[5] Liberation theologians attach relatively greater importance to the New Testament than did seventeenth-century radicals, though they have difficulties with the social conservatism present in some of St Paul's Epistles; they are happier with the Jesus who 'took on oppression in order to set us free'.[6]

'The God of the Bible', wrote Gutiérrez, 'is a God who not only governs history, but who orientates it in the direction of establishment of justice and right. He ... takes sides with the poor and liberates them from slavery and oppression'.[7] The historical memory of the poor will be restored to them by reading the Bible and interpreting it from their point of view. Gutiérrez wrote a book about Job, emphasizing the empathy with the poor which his own losses gave him.[8]

Liberation theologians make full use of the prophets, especially Ezra and Nehemiah, concentrating on their vigorous denunciation of injustice and vindication of the rights of the poor, and on God the liberator. They emphasize – more than English radicals wished or found it expedient to emphasize – armed uprising legitimated by pastors. And, like English radicals, they make much of Revelation as depicting an 'immense struggle of the people of God against all the monsters of history'. 'The rights of the poor are God's rights'.[9]

The situations are different in that twentieth-century liberation theologians wish to remain within the Roman Catholic church, whilst seventeenth-century Puritans totally rejected it, and many rejected the Church of England. Liberation theologians have to use a great deal of ingenuity and finesse when discussing the authority of the church hierarchy

---

4. Gutiérrez, *The Power of the Poor*, p. 197; cf. Ellis and Maduro, op. cit., pp. 67–8. In 1656 Milton's nephew Edward Phillips dedicated a translation of Las Casas's *Tears of the Indians* to Oliver Cromwell.

5. Gutiérrez, *The Power of the Poor*, pp. 45–6; Ellis and Maduro, op. cit., p. 56.

6. Clodovis Boff, *Introducing Liberation Theology* (English translation, 1987), p. 53.

7. Gutiérrez, *The Power of the Poor*, p. 7; cf. pp. 37, 211–13. The sentiments recall Bunyan. Cf. Gutiérrez, *A Theology of Liberation: History, Politics and Salvation* (New York, 1988), pp. 88–90.

8. Ellis and Maduro, op. cit., p. 506; Gutiérrez, *On Job: God-Talk and the Suffering of the Innocent* (1986; English translation 1987), esp. pp. 33–5, 41, 58. On p. 114 Gutiérrez quotes Tawney's *Religion and the Rise of Capitalism*, including his reference to Job.

9. C. Boff, op. cit., pp. 35, 60.

and the rights of individual members of congregations. Nevertheless, allowing for caution in expression, they also make use of the Bible to say substantially the same things in many cases as did seventeenth-century radical protestants. Liberation theologians, benefiting by three centuries of historical interpretation, emphasize more specifically than could be done in the seventeenth-century that 'Christianity is the fruit of an upheaval. ... The church's mission is revolutionary' since 'the dangerous and subversive mission of Jesus of Nazareth, crucified under Pontius Pilate'. Like seventeenth-century radicals, liberation theologians deplore the donation of Constantine and the consequent involvement of the church in politics and worldly wealth. They stand up to the hierarchy: 'authoritarian situations are unacceptable to gospel values (Luke XXII.25–8)'. 'The risen Christ tore down all barriers that separate people: Ephesians II.15–18'.[10]

Their resort is to the authority of the Bible, and their stress is on 'the entire church (communitas fidelium)' rather than on its hierarchical structure. 'Today it is the church itself that is being called in question', said Gutiérrez: the church is the people of God, not a building.[11] 'Through Jesus Christ the spirit is communicated to the community of the entire church'. 'New ecclesiastical structures are needed'. God's gift to the individual is his charisma, 'a manifestation of the Spirit's presence in the members of the community', 'the concrete function that each person exercises within the community for the good of all'.[12] 'There is no non-charismatic member'. Judges XIII.25 tells us how 'the spirit's power and services are exercised in favour of the people's liberation through Samson'.[13] The phraseology is different from that of the seventeenth-century radicals, but the essence is the same. William Bradshaw in James I's reign had said 'There was not the poorest Christian in Thessalonica but Paul himself did think himself the better for the grace that was in him'.[14]

Gutiérrez is well aware of the parallel between his ideas and early protestant theology. 'The vanguard of protestant theology', he wrote, 'became the great Christian theology of modernity'.[15] But he distinguishes

10. Leonardo Boff, *Church, Charism and Power: Liberation Theology and the Institutional Church* (English translation 1985), pp. 49–52, 115, 142.
11. Gutiérrez, *The Power of the Poor*, p. 25; Cardinal Stephen Kim, in Ellis and Maduro, op. cit., pp. 19–20.
12. L. Boff, *Church, Charism and Power*, pp. 138–9, 148–57.
13. Ibid., pp. 157–8.
14. Bradshaw, *A Plaine and Pithy Exposition of the Second Epistle to the Thessalonians* (1620), p. 16.
15. Cf. Joan S. Bennett, 'Milton's Radical Christian Humanism and Liberation', Millersville.

sharply between early protestantism and 'liberal protestant theology', which 'by the end of the nineteenth century . . . became the theology of a self-assured middle-class Christianity'.[16] The modern theologian of whom Gutiérrez speaks most warmly is Dietrich Bonhoeffer, the Lutheran victim of Nazism.[17]

Considerable emphasis is laid on Biblical texts which proclaim human equality, rejecting respect for persons. Exodus is especially valued for emphasizing the role of women in liberation and the creation of a free people. Liberation theologians not only stress the equality of women as members of the congregation:[18] they also raise the question of their ordination. 'Jesus chose eleven married apostles and only one bachelor', wrote Leonardo Boff with disarming simplicity. 'Either the right of equality is universal or one cannot speak of equality without cynicism'.[19]

Liberation theologians have also benefited from some of the ideas of Marxism. They recognize the importance of economic factors and the class struggle, and the mystifying power of ideologies, including religious ideology.[20] As Gutiérrez put it, echoing Marx, his is 'a theology which does not stop with reflecting on the world but rather tries to be part of the process through which the world is transformed'.[21] But Marxism is an instrument, not something swallowed whole. Leonardo Boff was agreeably ironical when he wrote 'there is a surprising parallel between the Church's forms of government and that of the Communist Party in Russia'. By implication he was criticizing the church hierarchy for its refusal of real power to congregations.[22]

The strength of the new theology is such that Pope John Paul II told the Brazilian bishops in 1986 that 'the theology of liberation is not only op-

16. Gutiérrez, *The Power of the Poor*, pp. 178, 223; cf. pp. 202, 213.
17. Ibid., Chapter 7, *passim*.
18. Ellis and Maduro, op. cit., pp. 47, 208–14, 494 and Chapter 48, 'Women in the Future of the Theology of Liberation', by Maria Clara Bingemer, Professor of Theology in the Pontifical Catholic University of Rio de Janeiro. Of the forty-two contributors to this volume, fourteen were women.
19. L. Boff, *Church, Charism and Power*, pp. 36, 167, and *passim*; cf. his *Ecclesio-Genesis: The base communities reinvent the church* (English translation, 1986), Chapter 7 *passim*. First published in Portuguese 1977.
20. L. Boff, *Introducing Liberation Theology*, p. 28.
21. Gutiérrez, *A Theology of Liberation*, pp. 15, 272–9; cf. pp. 9, 30, 90, 97, 220; Ellis and Maduro, op. cit., pp. 262–70.
22. L. Boff, *Church, Charism and Power*, p. 171.

portune but useful and necessary'.[23] Different views have been expressed by the local hierarchy (without of course disagreeing with the Pope) and Gutiérrez and his colleagues have had to be very selective in their use of quotations from official sources. One is reminded of Gerrard Winstanley's insistence that Parliament's declaration of a free commonwealth authorized the sort of communist society which the Diggers wished to see established. Both sides in Latin America, moreover, have to walk carefully in view of the American-financed influx of evangelical protestant missionaries, who have had some success in conversions to fundamentalist protestantism. Liberation theologians find themselves between the Pope and the deep blue sea of fundamentalism. The 'liberal protestant theology' of western capitalism is not an option.

23. Ellis and Maduro, op. cit., p. 284. But see Harvey Cox, *The Silencing of Leonardo Boff: The Vatican and the Future of World Christianity* (1988), and Linebaugh, 'Jubilating', p. 87.

Index of Biblical Persons and Places

General Index of Persons and Places